ENCYCLOPEDIA OF
COMMUNICATION and INFORMATION

ENCYCLOPEDIA OF
COMMUNICATION
and INFORMATION

Volume 1

Edited by Jorge Reina Schement

MACMILLAN REFERENCE USA

GALE GROUP
™
THOMSON LEARNING

New York • Detroit • San Diego • San Francisco
Boston • New Haven, Conn. • Waterville, Maine
London • Munich

Encyclopedia of Communication and Information

Macmillan Library Reference USA
300 Park Avenue South
New York, NY 10010

Macmillan Library Reference USA
27500 Drake Road
Farmington Hills, MI 48331–3535

Library of Congress Cataloging-in-Publication Data

Encyclopedia of communication and information/edited by Jorge Reina Schement.
      p. cm.
    Includes bibliographical references and index.
    ISBN 0-02-865386-6 (set : hardcover : alk. paper)-ISBN 0-02-865383-1 (v. 1 : hardcover : alk. paper)-ISBN 0-02-865384-X (v. 2 : hardcover : alk. paper)-
    ISBN 0-02-865385-8 (v. 3 :hardcover : alk. paper)
      1. Communication-Encyclopedias. I. Schement, Jorge Reina.
    P87.5.E53 2001
    302.2"03-dc21   2001031220

Printed in United States of America

10 9 8 7 6 5 4 3 2 1

Contents

Preface . . . . *vii*

List of Articles . . . . *ix*

List of Contributors . . . . *xix*

Encyclopedia of Communication and Information *1*

Index *1097*

Editorial and Production Staff

Linda Hubbard
Editorial Director

Brian Kinsey
Project Editor

Kathleen Edgar, Shanna Weagle
Proofreaders

Wendy Allex
Indexer

Margaret Chamberlain
Permissions

Robert Duncan
Imaging

GGS Information Services, Inc.
Line Art Program

Linda Mahoney-LM Design
Compositor

MACMILLAN REFERENCE USA

Elly Dickason
Publisher

Hélène G. Potter
Editor in Chief

Preface

Studies of communication and information have engaged people since classical times, if not even earlier. Socrates, Plato, and Aristotle taught communication skills and considered the nature of ideas to be a mark of being human. Yet, although language emerged sometime between 300,000 and 30,000 years ago, words that represent the ideas of communication and information arrived only in relatively recent times. In English, John Wyclif introduced the word "communication" in his 1382 English translation of the Bible and used the word to convey a sense of transferring. In the same decade (1386?), the word "information" surfaced in the "Tale of Melibee" (in Geoffrey Chaucer"s *Canterbury Tales*), with the denotation of an instruction. Six hundred years later, most people could not get through a day without using the words "information" and "communication."

Since the late nineteenth century, psychologists, sociologists, anthropologists, biologists, neurologists, linguists, computer scientists, communication researchers, and information scientists, have expanded our understanding of communication and information. Today, social workers, clinical psychologists, psychiatrists, and speech pathologists comprise some of the professions that help people improve their communication skills. Other professionals, such as librarians, archivists, and information systems managers, organize information for storage and retrieval. Still others, including writers, journalists, broadcasters, television producers and directors, and screenwriters, contribute communication information through the mass media. Indeed, today, the United States, Japan, most European nations, and several countries on the Pacific Rim have work forces where the information and communication occupations account for the largest group of workers.

The *Encyclopedia of Communication and Information* brings together an assemblage of international experts in order to summarize what we know about communication and information in all of their manifestations. The entries in the Encyclopedia are written by specialists who are themselves active researchers in the study of communication, information, or both. Moreover, an important strength of this Encyclopedia is that it is interdisciplinary, drawing contributors from across academic disciplines. The many perspectives that guide the study of communication and information are represented here, complete with the controversies and disagreements that sway the progress of scholarship.

The 280 entries in the Encyclopedia cover eight general topics:

1. Careers (e.g., journalist, librarian, publicist, researcher, teacher),
2. Information science (e.g., human-computer interaction, information storage and retrieval),
3. Information technologies (e.g., broadband, computers, the Internet, radio, telephony, television),
4. Literacy (e.g., computer literacy, media literacy, traditional literacy,),
5. Institutional studies (e.g., elections, government policy, information society, law, media history),
6. Interpersonal communication (e.g., groups, organizations, relationships, rhetoric),
7. Library science (e.g., cataloging, library functions, text-based literacy),

8. Media effects (e.g., advertising, alcohol, dependence, interventions, opinion formation, public health campaigns).

The entries are organized in a strict alphabetical sequence, with cross-references to related entries provided where appropriate. Almost every entry includes a brief bibliography. Illustrations have been chosen and inserted to maximize effectiveness of the entries. Accordingly, the overall scheme balances familiarity of presentation and organization with originality in bringing communication and information subjects together in one encyclopedia.

The *Encyclopedia of Communication and Information* is a reference resource meant for people, especially students, who want full, up-to-date, trustworthy information about all aspects of communication and information. This includes readers who want more information about a "hot" topic, such as violence in media, or an important piece of legislation, such as the Telecommunications Act of 1996. Readers will find biographies on important individuals such as Thomas Edison, Marshall McLuhan, and Nellie Bly. Furthermore, they will find articles that describe a variety of communication and information occupations and professions. High school and college students who need material for class discussions and papers for courses will be able to turn to the Encyclopedia for relevant information. Finally, it will be of use to scholars, who can consult it as a handy state-of-the-art review about topics on which they are not expert.

This Encyclopedia is a necessary source for these lay readers, students, and scholars because communication and information form part of the foundation of human society. The evolution of human communication created the basis for sharing thoughts. The ability to describe, interpret, and imagine, when expressed to another, transports human potential beyond the necessary and immediate to a domain where abstractness can take root and grow. In this realm, the raw data of nature can be collected into information, transformed into a new idea, and communicated to people. Humans overlay the immutable facts of birth, life, and death with explanations, stories, and exhortations—which, in turn, leads to systemic actions. By communicating information, individuals coordinate actions beyond sight of each other and change actions in response to new information. When shared information becomes a group vision, social hierarchy results, collective acceptance of supernatural beings emerges,

and the satisfaction of self-interest through the exchange of goods spreads. Experiences interpreted and shared through communication form the norms of culture, and, when translated through the lens of absurdity, they even become funny stories that live on for generations. Thus, in the broadest sense, communication and information create society. For this reason, it is important that a reference source such as the *Encyclopedia of Communication and Information* be made available to help further human understanding of these topics.

As a project, the Encyclopedia brought together hundreds of people, who worked together to produce a compendium of the most up-to-date information. I thank the contributors for their dedication to conferring a high standard of quality on the content of the Encyclopedia. The associate editors merit special recognition and my gratitude, for without them there would be no encyclopedia. Their scholarly expertise in identifying topics, selecting contributors, and reviewing the submitted manuscripts ensured that this project would be successful. I want to thank Hélène Potter and Brian Kinsey of Macmillan for their encouragement and guidance. Hélène saw us through the design of the Encyclopedia and helped us to become a smoothly working editorial team. Brian's project management skills facilitated the work of editors at five distant universities. Indeed, his patience is legendary. Finally, the work conducted by colleagues, staff, and students here at the Institute for Information Policy contributed an essential ingredient to the project's success. Richard D. Taylor and Dennis Davis served as tireless sounding boards. Billie Young, the institute's staff assistant, kept paper and e-mail flowing. Graduate assistants Janice Ascolese, Scott Forbes, Sheila Sager, and Sharon Stringer spent many odd hours providing editorial support.

This project provides proof that a work of this sort requires the smooth cooperation of many experts who contribute their years of knowledge for scant compensation. These experts represent the many sides of the scholarly issues, and they share a commitment to the popular dissemination of materials related to communication and information studies. If this Encyclopedia adds to a reader's knowledge, introduces a student to a career, or enhances a teacher's course materials, then we will have fulfilled our purpose.

JORGE REINA SCHEMENT

List of Articles

A

Academia, Careers in
Mary Anne Fitzpatrick

Academic Achievement and Children's Television Use
George Comstock

Advertising, Subliminal
Joel Saegert

Advertising Effects
David W. Stewart
Sarah E. Stewart

Alcohol Abuse and College Students
Linda Costigan Lederman

Alcohol in the Media
Linda C. Godbold

Alphabets and Writing
Bertram C. Bruce

Animal Communication
Brent D. Ruben

Antiviolence Interventions
Amy I. Nathanson

Apprehension and Communication
James C. McCroskey
Virginia P. Richmond

Archives, Public Records, and Records Management
Jennifer A. Marshall
Tywanna M. Whorley

Archivists
Robert M. Warner

Armstrong, Edwin Howard
John W. Owens

Arousal Processes and Media Effects
Dolf Zillmann

Artificial Intelligence
Antonios Michailidis
Roy Rada

Attachment to Media Characters
Cynthia A. Hoffner

Audience Researchers
Horst Stipp

B

Baker, Augusta Braxton
Janice M. Del Negro

Bell, Alexander Graham
Martin L. Hatton

Bennett, James Gordon
Ellen Williamson Kanervo

Bibliography
D. W. Krummel

Bly, Nellie
Ellen Williamson Kanervo

Body Image, Media Effect on
Kristen Harrison

Broadcasting, Government Regulation of
Francesca Dillman Carpentier

Broadcasting, Self-Regulation of
Francesca Dillman Carpentier

Bush, Vannevar
Linda C. Smith

C

Cable Television
Alan B. Albarran

Cable Television, Careers in
Hal Hughes

Cable Television, History of
Mark J. Pescatore

Cable Television, Programming of
Larry Collette

Cable Television, Regulation of
Timothy E. Bajkiewicz

Cable Television, System Technology of
Patrick R. Parsons

Carnegie, Andrew
Wayne A. Wiegand

Cataloging and Knowledge Organization
Clare Beghtol

Catharsis Theory and Media Effects
Brad J. Bushman
Colleen M. Phillips

Chaplin, Charlie
Stephen D. Perry

Chief Information Officers
José-Marie Griffiths

Children and Advertising
Dale Kunkel

Children's Attention to Television
Daniel R. Anderson

Children's Comprehension of Television
Shalom M. Fisch

Children's Creativity and Television Use
Patti M. Valkenburg

Children's Preferences for Media Content
Patti M. Valkenburg

Communications Act of 1934
Francesca Dillman Carpentier

Communications Decency Act of 1996
Patrick M. Jablonski

Communication Study
Brent D. Ruben

Community Networks
Douglas Schuler

Computer Literacy
Tonyia J. Tidline

Computer Software
Eric Johnson

Computer Software, Educational
Sandra L. Calvert

Computing
Christopher Brown-Syed
Terri L. Lyons

Conservators
M. E. Ducey

Consumer Culture
Emory H. Woodard

Consumer Electronics
David Sedman

Copyright
Matt Jackson

Cultivation Theory and Media Effects
Nancy Signorielli

Cultural Studies
Paul Grosswiler

Culture and Communication
Brent D. Ruben

Culture Industries, Media as
Ronald V. Bettig

Cumulative Media Effects
L. Rowell Huesmann
Angie C. Beatty

Curators
Tonyia J. Tidline

D

Database Design
Martha E. Williams

Databases, Electronic
Martha E. Williams

Democracy and the Media
Brian R. McGee

Dependence on Media
Robert Kubey

Desensitization and Media Effects
Daniel Linz

Dewey, John
Larry A. Hickman

Dewey, Melvil
Wayne A. Wiegand

Diffusion of Innovations and Communication
Ronald E. Rice

Digital Communication
Michael Silbergleid
Mark J. Pescatore

Digital Media Systems
Patrick R. Parsons

Disney, Walt
Tracy Lauder

Durkheim, Émile
Eric W. Rothenbuhler

E

Economics of Information
Sandra Braman

Edison, Thomas Alva
Stephen D. Perry

Editors
Ardis Hanson

Educational Media Producers
Kay F. Klubertanz

Elderly and the Media
Marie-Louise Mares

Election Campaigns and Media Effects
Holli A. Semetko

Electronic Commerce
Richard D. Taylor

Ethics and Information
Marsha Woodbury

Evolution of Communication
Brent D. Ruben

F

Families and Television
Jennings Bryant
J. Alison Bryant

Farnsworth, Philo Taylor
John W. Owens

Fear and the Media
Joanne Cantor

Federal Communications Commission
Francesca Dillman Carpentier

Feminist Scholarship and Communication
Lea P. Stewart

Film Industry
Robert V. Bellamy Jr.

Film Industry, Careers in
Carey Martin

Film Industry, History of
Stephen D. Perry

Film Industry, Production Process of
Lilly Ann Boruszkowski

Film Industry, Technology of
David Sedman

First Amendment and the Media
Francesca Dillman Carpentier

Franklin, Benjamin
Wayne A. Wiegand

Functions of the Media
Kimberly B. Massey

G

Gays and Lesbians in the Media
Peter M. Nardi

Gender and the Media
Mary Beth Oliver
Chad Mahood

Geographic Information Systems
Richard Beck

Globalization of Culture Through the Media
Marwan M. Kraidy

Globalization of Media Industries
Roger Cooper

Greeley, Horace
Susan Ross

Griffith, D. W.
Stephen D. Perry

Group Communication
Mark Aakhus

Group Communication, Conflict and
Mark Aakhus

Group Communication, Decision Making and
Mark Aakhus

Group Communication, Dynamics of
Mark Aakhus

Group Communication, Roles and Responsibilities in
Brent D. Ruben

Gutenberg, Johannes
Marcella Genz

H

Haines, Helen E.
Holly Crawford

Health Communication
Gary L. Kreps

Health Communication, Careers in
Gary L. Kreps

Hearst, William Randolph
Mark Reid Arnold

Home as Information Environment
Scott C. Forbes

Human-Computer Interaction
Michael Twidale

Human Information Processing
Brent D. Ruben

I

Information
Jorge Reina Schement

Information Industry
Michelle M. Kazmer

Information Society, Description of
Leah A. Lievrouw

Innis, Harold Adams
Paul Grosswiler

Instructional Communication
Gustav W. Friedrich

Intellectual Freedom and Censorship
Ann K. Symons
Charles Harmon

Intercultural Communication, Adaptation and
Young Yun Kim

Intercultural Communication, Interethnic Relations and
Young Yun Kim

Internet and the World Wide Web
Charles L. Viles

Interpersonal Communication
Jenny Mandelbaum

Interpersonal Communication, Conversation and
Jenny Mandelbaum

Interpersonal Communication, Ethics and
Lea P. Stewart

Interpersonal Communication, Listening and
Linda Costigan Lederman

Intrapersonal Communication
Linda Costigan Lederman

J

Journalism, History of
Hazel Dicken-Garcia

Journalism, Professionalization of
Nancy L. Roberts
Giovanna Dell'Orto

K

Knowledge Management
Chun Wei Choo

Knowledge Management, Careers in
Evelyn H. Daniel

L

Language Acquisition
Jean Berko Gleason
Elena Zaretsky

Language and Communication
Jenny Mandelbaum

Language Structure
Jenny Mandelbaum

Lazarsfeld, Paul F.
Everett M. Rogers

Librarians
Charles Harmon
Ann K. Symons

Libraries, Digital
Paul B. Kantor

Libraries, Functions and Types of
Michael H. Harris

Libraries, History of
D. W. Krummel

Libraries, National
Thomas D. Walker

Library Associations and Consortia
Terry L. Weech

Library Automation
Jamshid Beheshti

Licklider, Joseph Carl Robnett
Eric Johnson

Literacy
Margaret Mary Kimmel

Lumière, Auguste; Lumière, Louis
Stephen D. Perry

M

Machlup, Fritz
Robert F. Rich

Magazine Industry
Stacey Benedict

Magazine Industry, Careers in
Tracy Lauder

Magazine Industry, History of
Tracy Lauder

Magazine Industry, Production Process of
Stacey Benedict
Tracy Lauder

Management Information Systems
Lucas D. Introna

Marconi, Guglielmo
Stephen D. Perry

Marketing Research, Careers in
Eugenia Yew-Yen Peck

McLuhan, Herbert Marshall
Paul Grosswiler

Mead, George Herbert
John J. Pauly

Méliès, Georges
Ted C. Jones

Mills, C. Wright
Robert Faber

Minorities and the Media
Mary Beth Oliver
Dana R. Broussard

Models of Communication
Brent D. Ruben

Mood Effects and Media Exposure
Dolf Zillmann

Moore, Anne Carroll
Anne Lundin

Morse, Samuel F. B.
Martin L. Hatton

Murrow, Edward R.
Stephen D. Perry

Museums
Paul F. Marty

Music, Popular
Donald F. Roberts
Peter G. Christenson

N

National Television Violence Study
Barbara J. Wilson

Networks and Communication
Ronald E. Rice

News Effects
Dolf Zillmann

Newspaper Industry
Robert V. Bellamy Jr.

Newspaper Industry, Careers in
Coy Callison

Newspaper Industry, History of
Lawrence N. Strout

News Production Theories
Stephen D. Reese

Nonverbal Communication
Mark G. Frank

Nutrition and Media Effects
Katherine Battle Horgen
Kelly D. Brownell

O

Opinion Polling, Careers in
Michael W. Traugott

Organizational Communication
Ronald E. Rice

Organizational Communication, Careers in
Ronald E. Rice

Organizational Culture
Lea P. Stewart

Organizational Quality and Performance Excellence
Brent D. Ruben

P

Paley, William S.
Greg Pitts

Paradigm and Communication
Brent D. Ruben

Paranormal Events and the Media
Glenn G. Sparks

Parental Mediation of Media Effects
Amy I. Nathanson

Peirce, Charles Sanders
Richard L. Lanigan

Pirate Media
Stanley J. Baran

Political Economy
Ronald V. Bettig

Pornography
Richard Jackson Harris
Christina L. Scott

Pornography, Legal Aspects of
Steven G. Gey

Preservation and Conservation of Information
M. E. Ducey

Price, Derek John de Solla
Linda C. Smith

Printing, History and Methods of
D. W. Krummel

Privacy and Communication
Eric E. Harlan

Privacy and Encryption
Louise S. Robbins

Propaganda
Brian R. McGee

Provider-Patient Relationships
Gary L. Kreps

Psychological Media Research, Ethics of
Cynthia A. Hoffner

Public Broadcasting
Willard D. Rowland Jr.

Public Health Campaigns
Gary L. Kreps

Public Relations
Todd Hunt

Public Relations, Careers In
Todd Hunt

Public Service Media
Marc Raboy

Public Speaking
Lea P. Stewart

Public Speaking, Careers in
Lea P. Stewart

Publishing Industry
Lorna Peterson

Publishing Industry, Careers in
Lorna Peterson
Deborah J. Karpuk

Pulitzer, Joseph
Charles F. Aust

R
Radio Broadcasting
Alan B. Albarran

Radio Broadcasting, Careers in
Stephen D. Perry

Radio Broadcasting, History of
Greg Pitts

Radio Broadcasting, Station Programming and
John W. Owens

Radio Broadcasting, Technology of
Hal Hughes

Ranganathan, Shiyali Ramamrita
Pauline Atherton Cochrane

Ratings for Movies
Joel Federman
Joanne Cantor

Ratings for Television Programs
Joanne Cantor

Ratings for Video Games, Software, and the Internet
Donald F. Roberts

Recording Industry
Paul D. Fischer

Recording Industry, Careers in
Paul D. Fischer

Recording Industry, History of
Paul D. Fischer

Recording Industry, Production Process of
Richard D. Barnet

Recording Industry, Technology of
John M. Hoerner Jr.

Reference Services and Information Access
Nancy Huling

Relationships, Stages of
Lea P. Stewart

Relationships, Types of
Lea P. Stewart

Religion and the Media
Robert Abelman

Researchers for Educational Television Programs
Shalom M. Fisch

Research Methods in Information Studies
Bryce Allen

Retrieval of Information
P. Bryan Heidorn
J. Stephen Downie

Rhetoric
Amy R. Slagell

S
Sarnoff, David
Greg Pitts

Satellites, Communication
C. A. Tuggle

Satellites, History of
C. A. Tuggle

Satellites, Technology of
C. A. Tuggle

Schramm, Wilbur
Everett M. Rogers

Semiotics
Igor E. Klyukanov

Sesame Street
Rosemarie T. Truglio

Sex and the Media
Jane D. Brown
Susannah R. Stern

Soap Operas
Renée A. Botta

Social Change and the Media
Marwan M. Kraidy

Social Cognitive Theory and Media Effects
Albert Bandura

Social Goals and the Media
Marie-Louise Mares

Society and the Media
Stanley J. Baran

Sociolinguistics
Alla V. Yelyseieva

Sports and Media Effects
Edward R. Hirt
Nathan L. Steele

Standards and Information
David S. Dubin

Storytellers
Betsy Hearne

Storytelling
Betsy Hearne

Symbols
Brent D. Ruben

Systems Designers
Hong Xu

T
Talk Shows on Television
Marie-Louise Mares

Technology, Adoption and Diffusion of
Martin L. Hatton

Technology, Philosophy of
Charles F. Aust

Telecommunications, Wireless
Eric E. Harlan

Telecommunications Act of 1996
Eric E. Harlan

Telephone Industry
David H. Goff

Telephone Industry, History of
Martin L. Hatton

Telephone Industry, Regulation of
Martin L. Hatton

Telephone Industry, Technology of
David H. Goff

Television, Educational
Sandra L. Calvert

Television Broadcasting
Joseph Turow

Television Broadcasting, Careers in
Francesca Dillman Carpentier

Television Broadcasting, History of
Richard Landesberg
Mark J. Pescatore

Television Broadcasting, Production of
Francesca Dillman Carpentier

Television Broadcasting, Programming and
David Sedman

Television Broadcasting, Station Operations and
Francesca Dillman Carpentier

Television Broadcasting, Technology of
Mark J. Pescatore
Michael Silbergleid

Tobacco and Media Effects
Michael Pfau
Erin Alison Szabo

U
Use of Information
Heidi Julien

V
V-Chip
Joanne Cantor

Video and Computer Games and the Internet
Patti M. Valkenburg

Violence in the Media, Attraction to
Amy I. Nathanson

Violence in the Media, History of Research on
Glenn G. Sparks

Visualization of Information
Shaoyi He

W
Weber, Max
Eric W. Rothenbuhler

Webmasters
Michael Twidale

Welles, Orson
Lawrence N. Strout

Williams, Raymond
Bonnie S. Brennen

Wilson, Halsey William
Christine Pawley

Wittgenstein, Ludwig
Dale Jacquette

Writers
Betsy Hearne

List of Contributors

Mark Aakhus
Rutgers University, New Brunswick
Group Communication
Group Communication, Conflict and
Group Communication, Decision Making and
Group Communication, Dynamics of

Robert Abelman
Cleveland State University
Religion and the Media

Alan B. Albarran
University of North Texas
Cable Television
Radio Broadcasting

Bryce Allen
University of Missouri, Columbia
Research Methods in Information Studies

Daniel R. Anderson
University of Massachusetts, Amherst
Children's Attention to Television

Mark Reid Arnold
*California Polytechnic State University,
    San Luis Obispo*
Hearst, William Randolph

Charles F. Aust
Kennesaw State University
Pulitzer, Joseph
Technology, Philosophy of

Timothy E. Bajkiewicz
University of South Florida
Cable Television, Regulation of

Albert Bandura
Stanford University
Social Cognitive Theory and Media Effects

Stanley J. Baran
San Jose State University
Pirate Media
Society and the Media

Richard D. Barnet
Middle Tennessee State University
Recording Industry, Production Process of

Angie C. Beatty
University of Michigan, Ann Arbor
Cumulative Media Effects (with L. Rowell
    Huesmann)

Richard Beck
University of Illinois, Urbana-Champaign
Geographic Information Systems

Clare Beghtol
University of Toronto
Cataloging and Knowledge Organization

Jamshid Beheshti
McGill University
Library Automation

Robert V. Bellamy Jr.
Duquesne University
Film Industry
Newspaper Industry

Stacey Benedict
University of Alabama, Birmingham
Magazine Industry
Magazine Industry, Production Process of
    (with Tracy Lauder)

Ronald V. Bettig
Pennsylvania State University
Culture Industries, Media as
Political Economy

Lilly Ann Boruszkowski
Southern Illinois University
Film Industry, Production Process of

Renée A. Botta
Cleveland State University
Soap Operas

Sandra Braman
University of Alabama, Tuscaloosa
Economics of Information

Bonnie S. Brennen
University of Missouri, Columbia
Williams, Raymond

Dana R. Broussard
Pennsylvania State University
Minorities and the Media
  (with Mary Beth Oliver)

Jane D. Brown
University of North Carolina, Chapel Hill
Sex and the Media (with Susannah R. Stern)

Kelly D. Brownell
Yale University
Nutrition and Media Effects
  (with Katherine Battle Horgen)

Christopher Brown-Syed
Wayne State University
Computing (with Terri L. Lyons)

Bertram C. Bruce
University of Illinois, Urbana-Champaign
Alphabets and Writing

J. Alison Bryant
University of Southern California
Families and Television (with Jennings
  Bryant)

Jennings Bryant
University of Alabama, Tuscaloosa
Families and Television
  (with J. Alison Bryant)

Brad J. Bushman
Iowa State University
Catharsis Theory and Media Effects
  (with Colleen M. Phillips)

Coy Callison
Texas Tech University
Newspaper Industry, Careers in

Sandra L. Calvert
Georgetown University
Computer Software, Educational
Television, Educational

Joanne Cantor
University of Wisconsin, Madison
Fear and the Media
Ratings for Movies (with Joel Federman)
Ratings for Television Programs
V-Chip

Francesca Dillman Carpentier
University of Alabama, Tuscaloosa
Broadcasting, Government Regulation of
Broadcasting, Self-Regulation of
Communications Act of 1934
Federal Communications Commission
First Amendment and the Media
Television Broadcasting, Careers in
Television Broadcasting, Production of
Television Broadcasting, Station
  Operations and

Chun Wei Choo
University of Toronto
Knowledge Management

Peter G. Christenson
Lewis & Clark College
Music, Popular (with Donald F. Roberts)

Pauline Atherton Cochrane
*Syracuse University and University of Illinois,
  Urbana-Champaign (emerita)*
Ranganathan, Shiyali Ramamrita

Larry Collette
University of Denver
Cable Television, Programming of

George Comstock
Syracuse University
Academic Achievement and Children's
  Television Use

Roger Cooper
Texas Christian University
Globalization of Media Industries

Holly Crawford
Rutgers University, New Brunswick
Haines, Helen E.

Evelyn H. Daniel
University of North Carolina, Chapel Hill
Knowledge Management, Careers in

Giovanna Dell'Orto
University of Minnesota
Journalism, Professionalization of
    (with Nancy L. Roberts)

Janice M. Del Negro
University of Illinois, Urbana-Champaign
Baker, Augusta Braxton

Hazel Dicken-Garcia
University of Minnesota
Journalism, History of

J. Stephen Downie
University of Illinois, Urbana-Champaign
Retrieval of Information (with P. Bryan
    Heidorn)

David S. Dubin
University of Illinois, Urbana-Champaign
Standards and Information

M. E. Ducey
University of Nebraska, Lincoln
Conservators
Preservation and Conservation of
    Information

Robert Faber
Pennsylvania State University
Mills, C. Wright

Joel Federman
The Concord Project, San Francisco, CA
Ratings for Movies (with Joanne Cantor)

Shalom M. Fisch
Sesame Workshop, New York City
Children's Comprehension of Television
Researchers for Educational Television
    Programs

Paul D. Fischer
Middle Tennessee State University
Recording Industry
Recording Industry, Careers in
Recording Industry, History of

Mary Anne Fitzpatrick
University of Wisconsin, Madison
Academia, Careers in

Scott C. Forbes
Pennsylvania State University
Home as Information Environment

Mark G. Frank
Rutgers University
Nonverbal Communication

Gustav W. Friedrich
Rutgers University, New Brunswick
Instructional Communication

Marcella Genz
University of Alabama, Tuscaloosa
Gutenberg, Johannes

Steven G. Gey
Florida State University
Pornography, Legal Aspects of

Jean Berko Gleason
Boston University
Language Acquisition (with Elena Zaretsky)

Linda C. Godbold
East Carolina University
Alcohol in the Media

David H. Goff
University of Southern Mississippi
Telephone Industry
Telephone Industry, Technology of

José-Marie Griffiths
University of Michigan, Ann Arbor
Chief Information Officers

Paul Grosswiler
University of Maine
Cultural Studies
Innis, Harold Adams
McLuhan, Herbert Marshall

Ardis Hanson
University of South Florida
Editors

Eric E. Harlan
Mississippi University for Women
Privacy and Communication
Telecommunications, Wireless
Telecommunications Act of 1996

Charles Harmon
Neal-Schuman Publishers, Inc., New York City
Intellectual Freedom and Censorship (with
    Ann K. Symons)
Librarians (with Ann K. Symons)

Michael H. Harris
High Dakota Group, Palm Coast, Florida
Libraries, Functions and Types of

Richard Jackson Harris
Kansas State University
Pornography (with Christina L. Scott)

Kristen Harrison
University of Michigan, Ann Arbor
Body Image, Media Effect on

Martin L. Hatton
Mississippi University for Women
Bell, Alexander Graham
Morse, Samuel F. B.
Technology, Adoption and Diffusion of
Telephone Industry, History of
Telephone Industry, Regulation of

Shaoyi He
Pennsylvania State University
Visualization of Information

Betsy Hearne
University of Illinois, Urbana-Champaign
Storytellers
Storytelling
Writers

P. Bryan Heidorn
University of Illinois, Urbana-Champaign
Retrieval of Information (with J. Stephen
    Downie)

Larry A. Hickman
Southern Illinois University, Carbondale
Dewey, John

Edward R. Hirt
Indiana University, Bloomington
Sports and Media Effects
    (with Nathan L. Steele)

John M. Hoerner Jr.
University of Montevallo
Recording Industry, Technology of

Cynthia A. Hoffner
Georgia State University
Attachment to Media Characters
Psychological Media Research, Ethics of

Katherine Battle Horgen
Yale University
Nutrition and Media Effects
    (with Kelly D. Brownell)

L. Rowell Huesmann
University of Michigan, Ann Arbor
Cumulative Media Effects
    (with Angie C. Beatty)

Hal Hughes
University of Alabama, Tuscaloosa
Cable Television, Careers in
Radio Broadcasting, Technology of

Nancy Huling
University of Washington
Reference Services and Information Access

Todd Hunt
Rutgers University (emeritus)
Public Relations
Public Relations, Careers In

Lucas D. Introna
Lancaster University, England
Management Information Systems

Patrick M. Jablonski
University of Central Florida
Communications Decency Act of 1996

Matt Jackson
Pennsylvania State University
Copyright

Dale Jacquette
Pennsylvania State University
Wittgenstein, Ludwig

Eric Johnson
Lynne Gilfillan Associates, Fairfax, VA
Computer Software
Licklider, Joseph Carl Robnett

Ted C. Jones
Austin Peay State University
Méliès, Georges

Heidi Julien
Dalhousie University
Use of Information

Ellen Williamson Kanervo
Austin Peay State University
Bennett, James Gordon
Bly, Nellie

Paul B. Kantor
Rutgers University, New Brunswick
Libraries, Digital

Deborah J. Karpuk
State University of New York, Buffalo
Publishing Industry, Careers in
    (with Lorna Peterson)

Michelle M. Kazmer
University of Illinois, Urbana-Champaign
Information Industry

Young Yun Kim
University of Oklahoma
Intercultural Communication, Adaptation
    and
Intercultural Communication, Interethnic
    Relations and

Margaret Mary Kimmel
University of Pittsburgh
Literacy

Kay F. Klubertanz
Wisconsin Public Television, Madison
Educational Media Producers

Igor E. Klyukanov
Eastern Washington University
Semiotics

Marwan M. Kraidy
American University
Globalization of Culture Through the Media
Social Change and the Media

Gary L. Kreps
National Cancer Institute, Bethesda, MD
Health Communication
Health Communication, Careers in
Provider-Patient Relationships
Public Health Campaigns

D. W. Krummel
University of Illinois, Urbana-Champaign
Bibliography
Libraries, History of
Printing, History and Methods of

Robert Kubey
Rutgers University, New Brunswick
Dependence on Media

Dale Kunkel
University of California, Santa Barbara
Children and Advertising

Richard Landesberg
Morrisville, NC
Television Broadcasting, History of
    (with Mark J. Pescatore)

Richard L. Lanigan
Southern Illinois University, Carbondale
Peirce, Charles Sanders

Tracy Lauder
University of Alabama, Tuscaloosa
Disney, Walt
Magazine Industry, Careers in
Magazine Industry, History of
Magazine Industry, Production Process of
    (with Stacey Benedict)

Linda Costigan Lederman
Rutgers University
Alcohol Abuse and College Students
Interpersonal Communication, Listening and
Intrapersonal Communication

Leah A. Lievrouw
University of California, Los Angeles
Information Society, Description of

Daniel Linz
University of California, Santa Barbara
Desensitization and Media Effects

Anne Lundin
University of Wisconsin, Madison
Moore, Anne Carroll

Terri L. Lyons
London, Ontario
Computing (with Christopher Brown-Syed)

Chad Mahood
University of California, Santa Barbara
Gender and the Media (with Mary Beth Oliver)

Jenny Mandelbaum
Rutgers University, New Brunswick
Interpersonal Communication
Interpersonal Communication,
    Conversation and

Jenny Mandelbaum (cont.)
Language and Communication
Language Structure

Marie-Louise Mares
University of Wisconsin, Madison
Elderly and the Media
Social Goals and the Media
Talk Shows on Television

Jennifer A. Marshall
University of Pittsburgh
Archives, Public Records, and Records
   Management (with Tywanna M. Whorley)

Carey Martin
Barry University, Miami Shores
Film Industry, Careers in

Paul F. Marty
University of Illinois, Urbana-Champaign
Museums

Kimberly B. Massey
San Jose State University
Functions of the Media

James C. McCroskey
West Virginia University
Apprehension and Communication
   (with Virginia P. Richmond)

Brian R. McGee
Texas Tech University
Democracy and the Media
Propaganda

Antonios Michailidis
State University of New York, Stony Brook
Artificial Intelligence (with Roy Rada)

Peter M. Nardi
Pitzer College
Gays and Lesbians in the Media

Amy I. Nathanson
Ohio State University
Antiviolence Interventions
Parental Mediation of Media Effects
Violence in the Media, Attraction to

Mary Beth Oliver
Pennsylvania State University
Gender and the Media (with Chad Mahood)
Minorities and the Media
   (with Dana R. Broussard)

John W. Owens
University of Cincinnati
Armstrong, Edwin Howard
Farnsworth, Philo Taylor
Radio Broadcasting, Station
   Programming and

Patrick R. Parsons
Pennsylvania State University
Cable Television, System Technology of
Digital Media Systems

John J. Pauly
Saint Louis University
Mead, George Herbert

Christine Pawley
University of Iowa
Wilson, Halsey William

Eugenia Yew-Yen Peck
University of Wisconsin, Madison
Marketing Research, Careers in

Stephen D. Perry
Illinois State University
Chaplin, Charlie
Edison, Thomas Alva
Film Industry, History of
Griffith, D. W.
Lumière, Auguste; Lumière, Louis
Marconi, Guglielmo
Murrow, Edward R.
Radio Broadcasting, Careers in

Mark J. Pescatore
University of North Carolina, Chapel Hill
Cable Television, History of
Digital Communication
   (with Michael Silbergleid)
Television Broadcasting, History of
   (with Richard Landesberg)
Television Broadcasting, Technology of
   (with Michael Silbergleid)

Lorna Peterson
State University of New York, Buffalo
Publishing Industry
Publishing Industry, Careers in
   (with Deborah J. Karpuk)

Michael Pfau
University of Wisconsin, Madison
Tobacco and Media Effects
   (with Erin Alison Szabo)

Colleen M. Phillips
Iowa State University
Catharsis Theory and Media Effects
(with Brad J. Bushman)

Greg Pitts
Bradley University
Paley, William S.
Radio Broadcasting, History of
Sarnoff, David

Marc Raboy
University of Montreal
Public Service Media

Roy Rada
University of Maryland, Baltimore County
Artificial Intelligence
(with Antonios Michailidis)

Stephen D. Reese
University of Texas, Austin
News Production Theories

Ronald E. Rice
Rutgers University, New Brunswick
Diffusion of Innovations and
Communication
Networks and Communication
Organizational Communication
Organizational Communication, Careers in

Robert F. Rich
University of Illinois, Urbana-Champaign
Machlup, Fritz

Virginia P. Richmond
West Virginia University
Apprehension and Communication
(with James C. McCroskey)

Louise S. Robbins
University of Wisconsin, Madison
Privacy and Encryption

Donald F. Roberts
Stanford University
Music, Popular (with Peter G. Christenson)
Ratings for Video Games, Software, and the
Internet

Nancy L. Roberts
University of Minnesota
Journalism, Professionalization of
(with Giovanna Dell'Orto)

Everett M. Rogers
University of New Mexico
Lazarsfeld, Paul F.
Schramm, Wilbur

Susan Ross
Southwest Texas State University
Greeley, Horace

Eric W. Rothenbuhler
University of Iowa
Durkheim, Èmile
Weber, Max

Willard D. Rowland Jr.
*University of Colorado, Boulder, and
Colorado Public Television (KBDI-TV,
Channel 12), Denver*
Public Broadcasting

Brent D. Ruben
Rutgers University, New Brunswick
Animal Communication
Communication Study
Culture and Communication
Evolution of Communication
Group Communication, Roles and
Responsibilities in
Human Information Processing
Models of Communication
Organizational Quality and
Performance Excellence
Paradigm and Communication
Symbols

Joel Saegert
University of Texas, San Antonio
Advertising, Subliminal

Jorge Reina Schement
Pennsylvania State University
Information

Douglas Schuler
Evergreen State College
Community Networks

Christina L. Scott
Loyola University of Chicago
Pornography (with Richard Jackson Harris)

David Sedman
Southern Methodist University
Consumer Electronics
Film Industry, Technology of
Television Broadcasting, Programming and

Holli A. Semetko
University of Amsterdam
Election Campaigns and Media Effects

Nancy Signorielli
University of Delaware
Cultivation Theory and Media Effects

Michael Silbergleid
New York, NY
Digital Communication (with Mark J.
  Pescatore)
Television Broadcasting, Technology of (with
  Mark J. Pescatore)

Amy R. Slagell
Iowa State University
Rhetoric

Linda C. Smith
University of Illinois, Urbana-Champaign
Bush, Vannevar
Price, Derek John de Solla

Glenn G. Sparks
Purdue University
Paranormal Events and the Media
Violence in the Media, History of Research on

Nathan L. Steele
Indiana University, Bloomington
Sports and Media Effects
  (with Edward R. Hirt)

Susannah R. Stern
Boston College
Sex and the Media (with Jane D. Brown)

David W. Stewart
University of Southern California
Advertising Effects (with Sarah E. Stewart)

Sarah E. Stewart
University of Redlands
Advertising Effects (with David W. Stewart)

Lea P. Stewart
Rutgers University, New Brunswick
Feminist Scholarship and Communication
Interpersonal Communication, Ethics and
Organizational Culture
Public Speaking
Public Speaking, Careers in
Relationships, Stages of
Relationships, Types of

Horst Stipp
*Vice President of Primary and Strategic
  Research, National Broadcasting
  Company, Inc.*
Audience Researchers

Lawrence N. Strout
Xavier University of Louisiana
Newspaper Industry, History of
Welles, Orson

Ann K. Symons
Juneau Scool District, Juneau, Alaska
Intellectual Freedom and Censorship
  (with Charles Harmon)
Librarians (with Charles Harmon)

Erin Alison Szabo
University of Wisconsin, Madison
Tobacco and Media Effects
  (with Michael Pfau)

Richard D. Taylor
Pennsylvania State University
Electronic Commerce

Tonyia J. Tidline
University of Illinois, Urbana-Champaign
Computer Literacy
Curators

Michael W. Traugott
University of Michigan, Ann Arbor
Opinion Polling, Careers in

Rosemarie T. Truglio
Sesame Workshop, New York City
Sesame Street

C. A. Tuggle
University of North Carolina, Chapel Hill
Satellites, Communication
Satellites, History of
Satellites, Technology of

Joseph Turow
University of Pennsylvania
Television Broadcasting

Michael Twidale
University of Illinois, Urbana-Champaign
Human-Computer Interaction
Webmasters

Patti M. Valkenburg
University of Amsterdam
Children's Creativity and
    Television Use
Children's Preferences for
    Media Content
Video and Computer Games and
    the Internet

Charles L. Viles
University of North Carolina, Chapel Hill
Internet and the World Wide Web

Thomas D. Walker
University of Southern Mississippi
Libraries, National

Robert M. Warner
University of Michigan, Ann Arbor
Archivists

Terry L. Weech
University of Illinois, Urbana-Champaign
Library Associations and Consortia

Tywanna M. Whorley
University of Pittsburgh
Archives, Public Records, and Records
    Management (with Jennifer A. Marshall)

Wayne A. Wiegand
University of Wisconsin, Madison
Carnegie, Andrew
Dewey, Melvil
Franklin, Benjamin

Martha E. Williams
University of Illinois, Urbana-Champaign
Database Design
Databases, Electronic

Barbara J. Wilson
University of Illinois, Urbana-Champaign
National Television Violence Study

Emory H. Woodard
Villanova University
Consumer Culture

Marsha Woodbury
University of Illinois, Urbana-Champaign
Ethics and Information

Hong Xu
University of Pittsburgh
Systems Designers

Alla V. Yelyseieva
Georgetown University
Sociolinguistics

Elena Zaretsky
Boston University
Language Acquisition
    (with Jean Berko Gleason)

Dolf Zillmann
University of Alabama, Tuscaloosa
Arousal Processes and Media Effects
Mood Effects and Media Exposure
News Effects

A

■ ACADEMIA, CAREERS IN

A professor is a college or university teacher of the highest rank in a particular branch of learning. In Middle English, the word "professor" meant either one who had taken the vows of a religious order or a public lecturer. From the very beginning, a professor was an individual who had taken religious orders to defend and discover the truth. The distinctive task of a professor is the discovery and transmission of truth, just as the care and well-being of a patient is the task of the physician. Of course, the concept of truth is a very ambiguous one; its determination is a difficult matter. Truth is not static. It must be incessantly examined as truths are continuously challenged when new knowledge is discovered. The Middle English definition is also a reminder that professors are public lecturers or teachers. In other words, professors must share their knowledge and understanding of the truth with others. This sharing may be through teaching, writing, or community service. These underlying commitments of a professor have evolved into three interrelated and mutually reinforcing roles: (1) teaching and advising of students, (2) conducting research, and (3) providing public service.

Teaching and Advising

Within their particular areas of advanced training and knowledge, professors teach and advise students about academic and career issues. In the modern college and university, professors are expected to do a wide range of types of teaching, calling upon very diverse skills and abilities. The workload for a professor typically varies between conducting two and four group instruction sections a semester and leading a variety of individual instruction classes.

Group instruction sections are what students usually think of as classes. These are classes that meet at regularly scheduled times each week. There are small group instruction sections that usually range in size from twelve to forty students, where professors and students can discuss and debate the material in the course. In large institutions, a professor may teach a large group instruction course, which might involve teaching assistants, who are graduate students pursuing advanced degrees in the subject they teach. These large lecture classes often take the form of one or two weekly lectures followed by laboratory or small group recitation sessions. Professors are responsible for the complete design of the course, for the setting of the course standards and requirements, and for the training of the graduate student teaching assistants.

Many universities experiment with technology in these large group lectures. Students participate in web-based discussions and problem-solving exercises, try various experimental procedures, and sometimes watch lectures on video or on their laptop computers. In these technologically enhanced lectures, students may not need to attend a traditional class at a set time but may consult with the professor and other students over the Internet. Regardless of their field of expertise, professors are becoming versed in technology so they can design a number of learning experiences to supplement and even replace traditional classroom learning for their students.

Individual instruction sections are highly specialized courses where a student may pursue a thesis, a set of readings, or a special project under the guidance of the professor. The individual sections are the one-on-one courses where a professor works with a student on a specific research project or a given area that the student wants to study. These classes are worked out individually between the student and the professor and mutually satisfactory expectations are set for the amount of guidance and help that the student will receive as he or she moves through the material.

Professors also advise students about specific courses, majors, and interesting directions in which to take their work. Professors are often a good source of information about career opportunities within their own fields. Career information, in this sense, does not mean that professors necessarily help the student find a job, but they can be a valuable source of information about the kind of training and experience that students might need to succeed in a field. Professors can organize two types of courses to help students find and develop their interests. First, there are internships or field experiences. These are opportunities (either paying or volunteer) to experience what entry-level work is like in a given industry. The other type of course experience is service-based learning. Here, students use their talents to help a nonprofit group to accomplish its goals.

Conducting Research

Professors are expected to conduct research. Most students tend to think this means that professors read a few books or write a few papers. However, research involves much more than that. Research is the creation, accumulation, and transfer of new knowledge. The range of topics is very broad. Communication scholars might add new knowledge on topics as varied as children's enduring fright reactions to media, patterns of conflicts in different types of marriages, the early influences on the rhetoric of George Washington, audience reactions to women's television programming, government regulation of broadcasting in different countries, and so on. Research can involve activities as diverse as bringing children into a laboratory to watch television, videotaping a couple in their home as they discuss a difficult issue, analyzing the fan mail and script development of a successful television show, and reading archived letters and primary sources about a famous historical figure.

Some research is motivated by theoretical considerations where the current use of the findings may not be obvious. Research may also be motivated by solving a practical problem for society. Many communication researchers are called upon to conduct applied research on persuasion or the marketing of prosocial goals and ideas. For example, some communication researchers investigate how children can be persuaded not to start smoking.

In many research universities, students can become involved in faculty research from the very start of their academic careers. They can find out the type of research that a faculty member does and then become part of the research team. This work involves students closely in learning how knowledge about a topic is generated, so it can be a valuable part of a college or university education.

Providing Public Service

The final role for the professor is service. A professor must help to run his or her university and academic discipline. Running the university means serving on and chairing various committees that oversee the curriculum, the budget, and the tenure and promotion of individuals within the system. Some professors also become academic administrators, serving as deans of their colleges and even university presidents. Running one's discipline means editing journals and books and serving as an officer of national or regional academic or professional societies.

Because of the major public investments in the colleges and universities, the public expects the knowledge generated in the universities to be rapidly diffused through public service. Although their first and most important job is classroom teaching and serving the students in their classes, professors must do more than classroom teaching. Public service and community outreach are very important parts of the job of a professor. Professors have a responsibility to the public to use their talents for the betterment of their communities. Serving on commissions and public service forums, giving speeches, being active in community and political groups, consulting with business and nonprofit organizations, and serving as stewards of their community are important roles. The job of a professor is to form relationships with schools, government, businesses, and individuals across the nation, using their expertise to help solve the challenges that face society.

Career Stages

Professors are usually required to hold the highest degree in their chosen field of specialization. In most fields, this is the doctoral degree or the Ph.D. (Doctor of Philosophy), although the highest degree for artists can be the master's degree or the M.F. A. (Master of Fine Arts). These advanced degrees require many years of study beyond the four years that are spent in undergraduate school. The average doctoral degree usually takes at least five years of work beyond the baccalaureate degree, and it is not unusual for individuals to spend ten years in pursuit of that degree. The Master of Fine Arts degree requires an individual to develop a high degree of skill and proficiency in the chosen artistic field and demands that individuals produce acclaimed works (e.g., films, videos, paintings).

After completing the necessary education, individuals begin university employment as untenured assistant professors. As part of a probationary period that lasts six or seven years, assistant professors must work to develop a case for tenure. That is, the young faculty members must demonstrate that they can be effective and vital teachers and advisors, conduct excellent research, and serve their communities. Often, people outside of academia find the concept of tenure or "lifetime job security" hard to understand. Originally, however, tenure was not designed as a system for measuring performance; tenure arose out of a concern for political independence. In other words, tenure was designed to protect the academic freedom of the faculty. That is, with the sense that their basic position is protected, faculty members can feel much freer to teach and speak out about the important controversial issues of the day. Faculty members in communication departments, for example, often severely criticize the media and their content.

When tenure is granted, an assistant professor is promoted to the position of associate professor. Individuals usually remain at this rank for at least five years, and some remain their even longer. Promotion to the position of professor requires the individual to demonstrate significantly more accomplishments beyond those that were required

to gain tenure. The typical time that elapses between entering graduate school and attaining the rank of professor in a university is seventeen to twenty years. Clearly, choosing a career in academia involves a serious commitment on the part of the individual.

See also: COMPUTER SOFTWARE, EDUCATIONAL; EDUCATIONAL MEDIA PRODUCERS; INSTRUCTIONAL COMMUNICATION; RESEARCHERS FOR EDUCATIONAL TELEVISION PROGRAMS; TELEVISION, EDUCATIONAL.

MARY ANNE FITZPATRICK

ACADEMIC ACHIEVEMENT AND CHILDREN'S TELEVISION USE

The relationships between television viewing and the academic performance of children and teenagers have been the subject of great controversy. Popular opinion and some educators have held that television generally has had a detrimental effect—by taking up time that might be better spent acquiring basic skills or doing homework, by encouraging a preference for quick solutions and entertaining portrayals that is inconsistent with the sometimes frustrating demands of schoolwork, and by creating tastes and enthusiasms that draw young people away from intellectually demanding subject matter. In contrast, very sophisticated statistical analyses of amount of viewing and achievement scores among large samples seemingly have indicated that television has no effect when other contributing factors are taken fully into account. In fact, the actual findings of the many dozens of empirical research studies that bear on the topic do not conform perfectly to either of these perspectives.

Viewing and Achievement

There is absolutely no question that children and teenagers who spend greater amounts of time with television perform less well on standardized tests of achievement. This inverse relationship—the greater the viewing, the lower the achievement—holds for the three basic skills (i.e., reading, writing, and mathematics) and for other subjects as well (e.g., science, social science, and history). The controversy centers on why this should be so.

This inverse relationship has been observed consistently and repeatedly in samples ranging from a few hundred to more than a half million subjects, which taken together can be said to be representative of American children and teenagers. There are several important qualifications, however. The relationship is most severe among young people from households that are higher in socioeconomic status (where parents score higher on education, income, or occupational standing) and among those from households where there are greater educational and cultural resources, such as books, magazines, newspapers, and encyclopedias. The relationship between household socioeconomic status and achievement scores is markedly stronger than the relationship between television viewing and academic achievement, with young people from households of higher status performing much better.

A good example is the data produced by the 1980 California Assessment Program, which was sponsored by the state department of education. Tests and questionnaires were administered to all pupils present on a given day in the sixth and twelfth grades (about 282,000 and 227,000 students, respectively). The pattern among these more than half million young people displayed the inverse relationship between television viewing and scores on standardized tests devised by the department for the three basic skills of reading, written expression, and mathematics. The inverse relationship was less pronounced among students in the sixth grade than among those in the twelfth grade. The inverse relationship was also less pronounced among students from households that had a lower socioeconomic status.

Another good example is the 1990 study by Steven L. Gortmaker (of the Harvard University School of Public Health) and his colleagues. These researchers uncovered a set of very-high-quality data that would allow them to explore relationships between television viewing and achievement scores. The data had been collected by the U.S. government's Health Examination Program from a sample of about 1,750 young people. A first set of data was gathered between July 1963 and December 1965, when the respondents were between the ages of six and eleven, and a second set of data was gathered from the same people between March 1966 and March 1970, when the respondents were between the ages of twelve and seventeen. The advantages of these data were (1) that the sample was very large and representative of the noninstitutionalized population of the United States for the ages covered, (2) that the design permitted the examination of changes in test scores over time, and (3) that the measures included three widely recognized standardized tests of intellectual aptitude as well as amount of television viewing and a variety of background variables. The three standardized tests were the Wechsler Intelligence Scale for Children (WISC), the Wide Range Achievement Test in Arithmetic (WRAT-A), and the Wide Range Achievement Test in Reading (WRAT-R). The fact that the data were collected in the 1960s and early 1970s was not a serious impediment to their use because, in the absence of very large changes in television or in the way in which young people use the medium, one would not expect large changes over time in the relationship between television use and achievement. Certainly, the data would reflect circumstances for young people of those ages at that time.

In this example, Gortmaker and his colleagues embarked on the conventional path of using survey data to investigate the likelihood of a causal link between two variables. The strength of survey data, unlike those produced by laboratory experiments, is that they represent real-world occurrences, and when the sample is representative of the population as a whole, any outcomes can be said with great confidence to apply to the population represented. The weakness for causal inference is that surveys describe what occurs rather than linking a subsequent outcome to a prior event or treatment, while such a link is provided by an experiment. The logic of making a case for a causal link from survey data is (1) a demonstration that there is a relationship between two variables and (2) the documentation that the relationship persists after as many other variables as possible are controlled statistically so that the possibility can be ruled out that the relationship is actually attributable to another variable. Then, by careful reasoning or statistical analysis, a case must be made that the ostensible cause preceded the effect in time, since the logic of causation insists that a supposed cause cannot occur subsequent to an alleged effect.

The first step of these researchers was to examine the data in the second measurement, when the young people were between the ages of twelve and

Surveys

The survey is a research method that seeks to describe a population by the use of questionnaires, tests, interviews, and other methods by which the attributes of those making up the population can be recorded. Most often, the population is made up of people, but anything that occurs in aggregates can be surveyed—businesses, housing, manufacturers, radio and television stations, and schools and universities. Usually, a sample is drawn to represent a much larger population because this makes the collection of information about the population much less expensive than if every member were examined. Best known are the opinion polls of presidential choices and other public preferences that receive widespread news coverage and often are sponsored by the media. However, thousands of surveys are conducted each year in the United States under the sponsorship of the federal government, political candidates, businesses, and other organizations, as well as the media.

In the case of academic achievement and television viewing, surveys often have been used to determine whether there is a relationship between the two. For example, both the 1980 California Assessment Program and the 1990 Harvard School of Public Health study by Steven L. Gortmaker and his colleagues matched data from questionnaires about television viewing and other attributes of students with their scores on tests of achievement or mental ability. Both studies produced reliable and valid data for reaching conclusions about the populations represented—California public school students (and particularly those in the sixth and twelfth grades, from whom the data were obtained, but one would expect the findings to be similar for other grades) and children and teenagers nationwide (because the sample of about 1,750 was statistically representative of U.S. children and teenagers).

The three principal criteria by which surveys are evaluated are (1) the sample, (2) the measures, and (3) the analysis. The sample is judged on representativeness and appropriateness for the purpose at hand. A random or probability sample gives every member of a population an equal chance of being included, and it is statistically representative of the population. This means that conclusions can be drawn about the larger population with precise margins of possible error (i.e., in only

one out of twenty times would the actual percentage for the population vary from the survey by more than plus or minus a stated number of percentage points). Samples that are not random can still be useful if they are large and varied enough for the comparison of subgroups based on gender, age, socioeconomic status, or other attributes, such as beliefs, attitudes, or test scores of any sort. Measures must be reliable, in the sense that outcomes must not vary unless the variable being measured in fact has changed, and they must be valid, which means that they must represent accurately the intended variable whether it be demographic, a belief, an attitude, or something measured by a test. The analysis will become more useful with a greater effort to relate one variable (such as amount of television viewing) to another (such as achievement in written expression) and to examine the interrelationships of more than two variables at a time.

Surveys have three major uses in research. The first is simply to report on the attributes of a population (e.g., how many respondents come from households whose head is an unskilled worker, or how many respondents approve of the way in which the president is handling the job). The second is to explore relationships between variables (e.g., whether achievement test scores vary with amount of television viewing). The third is to detect evidence of causation by examining whether a necessary condition, an association between two variables, can be explained by the influence of another variable or variables and whether the time-order requirement that a cause must precede a consequence has been met (e.g., whether nontelevision factors explain the inverse association between viewing and achievement, or whether greater television viewing precedes lower academic achievement).

Even when a sample is not unambiguously representative of a much larger population, surveys are useful because their findings may be suggestive of what would be the case for such a population (and it is for this reason that academic researchers legitimately often pull a sample from a convenient population, such as the student body of their university, the enrollment of a nearby school, or the voters in a particular city). Surveys are thus one of the fundamental means of scientific inquiry.

seventeen, to determine the relationship between television viewing and test scores. They found a substantial inverse correlation, with scores for all three tests declining in a linear fashion as the amount of viewing increased. The researchers next addressed whether television viewing should be considered a cause of the lower scores. They turned to the relationships between test scores at the time of the second measurement and the amount of television viewed at the time of the first measurement. This would establish whether the necessary condition was met for an inference that television had a causal role—a time order in which viewing preceded the outcome. Indeed, television viewing stoutly remained inversely associated with the three test scores. The researchers then controlled for the earlier scores on the same three tests, which meant they now would be examining only changes in scores since both the earlier viewing and testing. The inverse associations dropped to a fraction of their original values. Next, the researchers controlled for other variables, such as time of year, region and size of place of residence, race, and household socioeconomic status, all of which have well-documented long-standing relationships with average amounts of viewing. The inverse associations essentially vanished.

Gortmaker and his colleagues concluded that the data "indicate no significant causal relationship between the amount of television viewed and the mental aptitude and achievement test scores of adolescents." However, this conclusion is limited to the type of tests they employed. The three tests, the WISC, WRAT-A, and WRAT-R, are essentially measures of traits that remain quite stable over time, and, in fact, people who take the tests at one point in time usually score about the same when they take the tests at a later point in time. As a result, when the researchers controlled for the earlier test scores, they also reduced strongly the plausibility of any inverse association remaining. Thus, these data only unambiguously confirm that those who score lower on standardized tests of intellectual ability on the average will watch greater amounts of television.

Logically correct in every aspect of its execution, this study by Gortmaker and his colleagues thus does not definitively establish that there is no causal relationship between the amount of television viewing and academic achievement. First, it does not cover the possibility of the displacement of time that might be spent acquiring the three basic skills of reading, written expression, and mathematics, which would occur at earlier ages. Second, it does not employ measures reflective of and sensitive to behavior that might more realistically be negatively affected by greater viewing (e.g., school grades, scores on homework assignments, tests designed to measure progress over a semester or a year, or, outside the classroom, choice of reading matter).

Interpretation

Inverse associations between viewing and achievement scores would not necessarily represent the effects of television use, and there are several reasons for this. First, young people from households that are lower in socioeconomic status on the average watch greater amounts of television. Also, because of the strong positive relationship between socioeconomic status and scholastic performance, young people from households that are lower in socioeconomic status on average score lower on achievement tests. Second, mental ability has a strong positive relationship with achievement, but it is inversely related to television viewing, so that those who on average watch greater amounts of television also on average will score lower on achievement tests. Third, those who are under stress (e.g., with troubling personal, family, or social problems) on average watch greater amounts of television as a means of flight from their difficulties, and these same stress factors are likely to hamper scholastic performance. Similarly, those students who are not performing well in school might, in their frustration, turn to television as an escape.

Thus, there are very good reasons for concluding that those students who watch greater amounts of television have attributes or are experiencing circumstances that are likely to be associated with lower levels of achievement. The explanation suggested by these patterns is that greater television viewing is the outcome of influences that themselves contribute to or are associated with lower achievement, and greater viewing is not a cause of that lower achievement.

However, additional evidence indicates that this explanation is too simplistic. There are many documented ways in which television use may interfere with success at school. First, academic tasks, such as reading and problem solving, have been shown to be less effectively done in the company of television—reading comprehension is lower and right answers are fewer. Second, during the first through third grades when children are learning the basic skill of reading, some students will use time that could be spent mastering this skill for another, less frustrating activity—television viewing. The same applies to the two other basic skills, written expression and mathematics. Third, those students who watch a great deal of television are more likely to scoff at the value of books and are less likely to read outside of assignments, while those who do such reading are more likely to perform well scholastically. Fourth, those who habitually watch a great deal of television also are less likely to expend as much cognitive attention and thought when they do read and are more likely to prefer (to a greater degree) to read undemanding nonfiction about celebrities and light fiction-fare that resembles television programming. As George Comstock and Erica Scharrer conclude in their assessment of the evidence in *Television: What's On, Who's Watching, and What It Means* (1999), most of these outcomes occur among both children and teenagers.

Thus, the evidence points toward a number of adverse influences—interference with learning the basic skills, lowered quality of effort when reading or completing academic tasks in the company of television, and, among those who watch large amounts of television, desultory concentration while reading, low esteem for books, and the nurturing of tastes for reading matter that resembles television in substance and style. The most reasonable interpretation of the inverse relationships between amount of television viewing and scores on standardized achievement tests is one that incorporates both perspectives; they in part reflect greater attention to television by those who are less likely to do well academically for other reasons and in part reflect the detrimental effects of television viewing on academic achievement.

Effect Size and Who Is Affected

It is important to recognize that the inverse relationships are quite modest, amounting (on the average) to only about a 10 percent decline in scores between those who view the least amounts of television and those who view the most. The detrimental effects that television viewing has on achievement scores are thus quite small. The addi-

tional consequences for intellectual activity in general are probably more serious. These include the lowered esteem for books, the reduced concentration while reading, the preferences for undemanding entertainment, and lesser ability in the three basic skills—all of which, for some, may be a consequence of greater television use. Those people who are most likely to be affected adversely are (1) those who voluntarily allow television to displace time that might have been spent learning the three basic skills, (2) those for whom opportunities foregone would have been of greater academic value, and, of course, (3) those who watch television for a very large amount of time.

See also: CHILDREN'S ATTENTION TO TELEVISION; CHILDREN'S CREATIVITY AND TELEVISION USE; PARENTAL MEDIATION OF MEDIA EFFECTS; TELEVISION, EDUCATIONAL.

Bibliography

California Assessment Program. (1980). *Student Achievement in California Schools. 1979–80 Annual Report.* Sacramento: California State Department of Education.

Comstock, George, and Scharrer, Erica. (1999). *Television: What's On, Who's Watching, and What It Means.* San Diego, CA: Academic Press.

Gaddy, Gary D. (1986). "Television's Impact on High School Achievement." *Public Opinion Quarterly* 50(3):340–359.

Gortmaker, Steven L.; Salter, Charles A.; Walker, Deborah K.; and Dietz, William H., Jr. (1990). "The Impact of Television Viewing on Mental Aptitude and Achievement: A Longitudinal Study." *Public Opinion Quarterly* 54(4):594–604.

Koolstra, Cees M., and van der Voort, Tom H. A. (1996). "Longitudinal Effects of Television on Children's Leisure-Time Reading. A Test of Three Explanatory Models." *Human Communication Research* 23(1):4–35.

Koolstra, Cees M.; van der Voort, Tom H. A.; and van der Kamp, Leo J. Th. (1997). "Television's Impact on Children's Reading Comprehension and Decoding Skills: A 3-Year Panel Study." *Reading Research Quarterly* 32(2):128–152.

MacBeth, Tannis M., ed. (1996). *Tuning in to Young Viewers: Social Science Perspectives on Television.* Thousand Oaks, CA: Sage Publications.

Neuman, Susan B. (1988). "The Displacement Effect: Assessing the Relation Between Television Viewing and Reading Performance." *Reading Research Quarterly* 23(4):414–440.

Neuman, Susan B. (1991). *Literacy in the Television Age.* Norwood, NJ: Ablex.

Van Evra, Judith (1998). *Television and Child Development,* 2nd edition. Mahwah, NJ: Lawrence Erlbaum.

Williams, Tannis MacBeth, ed. (1986). *The Impact of Television: A Natural Experiment in Three Communities.* New York: Praeger.

GEORGE COMSTOCK

ACCESS TO INFORMATION

See: Reference Services and Information Access; Retrieval of Information

ADDICTION

See: Dependence on Media

ADOPTION OF TECHNOLOGY

See: Diffusion of Innovations and Communication; Technology, Adoption and Diffusion of

ADVERTISING, CHILDREN AND

See: Children and Advertising

ADVERTISING, SUBLIMINAL

The notion of subliminal advertising, that is, that advertisers can influence the desirability or even purchase of a brand through using hidden, undetectable advertising stimuli, is one of the myths of twentieth-century popular culture. Martha Rogers and Kirk Smith (1993) have noted that while professional advertisers scoff at the idea and virtually no members of the academic advertising community give it credence, the general public seems to assume that subliminal advertising is widely and effectively practiced. Apparently, the initial claims in the 1950s of subliminal advertising influence, the proponents of which produced not the slightest scientific documentation or evidence, nevertheless instilled the assumption that advertisers use subliminal messages to influence individuals without the individuals being aware of it. As far as the public is concerned, it is a story that is too good not to be true.

Absence of Evidence

Examples of research reviews that conclude against the effectiveness of subliminal advertising include those by Timothy E. Moore (1982), Joel Saegert (1987), and John R. Vokey and J. Don Read (1985). One academic review by Kathryn Theus (1994) affords subliminal advertising mild plausibility, without claiming evidence for behavioral influence. While there has been much psychological research pertaining to the possibility of subliminal perception and persuasion (see, for example, Dixon, 1981), the results remain controversial as to the existence of subliminal effects, especially regarding the ability of subliminal stimuli to influence behavior. In the realm of advertising, the few academic researchers who have claimed effectiveness for subliminal stimuli are vulnerable on methodological or logical grounds (e.g., Kilbourne, Painton, and Ridley, 1985). Moreover, after Sharon Beatty and Del Hawkins (1989) failed to replicate the widely cited early claim by Del Hawkins (1970) of subliminal effects in advertising-like conditions, the claim was retracted. In fact, no successful replication of any study offered as evidence in support of subliminal effects in an advertising-like setting has been reported. Finally, a meta-analysis by Charles Trappey (1996) of studies of subliminal effects in advertising-like contexts found that the amount of variability accounted for (i.e., differences between results for subliminal versus control conditions) is negligible.

Probably the earliest and most-cited claim of subliminal advertising influence was made by James Vicary, reported by *Advertising Age* in "'Persuaders' Get Deeply 'Hidden' Tool: Subliminal Projection" (1957, p. 127):

> Mr. Vicary, head of the motivation research company bearing his name, said the commercial messages are superimposed on a film as "very brief overlays of light." They are so rapid—up to 1/3,000 of a second—that they cannot be seen by the audience.

> Mr. Vicary reported that he recently tested the "invisible commercial" in a (Fort Lee) New Jersey movie theater. The tests ran for six weeks, during which time some 45,000 persons attended the theatre. Two advertising messages were projected—one urging the audience to eat popcorn, the other suggesting, "Drink Coca-Cola."

> According to Mr. Vicary, the "invisible commercial" increased popcorn sales by 57.5% and Coca-Cola sales by 18.1%.

Absence of details for such a provocative claim is, of course, highly unsatisfactory and, without further information, no social scientist or advertising practitioner would take Vicary's account seriously. For example, not only is there no mention of an unexposed control group, there is no reference to a baseline of historical data during periods where conditions matched those pertaining during the test (e.g., day of week, composition of audience, hour of day, weather conditions, season of year, and stocks of product on hand). Furthermore, the claimed demonstration has not been replicated.

Absence of a Systematic Framework

More substantively, what claim is Vicary, in fact, making? Is he claiming that people who never before, or rarely, had bought refreshments during a movie, were now doing so; that people who regularly purchase refreshments were doing so more often, or earlier; or that people who normally chose Pepsi or other soft drinks found themselves drinking Coke? The findings are so inadequately specified as to be uninterpretable from the viewpoint of marketing analysis.

Such weaknesses are not peculiar to the Vicary story among proponents of effects from subliminal advertising. If the phenomenon is to be taken seriously and developed, it should be discussed in the context of a view of how advertising is assumed to work. The absence of a plausible rationale for how subliminal advertising messages might have their effect leaves the phenomenon a conceptual orphan and leaves advertisers without guidance about how to implement the device for best return.

Perhaps the widespread (but unsupported) popular belief in subliminal advertising stems from public misunderstanding of the role of advertising. The ubiquitous presence of advertising reflects the need of advertisers to communicate the availability and special applications or features of their brands to prospective customers who are widely dispersed and with whom personal contact is impractical. In a cluttered environment, advertisers face a daunting task of registering their message with their targets. The essential advertising strategy is to rely on elements in the message finding a resonance in the target of the advertisement (i.e., those individuals in the population who experience the condition(s) for which the

brand has been tailored). According to Moore (1982), attenuating the signal to a subliminal level offers no discernible advantage, given such an overriding strategy.

More likely, popular readiness to believe in the possibility, and even use, of subliminal advertising has an existence that is independent of the above critique. Without pausing to consider whether such influence is feasible, people doubtless abhor the idea of being made to act in the absence of the subjective experience of choosing to act. The depth of such distaste may explain the persistence of the belief, regardless of the absence of evidence for, or conceptual development of, subliminal influence or its relevance to the nature of the task of an advertiser.

Absence of Public License

However irritating the daily barrage of advertisements may be to some, especially those who are not "in the market" for the advertised brands, conventional advertising is largely accepted as unavoidable. Subliminal advertising, on the other hand, is not so accepted. Undoubtedly, if examples of effective or even attempted subliminal advertisements were to come to light, an outraged public would again demand that such practices be outlawed, as happened when Vicary first broached the concept. According to Rogers and Christine Seiler (1994), in general, industry professionals do not claim to use subliminal advertising and, when asked, deny that they do. Cynics who maintain that advertisers will, of course, keep successful subliminal campaigns secret fail to ask at what level and where such a decision is taken. Given the complex nature of the advertising business, the layers of approval through which an advertising campaign must pass, and the number of players (e.g., clients, advertising agency personnel, and network executives), such cynics will be hard pressed to suggest how subliminal advertising could be authorized and implemented. The chain from inception of an advertising strategy to its implementation in the broadcast medium is a long on. Presumably, the decision to insert a subliminal message would have to be made at the highest level, yet implemented down the line. The advertiser would likely have to include its corporate lawyers in the decision and then instruct its advertising agency to perform the necessary technical operations. Thus, there would be many opportunities for discovery of what was afoot. The uproar over allegations of subliminal shenanigans in the 2000 presidential campaigns serves as ample evidence that the media are more than willing to expose any promotional attempts that are deemed to be newsworthy.

The Bottom Line

Businesses are in business to achieve return on investment and do not knowingly invest resources in an enterprise that fails to promise return. In this regard, subliminal advertising has no credible evidence that it will yield return; moreover, proponents provide no rationale to guide its effective use. Finally, even if successful return on investment were forthcoming from subliminal advertisements, advertisers would quickly be precluded from attempting to use such approaches because of public disapproval. The bottom line, however, is that subliminal advertising is a myth.

See also: ADVERTISING EFFECTS.

Bibliography

Beatty, Sharon E., and Hawkins, Del I. (1989). "Subliminal Stimulation: Some New Data and Interpretation." *Journal of Advertising* 18(3):4–8.

Dixon, Norman F. (1981). *Preconscious Processing.* London: Wiley.

Hawkins, Del I. (1970). "The Effects of Subliminal Stimulation of Drive Level and Brand Preference." *Journal of Marketing Research* 8:322–326.

Kilbourne, William; Painton, Scott; and Ridley, Danny. (1985). "The Effect of Sexual Embedding on Responses to Magazine Advertisements." *Journal of Advertising* 14(2):48–55.

Moore, Timothy E. (1982). "Subliminal Advertising: What You See Is What You Get." *Journal of Marketing* 46:38–47.

"'Persuaders' Get Deeply 'Hidden' Tool: Subliminal Projection." (1957). *Advertising Age* 28(37):127.

Rogers, Martha, and Seiler, Christine A. (1994). "The Answer Is No: A National Survey of Advertising Industry Practitioners and Their Clients about whether They Use Subliminal Advertising." *Journal of Advertising Research* 34(2):36–45.

Rogers, Martha, and Smith, Kirk H. (1993). "Public Perceptions of Subliminal Advertising: Why Practitioners Shouldn't Ignore this Issue." *Journal of Advertising Research* 33(2):10–18.

Saegert, Joel. (1987). "Why Marketing Should Quit Giving 'Subliminal Advertising' the Benefit of the Doubt." *Psychology and Marketing* 4(2):107–120.

Theus, Kathryn T. (1994). "Subliminal Advertising and the Psychology of Processing Unconscious Stimuli: A Review of Research." *Psychology and Marketing* 11(3):271–290.

Trappey, Charles A. (1996). "Meta-Analysis of Consumer Choice and Subliminal Advertising." *Psychology & Marketing* 13(5):517–530.

Vokey, John R., and Read, J. Don. (1985). "Subliminal Messages: Between the Devil and the Media." *American Psychologist* 40:1231–1239.

JOEL SAEGERT

■ ADVERTISING EFFECTS

Advertising is paid, nonpersonal communication that is designed to communicate in a creative manner, through the use of mass or information-directed media, the nature of products, services, and ideas. It is a form of persuasive communication that offers information about products, ideas, and services that serves the objectives determined by the advertiser. Advertising may influence consumers in many different ways, but the primary goal of advertising is to increase the probability that consumers exposed to an advertisement will behave or believe as the advertiser wishes. Thus, the ultimate objective of advertising is to sell things persuasively and creatively. Advertising is used by commercial firms trying to sell products and services; by politicians and political interest groups to sell ideas or persuade voters; by not-for-profit organizations to raise funds, solicit volunteers, or influence the actions of viewers; and by governments seeking to encourage or discourage particular activities, such a wearing seatbelts, participating in the census, or ceasing to smoke. The forms that advertising takes and the media in which advertisements appear are as varied as the advertisers themselves and the messages that they wish to deliver.

The word "advertise" originates from the Latin *advertere*, which means to turn toward or to take note of. Certainly, the visual and verbal commercial messages that are a part of advertising are intended to attract attention and produce some response by the viewer. Advertising is pervasive and virtually impossible to escape. Newspapers and magazines often have more advertisements than copy; radio and television provide entertainment but are also laden with advertisements; advertisements pop up on Internet sites; and the mail brings a variety of advertisements. Advertising also exists on billboards along the freeway, in subway and train stations, on benches at bus stops, and on the frames around car license plates. In shopping malls, there are prominent logos on designer clothes, moviegoers regularly view advertisements for local restaurants, hair salons, and so on, and live sporting and cultural events often include signage, logos, products, and related information about the event sponsors. The pervasiveness of advertising and its creative elements are designed to cause viewers to take note.

The Functions of Advertising

Although the primary objective of advertising is to persuade, it may achieve this objective in many different ways. An important function of advertising is the identification function, that is, to identify a product and differentiate it from others; this creates an awareness of the product and provides a basis for consumers to choose the advertised product over other products. Another function of advertising is to communicate information about the product, its attributes, and its location of sale; this is the information function. The third function of advertising is to induce consumers to try new products and to suggest reuse of the product as well as new uses; this is the persuasion function.

The identification function of advertising includes the ability of advertising to differentiate a product so that it has its own unique identity or personality. One famous example of this is found in the long-running advertising for Ivory Soap. In the late 1800s, a soap maker at Procter and Gamble left his machine running during his lunch period and returned to find a whipped soap that, when made into bars, floated. The company decided to capitalize on this mistake by advertising Ivory Soap with the phrase "It Floats." This characteristic of Ivory Soap served to uniquely identify it and differentiate it from other bars of soap.

The information function of advertising can also be found in advertising for Ivory Soap. For more than one hundred years, advertisements for Ivory Soap have focused on such product characteristics as purity of ingredients, child care, and soft skin. These characteristics, in turn, were often related to key benefits that could be obtained from using Ivory Soap. Thus, various advertisements emphasized "That Ivory Look," which focused on

A 1917 advertisement for Ivory Soap features the famous statements that "It Floats" and indicates how "pure" the product is. (Bettmann/Corbis)

the relationships between product characteristics and the benefits of obtaining a fresh and healthy appearance.

The third and most important function of advertising, persuasion, is also evident in the long-running Ivory Soap advertising campaigns. The advertiser, Procter and Gamble, has linked Ivory Soap with obtaining benefits that are important to customers: a fresh and healthy appearance for women, a mild, nonirritating method for bathing babies, and a novelty for children in the tub (since it floats). The benefits of the product suggest reasons to buy and use Ivory Soap and thus provide a basis for persuading consumers. Different benefits are important to different customers. Thus, to realize its full potential as a persuasive tool, advertising must often be tailored to emphasize those benefits that are important and meaningful for a particular type of customer or a particular use of the product.

Advertising has a very long history. It existed in ancient times in the form of signs that advertised wares in markets. In Europe and colonial America, criers were often employed by shopkeepers to shout a message throughout a town. Medicine shows, in which there was a combination of entertainment and an effort to sell a product, usually a patent medicine or elixir, presaged modern advertising by creating an entertainment context in which advertising was embedded. Advertising became especially important in the second half of the nineteenth century as retailers began to advertise products and prices that would bring customers to their stores. Advertising for patent medicines also played a prominent role in the development of advertising, and by the end of the nineteenth century, the firms that would become advertising agencies had already begun to form.

Advertising and Psychology

Although advertising has a very long history, serious study of advertising and its effects on consumers did not begin until early in the twentieth century. Psychologists began to recognize that advertising was an important form of communication and began to apply the theories and methods of psychology to its study. Individuals such as Harlow Gale began to conduct experiments designed to determine the power of individual advertisements to attract attention and persuade consumers to buy. Walter Dill Scott of Northwestern University wrote the book *The Theory of Advertising* (1903), which sought to build a theoretical understanding of advertising based on the principals of psychological science. Scott suggested that advertisers should develop certain fundamental principles on which to construct a "rational theory of advertising." The work of these psychologists was noted by such advertising professionals as Stanley Resor of the J. Walter Thompson Agency, who, in 1912, commissioned a study of the demographics and purchasing patterns of consumers to understand better both what motivated consumers to buy and how to persuade better those same consumers. Since this early work, psychologists and other social scientists have played an important role in both the study and practice of advertising.

The application of psychological theories to advertising provides an understanding of how consumers process advertising messages and make purchase decisions. Theories of attention, information processing, attitude formation, and decision making all have relevance to understanding how advertising affects consumers. Another important application of psychological principals is to develop an understanding of consumer needs so that products can be developed, designed, and communicated in a manner that reflects the relevant and important needs of consumers.

How Advertising Works

Advertising is a form of communication. Like all forms of communication, it has many different effects and these effects are often related to one another. The message in an advertisement, no matter how strong and persuasive, will have no effect if the consumer does not see the advertisement or pay attention to it. One useful framework for understanding these multiple effects and their interrelationships is called the hierarchy of effects model. The hierarchy of effects model identifies different stages in the communication process. Effective communication must begin by obtaining the attention of the consumer. Then, the consumer must process the information carried in the advertisement. Such processing of information may be followed by an evaluation of the information, the source of the information, and ultimately the desirability of any actions suggested by the communication. This evaluation process may, in turn, give rise to the formation of attitudes, the development of intentions for future action, and, eventually, an action. Different characteristics of an advertisement have effects at different points in this hierarchy.

Getting Attention

In the context of advertising, the first hurdle for an advertiser is to obtain the attention of the consumer. This involves two important actions. First, it is important for the advertiser to know where a communication should be place to increase the odds of reaching a particular type of consumer; this is the media decision. Careful analysis of the consumer use of various media (e.g., what television shows they watch, what route they take to work, and what magazines they read) allows the advertisers to identify those media to which target consumers are most likely to be exposed. Placing an advertisement in a place where relevant consumers are unlikely to see it assures that the advertising will be ineffective.

However, just because a consumer happens to view a television show or read a magazine in which an advertisement is placed does not a guarantee that the consumer will see the advertisement. The consumer may have left the room when the television commercial aired or may not have read the particular part of the magazine in which the advertisement appeared. Advertisers solve this problem by repeating advertising in the same and in different media in order to increase the probability that a given consumer will actually be exposed to the advertising. Thus, a key task for the advertiser is to identify those media to which relevant consumers regularly attend and develop a schedule of repetition for the advertisement that maximizes the number of consumers who will be exposed to the advertising message. This is typically the responsibility of the media department in an advertising agency.

Exposure to an advertisement still does not mean that a consumer will attend to it. A consumer may simply turn the page of a magazine, look away from the television, or click on a banner advertisement on the Internet to make it go away without ever paying attention to the advertisement. Thus, obtaining the attention of consumers who are, in fact, exposed to an advertisement is a significant challenge for advertisers. Various characteristics of advertisements have been found to increase the likelihood that consumers will attend to an advertisement. Advertisements that include relevant information for the consumer, such as a product benefit that is important to the consumer, are especially likely to attract attention. Information that is new to the consumer is also likely to obtain the attention of the consumer. Various creative devices such as the use of humor, a well-known celebrity, or an especially entertaining presentation also tend to attract attention. The latter devices must be used carefully; if they are not well integrated with the primary message of the advertiser, the consumer may attend to the advertisement, but only focus on the creative device (the humor, the identity of the celebrity) rather the intended message of the advertiser. Advertisers often refer to characteristics of advertisements that gain attention but distract the viewer from the primary message as "creative clutter."

An especially challenging dimension of advertising revolves around balancing the repetition of an advertisement, which is intended to increase the probability of a consumer being exposed to it, with the likelihood the consumer will attend to the advertisement when exposed. Consumers are less likely to attend to advertisements they have already seen, and the more often an individual consumer has seen an advertisement previously the less likely they are to pay attention to it when exposed again. This phenomenon is referred to as "advertising wearout." Wearout can be a particular problem when advertising in markets where the likelihood of advertising exposure varies considerably across consumers. The number of repetitions of the advertisement needed to reach some consumers may be so great that the advertisement wears out among other consumers who are more readily exposed to the advertisement. To combat such wearout, advertisers will often use multiple advertisements that vary in terms of execution or presentation but carry similar messages. Such variation tends to reduce advertising wearout by providing something new to the consumer that serves as the basis for attracting attention.

Processing Information

Consumers may attend to advertisements for a variety of reasons. Attention alone is not sufficient to make the advertising successful. Advertisements that are interesting, entertaining, and even irritating can attract attention; however, such advertisements may not result in the consumer attending to or understanding the intended message of the advertiser. Assuring that consumers attend to and understand the intended message rather than peripheral characteristics (such as a joke or song) requires careful crafting of the advertising message. Advertising research has demonstrated that the message must be clear and meaningful to the consumer; if the consumer does not comprehend the message, it will not have the desired effect. Thus, it is important when creating the advertisement to understand how consumers think about products and product benefits and to use language that the consumer will understand. It is also important that the product and the product message be the focal point of the advertisement. Most of the time or space in the advertisement should be devoted to the product and the product message should be well integrated within the advertisement. Advertising that consists primarily of creative clutter and does not focus on the product is unlikely to be effective.

Spokespeople, such as supermodel Elizabeth Hurley for Estee Lauder, can be effective endorsers of products and can increase the likelihood that consumers will follow through by purchasing.
(Mitchell Gerber/Corbis)

variability exists among consumers with respect to their willingness to process information. Such an understanding not only indicates how much information to put in an advertisement, it also suggests which media may be most appropriate for delivering the message. Complex messages are generally better delivered in print advertising, while simple messages can generally be delivered on television or radio.

Information Evaluation

After a consumer has processed information, there is a need to evaluate it. The consumers will need to determine how believable the information is and how relevant it is to their individual situation in life and to their behavior as consumers. This evaluation phase poses significant problems for advertisers. Most consumers tend to discount the information in advertising because they understand that the purpose of the advertising is to persuade. Making an advertising message believable is not easy; though often it is sufficient to make the consumer curious enough to try the product. Such curiosity is often referred to as interested disbelief. Advertisers use a variety of devices to increase the believability of their advertising: celebrities or experts who are the spokespersons for the product, user testimonials, product demonstrations, research results, and endorsements.

Attitude Formation

In some cases, the objective of the advertiser is immediate action by the consumer; this is typical of direct-response advertising where the goal is to have the consumer do something immediately (buy a product, make a pledge, and so on). In most cases, however, there is a lag between advertising exposure and any action on the part of the consumer. In such cases, an important communication goal of an advertiser is to create a positive attitude toward their product. Attitudes are predispositions or tendencies to behave or react in a consistent way over time. There is an affect, or feeling, dimension associated with attitudes, and there are generally various beliefs that provide justification for the feeling and predisposition. The goal of advertising is to have a positive impact on attitudes; these attitudes, in turn, influence future behavior. When the consumer next goes to the store to buy a particular type of product, these attitudes influence the choice of the product.

Longer advertisements tend to facilitate better information processing, but the benefit of a longer advertisement may not always be sufficiently large enough to justify the additional costs of a longer advertisement.

An especially important issue in the creation of advertising is related to understanding how much information consumers want about a given product. For some products, consumers may want a great deal of information and may wish to exert a great deal of effort in processing the information. In many cases, however, especially for products of relatively low cost, consumers do not want very much information and are unwilling to process more than a modest amount of product information. In fact, consumers may differ with respect to the amount of information processing they are willing to do even for the same product. Thus, the advertiser must understand how much information individual consumers desire and how much

In some cases, the goal of advertising may be to create negative attitudes. For example, in various antidrug and antismoking public-service announcements, the objective of the communication is to reduce the likelihood that the viewer will use drugs or smoke.

Attitudes and attitude formation are among the most widely researched phenomenon in communication research. Various theories have been offered to explain how attitudes are formed and how they may be reinforced or modified. Advertising plays a role in attitude formation, but it is important to recognize that the advertised product itself is the most important determinant of attitude in the long term. A bad experience with a product will create a negative attitude that no advertising is likely to overcome. On the other hand, advertising can play an especially important role in inducing consumers to try a product for the first time, and if the product is satisfactory, a positive attitude will result. In addition, advertising can reinforce positive attitudes by reminding consumers of product benefits, desirable product characteristics, and positive product experiences.

Intentions and Behavior

Ultimately, the success of advertising rests on whether it influences behavior. Product advertisers want consumers to buy their product; political advertisers want voters to vote for their candidate; and sponsors of public-service announcements related to the harmful effects of smoking want the incidence of smoking to decline. While such effects are of primary interest for understanding the influence of advertising, advertising is only one of many factors that influence such behaviors. A consumer might want to buy an advertiser's product, but may not find it in the store, or another less-desirable product is so much less-expensive that the consumer chooses it instead. It is possible, in some cases, to identify the direct effects of advertising on behavior, but in most cases, there are simply too many other factors that can influence behavior to isolate the effects of advertising. It is for this reason that most advertising research focuses on other effects in the hierarchy of effects. When measuring the direct effect of advertising on behavior is of interest, it is necessary to design carefully controlled experiments to control for all factors other than advertising.

What Advertising Does Not Do

Some writers have argued that advertising can create needs and stimulate unconscious and deep-seated motives. This view has led some critics of advertising to argue that advertising is a persuasive tool with the dangerous potential to create consumer needs. John Kenneth Galbraith, in *The New Industrial State* (1985), suggests that the central function of advertising is to create desires—to bring into being wants that previously did not exist. It is certainly true that people frequently want things when they become aware that they exist and advertising does contribute to such awareness. It is also the case that people sometimes do not realize that they have a need until they become aware of a solution that meets this need. Advertising is not able to create needs that did not already exist, however. Indeed, advertising is a relatively weak persuasive tool. The evidence of this weakness is abundant and unambiguous. First, the failure rate for new products is very high (approximately 90%). This fact is not consistent with the claim that advertisers can actually mold people's needs. If advertisers could create needs, they should then be able to compel consumers to buy their products. Second, experts argue that advertising works best when it is working with, rather than counter to, the existing interests of the consumers. For example, for many years, low-calorie beer had not been able to find a consumer need to address and the product had limited sales. When the Miller Brewing Company introduced its Lite brand of beer and positioned it as the beer with fewer calories (which "makes it less filling"), it became an instant success.

Advertising has the power to create awareness, inform, and persuade. It is a communication tool of enormous complexity, however. Much advertising does not have its intended effect. The reasons for this failure lie in the variety and complexity of the effects of advertising. Like all successful communication, effective advertising is guided by a thorough understanding of its intended audience and how that audience will receive the intended message.

See also: ADVERTISING, SUBLIMINAL; CHILDREN AND ADVERTISING; ELECTION CAMPAIGNS AND MEDIA EFFECTS; INTERNET AND THE WORLD WIDE WEB; PUBLIC HEALTH CAMPAIGNS; PUBLIC RELATIONS; PUBLIC RELATIONS, CAREERS IN; PUBLIC SERVICE MEDIA.

Bibliography

Bly, Robert W. (1998). *Advertising Manager's Handbook.* Englewood Cliffs, NJ: Prentice-Hall.

Galbraith, John Kenneth. (1985). *The New Industrial State*, 4th edition. Boston: Houghton Mifflin.

Schumann, David W., and Thorson, Esther. (1999). *Advertising and the World Wide Web.* Hillsdale, NJ: Lawrence Erlbaum.

Scott, Walter Dill. (1903). *The Theory of Advertising.* Boston: Small, Maynard.

Stewart, David W. (1994). "How Advertising Works in Mature Markets." *American Demographics* 16(Sept.):40–47.

Stewart, David W., and Furse, David H. (1986). *Effective Television Advertising: A Study of 10,000 Commercials.* Lexington, MA: Lexington Books.

Tellis, Gerard. (1998). *Advertising and Sales Promotion Strategy.* New York: Addison-Wesley.

Wells, William D.; Burnett, John; and Moriarty, Sandra. (1998). *Advertising: Principles & Practice,* 4th edition. Englewood Cliffs, NJ: Prentice-Hall.

DAVID W. STEWART
SARAH E. STEWART

■ ALCOHOL ABUSE AND COLLEGE STUDENTS

One of the ways in which communication functions is in the creation and maintenance of the ways in which using and abusing substances, especially alcohol, are talked about and treated. When, for example, society considered the use of alcohol to be a social sin, its use was banned. "Prohibition" is the name given to the era during which it was illegal in the United States to buy, sell, and drink alcohol. After prohibition was repealed, alcohol once again became a legal substance, while other related drugs, such as marijuana, continued to be thought of as harmful. Words for the use of these substances and the meanings that are attributed to their use arise out of communication and are an area of study in health communication. Linda Lederman (1993) calls the ways of using and abusing alcohol on the college campus the "culture of college drinking." In the culture of college drinking, drinking to excess is considered to be an inherent part of the college years. Because of the attention that drinking on the campus receives, it is an important example of a broader subject: communication, health, and substance abuse.

While dangerous drinking concerns college health educators, administrators, and even some students and parents, most students (and their parents) consider drinking itself to be an integral part of college life. Because their perception is relative to those around them, students who drink dangerously often do not recognize that their drinking is problematic. Many of them think that no matter how much they drink, there are others who drink more.

This perception of a cultural norm of excessive drinking during the college years is created and/or reinforced on a daily basis by the media (including college newspapers that carry "All You Can Drink" and "Happy Hour" advertisements), major advertising that targets students (e.g., beer companies with Spring Break Drinking Campaigns), and interpersonal experience (e.g., sharing war stories about the "night before"; attending fraternity parties and other social events that encourage alcohol abuse). All of this occurs despite the fact that data consistently indicate that the percentage of students who actually drink excessively is far below the shared misperception that "everybody does."

Concern about dangerous drinking has led to a variety of studies and interventions on college campuses. Using focus group interviews, many researchers have explored the role that alcohol plays in the lives of students. While students articulate negative consequences (e.g., hangovers, vomiting, being taken advantage of physically and/or sexually), they report ignoring these factors because they see drinking as a rite of passage into adulthood (i.e., limits testing).

These qualitative analyses have also determined how alcohol consumption by undergraduates is used as a means of fulfilling social interaction needs. One focus group study conducted by Lederman (1993) centered on high- and low-risk female respondents. The study demonstrated how self-destructive alcohol consumption has been negotiated as an acceptable risk for the sake of making friends and creating social circles among undergraduates who are new to vast, overwhelming, and alienating environments such as very large college campuses. Incoming students use the inhibition-lowering effect of alcohol, along with its aid to perceived interpersonal competency, to make contact with new friends, colleagues, and sexual partners.

If simply getting drunk helps students to achieve their social and interpersonal goals, then

Spring Break activities often can serve to increase the likelihood of a college student abusing alcohol, as is the case in this particular situation, where a student is encouraged to drink more alcohol before participating in a game while on vacation in Daytona Beach, Florida. (Patrick Ward/Corbis)

students can be expected to keep getting drunk. Even if severe intoxication causes illness, the downside of drinking can be endured as long as it is not worse than the rewards that are gained. However, it has been shown that alcohol is no longer abused when students gain the pleasure of social contact and friendship without having to drink (Cohen and Lederman, 1998).

One pervasive and powerful environmental factor that is influential in creating and maintaining this cultural image of drinking as a fundamental part of college life is the social interactions of students. The myth that dangerous drinking is pervasive is perpetuated by students who share war stories about the "night before," faculty members who make jokes in class about students' partying, and social events that encourage alcohol abuse. If drinking and talking about getting drunk help students to achieve their social and interpersonal goals, then the data suggest that students can be expected to continue these behaviors. The

effect of these social situations is addressed by the socially situated experiential learning model. The model identifies three conceptual bases that can be used to understand the socially situated nature of college drinking: communication theory, social norms theory, and experiential learning theory.

Communication theory provides a basis on which to examine social behaviors on the college campus because communication is the process through which social institutions and the norms and customs embedded in those institutions are created and maintained. Using this understanding of communication to approach drinking-related behavior allows researchers to "enter socially situated scenes" in which the attitudes, beliefs, and behaviors of individuals can be examined both in relation to each other and as the product of the interpretive processes of the individual within the sociocultural community.

The basis of social norms theory is the assertion that students measure themselves against others in assessing the appropriateness or acceptability of their own behaviors. Often, these measures are based on false understandings of what is normative or misperceptions of the behavior of others. The notion that everyone drinks excessively in college, for example, is a misperception. Social norms theory is employed in prevention campaigns by (1) collecting data on the extent of misperceptions, (2) successfully communicating this information to a targeted campus population, (3) assisting them to understand the discrepancies that exist between fact and myth, and (4) making salient new behaviors and norms that are associated with the facts instead of the myths.

Experiential learning theory argues that learning is cyclical. A person has an experience, reflects on that experience, draws some conclusions about the lessons that can be learned from that experience, and then uses those lessons as part of his or her basis for reactions to future experiences. In terms of college drinking, for example, many students who engage in risky sexual behavior while drinking do not perceive themselves to be outcasts in their social circles because in their everyday "experience," their behaviors are the norm as they perceive them.

See also: ALCOHOL IN THE MEDIA; HEALTH COMMUNICATION; INTERPERSONAL COMMUNICATION; SOCIAL CHANGE AND THE MEDIA; SOCIAL COGNITIVE THEORY AND MEDIA EFFECTS; SOCIAL GOALS AND THE MEDIA; SOCIETY AND THE MEDIA.

Bibliography

Burns, David; Ballou, Janice; and Lederman, Linda C. (1991). "Perceptions of Alcohol Use and Policy on the College Campus: Preventing Alcohol/Drug Abuse at Rutgers University." U.S. Department of Education Fund for the Improvement of Post-Secondary Education (FIPSE) conference paper.

Burns, David, and Goodstadt, Michael. (1989). "Alcohol Use on the Rutgers University Campus: A Study of Various Communities." U.S. Department of Education Fund for the Improvement of Post Secondary Education (FIPSE) conference paper.

Cohen, Debra, and Lederman, Linda C. (1998). "Navigating the Freedom of College Life: Students Talk about Alcohol, Gender, and Sex." In Women and AIDS: Negotiating Safer Practices, Care, and Representation, eds. Nancy L. Roth and Linda K. Fuller. New York: Haworth Press.

Haines, Michael P. (1996). A Social Norms Approach to Preventing Binge Drinking at Colleges and Universi-

ties. Newton, MA: The Higher Education Center for Alcohol and Other Drug Prevention.

Jeffrey, Linda R., and Negro, Pamela. (1996). Contemporary Trends in Alcohol and Other Drug Use by College Students in New Jersey. Glassboro, NJ: New Jersey Higher Education Consortium on Alcohol and other Drug Prevention and Education.

Kolb, David. (1984). Experiential Learning: Experience as a Source of Learning. Englewood Cliffs, NJ: Prentice-Hall.

Lederman, Linda C. (1993). "Friends Don't Let Friends Beer Goggle: A Case Study in the Use and Abuse of Alcohol and Communication among College Students." In Case Studies in Health Communication, ed. Eileen Berlin Ray. Hillsdale, NJ: Lawrence Erlbaum.

Lederman, Linda C., and Stewart, Lea P. (1998). "Addressing the Culture of College Drinking through Correcting Misperceptions: Using Experiential Learning Theory and Gilligan's Work." Center for Communication and Health Issues Research Series: Report 4. New Brunswick, NJ: Rutgers University Center for Communication and Health Issues.

Lederman, Linda C., and Stewart, Lea P. (1999). "The Socially Situated Experiential Learning Model." Center for Communication and Health Issues Research Series: Report 13. New Brunswick, NJ: Rutgers University Center for Communication and Health Issues.

Lederman, Linda C.; Stewart, Lea P.; Kennedy, Lynn; Powell, Richard; Laitman, Lisa; Goodhart, Fern; and Barr, Sherry. (1998). "Self Report of Student Perceptions: An Alcohol Awareness Measure." Center for Communication and Health Issues Research Series: Report 2. New Brunswick, NJ: Rutgers University Center for Communication and Health Issues.

Perkins, Wesley, and Wechsler, Henry. (1996). "Variation in Perceived College Drinking Norms and Its Impact on Alcohol Abuse: A Nationwide Study." Journal of Drug Issues 26(4):961–974.

LINDA COSTIGAN LEDERMAN

ALCOHOL IN THE MEDIA

The presentation of alcohol and other drugs in the media has received both scrutiny and criticism. As a result, researchers have started to explore the types of portrayals of, in particular, alcohol use in television programs and advertisements and the influence of those portrayals on adolescents.

Television Depiction of Alcohol Use

Multiple studies indicate an abundance of alcohol use in entertainment programming. In their review of prime-time television content from

1976 to 1982, Warren Breed and his colleagues (1984) found that in the television world, alcohol was the most consumed beverage, followed by coffee, tea, soft drinks, and then water. In reality, the pattern of consumption is the opposite. Alan Mathios and his associates (1998) looked at almost three hundred prime-time programs during the 1994–1995 television season. They found that alcohol use was portrayed on television more frequently than the use of any other food or drink. Even music television portrays a great deal of alcohol use. Robert DuRant and his colleagues (1997) reviewed more than five hundred videos shown on VH1 (Video Hits 1), MTV (Music Television), BET (Black Entertainment Television), and CMT (Country Music Television). More than 25 percent of the videos included alcohol use.

Characters who drink on television tend to be well liked, professional, and wealthy. Mathios and his colleagues (1998) reported that characters in the high socioeconomic category were much more likely to drink than were those in the low socioeconomic category. Breed and his colleagues (1984) reported that characters who drank on television were mostly professionals, including doctors, lawyers, executives, and detectives.

Lawrence Wallack and his associates (1990) found that very few young people depicted on television drink; in their study of fictional prime-time network programming in 1986, less than 5 percent of the characters under twenty-one years of age were involved with alcohol use. The most common age range for characters preparing or ingesting alcohol was thirty to thirty-nine years of age. Mathios's study (1998) reported a slightly higher use of alcohol by teenage characters on television; almost 10 percent of the alcohol incidents in their sample occurred among teenage characters.

Depictions of alcohol use on television are rarely negative. Wallack and his colleagues (1990) categorized portrayals of alcohol use as attractive, unattractive, or neutral. Under this categorization, 60 percent of all alcohol-related activities were neutral and more than 25 percent were considered attractive. When adolescent characters were compared to adult characters, however, the incidents of alcohol use that involved the younger characters were more likely to be coded as unattractive than were the incidents involving the older characters. Mathios and his associates (1998) rated the personality of the characters in the programs they reviewed. Among adult characters, those who used alcohol were portrayed as being more positive than those who did not. On the other hand, among adolescent characters, those who drank tended to receive more negative ratings than those who did not.

Advertisements and Alcohol

Correlational research indicates that media exposure is associated with the perceptions, attitudes, and behaviors of young people. A questionnaire study conducted by Larry Tucker (1985) and involving high school males indicated that viewers who watched a great deal to television had significantly higher levels of alcohol use per month than did viewers who watched comparatively less television. Gary Connolly and his colleagues (1994), who were also interested in the link between television viewing and alcohol consumption, conducted a study that followed participants over several years. Respondents were queried about their television viewing habits at ages thirteen and fifteen and their alcohol consumption at age eighteen. The researchers found that the more television the female subjects watched overall at ages thirteen and fifteen, the greater were their reported beer, wine, and liquor consumption at age eighteen. For males, there was no significant relationship between viewing at ages thirteen and fifteen and consumption at age eighteen.

An area more widely researched than entertainment portrayals of alcohol use is alcohol advertising. Joel Grube (1993) points out that the major themes associated with advertisements for alcohol are sociability, elegance, physical attractiveness, success, relaxation, romance, and adventure. Donald Strickland and his associates (1982) reviewed alcohol advertisements from almost five hundred magazines published between 1978 and 1982 in search of themes that dominated these advertisements. While most advertisements focused on the products, some included human models. They found that the models in the advertisements were predominantly between twenty-five and thirty-four years of age and that the activities depicted in the advertisements included primarily drinking by itself; however, drinking after work and drinking related to a sports event were also depicted.

Patricia Madden and Grube (1994) looked at both the themes and the frequency of advertising beer on television. They found more than two alcohol commercials per hour during major professional sports programs, about one per hour during college sports and one every four hours during prime-time fictional entertainment. One of the concerns emerging from this study was related to the content of the advertisements. Cars and other vehicles were present in more than 15 percent of the advertisements and water activities were present in 25 percent of the advertisements. Although alcohol use while operating vehicles is not advocated, it is interesting that the advertisements include these and other activities that might be hazardous for those who have been drinking.

There have been several studies concerning the effects of alcohol advertisements on young people. Lisa Lieberman and Mario Orlandi (1987) asked almost three thousand New York City sixth-grade students to recall and describe alcohol advertisements that they had seen on television. Eighty-five percent of the children could recall at least one advertisement. When asked what types of people were in the advertisements, the most frequently cited types were sports figures, celebrities, models and actors, and wealthy people. Almost 90 percent of the participants said the people in the advertisements were young adults.

Grube and Wallack (1994) interviewed fifth- and sixth-grade students about their awareness of alcohol advertising and their perceptions, attitudes, and behavioral intentions regarding alcohol consumption. The researchers reported that the more aware students were of alcohol advertisements, the more positive their beliefs were about drinking. More positive beliefs about alcohol were associated with indications of likelihood to drink as an adult.

Because much of the alcohol advertising occurs during sporting events, some researchers have focused their attention on exposure to these events and attitudes toward alcohol. Paul Bloom and his colleagues (1997) surveyed individuals who were between thirteen and eighteen years of age. Those individuals who reported watching a large amount of professional football and professional baseball on television had greater intentions to drink than those who reported watching a smaller amount of these types of programs.

Conclusion

The research on the portrayal of alcohol use in entertainment programming and in commercial advertisements is fairly consistent. The image of

alcohol use presented by the media is one that shows it as a relatively problem-free activity. This is enhanced by the fact that the individuals shown using alcohol are celebrities, wealthy, professional, successful, and attractive. The survey research, which provides correlational data, thus far points to an association between exposure to these portrayals and positive perceptions, attitudes, and behaviors regarding alcohol. Further investigations into the effects of portrayals should include experimental as well as survey research.

See also: TOBACCO AND MEDIA EFFECTS.

Bibliography

Aitken, P. P.; Eadie, D. R.; Leathar, D. S.; McNeill, R. E. J.; and Scott, A.C. (1988). "Television Advertisements for Alcoholic Drinks Do Reinforce Under-Age Drinking." *British Journal of Addiction* 83:1399–1419.

Bloom, Paul N.; Hogan, John E.; and Blazing, Jennifer. (1997). "Sports Promotion and Teen Smoking and Drinking: An Exploratory Study." *American Journal of Health Behavior* 21:100–109.

Breed, Warren; De Foe, James R.; and Wallack, Lawrence. (1984). "Drinking in the Mass Media: A Nine-Year Project." *Journal of Drug Issues* Fall:655–663.

Connolly, Gary M.; Casswell, Sally; Zhang, Jia-Fang; and Silva, Phil A. (1994). "Alcohol in the Mass Media and Drinking by Adolescents: A Longitudinal Study." *Addiction* 89:1255–1263.

De Foe, James R.; Breed, Warren; and Breed, Lawrence A. (1983). "Drinking in Television: A Five-Year Study." *Journal of Drug Education* 13:25–37.

DuRant, Robert H.; Rome, Ellen S.; Rich, Michael; Allred, Elizabeth; Emans, S. Jean; and Woods, Elizabeth R. (1997). "Tobacco and Alcohol Use Behaviors Portrayed in Music Videos: A Content Analysis." *American Journal of Public Health* 87:1131–1135.

Fernandez-Collado, Carlos; Greenberg, Bradley; Korzenny, Felipe; and Atkin, Charles. (1978). "Sexual Intimacy and Drug Use in TV Series." *Journal of Communication* 28:30–37.

Grube, Joel W. (1993). "Alcohol Portrayals and Alcohol Advertising on Television." *Alcohol Health and Research World* 17:61–66.

Grube, Joel W., and Wallack, Lawrence. (1994). "Television Beer Advertising and Drinking Knowledge, Beliefs, and Intentions Among School Children." *American Journal of Public Health* 84(2):254–259.

Lieberman, Lisa R., and Orlandi, Mario A. (1987). "Alcohol Advertising and Adolescent Drinking." *Alcohol Health and Research World* 3:30–43.

MacDonald, Patrick T. (1983). "The 'Dope' on Soaps." *Journal of Drug Education* 13:359–369.

Madden, Patricia A., and Grube, Joel W. (1994). "The Frequency and Nature of Alcohol and Tobacco Advertising in Televised Sports, 1990 through 1992." *Public Health Briefs* 84(2):297–299.

Mathios, Alan; Avery, Rosemary; Bisogni, Carol; and Shanahan, James. (1998). "Alcohol Portrayal on Prime Time Television: Manifest and Latent Messages." *Journal of Studies on Alcohol* 59:305–310.

Slater, Michael D.; Rouner, Donna; Murphy, Kevin; Beauvais, Frederick; Van Leuven, James; and Domenech-Rodriguez, Melanie M. (1996). "Male Adolescents' Reactions to TV Beer Advertisements: The Effects of Sports Content and Programming Context." *Journal of Studies on Alcohol* 57:425–433.

Strickland, Donald E.; Finn, T. Andrew; and Lambert, M. Dow. (1982). "A Content Analysis of Beverage Alcohol Advertising." *Journal of Studies on Alcohol* 43:655–682.

Tucker, Larry A. (1985). "Television's Role Regarding Alcohol Use among Teenagers." *Adolescence* 20:593–598.

Wallack, Lawrence; Breed, Warren; and DeFoe, James R. (1985). "Alcohol and Soap Operas: Drinking in the Light of Day." *Journal of Drug Education* 15:365–379.

Wallack, Lawrence; Grube, Joel W.; Madden, Patricia A.; and Breed, Warren. (1990). "Portrayals of Alcohol on Prime-Time Television." *Journal of Studies on Alcohol* 51:428–437.

LINDA C. GODBOLD

■ ALPHABETS AND WRITING

This entry, in fact, this entire encyclopedia, would be a very different object if there were no alphabet. Although there are nonalphabetic writing systems and there are ways to communicate other than through writing, an alphabet is one of the most powerful tools for the easy expression of a diverse range of ideas.

An alphabet facilitates a print culture, one in which permanent records can be maintained and people can communicate with others across time and space. Even as people surf the World Wide Web for information in diverse media, they visit websites that are filled with displays of alphabetic characters. The source codes for these sites are even written in programming languages that rely on alphabets.

What exactly is an alphabet? How did the first ones arise? What was it like to communicate prior to the invention of the alphabet? What are the differences between alphabets and other writing systems? How does the use of an alphabet relate to a print culture? Questions such as these have been explored for more than two thousand years and have led to heated debates, arduous archaeological expeditions, and massive treatises on the development of writing.

Development of the Alphabet

Although the details are the subject of active research and scholarly debate, there is a rough consensus on the general development of writing and the series of stages that were involved. However, many scholars disagree about the precise dates or sources of the changes that moved writing from one stage to the next.

In the earliest stage, any culture possesses a system of meaning; in fact, that is usually a key component of any definition of "culture." People communicate that meaning through verbal means, gestures, and physical markings. Cultures throughout the world have placed these markings in the sand, on rocks and trees, and on individuals' bodies. A palm print on the wall of a cave is not usually considered to be "writing," but it may

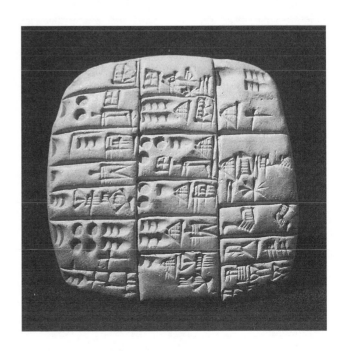

A Sumerian clay tablet from Ancient Mesopotamia features incised cuneiform characters that provide a tally of sheep and goats. (Gianni Dagli Orti/Corbis)

well qualify as such, given that it is an enduring representation of meaning.

Over time, these symbol systems evolve and begin to serve more complex functions in society. Denise Schmandt-Besserat (1989) has made the case that the use of tokens for accounting was a major precursor of writing in Sumeria. She presents evidence that simple tokens (e.g., spheres, disks, cones) indicating quantities of stored grain appeared with the development of agriculture in 8000–7500 B.C.E. More complex tokens representing manufactured goods appeared with elaborate markings at the time when cities and organized states developed, around 3500–3000 B.C.E. The earliest full-fledged writing systems then grew out of methods for representing these tokens in a linear form on tablets.

The early writing systems of Sumeria, Egypt, and neighboring countries were complex and difficult to learn. There were hundreds of distinct signs, or pictographs, to learn, each with multiple meanings. As a result, only a few scribes could read and write; literacy was essentially a monopoly of the rich and powerful. One might compare these systems to the Chinese writing, which originally developed around 1500 B.C.E. and now has thousands of characters.

It was once thought that the transition to alphabetic writing, to the forerunner of Greek, Hebrew, Arabic, and Latin alphabets that are in use today, occurred around 1700 B.C.E. in the Levant region, or what is now Syria, Lebanon, and Israel. However, in 1993 and 1994, John Darnell and Deborah Darnell made a discovery that changed previous thoughts. They were exploring in southern Egypt at a place called Wadi el-Hol (Gulch of Terror) when they discovered limestone inscriptions that appeared to be alphabetic. Returning in the summer of 1999, with early writing experts, they were able to show that the earliest known alphabet was probably invented around 1900–1800 B.C.E. by Semitic-speaking slaves who were working in Egypt. By reducing the set of symbols to a manageable thirty and by using these to represent consonants that appeared in the spoken language, the slaves had developed a system that anyone could learn relatively easily. This expanded greatly the possibilities for accumulating knowledge, manipulating it, preserving it, transmitting it to succeeding generations, and sharing it with others.

The Semitic alphabet then spread in various forms. Of most significance was its adoption by the Greeks (around 1000 B.C.E.), who eventually added symbols to the alphabet in order to represent vowels that appeared in their spoken language and to distinguish different words that might otherwise be represented by the same set of consonant symbols. Not long afterwards, this alphabet moved from the Etruscans (with influences from the Greek) to Rome, leading to the development of the Latin alphabet, which spread rapidly throughout the Western world.

The Origin of Print Culture

The shift to alphabetic writing made widespread literacy more attainable. It became easier to learn how to write and, perhaps more important, easier to learn how to read. With a writing system that could easily represent spoken language, it became possible to conceive of recording a lecture, a political speech, or a plan of action. Those permanent records led to many changes in society.

It overstates the case to mark the beginning of history by the beginning of an alphabet. Nevertheless, the movement from the oral narratives of Homer's day to the formal historical analysis of Herodotus and Thucydides depended on having the efficient, widely used writing system that the Greek alphabet provided. It is a similar overstatement to link the beginning of formal education, as in Plato's Academy, to the creation of an alphabet. Yet it is no accident that people speak of learning the ABCs; the modern educational system depends on alphabetic writing. Others have traced the origins of literature, philosophy, government, and science to the creation of alphabetic writing systems.

In the fifteenth century, the printing press was invented in Europe. Although a printing press had been developed in China, Johannes Gutenberg's innovation was to combine the press with typography, a technology that itself depended on an alphabetic system of writing. The possibility of wide dissemination of texts reshaped the church and the academy, extending a process of alphabetization that had begun more than twenty-five hundred years earlier.

A key aspect throughout this process of developing alphabets was the ability to represent knowledge in both permanent and mobile forms. As Bruno Latour (1988) argues, this made possible the development of both modern science and the Western European imperialist movement. The alphabet was a key element, facilitating typographic printing, which in turn allowed the easy reproduction of texts.

The great flowering of Greek culture appeared shortly after the adoption of alphabetic writing. Later, the Roman culture blossomed following its adoption of the alphabet from the Etruscans. Then, the full realization of the alphabet is observed through the printing press, which predates the Renaissance of these classic cultures. It is thus easy to adopt the innovation-driven view that the alphabet was necessary for, or even caused, these great changes in history. In *The Literate Mind* (1998), Jens Brockmeier cautions people about this kind of reasoning. He argues that before an alphabet can have the powerful effects attributed to it, there must be a literate mind ready to accept it and make use of it. More generally, that caution should lead people to be skeptical about any simple, one-step model of social change. Alphabets have certainly made a difference in the development of print culture, but it is necessary to look carefully at the processes of change to see the relations among literacy tools (such as alphabets), literacy practices, social organization, and literate modes of thought.

Alphabets Versus Other Writing Systems

It is impossible to ignore alphabets and their influence on the development of Western civilization. Alphabets can represent phonemes (i.e., units of speech that are distinguishable within a language) and, thus, alphabetic texts typically remain close to the familiar spoken language. This can make it relatively easy to learn to read and write. It also makes computing and printing easier. In contrast, nonalphabetic writing tends to represent concepts independent of their representation in speech. While there are a small number of phonemes in any language, there are thousands of concepts and, correspondingly, thousands of symbols. Thus, for example, in written Chinese there are thousands of characters to learn and remember. The huge number of symbols also makes printing and computer use more difficult.

The differences between alphabetic and other writing systems are important. On the other hand, one should be cautious in attributing too much to an alphabet. Consider, for example, its relation to

A nineteenth-century chart illustrates written Chinese, which is an example of a nonalphabetical writing system. (Historical Picture Archive/Corbis)

literature. Many would argue that alphabetic writing made possible literacy for everyone and mass distribution of texts through the printing press. Yet, a country such as China has achieved a high rate of literacy despite a writing system that few people, perhaps no one, can fully master. In fact, there are claims that the body of literature in Chinese is greater than that in European languages.

It is also argued that an alphabetic system is better because it is phonetic (i.e., the symbols can represent spoken sounds). This makes is easy to learn and easy to establish a connection between spoken and written language. However, linking the spoken and written language creates difficulties in multilingual contexts. In Europe, for example, there is no common written language in which one could write the charter for a European union. On the other hand, people throughout

China, even though they speak very different languages, can all read Chinese writing. This is true across other countries in Asia as well. In a time in which people seek global understanding, nonphonetic writing systems can meet the needs of diverse speakers and alphabets can seem obstacle.

Some people also argue that alphabets make possible the permanent representation of meaning; indeed, that is a key ingredient of a print culture. However, because the alphabetic representation corresponds to the spoken sounds, it must change rapidly to accommodate inevitable changes in the way in which people speak. Thus, it is difficult to read some words that were written by William Shakespeare and nearly impossible for most people to read the original words written by Geoffrey Chaucer. Using an ideographic language, which makes no attempt to represent sounds, it would be much easier to turn to the texts of long ago. A person who is literate in Chinese can still read with ease those texts that were written long before the time of Shakespeare and Chaucer. The ability to transcend phonemic changes must certainly contribute to a sense of history and an understanding of the origins of ideas.

Finally, the straightforward simplicity of alphabetic languages comes at another price. As William Jenner (1992) points out, it may be easier to express laws less ambiguously in an alphabetic language, but the possibilities for poetry may be inherently greater in a language that is less tied to precise replication of spoken forms. Ideographic and pictographic languages offer multiple readings of both the sounds and visualizations of language that are not possible with alphabets.

The Mythical Story of Alphabets

The student of alphabets and writing might be forgiven for starting with what might be called the Homeric myth of alphabets. It goes something like the following. Someone in Ancient Greece invented an alphabet. This made possible writing, as it is known it in the West, and consequently, literature, history, philosophy, schools, laws, and the other trappings of modern civilization. As a result, there was one of the most dramatic shifts in all of human history, from an oral to a print culture and from illiteracy to literacy. The shift marks the divide between history and prehistory.

Several specific (although not necessarily correct) ideas follow from this legend. First, because

alphabets developed long ago, their history is well established and noncontroversial; scholars know where and when the alphabets arose, and the unknown events that led to the development of alphabetic writing are lost forever in the desert sands. Second, the move to alphabetic writing represents the straightforward adoption of a useful new tool, and the origin of a print culture can be seen clearly as a consequence of the shift to alphabetic writing. Third, alphabets are clearly superior to other modes of writing. Fourth, alphabets and their use are fixed elements in the modern movements of technology and globalization.

As with any legend, there are elements of truth, but a long and continuing thread of scholarship has shown that the move to alphabetic writing, or what might better be termed a process of alphabetization, is far more complex, dynamic, far-reaching, and current than this discrete shift model suggests.

Modern Alphabets

It is easy to think of the development of the alphabet as a historical curiosity, one representing an important event, but an event with little relevance to modern concerns. That way of thinking would miss seeing some fascinating events and issues.

First of all, the field of study of early writing systems is undergoing changes that are typical of a new or emerging field, rather than one wherein the major questions have all already been answered. As mentioned above, one of the most significant events in this area of inquiry was the finding of the first sample of alphabetic writing, which was reported in the mass media only at the end of 1999. As with similar discoveries, it has raised more questions than answers. What did that first writer say? Was he or she really the first? How was that alphabet invented? How did the ideas get back to the Levant and later to Greece and Rome?

To investigate questions such as these, centers have been established, such as the West Semitic Research Project at the University of Southern California. This project uses large-format cameras or high-resolution digital imaging to photograph objects and manuscripts. Various kinds of film, including those that record only infrared light, are employed as well. These new technologies transform the kinds of questions that scholars are able to ask about ancient texts and artifacts.

Moreover, the actual processes of developing writing systems are continuing throughout the world. The well-known emoticons used in e-mail messages, such as the smiley face made up of a colon and a right parenthesis, are examples of people's continuing need to find better symbols for expression through writing. In some countries, this process is not so benign.

Toby Lester (1997) describes the situation in Azerbaijan. In 1991, the government had decreed that all Azerbaijan writing was to be in Latin letters instead of the Cyrillic alphabet, which had also been used for Russian. These changes are far more significant than, for example, the conversion to the metric system in the United States would have been. Changing alphabets in Azerbaijan is a traumatic process, but it happened before when they changed from Arabic to Latin in the 1920s, and then from Latin to Cyrillic in the 1930s.

Azerbaijan is not unique in this regard. Throughout the world, alphabets are a subject of politics, not just linguistics. They are also a way to express culture and social relations. Consider the ASCII system, which defines how computers encode characters. Few people may be aware of the fact that the system works perfectly well for the Latin alphabet but that it does not work at all for most of the languages in the world and that it requires more complicated coding for even the major European languages, such Spanish with its tilde, French with the cedilla, or German with the umlaut.

These issues are being played out in the World Wide Web. Major efforts have been devoted to building systems that can accommodate all writing systems, including even the nonalphabetic systems, but in practice, the user is still much better off if he or she can use the Latin alphabet. Will technologies be developed to permit communication across writing systems? Will the diversity in writing systems be preserved? Or, will participation in a global system lead to the dominance of a single alphabet? Will that alphabet itself change to meet new technological and political imperatives? These are questions that call for continued attention to the nature of the symbols that are used for writing.

See also: Animal Communication; Gutenberg, Johannes; Internet and the World Wide Web; Language Acquisition; Language and Communication; Nonverbal Communication; Printing, History and Methods of; Symbols.

Bibliography

Brockmeier, Jens. (1998). *Literales Bewusstsein: Schriftlichkeit und das Verhältnis von Sprache und Kultur* [*The Literate Mind: Literacy and the Relation Between Language and Culture*]. Munich: Fink.

Coulmas, Florian. (1989). *The Writing Systems of the World.* London: Blackwell.

Daniels, Peter T., and Bright, William, eds. (1996). *The World's Writing Systems.* New York: Oxford University Press.

Himelfarb, Elizabeth J. (2000). "First Alphabet Found in Egypt." <http://www.archaeology.org/0001/newsbriefs/egypt.html.>

Jenner, William J. F. (1992). *The Tyranny of History: The Roots of China's Crisis.* London: Penguin.

Latour, Bruno. (1988). "Drawing Things Together." In *Representation in Scientific Practice,* eds. Michael Lynch and Stephen Woolgar. Cambridge, MA: MIT Press.

Lester, Toby. (1997). "New-Alphabet Disease?" <http://www.theatlantic.com/issues/97jul/alphabet.htm>.

Ong, Walter. (1982). *Orality and Literacy: The Technologizing of the Word.* London: Routledge.

Schmandt-Besserat, Denise. (1989). "Two Precursors of Writing in One Reckoning Device." In *The Origins of Writing,* ed. Wayne M. Senner. Lincoln, NE: University of Nebraska Press.

Senner, Wayne M., ed. (1989). *The Origins of Writing.* Lincoln: University of Nebraska Press.

Wilford, John Noble. (1999). "Discovery of Egyptian Inscriptions Indicates an Earlier Date for the Origin of the Alphabet." <http://www.library.cornell.edu/colldev/mideast/alphorg.htm>.

BERTRAM C. BRUCE

ANIMAL COMMUNICATION

While it is customary to think of humans as being unique among life forms, humans have a number of basic characteristics in common with other animals. Similar to other animals, humans are "open systems." Open systems are entities that are able to function and survive through ongoing exchanges with their environment. James G. Miller (1965) was one of the first scholars to observe that there are two general ways in which these systems interact with their environment. One involves a give-and-take of matter, and the other involves a give-and-take of information. The first process consists of an intake of food and oxygen, the processing of these materials for energy, and finally an outflow of wastes and carbon dioxide. The second activity involves attending to and acting on information. This second process can be termed "communication."

Viewed in this way, communication is one of the two basic processes of all living—human and animal—systems. Communication is the critical life process through which animals and humans create, acquire, transform, and use information—in the form of messages to carry out the activities of their lives.

Forms of Animal Communication

Messages take a variety of forms—visual, tactile, olfactory, gustatory, and auditory. Visual messages are particularly important to humans, but they also play a necessary role in the lives of many other animals. Examples of visual messages that are useful in human communication include printed words or illustrations, a smile, a handshake, a tear, a new blue suit, or a stop sign. Movements, gestures, and colors have similar importance for animals. The color of birds and butterflies, the rhythmic light of fireflies, and the movement of head, ears, or tail by primates all serve as valuable sources of information. Types of visual messages include facial displays, movement of the body, spacing and position, dress, and other forms of adornment.

Tactile messages involve touch, bumping, vibration, and other types of physical contact. For humans, tactile messages are important from the time of conception to the end of life. This form of communication is at least as important for many other animals, for whom tactile messages play a role in biological as well as social development. Tactile communication is vital for many animal species in parent-young relations, courtship and intimate relations, social greetings and social interaction, and defense and aggression. Types of tactile messages include touch, vibration, stroking, rubbing, pressure, pain, and temperature-related information.

Olfactory and gustatory messages are chemical messages conveyed by smells and tastes. The technical term for these chemical messages is "pheromones." Pheromones are transported by water or air. Humans, of course, receive these messages by means of receptors that are sensitive to food and water-borne substances ingested by mouth and to air-borne scents that enter the nose. Insects receive these messages through sensors in their antennae, fish receive them through odor-sensitive cells on the body or in the nose, and vertebrates receive them through the nose.

Auditory messages take the form of sounds produced by speaking, whistling, drumming, or striking a part of the body against an object, the ground, or another portion of the body. Auditory messages can also be created as an extension of human activity, such as the squealing of brakes on a car or the firing of a gun.

In addition to speech by humans and vocalizations by birds, primates, dogs, and various other animals, other auditory messages play an important role in human and animal communication. In the case of humans, auditory signals, such as alarms, are used to alert and to warn, and more complex auditory forms of communication, such as music, are also important.

As with other forms of communication, auditory messages become significant to animal and human systems when they are detected by receptors and then processed by the brain. In the case of lower-order living systems, the response is generally either one of approach or avoidance; that is, animals may respond to auditory messages either by approaching the source of a message or distancing themselves from it.

Some messages that are of importance to animal and human systems are created intentionally by utterances, written messages, or gestures. Others are not. For a human's tear and an animal's color are examples of messages that are not sent intentionally. Regardless of whether messages are sent intentionally or unintentionally, they can be of equal communicative significance to those who attend to them.

Functions of Animal Communication

Visual, tactile, olfactory, gustatory, and auditory messages serve a variety of essential communication functions for animal and human systems. Some particularly significant categories of these functions include courtship and mating, reproduction, parent-offspring socialization, navigation, self-defense, and territoriality.

Courtship and Mating

Differences between courtship and mating practices are substantial across different animal groups. Nonetheless, communication plays a basic role for all species. Some aspects are straightforward. For example, an essential part of courtship and mating involves the identification of an appropriate mate. Depending on the species, this identification process requires the processing of visual, tactile, olfactory, gustatory, and/or auditory messages. Courtship and mating also involve attracting potential mates, and sometimes persuasion and negotiation, each of which is a communication process.

The specifics of how these communication processes take place vary widely. For example, grasshoppers and crickets use song, moths use pheromones, and fireflies use the visual messages created by their flashing light.

Reproduction

The biological aspects necessary for reproduction can also be understood as a communication process—actually life's most fundamental such process. The reproductive process begins at the moment of conception with the joining of a sperm cell and an egg cell. These cells contain all the information needed for the creation of a new living being that bears a remarkable resemblance to its parents. Thus, through the union of these cells, and the development that unfolds thereafter, genetic communication assures the creation of new offspring and, in a broader sense, the continuity of the species.

Parent-Offspring Relations

Many offspring are quite dependent on adults for survival. For example, the survival of social insects, birds, and mammals depends on interaction with their parents. This interaction may take the form of food providing and physical guidance from one point to another. For many more complex social animals, extended contact between the offspring and adults is critical. In his classical studies, Konrad Lorenz demonstrated how birds and some other animals learn, or imprint, their identity through communication:

> One of the most striking as well as pathetically comical instances . . . concerned an albino peacock in an Australian zoo, the lone survivor of a brood that had succumbed to a spell of bad weather. The peafowl was placed in the only warm room available. . . . Although the peacock flourished in these surroundings, the peculiar effect of its reptilian roommates on the bird became apparent not long after it had

A male frigate bird inflates its red throat in order to attract females during the courtship process. (Wolfgang Kaehler/Corbis)

attained sexual maturity and grown its first train: Beginning then and forever after, the peacock displayed his magnificent plumes in the famous "wheel" position only to giant tortoises, eagerly if vainly courting these reptiles while ignoring even the most handsome peahens with which the zoo supplied him [Simon, 1977, p. 23].

This observation illustrates the fact that communication, in addition to providing support and instruction necessary for survival, can, in some cases, even provide the basic identity of the offspring.

Navigation

The term "navigation" refers to an animal's goal-directed movement through space. Whether the intention is to locate food, avoid an enemy, follow a colleague, or arrive at a particular destination, the activity involves the processing of messages of one form or another. Again, the ways in which these processes take place varies greatly from one species to another. Humans make extensive use of visual messages. Ants find their way by following an odor trail put in place by other ants.

Some animals navigate using echolocation, whereby they send out auditory signals and then guide themselves by processing information that comes from the echoes that are created as the signals

A leopard stretches and scratches a small tree to sharpen its long claws and to mark its territory on the Maasai Mara plains of Kenya. (Barbra Leigh/Corbis)

bounce off nearby objects. Among bats, these communication skills are so finely tuned that a bat can pass between two black silk threads placed less than a foot apart without colliding with the threads. Dolphins also use echolocation for navigation; they transmit clicking messages through their forehead and receive and "interpret" returning messages through their jaw and throat.

A most amazing navigational communication process is that used by social bees. Researcher Karl von Frisch (1971) found that when a worker bee identifies a desirable food source, it announces the discovery to other bees in the hive by performing a kind of dance. The distance to the food is conveyed by a rhythmic tail wagging, and the direction of the food is indicated by the path traveled by the bee as it performs its dance routine. If the dance points upward, the food lies in the direction of the sun. If the dance runs 90 degrees to the left of the sun, the food is 90 degrees to the left of the sun, and so on.

Self-Defense

The way in which animals defend themselves also frequently involves communication. For example, when an animal detects the presence of a predator, it reacts by mobilizing itself to flee the situation. Communication is basic to this detection-mobilizing-flight activity. Moreover, the departure of the animal may well become a message to other animals nearby—and to the predator—who may all respond based on the messages that they detect and process.

The communication dynamics associated with self-defense among humans are quite complex. Humans react to the sense that they are physically threatened, but they also react when they believe they are symbolically or psychologically threatened. The detecting-mobilizing-reacting process that occurs in response to events such as criticism, a failing grade, or rejection by a friend or romantic interest involves communication. These communication dynamics can then trigger communication responses in others who witness the initial detecting-mobilizing-reacting process.

Territoriality

Communication can also play a role in establishing and maintaining home territories. Many animals—humans among them—become attracted to particular places and spaces where they were born, spent their early years, or mated. This attachment also leads to a desire to mark, maintain, and sometimes even defend the territory against intruders. Communication is a process through which territories are marked, and it is also the means by which animals detect and respond to invasions.

Birds provide one of the best examples of the importance of territoriality and the way in which territories are defined, maintained, and defended. Some birds take possession of an area, a hedge, or a portion of a meadow. Once this has occurred, male birds go to great efforts of using songs to keep out other males. Some birds actually create songs with two distinct forms. They use one song to maintain communication with their partners, and they use another version to define and display their territory. Obviously, humans also go to great efforts to define and defend their territories—homes, neighborhoods, communities, or countries against "outsiders."

Some animals, humans among them, establish temporary or transitory territories. Examples are provided by fish and birds that travel or rest in groups. Temporary personal space is also a major issue for humans. Individuals, for example, claim temporary space at the beach by using towels and other miscellaneous items as messages to others that the space is already taken. Newspapers or a folded coat on an empty seat on a bus or in the movie theater similarly serve as messages about spaces being claimed. Perhaps most sacred is the "bubble" of personal space that exists around individuals. When this space is violated by someone who is standing or sitting "too close" to an individual, it results in discomfort and, generally, a physical response in which the individual moves away in a direction that reclaims the amount of space to which he or she feels entitled.

Summary

Communication plays a major role in the most fundamental life processes of animals. This perspective provides a reminder that communication is one of the two means through which all animals adapt to and survive in their environment. Communication takes many forms and serves a variety of functions, but amid all this diversity, there is still a good deal of commonality in terms of the basic communication dynamics and the functions they serve for living systems.

The study of animal communication, beyond being of interest in its own right, helps to further an understanding of human behavior and the role communication plays in human affairs more generally. It provides a source of reflection on human behavior and activities, and it provides a reminder that humans share a great deal in common with other animals. At the same time, these studies serve to highlight the complexity and special character of human communication, which involves the use of symbols. Symbols are messages that stand for things other than themselves, and their use is fundamental to human communication and human life.

Words are symbols, as are flags, dates on the calendar, dollar bills, and stop lights. Each message serves as a signal for a set of meanings that have been created, taught, and maintained through communication. To illustrate, a flag of a country has no inherent, natural meaning. It is simply a piece of colored cloth. However, through time and use, flags become symbols that are capable of conveying many rich meanings. Using sym-

bols in communication allows humans to have much more flexibility than other animals, whose communication essentially involves signals with far more limited ranges of meaning. At the same time, human symbolic communication is far more complex than animal communication and carries with it possibilities for misunderstanding, error, and misinterpretation.

See also: NONVERBAL COMMUNICATION; SYMBOLS.

Bibliography

Behrencamp, Sandra L., and Bradbury, Jack W. (1998). *Principles of Animal Communication.* Sunderland, MA: Sinauer Associates.

Brothers, Leslie. (1997). *Friday's Footprint: How Society Shapes the Human Mind.* Oxford, Eng.: Oxford University Press.

Frings, Hubert, and Frings, Mabel. (1975). *Animal Communication.* Norman: University of Oklahoma Press.

King, Barbara J. (1999). *Origins of Language: What Nonhuman Primates Can Tell Us.* Santa Fe, NM: School of American Research Press.

Landauer, Martin. (1961). *Communication among Social Bees.* Cambridge, MA: Harvard University Press.

Méry, Fernand. (1975). *Animal Languages*, tr. Michael Ross. Westmead, Eng.: Saxon House.

Miller, James G. (1965). "Living Systems." *Behavioral Science* 10:193–237.

Prince, Jack H. (1975). *Languages of the Animal World.* Nashville, TN: Thomas Nelson.

Ruben, Brent D., and Stewart, Lea P. (1998). *Communication and Human Behavior,* 4th edition. Needham Heights, MA: Allyn & Bacon.

Simon, Hilda. (1977). *The Courtship of Birds.* New York: Dodd, Mead.

Trefil, James S. (1997). *Are We Unique?: A Scientist Explores the Unparalleled Intelligence of the Human Mind.* New York: Wiley.

von Frisch, Karl. (1971). *Bees: Their Vision, Chemical Senses, and Language.* Ithaca, NY: Cornell University Press.

Wilson, Edward O. (1971). *The Insect Societies.* Cambridge, MA: Belknap Press.

BRENT D. RUBEN

ANTIVIOLENCE INTERVENTIONS

Concern over the harmful effects of televised violence on children has prompted the development of antiviolence interventions to prevent these negative outcomes. These interventions have taken many different forms, from formal television literacy curricula implemented by schools to smaller-scale research efforts designed by individual researchers.

Television literacy curricula were first developed in the late 1960s and early 1970s to provide systematic instruction in how to watch television. Since then, many different organizations and individuals have developed television literacy materials, including the major television networks and organizations funded by the U.S. Office of Education. Television literacy programs have been used with children as early as kindergarten and as late as high school. They have been implemented in many different locations around the globe, including the United States, Sweden, South Africa, Great Britain, France, Canada, and Australia.

Advocates of television literacy curricula argue that, just as children need schooling to learn how to read, children must be taught how to watch television so they can become literate television viewers. According to this perspective, children who lack television literacy are at a greater risk of misunderstanding television and experiencing negative effects from exposure to it. As a result, they require intensive instruction in television literacy.

To prevent negative effects (including the imitation of televised violence) from occurring, television literacy curricula involve teaching children a number of skills and lessons regarding television. For example, children are often taught about the technical and economic aspects of producing television programs, the purpose of televised commercials, and the difference between the fantasy world of television and the real world. Some curricula may also include units that address certain types of televised portrayals, such as those featuring stereotypes and violence.

Often, the effectiveness of television literacy curricula is not empirically tested. As a result, it is difficult to determine how well the various programs work in protecting children from the negative effects of television. However, as Dorothy G. Singer and Jerome L. Singer (1998) noted, the empirical assessments that have been made indicate that television literacy curricula do help in successfully teaching children about television. For example, children who have participated in these kinds of programs can identify special effects, more easily distinguish between reality and the fantasy world of television, know more

about advertising, and understand more television-specific vocabulary (e.g., "sponsor," "animation") than other children. It is often assumed that children who have developed these kinds of critical viewing skills will be less vulnerable to experiencing negative effects from viewing harmful media content, such as violence.

Unfortunately, many of the television literacy programs do not assess whether participating children are less affected by the violent television they view. However, there is some limited evidence that children who receive in-school lessons about television violence are less likely to be affected by this content than other children. For example, Marcel W. Vooijs and Tom H. A. van der Voort (1993) found in their study that children who are taught about the seriousness of violence became more critical viewers of televised violence. Likewise, L. Rowell Huesmann and his colleagues (1983) found in their study that children who participate in television literacy programs that highlight the undesirability of watching and imitating violent acts shown on television have more negative attitudes toward television violence and are less aggressive than other youngsters. It could be, then, that curricula aimed at decreasing the negative effects of televised violence need to encourage teaching children explicitly about this content rather than simply providing instruction about television in general.

Other efforts to intervene in the media violence-aggression relationship among children have taken different forms. For example, some efforts target parents rather than children and involve workshops, brochures, and videos. These materials often seek both to educate parents about the potential negative effects of television and to teach parents strategies for promoting critical viewing skills among their children. The assumption is that by educating parents about the harmful effects of television and teaching them skills for mitigating these effects, parents will "mediate" their children's television viewing. Unfortunately, as Singer and her colleagues (1980) noted, many parents are not interested in this kind of instruction, perhaps because they perceive television to be a problem for other children, not their own.

Although relatively few of the major efforts at teaching television literacy have included specific instruction about television violence, smaller-scale interventions designed to combat the effects of this particular content have been developed. These interventions are typically implemented by individual researchers who have designed very brief messages that they believe will counteract the negative effects of violent television on children. During the experiment, one group of children usually watches a clip from a violent television program with an experimenter who makes negative comments during the program, and another group usually watches the clip with an experimenter who either does not make any comments or makes very neutral comments. In both cases, after the program has been shown, the aggression levels of all of the children are assessed. It is expected that children who hear the negative comments during viewing will be less aggressive after exposure than will be children who do not hear negative comments. The assumption of this research appears to be that children need an adult to condemn the glamorous depiction of violence on television so that they will not experience negative effects from viewing this content. It should be noted that many of these experiments are conducted with the goal of developing strategies that parents could use when they watch violent television with their children. As a result, this research is very relevant to the work conducted on parental mediation.

Although there have only been a handful of studies that evaluate the effectiveness of these smaller-scale interventions, the research that has been conducted has yielded promising results. For example, David J. Hicks (1968) found in his experiment that children who hear an experimenter make negative comments about the television violence they are watching (e.g., "He shouldn't do that," "That's wrong," and so on) have less-aggressive attitudes and display less-aggressive behavior than do other children. Further, Amy I. Nathanson and Joanne Cantor (2000) found from their experiment that asking children to empathize with the victims of televised violence is also successful in reducing the likelihood that children will experience negative effects from watching television violence. It seems, then, that children can benefit from hearing very simple, straightforward messages regarding television violence.

Overall, research on antiviolence interventions suggests that children can learn to resist the negative messages they receive from violent television. Although the effectiveness of many of the formal television literacy programs is unknown, the available research indicates that instruction—whether it occurs as part of a formal curriculum or whether it occurs only as children view televised violence—should highlight the undesirability of the behavior that is being depicted. When faced with the often glamorous depictions of television violence, children may need adults to help them critically view this material and process it in a way that reduces the harmful effects.

See also: CHILDREN'S COMPREHENSION OF TELEVISION; PARENTAL MEDIATION OF MEDIA EFFECTS; VIOLENCE IN THE MEDIA, ATTRACTION TO; VIOLENCE IN THE MEDIA, HISTORY OF RESEARCH ON.

Bibliography

Anderson, James A. (1983). "Television Literacy and the Critical Viewer." In *Children's Understanding of Television: Research on Attention and Comprehension,* eds. Jennings Bryant and Daniel R. Anderson. New York: Academic Press.

Corder-Bolz, Charles R. (1980). "Mediation: The Role of Significant Others." *Journal of Communication* 30(3):106–118.

Dorr, Aimee; Graves, Sherryl B.; and Phelps, Eric. (1980). "Television Literacy for Young Children." *Journal of Communication* 30(3):71–83.

Hicks, David J. (1968). "Effects of Co-Observer's Sanctions and Adult Presence on Imitative Aggression." *Child Development* 39:303–309.

Huesmann, L. Rowell; Eron, Leonard D.; Klein, Rosemary; Brice, Patrick; and Fischer, Paulette. (1983). "Mitigating the Imitation of Aggressive Behaviors by Changing Children's Attitudes about Media Violence." *Journal of Personality and Social Psychology* 44:899–910.

Nathanson, Amy I., and Cantor, Joanne. (2000). "Reducing the Aggression-Promoting Effect of Violent Cartoons by Increasing Children's Fictional Involvement with the Victim: A Study of Active Mediation." *Journal of Broadcasting and Electronic Media* 44:125–142.

Rapaczynski, Wanda; Singer, Dorothy G.; and Singer, Jerome L. (1982). "Teaching Television: A Curriculum for Young Children." *Journal of Communication* 32(2):46–54.

Singer, Dorothy G., and Singer, Jerome L. (1998). "Developing Critical Viewing Skills and Media Literacy in Children." *Annals of the American Academy of Political and Social Science* 557:164–179.

Singer, Dorothy G.; Zuckerman, Diana M.; and Singer, Jerome L. (1980). "Helping Elementary School Children Learn about TV." *Journal of Communication* 30(3):84–93.

Vooijs, Marcel W., and van der Voort, Tom H. A. (1993). "Learning about Television Violence: The Impact of a Critical Viewing Curriculum on Children's Attitudinal Judgments of Crime Series." *Journal of Research and Development in Education* 26:133–142.

AMY I. NATHANSON

■ APPREHENSION AND COMMUNICATION

Communication apprehension (CA) is the fear or anxiety associated with either real or anticipated communication with another person or persons. Although some people desire to communicate with others and see the importance of doing so, they may be impeded by their fear or anxiety. People who do not have appropriate communication skills or whose communication is ethnically or culturally divergent may also develop communication apprehension. Most people who are communication apprehensive, however, are neither skill deficient nor different from others in the general culture. Typically, they are normal people who are simply afraid to communicate. Because it is natural for people to avoid things that they fear, communication-apprehensive people tend to be less willing to communicate. Therefore, they may be labeled shy by others around them. It is important to note, also, that many communication-apprehensive people do not feel restricted by their feelings about communicating—they can be as happy and as productive as nonapprehensive communicators. Most of the social problems that are experienced by these individuals stem from how they are perceived by others and how others respond to them.

This entry focuses on the discussion of communication apprehension on norms from the Personal Report of Communication Apprehension (PRCA) 24 scale. Completing the scale allows the user to know where he or she falls within the normative range of scores. Scores on the PRCA24 scale should range between 24 and 120 (if they are below 24 or more than 120, a computational error has been made). The PRCA24 scale is designed to measure a general trait of communication apprehension—how a person typically reacts to oral communication with others. The higher a person scores on the PRCA, the more apprehension that person generally feels about communicating.

Between 60 percent and 70 percent of the people who have completed the PRCA scale have scores ranging from 50 to 80. This is called the "normal" range. If one's score falls anywhere outside this range, the idea of communication apprehension may be especially relevant to that person. If one's score is between 24 and 50, that person is among those people who experience the least communication apprehension. This individual is apt to be higher talkers and may actively seek out opportunities to interact with others. Very few, if any, communication situations cause this individual to be fearful or anxious. If one's score is somewhere between 50 and 60, that person experiences less communication apprehension than most people. However, he or she is likely to feel some fear or anxiety about a few situations. If one's score falls between 60 and 70, that person's level of communication apprehension is similar to that of most people. There are some communication situations that may cause this person to feel anxious or tense; in others, he or she will feel quite comfortable. If one's score is between 70 and 80, that person experiences more communication apprehension than most people. Probably, many communication situations cause this person to be fearful and tense, but some do not. If one's score falls between 80 and 120, that person is among those who experience the most communication apprehension. This individual is likely a low talker, one who actively avoids many communication situations because he or she feels much anxiety and tension in those situations.

Those people who fall within the various score ranges on the PRCA scale will now be examined more closely. People in the "normal" range (50 to 80) tend to respond quite differently in different situations. They may be very tense in one situation (when giving a speech) but quite comfortable in another (when out on a date). Those who score in the "low" (below 50) and "high" (above 80) ranges tend to respond to most communication situations in the same way. Researchers consider both extremes to be abnormal. The "low" communication-apprehensive person is considered abnormal because this person is unlikely to feel any fear or anxiety about communicating, even in situations in which he or she should be anxious (e.g., when entering his or her very first job interview). Although it is often an advantage not to be bothered by oral communication, it is also normal

FIGURE 1. *The PRCA24 scale.*

Personal Report of Communication Apprehension (PRCA24)

Directions: This instrument is composed of twenty-four statements concerning feelings about communicating with other people. Please indicate the degree to which each statement applies to you by marking whether you (1) strongly agree, (2) agree, (3) are undecided, (4) disagree, or (5) strongly disagree. Work quickly; record your first impression.

___1. I dislike participating in group discussions.
___2. Generally, I am comfortable while participating in group discussions.
___3. I am tense and nervous while participating in group discussions.
___4. I like to get involved in group discussions.
___5. Engaging in a group discussion with new people makes me tense and nervous.
___6. I am calm and relaxed while participating in group discussions.
___7. Generally, I am nervous when I have to participate in a meeting.
___8. Usually, I am calm and relaxed while participating in meetings.
___9. I am very calm and relaxed when I am called on to express an opinion at a meeting.
___10. I am afraid to express myself at meetings.
___11. Communicating at meetings usually makes me uncomfortable.
___12. I am very relaxed when answering questions at a meeting.
___13. While participating in a conversation with a new acquaintance, I feel very nervous.
___14. I have no fear of speaking up in conversations.
___15. Ordinarily, I am very tense and nervous in conversations.
___16. While conversing with a new acquaintance, I feel very relaxed.
___17. Ordinarily, I am very calm and relaxed in conversations.
___18. I am afraid to speak up in conversations.
___19. I have no fear of giving a speech.
___20. Certain parts of my body feel very tense and rigid while I am giving a speech.
___21. I feel relaxed while giving a speech.
___22. My thoughts become confused and jumbled when I am giving a speech.
___23. I face the prospect of giving a speech with confidence.
___24. While giving a speech, I get so nervous I forget facts I really know.

Scoring: To compute context subscores, begin with a score of 18 for each context and follow the instructions below:
  1. Group discussion: Add scores for items 2, 4, and 6. Subtract scores for items 1, 3, and 5.
  2. Meetings: Add scores for items 8, 9, and 12. Subtract scores for items 7, 10, and 11.
  3. Interpersonal: Add scores for items 14, 16, and 17. Subtract scores for items 13, 15, and 18.
  4. Public speaking: Add scores for items 19, 21, and 23. Subtract scores for items 20, 22, and 24.

To compute the total score for the PRCA24, add the four subscores (which should each range from 6 to 30). Total scores can range from 24 to 120. Scores above 80 = high communication apprehension; below 50 = low communication apprehension.

---

to feel some fear in response to a threatening situation. The person who experiences no fear in such situations usually makes poor decisions about when to communicate and when not to communicate. The "high" communication-apprehensive person is considered abnormal because this person usually experiences fear and anxiety about communicating—even in presumably nonthreatening situations such as calling a friend on the phone. Such people are likely to avoid communication in many, even most, situations. This avoidance can be quite costly when communicating would be advantageous. A common example is the student who never participates in class discussion even when participation is a criterion for a higher grade.

Communication Apprehension as a Trait

By the phrase "as a trait," it is meant that communication apprehension is a part of the person-

ality of an individual. Such a trait is most important for those people who have either very high or very low levels of communication apprehension. It is this trait that the total score on the PRCA scale was designed to measure. An extreme score on this measure suggests that the behavior of an individual is influenced as much, if not more, by general fear or anxiety about communication as by any specifics of a communication situation in which the individual find him- or herself. At the extremes of the trait, an individual either experiences high degrees of anxiety in most communication situations or experiences very low degrees of anxiety in most communications situations.

From 15 percent to 20 percent of the population falls within each extreme category. Thus, if an individual scores very low or very high on the PRCA scale, that person is outside the normal range of scores where about two-thirds of the population score. At one end are the people who are called "high CAs" (those who have high communication apprehension), and at the other end are the people who are called "low CAs" (those who have low communication apprehension). The people who are called "moderate CAs" (those who have moderate communication apprehension) are those who fall in the normal range. All three of these terms refer to trait communication apprehension.

Communication Apprehension in Generalized Contexts

This view of communication apprehension recognizes those individuals who experience high levels of anxiety about communicating in a particular context or situation but have much less or even no anxiety about communicating in other contexts. The PRCA scale, besides giving a measure of trait communication apprehension, can be broken down to yield measures of communication apprehension in four generalized contexts: talking within small groups, speaking in meetings or classroom situations, talking in dyadic interpersonal encounters, and presenting public speeches.

The level of apprehension that a person experiences in each of these generalized contexts can be computed by using the following formulas that are based on how the individual completed the PRCA:

Group CA = 18 + (Item 2 + Item 4 + Item 6 - Item I - Item 3 - Item 5)

Meeting CA = 18 + (Item 8 + Item 9 + Item 12 - Item 7 - Item 10 - Item 11)

Dyadic CA = 18 + (Item 14 + Item 16 + Item 17 - Item 13 - Item 15 - Item 18)

Public Speaking CA = 18 + (Item 19 + Item 21 + Item 23 - Item 20 - Item 22 - Item 24)

For these scales, a score above 18 is high, and a score above 23 shows an extremely high level of communication apprehension about that generalized context. It is quite possible for a person to score very high in one context but relatively low in another or even all of the others. If this is the case, it indicates that the person is highly apprehensive about some but not all generalized contexts.

Some people score high on the measure for group communication but low on the others. Here, a person would feel apprehensive about communicating in situations that involve a small group. Two types of groups are important here. One type is the task-oriented group. This type of group is one in which the participants meet for solving one or more problems (e.g., a group of students who meet to study for an exam). The other type of small group is the social group. This type of group formed for enjoyment, amusement, and/or sharing friendship.

A person could feel apprehensive about communicating in either type of group for many reasons. Perhaps the person feels that other group members are too critical of her or his ideas or suggestions. Perhaps the person feels that her or his own contributions are not important to the other members. Alternatively, the attitude of the person could be "More than two people cannot carry on a meaningful and effective oral exchange, so why get involved?" For the person who is highly apprehensive in small-group contexts but not in others, there is simply some aspect of small-group situations that causes the individual much discomfort when participating in them.

Some people have a higher level of communication apprehension in a meeting than in other situations. Meetings are similar to the group situation. Here the group is larger, and communication among participants is relatively formal and stylized. A good analogy is the typical college classroom. A person may be very talkative when with friends, when on a date, or even when meeting a new acquaintance. However, the formal structure of the classroom, combined with the pressure of having to display knowledge orally, may cause much anxiety. Most people can communicate quite openly and easily when they feel free to say what they want when they want to say it. When they confront a context such as a classroom or committee meeting where communication is restricted by explicit rules, they can become very apprehensive.

If one's level of communication apprehension is higher for dyadic interpersonal contexts than for the others, that person experiences anxiety when interacting with others on a one-on-one basis. There are several interpersonal contexts in which one might feel highly apprehensive about communicating. One context is when someone is interacting with a peer. The person may be so concerned with trying to make a good impression that it leads to much tension and anxiety. Another interpersonal context in which many people feel anxious is in interacting with a teacher. The individual may be very talkative in class. However, when facing a teacher one-on-one, the person experiences anxiety because of uncertainty about how to react to the teacher or about how the teacher might respond. A third anxiety-producing dyadic context is that involving encounters with the opposite sex. Some people approach communication with the opposite sex with confidence. Others, however, because of past negative experiences or anticipated negative consequences, find communicating with the opposite sex to be quite traumatic.

Feeling some anxiety about interpersonal situations such as a job interview is common to the majority of people. A job interview, particularly the first one, is a very strange and novel experience, and few people really know how to deal with it. Communication is the key to a successful interview. Being uncertain and fearful about what to say in a job interview and how to respond to the interviewer can result in high levels of communication apprehension. Many people feel apprehensive when communicating with their supervisors at work. This feeling may stem from a need to make a good impression on the supervisor. Perhaps it stems from a fear of having the ideas that one puts forth to the supervisor explicitly rejected. Conversely, many supervisors have a high level of anxiety about communicating with subordinates. Their apprehension could stem from anticipating complaints about how matters that involve subordinates are being handled. Their apprehension could stem from not having the information that subordinates want or need to carry out their jobs in an effective way. Whether the situation is formal or informal, whether it involves friends or strangers or people of equal or different status, many individuals find dyadic interpersonal contexts to be anxiety-producing situations.

Public speaking is the generalized context that causes the most problems for the most people. In fact, several national studies have indicated that the fear of public speaking is the number one fear of Americans. Public speaking places a person in a conspicuous position in front of others who will be critically evaluating both the person and what the person has to say. Many people have little experience and little or no training in effective speech making. Thus, it is not surprising that so many people find this context threatening.

Communication Apprehension with a Given Individual or Group

Nearly 95 percent of the American population has felt apprehension at least once when communicating with some specific person or group. It is not the communication context that triggers the problem; it is the other people. Some people simply cause others to be apprehensive. It may be a parent, a teacher, a certain salesperson, the IRS agent, the principal, or the boss. This anxiety may be a function of how others behave toward one (e.g., "Bring home an F, and you're on your own.") or perhaps the role they play in one's life (e.g., "Hello. I'm here to audit your tax returns for the past five years"). For most of people there is someone, such as a friend or relative, who makes them feel totally relaxed during interactions. It also is quite normal for individuals to find talking with some specific person or group, such as a police officer or a doctor, to be anxiety-producing.

Virtually all people experience communication apprehension with a given individual or group in a given *situation*. Most examples of this seem extreme—such as a person who is forced to apologize to a friend for offending that person, a person who arrives home to find a message that a date has had a last-minute change of heart, or a person being confronted by a teacher after class with the accusation of cheating. What separates communication apprehension in these situations from the other forms of communication apprehension is that these situations are unique encounters with a specific individual. Thus, although one generally would not be apprehensive about communicating with the other person, the specific situation arouses anxiety. Most people can communicate quite easily with their mothers, but forgetting their mother's birthday can lead to quite a hair-raising communicative event.

Communication apprehension, therefore, is a fear or anxiety about communicating that can stem from one's basic personality, from the type of communication expected, from the person or persons with whom one anticipates communicating, or from the unique circumstances that surround a given interaction. No matter what its source is, communication apprehension causes people discomfort, it may lead people to avoid communication, and it can result in people being ineffective in their communication with others.

Causes of Communication Apprehension

Trait-like communication apprehension is thought to be a matter of personality. Thus, the causes of this type of communicative anxiety are much like those of any personality variable; namely, it is a function of either the environment or genetic factors, or most likely a combination of the two. The discussion that follows focuses on potential environmental causes of generalized apprehension. As for situational communication apprehension, many causes are possible. Some of these have to do with the nature of specific interactions, the relationships between the participants in the interaction, and past experience—all functions of the environment.

Generalized Communication Apprehension

Research has failed to find out with absolute certainty the causes of trait-like communication apprehension. Research has been able to show statistical correlations between communication apprehension and theoretically proposed "causes." One particular theory, however, does permit a causal explanation of generalized communication apprehension because it takes into account both personality traits and situational constraints. The theory is expectancy learning, or, more specifically, a type of expectancy learning known as learned helplessness.

The underlying assumption of expectancy learning, as applied to communication apprehension, is that people develop expectations about other people and situations and about the probable outcomes of communication with those people and/or in those situations. A person develops confidence in his or her communication to the extent that such expectations are fulfilled. When expectations are not met, the individual develops a need to form new expectations. If expectations continually are not met, the person may develop a lack of confidence. Anxiety is produced when no appropriate expectations can be formed. Fear is produced when expectations lead to negative outcomes that are difficult or impossible to avoid. These two occurrences, according to expectancy-learning theory, are the foundation of communication apprehension.

An example will illustrate this point. Heather had recently made a new acquaintance, Mike. At their first meeting, Heather was quite attracted to Mike and felt that the interest was reciprocal.

After crossing paths a few more times, she was certain that Mike liked her and that he would soon call. At this point, Heather had formed two expectations: (1) Mike liked her and (2) he was likely to ask her out. After many more meetings, Heather began to wonder why Mike had not called her. Later, at a movie, Heather saw Mike with another woman and discovered that the couple had been dating for several weeks. At this point, Heather developed a lack of confidence in her predictions about Mike and his feelings for her. Having failed to form any appropriate expectations about their actual and potential relationship, Heather became anxious about her interactions with the opposite sex. If this happens to Heather with several different male acquaintances, she could very well develop a fear of interacting with men and experience communication apprehension when placed in that type of situation.

The example of Heather is greatly oversimplified and perhaps overdramatized. The process portrayed would require a great amount of time and more than one relationship and situation. It does help to illustrate, however, how expectations can serve to heighten apprehension about communication. Regularity of appropriate expectations is the key. One of the most general expectations in life is to have regularity in one's environment. People expect to be reinforced for some behaviors and not reinforced for others. Reinforcement, or the lack of it, is the outcome that people learn to expect by continually engaging in certain behaviors over time and across situations. From this process, three things can happen: (1) people develop new positive expectations, (2) people develop new negative expectations, or (3) people become helpless.

When a person engages in communicative behaviors that work i.e., when he or she receives reinforcement for the communication), that person develops positive expectations for those behaviors. The behaviors become a regular part of the person's communicative "storehouse." Had Mike called Heather for a date, she would have developed positive expectations for her communicative behavior that led to the date. She would have continued engaging in them since Mike reinforced them. Neither anxiety nor fear is associated with such positive expectations. Negative expectations are developed in much the same way as positive expectations. People discover that some communicative behaviors lead to punishment or lack of reinforcement, and they tend to reduce those behaviors. This is what happened to Heather in the above example. Mike offered no reinforcement for how Heather communicated with him (at least as she saw it). Thus, Heather began to question the appropriateness of her behavior. The next time that she meets a new potential date, having no other behaviors readily available from which to choose, Heather's fear will be her natural response.

Learned helplessness results from irregular or inconsistent reward and punishment. Perhaps the last young man whom Heather met was very responsive to her and they had a good relationship for quite some time. Now Mike comes along and offers no reinforcement for her behaviors. If this inconsistency were to occur through several relationships for Heather, and if she were unable to determine the appropriate (reinforced) behaviors from the inappropriate, she would become literally "helpless" in her relationships with males. Learned helplessness and negative expectations are the primary components of communication apprehension. The more general the helplessness or negative expectations, the more trait-like the apprehension. In other words, if an individual constantly forms negative expectations about and becomes helpless in her or his communication with others, then he or she is more likely to have communication apprehension as a trait.

Situational Communication Apprehension

The causes of situational apprehension may be generated by the following eight elements: novelty, formality, subordinate status, conspicuousness, unfamiliarity, dissimilarity, excessive attention, and evaluation from others.

The first day of a new class or a new job can be a difficult situation to deal with initially. It is the novelty of the situation that causes the anxiety. In fact, such novel situations may prevent people from being comfortable communicating with others.

Formal situations are associated with highly prescribed behaviors. In these situations, the prescribed behaviors are deemed appropriate and there is little latitude for deviation from them.

The same is true for subordinate status. In this situation, the person holding the higher status

Apprehension can increase in relation to an individual's shyness, which, in the case of Leilani Tassillo, resulted in her covering her face in an awkward moment during a White House media event held in August 1999 to address the issue of youth violence.
(Reuters NewMedia Inc./Corbis)

(e.g., an instructor to a student) defines what is appropriate behavior.

Being conspicuous can increase a person's communication apprehension. For example, when a person is put "on the spot," such as when giving a speech or introducing a speaker to an audience, the person can experience heightened anxiety.

Unfamiliarity is involved when a person attends a social gathering and only know one or two other people. Generally, the more unfamiliar the people and situation around one, the more apprehensive a person feels.

In much the same way, dissimilarity of those around one causes communication apprehension to increase. For the most part, talking to people who are similar to oneself is easier than talking to people who are different. For example, if an individual is an English major, he or she may find it hard to carry on a conversation with a person who is a diehard engineering major. There are exceptions. Some people are less comfortable when they are talking to people who are like themselves than when they are talking to people who are very different, or even strangers. This happens because the former is more likely to make evaluations that may prove threatening.

Most people do not like others staring at them. Neither do they care to be ignored by others. A moderate degree of attention from others is usually the most comfortable situation. Excessive attention, such as staring or having someone probe into one's private thoughts, can cause the level of communication apprehension to rise sharply.

Many students have little trouble conversing with their teachers—until the teacher begins evaluating the student's classroom performance. The same holds true for workers in relation to their supervisors. When people are evaluated, they tend to become more anxious than they would otherwise be. As the intensity of the evaluation increases, so might the level of apprehension.

Of all of the causal elements of communication apprehension that have been discussed, the most important may be previous failure. When a person fails at something once, he or she will probably fear failing again. It is a case of expectations. If one expects to fail and does so, the negative expectations are reinforced. If a person is unable to decide the successful behavior to engage in, he or she is quite apt to develop apprehension. Of course, success causes confidence, which leads to more success, which reduces apprehension.

Effects of Communication Apprehension

The most obvious effects of communication apprehension are internal discomfort, avoidance or withdrawal from communication situations, and communication disruption. People experience communication apprehension internally. That is, the experience of communication apprehension is a mental one—it is felt psychologically. Thus, while some individuals may experience communication apprehension to greater or lesser degrees than other individuals, or only with certain people or in certain situations, the one thing that people all share when they are anxious about communicating is an internally experienced feeling of discomfort. Typically, the lower the communication apprehension, the lower the discomfort.

People tend to differ in their individual responses to communication apprehension. Some handle it well and can communicate effectively despite their internal discomfort. However, most people who experience communication apprehension, particularly those who experience high levels of it, communication is a problem. Three typical response patterns emerge when communication apprehension is experienced: communication avoidance, communication withdrawal, and communication disruption.

When people are confronted with a situation that they expect will make them uncomfortable and they have a choice of whether or not to enter the situation, they can decide either to confront the situation and make the best of it or to avoid it and thus avoid the discomfort. An analogy is the student who receives poor midterm grades and decides not to go home for spring break. By not going home, the student avoids the discomfort of having to face his or her parent's wrath about the grades (this assumes, of course, that the student has a choice of whether to go home). Frequently, people who have high communication apprehension will avoid situations that require them to communicate orally with others.

It is not always possible for a person to avoid communication. Sometimes there is no reason to expect a situation to cause discomfort, so a person may enter it with her or his psychological guard down. When situations such as these arise, withdrawal is the typical response for the person who is experiencing communication apprehension. The withdrawal may be total (e.g., absolute silence) or partial (e.g., talking only when absolutely necessary). An example of possible withdrawal is the student who speaks in class only when directly called on by the teacher. Another is when a person in a one-on-one interaction only answers questions and gives responses but never initiates conversation. When unable to avoid a communication situation, the communication-apprehensive person usually will, if possible, withdraw from interaction.

A third typical response to communication apprehension is communication disruption. This disruption can take two forms. One form is disturbed or nonfluent communication. Examples include stuttering, stammering, speaking too softly, increased pauses, use of inappropriate gestures and expressions, and poor choices of words and phrases. The other form of disruption is overcommunication. This is an overcompensation reflected in one's attempt to succeed in the situation despite the internal discomfort it causes. An example is the person who, in spite of her or his apprehension, attempts to dominate interactions with others, refuses to acknowledge cues that others want to leave, or tries to answer every question a teacher poses in a class. Thus, the highly communication-apprehensive individual is likely to use inappropriate behaviors in a discomforting communication situation. It is important to note, however, that disruption is also characteristic of people with inadequate communication skills and that overcommunication is often mistaken for low apprehension.

Perceptions about Quiet People

As noted earlier, society places a great deal of importance on communication. It is no surprise, then, that low talkers are usually perceived as being unfriendly. Low talkers are also viewed as being less attractive than talkative people. Moreover, even low talkers perceive other low talkers to be less attractive than talkative people. Low talkers are perceived as being less competent than talkative people. Research has found people to have a stereotype of a quiet person as being less competent and less intelligent. Fortunately, this is only a stereotype (i.e., a generalization that generally does not hold true for all members of a group). There are just as many intelligent low talkers as there are intelligent high talkers. Nevertheless, the general perception of low talkers is that they are less competent and less intelligent.

A frequently accurate perception of low talkers is that they are generally more anxious than talkative people. Although not all low talkers are apprehensive about communication, many are apprehensive. Their tendency for apprehension is generalized to other low talkers. This leads to another stereotype: that low talkers are anxious people.

The role of leader in most situations requires at least a moderate degree of communication with other people. Thus, low talkers are perceived to be poor leaders. This perception is very often correct. There are, of course, instances in which quiet people provide leadership functions. For example, they might provide some necessary information that helps a group reach a decision. However, even in these situations, the low talker is unlikely to be perceived as a leader.

Perceptions such as the ones just presented are important for several reasons. How people perceive others determines the nature of the relationship between them. In addition, how people perceive others will have a significant effect on interactions in certain settings. Three of these settings are school, social environment, and the workplace.

School

The perception of low talkers as less competent and less intelligent than talkative people greatly affects how they are responded to in school. For example, since teachers tend to expect low talkers to do less well in school, they treat low talkers as if they were less intelligent. Low talkers are less likely to be called on in class, receive less attention from teachers, and ask for help less frequently than do talkative people. Therefore, with so little interaction, the low talker has fewer opportunities to correct mistakes and to receive reinforcement.

Does this affect their achievement? Research suggests that it does. Take, for example, the classroom in which much of the final grade depends on "participation": the low talker is less likely to participate in class activities, and this student's grade is apt to be lower than that of talkative students. As this type of evaluation affects the achievement of the low talker throughout school, it ultimately has an effect on the student's general learning. Lack of opportunity and even discrimination lead to less learning for the low talker in the long run, although the low talker is no less intelligent than the talkative person. In short, low talkers tend to fare poorly in school while talkative people tend to fare well.

Social Environment

Social relationships require communication for their establishment and maintenance. Typically, when someone does not want to talk, people disregard that person and move on to someone else. As noted earlier, low talkers are perceived as being both less friendly and less attractive than talkative people. Low talkers have fewer dating relationships than talkative people, and, to some extent, they have fewer people whom they can call "friends."

In one study that asked high communication-apprehensives and low communication-apprehensives to indicate how many people they knew that they could classify as "good friends," the high apprehensives indicated a range from zero to two, with more than one-third indicating none. More interesting was the finding that, when asked to list the names of their good friends, the high apprehensives most often named relatives while the low apprehensives seldom listed relatives. Just as in school, then, it seems that low talkers tend to fare less well in the general social environment than do talkative people.

Workplace

The many perceptions that people have of low talkers are perhaps most felt in the work setting. Low talkers are less likely than talkative people to be given job interviews, especially when their qualifications are equal. Even when an interview is granted, the low talker will garner negative perceptions from the interviewer because of her or his likelihood of engaging in dysfunctional communication behaviors. This is not to suggest that low talkers never get job interviews or obtain employment. Most do, but it is much harder for them than it is for talkative people.

Similarly, low talkers and talkative people are not equally successful once employment is gained. Research in a variety of occupations has found low talkers to be less satisfied with their jobs than are talkative people. The most dramatic work-related difference between low talkers and high talkers, however, appears at promotion time. Not only are low talkers less frequently promoted than talkative people, but they often report not anticipating or even wanting to be promoted. This is because promotions to higher positions typically require greater communicative responsibilities. In short, then, as in the school setting and social environments, life at work seems much more difficult for low talkers than it is for more talkative people.

People have perceptions about low talkers being incompetent and, therefore, being in a highly undesirable condition. Is this necessarily true? Fortunately, it is not. Many quiet people are most happy and content with their lives, and they are successful at what they do. When offered help to overcome communication apprehension, many quiet people decline. Many have adjusted well to their lifestyle and have no desire to change. Nevertheless, people who are highly willing to communicate and happily engage in communication with others generally have a major advantage over those who are less willing to communicate.

Conclusion

Willingness to communicate can be a dominant force in a person's behavior. This is particularly true when the person's low willingness to communicate is generalized, or trait-like. In such cases, any communication situation may cause discomfort. As a result, the person is likely to avoid the situation or withdraw from it if he or she cannot avoid it. Perhaps, at worst, an inability to avoid or withdraw will lead the source to engage in dysfunctional communication. Essentially, if communication is dysfunctional for the person, it will be dysfunctional for the person with whom he or she is trying to communicate, thereby resulting in an ineffective encounter.

The willingness to talk is central to the outcomes of communication. Through talk people realize the fulfillment of their expectations for a given communication situation. Through talk people reduce the uncertainties that they have about various situations, other people, and themselves. Through talk people establish, maintain, and, when necessary, terminate relationships. Too little talk is usually an inappropriate form of communication. Too much talk can be too, but if the quality of that talk is high, it probably will not be perceived as being too much. The effective communicator is one who knows when to talk, when to be silent, and what are the appropriate responses to communications from another person.

See also: GROUP COMMUNICATION; GROUP COMMUNICATION, CONFLICT AND; GROUP COMMUNICATION, DECISION MAKING AND; GROUP COMMUNICATION, DYNAMICS OF; GROUP COMMUNICATION, ROLES AND RESPONSIBILITIES IN; INTERPERSONAL COMMUNICATION; INTERPERSONAL COMMUNICATION, CONVERSATION AND; INTERPERSONAL COMMUNICATION, LISTENING AND; INTRAPERSONAL COMMUNICATION; PUBLIC SPEAKING.

Bibliography

Beatty, Michael. J. (1988). "Situational and Predispositional Correlates of Public Speaking Anxiety." *Communication Education* 37:29–39.

Beatty, Michael J., and McCroskey, James C. (1998). "Interpersonal Communication as Temperamental Expression: A Communibiological Paradigm." In *Communication and Personality Trait Perspectives*, eds. James C. McCroskey, John A. Daly,

Matthew M. Martin, and Michael J. Beatty. Cresskill, NJ: Hampton Press.

Daly, John A.; McCroskey, James C.; Ayres, Joe; Hopf, Tim; and Ayres, Debbie, eds. (1997). *Avoiding Communication: Shyness, Reticence, and Communication Apprehension,* 2nd edition. Cresskill, NJ: Hampton Press.

McCroskey, James C. (1977). "Oral Communication Apprehension: A Summary of Recent Theory and Research." *Human Communication Research* 4:78–96.

McCroskey, James C. (1997). *An Introduction to Rhetorical Communication,* 7th edition. Boston, MA: Allyn & Bacon.

McCroskey, James C., and Richmond, Virginia P. (1996). *Fundamentals of Human Communication: An Interpersonal Perspective.* Prospect Heights, IL: Waveland Press.

Richmond, Virginia P. (1997). "Quietness in Contemporary Society: Conclusions and Generalizations of the Research." In *Avoiding Communication: Shyness, Reticence, and Communication Apprehension,* 2nd edition, eds. John A. Daly, James C. McCroskey, Joe Ayers, Tim Hopf, and Debbie Ayers. Cresskill, NJ: Hampton Press.

Richmond, Virginia P., and McCroskey, James C. (1998). *Communication: Apprehension, Avoidance, and Effectiveness,* 5th edition. Boston, MA: Allyn & Bacon.

JAMES C. MCCROSKEY
VIRGINIA P. RICHMOND

ARCHIVES, PUBLIC RECORDS, AND RECORDS MANAGEMENT

Archives have existed since ancient times. According to James O'Toole (1990), the term "archives" was originally used to "designate all collections of written records" (p. 28). In the modern world, however, the word "archives" is commonly used in three different senses. First, archives are documents that are created or accumulated by an individual or an organization in the normal course of business. Second, archives are the independent agencies or programs within institutions that are responsible for selecting, preserving, and providing access to archival documents. Finally, archives are the buildings or repositories that house collections of archival documents.

To understand the nature of archival documents in the first sense of the word, it is helpful to make a distinction between records and archives. Records are all information, regardless of format, that is produced or accumulated in the normal course of affairs by an individual or an organization and is maintained in order to provide evidence of specific transactions. Archives are those records that are deemed to have continuing value and are therefore retained beyond the period in which they are actively used. (The archives of individuals are sometimes referred to as "personal papers" or "manuscripts.") Thus, archives constitute a smaller portion of the entire documentary universe than do records.

Like records, archives can exist in any format on which information has been recorded. Archival collections frequently consist of a wide variety of media. In addition to traditional textual materials, archivists care for materials such as photographs, films, videotapes, sound recordings, and magnetic tapes and disks. The many issues posed by archival materials recorded in electronic format are among the greatest challenges facing the archival profession.

Archival materials, like library materials, are important cultural resources. Several characteristics, however, distinguish the types of materials generally held in library collections from those found in archival collections. Alternate copies of the materials housed in a given library can often be found in the collections of other libraries. Archival materials, in contrast, are often unique and are found only in a single repository. Sue McKemmish (1993) provides an overview of the key distinctions between library and archival materials. She describes the materials held in libraries as information products, which have been consciously authored for dissemination or publication "to inform, perpetuate knowledge, convey ideas, feelings, and opinions; to entertain, [and] to provide information about their subject" (p. 7). She characterizes materials found in archives, on the other hand, as information by-products of activity, which are accumulated or created in the course of doing business in order to facilitate the business process of which they are a part. McKemmish further notes that while library materials are often discrete items, archival materials are usually part of a larger group of related records.

Importance of Archival Materials and Archival Institutions

Archival institutions select, preserve, and make their records accessible for a number of reasons, including legal, financial, and administrative purposes. Government archives (at the federal, state or local level) that administer public records, for example, maintain records as evidence of the government's policies and operations. Thus, public archives help ensure that the government is held accountable to the public by preserving records that enable citizens to monitor the conduct of government agencies and public servants. In addition, the records that are held by public archives document the rights of citizens, such as entitlement to social security benefits or ownership of property. Private organizations, such as businesses, churches, universities, and museums, also establish institutional archives to care for their records. The archival records that are maintained by these repositories document the organizations' origins, structures, policies, programs, functions, and vital information over time.

In addition to the legal, fiscal, and administrative purposes for which records are originally created and used, archival records are useful for historical or research purposes. Archives provide a key with which to examine past and present events. In addition to the administrative users of archives, a variety of researchers take advantage of archival sources. These researchers may include scholars, genealogists, students at all levels, local historians, biographers, independent writers, and documentary filmmakers. Since archival documents can be used for many purposes by diverse audiences, the records of organizations that do not have their own institutional archives, as well as the personal papers of individuals, are often actively sought by archival programs such as collecting repositories or historical societies. These types of institutions, rather than documenting the activities of a parent organization, focus on collecting records that document a particular topic (e.g., a person, subject, or geographical area).

Records Management and Archives

Records management and archives are closely related. Indeed, the existence of strong archives relies on the implementation of sound records management techniques. In the United States, most records professionals credit the National Archives with originating records management in the 1940s. While the National Archives was indeed influential in the evolution of modern records management in America and was responsible for much of the development of modern records management techniques in the United States, it is important to note that, historically speaking, records management is hardly a new development. Records management, in various forms, has been a concern across many cultures for centuries.

In 1989, the National Archives and Records Administration produced *A Federal Records Management Glossary*, which offered the following definition of records management: "The planning, controlling, directing, organizing, training, promoting, and other managerial activities related to the creation, maintenance and use, and disposition of records to achieve adequate and proper documentation of . . . policies and transactions and effective and economical management of agency operations" (p. 32). A core principle of records management is that of the life cycle of records. This concept holds that all records have a common life cycle, which is often divided into three phases: active, semi-active, and inactive.

During the active life of records, employees or records managers within an agency create and use records. In the semi-active phase, during which records are used less frequently but are occasionally necessary for the conducting of business, records may be transferred to a central records management office or an off-site facility for storage. When those records are no longer needed by the agency, they enter an inactive phase, at which time archivists are called in to make judgments about the disposition of records. Depending on the form of disposition that is selected, records may be retained for a designated period of time (in which case they are generally transferred to a records storage center), they may be retained indefinitely (in which case they are transferred to an archives), or they may be destroyed.

Ironically, while the modern records management profession in the United States emerged from the archival profession, a schism soon developed between the two fields. The roots of this rift may well lie in the very concept of the life cycle, which essentially makes the active phase of a record's life the domain of the records manager and the inactive phase the domain of the archivist. Perhaps in consequence of this distinction, records managers and archivists have often taken antagonistic attitudes toward each other rather than developing cooperative relationships to ensure the documentation of organizations and of society. As Terry and Carol Lundgren (1989) point out, "[In] records

The Central Intelligence Agency uses a robotic arm to handle magnetic tapes that are part of the information storage system. (Roger Ressmeyer/Corbis)

management circles, archivists are sometimes unkindly referred to as pack rats, since their primary concern is the permanent preservation of all records that have or may have historical value" (p. 153). In archival circles, on the other hand, records managers might well be seen uncharitably as philistines who are devoid of any sense of history and whose primary concern is ensuring the economy and efficiency of their parent organizations by disposing of as many records as possible.

The rapid proliferation of electronic media has caused archivists and records managers alike to rethink the concept of the life cycle and the division between their closely related professions. The Australian archival community in particular has been especially active in advocating the replacement of the concept of the life cycle with that of a records continuum that recognizes the interconnectedness of managing a record at all phases of its life, from its creation to its disposition. Indeed, the continuum concept recognizes that, with electronic documents, it is necessary to plan for records management prior to the creation of

records. This can be accomplished through the development of adequate recordkeeping systems that will ensure the continued preservation of and access to electronic documents. Thus, in order to manage documents effectively in electronic format, archivists and records managers need to work together and they need to collaborate closely with other information professionals, such as computer specialists and systems analysts.

The 1990s saw the emergence of the knowledge management field, which is another information field that is related to records management. Knowledge management is most prevalent in corporate, rather than government or nonprofit, settings. Bruce Dearstyne (1999) offers the following working definition for this emerging area: "Knowledge management is an evolving set of strategic approaches, management skills, and technologies to enhance the application of information resources and individuals' knowledge to the business purposes of an organization and to strengthen its capacity to improve its operations and services" (p. 2).

This articulation of knowledge management suggests that this field differs from records management in at least two significant ways. First, knowledge management incorporates implicit knowledge, such as people's expertise, experience, and insights, as well as the explicit knowledge, in the form of recorded information, that is the realm of records management. Second, the primary goal of knowledge management is to enhance business operations and services, while the primary objectives of records management are to provide adequate documentation of an organization's policies and transactions and to demonstrate effective management of organizational operations.

Archival Management

The management of archival materials can be roughly categorized into the following functions: appraisal, accessioning, arrangement, description, preservation, access, outreach, and advocacy. Although these functions will be discussed separately here, in practice they overlap, since the decisions that are made at each stage necessarily affect management of the materials in other stages.

Appraisal

The initial step in the management of archival materials is appraisal, in which the archivist makes a judgement as to whether particular records should be acquired by the archival repository. Appraisal is the process of determining the value, and thus the disposition, of records. During this process, decisions are made about whether and for how long records should be preserved based on criteria such as their current administrative, legal, and fiscal use, their evidential and informational value, their arrangement and condition, their intrinsic value, and their relationship to other records. Archivists often use the terms "appraisal" and "selection" interchangeably to describe this process. It is important to note that when used in the archival context, appraisal does not have anything to do with monetary value.

The Society of American Archivists' Task Force on Goals and Priorities (1986) emphasizes that an archivist's first responsibility is the selection of records that have enduring value. The other responsibilities of an archivist depend on wise selections being made at this stage. Despite the centrality of this function to archival management, archivists continue to debate the role of the archivist in appraisal and the best criteria on which to base appraisal decisions. Archivists have adopted various criteria for appraisal based on the value of the records, the use to which the records might be put in the future, the policy of the archival repository, and the goal of creating an image of the institution or the society to which the records pertain.

The writings of Theodore Shellenberg (1949, 1956) with regard to appraisal represent a codification of appraisal practice at the National Archives, and they designate various types of values that are found in records as the basis for selection decisions. Shellenberg postulated that records possess primary values that are related to the purposes for which they were originally created (e.g., administrative, legal, fiscal, research, or historical). In addition, records have secondary value when they are used for any purpose other than that for which they were originally created. This secondary value may be informational (i.e., related directly to the data found in the records) or evidential (i.e., related to the degree to which the records reflect an organization's functions and policies over time).

The potential use to which archival materials may be put has also been advanced as a criterion on which to base, and test, appraisal decisions. The application of this criterion is particularly problematic, however, because it requires the archivist to become a soothsayer, predicting the research needs of the future users of archives. Nonetheless, use has been accepted by many archivists as a strong qualifier for the selection and appraisal of records.

During the 1980s, a new approach to the appraisal of archival materials began to emerge. Drawing on the library literature about collection management, archivists began to argue that selection decisions should be made within the context of a clearly defined collecting policy. While, in practice, many archival repositories had been guided in their appraisal choices by institutional policy for some time, Faye Phillips's 1984 article "Developing Collecting Policies for Manuscript Collections" provided a detailed model policy that different types of archives could adapt to their needs.

Subsequent discussions of appraisal in the archival literature have focused on documentation strategies, institutional functional analysis, and macro-appraisal. Collectively, these approaches adopt a "top down" rather than a "bottom up" orientation to appraisal. More traditional approaches, based on value, use, and policy, have focused on records themselves. Advocates of the emerging methods of appraisal argue that careful research and analysis of the records creators and the records creating processes should precede the examination or appraisal of any actual records. By approaching appraisal in this manner, archivists can identify the most important records creators and records producing functions within an organization, thereby placing themselves in a better position to create a more complete image of the institution or society that is being documented.

Accessioning

Once archives make the decision to acquire a collection of records, the next step in the management process is for the archival institution to accession the records. Accessioning is the procedure through which an archival repository takes administrative, legal, and physical custody of a group of records. The means by which archives acquire administrative and legal control of records is slightly different for institutional archival programs than it is for collection repositories. Within institutional archives, records are generally transferred by means of a transmittal form, in which the office that created the records grants custody to the archival program of the same institution. For collecting repositories, which acquire records not from a parent organization but from private donors or external institutions, a deed of gift is the primary instrument by which the archives gain legal and administrative control over the records.

During accessioning, the archivist collects basic information about the records on the basis of a preliminary examination. Generally, an accession form is created, which includes data such as the creator of the records, the quantity, condition, and current location of the records, any restrictions on the records, a list of contents and brief descriptions of the records. The information that is gathered during the accessioning process provides essential information about the newly acquired records and later serves as the basis for the arrangement and description functions.

Arrangement and Description

The arrangement and description of archives serve the dual functions of preserving records and making them available for use. Collectively,

arrangement and description are often referred to as the "processing" of archival collections. Fredric Miller (1990) notes that "[by] making possible the use of records, processing gives meaning to their acquisition and preservation. At the same time, processing is the key method by which archivists control and administer the records in their custody" (p. 3). In the arrangement of archival records, archivists organize and order their collections, thereby bringing archives under physical control. In the description of archival collections, archivists bring together information that provides a context for the records, thereby bringing them under intellectual control.

The arrangement of archival collections is governed by two key concepts: provenance and original order. According to the principle of provenance, which emerged from nineteenth-century European archival practice, records are maintained according to their creator or source, rather than by subject or classification systems. Records produced by different creators are not intermingled, even though they might share a common subject. The second important concept for archival arrangement, original order, holds that whenever possible, records should be maintained according to the filing structures that were used by their creators. In some cases, however, records come to archives in such a state of disorganization that to maintain them in their original order would be a detriment to subsequent use. In these cases, the archivist may choose to arrange the records in a logical way (e.g., alphabetically, chronologically, or topically) in order to facilitate access. By arranging archival collections according to the principles of provenance and original order, archivists maintain important contextual information about how the materials were initially created and used.

Archival materials can be arranged (and subsequently described) at a variety of levels. Ranging from the broadest to the most specific, these levels include the following: the repository, the record group or collection, the series, the file unit, and the item. Professional practice holds that archives should gain physical and intellectual control over all of the records at a broad level before proceeding to progressively refined, more specific, levels of arrangement and description.

Unlike library materials, which are generally cataloged at the item level, collective description of groups of records is the norm for archival description. Collective description emerged in the organization of archival materials for practical as well as intellectual reasons. Many archival collections are quite large, composed of hundreds, thousands, or even millions of items. To create individual records for each item in these collections would be an overwhelming, if not an impossible, task. Moreover, archival documents can generally be used more effectively in the aggregate, since the value of an archival record is often enhanced by the relationships that connect it to other records within the collection. There are, of course, situations in which an individual item (e.g., the Declaration of Independence) possesses an intrinsic value and therefore merits description at the item level, but these cases are the exception rather than the rule.

Archives produce a variety of information surrogates to represent their holdings. These surrogates range from guides to the collections of several institutions in an area, to guides to the holdings of a single institution, to guides to a particular subject area, to inventories of specific collections, to brief catalog records. The primary descriptive tool that is produced by most archives is the inventory, or finding aid, which provides a detailed, narrative account for a collection of records that is held by a repository. Finding aids typically consist of two types of information: explanatory notes and an inventory. The description of the records might include the creator, the dates covered by the records, the quantity of the records, the title for the collection or series, the location of the records, the restrictions to access of the records, the information about the arrangement of the records, a narrative account of the records creator, information about the contents, and information that notes the existence of related materials. The inventory portion of a finding aid includes a brief list of the contents of each container, file, volume, or item, depending upon the level to which the collection is processed.

Since archival materials are so diverse, archival institutions have not been able to take advantage of standards for the exchange of information about their holdings in the same way that libraries have. However, the archival profession has begun to explore more standardized methods by which archival programs can exchange information with other archives and with other cultural institutions. There have been two promising advances in

this area. The first was the development in the 1980s of an archival format for Machine Readable Cataloging (MARC), by which archivists can enter brief descriptions of their collections into national bibliographic utilities. The second, Encoded Archival Description (EAD), was introduced in 1993 and has slowly begun to be accepted by the archival community. EAD defines common elements that are found in finding aids and prescribes an order in which they should appear. It designates a few elements that are required for providing a minimally acceptable level of information about a collection, but it is flexible enough to be applied in a wide variety of archival settings. Since EAD is still in its infancy, relatively speaking, its long-term effect on archival description remains to be seen.

Preservation

Records on all forms of media located in archives need protection in order to minimize the wear and tear that are inherent in handling, copying, loaning, and exhibiting them. Preservation refers to the management activities that are associated with maintaining materials in their original form or other format. Preservation of archival materials encompasses a number of technical and administrative processes that should be comprehensive and integrated within the overall archival program. Archivists are concerned with a number of preservation issues, including the following:

- environment (i.e., temperature, relative humidity, light, dust, mold, pests, and gases),
- storage space,
- disaster preparedness (i.e., preparing contingency plans for use in case of fire, flood, storms, and other natural or man-made disasters),
- assessing the scope and nature of deterioration and damage to records (i.e., brittle paper and/or technological obsolescence), and
- use (i.e., establishing policies about the use of holdings by patrons and staff and about the public display of holdings).

A well thought out archival preservation program would consist of installing equipment to monitor and stabilize environmental conditions, maintaining the physical facilities routinely, enforcing security procedures for staff, patrons and others, and implementing routine holdings maintenance actions, including removing or replacing damaged or deteriorated items.

Access

If people are to use archives, then they must have intellectual, legal, and physical access to them. The term "access" encompasses all three concepts. Intellectual access is provided through the arrangement and description of records and reference assistance from an archivist. Archivists create and rely on finding aids as reference tools to assist users. Finding aids help users locate needed records and information.

Access is also related to whether or not users have permission or authority to use archives. Records created and maintained for personal or internal use may include private or confidential information. Archivists are legally and ethically bound to ensure equitable access to records that are in their care. Maintaining fair use, however, is a problem because archivists have to deal with such issues as privacy, confidentiality, copyright, preservation, and freedom of information.

Repositories provide physical access by maintaining standard operating hours that allow users to visit the archives to study and copy records for private or educational purposes. The World Wide Web, however, has redefined physical access to records. Repositories are making many of their records available online. Thus, users can access finding aids and records from their personal computers. Users have the opportunity to examine finding aids and to exchange e-mail messages with reference archivists before deciding if a visit to the actual archives is necessary.

Outreach and Advocacy

Outreach and advocacy represent the culmination of archival work. Archivists use advocacy and outreach to help the general public understand archives and build support for archival programs. Outreach is any effort to generate or gain public interest in the archives through a variety of mechanisms such as lecture and film series, fundraisers, brochures, media coverage, exhibits, and publications. Advocacy builds on outreach. It involves archivists, records professionals, and manuscript curators engaging in activities, such as lobbying on behalf of specific legislation or influencing public policy, that affect some aspect of archives or records. Outreach and advocacy are crucial func-

tions because archivists have to vie with other information providers and because technological changes have transformed delivery methods for archives and historical records.

Conclusion

Archives are vital to society for many reasons. Among the most important functions that archival records fulfill is that they serve as instruments of accountability and as building blocks of collective memory. John McDonald (1998) succinctly expresses the relationship between records and accountability as follows: "Without records, there can be no demonstration of accountability. Without evidence of accountability, society cannot trust in its public institutions." In addition to providing for accountability, archival collections constitute an important part of society's cultural and intellectual heritage, thereby contributing to the formation of a nation's collective memory. To ensure the preservation of this valuable legacy and to provide for democratic accountability, archivists and records managers (including public records officers) from diverse organizations must work together to administer the records that they hold in trust for future generations.

See also: ARCHIVISTS; CATALOGING AND KNOWLEDGE ORGANIZATION; CONSERVATORS; CURATORS; KNOWLEDGE MANAGEMENT; KNOWLEDGE MANAGEMENT, CAREERS IN; LIBRARIES, FUNCTIONS AND TYPES OF; MUSEUMS; PRESERVATION AND CONSERVATION OF INFORMATION; REFERENCE SERVICES AND INFORMATION ACCESS; STANDARDS AND INFORMATION.

Bibliography

Bellardo, Lewis, and Bellardo, Lynn Lady, comps. (1992). *A Glossary for Archivists, Manuscript Curators, and Records Managers.* Chicago: Society of American Archivists.

Berner, Richard C. (1983). *Archival Theory and Practice in the United States: A Historical Analysis.* Seattle: University of Washington Press.

Cox, Richard J. (2000). *Historical Perspectives on Modern Archives and Records Management.* Westport, CT: Greenwood Press.

Dearstyne, Bruce. (1999). "Knowledge Management: Concepts, Strategies, and Prospects." *Records and Information Management Report* 15(7):1–14.

Fox, Michael J., and Wilkerson, Peter. (1999). *Introduction to Organization and Description: Access to Cultural Heritage.* Los Angeles: Getty Institute.

Ham, F. Gerald. (1992). *Selecting and Appraising Archives and Manuscripts.* Chicago: Society of American Archivists.

Lundgren, Terry, and Lundgren, Carol. (1989). *Records Management in the Computer Age.* Boston: PWS-Kent Publishing.

McDonald, John. (1998). "Accountability in Government in an Electronic Age." <http://www.irmt.org/education/malpaper2.html.>

McKemmish, Sue. (1993). "Introducing Archives and Archival Programs." In *Keeping Archives*, 2nd edition, ed. Judith Ellis. Port Melbourne, Australia: D. W. Thorpe.

Miller, Fredric M. (1990). *Arranging and Describing Archives and Manuscripts.* Chicago: Society of American Archivists.

National Archives and Records Administration. (1989). *A Federal Records Management Glossary.* Washington, DC: National Archives and Records Administration.

O'Toole, James M. (1990). *Understanding Archives and Manuscripts.* Chicago: Society of American Archivists.

Penn, Ira. (1983). "Understanding the Life Cycle Concept of Records Management." *Records Management Quarterly* 17(3):5–8, 41.

Phillips, Faye. (1984). "Developing Collecting Policies for Manuscript Collections." *American Archivist* 47(1):30–42.

Pugh, Mary Jo. (1992). *Providing Reference Services for Archives and Manuscripts.* Chicago: Society of American Archivists.

Ritzenhaler, Mary Lynn. (1993). *Preserving Archives and Manuscripts.* Chicago: Society of American Archivists.

Schellenberg, Theodore R. (1949). *Disposition of Federal Records: How to Develop an Effective Program for the Preservation and Disposal of Federal Records.* Washington, DC: National Archives.

Schellenberg, Theodore R. (1956). *The Appraisal of Modern Public Records.* Washington, DC: National Archives.

Society of American Archivists Task Force on Goals and Priorities. (1986). *Planning for the Archival Profession: A Report of the SAA Task Force on Goals and Priorities.* Chicago: Society of American Archivists.

Wilsted, Thomas, and Nolte, William. (1991). *Managing Archival and Manuscript Repositories.* Chicago: Society of American Archivists.

JENNIFER A. MARSHALL
TYWANNA M. WHORLEY

ARCHIVISTS

Archivists, people who look after the records of businesses, organizations, or governments, probably have been around since the fourth millennium B.C.E. At that time, cuneiform clay tablets and hieroglyphics on papyrus came into use in the Middle East and Egypt, and with the creation of such records came the need for people to look after them. As civilization developed and advanced in Greece, Rome, and China, more records were produced in a variety of formats and these records required care.

This early recordkeeping continued and accelerated during the rise of nation-states, which in turn brought their recordkeeping practices to their colonies. As early as 1626, the English colony of Jamestown in North America had systematic land records. And records were so important to the rebellious colonists during the American Revolution that they were mentioned in the *Declaration of Independence.*

But in the new United States of America, archives and the archival profession did not grow rapidly. To be sure, recordkeeping developed apace with the new federal government, but the care of these governmental records was largely unsystematic and lacking any real archival identity. Fortunately, by the eighteenth century, records of special historical value began to be systematically preserved by privately supported state and local historical societies—an archival movement that eventually took many forms and steadily expanded in the nineteenth and early twentieth centuries.

The establishment in 1934 of the National Archives of the United States gave great impetus to archival growth and defined more clearly the archival profession. This was a major step, albeit a rather tardy one if compared to similar development in other countries. Nonetheless, this new governmental institution quickly proved to be a major force in promoting archives and what was to become the archival profession.

Initially, the National Archives drew heavily from the history profession. Most early National Archives staff members had master's degrees or doctorates in history. Gradually, the archivist developed a separate professional identity that led to the establishment of the first professional organization of archivists. Founded in 1936, the

Society of American Archivists continues to this day and is supplemented by many regional, state, and local archival organizations.

The years of the New Deal and World War II (approximately 1932 to 1945) sparked a vast expansion of records in both the public and private sectors, leading to the creation of a new discipline known as records management. Records managers did not come from either the historical or the archival profession; they were in essence people who were more interested in the efficient and economical arrangement of documents than in their historical value. These new records managers inherited an ancient tradition of efficient custodial care of records. Reflecting this new discipline closely allied with that of archivist, the National Archives became the National Archives and Records Service.

In the postwar years, the archival movement accelerated, and in the late 1950s, a national study showed that there were about 1,300 archives and archival-related agencies in the United States. In 1988, a successor survey reported the existence of 4,200 such agencies. As the agencies grew, so did the number of people staffing them. The Society of American Archivists has grown from its original membership of 125 in 1936 to a membership of 3,600 in 1999. This figure still falls far short of the actual number of people who are employed in archives or archival-related agencies.

Archivists perform a wide variety of professional assignments in a broad range of settings. They seek out and acquire historical and/or current records, including electronic records. They devise systems to bring records into the archives, a process known as "accessioning." They must then decide what records to save and how to fit them into the overall plan, a process known as "appraisal." They then must preserve the original arrangement of the records or organize them systematically, a process known as "arranging the records." After the newly acquired records are accessioned, appraised, and arranged, they must then be described through the creation of catalogs, finding aids, or computer-based access systems. And finally, the acquired, accessioned, appraised, arranged, and described records must be preserved by a variety of methods that range from simple repairs to complex laboratory preservation procedures. It should be kept in mind that paper records, traditionally the major concern of

An archivist in New York City looks through files that are part of a print archive. (Timothy Fadek/Corbis)

archivists, have become but one part of modern archives, which commonly include photographs, motion pictures, microfilms, videotapes, sound recordings, and other electronic media products. All of these records, in no matter what form, must be acquired, accessioned, appraised, arranged, described, and preserved.

Archivists perform their activities in widely varied institutional settings, ranging in size from a one-person single operation to the National Archives and Records Administration (NARA) with its two major buildings in Washington, D.C., its ten presidential libraries, its twelve regional archives branches scattered across the country (usually located in NARA records centers), and its additional centers that are used for records-management functions. Archivists may find themselves working in federal, state, or local governmental units or in archives that are connected with colleges or universities, public or private libraries, churches and religious organizations, corporations, or other business enterprises. A single archivist in a small unit may be responsible for all of "archiving" functions in addition to administrative duties, which might include developing budgets, overseeing expenditures, perhaps even fund raising, as well as hiring and overseeing staff. People working in larger units will see a division of labor among all of the functions traditionally ascribed to archivists. As a result, the larger the archival staff, the higher the degree of specialization (and usually the higher the salaries).

How do people become archivists? In the nineteenth century and the early years of the twentieth century, archivists in the United States came primarily from a history background, a not-surprising development considering that historians were the primary users of archives and historical manuscript collections. It was historians who took the lead in establishing many state archival agencies, and it was historians who provided the leadership in the movement to create the National Archives. It was historically oriented personnel at the National Archives who pioneered the earliest formal training of archivists in their own archival institutes and in conjunction with American University. In time, a scattering of universities throughout the United States offered formal courses in archival management, often as components of a master's degree program in history or in library science. These courses were usually introduced and taught by archivists who saw the need for more formal training for those entering the profession. These meager attempts at formal archival education lagged far behind the archival training programs in a number of European nations.

In the 1990s, a few archival educational ventures evolved into multicourse archival programs generally culminating in a master's degree. Some of these programs are still a part of history departments, although as a result of the new technology they are more commonly associated with schools of library and information studies. Schools of librarianship changed dramatically in the 1980s and 1990s. Archivists and librarians were brought closer together by new technology. Two professions that were quite different were brought into closer alignment. Two professions that formerly differed in their practices and procedures began to share common preservation problems and the new world of information technology. Archival programs that lead to a master's degree are in operation at the University of Michigan, the University of Pittsburgh, the University of Maryland, the University of Texas, Wayne State University, the University of California at Los Angeles, and New York University. The Society of American Archivists, which has its headquarters in Chicago and itself conducts many short-term seminars and workshops that focus on continuing education for archivists, provides information about the programs offered by these universities, as well as other education programs in the field.

Clearly archivists, along with librarians and records managers, play an important role in the fast-changing, interrelated information world. Archivists are handling an increasing volume of computer-generated record material. Paper records will continue to occupy their attention, but the profession must now use the new information technology to control and make accessible the archival holdings. This new dimension of archival practice is requiring revised theories, practices, and education to ensure the survival of the records of modern civilization and those of future societies. Archivists hold the records of the past and the future in their hands.

See also: ARCHIVES, PUBLIC RECORDS, AND RECORDS MANAGEMENT; CATALOGING AND KNOWLEDGE ORGANIZATION; LIBRARIANS.

Bibliography

Bantin, Philip C. (1998). "Strategies for Managing Electronic Records: A New Archival Paradigm? An Affirmation of Our Archival Traditions?" *Archival Issues* 23(1):17–34.

Daniels, Maygene F., and Walch, Timothy, eds. (1984). *A Modern Archives Reader: Basic Readings on Archival Theory and Practice.* Washington, DC: National Archives and Records Service.

Evans, Frank B. (1975). *Modern Archives and Manuscripts: A Select Bibliography.* Chicago: Society of American Archivists.

Ham, F. Gerald. (1992). *Selecting and Appraising Archives and Manuscripts.* Chicago: Society of American Archivists.

Miller, Frederic. (1990). *Arranging and Describing Archives and Manuscripts.* Chicago: Society of American Archivists.

O'Toole, James M. (1990). *Understanding Archives and Manuscripts.* Chicago: Society of American Archivists.

Pugh, Mary Jo. (1992). *Providing Reference Services for Archives and Manuscripts.* Chicago: Society of American Archivists.

Ritzenthaler, Mary Lynn. (1993). *Preserving Archives and Manuscripts.* Chicago: Society of American Archivists.

Wilsted, Thomas, and Nolte, William. (1991). *Managing Archival and Manuscript Repositories.* Chicago: Society of American Archivists.

ROBERT M. WARNER

▪ ARMSTRONG, EDWIN HOWARD (1890–1954)

Millions of radio listeners each day tune in their favorite FM (i.e., frequency modulation) stations to hear crystal clear, high-fidelity music and other programming. FM radio offers clarity and a dynamic range that cannot be matched by AM (i.e., amplitude modulation) broadcasting. Many people cannot explain how the signals reach their radios or why the FM stations sound so much better than their AM equivalents. However, if people enjoy the programming that FM stations provide, then they owe a debt of gratitude to the inventor of the technology that made it all possible: Edwin Howard Armstrong.

Armstrong was born on December 18, 1890, in New York City, the first child of Emily and John Armstrong. Young Edwin grew up in a family that was well to do, well educated, and a cornerstone of their Yonkers, New York, community. A quick mind was highly valued in the Armstrong household, as well as a strong body. John Armstrong taught his children the game of tennis, which Edwin would retreat to later in life as a reprieve from his struggles in the laboratory.

Armstrong developed his interest in wireless telephony from books that his father brought back from annual business trips to London. He was fascinated by the tales of inventors such as Guglielmo Marconi and his efforts to send wireless signals across the Atlantic. Soon, with the help of a family friend, Armstrong was building his own wireless apparatus in the attic and communicating with other young boys who were bitten by the wireless "bug."

The long hours in his attic continued throughout his childhood and through adolescence. Upon graduation from Yonkers High School, Armstrong set out for Columbia University and its prestigious program in electrical engineering; however, the tinkering in the attic never ceased. Armstrong's professors recognized his brilliant mind, but his dedication to coursework paled in comparison with his love of the laboratory.

In 1912, with the help of Professor John Morecroft, Armstrong began investigating the properties of the audion tube, a tri-element vacuum tube invented by Lee De Forest that was used to detect an electromagnetic signal. Even De Forest himself, however, was unclear as to how the audion worked. Armstrong discovered, according to Tom Lewis

(1991, p. 70), that "[the] audion was essentially a device that relayed electrons. . . . Acting on this discovery, Armstrong then thought of feeding the oscillating current from the plate back into the grid circuit to have it amplified over again." The result, in September 1912, was Armstrong's first invention: the regenerative circuit.

As was often the case in this era of invention, Armstrong's invention was challenged in the courts. De Forest claimed to have invented the regenerative circuit in 1912, a year before Armstrong had applied for his patent. After several early convincing victories for Armstrong in the courts, many felt that De Forest was "throwing in the towel" when he requested a license to manufacturer the regenerative circuit. However, convinced that De Forest had attempted to steal his invention, Armstrong blocked the request. While Armstrong's focus and determination had served him well as an attic inventor, his stubbornness in his dealings with De Forest cost him dearly. De Forest continued his interference application in the U.S. Patent Office, won a few key victories, and finally, in 1934, had his claim as the inventor of the regenerative circuit upheld by the U.S. Supreme Court. Although the courts named De Forest the victor, most of the radio engineering community maintained Armstrong as the true founder of regeneration. At the 1934 meeting of the Institute of Radio Engineers (IRE), Armstrong attempted to give back a Medal of Honor that he had received years earlier from this organization for his work in relation to regeneration. The board of directors of the IRE refused to take back his medal and instead publicly affirmed the spirit of their original citation.

Armstrong's greatest accomplishment, however, was yet to come. For years, radio engineers had struggled with the static associated with an AM signal. Attempts at solving this problem included increased amplification (increasing noise at the same time) and restricting the frequency range of the signal (resulting in a loss of fidelity). All of these attempts, however, were made with the existing transmission method of amplitude modulation. Armstrong's approach to this significant problem typified his innovative style. He broke from traditional theory and experimented with an entirely new system of broadcasting: frequency modulation.

In brief, radio signals are piggybacked on a carrier wave, which is an electromagnetic signal that is characterized by consistent wave height (amplitude) and cycles per second (frequency). From

This amplifier was invented by Edwin H. Armstrong to reduce static, tube noises, fading, and interference in radio broadcasts. (Bettmann/Corbis)

the beginning, radio stations were transmitting their information by amplitude modulation, wherein the frequency is kept constant while the height of the wave is adjusted. Armstrong thought that frequency modulation (adjusting the cycles per second rather than the height of the wave) might hold the key to the elimination of static.

Others had experimented with frequency modulation as a transmission method; however, none had attempted to change the whole system, from transmitter to receiver. Some, including noted theoretical mathematician John Carson, thought static would always be a part of radio. Armstrong, with help of assistants Thomas Styles and John Shaughnessy, set about creating this new system by confronting one of the key principles of traditional AM broadcasting: narrow bandwidth.

Bandwidth is the space a signal occupies when it is imposed upon a carrier wave. A wide bandwidth can carry a better signal, but it also is more susceptible to interference. The solution to this interference, in the AM model, was to narrow the bandwidth, thus reducing the noise in the transmission. When early experiments with frequency modulation applied this commonly held principle of narrow bandwidth, static was not reduced. The result was that many scientists abandoned FM as a viable transmission method, but Armstrong believed that widening the bandwidth could dramatically improve the signal-to-noise ratio.

The key component of Armstrong's system was his ingenious receiver that captured the FM signal, amplified it, strained out amplitude variations, converted the signal to amplitude modulation, and prepared it for conversion to acoustic energy through a loudspeaker. Armstrong received multiple patents for this new system in 1933 and it was publicly demonstrated for the first time at the Institute of Radio Engineers meeting in New York City on November 5, 1935. According to Lawrence Lessing (1956), the demonstration went off without a hitch, transmitting music and other sounds at fidelity not heard before. Not only did the "wide band" FM system offer improved quality, it operated with much less power than a typical AM transmitter. Business reality, however, kept Armstrong's innovation from being adopted immediately.

In 1935, the Radio Corporation of America (RCA) was heavily invested in the existing AM broadcasting system, owning every major patent. In addition, they were also spending millions of dollars to develop what they believed to be the next great innovation in broadcasting: television. Both FM and television were completely new systems and RCA was reluctant to ask the public and broadcasters to invest in two new technologies at once. Nevertheless, it was not only industry powers that halted the advance of FM. The Federal Communications Commission (FCC) waited until March 1940 before they authorized FM broadcasting. Armstrong was further thwarted by World War II, which delayed the construction of new FM stations until 1946.

The final blow for Armstrong came from his former friend, David Sarnoff, and RCA. In the early 1950s, RCA, in an attempt to circumvent Armstrong's patents, claimed to have invented an FM broadcasting system superior and markedly different from Armstrong's. This set in motion litigation that lasted more than a decade and led to the ultimate unraveling of Edwin Armstrong's life. His fortune, amassed from royalty payments from his previous patents, dwindled during this court battle. His marriage of some thirty years to his wife Marion was crumbling while he obsessed with professional redemption. Finally, after rejecting a settlement proposal from RCA, and with his wife away with her sister in Connecticut, Armstrong committed suicide on January 31, 1954, by jumping from the window of his thirteenth-floor apartment in New York City.

Unfortunately, Armstrong did not live to see the fruits of his greatest invention and his final victory in the courts. FM listenership expanded greatly in the 1960s and 1970s, in large part because of the demand for the high-fidelity stereo sound that only FM broadcasting could deliver. By 1980, the audience for FM stations was larger than the one for AM stations, and by the end of the 1990s, FM stations were attracting more than 80 percent of the radio listeners.

Possibly because of the tragic nature of his death, Armstrong's fame has never been commensurate with the influence that he had on the communication industry. However, while he may never be a household name, the effect that he had on the radio industry will last forever.

See also: MARCONI, GUGLIELMO; RADIO BROADCAST-ING, HISTORY OF; RADIO BROADCASTING, TECH-NOLOGY OF; SARNOFF, DAVID.

Bibliography

Dunlap, Orrin E., Jr. (1944). *Radio's 100 Men of Science.* New York: Harper.

Erickson, Don V. (1973). *Armstrong's Fight for FM Broadcasting: One Man vs. Big Business and Bureaucracy.* University: University of Alabama Press.

Keith, Michael, and Krause, Joseph. (1993). *The Radio Station.* Boston: Focal Press.

Lessing, Lawrence. (1969). *Man of High Fidelity: Edwin Howard Armstrong.* New York: Bantam.

Lewis, Tom. (1991). *Empire of the Air: The Men Who Made Radio.* New York: HarperCollins.

JOHN W. OWENS

■ AROUSAL PROCESSES AND MEDIA EFFECTS

"Arousal" refers to a state of physical excitation that accompanies all emotions that are linked to action. The biological function of such excitation is to energize the organism for a bout of activity.

According to the classic fight-flight theory, arousal occurs when someone is confronted with danger and readies the person for escape (flight) or attack by vigorous action (fight), thereby increasing the chance for survival in either case. In modern times, arousal in response to signs of danger (or incentive opportunities) may prove largely non-adaptive (i.e., fail to serve safety and wellness), or even foster counterproductive reactions, because vigorous action often does not lead to an advantageous resolution. Although the fight-flight response is generally an outdated reaction, the tendency to become aroused is nonetheless triggered when people are faced with numerous situations that relate to coping with danger (or the attainment of incentives)—or when exposed to media representations of such situations.

Cognition-Excitation Interplay

Stanley Schachter (1964) focused attention on the unique interplay of cognition (i.e., thought) and arousal in the experiencing of emotion. He proposed that arousal is essentially the same in all emotions and that cognition, by furnishing instant appraisals of circumstances, lets individuals understand the emotions that are being experienced. In this conceptualization, arousal (or excitation) is blind to the hedonic valence of emotions (i.e., to their degree of pleasure or displeasure) and simply intensifies each and every emotion. Through intero- and exteroceptive feedback (e.g., muscle tension, heavy breathing, heart pounding, palm sweating), individuals have some cognizance of the intensity of their various emotions.

Excitation Transfer

Based on the premise that arousal is not emotion specific, Dolf Zillmann (1996) developed an excitation-transfer theory that considers summations and alternative integrations of sympathetic excitation. In this theory, he suggests that excitations caused by different sources combine to intensify both the feelings and the actions that are cognitively determined and directed by circumstances in the immediate environment of an individual. For example, a person who steps on a snake in the grass is bound to get excited and appraise the reaction as fear, possibly intertwined with disgust. Recognizing that the snake is a rubber dummy planted by a mischievous child, the person is bound to experience a quasi-instantaneous reappraisal of the emotional reaction as anger that, after a while, is likely to turn into amusement. These later reactions, due to the fact that chemically mediated excitation (i.e., mediation by the systemic release of catecholamines that function as neurotransmitters and whose effect diminishes only slowly) cannot decay instantly and lingers for some time, are intensified by residual excitation from the initial fear reaction. In principle, residual excitation from any kind of prior emotion will "artificially" intensify the experience of any kind of subsequent emotion.

The transfer of residual excitation into subsequent emotional reactions is particularly relevant for the emotional experience of fictional and nonfictional events of audiovisual media presentations. The reason for this is the compact presentation of emotion-inducing scenes. Because the material that is not immediately relevant to the emotional core of the presentation is eliminated by editing, the elicitation of different emotional experiences comes closer together. This condition is ideal for the intensification of emotional reactions because of the transfer of residual excitation from preceding arousal-inducing events.

Dramaturgy of Transfer

Excitation-transfer theory has been used to explain the seemingly paradoxical enjoyment of drama that predominantly features distressing events. For example, the enjoyment of satisfying resolutions of suspenseful drama has been found to be more intense when the preceding events of the drama are more torturous. It also has been observed that the more frightening the preresolution portions of drama, the more it is likely to be enjoyed in the end. Even tragic drama tends to be more enjoyed when the initially featured suffering is more severe. Residual excitation from hedonically negative (i.e., displeasing) experiences is thus capable of intensifying subsequent enlightenment and euphoric experiences. This relationship, moreover, has been ascertained for the enjoyment of competitive sports. Suspenseful, close contests tend to trigger more intense enjoyment than lopsided contests. Hedonically reversed emotion intensification is in evidence as well. Residues from exposure to pleasant erotic scenes, for example, have been found to intensify experiences of anger and hostile inclinations. However, emotion facilitation also can occur within hedonically compatible conditions. The interspersion of pleasant sexual imagery in music videos, for example, has been found to intensify the enjoyment of the music. The excitation-transfer theory thus can be seen as a dramaturgic script for the manipulation of emotional reactions to drama and other media presentations by specific arrangements of narrative elements (cf. Zillmann, 1996).

Outside fiction, transfer effects have been observed in advertising. Residual excitation from pleasant and unpleasant experiences was found to enhance the appeal of products and activate purchase intentions. Regarding news programs, highly arousing images of catastrophes like famine and epidemics are known to move viewers to various civic actions.

Arousal Seeking

Marvin Zuckerman (1979) examined individual differences in excitement seeking and attempted to explain them as a result of varying needs for neuroendocrine stimulation. People who had a self-proclaimed high need for excitement were found to be drawn more strongly than others to sex-laden and violent, even morbid, media entertainments. They also showed a stronger preference for contact sports and hard-rock music, whether live or featured in the media.

Mood Management

Zillmann (1988), in the context of mood-management theory, proposed that media content is selectively used to maximize arousal that is pleasantly experienced (eustress) and to minimize arousal that is unpleasantly experienced (distress). This implies that the content selections serve to move from distress to eustress, rather than to maximize arousal regardless of hedonistic considerations (i.e., pleasure-displeasure). Consistent with this proposal are findings showing that stressed persons, compared to relaxed ones, are drawn to media programming that holds a promise of cheering them up, such as comedies, while avoiding programming that does not hold this promise, such as conflict-laden news reports.

Considering arousal specifically, it has been observed that understimulated, bored people prefer exciting programs over relaxing programs, whereas overstimulated, stressed people prefer relaxing programs over exciting programs. Such choices, by bringing "down" people "up" and "up" people "down," serve excitatory homeostasis (i.e., the return to excitatory normalcy).

Habituation of Arousal

Excitatory habituation refers to the waning of arousal reactions that results from repeated, extensive exposure to particular stimuli. Media portrayals of violent and sexual events, for example, may initially evoke strong emotions, but as the excitatory response habituates (i.e., diminishes) with repeated and potentially massive exposure, emotional reactions become shallow and may vanish altogether. This phenomenon is often discussed as desensitization.

There is no doubt that habituation to violent and sexual media presentations occurs. It has been demonstrated, for example, that prolonged exposure to erotica diminishes arousal reactions until they become negligible. On occasion, desensitization is intended. For example, adolescents seek it in response to horror in order to prove their toughness (i.e., emotional insensitivity) to peers. As a rule, however, strong emotional reactivity is the object of most entertainments, often also of informative, nonfictional programs.

Arousal Retention

On the premise that both curiosity about, and the enjoyment of, media presentations tend to increase with the degree to which these presentations are emotionally engaging, techniques are sought to counteract the excitatory habituation to media offerings. As self-imposed media abstinence is not an option, the remedy lies in the employment of novel and potentially stronger material. A habituation-based shift to unfamiliar material has been demonstrated for erotica. It was found that consumers, after excitatory habituation to common fare, selected exposure to depictions of unusual sexual behaviors, apparently in efforts to sustain the intensity of pleasurable reactions (cf. Zillmann, 1991). More generally, this shift is prominent in the escalation of dramatic media content toward increasingly graphic displays of increasingly uncommon violent and sexual behaviors. It is also evident in the growing success of reality programs with extreme, shocking content. Reality programs ensure strong arousal reactions because the depicted events cannot be dismissed as fictional.

See also: ADVERTISING EFFECTS; MOOD EFFECTS AND MEDIA EXPOSURE; PORNOGRAPHY; TELEVISION BROADCASTING, PROGRAMMING AND; VIOLENCE IN THE MEDIA, ATTRACTION TO; VIOLENCE IN THE MEDIA, HISTORY OF RESEARCH ON.

Bibliography

Schachter, Stanley. (1964). "The Interaction of Cognitive and Physiological Determinants of Emotional State." In Advances in Experimental Social Psychology, Vol. 1, ed. Leonard Berkowitz. New York: Academic Press.

Zillmann, Dolf. (1988). "Mood Management through Communication Choices." American Behavioral Scientist 31(3):327–340.

Zillmann, Dolf. (1991). "The Logic of Suspense and Mystery." In Responding to the Screen: Reception and Reaction Processes, eds. Jennings Bryant and Dolf Zillmann. Hillsdale, NJ: Lawrence Erlbaum.

Zillmann, Dolf. (1994). "The Regulatory Dilemma Concerning Pornography." In Problems and Conflicts between Law and Morality in a Free Society, eds. James E. Wood and Derek Davis. Waco, TX: Baylor University.

Zillmann, Dolf. (1996). "Sequential Dependencies in Emotional Experience and Behavior." In Emotion: Interdisciplinary Perspectives, eds. Robert D. Kavanaugh, Betty Zimmerberg, and Steven Fein. Mahwah, NJ: Lawrence Erlbaum.

Zuckerman, Marvin. (1979). Sensation Seeking: Beyond the Optimal Level of Arousal. Hillsdale, NJ: Lawrence Erlbaum.

DOLF ZILLMANN

ARTIFICIAL INTELLIGENCE

Artificial intelligence (AI) is a scientific field whose goal is to understand intelligent thought processes and behavior and to develop methods for building computer systems that act as if they are "thinking" and can learn from themselves. Although the study of intelligence is the subject of other disciplines such as philosophy, physiology, psychology, and neuroscience, people in those disciplines have begun to work with computational scientists to build intelligent machines. The computers offer a vehicle for testing theories of intelligence, which in turn enable further exploration and understanding of the concept of intelligence.

The growing information needs of the electronic age require sophisticated mechanisms for

In 1980, John McCarthy explained the pictured equation that represented the process of extended logic with the following: "The computer must be able to jump to the conclusion that the only blocks on the table are the ones it knows about." (Roger Ressmeyer/Corbis)

information processing. As Richard Forsyth and Roy Rada (1986) point out, AI can enhance information processing applications by enabling the computer systems to store and represent knowledge, to apply that knowledge in problem solving through reasoning mechanisms, and finally to acquire new knowledge through learning.

History

The origin of AI can be traced to the end of World War II, when people started using computers to solve nonnumerical problems. The first attempt to create intelligent machines was made by Warren McCulloh and Walter Pitts in 1943 when they proposed a model of artificial networked neurons and claimed that properly defined networks could learn, thus laying the foundation for neural networks.

In 1950, Alan Turing published "Computer Machinery and Intelligence," where he explored the question of whether machines can think. He also proposed the Turing Test as an operational measure of intelligence for computers. The test requires that a human observer interrogates (i.e., interacts with) a computer and a human through a Teletype. Both the computer and the human try to persuade the observer that she or he is interacting with a human at the other end of the line. The computer is considered intelligent if the observer cannot tell the difference between the computer responses and the human responses.

In 1956, John McCarthy coined the term "artificial intelligence" at a conference where the participants were researchers interested in machine intelligence. The goal of the conference was to explore whether intelligence can be precisely defined and specified in order for a computer system to simulate it. In 1958, McCarthy also invented LISP, a high-level AI programming language that continues to be used in AI programs. Other languages used for writing AI programs include Prolog, C, and Java.

Approaches

Stuart Russell and Peter Norvig (1995) have identified the following four approaches to the goals of AI: (1) computer systems that act like humans, (2) programs that simulate the human mind, (3) knowledge representation and mechanistic reasoning, and (4) intelligent or rational agent design. The first two approaches focus on studying humans and how they solve problems, while the latter two approaches focus on studying real-world problems and developing rational solutions regardless of how a human would solve the same problems.

Programming a computer to act like a human is a difficult task and requires that the computer system be able to understand and process commands in natural language, store knowledge, retrieve and process that knowledge in order to derive conclusions and make decisions, learn to adapt to new situations, perceive objects through computer vision, and have robotic capabilities to move and manipulate objects. Although this approach was inspired by the Turing Test, most programs have been developed with the goal of enabling computers to interact with humans in a natural way rather than passing the Turing Test.

Some researchers focus instead on developing programs that simulate the way in which the human mind works on problem-solving tasks. The first attempt to imitate human thinking was the Logic Theorist and the General Problem Solver programs developed by Allen Newell and Herbert Simon. Their main interest was in simulating human thinking rather than solving problems correctly. Cognitive science is the interdisciplinary field that studies the human mind and intelligence. The basic premise of cognitive science is that the mind uses representations that are similar to computer data structures and computational procedures that are similar to computer algorithms that operate on those structures.

Other researchers focus on developing programs that use logical notation to represent a problem and use formal reasoning to solve a problem. This is called the "logicist approach" to developing intelligent systems. Such programs require huge computational resources to create vast knowledge bases and to perform complex reasoning algorithms. Researchers continue to debate whether this strategy will lead to computer problem solving at the level of human intelligence.

Still other researchers focus on the development of "intelligent agents" within computer systems. Russell and Norvig (1995, p. 31) define these agents as "anything that can be viewed as perceiving its environment through sensors and acting upon that environment through effectors." The goal for computer scientists working in this area is to create agents that incorporate information about the users and the use of their systems into the agents' operations.

Fundamental System Issues

A robust AI system must be able to store knowledge, apply that knowledge to the solution of problems, and acquire new knowledge through experience. Among the challenges that face researchers in building AI systems, there are three that are fundamental: knowledge representation, reasoning and searching, and learning.

Knowledge Representation

What AI researchers call "knowledge" appears as data at the level of programming. Data becomes knowledge when a computer program represents and uses the meaning of some data. Many knowledge-based programs are written in the LISP programming language, which is designed to manipulate data as symbols.

Knowledge may be declarative or procedural. Declarative knowledge is represented as a static collection of facts with a set of procedures for manipulating the facts. Procedural knowledge is described by executable code that performs some action. Procedural knowledge refers to "how-to" do something. Usually, there is a need for both kinds of knowledge representation to capture and represent knowledge in a particular domain.

First-order predicate calculus (FOPC) is the best-understood scheme for knowledge representation and reasoning. In FOPC, knowledge about the world is represented as objects and relations between objects. Objects are real-world things that have individual identities and properties, which are used to distinguish the things from other objects. In a first-order predicate language, knowledge about the world is expressed in terms of sentences that are subject to the language's syntax and semantics.

Reasoning and Searching

Problem solving can be viewed as searching. One common way to deal with searching is to develop a production-rule system. Such systems use rules that tell the computer how to operate on data and control mechanisms that tell the computer how to follow the rules. For example, a very simple production-rule system has two rules: "if A then B" and "if B then C." Given the fact (data) A, an algorithm can chain forward to B and then to C. If C is the solution, the algorithm halts.

Matching techniques are frequently an important part of a problem-solving strategy. In the above example, the rules are activated only if A and B exist in the data. The match between the A and B in the data and the A and B in the rule may not have to be exact, and various deductive and inductive methods may be used to try to ascertain whether or not an adequate match exists.

Generate-and-test is another approach to searching for a solution. The user's problem is represented as a set of states, including a start state and a goal state. The problem solver generates a state and then tests whether it is the goal state. Based on the results of the test, another state is generated and then tested. In practice, heuristics, or problem-specific rules of thumb, must be found to expedite and reduce the cost of the search process.

Learning

The advent of highly parallel computers in the late 1980s enabled machine learning through neural networks and connectionist systems, which simulate the structure operation of the brain. Parallel computers can operate together on the task with each computer doing only part of the task. Such systems use a network of interconnected processing elements called "units." Each unit corresponds to a neuron in the human brain and can be in an "on" or "off" state. In such a network, the input to one unit is the output of another unit. Such networks of units can be programmed to represent short-term and long-term working memory and also to represent and perform logical operations (e.g., comparisons between numbers and between words).

A simple model of a learning system consists of four components: the physical environment where the learning system operates, the learning element, the knowledge base, and the performance element. The environment supplies some information to the learning element, the learning element uses this information to make improvements in an explicit knowledge base, and the performance element uses the knowledge base to perform its task (e.g., play chess, prove a theorem). The learning element is a mechanism that attempts to discover correct generalizations from raw data or to determine specific facts using general rules. It processes information using induction and deduction. In inductive information processing, the system determines general rules and patterns from repeated exposure to raw data or experiences. In deductive information processing, the system determines specific facts from general rules (e.g., theorem proving using axioms and other proven theorems). The knowledge base is a set of facts about the world, and these facts are expressed and stored in a computer system using a special knowledge representation language.

Applications

There are two types of AI applications: standalone AI programs and programs that are embedded in larger systems where they add capabilities for knowledge representation, reasoning, and learning. Some examples of AI applications include robotics, computer vision, natural-language processing; and expert systems.

Robotics

Robotics is the intelligent connection of perception by the computer to its actions. Programs written for robots perform functions such as trajectory calculation, interpretation of sensor data, executions of adaptive control, and access to databases of geometric models. Robotics is a challenging AI application because the software has to deal with real objects in real time. An example of a robot guided by humans is the Sojourner surface rover that explored the area of the Red Planet where the Mars Pathfinder landed in 1997. It was guided in real time by NASA controllers. Larry Long and Nancy Long (2000) suggest that other robots can act autonomously, reacting to changes in their environment without human intervention. Military cruise missiles are an example of autonomous robots that have intelligent navigational capabilities.

Computer Vision

The goal of a computer vision system is to interpret visual data so that meaningful action can be based on that interpretation. The problem, as John McCarthy points out (2000), is that the real world has three dimensions while the input to

The final prototype of the Mars Pathfinder, a six-wheeled vehicle controlled remotely by NASA technicians, was tested in a large sandbox at the Jet Propulsion Laboratory in February 1993. (James A. Sugar/Corbis)

cameras on which computer action is based represents only two dimensions. The three-dimensional characteristics of the image must be determined from various two-dimensional manifestations. To detect motion, a chronological sequence of images is studied, and the image is interpreted in terms of high-level semantic and pragmatic units. More work is needed in order to be able to represent three-dimensional data (easily perceived by the human eye) to the computer. Advancements in computer vision technology will have a great effect on creating mobile robots. While most robots are stationary, some mobile robots with primitive vision capability can detect objects on their path but cannot recognize them.

Natural-Language Processing

Language understanding is a complex problem because it requires programming to extract meaning from sequences of words and sentences. At the lexical level, the program uses words, prefixes, suffixes, and other morphological forms and inflections. At the syntactic level, it uses a grammar to parse a sentence. Semantic interpretation (i.e., deriving meaning from a group of words) depends on domain knowledge to assess what an utterance means. For example, "Let's meet by the bank to get a few bucks" means one thing to bank robbers and another to weekend hunters. Finally, to interpret the pragmatic significance of a conversation, the computer needs a detailed understanding of the goals of the participants in the conversation and the context of the conversation.

Expert Systems

Expert systems consist of a knowledge base and mechanisms/programs to infer meaning about how to act using that knowledge. Knowledge engineers and domain experts often create the knowledge base. One of the first expert systems, MYCIN, was developed in the mid-1970s. MYCIN employed a few hundred if-then rules about meningitis and bacteremia in order to deduce the proper treatment for a patient who showed signs of either of those diseases. Although MYCIN did better than students or practicing doctors, it did not contain as much knowledge as physicians routinely need to diagnose the disease.

Although Alan Turing's prediction that computers would be able to pass the Turing Test by the year 2000 was not realized, much progress has been made and novel AI applications have been developed, such as industrial robots, medical diagnostic systems, speech recognition in telephone systems, and chess playing (where IBM's Deep Blue supercomputer defeated world champion Gary Kasparov).

Conclusion

The success of any computer system depends on its being integrated into the workflow of those who are to use it and on its meeting of user needs. A major future direction for AI concerns the integration of AI with other systems (e.g., database management, real-time control, or user interface management) in order to make those systems more usable and adaptive to changes in user behavior and in the environment where they operate.

See also: COMPUTER SOFTWARE; COMPUTING; HUMAN–COMPUTER INTERACTION; LANGUAGE ACQUISITION; LANGUAGE STRUCTURE; SYMBOLS.

Bibliography

Forsyth, Richard, and Rada, Roy. (1986). *Machine Learning: Expert Systems and Information Retrieval.* London: Horwood.

Gardner, Howard. (1993). *Multiple Intelligences: The Theory in Practice.* New York: Basic Books.

Long, Larry, and Long, Nancy. (2000). *Computers.* Upper Saddle River, NJ: Prentice-Hall.

McCarthy, John. (2000). *What is Artificial Intelligence?* <http://www-formal.stanford.edu/jmc/whatisai/whatisai.html.>

Russell, Stuart, and Norvig, Peter. (1995). *Artificial Intelligence: A Modern Approach.* Englewood Cliffs, NJ: Prentice-Hall.

Turing, Alan M. (1950). "Computing Machinery and Intelligence." *Mind* 59:433–460.

ANTONIOS MICHAILIDIS
ROY RADA

■ ATTACHMENT TO MEDIA CHARACTERS

The many forms of mass media that were developed during the twentieth century have challenged the assumption that relationships occur only between "real" people who know each other personally. Mass media creators, as well as researchers, have long recognized that media consumers are drawn to compelling media characters and personalities. In 1956, Donald Horton and R. Richard Wohl wrote a seminal article entitled "Mass Communication and Para-Social Interaction." They coined the term "parasocial interaction" to describe the imaginary interactions between television variety show hosts and their home audiences, as well as the "seeming face-to-face relationship" that viewers developed with these personalities. Horton and Wohl argued that a sense of "interaction" was conveyed to viewers because hosts appeared as themselves and often directly addressed the audience. In fictional programming, performers rarely "break the fourth wall" and speak directly to the audience. Yet viewers still typically feel as though they are involved to some extent in fictional events that are depicted on screen, and they sometimes have the sense that they are participating in imaginary interactions with the characters.

Horton and Wohl's article did not stimulate much research until the late 1970s and early 1980s, when media scholars showed renewed interest in the topic. In 1985, Alan Rubin, Elizabeth Perse, and Robert Powell developed a self-report parasocial interaction scale to measure the perceived bond that viewers have with local television news personalities. Many researchers now use the term "parasocial relationship" to describe the affective bond that individuals develop with characters and personalities in a variety of media genres, including news programs, talk shows, soap operas, dramas, and situation comedies.

Theoretical Approaches

Parasocial relationships have often been examined from the perspective of motivations. The "uses and gratifications" perspective contends that people are not passive recipients of media messages; rather, they seek out particular media content because they are motivated by goals, needs, desires, and/or preferences. Parasocial relationships have been conceptualized as a form of audience involvement that provides social and emotional gratifications, motivates further viewing, and may help to satisfy the affiliative needs of audience members.

Star Trek, with its movie and television spin-offs, has demonstrated the possibility of character attachments that endure over long periods. This feat was rewarded with the issuing of a special postage stamp in 1999, more than twenty years after the original television series was first aired. (AFP/Corbis)

The study of parasocial relationships has also been guided by efforts to explore the "interface" between mass communication and interpersonal communication. Early research on parasocial relationships recognized that these relational bonds were similar in many ways to the social relationships that people develop through face-to-face contact with others. Calls to synthesize theory in mass and interpersonal communication escalated in the 1980s, motivated in part by changing communication technologies that markedly altered the nature of mediated communication. For example, Robert Hawkins, John Wiemann, and Suzanne Pingree edited a volume in 1988 that was entitled *Advancing Communication Science: Merging Mass and Interpersonal Processes*. Individual chapters in this book addressed such issues as the similarities and differences between face-to-face and mediated communication, the activity and interactivity of media audiences, and the role of mass media in interpersonal relationships. Consistent with these efforts toward creating a synthesis,

theoretical approaches from interpersonal communication and psychology (e.g., implicit personality theory, theories of interpersonal attraction, attribution theory, uncertainty reduction theory, attachment theory, and social cognitive theory) have been applied to the understanding of parasocial relationships. Consequently, much of the research on parasocial relationships has used terms and concepts that have traditionally been associated with interpersonal relationships, and it has furthered researcher's understanding of the nature of the psychological bonds that individuals form with others.

Components of Attraction

In the initial stages of any relationship, including parasocial relationships, individuals engage in the process of impression formation. In forming impressions of others, people use a wide range of observable information, including physical appearance, behaviors, and emotional reactions. Media creators often rely on particular physical attributes, such as attractiveness, physique, or manner of dress, to convey certain impressions quickly. Impressions also develop over time, as audience members learn more about the background, personality, behavioral tendencies, and emotional makeup of media characters and personalities. Although all individuals are responsive to physical appearance cues, the weight that is given to these cues in relation to other information changes developmentally. Young children rely heavily on appearance when they are evaluating others, but older viewers rely to a greater extent on less visually salient cues such as personality and behavior.

As a function of forming impressions of others, viewers are attracted to media characters and personalities to varying degrees. Research confirms that media characters and personalities whose personal attributes and behaviors are perceived favorably are generally liked more. Viewers also tend to be more attracted to characters and personalities who (they perceive) are similar to themselves. Perception of similarity is enhanced by shared characteristics such as sex, ethnicity, social class, and age, but it may also be influenced by other factors such as personality traits, feelings, beliefs, and experiences.

Many media characters and personalities, however, are extremely good-looking, unusually talented, or highly successful in their endeavors, and they are undoubtedly dissimilar in important ways to most audience members. Viewers are attracted to such individuals, but rather than feeling similar, they often view them as being role models—people they want to be like. The desire to be like another individual has been referred to as "wishful identification." This process is promoted during media exposure by the tendency to identify with or share the perspective of a media character and by vicariously participating in his or her experiences.

Most of the research that is related to wishful identification has been conducted with children. It is not surprising that the television characters children want to be like possess a variety of desirable attributes. Children often wish to be like successful characters, regardless of whether they approve of the behaviors of the characters. On television, good characters are not necessarily popular or successful, and violence is often used successfully or for prosocial ends. In general, the positive or negative consequences that are experienced by the characters may be more important than their social behavior *per se* in determining wishful identification. There is also evidence that a certain subgroup (mostly males) identifies strongly with violent characters.

The character attributes that are associated with wishful identification vary based on both the sex of the viewer and the sex of the character. Although there are some differences across studies, boys tend to prefer same-sex role models that are perceived as being strong, active, and intelligent. In contrast, girls choose role models of both sexes, but the traits that influence their choices differ for male and female characters. Girls choose male role models that they regard as being intelligent and funny, whereas their choice of female role models is based primarily on the physical attractiveness of the characters. These results may reflect both gender-role stereotypes in society and the nature of male and female portrayals on television.

Parasocial Attachment

There is much evidence that audience members form strong affective attachments to mass media characters and personalities and that these relationships tend to be stronger for individuals who are active, involved viewers. Researchers have used the term "parasocial relationship" to describe this type of affective bond, which develops over time. While viewing a media presentation, audience members often feel as though they are involved in the events, and they respond in some ways as if they were witnessing or participating in real interactions with people they know. Over time, they may come to feel that they know these individuals as well as they know their real-world friends or neighbors. This type of involvement and familiarity leads to the formation of emotional attachments or parasocial bonds. Many viewers become so emotionally tied to fictional characters in television series that the disappearance of these characters—either through the plot of the program or because the series ends—is emotionally upsetting. Audience members also develop close emotional ties to real people who appear in the mass media, such as actors, talk show hosts, and other celebrities. The death of Diana, Princess of Wales, in 1997 provided a vivid example of the power of parasocial bonds. Millions of people whose only contact with the princess had been through the mass

One of the most prominent media celebrities of the 1990s was Princess Diana, which was illustrated by the fact that her death led to a worldwide public response that included the gathering of crowds and the leaving of floral tributes outside the gates of Kensington Palace, which had been her home in London. (Jeremy Horner/Corbis)

media apparently had felt a deep emotional attachment to her, as exemplified by worldwide public displays of mourning.

Researchers have likened the development of parasocial relationships to the process by which people form interpersonal relationships. Communication to reduce uncertainty and to increase knowledge of another person has been shown to play an important role in this process. In parasocial relationships, uncertainty may be reduced through passive strategies, such as observing media characters or personalities in a variety of situations, and through active strategies, such as talking with others about the characters. Studies suggest that initial attraction to media characters motivates further efforts to "get to know" them, leading to increased confidence in predicting their behaviors, greater intimacy or parasocial attachment, and an increased sense of relationship importance. Although most research on parasocial relationships has been done with adults, there is

evidence that children and adolescents also develop affective attachments to characters.

Audience Characteristics that Affect Parasocial Attachment

The social relationships and personal characteristics of audience members have been examined in relation to their parasocial attachments. Initially, it was believed that parasocial relationships compensated for a lack of social connections. Jan-Erik Norlund, for example, advanced this argument in 1978. However, evidence regarding this hypothesis has been mixed. Some research suggests that individuals who have less social involvement are more likely to use television for companionship and parasocial relations. Several other studies, however, have found no association between chronic loneliness and the tendency to form parasocial relationships. However, evidence does indicate that the interpersonal attachment style of an individual influences his or her formation of parasocial relationships. A study by Tim Cole and Laura Leets (1999), for example, found that individuals who had an anxious-ambivalent attachment style were most likely to form parasocial bonds, possibly as a way of fulfilling their unmet emotional needs. Individuals who had an avoidant attachment style were least likely to form parasocial bonds, and those who had secure interpersonal attachments fell in the middle.

Individual differences in empathy are also important. Although there are many definitions of empathy, it has been defined broadly as an individual's responses to the observed experiences of another person. Empathy plays an important role in interpersonal relations and contributes to short-term emotional responses to media characters. There is some evidence that empathy also facilitates the development of long-term affective attachments to characters. Empathy increases a viewer's tendency to recognize and share a character's perspective and emotional experiences, which in turn should facilitate knowledge and understanding of the character and lead, over time, to the sense of a close parasocial bond. A study by John Turner (1993) has found that self-esteem was related to the development of parasocial relationships, but the nature of this association depended on the role of the media performer. For example, individuals who had difficulty communicating with others because of low self-esteem formed strong parasocial bonds with soap opera characters, but not with real media personalities. Finally, many studies have found that females tend to develop stronger parasocial attachments than do males.

Media Characteristics that Affect Parasocial Attachment

As Joshua Meyrowitz argued in 1979, formal aspects of television and film productions can shape the viewers' responses and their tendency to develop parasocial relationships with media characters or personalities. Camera angles, close-ups, and editing techniques influence the viewers' selection and interpretation of information, and they may affect the sense of closeness between the viewer and a character or performer, in much the same way as spatial distance affects interpersonal relations. Several studies indicate that parasocial relationships are enhanced when media characters or performers directly address the audience, thereby simulating the process of face-to-face interaction.

The content of media presentations may contribute to uncertainty reduction, and in some cases, it may resemble the process of self-disclosure. For example, the information that viewers receive about a fictional character is scripted and designed to reveal quickly the key aspects of the character's background and personality. Programs depict characters' interactions with others in a variety of contexts, their solitary activities, and even their innermost thoughts and feelings (e.g., via dream sequences). This type of information permits viewers to know more about media characters than they may know about the people with whom they have close interpersonal relationships. Similarly, celebrities, such as the hosts and guests on talk shows, often reveal personal information about themselves and share emotional experiences. Perhaps one of the factors that contributes to people's intense attachments to celebrities such as Princess Diana or Oprah Winfrey is the public's access to their so-called backstage behaviors—behaviors that reveal how these individuals act in their private lives. Furthermore, audience members can obtain extensive information about media personalities and fictional characters from many sources, including print and television interviews, magazines that are devoted to particular series or genres (e.g., soap operas), and Internet chat rooms and message boards.

Long-Term Consequences of Parasocial Attachment

Parasocial relationships can be emotionally gratifying, they can provide viewers with a sense of companionship and pseudo-friendship, and they may enable viewers to participate vicariously in relationships as preparation for real-life social roles. Research also shows that parasocial relationships foster reliance on media characters and personalities for personally relevant information such as how to behave or how to cope with problems. Dependence on individuals who are known only through the media for behavioral guidance has the potential to affect people's lives positively or negatively, depending on the nature of the media portrayals. For example, fictional characters and celebrities who successfully confront personal problems may encourage safe and socially appropriate behaviors, but those who act antisocially, with few sanctions or adverse effects, may promote the acceptance of such behaviors.

See also: CHILDREN'S PREFERENCES FOR MEDIA CONTENT; GENDER AND THE MEDIA; INTERPERSONAL COMMUNICATION; RELATIONSHIPS, TYPES OF; SOAP OPERAS; SOCIAL COGNITIVE THEORY AND MEDIA EFFECTS; TALK SHOWS ON TELEVISION; VIOLENCE IN THE MEDIA, ATTRACTION TO.

Bibliography

Alperstein, Neil M. (1991). "Imaginary Social Relationships with Celebrities Appearing in Television Commercials." *Journal of Broadcasting & Electronic Media* 35:43–58.

Auter, Philip J. (1992). "TV that Talks Back: An Experimental Validation of a Parasocial Interaction Scale." *Journal of Broadcasting & Electronic Media* 36:173–181.

Cohen, Jonathan. (1997). "Parasocial Relations and Romantic Attraction: Gender and Dating Status Differences." *Journal of Broadcasting & Electronic Media* 41:516–529.

Cole, Tim, and Leets, Laura. (1999). "Attachment Styles and Intimate Television Viewing: Insecurely Forming Relationships in a Parasocial Way." *Journal of Social and Personal Relationships* 16:495–511.

Hawkins, Robert P.; Wiemann, John M.; and Pingree, Suzanne, eds. (1988). *Advancing Communication Science: Merging Mass and Interpersonal Processes.* Newbury Park, CA: Sage Publications.

Hoffner, Cynthia. (1996). "Children's Wishful Identification and Parasocial Interaction with Favorite Television Characters." *Journal of Broadcasting & Electronic Media* 40:389–402.

Hoffner, Cynthia, and Cantor, Joanne. (1991). "Perceiving and Responding to Mass Media Characters." In *Responding to the Screen: Reception and Reaction Processes*, eds. Jennings Bryant and Dolf Zillmann. Hillsdale, NJ: Lawrence Erlbaum.

Horton, Donald, and Wohl, R. Richard. (1956). "Mass Communication and Para-Social Interaction." *Psychiatry* 19:215–229.

Meyrowitz, Joshua. (1979). "Television and Interpersonal Behavior: Codes of Perception and Response." In *Inter/media: Interpersonal Communication in a Media World*, eds. Gary Gumpert and Robert Cathcart. New York: Oxford University Press.

Norlund, Jan-Erik. (1978). "Media Interaction." *Communication Research* 5:150–175.

O'Sullivan, Patrick B. (1999). "Bridging the Mass-Interpersonal Divide: Synthesis Scholarship in HCR." *Human Communication Research* 25:569–588.

Perse, Elizabeth M., and Rubin, Rebecca B. (1989). "Attribution in Social and Para-Social Relationships." *Communication Research* 16:59–77.

Rubin, Alan M., and Perse, Elizabeth M. (1987). "Audience Activity and Soap Opera Involvement: A Uses and Effects Investigation." *Human Communication Research* 14:246–268.

Rubin, Alan M.; Perse, Elizabeth M.; and Powell, Robert A. (1985). "Loneliness, Parasocial Interaction, and Local Television News Viewing." *Human Communication Research* 12:155–180.

Rubin, Rebecca B., and McHugh, Michael P. (1987). "Development of Parasocial Interaction Relationships." *Journal of Broadcasting & Electronic Media* 31:279–292.

Turner, John R. (1993). "Interpersonal and Psychological Predictors of Parasocial Interaction with Different Television Performers." *Communication Quarterly* 41:443–453.

CYNTHIA A. HOFFNER

ATTENTION TO TELEVISION
See: Children's Attention to Television

AUDIENCE RESEARCHERS

"Research" in a media organization can mean checking sources for news programs, and it can mean conducting market research for advertisers. "Audience research," however, means only one thing: research that seeks to answer questions about the size and nature of the audience of television programs, radio stations, newspapers, magazines, and Internet websites. Because of the size of the television business and the important role of audience measurement, most audience researchers work at broadcast and cable networks and at local television stations. Therefore, this entry will focus on television audience research. (Audience research at the various media companies differs somewhat, but there are many similarities.)

The Famous "Nielsen Ratings"

Most people outside of the media business have some idea about audience research at the television networks because of the so-called Nielsen ratings, which are widely reported as measures of television program popularity. However, these ratings are frequently misunderstood and misinterpreted. For example, it is often said that Nielsen data shows that Americans watch seven hours of television each day. They do not; that is, Nielsen does not say that, and Americans watch much less. Nielsen finds that, in the average home, television sets are turned on for seven hours, but that does not mean that any one person in the average household watches that many hours of television programs.

Nielsen data are quite complex and not always easy to interpret. There are a variety of measures: household data (which are most widely reported, even though they are quite unimportant); "PUTs" (persons using television); "ratings" and "shares" (a share is a rating relative to the overall viewing level at the time); and "demo ratings" (demographic ratings, such as "18-49"). All of these provide information that is very important to most advertisers.

The complexity of the measures and the skills needed to interpret them accurately are not the main reasons why an audience researcher has a very important job. Audience research data are the "currency" of the commercial television business. While the Nielsen ratings are important measures of program popularity and help programmers decide which shows to keep on the air and which to cancel, their main function is to provide information for advertisers. For most networks and stations, advertising revenue is the main source of income, and that revenue depends on the size and quality of the audience. The more people watch a program, and the more those people watching the program are likely customers of the advertiser, the higher the revenue the broadcaster can expect to receive from commercials shown during that program. And since there is no other objective measure of the value of the programs to the advertiser, the Nielsen ratings are the currency of the television business. In a way, the audience numbers—and not the programs—are the products of television. (This is also true of radio and, to a large extent, the Internet. Magazines and newspapers also have circulation numbers that indicate how many "eyeballs" may have been reached by an advertisement.)

In short, audience researchers analyze the numbers that have a huge influence on television programming and determine the placement of billions of advertising dollars each year. A change of one point in the rating of a program can make a difference of $20,000 in the price of one thirty-second commercial; a change of one-tenth of a rating point for a television season could mean $30 million more or less revenue for the networks.

Becoming an Audience Researcher

When television was in its infancy, most audience researchers learned on the job. Today, many colleges and universities offer courses and degrees related to the business of the media; some have programs specifically designed to prepare students for a career in this field. Not very many institutions, however, have courses on audience measurement, and there is no up-to-date textbook on this topic.

Essential skills for this job include research methods, statistics, and familiarity with computer programs. Just as important is an interest in and knowledge of television, advertising, and marketing. To supplement the college curriculum, students may want to try spending some time as interns at a television station and/or with media planners of an advertising agency. (The latter might provide an understanding of all media, not just television.) The more knowledge and the deeper the understanding of those areas, the greater the opportunities a person will have to advance beyond the level of an analyst (who conducts important, but more routine and repetitious analyses of data), to a level where he or she gets involved in all aspects of audience measurement. This might include preparing reports that decide the fate of a major television program, conducting an analysis that might help the sales department bring in an extra $50 million of advertising revenue, working with Nielsen on methodological issues, or analyzing Internet usage in relationship to television usage.

On the Job as Audience Researcher

What does the day of a media researcher at a network look like? The first ratings are released each morning. Many programming executives get up quite early and want to find out immediately how their programs performed on the previous night. These clients also want trend analyses and other special reports that are geared toward their specific needs.

The other group of clients are the marketing and sales people who need the audience numbers to use in selling advertising time and making presentations on the quality of the audience. They may want information about the same programs as the programmers, but from a very different perspective. For example, they are primarily interested in positive data and information that will be useful for specific advertisers.

Beyond these daily, "normal" aspects of these kinds of jobs, there is an ever-changing array of special circumstances that often involves changes in Nielsen procedures or computer programs. Of growing importance is the arrival of new technologies—from high-definition television (HDTV) to digital video recorders (such as TiVo), and WebTV—that are difficult or impossible to measure with current hardware and methods. Thus, the job of an audience researcher will evolve, but it will continue to challenge and offer great opportunities to those who continue to learn on the job.

See also: TELEVISION BROADCASTING; TELEVISION BROADCASTING, CAREERS IN; TELEVISION BROADCASTING, PROGRAMMING AND.

Bibliography

Gannett Center for Media Studies. (1988). "Measuring the Audience." *Gannett Center Journal* 2(3), special issue.

Stipp, Horst. (1997). "How to Read TV Ratings." *American Demographics* 19(3):28–29.

HORST STIPP

AUTOMATION

See: Library Automation

B

BAKER, AUGUSTA BRAXTON (1911–1998)

Augusta Braxton Baker, an African-American librarian, storyteller, and activist, was born on April 1, 1911, in Baltimore, Maryland. Her school-teacher parents put strong emphasis on the importance of education and the joys of reading, and after high school graduation, Baker began attending the University of Pittsburgh in 1927. At the end of her sophomore year, she married fellow student James Baker, and together they moved to Albany, New York. She attended New York State Teacher's College, from which she earned a B.A. in education (1933) and a B.S. in library science (1934). Soon afterwards, the couple moved to New York City, where Baker worked briefly as a teacher, and her son, James Henry Baker III, was born.

In 1937, Baker was hired by Anne Carroll Moore, formidable supervisor of youth services for the New York Public Library, to be a children's librarian at what was then the 135th Street Harlem Branch (now the Countee Cullen Regional Branch). The library had a sizable collection of books on African-American history and culture; unfortunately, Baker found the fiction not only inadequate but insulting, and her career as a velvet-gloved revolutionary began. In 1939, an inspired if exasperated Baker began assembling a special collection of titles that would fairly represent African-American culture and give children of all races a realistic picture of African-American life. To draw attention to the need for accurate portrayals of African Americans in literature for young people, and to promote the visibility of the slowly burgeoning collection, Baker wrote letters and gave speeches to publishers and editors at professional meetings. Her influence motivated several leading publishers to identify authors and illustrators who could produce stories with positive images of African Americans. Baker inspired a number of distinguished authors and illustrators, including Julius Lester, Ezra Jack Keats, Maurice Sendak, John Steptoe, and Madeleine L'Engle. Baker's recognition of a deficit in juvenile library collections and her professional and personal responsibility to fill that gap resulted in what was ultimately christened The James Weldon Johnson Memorial Collection. Baker published the first edition of her groundbreaking bibliography, *Books about Negro Life for Children*, in 1946, and a number of revised editions followed. In 1971, the bibliography was updated, and the title was changed to *The Black Experience in Children's Books*.

It was during the 1940s that the dynamic Baker began to gain a reputation as a spellbinding storyteller. A traditional mainstay of programming for young people at the New York Public Library, storytelling became for Baker a lifelong journey. In 1953, she was appointed storytelling specialist and assistant coordinator of children's services. She was the first African-American librarian to have an administrative position in the New York Public Library. Her love of traditional folktales and her desire to promote them among both children and other storytellers spurred Baker to compile four collections of stories: *The Talking Tree* (1955), *The Golden Lynx* (1960), *Young Years: Best Loved Stories and Poems for Little Children* (1960), and *Once Upon a Time* (1964). Two of these titles,

Famed storyteller Augusta Baker reads a book to a group of children.
(Granger Collection)

The Talking Tree and *The Golden Lynx*, are recognized by library professionals as classic world folktale collections.

In 1961, Baker became the first African-American coordinator of children's services for the New York Public Library, a position that put this gifted librarian in charge of both programming for young people and policies governing that programming in all eighty-two branches of the library. Baker seized the opportunity to improve the quality of the youth collections in the library, emphasizing culturally inclusive books and audiovisual materials. Her growing influence did not stop at the library walls, but spread to schools, community groups, and professional organizations. She taught courses, gave workshops, spoke at conferences, and lectured on storytelling and children's literature. She was a consultant for the television program *Sesame Street;* an advisor to Weston Woods Media Company; and a moderator of the weekly radio program *The World of Children's Literature.* Baker participated in high-profile professional activities, serving the Children's Services Division of the American Library Association in various capacities, including president of the Association for Library Service to Children (ALSC) and chair of what was then the combined Newbery/Caldecott Awards Committee. Throughout a productive and respected career, the indefatigable Baker told stories, influenced public library policy, and altered the course of American publishing for children.

In 1974, after thirty-seven years with the New York Public Library, Baker retired as children's coordinator, but she did not retire from storytelling, libraries, or professional life. She was a sought-after speaker, and continued to lecture at universities, conduct workshops, and tell stories. In 1977, with coauthor Ellin Greene, Baker published *Storytelling: Art and Technique,* an authoritative handbook on storytelling in libraries.

In 1980, Baker was offered a position as storyteller-in-residence at the University of South Carolina, the first such position at any university. In 1986, the University of South Carolina College of Library and Information Science and the Richland County Public Library established the annual "A(ugusta) Baker's Dozen: A Celebration of Stories" in her honor. Among Baker's many additional awards are two honorary doctorates, the Grolier Foundation Award, the Regina Medal from the Catholic Library Association, the Constance Lindsay Skinner Award from the Women's National Book Association, and the Circle of Excellence Award from the National Storytelling Network.

Baker retired from her University of South Carolina position in 1994 and died on February 23, 1998. Her son donated her papers to the University of South Carolina. The Augusta Baker Collection of African-American Children's Literature and Folklore is located at the Thomas Cooper Library of the University of South Carolina. The Baker Collection contains more than 1,600 children's books (many inscribed), together with papers and illustrative material that provide an in-depth, microcosmic look at the history of children's literature and librarianship in the United States.

See also: LIBRARIANS; MOORE, ANNE CARROLL; STORYTELLERS; STORYTELLING.

Bibliography

American Library Association. (1980). *ALA World Encyclopedia of Library and Information Services.* Chicago: American Library Association.

Baker, Augusta. (1971). *The Black Experience in Children's Books.* New York: New York Public Library.

Baker, Augusta, with Greene, Ellin. (1996). *Storytelling: Art and Technique*, 3rd edition. New York: Bowker.

Glick, Andrea. (1998). "Storyteller Leaves Lasting Legacy." *School Library Journal* 44(4):13.

Josey, E. J., ed. (1970). *The Black Librarian in America.* Metuchen, JN: Scarecrow Press.

Smith, Henrietta M. (1995). "An Interview with Augusta Baker." *Horn Book Magazine* 71(3):292.

South Carolina University. (1996). "The Augusta Baker Papers." <http://www.sc.edu/library/socar/uscs/1993/baker93.html>.

South Carolina University. (1999). "The Augusta Baker Collection of African-American Children's Literature & Folklore." <http://www.sc.edu/library/spcoll/kidlit/baker.html>.

Thompson, Jennifer R. (1998). "Augusta Baker: A Master Storyteller." <http://www.libsci.sc.edu/baker/baker.htm>.

Women's Stories. (2000). "Children's Book Champion Augusta Baker (1911–1998)." <http://writetools.com/women/stories/baker_augusta.html>.

JANICE M. DEL NEGRO

BELL, ALEXANDER GRAHAM (1847–1922)

In 1876, Alexander Graham Bell was granted U.S. patent 174,465 for the telephone. Bell's developments in telephony, however, were a consequence of his research and devotion to the hearing impaired.

"Alec" Bell (as he was known to family and close friends) was born in Edinburgh, Scotland, to Eliza Grace Symonds Bell and Alexander Melville Bell on March 3, 1847. Bell's paternal grandfather, also named Alexander, had worked as an elocution teacher and had published several books, including *The Practical Elocutionist* (1834), *Stammering and Other Impediments of Speech* (1836), and *A New Elucidation of the Principles of Speech and Elocution* (1849). Bell's father continued the family's work in this area, and the efforts of Bell and his father to teach speech to the hearing impaired was greatly influenced by the fact that Bell's mother was deaf.

In London in 1863, Bell and his father met with Charles Wheatstone, who had patented an electric telegraph in England in 1837 and made improvements to a mechanical speech-recording device. One consequence of the Bells' study of Wheatstone's device was an improved understanding of the physiology of speech. In 1864, Bell's father began developing the first universal phonetic alphabet, which eventually led to the publication of *Visible Speech: The Science of Universal Alphabets* (1867). Bell began studying phonetics by himself in 1865 and then physiology at London University in 1868. Alec also began teaching in 1868 at Susanna Hull's school for the deaf in South Kensington. The lackluster reception of *Visible Speech* in Europe and the deaths of Bell's brothers due to tuberculosis motivated his father to move the family to Canada in 1870.

Bell began teaching at Sarah Fuller's school for the deaf in Boston in 1871. It was there that he met Gardiner Hubbard, who shared similar interests with Bell since Hubbard's daughter, Mabel, was deaf. She and Bell were married on July 11, 1877, and they eventually reared two daughters together.

Bell lived in Salem, Massachusetts, at the home of one of his students, George Sanders, while he taught in Boston. Bell developed his idea for a "musical telegraph," a device based on the principle of sympathetic resonance, while living with the Sanders family. From this research, Bell concluded that a telegraph wire could carry several different tones at one time, thus leading to his experiments in multiplex telegraphy.

In 1874, shortly after he began teaching elocution at Boston University, Bell began working with Clarence Blake on experiments to replicate the effects of sound on the human ear. Bell intended to teach the deaf by re-creating exact visual representations of speech learned from these experiments. One by-product of the experiments of Blake and Bell was the phonautograph, a device that recorded the vibrations of sound and that led to Bell's development of the membrane, or diaphragm, telephone.

Also in 1874, Elisha Gray, an employee of Western Electric Company, was working on his own version of a telephone. Bell was being encouraged by both Hubbard and Thomas Sanders to file for patents for his ideas. Hubbard and Sanders became financiers and founding members of the Bell Telephone Company, as did Thomas Watson. Bell began working with Watson in January 1875 while preparing to patent the harmonic telegraph. Bell filed for three patents for his invention on February 25, 1875, but he lost the first two, in part to Gray, who had filed two days earlier for a similar device. Bell and Gray filed for legal rights similar inventions again on February 14 Gray filed for a caveat, and Bell filed for the telephone on the same day. Th

Alexander Graham Bell speaks into the Centennial telephone around 1876. (Bettmann/Corbis)

speculation that the patent officer, Zenas Fisk Wilber, may have allowed Bell to view Gray's caveat, which had been filed earlier that day.

Bell was granted the telephone patent on March 7, 1876. Watson was the first to hear a human voice via the telephone three days later, and the message generally is accepted to have been, "Mr. Watson, come here, I want you!" Bell's first significant public demonstration of the telephone was at the 1876 Centennial Exposition in Philadelphia, which provided the national and international exposure needed for marketing the telephone.

The first of more than six hundred lawsuits that challenged the Bell telephone patent began in March 1878. Peter Dowd, representing Western Union, challenged Bell's claim to the telephone. The Dowd lawsuit was settled in 1879 with the Bell Company acquiring Western Union's networks, customer base, and several enhancements to the device. Bell appeared in court to defend his patent on two other occasions. The second case took place in 1883 and dealt with Daniel Drawbaugh's claims of inventing the telephone. The third case, especially taxing to Bell, was initiated by James Rogers of Tennessee. Rogers anticipated tying up the Bell patent in litigation until its expiration, at which time Rogers assumed he could freely enter the telephone market. Rogers encouraged the U.S. government to file a suit against Bell

in January 1887, a case that took nine years before a settlement was reached in Bell's favor.

After the telephone, Bell continued his research, inventing both the telephonic probe and photophone. Legal battles over the telephone, however, discouraged Bell from seeking patents for his work. Bell's wife urged his reluctant patent application for the tetrahedral space frame, which was a concept he developed as a by-product of his interest in flight but which became more valuable in the fields of architecture and structural engineering.

Bell's advocacy led to better treatment of the hearing impaired, which drew the admiration of many of Bell's acquaintances, including Helen Keller. Bell's own Volta Bureau was merged with the American Association for the Promotion of the Teaching of Speech to the Deaf in 1956 to form the Alexander Graham Bell Association for the Deaf.

Bell died at his Beinn Breagh estate in Nova Scotia, Canada, on August 2, 1922. The patent for the invention of the telephone went to Bell in 1876, and the U.S. legal system upheld that decision throughout years of patent litigation. While several individuals, including Gray, deserve credit for inventing much of the technology of the telephone, it was Bell's conceptual development of the transmission of speech that best represents his achievement. Nevertheless, Bell's developments in telephony represent one period only of a career that was devoted to understanding the physiology of human speech.

See also: RECORDING INDUSTRY, HISTORY OF; TELEPHONE INDUSTRY, HISTORY OF; TELEPHONE INDUSTRY, REGULATION OF; TELEPHONE INDUSTRY, TECHNOLOGY OF.

Bibiliography

Coe, Lewis. (1995). *The Telephone and Its Several Inventors.* Jefferson, NC: McFarland & Company.

Mackay, James. (1997). *Sounds Out of Silence: A Life of Alexander Graham Bell.* Edinburgh: Mainstream Publishing.

Pound, Arthur. (1926). *The Telephone Idea: Fifty Years After.* New York: Greenberg.

Snyder, Charles. (1974). *Clarence John Blake and Alexander Graham Bell: Otology and the Telephone.* St. Louis, MO: Annals Publishing Company.

Winefield, Richard. (1987). *Never the Twain Shall Meet: Bell, Gallaudet, and the Communications Debate.* Washington, DC: Gallaudet University Press.

MARTIN L. HATTON

■ BENNETT, JAMES GORDON (1795–1872)

When James Gordon Bennett Sr. died on June 1, 1872, his old rival Horace Greeley's *New York Tribune* eulogized: "He developed the capacities of journalism in a most wonderful manner, but he did it by degrading its character. He made the newspaper powerful, but he made it odious."

Bennett founded the *New York Herald* on May 6, 1835, with five hundred dollars and a cellar office. In the ensuing thirty-seven years, he guided the *Herald* into one of the world's most powerful newspapers, with circulation and advertising revenue second only to the *London Times.* Along the way, he helped create the modern newspaper. Bennett's credits include being the first Washington correspondent; first to publish a direct news interview (with a brothel madam); and first American editor to use news illustrations, print weather reports, cover sports regularly, and hire foreign correspondents.

Born September 1, 1795, in Keith, Banffshire, Scotland, Bennett was the son of one of the area's few independent farmers. At fifteen years of age, he attended seminary in Aberdeen to prepare for the priesthood. He was an eager student but experienced a crisis in faith and left college in 1814. During the next five years he traveled and read extensively and sold his first freelanced article. Fascinated by Benjamin Franklin's *Autobiography,* he decided on impulse to visit America.

On New Year's Day 1820, Bennett arrived in Boston, Massachusetts. A fellow Scot hired him to clerk for booksellers/publishers Wells and Lilly. Though he worked hard, his appearance, accent, and sarcasm annoyed customers. One contemporary described Bennett as "so terribly cross-eyed that when he looked at me with one eye, he looked out at the City Hall with the other." Wells and Lilly moved him to proofreading, a job he excelled at, but which may have exacerbated his eye problems.

He soon moved on to New York and worked at odd jobs until Aaron Smith Willington, editor of the Charleston, South Carolina, *Courier,* hired him. Bennett spent ten months translating for *Courier* readers the French and Spanish newspaper articles that were brought by ships into Charleston's harbor. Returning to New York, he freelanced, failed in an attempt to found a com-

James Gordon Bennett. (Bettmann/Corbis)

mercial school, bought and sold the unprofitable *Sunday Courier,* and in 1827 obtained a job on Mordecai M. Noah's *Enquirer.* Like the *Courier,* the *Enquirer* was a mercantile newspaper primarily offering news for merchants. Also like its fellows, the *Enquirer* had a political position—it supported the Democratic party and Andrew Jackson—and in turn was supported by party members. Bennett actively entered party politics and rose to member of the Democratic Ward Committee in 1831, but his attempts to secure higher positions failed.

Though Bennett and Noah were both strong Jackson supporters and Noah appreciated Bennett's talents, he did not like Bennett personally. When Bennett proposed writing from Washington, Noah obliged and Bennett became New York's first Capitol Hill correspondent. He soon earned a national reputation for breezy, witty reporting as other Jacksonian papers picked up his stories.

In 1832, he started his own newspaper in New York, the *Globe,* but it failed. He bought shares in and edited the *Pennsylvanian* in 1833. He applied to Martin van Buren for a $25,000 loan but was turned down. After a year, he returned to New York, professing disillusion with the "hollow-heartedness and humbuggery" of politicians.

While Bennett was in Pennsylvania, Benjamin H. Day had founded the New York *Sun,* an apolitical paper aimed at the newly literate masses. At that time, the twelve New York City dailies had average circulations of around two thousand each. By 1835, the *Sun,* which sold for a penny, had a daily circulation of nearly twenty thousand, more than the *London Times.* Bennett made overtures to Day but was not hired. He next tried to interest Horace Greeley in a partnership but was turned down. Then at forty years of age, after a string of political, business, and publishing failures, he launched the *New York Herald,* declaring, "We shall support no party . . . and care nothing for any election or candidate from president down to constable" and boasting that through "intelligence, good taste, sagacity, and industry," the *Herald* would soon have a circulation of "twenty or thirty thousand."

The *Herald* had something for everyone: concise news summaries; local stories emphasizing the humorous and tragic, especially police court; lively accounts of sporting events; reviews of plays and musicals; and economic news, including a financial feature, "Money Market," that brought Wall Street news to a general audience for the first time. Even advertising was checked daily to maintain its reader appeal. Unlike the *Sun,* the *Herald* from the beginning covered world and national news and economic developments as fully as its four pages allowed. It went after not only the blue-collar readers of the *Sun,* but also the middle- and upper-class readers of the mercantile press.

Bennett wrote about events vividly, intimately, and controversially. His sensational journalism did attract readers, but it also attracted enemies. From Wall Street businessmen to society *doyennes,* the upper crust resented having their private bankruptcies and dinner parties laid out for the *hoi polloi.* Bennett took advantage of his enemies, especially editors, by attacking them in the *Herald,* hoping they would print counterattacks, thereby publicizing the *Herald* to their own readers. Benjamin Day obliged, writing that Bennett's "only

chance of dying an upright man will be that of hanging perpendicularly from a rope." In 1836, Bennett's former employer, James Watson Webb, responded by severely caning him one day on Wall Street. Bennett regaled the next day's *Herald* readers with an account of the attack, noting Webb had "cut a slash in my head about one and a half inches in length. . . . The fellow, no doubt, wanted to let out the never failing supply of good humour and wit . . . and appropriate the contents to supply the emptiness of his own thick skull."

Bennett accumulated powerful enemies, from politicians (he once wrote that his crossed eyes came from watching "the winding ways of Martin Van Buren") to clergymen (New York's Roman Catholic bishop excommunicated him for dubbing transubstantiation "religious cookery"). In 1840, these leaders declared a "Moral War" on him, organizing boycotts and attacking him viciously in the press. The war did not drive away *Herald* advertisers, but it did pull perhaps one-third of the readers; the paper took five years to regain its pre-1840 circulation. It also forced Bennett to promise publicly to improve the tone of the *Herald.* Never again was the paper quite so impishly egotistical, so crudely defiant. As Greeley later sneered, it gained some decency if not principle.

A consummate newsman, Bennett spent whatever it took to scoop others in reporting the day's events. He deployed the fastest boats to relay news from ships in New York Harbor, made early and frequent use of the telegraph, and organized a consortium of newspapers to pay for a pony express from New Orleans that regularly beat the post office by as much as four days. Bennett had long championed the South editorially, but when the U.S. Civil War came, he strongly supported the Union. The *Herald* sent sixty-three correspondents to cover the war and often published news from the front before it had reached the U.S. War Department.

By 1865, the *Herald* had a circulation of 110,000 with an annual revenue of $1,095,000. Bennett officially handed the *Herald* over to his son James Gordon Bennett Jr. in 1867. While the son had Bennett's nose for news—he sent Henry M. Stanley to Central Africa to find Dr. David Livingstone—he lacked his business sense and capacity for hard work. After his death in 1918, the *Herald* was bought by the owners of the *New York Tribune,* who merged the papers of rivals and enemies Bennett and Greeley into the *New York Herald Tribune* in 1924.

See also: GREELEY, HORACE; JOURNALISM, HISTORY OF; NEWSPAPER INDUSTRY, HISTORY OF.

Bibliography

Crouthamel, James A. (1989). *Bennett's New York Herald and the Rise of the Popular Press.* Syracuse, NY: Syracuse University Press.

Fermer, Douglas. (1986). *James Gordon Bennett and the New York Herald: A Study of Editorial Opinion in the Civil War Era 1854–1867.* New York: St. Martin's Press.

Gordon, John Steele. (1996). "The Man Who Invented Mass Media." *St. Louis Journalism Review* 26(184):10–13.

Herd, Harold. (1977). *Seven Editors.* Westport, CT: Greenwood Press.

Pray, Isaac C. (1855). *Memoirs of James Gordon Bennett and his Times.* New York: Stringer and Townsend. (Reprinted by Arno Press, 1970.)

Seitz, Don C. (1928). *The James Gordon Bennetts: Father and Son, Proprietors of the New York Herald.* Indianapolis, IN: Bobbs-Merrill.

ELLEN WILLIAMSON KANERVO

BIBLIOGRAPHY

Bibliography is the study of books as conceptual content and as physical objects. The books in question, once limited to hardbound objects available in bookstores, are today generally defined more broadly. The term "book" is now generally applied to all texts (be they published or in manuscript) that are meant to be permanent, including periodicals, maps, music, pictures, and ephemera, as well as materials preserved in the audiovisual and electronic media. The conceptual and physical aspects of these objects involve the two specialties of reference bibliography and analytical bibliography.

Reference Bibliography

Lists, inventories, footnotes, and prose essays are all ways in which readers and books can be brought together. To make these tools more useful to the reader, standard citations have been formulated for each situation. These citations emphasize content, even though the physical embodiment is inseparable.

A bibliographical citation typically consists of an entry that names

1. the creator of the text,
2. the title of the text, either as formally presented or in common usage,
3. a source where the text is available (i.e., an imprint statement that names the publisher or a statement that identifies the larger work, such as a periodical, in which the text appears), and
4. other specifics (such as date and place of publication, volume number, and pagination) that can be fitted into an established formula.

In some cases, an annotation or abstract, describing the content in a free-form prose statement, is appended to the above elements in a bibliography citation.

Systematic bibliography is the study of the compiling of lists; enumerative bibliography is the study of the use of those lists. The lists themselves, generally referred to as bibliographies, are often qualified by adjectives that designate a topic, genre, or approach. Examples of this include subject or national bibliographies (e.g., French bibliographies), author bibliographies (e.g., Milton bibliographies), and critical bibliographies. Among the offspring of bibliographies are discographies, for sound recordings in whatever physical form, and filmographies, for motion pictures in whatever physical form. Archival finding aids and calendars, museum inventories, and many merchandise displays are often closely modeled on bibliographical lists. Although bibliographies are usually thought of as things to be consulted, people do *read* them as well. For example, browsers who are in search of perspectives on a topic would read through complete bibliographies, as would browsers who are interested in surveying a topic's literature in its entirety.

Lists may be organized either in linear sequence on paper or randomly in computers. With printed lists, additional access often needs to be provided through the inclusion of indexes, classified lists, and tables of contents. With online lists, access depends on the vocabulary of searchable terms. Printed lists have the advantage of a structure that is visible to the reader. Online lists, however, may provide more current information. Each type depends on establishment of its credibility. Inevitably, bibliographies reflect their compilers' conceptions of the unity, totality, and structure of the topic they cover; along the way, the compilers define the topic itself and aspire to canonize their literature. Bibliographies at once both describe and prescribe—their statements inevitably promote the texts in the process of referring to them. At the same time, the precise uses of bibliographies are inevitably determined by their readers.

The difference between a catalog and a bibliography is still widely seen as one of function. While catalogs identify specific copies (e.g., of a book held by a library), bibliographies refer to writings in general (e.g., all books published on a topic). This distinction is now becoming obsolete, thanks to union catalogs that bring together writings or other media from many different library collections. These new types of catalogs can then work as bibliographies.

Bibliographic control (a concept that underlies the concern of the librarian for universal bibliographic control), along with its counterpart, bibliographical organization, involves strategies for making the entire world of books better available to readers. In the study of citation analysis, bibliometrics employs statistics to evaluate bibliographical references and measure the patterns involved in the use of texts. As it offers gateways to the written literature of society, reference bibliography is obviously crucial to the communities of readers and to the use of books.

Analytical Bibliography

Books, in addition to being studied for their content, can be studied as physical objects, in terms of both the materials used in them (paper, type, ink) and the activities involved in producing them (type design and composition, illustration, house practices of layout and presswork, printing processes, as well as binding and preservation). Among its interrelated specialties, textual bibliography (sometimes considered to be the same as textual criticism) is the study of the relationship between the content of the text and the physical form of the text as it is envisioned by those who create its conceptual and physical artifacts. The physical presentation of a book—its typeface, paper quality, and overall design, for example—subtly affects the way the message is read. In overt ways, the text itself thus often comes to be distorted through misreadings, editorial changes, or printing errors. Descriptive bibliography then for-mulates in scrupulous detail the statements that identify the physical book. This type of bibliography allows the user to compare a particular copy of a book with other copies of the same title in order to spot the differences and to determine what the ideal copy was meant to look like.

The study of physical evidence ranges from the work of historians who confirm what exactly the text consisted of to the work of forensic specialists who uncover evidence of either authenticity or of tampering. Increasingly, this latter activity involves the scientific laboratory. The graphic arts, concerned with the visual presentation of words and/or pictures, are generally not seen as a branch of bibliography, although they are nonetheless essential to bibliography. Emphasizing printing as it does, physical bibliography has counterparts in the disciplines of paleography, which is concerned with manuscripts (those from the eras before printing in particular), and epigraphy, which is concerned with inscriptions and other writings on hard surfaces.

The study of physical bibliography has long been the specialty not only of printing historians but also of bibliophiles and antiquarian book dealers, whose concerns for authenticity are closely related to the use of books as historical evidence. The work of these individuals is of basic importance in the study of the historical role of communication in society, and the interrelationships between its written, electronic, and oral forms. Historical bibliography, since it recognizes names, places, titles, and events, involves the study of the tastes and cultural dynamics of physical books to uncover the relationships between books and history. The term "book history" is also coming to be used for this field of study; a fascination with French *annales* historians has also inspired the term "*histoire du livre*." Recorded knowledge, in its iconic and symbolic forms, is abundantly in evidence today, thanks in large part to physical bibliography.

See also: Cataloging and Knowledge Organization; Library Automation; Printing, History and Methods of.

Bibliography

Krummel, Donald W. (1984). *Bibliographies: Their Aims and Methods.* London: Mansell.

Stokes, Roy. (1969). *The Function of Bibliography.* London: André Deutsch.

D. W. Krummel

BLY, NELLIE
(1864–1922)

"Nellie Bly" was the pen name of Elizabeth Jane Cochrane Seaman, a pioneer of "stunt" journalism (an early form of investigative reporting). Bly's most important investigative pieces included detailing the miserable conditions of a mental asylum, exposing corruption in New York state government, and publicizing the plight of the families of workers during the Pullman Palace Car Company strike of 1894. She is perhaps most famous for her dash around the world in seventy-two days, a feat that boosted the circulation of Joseph Pulitzer's *New York World* and made "Nellie Bly" a household name. She was the first woman to report from the Eastern Front in World War I, and she wrote an advice column chronicling her charitable efforts.

In 1885, *The Pittsburgh Dispatch* ran a series of columns by Erasmus Wilson decrying "restless dissatisfied females" and longing for women who make "home a little paradise." Among women across the city chastising Wilson, one signed herself "Lonely Orphan Girl." The *Dispatch* advertised for the writer to present herself, and the next day Nellie Bly's career was launched. During the next year, Bly wrote pieces on divorce, working girls, and factory conditions—before being moved to cover fashion, society, gardening, and arts. Bly disliked these softer stories and, when she failed to break out of women's news, quit the *Dispatch* in December 1885.

On February 24, 1886, she reappeared in the *Dispatch* under the headline "Nellie in Mexico." This article was the first installment in a series of more than thirty articles chronicling her adventures south of the border. Bly later turned these pieces into her first book, *Six Months in Mexico*, but when she returned to Pittsburgh, the editors at the *Dispatch* again assigned her to cover the arts. She chaffed under these assignments, the last of which appeared March 20, 1887. Soon after, she left the staff this note: "I am off for New York. Look out for me."

Four months and her life savings later, she was desperate. After borrowing cab fare from her landlady, Bly talked her way into the private office of the managing editor of Pulitzer's *New York World* and into an assignment to get herself committed to the Women's Lunatic Asylum on Blackwell's Island. The resulting story ran as the lead Sunday features on October 9 and 16, 1887. Bly's byline appeared at the end of the first story, an honor rarely accorded veteran writers, and her name made the headline of the second installment, indicating that Bly had catapulted to journalistic stardom. Two months later, her book, *Ten Days in a Mad-House,* was published.

For the next two years, Bly became the leading "stunt girl" for the *World*, posing as a sinner needing reform to investigate the Magdalen Home for Unfortunate Women, pretending to be a patent medicine manufacturer's wife to uncover corruption in state government, and getting herself arrested to spend the night in a co-ed jail. While many of her stunts were titillating and sensational, she often took the role of reformer, pointing out the needs of the downtrodden, unmasking con artists, and exposing legal and political biases. She was not a polished writer, but she had good instincts for framing questions to elicit powerful quotes and for telling compelling stories. Bly also usually managed to inject herself into her stories, frequently including quotes (provided by those people whom she interviewed) about her own winsome smile, pluck, and bravery.

On November 14, 1889, Bly set out to beat the fictional record of Jules Verne's Phileas Fogg by circling the world in less than eighty days. Along the way, she charmed the French novelist—and the rest of the world—with accounts of danger, frustration, and exotic adventures. She completed her trip on January 25, 1890, in seventy-two days, six hours, eleven minutes, and fourteen seconds, arriving back in New York City amid cheers from thousands of well-wishers. On the Saturday that she returned, the *World* sold ten thousand more papers than it had on the previous Saturday. However, Bly thought that the newspaper failed to acknowledge her contribution to its popularity. She signed a three-year contract with Norman L. Munro to write serial fiction for his weekly *New York Family Story Paper.* No known record exists of Bly's stories or their reception, but Bly's letters to Erasmus Wilson indicate that she battled depression over the next three years.

On May 10, 1893, the *World* celebrated its tenth anniversary with synopses of its most memorable stories. The accounts mention only one reporter by name, Nellie Bly. Perhaps this retrospective caused the editors of the *World* to seek out Bly. On September 17, 1893, under the front-

The success of Nellie Bly's record-breaking trip around the world was given full front-page coverage upon its completion. (Bettmann/Corbis)

page headline "Nellie Bly Again," she returned to the stable of stunt reporters for the *World*. Among her best reporting was her coverage of the Pullman Palace Car Company strike of 1894, in which she sympathetically outlined the plight of workers who were living in company towns and at the mercy of company salaries and prices.

By 1895, still battling depression, Bly left the *World* for a five-week stint at the *Chicago Times-Herald,* and on April 5, 1895, Bly secretly wed Robert Livingston Seaman, a seventy-year-old New York industrialist. She was thirty-one. The couple's first year together was stormy. His relatives opposed the match and caused enough trouble over money that Bly decided to reenter journalism, interviewing political figures about their views on marriage, covering the National Woman Suffrage Convention in Washington, D.C., and, in March 1896, proposing to recruit a regiment to fight for Cuba against Spain. The last story may have shaken Seaman enough to save her marriage. Her plan faded into oblivion, and by August, the Seamans had sailed for Europe, where

they remained for the next three years, with Bly nursing her husband through deteriorating eyesight and Seaman changing his will to make her sole beneficiary. They returned to the United States in 1899 and lived quietly until Seaman died in 1904. By that time, Bly was immersed in running Seaman's Iron Clad Manufacturing Company. By 1905, she held twenty-five patents in her own name. She designed, manufactured, and marketed the first successful steel barrel produced in the United States in a factory she strove to make a model of social welfare for her fifteen hundred employees. But she failed as a financial overseer. The Iron Clad Manufacturing Company fell prey to employees who embezzled perhaps as much as $1.6 million. In 1911, Bly faced a bankruptcy fight that would last for three years. To make ends meet, she worked intermittently for William Randolph Hearst's *New York Journal.*

In 1914, four days after Austria declared war on Serbia, Bly set out for Vienna, seeking financing for her Iron Clad offshoot, American Steel Barrel Company, from wealthy Austrian friend Oscar

Bondy. While her mission began as business, she recognized her journalistic opportunity and covered the early part of the war for the *Journal*. She became an Austrian supporter and stayed in Vienna until the end of the war, working for the welfare of widows and orphans.

In 1919, she returned to New York, where she wrote, for the *Journal*, an advice column that publicized her efforts to help unwed mothers and their children. By 1921, she told readers she had placed thousands of children in happy homes and provided thousands of unwed mothers with new chances. Bly died January 27, 1922.

See also: HEARST, WILLIAM RANDOLPH; JOURNALISM, HISTORY OF; NEWSPAPER INDUSTRY, HISTORY OF; PULITZER, JOSEPH.

Bibliography

Kroeger, Brooke. (1994). *Nellie Bly: Daredevil, Reporter, Feminist.* New York: Times Books.

Marks, Jason. (1993). *Around the World in 72 Days: The Race Between Pulitzer's Nellie Bly and Cosmopolitan's Elizabeth Bisland.* New York: Gemittarius Press.

Ross, Ishbel. (1936). *Ladies of the Press.* New York: Harper & Brothers.

Wildemuth, Susan. (1999). "Nellie Bly and the Power of the Press." *Cobblestone* 20(1):16.

ELLEN WILLIAMSON KANERVO

BODY IMAGE, MEDIA EFFECT ON

According to Judith Rodin, Lisa Silberstein, and Ruth Striegel-Moore (1984), the concern American women have with weight has become "a normative discontent." Consider the mother, sister, or friend who is perpetually on a diet to lose "those last five pounds." Such widespread concern with body shape (or "body-image disturbance") is a relatively new historical development that mirrors the increasing tendency for media outlets to feature dieting information and images of extremely thin characters and models.

Eating disorders such as anorexia nervosa and bulimia nervosa are less common than body-image disturbances, but they too are increasing in prevalence. Rates of occurrence of eating disorders among females in the United States range from as little as 1 percent (for anorexia) to more than 20 percent (for bulimia). Rates of occurrence of eating disorders among males in the United States are smaller (about one-tenth that for females), but they are growing too. As these numbers increase, the population of people with eating disorders is becoming more diverse. Early research suggested that young, white, upper-middle-class, college-educated women were at highest risk for developing eating disorders, but more recent research shows that eating disorders are quickly becoming an affliction of equal opportunity, affecting women of color, children, men, older people, and, as research by Anne E. Becker (1991) suggests, people in countries that previously had little problem with eating disorders until they began importing American media.

Trends in Media Depictions of the Ideal Body

Some feminist theorists have argued that when women gain ground politically, thinness as a female ideal becomes fashionable because American society is uncomfortable with voluptuous women in powerful positions. This is meant to explain why the long, lean "flapper" style was popular during the women's suffrage movement, why British model Twiggy gained fame during the women's liberation movement of the 1960s and 1970s, and why the "heroin chic" waif look became appealing when the Clinton administration began in the early 1990s.

Whatever the reason for these trends, it is clear that the women depicted in the U.S. media have steadily grown thinner since the 1950s. A 1980 study by David M. Garner, Paul E. Garfinkel, Donald Schwartz, and Michael Thompson reported a significant decrease in the body measurements and weights of *Playboy* centerfold subjects and Miss America Pageant contestants from 1959 to 1978. Updates of this study show a continued trend toward the slimming of both centerfold subjects and pageant contestants. Dozens of other analyses of magazines, television, and movies show that there are more dieting and exercise articles being published than ever before and that the models and characters—especially females—featured in these media are disproportionately skinny when compared to the population at large.

Media Effects on Body Image

Given that the slimming trend in the media parallels the increasing obsession with thinness in real life, researchers have been compelled to study the effects of exposure to thin-ideal media.

Many people object to beauty pageants, including the Miss Universe competition, because the pageants foster the image of an "ideal" body type that many, if not most, young women cannot attain. (AFP/Corbis)

Research here is split into two domains: (1) media effects on body image and (2) media effects on disordered eating.

Research generally shows that exposure to the thin-body ideal leads to temporary decreases in self-esteem and increases in body and weight dissatisfaction, depression, and anxiety. But which audience members are most vulnerable? In a 1993 study by Kate Hamilton and Glenn Waller, research participants who did not have eating disorders were not affected by viewing a set of thin-ideal photographs, but when participants who did have eating disorders viewed the photographs, they subsequently overestimated their own body size by an average of 25 percent. These results are echoed in a study by Heidi D. Posavac, Steven S. Posavac, and Emil J. Posavac (1998), which showed that the adverse effects of exposure to thin-ideal media were especially strong for young women who were initially more dissatisfied with their bodies, as compared to women who were less dissatisfied with their bodies.

Much of the research on media effects on body image has been guided by the social comparison theory of Leon Festinger (1954), which holds that people are driven to evaluate themselves through comparison with others. This is a risky business, because unfavorable comparisons can make individuals feel inadequate and worthless. A study by Mary C. Martin and Patricia F. Kennedy (1993) showed that the tendency to compare the self to thin models was strongest for participants who initially felt the least personally attractive and who had the lowest self-esteem. In addition, a study by Renée Botta (1999) showed that the tendency to compare the self to thin media personalities (a tendency she calls "body-image processing") is important in predicting internalization of the thin-body ideal. These studies, as well as those summarized above, suggest that people who have the most to lose as a result of comparison are, unfortunately, those most likely to compare themselves to thin-ideal models and characters.

Media Effects on Eating Disorders

Research has shown convincingly that thin-ideal media exposure is related not only to body-image disturbances but also to disordered eating. Kristen Harrison and Joanne Cantor (1997) have shown that this correlation exists even for people who say they have no interest in dieting and fitness as media topics. Like body-image disturbance, disordered eating as an outcome of thin-ideal media exposure is dependent on the audience members' individual differences, such as sex (females exhibit stronger correlations than males) and interpersonal attraction to thin media personalities (people who are attracted to thin media personalities exhibit stronger correlations than people who are attracted to average or heavy media personalities). Several possible mediators of the media-disorder link include negative affect, thin-ideal body stereotype internalization, and body dissatisfaction.

Researchers including Michael P. Levine and Linda Smolak (1998) have been working on media literacy campaigns to arm vulnerable children against the onslaught of thin-ideal messages they encounter through media exposure. It is hoped that these campaigns, informed by continued work on individual differences in vulnerability, will help researchers develop prevention programs that can be tailored to audience members based on their own particular vulnerabilities.

See also: FEMINIST SCHOLARSHIP AND COMMUNICATION; GENDER AND THE MEDIA; NUTRITION AND MEDIA EFFECTS.

Bibliography

Becker, Anne E. (1991). "Body Image in Fiji: The Self in the Body and in the Community." *Dissertation Abstracts International* 51:2793.

Botta, Renée A. (1999). "Television Images and Adolescent Girls' Body Image Disturbance." *Journal of Communication* 49:22–41.

Festinger, Leon. (1954). "A Theory of Social Comparison Processes." *Human Relations* 7:117–140.

Garner, David M.; Garfinkel, Paul E.; Schwartz, Donald; and Thompson, Michael. (1980). "Cultural Expectations of Thinness in Women." *Psychological Reports* 47:483–491.

Hamilton, Kate, and Waller, Glenn. (1993). "Media Influences on Body Size Estimation in Anorexia and Bulimia: An Experimental Study." *British Journal of Psychiatry* 162:837–840.

Harrison, Kristen, and Cantor, Joanne. (1997). "The Relationship Between Media Exposure and Eating Disorders." *Journal of Communication* 47:40–67.

Levine, Michael P., and Smolak, Linda. (1998). "The Mass Media and Disordered Eating: Implications for Primary Prevention." In *The Prevention of Eating Disorders,* eds. Walter Vandereycken and Greta Noordenbos. New York: New York University Press.

Martin, Mary C., and Kennedy, Patricia F. (1993). "Advertising and Social Comparison: Consequences for Female Preadolescents and Adolescents." *Psychology and Marketing* 10:513–530.

Posavac, Heidi D.; Posavac, Steven S.; and Posavac, Emil J. (1998). "Exposure to Media Images of Female Attractiveness and Concern with Body Weight among Young Women." *Sex Roles* 38:187–201.

Rodin, Judith; Silberstein, Lisa; and Striegel-Moore, Ruth. (1984). "Women and Weight: A Normative Discontent." *Nebraska Symposium on Motivation* 32:267–307.

KRISTEN HARRISON

■ BROADCASTING, GOVERNMENT REGULATION OF

The system of broadcast regulation by the U.S. government evolved from the early twentieth century into an intricate web of influences that include government agencies, courts, citizen groups, and the industry itself. These entities work in concert to shape the regulation of broadcast content, networking, technology, advertising, ownership, public-interest obligations, community relations, and other aspects of the broadcast business.

Entities Involved in Broadcast Regulation

Operating under the Communications Act of 1934 as amended by the Telecommunications Act of 1996, the Federal Communications Commission (FCC) is the major independent regulatory agency that sits in the heart of the regulatory web. The FCC is primarily responsible for issuing operating licenses, managing the use of the airwaves, and creating rules and regulations that all nongovernment broadcasters must follow, both commercial and noncommercial. The FCC holds rule-making proceedings and inquiries to gather information needed to create, change, or abolish regulations. It also enforces existing rules and regulations using such measures as consent orders, forfeitures (fines), conditional license renewal, denial or revocation of license, or letters and other "raised eyebrow" actions. However, despite its position as the main regulatory agency for the broadcast medium, it must listen to the demands of the U.S. Congress, the president of the United States, the courts, the broadcasting industry, the general public, and other regulatory agencies.

Because Congress was responsible for creating the FCC as part of the Communications Act of 1934, Congress holds substantial power over the agency, including appropriation of the budget, approval of the five FCC commissioners, and reauthorization every two years of the agency's very existence. Congress can also appoint special committees to investigate FCC decisions or operations if it so chooses. However, the greatest power that Congress has over the FCC is that Congress may amend the Communications Act of 1934 at any time, thereby changing the rules, regulations, or organization of the agency.

Like Congress, the president of the United States also has some control over the FCC. The president nominates each of the five FCC commissioners, although they must be approved by Congress. Furthermore, the president may select which commissioner will become the FCC chairman. Other powers of the president include control of the airwaves during wartime and assignment of frequencies for government use.

In order to keep abreast with telecommunication matters, the president must have telecommunication advisors. The National Telecommunications and Information Administration (NTIA) fills this capacity. The NTIA advises the president on domestic and international communication policy and competitiveness, conducts telecommunication research, and encourages the development of various educational and public services. In addition, the NTIA promotes presidential policy to the FCC, Congress, and the general public.

The Federal Trade Commission (FTC), another independent regulatory agency, enters the web of broadcast regulation as a watchdog for false advertising and antitrust violations. The FTC, for example, may declare an advertisement to be misrepresentative or deceptive, and then charge the respective broadcaster and advertising agency to either cease, alter, or correct the faulty ad.

The Equal Employment Opportunity Commission (EEOC) enforces federal discrimination laws as well as affirmative action for all businesses in the United States. The broadcasting industry is not exempt from scrutiny by the EEOC. Therefore, all broadcast stations, networks, and affiliated offices must follow the equal employment opportunity guidelines and record their compliance in public inspection files.

Whenever an FCC decision is appealed, that appeal is taken to the federal courts. The U.S. Court of Appeals for the District of Columbia usually hears FCC-related appeals, reviews the various FCC decisions in question, and declares its findings. In certain situations, the U.S. Supreme Court may review a lower court's decision. Depending on the outcomes of the court decisions, the FCC must take the appropriate action, whether it is to abandon an initiative or try again.

The general public gained some influence over broadcast regulation during the twentieth century. For example, citizen groups and public-interest organizations took broadcasters to court, pressured local broadcast stations with petitions to deny license renewal, and negotiated settlements. Citizen groups also influenced the FCC directly by petitioning the agency to enforce its existing policies or to create new policies that would further broaden the scope of broadcast regulation.

Broadcast Industry Self-Regulation

In order to keep outside regulation at a minimum, the broadcasting industry undertakes measures of self-regulation, including voluntary programming ratings; voluntary screening of violent, indecent, and otherwise inappropriate program content; and refusal to accept advertising selling such items as cigarettes and hard liquor. These actions, like those taken under the Codes of Practice of the National Association of Broadcasters in the mid-1900s, have served to restrain the government from regulating what the industry has already been self-regulating.

Historical Development of Broadcast Regulation

The first official attempt by the United States to regulate broadcasting occurred in 1910, when Congress enacted the Wireless Ship Act to ensure maritime safety. The Wireless Ship Act required a radio and an accompanying skilled operator to be on board every passenger vessel. However, the legislation did not require the operator to be on duty

The original members of the Federal Radio Commission, which first met on April 2, 1928, to begin the task of unscrambling the air lanes according to the Radio Act of 1927, were (left to right) Sam Pickard, Orestes H. Caldwell, Eugene O. Skyes, Harold A. Lafount, and Ira E. Robinson; Carl H. Butman, secretary of the commission, is standing. (Underwood & Underwood/Corbis)

twenty-four hours a day, an oversight that became tragically evident when an operator on a nearby ship was not on duty to receive distress calls from the *Titanic* on April 14, 1912. Consequently, Congress tried again.

The Radio Act of 1912 followed the Wireless Ship Act and introduced the idea of assigning frequencies and issuing operating licenses to potential radio operators. Now, anyone wishing to transmit could apply for a broadcast license, and many people did. The result was an overcrowding of the airwaves and problems with signal interference. Unfortunately, the 1912 act gave the government no authority to reject license applications or fix the interference problems. Therefore, in an attempt to control the burgeoning field of broadcasting, Congress created a new act.

This new act was the Radio Act of 1927. This act solved the interference and licensing problems and provided the foundation on which the Communications Act of 1934 would be built. First, the

1927 act created a five-member Federal Radio Commission (FRC) to govern licensing, frequency assignments, and station operations, as well as to oversee network broadcasting and prohibit monopolization. Second, licensing standards became more stringent. An applicant had to meet certain criteria to be granted a license. Furthermore, licensing periods, which were indefinite under previous legislation, were now limited. Third, and perhaps most important, broadcasting was redefined and reconceptualized. For example, broadcasting was considered interstate commerce, which Congress had the authority to control under the U.S. Constitution (Article I, Section 8), and broadcast messages were granted First Amendment protection. Fourth, broadcasting was recognized as a unique form of communication that would require a different regulatory framework than that of common carriers such as telephony and telegraphy. All of this was then packaged with the philosophy that the broadcast media should serve "the public interest, convenience, and necessity."

Many of the changes, both operational and conceptual, that resulted from the Radio Act of 1927 were soon challenged in court by various broadcasters. At the heart of many challenges was the commission's authority to deny or revoke a license. These challenges eventually led to the birth of the Communications Act of 1934.

The Communications Act of 1934 became the first comprehensive legislation to regulate both wire and wireless communication. It enhanced the concepts introduced in the 1927 act, including the principles that the public owns the airwaves and that broadcasting is a legally unique form of communication. The 1934 act also created the FCC, which was charged with ensuring that broadcasters acted "in the public interest, convenience, and necessity."

In 1941, the FCC initiated the chain broadcasting rules, which limited the programming power and economic influence that radio networks could have over affiliated local stations. Later, the FCC responded to the introduction of television by applying similar limitations to television networks.

It was not long after its action limiting network influence over local affiliates that the FCC sought to clarify its public-interest standard for broadcasters. In 1946, the FCC issued its *Blue Book*, which suggested that stations should air certain types of programs in order to serve the public interest. Specifically, the 1946 *Blue Book*, officially titled *Public Service Responsibility of Broadcast Licenses*, urged stations to serve the public interest by airing nonsponsored programs, local live programs, and programs that discussed public issues. The *Blue Book* also called for the elimination of advertising excesses.

Three years later, in 1949, the broadcast industry was confronted with a document titled *In the Matter of Editorializing by Broadcast Licensees*. This document created a ban on station editorializing and produced the Fairness Doctrine, which required stations to devote a reasonable amount of time to the discussion of controversial issues of public importance and to present contrasting views on such issues. The 1960 Programming Policy Statement (officially *Report and Statement of Policy re: Commission en banc Programming Inquiry*) further defined the public-interest programming obligations of broadcasters by requiring stations to ascertain the needs and interests of their communities and then demonstrate how those needs were being met. However, broadcasters did get relief in 1959 and 1960 when two amendments to the Communications Act of 1934 were passed.

The 1959 and 1960 amendments applied to section 315 of the Communications Act of 1934. This section required that if broadcasters allowed a political candidate to express views on the air, then the stations had to provide an equal opportunity for opposing candidates to present their views. The 1959 amendment exempted *bona fide* newscasts, news interviews, news documentaries, and on-the-spot news coverage from this requirement. The 1960 amendment, a reaction to the Nixon-Kennedy debates, included coverage of debates as another type of exempted program.

The 1960s also saw the influence of new technologies on legislation. The Communications Satellite Act of 1962 was created to control the long-term commercial use of satellites. The 1962 All Channel Receiver Law added section 303 to the 1934 act, requiring all television receivers sold in the United States to be capable of receiving both VHF and the new UHF signals. In public broadcasting, the Educational Television Facilities Act of 1962 provided a monetary jumpstart for the construction of educational television stations, and in 1967, the Public Broadcasting Act was passed, which created the Corporation for Public Broadcasting and provided direct appropriations for noncommercial programming. Also, citizens gained the means to influence station licensing and renewal directly when the U.S. Court of Appeals for the District of Columbia Circuit established—in *Office of Communication of the United Church of Christ v. Federal Communications Commission* (1966)—the right of the public to participate legally in broadcast licensing proceedings.

The 1970s began with stricter rules on networks. The first of three tries at Prime-Time Access rules was introduced in 1970 and limited network programming to three hours per day between 7:00 P.M. and 10:00 P.M. Central Time. The Financial Interest and Syndication Rules, also known as the Fin-Syn Rules, were also passed in 1970. These rules prohibited networks from holding any financial interest in syndication or from syndicating their own programs. By the end of the decade, regulation began to relax, with such repeals as the 1977 elimination of the chain broadcasting rules for radio.

The 1980s carried the wave of deregulation to new heights. This can be attributed to the FCC's adoption of a marketplace philosophy, which advocated that a station's service to the public could best be determined by that station's performance in the marketplace. Under President Ronald Reagan and the new marketplace philosophy, the FCC repealed a number of rules, including the community ascertainment requirements of the 1960 Programming Policy Statement (eliminated in 1984) and the Fairness Doctrine (repealed in 1987). License terms and renewal periods were extended from three years to eight years. Ownership rules were also relaxed, a trend that carried into the 1990s. Another deregulatory measure was the repeal of the Fin-Syn rules in 1993.

In 1990, the U.S. Congress passed the Children's Television Act. This act limits advertising time and usage during children's programming, and it places requirements on the amount and type of children's programming that a station must broadcast.

The Telecommunications Act of 1996 was enacted to amend the Communications Act of 1934. It included regulations for new technologies and public-service requirements for communications. Most important, however, the Telecommunications Act of 1996 provided new initiatives for the United States as it began to enter a digital era where future technologies and possibilities would once again reshape the history of broadcast regulation.

Rationales for Broadcast Regulation

Broadcast regulation, despite basic First Amendment protection for the press, grew and evolved as each succeeding act of legislation attempted to shape and control the burgeoning industry. Five rationales for regulating broadcasting introduced in the Radio Act of 1927 and carried forward in the Communications Act of 1934 have endured.

The first rationale for broadcast regulation is the notion that the public owns the airwaves. Therefore, the public, represented by its government, is entitled to demand that the airwaves be used in the public interest. The second rationale, consequently, is that a licensed broadcaster is merely a trustee of the publicly owned airwaves and therefore must act as the public's proxy while using the public resource.

The third rationale, scarcity of the airwaves, suggests that the government must regulate the assignment and use of the airwaves because there are a limited number of useable frequencies in the electromagnetic spectrum. From this, it follows that government has the right to deny or revoke a broadcaster's license to use a frequency, so long as that action is in the public interest.

Media uniqueness, the fourth rationale, claims that the broadcast media have a more "captive" audience than do print media. Behind this rationale is the assumption that users of broadcast media will be less likely to actively select and scrutinize the messages that are received via broadcasting. Therefore, it is important that the government ensure that these unique media are programming in the public interest.

The fifth rationale for broadcast regulation addresses the very nature of the airwaves. It states that the airwaves do not have the traditional physical boundaries that other, more tangible means of communication share. Consequently, because broadcast messages are more pervasive, their potential for social influence is great. It is this potential that allows the government to regulate broadcasting and limit, to some extent, its First Amendment protection.

See also: BROADCASTING, SELF-REGULATION OF; CABLE TELEVISION, REGULATION OF; COMMUNICATIONS ACT OF 1934; FEDERAL COMMUNICATIONS COMMISSION; FIRST AMENDMENT AND THE MEDIA; PUBLIC BROADCASTING; RADIO BROADCASTING; TELECOMMUNICATIONS ACT OF 1996; TELEVISION BROADCASTING.

Bibliography

Barnouw, Erik. (1966). *A Tower in Babel: A History of Broadcasting in the United States to 1933*. New York: Oxford University Press.

Barnouw, Erik. (1968). *The Golden Web: A History of Broadcasting in the United States 1933–1953*. New York: Oxford University Press.

Barnouw, Erik. (1970). *The Image Empire: A History of Broadcasting in the United States from 1953*. New York: Oxford University Press.

Kahn, Frank J., ed. (1978). *Documents of American Broadcasting*, 3rd edition. Englewood Cliffs, NJ: Prentice-Hall.

Quello, James H. (1997). "Commissioner Quello's Statement, June 12, 1997, Re: Proposed Notice of Inquiry on Broadcast Advertisement of Distilled Spirits." <http://www.fcc.gov/Speeches/Quello/liquor.html>.

Smith, F. Leslie; Meeske, Milan; and Wright, John W., II. (1995). *Electronic Media and Government: The Regulation of Wireless and Wired Mass Communication in the United States.* White Plains, NY: Longman.

FRANCESCA DILLMAN CARPENTIER

BROADCASTING, SELF-REGULATION OF

As with many other industries, the broadcasting industry practices a form of self-regulation in addition to following the regulations imposed by the government. Self-regulation is attractive for several reasons. First, an industry that regulates itself in certain areas can avoid potentially harsher regulations by the government because the government will often refrain from entering the realm that is already being adequately controlled by the industry itself. Second, self-regulation can expedite the development of standards and practices that can be voluntarily accepted by the industry. Third, and perhaps most valuable, industries that practice self-regulation can gain more public favor than do industries that only rely on government regulation. Therefore, self-regulation can be a good image builder as well as good business practice. This is why the broadcasting industry created the now-defunct National Association of Broadcasters Codes of Practices in the early 1900s and continues to follow many of its tenets.

The National Association of Broadcasters Codes of Practices

In 1929, the National Association of Broadcasters (NAB), the major professional and political organization of the broadcasting industry, created the radio Codes of Practices, which it expanded in 1952 to include television. These codes, inspired by previous court decisions, government urging, and public opinion, were completely voluntary—so much so that fewer than half of the radio stations and two-thirds of the television stations subscribed to them. However, the codes had a great enough presence to gain the attention of the U.S. Department of Justice and eventually be dissolved in 1982.

Among the code provisions were advertising limitations and programming standards. For example, limits were placed on the total amount of advertising time a station could sell, especially during children's programming times. Limits were also placed on the amount of medical-product advertising and the number of contest and other promotional offers that could be accepted. The programming standards suggested by the codes encouraged educational, cultural, children's, and news programming. Alternately, the codes discouraged editorializing as well as the sale of airtime for controversial issues. A third provision was the Family Viewing Time block, which allotted certain evening hours for family-friendly programming that, consequently, contained fewer advertisements.

Several of these provisions, though seemingly altruistic, were questioned by the U.S. Department of Justice. Family Viewing Time, for example, was considered in *Writers Guild of America v. Federal Communications Commission* (1976) to be a violation of the broadcasters' First Amendment rights because its existence was the product of government pressure. The discouragement of selling time for the presentation of controversial viewpoints was also questioned because of possible intentions to bypass the Fairness Doctrine (as officially outlined in the 1949 document *In the Matter of Editorializing by Broadcast Licensees*, issued by the Federal Communications Commission). The Fairness Doctrine, created in 1949 and repealed in 1987, required broadcasters to deal with controversial issues of public importance in a fair and even-handed manner; in other words, they had to grant airtime to all sides of a controversial issue if one side of that issue received airtime. By discouraging the sale of airtime for controversial viewpoints, it was presumed that broadcasters were seeking to avoid controversial issues, and thus the provisions of the Fairness Doctrine altogether. However, this presumed avoidance was not the most controversial point of the codes.

The most controversial point of the codes concerned the advertising limits. Broadcasters were accused of limiting their advertising time to increase demand artificially, which would therefore raise the price of that advertising time. This was seen in *United States v. National Association of Broadcasters* (1982) as a violation of section 1 of the Sherman Antitrust Act. It was the ultimate downfall of the NAB codes.

These threats of legal action by the U.S. Department of Justice put tremendous pressure on the NAB and those stations that subscribed to the codes. The resulting action was the dissolution of the Codes of Practices for both radio and television in 1982 and the end of an industry-sponsored code of ethics. However, the ideals of the codes and, indeed, some of their practices would remain, absorbed in the standards and practices departments of the networks.

Broadcast Standards and Practices

Among the many departments of a major television network is the department of broadcast standards and practices. This department houses censors who judge potential programs and advertisements in order to determine which program and advertising content is appropriate to air as well as when it is appropriate to air. A hypothetical example of this might be the approval of a made-for-television movie on the condition that it airs only after 9:00 P.M. and that two scenes are eliminated.

In addition to specific program evaluation, the department establishes, alters, and implements network policies regarding programming content, and it ensures that other network departments and production affiliates acknowledge or comply with the various policies. Another arm of the standards and practices department collects comments, complaints, and other feedback from the general public. This enables the department to monitor public opinion and review or change its policies accordingly.

Industry-wide standards also exist, the most visible of which are advertising practices and television content ratings. For example, regarding advertising practices, television stations continue to refrain from airing commercials for hard liquor or cigarette products. It is necessary to note that the Federal Trade Commission has regulations that address the advertising of alcoholic beverages on television. However, this regulation is lenient enough to allow the broadcasting industry to place further restrictions on itself regarding the acceptance of alcohol advertisements. Therefore, this practice is included as a voluntary commitment by the industry, a commitment that has thus far succeeded in circumventing a harsher government regulation.

Television content ratings are also voluntary, although their establishment was caused by government pressure. The pressure came in June 1995, when the U.S. Senate voted to add a provision to the Telecommunications Reform Bill (later the Telecommunications Act of 1996) that would create a Television Ratings Commission to rate television programming in the absence of an industry-crafted system. Naturally, the industry crafted a system.

The industry system for rating television programs contains six labels (TV-Y, TV-Y7, TV-G, TV-PG, TV-14, and TV-MA) with accompanying descriptions of specific content. TV-Y indicates that the program is appropriate for young children. TV-Y7 indicates that the program is suitable for children over the age of six. TV-G indicates that the program is suitable for a general audience. TV-PG indicates that parental guidance is suggested because of inappropriate language, violence, or sexual situations. TV-14 indicates that the program is inappropriate for children under age fourteen because it contains mature language, violence, or sexual situations. TV-MA indicates that the program is unsuitable for anyone under age seventeen. These voluntary ratings, compatible with V-chip technology, enable parents to evaluate programming for their children—without government regulation.

See also: BROADCASTING, GOVERNMENT REGULATION OF; CABLE TELEVISION, REGULATION OF; RADIO BROADCASTING; RADIO BROADCASTING, STATION PROGRAMMING AND; RATINGS FOR TELEVISION PROGRAMS; TELECOMMUNICATIONS ACT OF 1996; TELEVISION BROADCASTING, PROGRAMMING AND; V-CHIP.

Bibliography
Kahn, Frank J., ed. (1978). *Documents of American Broadcasting*, 3rd edition. Englewood Cliffs, NJ: Prentice-Hall.

Quello, James H. (1997). "Commissioner Quello's Statement, June 12, 1997, Re: Proposed Notice of Inquiry on Broadcast Advertisement of Distilled Spirits." <http://www.fcc.gov/Speeches/Quello/liquor.html>.

Smith, F. Leslie; Meeske, Milan; and Wright, John W., II. (1995). *Electronic Media and Government: The Regulation of Wireless and Wired Mass Communication in the United States*. White Plains, NY: Longman.

FRANCESCA DILLMAN CARPENTIER

BUSH, VANNEVAR
(1890–1974)

Vannevar Bush was born March 11, 1890, in Everett, Massachusetts, son of Universalist minister Richard Perry Bush and Emma Linwood Paine Bush. As a boy, he loved to tinker. He received bachelor's and master's degrees in engineering from Tufts University in 1913, earning the first of his many patents while he was still in college. In 1913, he was employed by General Electric in Schenectady, New York, but returned to Tufts in 1914 as an instructor in mathematics. He earned a doctorate in engineering from the Massachusetts Institute of Technology (MIT) and Harvard University in 1916 and became an assistant professor of electrical engineering at Tufts. He married Phoebe Davis in 1916, and they had two sons. In 1919, he joined MIT as associate professor of power transmission, became a full professor in 1923, and served as vice-president and dean of the School of Engineering beginning in 1932. His most notable research achievements in this period involved advances in analog computing which greatly facilitated the solution of complex mathematical problems using the differential analyzer, a machine for solving differential equations. In 1939, he moved to Washington, D.C., as president of the Carnegie Institution. He subsequently became director of the federal Office of Scientific Research and Development, where he was responsible for coordinating the work of scientists who were involved in the war effort. Following the end of World War II, he advocated continuing national support for basic scientific research, which eventually led to the establishment of the National Science Foundation. He retired from the Carnegie Institution in 1955 and returned to Massachusetts, where he died on June 28, 1974. He was the recipient of numerous awards including the National Medal of Science and was named a member of the National Academy of Sciences in 1934.

The most persistent line of Bush's inventive endeavors involved technology for processing information. The differential analyzer, an analog computer, was the most important product of this activity. Other, less successful efforts included a decoding machine for the U.S. Navy and the Rapid Selector, both limited by the state of available technology at the time of their invention. The latter device employed 35-mm film, on which microphotographed texts could be made quickly

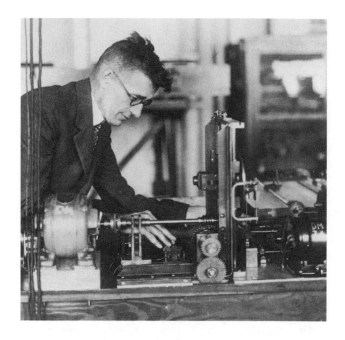

Vannevar Bush examines one of his inventions in 1927 at the Massachusetts Institute of Technology. (Bettmann/Corbis)

available by the use of photoelectric cells scanning a coded index.

Bush is best remembered by information scientists for the visions of devices that were described in his 1945 essay "As We May Think." This was first published in *Atlantic Monthly,* followed by a summary of the major points in a brief article in *Time* and a condensed and illustrated version in *Life.* Reflecting on what direction science and technology might take following the end of World War II, Bush indicated ways in which existing photographic, controlling, and electronic techniques and their reasonable extrapolations might be applied to recording, transmitting, and reviewing the results of research. Devices described included a compact cyclops camera for capturing images, high-capacity microfilm for compact storage, a machine that could type when talked to, and high-speed computational devices. Writing in his autobiography, *Pieces of the Action* (1970), Bush commented in particular on his concept for the memex, the most notable device proposed in his groundbreaking essay. It would be "a machine that should be an extension of the personal memory and body of knowledge belonging to an individual, and should work in a fashion analogous to the working of the human brain—by association rather than by categorical classification"; essentially, "a memex is a filing system, a repository of information, and a scheme of searching and speedily finding a desired piece of information" (p. 190).

The analog technologies of Bush's day made it impossible to turn the memex idea into a functioning machine, but memex is often cited by others as an inspiration for their subsequent work in information retrieval and hypertext development. Memex suggested both the possibility of a device that could serve as a personal tool in support of information work and the potential value of trails connecting pieces of information. In the conclusion of his 1945 essay, Bush forecast that "wholly new forms of encyclopedias will appear, readymade with a mesh of associative trails running through them, ready to be dropped into the memex and there amplified" (p. 108).

Bush remained more comfortable with analog devices and made no technical contribution to modern digital computers. However, his analysis of the problem—that existing ways of handling information were inadequate—and his solution— a device that stored and organized information that was of value to an individual—were widely accepted. It took more than fifty years for Bush's vision of memex to become fully realized with the development of personal computers, the World Wide Web, and search engines. Bush's widely read and reprinted essay made him for decades the best-known advocate in the United States for information retrieval systems that both responded to and expanded on human inquiries.

See also: INTERNET AND THE WORLD WIDE WEB; RETRIEVAL OF INFORMATION.

Bibliography

Burke, Colin. (1994). *Information and Secrecy: Vannevar Bush, Ultra, and the Other Memex*. Metuchen, NJ: Scarecrow Press.

Bush, Vannevar. (1945). "As We May Think." *Atlantic Monthly* 176(July):101–108.

Bush, Vannevar. (1970). *Pieces of the Action*. New York: William Morrow.

Nyce, James M., and Kahn, Paul, eds. (1991). *From Memex to Hypertext: Vannevar Bush and the Mind's Machine*. Boston: Academic Press.

Wiesner, Jerome B. (1979). "Vannevar Bush, March 11, 1890–June 28, 1974." *Biographical Memoirs of the National Academy of Sciences* 50:88–117.

Zachary, G. Pascal. (1997). *Endless Frontier: Vannevar Bush, Engineer of the American Century*. New York: Free Press.

LINDA C. SMITH

C

■ CABLE TELEVISION

The cable television industry provides multichannel video services to approximately two-thirds of all television households in the United States. In addition to offering different tiers of programming, many cable systems offer ancillary services, such as high-speed Internet access and local telephone services. There are approximately 10,700 cable systems in operation in the United States. Many companies own more than one system, and are known in the cable industry as multiple system operators (MSOs).

Major Players in the Cable Industry

Ownership of cable television systems has changed considerably since 1980, resulting in a rapidly consolidated industry. Five companies dominate the cable industry. AT&T, Time Warner, Comcast, Cox Communications, and Adelphia are the leading MSOs. These companies account for 70 percent of all cable television customers. There are a number of smaller companies that serve the remainder of the cable audience. Several companies also hold ownership interests in cable television service in foreign markets.

While large media companies dominate cable ownership at the national level, cable is in reality a local service. Cable operators are awarded a franchise to serve a specific community or geographical area. The local governing board (e.g., city council) actually awards a franchise for cable service, usually for a ten- to fifteen-year period. In exchange for the right to provide service to the community, the operator normally pays a franchise fee equal to a maximum of 5 percent of the revenues derived from operating the system. In many cases, the operator also agrees to provide a number of public, educational, or governmental access channels (also known as PEG channels) as part of the franchise agreement. The operator, often in consultation and negotiation with the franchising body, sets rates for cable service.

In September 1999, the Federal Communications Commission (FCC) revised its limit on the number of households a single cable operator could serve at the national level. The FCC had previously established 30 percent of all television households as the benchmark, but the commission revised its definition to include households also served by various satellite carriers. The new ruling thus increased the ownership limit to 38 percent, allowing industry operators to engage in further consolidation.

Industry Organization

The cable operator offers packages of broadcast (i.e., over-the-air) channels and satellite-delivered channels—such as the Cable News Network (CNN), Music Television (MTV), ESPN, and the USA Network—to customers in the franchise area. Services range from basic cable (usually broadcast signals in the market, along with PEG channels) to expanded basic (the basic package plus an offering of satellite-delivered channels). Additionally, operators provide a number of subscription or pay channels, such as Home Box Office, Showtime, Cinemax, and Encore, for an additional monthly fee. Finally, the operator offers unedited movies and special events (e.g., concerts, sporting events, and

A view of the Atlanta, Georgia, newsroom of the Cable News Network (CNN) gives a glimpse inside the workings of what was the first all-news channel to be broadcast on cable television. (Mark Gibson/Corbis)

other types of entertainment) through a number of pay-per-view channels. The customer pays for each of these items on a per-event basis, in addition to the payment for basic and expanded service.

In building different packages of services to attract customers, the cable operator negotiates carriage fees with local broadcast stations and other program suppliers. The FCC's "must carry" provision requires that cable systems carry local, over-the-air television broadcast signals, but operators must still obtain the rights to carry these local signals. Broadcasters usually negotiate for another cable channel on the system as part of granting retransmission consent; in rare cases, the station may ask for cash compensation. Among the broadcast networks, Fox, NBC, and Disney (ABC) have successfully launched several cable channels (FX, MSNBC, ESPN2) through retransmission consent negotiations using their owned and operated broadcast stations.

National program suppliers such as CNN, ESPN, MTV, and Nickelodeon charge local cable operators fees based on the number of subscribers to the system. The operator pays these fees to the program supplier in exchange for permission to carry their programming. Consolidation helps negotiations with program suppliers, as it limits the number of potential agreements in which an MSO must be involved. By owning large numbers of cable systems, an MSO can realize greater efficiency in program negotiations and, ultimately, economies of scale. Programming is the greatest expense of any cable system operator. According to the National Cable Television Association (NCTA), program expenses in 1998 totaled $7.46 billion.

Cable systems also draw revenues from the sale of national and local advertising, and Internet and telephone services. Local advertising varies from market to market, but overall local advertising accounts for about 24 percent of cable television advertising revenues, according to data compiled by the Cable Advertising Bureau. Internet connection services, available through the rental of high-speed cable modems, is a growing revenue stream for cable operators. Many systems are planning to offer local telephone service in hopes of bundling voice, video, and data services in a single package to consumers.

Ultimately, all of the expenses charged for programming are eventually passed on to consumers in the way of monthly subscriber fees. Subscriber fees represent the primary source of revenue for cable operators. The cable industry is unique in that it derives revenues from a number of sources, whereas broadcast stations depend primarily on advertising revenues.

Industry Evolution

The cable television industry has experienced considerable change over the years. Originally, cable television service was initiated as a retransmission service for broadcast television signals in the 1940s and 1950s in areas where television signals were difficult to receive due to complications related to surrounding terrain. In fact, in its infancy, cable was known as CATV (community antenna television), reflecting the fact that it brought television signals to households in a specific geographical area.

Broadcasters, fearing the loss of audience, fought the introduction of cable television in urban markets. The broadcast industry was able to delay the diffusion of cable for several years, arguing that the presence of cable would cause economic harm to over-the-air broadcasting. The industry was most concerned with the possible importation of signals from outside the local market, which would provide competing programming that might siphon off some of the television audience available for local stations.

Following a series of court decisions, the industry was finally able to offer cable service in urban areas. In the 1970s, a number of different program services began to emerge. Home Box Office (HBO), originally conceived as a regional pay service in 1973, went national in 1975, becoming the first channel to offer unedited movies to television audiences. The introduction of HBO became a bellwether of change for the industry, providing qualitatively different content from regular television channels.

Other channels that debuted during the late 1970s and early 1980s further promoted interest in cable television among consumers. The USA Network became the first national advertising-supported cable channel in 1977. A year later, ESPN began operation. In 1980, CNN was launched by Turner Broadcasting to become the first all-news channel on cable. On August 1, 1981, MTV appeared.

In 1984, Congress passed the Cable Television Act, which deregulated many industry policies, especially in regard to rate regulation. Rates for services mushroomed between 1986 and 1990, prompting outrage from consumer groups and policymakers. The 1984 act also prohibited cable ownership by the broadcast networks and limited telephone companies to ownership of cable services that were outside of their regions of telephone service.

Despite the controversy over rate deregulation, cable systems and subscribers grew at an unprecedented rate. Not only did the audience enjoy a growing number of programming services, cable service also provided a higher quality picture than most television antennas. The evolution of cable television had drastic effects on broadcast television audiences, especially during the lucrative evening or prime-time hours when audience levels are the highest. Network television programming prior to the advent of cable would routinely draw 80 percent to 90 percent of the available television audience. As cable matured, audience shares for the networks would fall into the 45 percent to 50 percent range by the 1990s.

Rate regulation has not been the only subject of customer complaints. Customer service has been an ongoing complaint, especially with regard to service technicians missing or being late for appointments. Customers have also had concerns over the quality of service and unannounced "switchouts" of one channel for another. In a switchout, one channel is replaced by another at the discretion of the operator. During the 1990s, the industry worked hard to improve customer service and become more responsive to complaints.

In 1992, Congress reestablished rate regulation in the cable industry with the passage of the Cable Television Consumer Protection and Competition Act. The legislation required a rollback of rates for basic service in an effort to limit the monopoly power of cable operators. The results were short-lived; the Telecommunications Act of 1996 wiped out rate regulation at the federal level and opened the industry to competition from other industries.

The cable industry began to experience competition from the emerging DBS (direct broadcast satellite) industry during the 1980s. Satellite services primarily attracted rural customers who could not receive cable television. The early home satellites required large dish-type receiving antennas, which were bulky and considered by many to be eyesores. By the 1990s, technology enabled the diffusion of smaller home dishes, which could receive digital transmissions. Companies such as DSS, EchoStar, and the Dish Network were able to lure away cable customers, and together they accounted for approximately fifteen million subscribers by the end of the 1990s.

The 1996 act stimulated interest in cable system ownership among the various telephone companies ("telcos"). Freed from restrictions barring ownership of cable services within regions of telephone service, the telcos were interested in acquiring cable systems as a way to expand their base of telephone customers and to achieve the goal of providing multiple services (e.g., voice, data, video, broadband) to businesses and consumers. Several acquisitions happened within a few months. Southwestern Bell (now SBC) became one of the first telcos to acquire cable systems. Bell Atlantic and Tele-Communications Inc. (at the time the largest cable operator in the country) announced plans to merge, but the deal never happened. U.S. West acquired all the holdings of Continental Cablevision and renamed its cable unit Media One.

Following the 1996 act, the cable industry began a heavy period of consolidation. AT&T shocked the cable industry with its acquisition of TCI in 1998, followed just a few months later by another key acquisition, Media One. In less than a year, AT&T had moved from its position as the number one long-distance telephone company in the United States to also being the leading cable operator. Other competitors to cable include wireless telephone services, "wireless cable" services such as multichannel multipoint distribution services (MMDS) and satellite master antenna television (SMATV), and utility companies (power companies).

Issues Facing the Cable Industry

The cable industry faces a number of challenges. One key issue of concern among operators is the continual upgrading of the system's physical plant. With the conversion to digital transmission, many systems are investing millions of dollars in converting their analog transmission systems to a hybrid coaxial-fiber optic system. Fiber optic cable provides a much larger carrying capacity than coaxial cable, enabling the bundling of different types of services (e.g., voice, data, broadband). Furthermore, fiber is easier to maintain and provides greater reliability of service.

Upgrading of systems will result in faster deployment of cable modems that can provide high-speed Internet access to homes. However, competition for Internet service is extremely intense, with America Online, Earthlink, and Microsoft's MSN service already holding dominant shares of the ISP (Internet service provider) market. The cable industry will have to market cable modems aggressively as an alternative to traditional types of Internet service.

Controlling costs is another key issue for the cable industry. The costs to maintain and upgrade the physical plant pale in comparison to the rising cost of program services. Every year, new programming services continue to be introduced in the marketplace. As consumers learn of new services, they expect their cable operator to carry those services they deem most important. Every new program service added results in increasing program costs. In time, the industry may be forced to move to providing services on an *a la carte* basis, allowing subscribers to choose the specific services that they want and pay only for those services.

Competition will continue to be a concern in the cable industry. DBS services have already shown they are capable of luring existing cable subscribers. DBS services can now offer local broadcast signals as part of their program packages, placing further competitive pressure on the cable industry. No one is certain how the Internet will affect competition for multichannel services. Clearly, the Internet is capable of delivering video, but watching streaming video on a computer display is not the same experience as watching television programming on a large screen.

In addition to competition for services, competition for advertising remains intense. As an industry, cable television has done very well at attracting national advertising on the most popular cable channels (e.g., CNN, MTV, ESPN). Locally, competition for advertising is typically very strong, in that cable competes with newspapers, local radio and television, outdoor (e.g., billboards and transit media), and other advertising vehicles for revenues. Local revenues are important, and the industry recognizes more growth is needed at the local level.

Ancillary revenue streams in the form of Internet services (cable modems) and telephone service are also needed for the industry to maintain a strong competitive position. The latter will be much more difficult to obtain, especially with regard to local exchange or local telephone service. Most customers are not used to competition for local phone service, and they may be apprehensive about switching service to a provider that has a limited history. There are also questions concerning how responsive customers will be in accepting the bundling of voice, data, and broadband services from a single operator.

See also: BROADCASTING, GOVERNMENT REGULATION OF; CABLE TELEVISION, HISTORY OF; CABLE TELEVISION, PROGRAMMING OF; CABLE TELEVISION, REGULATION OF; CABLE TELEVISION, SYSTEM TECHNOLOGY OF; FEDERAL COMMUNICATIONS COMMISSION; SATELLITES, HISTORY OF; SATELLITES, TECHNOLOGY OF; TELECOMMUNICATIONS, WIRELESS; TELECOMMUNICATIONS ACT OF 1996; TELEVISION BROADCASTING; TELEVISION BROADCASTING, HISTORY OF.

Bibliography

Albarran, Alan B. (1996). *Media Economics: Understanding Markets, Industries and Concepts.* Ames: Iowa State University Press.

Albarran, Alan B. (1997). *Management of Electronic Media.* Belmont, CA: Wadsworth Publishing Company.

Baldwin, Thomas F., and McVoy, D. Stevens. (1991). *Cable Communications,* 2nd edition. Englewood Cliffs, NJ: Prentice-Hall.

Cable Advertising Bureau. (1999). *Cable TV Facts.* New York: Cable Advertising Bureau.

Carroll, Sidney L., and Howard, Herbert H. (1998). "The Economics of the Cable Industry." In *Media Economics: Theory and Practice,* 2nd edition, eds. Alison Alexander, James Owers, and Rod Carveth. Mahwah, NJ: Lawrence Erlbaum.

Chan-Olmsted, Sylvia, and Litman, Barry. (1988). "Antitrust and Horizontal Mergers in the Cable Industry." *Journal of Media Economics* 1:63–74.

National Cable Television Association. (1999). *Cable Television Developments.* Washington, DC: National Cable Television Association.

Owen, Bruce M., and Wildman, Steven. (1992). *Video Economics.* Boston: Harvard University Press.

Veronis Suhler & Associates. (1999). *Communications Industry Forecast.* New York: Veronis Suhler & Associates.

ALAN B. ALBARRAN

CABLE TELEVISION, CAREERS IN

The National Cable Television Association reported in 1999 that there was a 500 percent increase in the cable industry workforce between 1975 and 1998—from 25,000 full-time employees to more than 125,000 (Lacey et al., 1999). This major trade organization predicts further expansion of employment opportunities as a result of the need to rebuild and upgrade systems and as new service offerings such as digital video, data delivery, and high-speed cable Internet access are made available across the country.

Most of these jobs will be within one of the three segments that serve as the primary employers of the cable industry. The local cable system directly provides cable service to homes and communities. Multiple-system operators (MSOs) own and operate more than one cable television system. Cable networks provide some of the programming offered by the cable system. Joseph Dominick, Barry Sherman, and Gary Copeland (1996) report that cable is a decidedly blue-collar industry with most jobs falling into the technical or office/clerical category. The number of subscriber households basically determines the size of the staff needed. The vast majority of workers are employed by the thousands of operating systems around the nation.

Local cable systems require the combined efforts of a variety of skilled persons in providing subscribing customers with a clear television signal delivered directly to the home via cable. In smaller systems, one person may perform more than one function. These functions fall primarily into five areas: management, technical staff, administrative staff, marketing/public relations and advertising staff, and programming and production staff.

Management oversees all aspects of the operation. The general manager, as head of the cable system office, is responsible for conducting the operational affairs, interpreting and applying the policies of corporate management, and coordinating all functions of the system. The general manager's duties include recommending policies for system growth, overseeing budget and fiscal procedures, and developing employment and personnel policies. Department heads from the other four divisions report directly to the general manager and comprise the upper-level management of the local cable system. Qualifications for the position of general manager include a college degree in business administration and industry management experience.

The chief engineer is the head of the technical department, a position that requires superior management skills as well as first-rate technical knowledge. The chief engineer oversees all technical aspects of the cable system and supervises all the activities of the engineering staff. These responsibilities include equipment planning and installation, construction of facilities, specification of standards for equipment and material, proposing new technical services and developing new products for use by the system, directing construction activity, and giving technical advice to the various staff system-operating managers. Because the majority of the capital outlay and operating expense of a cable system involves the purchase and installation of costly equipment, the chief engineer also assists in preparing the capital budget and general development plans of the system. Qualifications for the position of chief engineer include a degree in electrical engineering and/or equivalent experience.

A number of technicians serve in the technical department under the direction of the chief engineer. Among these are the chief technician, trunk technician, service technician, and bench technician. The chief technician is the most highly skilled member of the technical staff and supervises all of the other technicians. This person is primarily responsible for maintaining equipment at the headend, that point at which all program sources are received, assembled, and processed for transmission. In addition to technical duties, some administrative chores such as setting performance standards, conducting salary reviews, and handling personnel matters are required. The trunk technician is responsible for the trunk line or main artery of the cable system. The service technician works more directly with the customer, either in the home or on the poles, lines, and amplifiers. The bench technician operates the repair facility of the cable system. Qualifications

for the position of chief technician include an industrial background and electronic training plus extensive hands-on experience. All of the other positions require some electronic training, and a strong electronics background is certainly helpful.

Generally, the position of installer is considered the entry-level step for a cable technician's career. This person prepares a customer's home for cable reception. At least some trade school background with demonstrated mechanical aptitude is desirable.

The office manager heads the administrative staff and is responsible for the smooth operation of daily business activities. This person monitors the customer service department and supervises office staff training, hiring, and work assignments. Experience in office administration and personnel management is a plus for this position.

The customer service representative and the service dispatcher provide a direct link between the technical staff and the customer by monitoring and coordinating communication between the two. These positions may require no more than a high school diploma and good communication skills.

The same person may fill the accounts payable, accounts receivable, and billing clerk positions in a smaller cable system. Regardless, these positions are fundamental to the successful financial operation of a system. Qualifications include two years of college with a strong bookkeeping and business background. Some larger systems hire a full-time accountant/bookkeeper, while smaller systems often use an outside accounting firm.

Cable systems often have a public-affairs director and a marketing director as part of the upper-level management. The public-affairs director represents the cable system within the community, working with local government officials and civic groups. The marketing director is responsible for increasing the number of subscribers to the system. Qualifications for these positions include a degree in public relations or marketing and related experience. Research is a valuable component of many marketing departments. The person holding the position of researcher should also have a degree in marketing.

Sales representatives work on two levels within a cable system. The first is to sell the services of the cable system to homes, apartment complexes, and hotels and motels. The advertising sales representatives market the cable system as an effective medium for advertising the products and services of other businesses. Qualifications for these positions include at least a high school diploma and a public relations, advertising, or sales background.

The fields of programming and production have shown substantial growth within many cable systems. The areas of local origination, public access, and governmental or educational access provide career opportunities for persons with a degree in communications and hands-on experience in production. In those systems that produce their own programming, a staff is usually necessary to handle the production. This staff would likely include a producer, assistant director, and various studio technicians to handle audio, lighting, and editing. Qualifications would include a degree in communications and/or an electronics background and hands-on experience in the respective fields. Some large cable systems maintain their own construction crew for ongoing work on new systems or expanding and upgrading existing systems.

Multiple system operators (MSOs) own and operate more than one cable system, sometimes as many as several hundred. For the most part, but on a much bigger scale, their personnel structure is quite similar to that of the individual cable system. On a corporate level, these larger systems consist of various department heads and staffs in administration and management, engineering, sales and marketing, public affairs, human resources, finance, and legal affairs. The qualifications for these positions, while similar to those in the individual cable system, do tend to have higher requirements in terms of educational background (in some cases an advanced degree) and in terms of more related experience in the respective field of employment.

One of the fastest growing segments of cable television is production and programming. Career opportunities with cable programming networks (such as basic cable, pay-TV, and pay-per-view) include many technical positions, as well as positions in the sales, legal, communications, and administration divisions. There are two types of programming: original and purchased. Original programs are those that are produced either in-house or contracted to an independent production company. The purchased programs include feature films that have already had a theatrical release and television series that have previously been aired

on broadcast television. Again, personnel requirements are very similar to those in local cable systems and in MSOs. Qualifications tend to include college degrees and job-related experience, often garnered in an individual cable system.

The number of American households being served by cable television is more than 70 percent and growing daily. It is, therefore, no surprise that career opportunities in this exciting industry continue to expand at an equal pace.

See also: CABLE TELEVISION; CABLE TELEVISION, HISTORY OF; CABLE TELEVISION, PROGRAMMING OF; CABLE TELEVISION, SYSTEM TECHNOLOGY OF; EDUCATIONAL MEDIA PRODUCERS; PUBLIC BROADCASTING; PUBLIC RELATIONS, CAREERS IN; TELEVISION BROADCASTING, CAREERS IN.

Bibliography

Dominick, Joseph R.; Sherman, Barry L.; and Copeland, Gary A. (1996). *Broadcasting/Cable and Beyond: An Introduction to Modern Electronic Media,* 3rd edition. New York: McGraw-Hill.

Lacey, Amy; Hopkins, Ryan; Barrows, Allison; Green, Richard; and Kirchenbaum, Adam, eds. (1999). *Careers in Cable.* Washington, DC: National Cable Television Association.

HAL HUGHES

CABLE TELEVISION, HISTORY OF

Cable television has its roots in community antenna television (CATV), which was developed to bring television to communities that did not have their own channels in the early days of television broadcasting. Just as television was starting to grow in popularity, the Federal Communications Commission (FCC) pulled the plug. In 1948, the FCC initiated a television broadcast license freeze in an effort to cope with the demand for frequencies. For four years, no new television stations were authorized to begin operation, and with only 108 stations already established, many communities were left without stations. The solution was CATV.

Early Development of Cable Television

One of the first CATV systems was established in 1950 by Robert J. Tarlton in Lansford, Pennsylvania. Because they were cut off by the

Allegheny Mountains, the community had extremely weak signals from Philadelphia-based stations. Tarlton, an appliance salesman who was looking for a way to cash in on the television business, convinced some friends to invest in his company, Panther Valley Television. At the top of a mountain, he erected a master antenna that was able to receive the television signals from Philadelphia and amplify them. Signals were distributed to subscribing households via coaxial cable. Subscribers paid an initial $125 hook-up fee and a $3 monthly charge.

Industry experts did not expect CATV to survive long after the FCC licensing freeze was lifted in 1952. Interference remained problematic, however, so the FCC limited the number of stations that could operate in a community. As a result, cable suddenly served a dual purpose; it became a service that would both provide clear reception of stations for communities that did not have stations, and it increased the number of stations that could be received in a community that already had stations.

In 1952, when the FCC lifted the license freeze, seventy CATV systems were serving close to fourteen thousand subscribers across the country. Cable had been the answer for many appliance dealers who were missing out on the booming television business because their communities were not serviced by local channels. By 1961, there were approximately seven hundred cable television systems across the United States.

At first, broadcasters welcomed the CATV systems; after all, cable extended their service area, and a larger audience could justify increased advertising rates. The FCC was also pleased since cable helped expand the audience of the fledgling television industry. In fact, the FCC declared in its decision in *Frontier Broadcasting Company v. Collier* in 1956 that the commission had no jurisdiction over CATV systems (because they were not broadcasters or common carriers).

By the 1960s, however, opinions began to change. Cable television services began to enter larger markets, providing channels from other markets to subscribers using microwave transmission. These imported channels sometimes duplicated the programming of local network affiliates, and neither affiliates nor independent stations wanted the additional competition. In 1962, the FCC stepped in with regulations for cable systems that brought in distant signals. By 1966, the FCC declared regulatory control over all cable systems. In 1972, the commission enacted its first comprehensive regulations of the cable industry, which were designed to protect broadcasters from competition from cable.

The Growth of Cable Television

Despite legal complications, cable continued its slow growth. Cable had about 2 percent of U.S. household penetration in the early 1960s and had grown to about 8 percent in 1970. Most early cable systems had a limit of twelve channels, but Ronald Mandell patented a converter in 1967 that was placed on the subscriber's television set and broke the twelve-channel barrier. This set-top converter also solved the interference problems that plagued many of the systems.

Still, industry experts began to question the further growth of cable, especially when they considered the potential infrastructure costs in urban areas. How could cable companies hope to attract the necessary subscribers to justify financially the massive start-up costs in an area that received clear local signals?

The answer was a rented transponder on a geostationary satellite named *Satcom I* that was launched in 1975 and was used to transmit a new television service to cable systems across the country. This service, Home Box Office (HBO), did nothing less than change the face of cable and spark unprecedented growth in the industry. (Time, Inc. had introduced HBO as a pay service on the cable system in Wilkes-Barre, Pennsylvania, in 1972, but its satellite delivery and potential national distribution were new developments.)

On September 30, 1975, HBO launched its service (on only a handful of cable systems) with coverage of a boxing match between Muhammad Ali and Joe Frazier. The new program service also offered commercial-free motion pictures that were not edited for television. HBO started slowly because cable systems had to buy an expensive satellite receiving dish to pull down signals that were transmitted by satellite, but HBO soon revolutionized the industry. Finally, cable television could provide something other than retransmitted broadcast signals. In addition, HBO was a pay-TV service (i.e., a premium service), which meant a new source of revenue for cable companies.

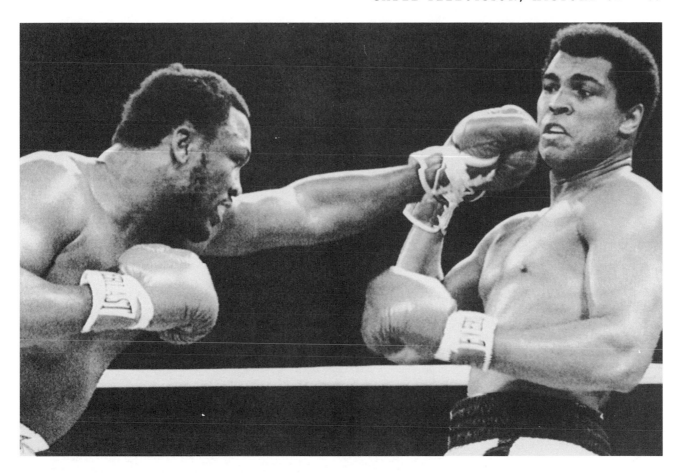

This 1975 fight between Joe Frazier and Muhammad Ali for the middleweight championship served as the launching point for Home Box Office (HBO). (Bettmann/Corbis)

To further improve matters, the FCC had also realized that its 1972 regulations were severely limiting the growth of the cable industry. As a result, the FCC essentially reversed its earlier thinking and decided to encourage competition between cable and broadcast stations. In 1984, the U.S. Congress passed the Cable Communications Policy Act, which gave cable system operators fewer regulations regarding rates and programming. Local communities were given clearer control over cable through the franchise process.

Cable companies cannot simply decide to build a system in a particular city; the company must be awarded a cable franchise by city officials. Usually, systems must pay a monthly franchise fee to the municipality and often negotiate other concessions, such as community studio facilities, free cable for local schools and government agencies, and a government information channel.

The combination of satellite program distribution and less regulation led to a period of explosive growth in cable. Within twelve years, from 1975 to 1987, the number of cable systems tripled and the percentage of U.S. homes with cable jumped from 14 percent to 50 percent. The booming industry attracted big-business investors, and the cable television landscape became dominated by multiple system operators (MSOs). By 1988, the five largest MSOs serviced more than 40 percent of cable subscribers in the nation. In the wake of the success of cable, as well as the increased popularity of videocassette recorders (VCRs) and independent stations, broadcast networks watched their audiences erode.

Expanding Cable Channels and Programming

In 1983, HBO's *The Terry Fox Story* was the first made-for-cable film, while Showtime ran original episodes of *The Paper Chase,* a critically acclaimed drama that had been dropped by the broadcast networks. Cable-originated programming became eligible for Emmy Award consideration in 1988 and has since become a regular contender. Original series and films, though not always of award-winning caliber, are common on both cable networks and premium services.

HBO's successful use of satellite delivery opened the floodgates for premium services and cable networks, many of which continue to remain popular. Of course, not every new cable service was a national network. In 1976, Cablevision Systems Corporation founder Charles Dolan created the first regional cable sports service, SportsChannel New York (now FOX Sports Net New York). Several regional sports channels still service selected markets across the country.

Ted Turner launched his Atlanta-based independent station (WTCG, later WTBS) as a "superstation" in 1976, using satellite distribution to reach a national audience. As president of Turner Broadcasting Systems, Turner continued to paint the cable network landscape with a number of national networks. For example, his Cable News Network (CNN), the first live, all-news channel, was launched in 1980. Less than two years later, CNN was followed by CNN Headline News, which provided highly structured thirty-minute newscasts around-the-clock.

Many industry executives predicted a quick death for CNN, which was referred to as "Chicken Noodle News" in its early days. The network, however, proved early critics wrong. Its twenty-four-hour schedule and continuous coverage of breaking news provided unparalleled coverage of several events, including the assassination attempt on President Ronald Reagan in 1981, the *Challenger* space shuttle disaster in 1986, and the Gulf War in 1991. Its extensive coverage of these and other "big" stories has helped make CNN a popular and respected source for news.

CNN also gained the respect of broadcast and cable networks through its budgetary efficiency. After almost ten years on the air, CNN and CNN Headline News shared an annual budget of approximately $100 million for around-the-clock coverage, while ABC, CBS, and NBC were each spending two or three times as much for only thirty minutes of news per day. The discrepancy resulted in layoffs and reorganization at the broadcast networks in the late 1980s.

While CNN was redefining television news, Music Television (MTV) was redefining television itself. The music video cable network debuted in 1981, essentially re-creating the album-oriented rock (AOR) radio format for television. It was a radical concept; MTV was programmed more like a radio station than a television network, and it had few regularly scheduled shows.

Filled with rock music videos, unique contests, and a generous helping of rebellious attitude, the channel was designed to appeal to males who were between eighteen and thirty-four years of age. MTV not only made music videos popular (and some say legitimized music video as an art form), it quickly spawned imitators, with more than three hundred music video programs on broadcast and cable networks competing for its audience in 1983.

Rock performers such as Rod Stewart and Journey were typical early MTV stars. Artists such as Michael Jackson, who would become a huge influence in music video, were not part of MTV's original play list. Jackson's videos, in fact, did not debut on MTV until 1983. Later, MTV's play list would become more diversified, welcoming rap, hip-hop, and alternative music. In the 1990s, the network became more structured, with "reality-based" original series and other regularly scheduled programs. MTV reaches more than 200 million households worldwide and is available in dozens of countries on every continent but Antarctica.

Most early cable networks employed a programming concept called narrowcasting, targeting their content to specific niche audiences. The Christian Broadcasting Network (CBN) began its national cable network in 1977. Viacom followed the movie formula in 1978 when it created Showtime, another premium service. A year later, the first network targeting children, Nickelodeon, debuted. Chicago's WGN and New York's WOR became superstations, and sports took center stage on the Entertainment and Sports Programming Network (ESPN).

From 1979 to 1985, more new networks established additional choices for viewers. In 1980, Bravo gave voice to high culture, while the Home Shopping Network (HSN) provided viewers with an alternative to the mall in 1985. Other additions to the cable network ranks included American Movie Classics (AMC), Arts & Entertainment (A&E), Black Entertainment Television (BET), The Discovery Channel, The Disney Channel, Eternal Word Television Network (EWTN), Lifetime, The Nashville Network (TNN), the Playboy

Channel, USA Network, and The Weather Channel. The 1990s saw the launch of several more successful cable networks, including the Sci-Fi Channel and Cartoon Network in 1992. Many of these channels have expanded their programming for international audiences.

As new cable networks were being developed in the early 1980s, smart executives learned to follow the "rule of one." Due to limited channels and advertising dollars, if two cable networks tried to narrowcast to the same target audience, one was doomed to fail. Turner's Cable Music Channel (CMC), for example, tried to duplicate the success of MTV with adult contemporary music, but it was shut down after only thirty-four days of programming in 1984. Even MTV's sister station, Video Hits One (VH1), took years to build a respectable audience after its 1985 debut. Increased channel capacities and viewership have made the rule of one obsolete and allowed cable networks to include multiple choices for music, sports, and news.

Cable also expanded its services to include event programming, also known as pay-per-view (PPV). Addressable converters allow subscribers to order specific, one-time programming without a technician visiting the premises. Warner Amex's Qube system in Columbus, Ohio, was the first to offer PPV to its subscribers. The system featured five interactive channels but failed to generate a profit from 1977 to 1984. Still, national PPV services began to appear by 1985, and more than seventeen million homes were equipped with addressable converters by 1991.

The Cable Television Consumer Protection and Competition Act of 1992

After years without government regulation, cable rates had increased swiftly in some areas, prompting Congress to approve the Cable Television Consumer Protection and Competition Act of 1992. The law reintroduced rate regulation for the industry and provided a new wrinkle with local broadcasters.

While the FCC's 1972 rules required cable systems to carry local channels, the U.S. Court of Appeals for the District of Columbia threw out the rule in 1985. Most cable systems, however, kept local channels in their lineup, since clear reception of local channels was (and remains) a major draw for many subscribers. The Cable Act of 1992, however, provided the option of "must-carry" or

"retransmission consent" to local broadcasters. As a result, broadcasters could either choose guaranteed carriage on a cable system or demand compensation from the cable system to carry their signal. Some local channels had to be dropped from cable lineups because agreements could not be reached.

Conclusion

The new cable systems of the 1980s had offered thirty-five or more channels, and operators were experimenting with fiber-optic technology. By 1995, the cable industry was looking to integrate high-speed Internet access into their services, as cable modems can provide data transfer rates thousands of times faster than conventional phone lines. Six of the ten largest MSOs launched cable modem services in limited areas in 1996. Within a year, nearly 100,000 customers across the country subscribed to the service. Cable telephony service was also launched in limited communities in 1997.

Despite increased competition from direct broadcast satellite (DBS), the cable industry remains prosperous and ratings continue to rise. In 2000, the cable landscape featured more than eleven thousand cable systems across the country serving more than seventy-three million homes. The industry has also begun preparations for digital television (DTV).

See also: BROADCASTING, GOVERNMENT REGULATION OF; CABLE TELEVISION; CABLE TELEVISION, CAREERS IN; CABLE TELEVISION, PROGRAMMING OF; CABLE TELEVISION, REGULATION OF; CABLE TELEVISION, SYSTEM TECHNOLOGY OF; FEDERAL COMMUNICATIONS COMMISSION; TELEVISION BROADCASTING; TELEVISION BROADCASTING, HISTORY OF.

Bibliography

Baldwin, Thomas F., and McVoy, D. Stevens. (1988). *Cable Communication,* 2nd edition. Englewood Cliffs, NJ: Prentice-Hall.

Denisoff, R. Serge. (1988). *Inside MTV.* New Brunswick, NJ: Transaction Publishers.

Dominick, Joseph R.; Sherman, Barry L.; and Copeland, Gary A. (1996). *Broadcasting/Cable and Beyond: An Introduction to Modern Electronic Media.* New York: McGraw-Hill.

Folkerts, Jean; Lacy, Stephen; and Davenport, Lucinda. (1998). *The Media in Your Life: An Introduction to Mass Communication.* Boston: Allyn & Bacon.

Negrine, Ralph M., ed. (1985). *Cable Television and the Future of Broadcasting*. London: Croom Helm.

Roman, James. (1996). *Love, Light, and a Dream: Television's Past, Present, and Future*. Westport, CT: Praeger.

Singleton, Loy. (1989). *Global Impact: The New Telecommunication Technologies*. New York: Harper & Row.

Sloan, Wm. David, and Startt, James D. (1996). *The Media in America: A History*, 3rd edition. Northport, AL: Vision Press.

MARK J. PESCATORE

CABLE TELEVISION, PROGRAMMING OF

One of the more challenging tasks faced by cable operators is selecting programming services that meet the particular needs of their cable systems. It is an ongoing concern, one that affects nearly every aspect of a cable system's business operations. The majority of cable subscribers in the United States have fifty-four or more channels from which to choose (NCTA, 2000). This means the cable operator must make fifty-four or more well-reasoned business decisions concerning how best to use a cable system's channel capacity. Channel capacity for the operator is very much like shelf space in the supermarket. It is a finite, limited "good"; once it is dedicated to a product, all other possibilities for uses of that space are eliminated. The cable operators generally seek to use that channel capacity in a way that helps to maximize company profits, adds quality to the overall programming mix, and delivers programming services that are at once desired and enjoyed by cable subscribers.

For the most part, when subscribers buy a multichannel television service, they are primarily concerned with the content or programming that it brings; they are largely indifferent to the technology that is used to deliver it. Cable television has introduced a strong measure of consumer sovereignty into the television programming equation, which means that the consumer has a greater range of choice and influence and that cable companies must respond to this. Unlike "free" local over-the-air broadcast television, cable subscription requires a conscious decision by the consumer to "renew" the cable service each month through a direct payment. When television programming falls short of consumer expectations, this invites the subscriber to begin questioning the wisdom of keeping the cable service. Disconnection then becomes a more attractive option. In cable industry terms, the problem of cable disconnects is referred to as "churn." Developing a quality programming mix is essential for keeping the cable subscriber from churning away from cable.

From the cable operator's perspective, the most important concerns surrounding information and entertainment program selection include: (1) using cable system channel capacity to help maximize returns, (2) creating a proper programming mix for service in their franchise area, (3) obtaining a fair price from programmers for their cable programming networks, (4) promoting a local identity and meeting requirements of the franchise agreement, (5) maximizing company profits on a per channel basis, and (6) maximizing company profits on an overall channel lineup basis.

Programming Tiers

The world of cable programming is divided into separate tiers of service on the local cable system. The basic cable tier generally consists of retransmissions of local over-the-air (broadcast) channels and Public Education Government (PEG) Access channels, along with whatever other channels the operator may wish to include. The extended or enhanced basic tier generally consists of a mix of advertiser-supported, cable-delivered network services (e.g., Lifetime, ESPN, MTV) and other services that may not rely on advertiser support (e.g., American Movie Classics, C-SPAN, Disney). By the end of the 1990s, there were around 150 basic cable channels for operators to choose from; this number continues to change periodically as new networks both appear (e.g. Oxygen) and disappear (e.g., The Military Channel).

In addition to the basic and extended services, there are premium or pay services that require an additional monthly subscription fee. There are more than forty-three premium or pay services, including Home Box Office (HBO), Showtime, and Encore, from which a cable operator may choose. Another type of service is pay-per-view (P-P-V), where viewers pay a separate fee for the one-time viewing of a program. This may involve a motion picture, a concert by a featured performer, or a sporting event, such as a championship-boxing match.

The Economics of Cable Programming

All cable networks have affiliation agreements with cable operators. Cable operators generally compensate the programmer from subscription revenues that come from their customers. In 1999, the average monthly rate for basic cable was $28.92 per month (NCTA, 2000). Income from basic and expanded basic cable accounts for nearly 63 percent of cable's revenue. It is important to remember that cable operators have two separate revenue streams: subscription fees from subscribers and revenue that comes from the sale of advertising.

Until the early 1980s, programmers actually paid cable operators to carry their networks. This circumstance changed as popular, branded networks became key features of cable services in a maturing industry. In addition, as the costs of obtaining and producing more desirable, higher quality programs rose, programmers needed a reliable revenue stream to offset the higher production costs. Some new cable channels still offer cable operators a fee to obtain a channel position on the cable system; a portion of these channels also continue to pay reduced fees for a prescribed time period. This is all done as an incentive to get operators to commit to new, untested program networks in hopes of the programmer acquiring enough cable affiliates to make the new network viable.

A cable operator pays the programmer on a cost-per-subscriber basis for each cable network that is received. These fees can range from a few cents a month for some channels to more than $1 for other channels. Cable systems' programming expenditures in 1999 topped the $8 billion mark (NCTA, 2000). The sports channels (e.g. ESPN, Fox Regional Sports) typically tend to be the most costly because of the high rights fees that must be paid to sports leagues (e.g., Major League Baseball, National Football League).

Deals struck between cable operators and premium service networks usually involve a negotiated split of revenues between the programmer and the operator. For example, if the subscriber cost for a premium service is $12 per month and the negotiated split is 50/50, the operator gets $6 and the programmer gets $6. Certain incentives aimed at increasing the marketing efforts of the operator and increasing the number of subscriptions may also be negotiated between the parties and result in an increased percentage of the "take" for the operator. Around 13 percent of cable's revenues come from pay cable or premium cable (NCTA, 2000).

The larger multiple system operators (MSOs), such as AT&T, Time Warner, and Comcast, can get more favorable terms from programmers in relation to the fees that are paid for affiliation. Large MSOs' program costs tend to be around 10 percent to 20 percent lower than those of smaller operators. MSOs carry clout because in some cases they may deliver ten million or more subscribers/potential viewers for the programmer's network in one fell swoop. This can substantially reduce the transaction costs of the programmer in selling a network service, while it adds to the potential viewer base that the network advertising will reach.

Discounts in affiliation fees are usually granted if the cable operator agrees to carry multiple programming services from the same programmer. For example, an operator that signs on for CNN, CNN Headline News, and Turner Network Television (TNT) from Time Warner Entertainment is likely to receive a "volume discount" that reduces the cost-per-channel amount that is paid. This then becomes part of the programming equation for the cable operator.

In addition, some large media/communications companies are vertically integrated, which means that they are involved in two or more stages of the cable industry. These stages include production, distribution, and exhibition. Production includes those entities that are responsible for producing the television programs (e.g. Paramount Pictures). Distribution includes the programmers, those networks that are responsible for distributing the programs (e.g. Nickelodeon, Lifetime, HBO). Exhibition includes the local cable operation (e.g. Time Warner Cable, AT&T, Cox Communications).

If the company owns cable systems (the exhibition stage) and programming networks (distribution), it is vertically integrated. Vertically integrated companies have obvious incentives for carrying their own programming networks on their own cable systems. These program selections are sometimes referred to as "corporate must carry" channels.

The Windowing Concept

Cable programming categories, especially for pay services, are very often related to the "currency" of the programming (Baldwin, McVoy, and Steinfield, 1996). The windowing process in the case of motion picture products provides a good illustration. Motion pictures are the principal content of premium cable services and P-P-V.

A motion picture is first released to theaters; this is considered to be the initial release window. The home video window, which involves the release of the videocassette and the DVD for the movie, follows the initial release window. Sixty to ninety days after the home video window, the motion picture enters the pay-per-view release window for cable and in-home satellite viewers. The next release window is premium or pay cable services. Later, the same motion picture will move to the broadcast television window and eventually into the syndication market window. As a film moves through each window, time advances and the likelihood of an interested viewer having already seen the motion picture increases.

Premium or pay services are increasingly producing their own original content for use on their networks. These programs supplement the traditional offering of motion pictures. For example, HBO, the first and largest of the pay cable services, produces not only feature films but also regularly scheduled television series such as *The Sopranos* and *Arliss*.

There are two distinct kinds of basic cable networks. There are general interest cable networks, which tend to appeal to more broad ranging audience tastes, and there are specialty networks. The general interest programming approach includes movies, drama, off-network reruns, and sports. The USA Network and TNT are two examples of general interest programmers. Specialty networks, as the name suggests, deal with more specialized forms of content. For example, Animal Planet programs mostly animal and pet-related content, and ESPN supplies sports and sports-related programming.

Where do the basic cable channels get their programming content? Programmers have two choices when it comes to obtaining programs: acquire material or produce it themselves. In the acquisition marketplace, networks shop around for content ranging from off-network broadcast reruns (e.g., *The Cosby Show*, *E.R.*) to original programs (e.g., *South Park*) or motion pictures (e.g., Lifetime's movies) from outside producers. Self-produced material involves "in-house" production

done by the programmers themselves. For example, MTV uses its production resources to produce such shows as *The Real World* and *Road Rules*. Most basic cable networks use a combination of acquisition and self-production to fill program schedules.

The Major Cable Programmers

According to National Cable Television Association figures, the basic cable channels that reached the greatest number of subscribers in the year 2000 are the following:

1. TBS (78,000,000 subscribers)
2. Discovery Channel (77,400,000 subscribers)
3. USA Network (77,181,000 subscribers)
4. ESPN (77,181,000 subscribers)
5. C-SPAN (77,000,000 subscribers)
6. CNN (77,000,000 subscribers)
7. TNT (76,800,000 subscribers)
8. Nickelodeon/Nick at Night (76,000,000 subscribers)
9. Fox Family Channel (75,700,000 subscribers)
10. TNN (75,000,000 subscribers)

The largest pay service programmers in 1999 (according to *Cablevision Magazine*) were the following:

1. HBO (26,659,000 subscribers)
2. Cinemax (14,820,000 subscribers)
3. Showtime (13,554,000 subscribers)
4. Encore (13,170,000 subscribers)
5. Starz! (9,160,000 subscribers)

In the P-P-V marketplace, In-Demand is the largest programmer and claims more than twenty million subscribers and seventeen hundred affiliated cable systems.

Programming Through the Years

Cable television's earliest programming consisted largely of retransmissions of over-the-air television stations in rural areas that were unable to receive adequate signals. Early on, cable had difficulty making inroads into large, metropolitan areas because of a lack of programming that could substantially differentiate it from already available broadcast television. A series of restrictive regulations from the Federal Communications Commission (FCC) and a number of court rulings that were adverse to the cable industry made it difficult to provide different programming that would attract new subscribers. Eventually, cable was allowed to bring distant independent television stations into certain markets, thereby bringing something "unique" to the market.

The first critical event in creating a unique programming identity that would propel cable to new heights occurred with the creation of HBO in 1972. The service was unique to cable and provided feature films and other programming. The network at first used a series of microwave repeater towers to distribute its signal, but this system was later replaced by satellite distribution via Satcom I in 1975. The use of satellite distribution was a technological breakthrough that pioneered the distribution of cable programming services on a national basis. The costs associated with networking fell precipitously because distance was no longer a major barrier.

Another important milestone occurred when Ted Turner made WTBS in Atlanta a "superstation" in 1975 by putting its signal on the satellite. This made the signal retrievable by cable operators on a national basis. Cable was gaining its own programming identity.

In time, other programming services would be formed. ESPN was launched in 1978, at a time when many people questioned the viability of an entire network dedicated to sports. However, the success of ESPN highlighted the ability of cable to service specialty or niche markets. In 1980, USA Network, a general interest programmer, was created, Black Entertainment Television (BET) was launched, and CNN went on the air as the first twenty-four-hour news channel. CNN had a profound effect on the way in which television news was gathered and presented. It led the way for other news services such as MSNBC (the result of a partnership between NBC and Microsoft) and Fox News (created by the News Corp.). MSNBC and Fox News were both launched in 1996. MTV, aimed at a younger generation, and often cited as the epitome of demographically targeted, specialty cable, began in 1981. It has since evolved from a video music service into a varied programming network that has added youth-oriented original programming. Shopping channels (e.g., QVC, Home Shopping Network) also represent a programming service that grew largely out of cable initiatives.

The range and depth of basic cable programming has grown dramatically since the early 1980s. As channel capacity increases with new digital technologies, the need for even more programming content is likely to create a boom in new networks. Already, familiar brand name networks have cloned new "branded" versions of themselves. For example, the Discovery Channel has created Discovery Kids, Discovery Science, and Discovery Health, further segmenting and targeting its programming strategy to reach new viewers in different ways. The same sort of "multiplexing" has taken place in the pay cable market as well. Each of the major players in that market space has multiplexed their offerings. For example, HBO has HBO Family, HBO Comedy, and others, while the Starz Encore Group offers a Super Pak made of twelve channels.

Cable Programming and the Future

The technology that makes true video-on-demand (VOD) possible exists and will be increasingly deployed as cable systems are upgraded and digital services flourish. This will mean that subscribers will be able to order entertainment or informational programming from vast libraries. Programming will be delivered when and in what manner the customer wants. The viewer at home will have videocassette recorder-like functionality, allowing him or her to edit, store, and retrieve programs at will. The television viewing experience will be changed, but the need for program content will remain.

Cable will be forced to deal with greater competition on all fronts, including direct broadcast satellite. It is likely that the Internet will evolve in some fashion to offer video-streamed content on its own. It could be that the programmer services will evolve into new digital forms across new platforms. The cable industry has created a programming culture of its own, one that will likely serve the varied interests of future information/entertainment seekers quite well.

See also: BROADCASTING, GOVERNMENT REGULATION OF; CABLE TELEVISION; CABLE TELEVISION, CAREERS IN; CABLE TELEVISION, HISTORY OF; CABLE TELEVISION, REGULATION OF; CABLE TELEVISION, SYSTEM TECHNOLOGY OF; DIGITAL

COMMUNICATION; RATINGS FOR TELEVISION PRO-
GRAMS; SATELLITES, COMMUNICATION; SATELLITES,
HISTORY OF; SATELLITES, TECHNOLOGY OF; TELE-
VISION BROADCASTING; TELEVISION BROADCAST-
ING, PROGRAMMING AND; TELEVISION
BROADCASTING, TECHNOLOGY OF.

Bibliography

Baldwin, Thomas F.; McVoy, D. Stevens; and Steinfield, Charles. (1996). *Convergence: Integrating Media, Information & Communication.* Thousand Oaks, CA: Sage Publications.

Cahners Business Information. (2001). "Cablevision Magazine." <http://www.tvinsite.com/cablevision/index.asp?layout=webzine>.

National Cable Television Association. (2000). *Cable Developments.* Washington, DC: NCTA.

Parsons, Patrick R., and Frieden, Robert M. (1998). *The Cable and Satellite Television Industries.* Boston: Allyn & Bacon.

LARRY COLLETTE

◼ CABLE TELEVISION, REGULATION OF

Television has proven to be one of the most powerful media of all time. Newspapers, magazines, radio, and the Internet have made substantial contributions to the sharing of ideas and providing entertainment, but none was so immediately pervasive and hypnotic as "the tube," which is able to deliver breaking news and weather, movies, concerts, and sporting events directly into people's living rooms.

Beginnings of Cable Television

When television began to be widespread in the late 1940s and early 1950s, one only had to put up an antenna (after purchasing a television) to receive the free, over-the-air broadcasts. However, not everyone could receive a clear signal. Living in hilly regions, the mountains, or dense cities could all lead to poor signal reception, as could living too far away from a major city that had a television station. In response, people set up antennas in areas that had good signal reception and then sent that signal over cables into those areas where signal reception was poor. Thus began cable television. Cable has also been called community antenna, or community access, television (CATV).

The history of cable is intertwined with television and broadcasting, which provide the basis for understanding government regulation of the cable industry. By passing the Communications Act of 1934, the U.S. Congress created the Federal Communications Commission (FCC) to regulate the then-expanding world of radio broadcasting. The FCC was mandated to regulate all radio-wave communications "in the public interest, convenience, and necessity." Although no clear definition exists for what is or is not in the "public interest" (the debate has raged since then), the public interest doctrine is a pillar upon which all FCC regulations stand.

As discussed by Daniel J. Smith (1997), two other ideas are fundamental to the regulatory philosophy of the commission: scarcity and localism. Scarcity refers to the portion of the electromagnetic spectrum (the "airwaves") that is used by broadcasters to send signals. The airwaves are considered to be owned by the public, so regulating their use is in the public interest. Because only so many frequencies physically exist for use by radio and television stations, they are said to be scarce. The FCC plays "traffic cop" and chooses who is able to use them and sets technical standards. The second concept, localism, refers to the distribution of broadcast stations around the United States. Unlike most European nations, which chose to have fewer but more powerful (and therefore more far-reaching) regional broadcast stations, the FCC maintains that it is preferable to have more numerous but less powerful local broadcast stations. The commission claims that this will allow a given station to reflect better the flavor and opinions of those in the local community of a broadcaster. Together, the ideas of public interest, scarcity, and localism have guided how and why the commission has made certain regulatory decisions and refused others.

In general, the legal rationale for regulating cable has never been clear, because cable does not neatly fit any of the known regulatory models. Print communication, such as books and newspapers, had existed for centuries; by the time that television was developed, the rights of journalists and authors were fairly well defined, but cable was very different from a newspaper or magazine. Cable could be considered to be closer to a telephone system because both have networks of wires to send their signals. However, telephone systems such as Bell Telephone and AT&T, were "common carriers," which means that they had no control over what was sent out over their systems. Cable operators, on the other hand, chose what went out on their systems, so they were not common carriers. Cable had much in common with broadcasting, but cable did not use over-the-air spectrum space. Therefore, it was not a perfect match because scarcity was not an issue for cable. Since cable did not fit into the existing models, a new regulatory model was needed for cable.

During the last half of the twentieth century, the FCC, Congress, the courts, broadcasters, cable operators, and the public all participated in forging this new path for the popular and promising communication medium. As the following discussion will illustrate, regulation of the cable industry has been dominated by the need to protect traditional over-the-air broadcasters from the growing influence of cable and by the desire for local governments to maintain some control over what was essentially considered a public utility.

The History of Cable Regulation

According to Robert W. Crandall and Harold Furchtgott-Roth (1996, p. 1), the first cable system was "either in Mahoney City, Pennsylvania, in 1948, or Astoria, Oregon, in 1949. The first subscription cable system was established in Lansford, Pennsylvania, in 1950." When the 1948 FCC-imposed freeze on new broadcast television stations ended in 1952, the number of television stations rapidly increased, and cable had been established (see Table 1). At first, broadcasters liked the idea of cable, because it increased the reach of their signals and, most important, the size of their audience, which determined how much they could charge advertisers. By the mid-1950s, cable operators could use a new technology, microwave transmission, to beam signals from distant television stations to their subscribers. Anything that involved communications fell under the jurisdiction of the FCC, and in 1954, the commission authorized cable operators to build such microwave transmission facilities so long as the general public could also use them.

Local broadcasters feared that viewers would prefer these out-of-town stations to their local stations. However, the FCC had not established jurisdiction over cable. In *Frontier Broadcasting Company v. Collier* (1958), the first major FCC rul-

TABLE 1.

Cable Statistics for Selected Years Between 1952 and 2000		
Year	Number of Systems	Total Subscribers
1952	70	14,000
1954	300	30,000
1956	450	300,000
1958	525	450,000
1960	640	650,000
1962	800	850,000
1964	1,200	1,085,000
1966	1,570	1,575,000
1968	2,000	2,800,000
1970	2,490	4,500,000
1972	2,841	6,000,000
1974	3,158	8,700,000
1976	3,681	10,800,000
1978	3,875	13,000,000
1980	4,225	16,000,000
1982	4,825	21,000,000
1984	6,200	29,000,000
1986	7,500	37,500,000
1988	8,500	44,000,000
1990	9,575	50,000,000
1992	11,035	53,000,000
1994	11,214	55,300,000
1996	11,119	60,280,000
1998	10,845	64,170,000
2000	10,400	66,500,000

SOURCE: Warren Communication News (2000, p. I-96)

ing to involve cable, broadcasters argued that cable was a common carrier, which meant the FCC could regulate it. The FCC ruled that cable was not a common carrier, but the commission also ruled that cable was officially not like broadcasting. The following year, the commission said it could find no authority with which to regulate cable.

The Beginnings of Regulation

Although cable could not be defined, it was a different matter if the success of a local broadcaster was directly threatened by cable, especially if it was the only station in the area. When this happened in *Carter Mountain Transmission Corporation v. FCC* in 1962, the FCC denied a cable operator a permit to build a microwave station. This set a precedent for supporting local television stations in conflicts between local stations and cable operators.

The first substantial cable regulation began in 1965 and established a policy that would affect the industry into the twenty-first century. The FCC outlined rules for those cable operators who used microwave systems (which were almost all of them), since FCC jurisdiction over microwave was already established. Cable was ordered to carry the signals of local broadcast stations, termed "must-carry," and was restricted from importing the same program as a local broadcaster, termed " nonduplication." Therefore, local broadcasters were always represented on their community's cable system, and they did not face competition from distant stations. The FCC also mandated that distant signals could not be imported into the top one hundred television markets. (There are about two hundred such markets, ranked by population. The two largest markets are New York and Los Angeles.)

Arguing that cable was interstate communication by wire, the FCC extended these regulations to all cable systems in 1966. In the public interest, cable outlets were also expected to offer "local origination," or the capacity for the general public to produce television programs and air them on special access channels. In the first cable-related U.S. Supreme Court case (*United States v. Southwestern Cable Company*, 1968), a cable company questioned the authority of the FCC to limit the signals that company could carry. The Court affirmed FCC authority over cable, but not directly, calling such authority "reasonably ancillary" to the tasks of the FCC. In *United States v. Midwest Video Corporation* (1972), the Court upheld must-carry and local origination. These new regulations limited the growth of cable and, accordingly, investment in the new industry.

By 1970, concerns existed with regard to the cross-ownership of various media and the number of media outlets that were owned by any one person or company. The FCC had already established limits on radio and television station ownership and forbidden a telephone company from owning a broadcast outlet. The commission extended this ruling to cable and prohibited a telephone network or local television station from owning a cable outlet. In 1975, the FCC decided not to impose a cross-ownership ban on cable and newspapers because a problematic situation did not exist. However, there was no restriction on companies that owned several cable outlets—multiple-system operators (MSOs)—to prevent them from buying interest in cable channels on their systems; this is known as vertical integration.

Concerns were also raised about cable's use of copyrighted programming, which prompted the commission to detail their regulations in 1972. Must-carry was extended to all local and educational television stations within thirty-five miles of the cable operator. Depending on the market size, cable was expected to carry a minimum of three network stations (there were only three television networks then) and one independent station. The nonduplication rule was also extended to syndicated programs, termed "syndicated exclusivity." As a result, cable was regulated as it had never been regulated before.

Cable operators were especially frustrated about the new and complex rules for premium (e.g., movies) and pay (e.g., sporting events) programming. Such shows had the potential to bring in substantial profits beyond just subscriptions, and new satellite technology could deliver signals all over the country much easier than microwave networks. However, the regulations made it almost impossible, and certainly unprofitable, to offer such fare. This changed in 1977 with *Home Box Office, Inc. v. FCC*. The U.S. Court of Appeals for the District of Columbia struck down the programming restrictions and adopted a standard to apply to future FCC cable regulations. This paved the way for some of the most popular and profitable pay services in cable history, such as Home Box Office and Showtime. That same year, the commission eased a technical requirement, which made "superstations" such as WTBS and WGN available to more cable outlets.

By the end of the 1970s, cable had more programming to offer, but there were also many more regulations to follow. In the 1979 decision *FCC v. Midwest Video Corporation*, the U.S. Supreme Court said that the commission had gone too far with local origination, but by then the FCC had already eased the rules. Foreshadowing the deregulation of the next decade, a 1979 FCC study found that, contrary to popular opinion, cable did not have an adverse effect on the growth and incomes of local television broadcasters. Partially based on that study, the FCC decided to drop all syndicated exclusivity regulations in 1980, in the interest of delivering more programming to the public. However, another version of the rules was instituted in 1988.

Deregulation and Re-regulation

With the administration of President Ronald Reagan came overall deregulation, and the cable industry was no exception. The Cable Communications Policy Act of 1984 stands as one of the most wide-sweeping regulatory efforts in cable television; it addressed several aspects of the industry, including subscription rates, service delivery, and programming. Up until that time, the local community that granted the cable franchise also regulated cable rates. With the 1984 act, if a cable company faced "effective competition," they decided basic cable rates. As defined, this effectively included all cable systems. Rates for pay services were also left to their discretion. Cable operators were ordered to provide service to their entire service area, not only the more profitable neighborhoods. Local governments could require channels for public, educational, and government use (PEG channels) to carry city council meetings and the like; however, franchises could only request broad categories of programming, not specific channels. The 1984 act also banned the entry of telephone companies into the video-delivery business.

Although the 1984 act gave cable operators authority in assigning rates, they resented being forced to dedicate channels to local stations under the must-carry provisions. Turner Broadcasting had asked the FCC to abolish the regulations as early as 1980. In *Quincy Cable TV, Inc. v. FCC* (1985), cable operators challenged must-carry as a violation of their First Amendment rights by restricting and forcing speech. The U.S. Court of Appeals for the District of Columbia said the FCC failed to justify the regulation and ordered it dropped. The same court struck down the commission's revised must-carry rules in *Century Communications Corporation v. FCC* (1987).

Increasing the presence of cable in households was an objective of the Cable Communications Policy Act of 1984. As seen in Table 1, this was apparently achieved, with a 186 percent increase in total subscribers from 1984 to 1992. However, as cable rates increased, so did public pressure on Congress to do something about it. The result was the Cable Television Consumer Protection and Competition Act of 1992. The definition of effective competition was again changed, this time such that almost all systems would be regulated. A crucial goal was to lower rates, but this did not occur. The 1992 act mandated regulating basic cable, but in response, operators created *a la carte* pricing by offering channels that used to be part of basic in packages. Generally, after the 1992 act, people paid more for the same number of channels than they had paid before.

The 1992 act included much more specific must-carry provisions and introduced an option for broadcasters: every three years they could either demand must-carry or they could negotiate to be paid for their programming under "retransmission consent." Many cable operators said they would never pay cash for something available for free, but they often did arrange trades of promotional time on other cable channels. Retransmission consent did not apply to educational stations or superstations. From 1993 to 1997, must-carry was again challenged, this time in *Turner Broadcasting System, Inc. v. FCC* (1993). In a reversal, must-carry was upheld as constitutional.

The 1992 act also addressed ownership issues, especially vertical integration. By that time, many MSOs owned all or large portions of many programming channels carried on their systems. Industry analysts worried that cable channels that were not owned by cable operators would not be carried and, thus, not survive. This legislation prevented the owners of any video-delivery system, such as cable, from taking such financial and business interests into consideration as a condition for carriage.

Heralded as an overhaul of the original Communications Act of 1934, the Telecommunications Act of 1996 deregulated aspects of the entire communications industry, including radio, television, and cable, in an effort to introduce increased competition and, hopefully, market-driven high-quality service. For the first time, telephone companies were allowed to enter the video-delivery market, although the ban on telephone-cable cross-ownership was retained. It was the hope of the FCC that the 1996 act would give a competitive boost to developing video technologies, such as direct broadcast satellite (DBS). Rate regulations for all cable programming tiers were eliminated after March 1999, as was the need for a uniform rate structure. This time, effective competition for cable meant the presence of any other video provider. This applied to almost all systems and, therefore, gave rate-setting authority back to cable operators.

Cable Franchises

Unlike broadcast television stations, which transmit over the air, cable systems use networks of wires to deliver signals. This involves miles of cable and assorted technical gadgets, as well as facilities to coordinate transmissions. It takes the cooperation of the local government to install and maintain this equipment successfully.

In the franchising process, municipalities choose among bids from cable-system operators who wish to build in the area. Bids often include promises of maximum channel delivery and public-service projects in exchange for a negotiated fee to the government. Typically, only one cable operator is selected, essentially granting a natural monopoly. Through the late 1950s and early 1960s, state courts generally ruled that because cable systems used public right-of-ways to install cable, they were public utilities and could, therefore, be regulated. In 1978, the FCC was given authority to regulate telephone-pole attachments that were used by cable operators.

The FCC did not mandate formal franchise processes until the Communications Policy Act of 1984. Before then, local franchise authorities regulated rates and often dictated programming, including channel selection. With the 1984 act, basic cable rates were deregulated, and franchises were limited to specifying only broad categories of programming. Franchise authorities were also limited in how much they could charge cable systems, not to exceed 5 percent of gross revenues. This act also addressed franchise renewal, which became a concern as the importance of cable increased and thirty-year-old franchise agreements were ending. Basically, cable operators could not assume automatic renewal.

The U.S. Supreme Court became involved with the franchising process in *Los Angeles v. Preferred Communications, Inc.* (1986). Los Angeles refused to authorize another cable system on the grounds that it was too disruptive. Ultimately, franchising was supported, but in a competitive situation, a city could not limit the number of systems to one.

With the Cable Television Consumer Protection and Competition Act of 1992 and a return to regulation, local franchises regulated with the cooperation of the FCC. Cable operators were also mandated to provide written notice to initiate renewal proceedings. At that time, franchising authorities could consider the efforts of a cable operator to expand cable and community services. Rates were again deregulated under the Telecommunications Act of 1996. By the end of the twentieth century, concern had switched from the building of cable systems to overbuilds, where capacity exceeds demand.

See also: BROADCASTING, GOVERNMENT REGULATION OF; BROADCASTING, SELF-REGULATION OF; CABLE TELEVISION; CABLE TELEVISION, HISTORY OF; CABLE TELEVISION, PROGRAMMING OF; COMMUNICATIONS ACT OF 1934; FEDERAL COMMUNICATIONS COMMISSION; FIRST AMENDMENT AND THE MEDIA; SATELLITES, COMMUNICATION; TELECOMMUNICATIONS ACT OF 1996; TELEVISION BROADCASTING.

Bibliography

Birinyi, Anne E. (1978). *Chronology of Cable Television Regulation: 1947–1978.* Cambridge, MA: Harvard University Press.

Crandall, Robert W., and Furchtgott-Roth, Harold. (1996). *Cable TV: Regulation or Competition?* Washington, DC: The Brookings Institution.

Duesterberg, Thomas J., and Pitsch, Peter K. (1998). *The Role of Competition and Regulation in Today's Cable TV Market.* Indianapolis, IN: Husdon Institute.

Ginsburg, Douglas H.; Botein, Michael H.; and Director, Mark D. (1991). *Regulation of the Electronic Mass Media: Law and Policy for Radio, Television, Cable and the New Video Technologies,* 2nd edition. St. Paul, MN: West Publishing.

Johnson, Leland L. (1994). *Toward Competition in Cable Television.* Cambridge. MA: MIT Press.

Middleton, Kent R.; Chamberlin, Bill F.; and Bunker, Matthew D. (1997). *The Law of Public Communication,* 4th edition. New York: Addison Wesley Longman.

Prohias, Rafael G. (1994). "Comments: Longer Than the Old Testament, More Confusing Than the Tax Code: An Analysis of the 1992 Cable Act." *CommLaw Conspectus* 2:81–93.

Sidak, J. Gregory, ed. (1999). *Is the Telecommunications Act of 1996 Broken? If So, How Can We Fix It?* Washington, DC: AEI Press.

Smith, Daniel J. (1997). "Note: Stay the Course: A History of the FCC's Response to Change in the Cable Industry." *Journal of Law & Politics* 13:715–740.

Wakeford, Kent D. (1995). "Cable Franchising: An Unwarranted Intrusion into Competitive Markets." *Southern California Law Review* 69:233–286.

Warren Communications News. (1998). *TV & Cable Factbook.* Washington, DC: Warren Communications News.

Watterman, David, and Weiss, Andrew W. (1997). *Vertical Integration in Cable Television.* Cambridge, MA: MIT Press.

Wiley, Richard E., and Wadlow, R. Clark. (1996). *The Telecommunications Act of 1996.* New York: Practising Law Institute.

TIMOTHY E. BAJKIEWICZ

■ CABLE TELEVISION, SYSTEM TECHNOLOGY OF

In its concept, the technology of cable television is relatively simple. It is a system of wires and amplifiers used to gather television and radio signals from a variety of sources and deliver them to the homes in a given geographic area. It is sometimes compared with the water system of a city, which takes water from one or two primary sources and distributes it to customers throughout the city. Cable television similarly distributes a roster of television channels to all the residents of an area who connect to its wire. Cable systems are expanding their services to include high-speed Internet access and traditional telephone service as well. The fundamental components of a cable system include the main office of the local system, called a "headend," where the various signals are gathered, combined, and fed out into the system; fiber-optic lines and coaxial cables, the wires that carry the information; amplifiers that boost the signal at regular intervals and maintain signal strength; and often set-top boxes, which translate the cable signals into electronic information that the home television set can use.

The Headend

The process of getting programming to the home begins far from the headend of the local system. National and multinational corporations such as AOL-Time Warner and Disney create the programming and operate familiar channels such as CNN, ESPN, HBO, Discovery, and MTV. These companies distribute the program signals, usually by satellite, from a few main origination points, beaming the material to the more than ten thousand individual cable systems in the United States, as well as to cable systems around the globe. Large dish antennas at the headend of the local system receive these signals. The programming companies simultaneously feed their signals to other multi-channel television providers such as direct broadcast satellite (DBS) companies (e.g., DirecTV).

In addition to the basic and premium cable packages, systems carry local and regional broadcast television stations, radio stations, and national audio services. Often, they also produce their own programming or carry programs that are produced by others in the community. Local radio and television stations are picked up by powerful

Large dish antennas have been used by local systems, such as Bethel Cablevision in Bethel, Alaska, to receive the signals from the major cable systems. (Yogi, Inc./Corbis)

versions of home television antennas, or they are sometimes sent to the headend via microwave link (a specialized broadcast technology) or wire. Typically, these local broadcasters will be affiliated with and carry the major national networks (e.g., NBC, CBS, ABC, PBS, Fox, WB, and UPN). Broadcast stations that are not affiliated with national programmers, including religious stations, will also be included in the package. National audio services that feature scores of digital music channels are fed by satellite in the same manner as national video programming.

Signals from television and radio stations that are outside of the normal reception range of the system, such as stations from another part of the state, can be picked up near that station's transmitting antenna and imported by microwave or landline. Programs that are created in television studios (usually small ones) at the headend are videotaped for later playback using professional-grade videotape machines. Those machines can

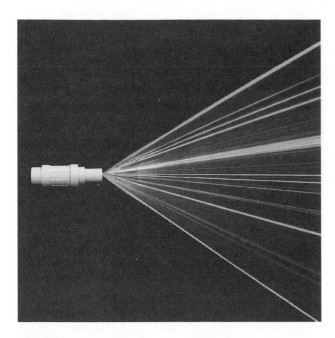

The adoption of fiber optic cable, with its ability to transmit information through laser-generated light, was a major advancement for the cable industry in the 1980s. (Charles O'Rear/Corbis)

also play back tapes that are created by others in the community to be carried on the public or governmental access channels of the system. Sometimes, programming will be fed by wire to the headend from a local government television facility or a television studio at an area high school or college. Many modern cable television systems also store and play back programming, usually commercials, using high-capacity digital servers.

All of this program material is electronically organized, and each signal is then imposed on a separate carrier wave, or channel. The combined signal is then sent out onto the system toward the subscriber's home.

The Wired System

There are three types of wire that are used in modern telecommunications: the so-called twisted pair, the fiber-optic cable, and the coaxial cable. The twisted pair is the familiar wire that is used by telephone companies to carry voice and data. Compared to fiber-optic and coaxial cables, twisted pair, without special conditioning, is quite limited in the amount of information that it can carry, and it is far too narrow an electronic pipe to transmit multichannel television programming. Cable operators therefore use coaxial and fiber-optic cables.

The cable television industry derives its name from the coaxial cable. Prior to the adoption of fiber optics in the 1980s, a cable system consisted almost entirely of "coax." The term "coaxial" refers to the two axes of the cable, a solid copper center wire (the first axis) surrounded by a metal sheath or tube (the second axis). The two axes are separated with either donut-shaped spacers or a solid, plastic-like material that is transparent to radio waves. A durable, plastic outer layer covers the cable.

Fiber is basically a thin glass thread that is about the width of a human hair. Instead of carrying information in the form of radio waves, fiber optics transmits information on beams of laser-generated light. Because it is made primarily of glass (the raw ingredients of which are plentiful) instead of copper, fiber is cheaper than coaxial cable. It can also carry significantly more information than coax and is less prone to signal loss and interference.

Both fiber and coax can carry a large number of television channels, along with other information, in part because of the way they harness the electromagnetic spectrum. The electromagnetic spectrum is the medium through which and within which television and radio signals are transmitted; it is an invisible part of the natural environment and includes such things as visible light, x-rays, gamma rays, and cosmic rays. A large portion of this natural spectrum can be employed to transmit information, and the U.S. government has allocated certain parts of it for many different types of wireless communication. This includes military communications, two-way radios, cellular telephones, and even garage-door openers. Commercial broadcasters, such as the hometown television and radio stations, therefore share this limited resource with other users.

Wired systems such as cable television, on the other hand, replicate the natural spectrum in an isolated and controlled environment. They can use all the available spectrum space that is created by that system without having to share it with other services. The amount of spectrum space that is available in a given system or for a particular application is called "bandwidth" and is measured in hertz, or more commonly, kilohertz (kHz) and megahertz (MHz). The phone line into a home is slightly more than 4 kHz, and it is termed "narrowband." A broadcast television signal requires 6

MHz, and most modern "broadband" cable systems operate at 750 to 860 MHz, or 110-plus analog television channels.

Amplifiers

As the television signal passes through the cable lines, both fiber and coaxial, that signal loses its strength. Resistance in the coaxial cable or impurities in the fiber cause the signal to deteriorate and fade over distance. The signals, therefore, have to be amplified at regular intervals. In contemporary cable systems, these amplifiers are placed about every two thousand feet for coaxial lines; a series of amplifiers is called a "cascade." The superior carrying power of fiber means that fewer amplifiers are needed to cover the same distance. The total number of amplifiers that can be used in a cascade or in a system is limited because every amplifier introduces a small amount of interference into the line. This interference accumulates and, with too many amplifiers, will reach a point of unacceptable distortion. The number of amplifiers that are used and the spacing between them in an actual system is depends on the system bandwidth and the medium (i.e., coaxial or fiber). A given cable system can have hundreds, even thousands, of miles of fiber and coax and hundreds of amplifiers.

The sophistication of the amplifier is also chiefly responsible for the exploitable bandwidth in the system, or the number of channels that a system can carry. The earliest cable television amplifiers could retransmit only one channel at a time, and a three-channel cable system had to have a separate set of amplifiers for each channel. Modern broadband amplifiers carry scores of channels simultaneously.

Network Architectures

The pattern in which a cable system is arranged (i.e., the configuration of wires from the headend to the subscriber's home) is the system architecture. From the earliest days of cable in the late 1940s, the classic architecture for a cable system was known as "tree and branch." Picture a family-tree diagram, with ancestral branches of the family coming off the trunk, and those large branches dividing and spreading out into finer and more numerous offshoots. The classic cable system is designed in this fashion. Signals leave the headend over high-capacity "trunk lines,"

usually fiber optic, which wind their way through the main arteries of the community, down city streets toward local neighborhoods. "Feeder," or distribution, cables branch off from the fiber trunk, or backbone, and spread down neighborhood streets toward hundreds, sometimes thousands, of homes. Finally, smaller coaxial "drop lines" sprout off the feeder cables to link to individual houses. All of the lines are either buried underground or strung on poles that are usually rented from the local telephone or power company. Because the trunk and feeder lines cannot support their own weight, they are lashed to heavy steel wires called "strand," which also carry the weight of the amplifiers.

With the development of cost-effective fiber-optic technology in the 1980s, cable systems began replacing much of their coaxial line with the new, higher capacity technology, starting with the trunk lines and moving toward the feeder lines. With the change in the hardware came a change in the system architecture. Use of fiber meant reduced costs over the long term, a decrease in the number of amplifiers needed, and an increase in the overall quality of the signal. Fiber could be run directly from the headend to hubs, or nodes, serving large clusters of homes. From these fiber hubs, mini tree and branch coax systems would service area customers. This combination of fiber and coaxial cable is the hybrid fiber coax (HFC) architecture.

Set-Top Boxes

Many cable subscribers, even those who have contemporary "cable-ready" television sets, have additional cable set-top boxes, or converters, that are sitting on or next to their sets. Set-top boxes perform several important tasks for the cable system. For some television sets, especially older or non-cable-ready sets, they act as the television tuner, the device that selects the channels to be viewed. Because the wired spectrum is a closed universe, cable operators can place their channels on almost any frequency that they want, and they do so to make the most efficient use of the space and technology. Operators, for example, carry the broadcast VHF channels 2 through 13 in their "normal" place on the dial, but the UHF channels 14 through 69, which in the open spectrum are higher than and separate from the VHF channels, have been moved in "cable space." The full cable spectrum is, in fact, divided into its own bands. Channels 2 through 6 are carried in the low band, channels 7 through 13 in the high band, and other cable network programming is distributed across the midband, superband, and hyperband channels. Part of the low band (i.e., 0 to 50 MHz) is often used to carry signals from the consumer's home "upstream" and back to the cable company headend. Television sets that are not set up to receive the many special bands of cable require set-top boxes for the conversion.

While cable-ready television sets have taken over most of the simple functions of signal reception in modern systems, converters remain a staple in the industry for the provision of more advanced services such as premium programming and "pay-per-view" movies. The boxes help control the distribution of such programming to subscriber homes. Many cable systems are "addressable," which means that each subscriber has an electronic address, and operators can turn a signal to that home on or off from the headend. The technology that helps make addressability possible is often housed in the set-top box. Finally, as cable moves into the digital era, set-top boxes are being used to convert the digital channels and services to signals that the standard analog television set can use.

Cable Interactivity and Advanced Services

While most cable systems are addressable, true interactivity remains limited in most systems. Interactivity has no set definition and can take many forms, including ordering movies when the customer wants to view them (video on demand) or having the cable system monitor the home smoke alarm. In all cases, it requires some means of getting a signal from the home back to the headend. Cable television systems were originally configured for the efficient delivery of large amounts of programming from one point (the headend) to multiple users—a point-to-multipoint distribution scheme. The arrangement has been very successful for one-way mass distribution of content, but it is limited in its two-way capacity. As noted, cable television systems designate a small portion of their spectrum space for upstream communication, but that bandwidth has been historically underexploited by the cable industry.

In contrast, telephone systems, despite their limited bandwidth, are configured for full two-way, point-to-point communication. Unlike cable, tele-

phone companies use a switching system to create a dedicated line between two callers. Traditional cable systems do not have the architecture or the switch to provide such service. Cable companies are seeking to overcome this technical handicap by developing techniques, using both hardware and software, to make their systems more interactive. The conversion to digital technology is especially seen as a way to provide additional and enhanced services, including interactive television, telephone service, and Internet access.

An early example of this effort is the cable modem. By distributing computer data, such as Internet web-pages, over the cable system, cable operators are able to exploit their broadband capacity and dramatically increase modem speeds. Customers who hook their computers to a cable system instead of using a standard telephone modem can download pages in seconds instead of minutes, and the cable modem is on all of the time—so there is no waiting for the computer to "dial up" an Internet connection.

Cable operators are also developing techniques that will allow them to offer telephone service using their cable plant. Ultimately, the broadband capacity of cable will provide one of the major distribution platforms for the high-speed interactive digital era—the information highway—and help create a seamless integration of video, voice, and data.

See also: CABLE TELEVISION; CABLE TELEVISION, CAREERS IN; CABLE TELEVISION, HISTORY OF; CABLE TELEVISION, PROGRAMMING OF; CABLE TELEVISION, REGULATION OF; DIGITAL COMMUNICATION; INTERNET AND THE WORLD WIDE WEB; SATELLITES, COMMUNICATION; TELEPHONE INDUSTRY, TECHNOLOGY OF; TELEVISION BROADCASTING, TECHNOLOGY OF.

Bibliography

Baldwin, Thomas; McVoy, D. Stevens; and Steinfeld, Charles. (1996). *Convergence: Integrating Media, Information, and Communication.* Thousand Oaks, CA: Sage Publications.

Bartlett. Eugene. (1999). *Cable Television Handbook: Systems and Operations.* New York: McGraw-Hill.

Ciciora, Walter; Farmer, James; and Large, David. (2000). *Modern Cable Television Technology: Video, Voice, and Data Communications.* San Francisco, CA: Morgan Kaufmann.

CARNEGIE, ANDREW • 115

Crisp, John. (1999). *Introduction to Fiber Optics.* Woburn, MA: Butterworth-Heinemann.

Jones, Glen. (1996). *Jones Dictionary of Cable Television Terminology.* Boston: Information Gatekeepers.

Maxwell, Kim. (1998). *Residential Broadband: An Insider's Guide to the Battle for the Last Mile.* New York: Wiley.

O'Driscoll, Gerard. (1999). *The Essential Guide to Digital Set-Top Boxes and Interactive TV.* Paramus, NJ: Prentice-Hall.

Parsons, Patrick R., and Frieden, Robert M. (1998). *The Cable and Satellite Television Industries.* Boston: Allyn & Bacon.

Southwick, Thomas. (1998). *Distant Signals: How Cable TV Changed the World of Telecommunications.* Overland Park, KS: Primedia Intertec.

PATRICK R. PARSONS

■ CARNEGIE, ANDREW (1835–1919)

Andrew Carnegie. (Corbis)

An industrialist and philanthropist, Andrew Carnegie was born in Dumferline, Scotland, to William and Margaret Morrison Carnegie. Economic reverses led the family to emigrate in 1848 to Allegheny, Pennsylvania, where for $1.20 per week Andrew took a job as a bobbin boy in a textile factory. Hungry for knowledge, he also became the heaviest user of Colonel J. Anderson's personal library, which was open to all Allegheny working boys. A year later, Carnegie hired on as a telegraph messenger boy, where he so distinguished himself that Thomas Scott, superintendent of the western division of the Pennsylvania Railroad, hired him as his personal telegrapher for $35 a month.

Under Scott, Carnegie learned business methods quickly, and when Scott became the general superintendent of the railroad in 1859, Carnegie took over the position of superintendent of the western division. The new salary enabled Carnegie to expand his investments, all of which turned substantial profits. In 1865, he resigned from the railroad to devote full attention to his growing business interests. When investments generated a comfortable income, he wrote himself a note in 1868: "Thirty-three and an income of $50,000 [sic] per annum. . . . Beyond this never earn—make no effort to increase fortune, but spend surplus each year for benovolent [sic] purposes." For the next twenty years, he generally ignored this commitment while he built a huge fortune in the steel industry.

In 1887, Carnegie married Louise Whitfield, and they had one daughter (born in 1897). By the end of the 1880s, however, the sentiment expressed in his 1868 note began to gnaw on Carnegie's conscience. In 1889, he published two essays in the *North American Review* outlining a "gospel of wealth" philosophy. Wealthy people, he said, had a responsibility to live moderately and give their excess wealth to needy people who would help themselves. In an essay entitled "The Best Fields for Philanthropy," he specifically identified seven institutions worthy of attention: universities, public libraries, medical centers, public parks and arboretums, concert halls, public swimming pools and baths, and churches. (Carnegie had foreshadowed some of these priorities earlier in the decade with gifts of a library and swimming bath to Dumferline, a library to Braddock, Pennsylvania, and an organ to an Allegheny church.) Much of this rhetoric, however, was tarnished by the Homestead Strike of 1892, in which seven steelworkers lost their lives in a fight with Pinkerton detectives who had been hired to help Carnegie break the union.

After selling his steel interests to J. P. Morgan for nearly $500 million in 1901, Carnegie turned his full attention to implementing his gospel of wealth. By the time of his death eighteen years later, he had donated more than $333 million to underwrite such causes and organizations as the Simplified Spelling Board, 7,689 church organs, the Carnegie Hero Fund, the Church Peace Union, the Carnegie Institute of Pittsburgh (which included an art gallery, library, concert hall, and the Carnegie Institute of Technology), the Carnegie Institute of Washington, D.C., the Carnegie Foundation for the Advancement of Teaching, and the Carnegie Endowment for International Peace. He also provided the money to construct the Pan American Union building in Washington, D.C. (to promote peace in the Western Hemisphere), a Court of Justice in Costa Rica (to arbitrate disputes between Central American countries), and The Hague Peace Palace in the Netherlands (to house the World Court). In 1911, Carnegie endowed the Carnegie Corporation with $125 million, and over time, he relinquished control of his philanthropy to the directors of the corporation.

Among all his philanthropic interests, Carnegie particularly liked libraries. He often boasted that around the world the sun always shone on at least one Carnegie library. Between 1890 and 1919, he donated $56 million to construct 2,811 libraries in the English-speaking world (including $41 million to construct 1,679 American public libraries in 1,412 communities and $4.3 million to erect 108 academic libraries in the United States). In 1917, Carnegie also donated the money to erect 36 libraries in camps located throughout the United States that trained soldiers for participation in World War I. The sheer size of Carnegie's philanthropy generated a competition between communities to establish libraries; it also helped create a climate of giving that encouraged other library philanthropists.

A typical Carnegie grant first required communities to provide a suitable site for the library. Once that had been established, Carnegie would agree to donate a sum (usually $2.00 per capita of the local population) to be used in the erection of a building—as long as the community promised to fund the library annually at a rate of 10 percent of the original gift.

Not all communities welcomed Carnegie grants, however. In Wheeling, West Virginia, for example, local labor leaders who remembered the Homestead Strike of 1892 rejected efforts by city fathers to accept a grant. "There will be one place on this great green planet where Andrew Carnegie can't get a monument with his money," steelworker Mike Mahoney told labor delegates at a meeting called to defeat the library levy in 1904. (Seven years later, Wheeling opened a public library with labor support, but without Carnegie money.) In scores of other communities, Carnegie grants were rejected for gender and race reasons. In some, the male elite rejected efforts by local ladies' clubs to add yet another institutional responsibility to the local tax burden. In others (especially in the South), the local white elite worried that to accept a "free" library would force them to offer racially integrated services.

Communities that successfully solicited Carnegie grants were often inexperienced in library design and architecture. To address this problem, James Bertram, Carnegie's private secretary, commissioned a set of six model library blueprints. In part, this had the effect of homogenizing public library architecture in small- to medium-sized communities. A typical classically designed Carnegie building required a library user to climb ten or more steps to enter through (usually) double doors. At that point she (the large majority of patrons were women and children) could turn left and descend to a lower level, where she generally found a restroom, heating plant, and meeting room available for community groups such as the local women's club and the Rotary Club. If the patron chose not to descend to the lower level, she could step forward to the circulation desk. Located in the middle of an open space (and often under a dome), the U-shaped circulation desk stood waist high and functioned as the command post of the librarian. From behind the desk, the librarian (almost always a woman) could, without moving, look right and monitor activities in the children's wing. The librarian could also look left into the adult reading room, where periodicals and newspapers were available. Behind the librarian were stacks filled with books that the American Library Association (ALA) had recommended in bibliographical guides (e.g., *Booklist* magazine, the ALA *Catalog*). These guides were funded in part by the interest that accrued on a $100,000 endowment made by Carnegie in 1902.

After Carnegie's death on August 11, 1919, in Lenox, Massachusetts, the Carnegie Corporation continued to favor most of his philanthropic interests, especially librarianship and higher education. The legacy of Carnegie's philanthropy was significant. Organizations that he founded and institutions that he helped to build during his lifetime evolved into essential agencies for creating, acquiring, organizing, and disseminating multiple forms of communication and information.

See also: LIBRARIES, HISTORY OF.

Bibliography

Carnegie, Andrew. (1889). *The Gospel of Wealth*. New York: Jenkins & McGowan.

Carnegie, Andrew. (1920). *The Autobiography of Andrew Carnegie*. New York: Houghton Mifflin.

Hendrick, Burton J. (1932). *The Life of Andrew Carnegie*. Garden City, NJ: Doubleday, Doran & Company.

Lagemann, Ellen Condliffe. (1989). *The Politics of Knowledge: The Carnegie Corporation, Philanthropy, and Public Polity*. Middletown, CT: Wesleyan University Press.

Livesay, Harold. (1975). *Andrew Carnegie and the Rise of Big Business*. Boston: Little, Brown.

Martin, Robert Sidney, ed. (1993). *Carnegie Denied: Communities Rejecting Carnegie Library Construction Grants, 1898–1925*. Westport, CT: Greenwood.

Van Slyck, Abigail. (1995). *Free to All: Carnegie Libraries & American Culture, 1890–1920*. Chicago: University of Chicago Press.

Wall, Joseph Frazier. (1970). *Andrew Carnegie*. New York: Oxford University Press.

WAYNE A. WIEGAND

CATALOGING AND KNOWLEDGE ORGANIZATION

If information cannot be found when it is wanted, it cannot be integrated into the world of human knowledge or into an individual's personal knowledge base. Whether people want to write a newspaper article, complete a project, or learn about a new hobby, they need to be able to find information that relates to what they are doing and to what they want to know. The overall purpose of cataloging and knowledge organization is to help people achieve the goal of finding information as easily as possible when they need it. This goal may seem to be a simple one, but accomplishing it is not necessarily easy or straightforward. For example, the way in which information is described and organized should ideally be consistent within one information medium, compatible with other information media, and predictable and appropriate for different kinds of information in different media. In addition, description and organization of information should be flexible enough to accommodate all the different assumptions, views of the world, and natural languages that human beings currently employ, as well as those that they have employed throughout the history of recorded information.

People have recorded information in many ways and in many forms. One general term for all of these information containers is "item." Information items can be textual (e.g., books or magazines), nontextual (e.g., paintings or sculptures), or a combination of the two (e.g., musical scores or maps). In addition, these information items can be physically stored in institutions such as libraries, museums, or archives, and/or they can be virtually stored in databases (textual or nontextual) for private use (e.g., within an organization) or for public use (e.g., through the Internet). This variety of possibilities has motivated information professionals to develop standardized and nonstandardized ways of helping people find what they want.

Recording Data about Information Items

Three processes help information professionals create access for users. These are the description of an item, the choice of descriptive elements as access points (i.e., data that may be searched), and the entry of the description into a file that is either manually or electronically searchable.

The description of an information item is a surrogate representation for it. A surrogate record stands for the information item in a manual or an electronic file. The purpose of the description is to allow people to decide whether they want to look at the thing itself. For example, the surrogate description for a book includes both physical characteristics (e.g., number of pages and dimensions) and intellectual characteristics (e.g., title and subject). These and other data elements (e.g., author, publisher, date of publication) help people decide whether they want to read the book. In general, the process of creating a description and assigning access points is known as "cataloging." The process of creating "metadata" has roughly the same meaning, but it may include how the description is put into machine-readable form, where the item may be found, and/or its relationship with other items. "Resource description" is a similarly broad term for methods of creating surrogates for any kind of item. The surrogate might be a cataloging record, an abstract or summary, or a thumbnail picture of the item. Clearly, if descriptions of items are standardized and predictable, people will more easily find the information they are looking for because they can make a comprehensive and complete search of an information file.

Charles Cutter (1904) identified three purposes for cataloging: (1) to allow someone to find an item with a known creator, title, or subject, (2) to allow someone to discover what an institution has about a certain topic, and (3) to allow someone to select an appropriate item from among a number of similar ones. These three goals still guide any catalog or other finding aid. The first objective is met by cataloging rules and codes, the second is met by knowledge organization systems, and the third is met by both kinds of systems.

Cataloging Rules and Codes

Standardized rules for cataloging have a long history. The most widely used cataloging code in the English-speaking world is the second revised edition of the *Anglo-American Cataloguing Rules* (AACR2, 1998). These rules were developed by an international Joint Steering Committee that included members from the United States, Canada, Australia, and Great Britain. AACR2 descriptions conform to a more general standard, the International Standard Bibliographic Description (ISBD), which was produced by a 1969 meeting of cataloging experts in Copenhagen, Denmark. The ISBD had three general goals. Its creators wanted to ensure (1) that records produced in one country in one language could be understood in other countries that might use other languages, (2) that records produced in one country could be integrated into files produced elsewhere, and (3) that records could be converted into machine-readable form. The first ISBD standard was developed for monographs, and

since then standards have been developed for printed music, nonbook materials, maps, computer files, and antiquarian materials, among others. Similarly, AACR2 contains rules for describing items in these different formats.

AACR2 is divided into two parts. Rules in the first part prescribe how to record data about the item using eight different areas or fields. These eight areas are either preceded or surrounded by punctuation marks that differentiate among the various roles a person or an institution played in the creation of the item. For example, in the area for the title and statement of responsibility for the item, the statement from the item that names its creator(s) is preceded by "/" (i.e., character space-slash-character space). Different punctuation marks are used for different information elements in the cataloging record. This kind of standardized punctuation allows people (or computers) to understand the information in the record without necessarily being able to read the language in which the record is written.

The second part of AACR2 contains rules for choosing access points and for standardizing the information content in a surrogate description. For example, a creator often uses a different name for different works. People may use different forms of the same name, or they may use entirely different names. Sometimes, people change their names or write under pseudonyms. First, a cataloger needs to decide which of these names to use in the surrogate record. Next, the cataloger needs to decide which form of that name to use in the surrogate. The purpose of these decisions is to establish a standardized name in a standardized form based on which name is likely to be known to the most people. For example, *The Adventures of Huckleberry Finn* was written under the pseudonym Mark Twain, but the author's real name was Samuel Clemens. Because Samuel Clemens never wrote under his real name, the cataloger will choose Mark Twain as the name most people are likely to know and use for a search.

In addition, different people can have the same name, and the cataloger needs to distinguish among people who have the same name in order to separate items created by one person from those created by another. For example, works by the nineteenth-century American novelist Winston Churchill need to be distinguished from works by the twentieth-century British prime minister with the same name. One way to make this distinction is to add a person's birth and/or death dates to the name. Another way is to add extra elements (e.g., a middle name). For names in English, the surname is usually listed first followed by the forename(s). This practice is familiar through, for example, telephone books. The process of choosing names and other access points and of establishing standardized forms for them is called "authority work." Authority work includes making references from unused names and from unused forms of a name to the standardized name and form so that, for example, people who look up one name (e.g., Clemens, Samuel) are directed to the chosen name (e.g., Twain, Mark). In this way, authority work ensures that people who are interested in works by the novelist Winston Churchill do not retrieve works by the prime minister Winston Churchill.

Various other sets of standards and rules that have been developed for generating surrogates in both manual and electronic information environments include *Archives, Personal Papers, and Manuscripts,* the *Dublin Core Elements,* and *Encoded Archival Description.* Each of these systems is appropriate for a particular kind of information item, and each has its own set of useful data elements for describing an item and establishing appropriate access points for it. Tools (called "crosswalks") for comparing the various standards have been developed to help information professionals understand differences and similarities among different standards, such as the different definitions each standard may give to the title or the creator of a work. Crosswalks establish which field(s) from one standard map onto which field(s) in another. Similar to translating between different natural languages, translating between different standards is not automatic, but it is an important activity because it allows one to merge files that contain records using different standards. In this way, records can be shared, and more people have access to the record for an item they are interested in retrieving.

Knowledge Organization Systems

One of the objectives that Cutter (1904) had for a surrogate system was to allow people to find items that have the same topic or subject. The topic of an item is what it is about (e.g., landscape painting, theoretical astrophysics, gardening, or how to fly an airplane). The term "knowledge organization" encompasses different methods for organizing information, but the term is sometimes used for information about a topic or subject. Standardized (i.e., alphabetical systems, classification systems) and nonstandardized methods of specifying subjects have been developed, all of which can be used in both manual and electronic environments to help people retrieve the information they want.

Standardized Methods

A cataloger analyzes an information item to determine its topic and the concepts it uses and then translates the concepts in the analysis into a standardized or controlled vocabulary. Standardized methods of knowledge organization include systems that are primarily displayed alphabetically (e.g., subject-heading systems and thesauri) and systems that are primarily displayed systematically (e.g., classification and ontological systems). These two types of systems are not mutually exclusive because alphabetical systems include classificatory elements, and classificatory systems include alphabetical elements. Both kinds of system are used to organize resources on the Internet (e.g., Beyond Bookmarks) and in nonelectronic information environments.

Subject-heading and thesaural systems are called "controlled vocabularies" because the particular terms the system prefers for expressing each concept are chosen in advance and controlled by the system developers. Searchers are guided to these preferred terms by networks of references that are called the "syndetic structure" of the system. Assigning subject headings to information items is usually called "subject cataloging" and assigning thesaurus terms is usually called "indexing."

Subject-heading lists provide words and/or phrases that may be used as access points for subjects. Subject-heading lists are often used in libraries and are usually created for knowledge in general. These systems provide networks of terms to describe the subjects in a document. *Library of Congress Subject Headings,* first published in 1914, is used in many large academic and national libraries in English-speaking countries. Usually, a cataloger gives a book more than one subject heading, and in an online system subject headings can be searched by keywords. That is, the searcher does not have to know the exact form of the subject heading in order to use it for searching.

Thesauri began to be developed in the 1950s. Thesaural systems are similar to subject-heading systems in providing lists of consistent terms that are assigned to an information item by an indexer. Unlike subject-heading systems, however, thesauri are usually created for a particular field. For example, the *Art & Architecture Thesaurus*, published by the Getty Information Institute, provides access to all kinds of heritage information items (e.g., texts, images, museum materials). In addition, the syndetic structures of thesauri are usually more strictly controlled than those of subject-heading systems, and the terms in them are defined for the particular purposes of that field of knowledge.

Both subject-heading and thesaural systems include codes that describe the relationships of one term to other terms. The most common relationships are "broader term" (BT), "narrower term" (NT), and "related term" (RT). A broader term names a concept that is wider in scope than another. For example, the concept "precipitation" is broader than "snow." A narrower term names a concept that is more specific. For example, the concept "oak tree" is narrower than "tree." A related term is associated in some way to the term in question but is neither broader nor narrower in scope. For example, "light" is related to "color" and may interest a searcher who has looked up "color," but the two terms do not have a broader/narrower hierarchical relationship. In addition, some terms are preferred terms (called "used terms"). Terms not preferred by the system are called "unused terms." Unused terms are considered synonyms for used terms and cannot be used for searching. For example, "wig" may be a synonym for "hair." People who look up an unused term (e.g., "wig") are directed to search with a used term instead (e.g., "hair").

Controlled vocabularies are useful in information retrieval systems because the terms assigned to information items can be used to search a database. Searching with an assigned term ensures that all the records that have been indexed with that term are retrieved. Certainty that all the relevant records have been found means that a searcher can feel confident that the search was comprehensive. Otherwise, the searcher would have to think of all the possible synonyms of a term in order to be sure that the search was complete.

Classification systems are structured systems that divide some knowledge domain into groups on the basis of likenesses and/or differences among the members of each group. The study of classification dates back at least to the philosophers of ancient Greece. Modern bibliographic classification systems started to appear in the late nineteenth century. In an ideal classification system, the classes are both mutually exclusive and jointly exhaustive. That is, the classes do not overlap (i.e., mutually exclusive), and all the classes taken together encompass all possible content so that nothing is left out (i.e., jointly exhaustive). This ideal cannot be fully achieved because new members of the classes can be discovered or invented at any time. Nevertheless, the ideal can be used to help evaluate classification systems because one can assess the classes for mutual exclusivity and joint exhaustivity.

In North America, most libraries use either the *Dewey Decimal Classification* or the *Library of Congress Classification* (in which each class is published separately). Both of these classification systems are called "enumerative systems" because they seek to list all of the possible topics that documents may have. In libraries, classification systems are used both to show the place of a particular topic in the context of the world of knowledge and also to provide a shelf address for each document. On the Internet, classification systems (e.g., DESIRE) often provide an address or hyperlink to the relevant site. Researchers into artificial intelligence have begun to create ontologies (i.e., classification systems) for real-world knowledge so computers can represent contexts, understand human languages, and recognize how things in the world are related to each other.

Most classification systems have a hierarchical structure in which the attributes of a class on a higher level are shared by those on the lower levels. For example, a document about Canadian history in general will not be as detailed on each of its constituent topics (e.g., the Canadian constitution) as a document that deals only with that topic, but a document about the narrower topic will also contain elements of the broader topic. For example, a document about the Canadian constitution will also deal to some extent with Canadian history in general. Unlike subject-heading systems and thesauri, classification systems are displayed structurally, not as an alphabetical list. Each class has a notation that represents the place of the class in the world of knowledge and in the system and that shows its relationships to a hierarchy of other classes. For example, part of the *Dewey Decimal Classification* schedules for "technology" (with growing specificity) is 600 for technology (applied sciences), 630 for agriculture and related technologies, 636 for animal husbandry, 636.7 for dogs, and 636.8 for cats.

Notation can be numeric, alphabetical, or mixed alphanumeric. For example, the notation for the topic "economics of education" is 338.4337 in the *Dewey Decimal Classification* and LC65 in the *Library of Congress Classification.* Hierarchical relationships may also be shown in the notation. For example, in the *Dewey Decimal Classification,* "Canadian history" is notated as 971, where the 9 stands for "history," the 7 stands for "North America," and the 1 stands for "Canada." The *Dewey Decimal Classification* notation 971 thus shows that history is a broader concept than North America and that North America is a broader concept than Canada.

One relatively recent development in the creation of classification systems is the construction of faceted systems. Facet theory was developed by Shiyali R. Ranganathan in India and refined in his *Colon Classification* (1964). Facet analysis divides a subject field into mutually exclusive groups called "facets" and then divides each facet into its constituents. For example, the material facet for furniture would contain terms for the various kinds of materials from which furniture can be made (e.g., wood, metal, cloth, plastic). Each of these terms has its own notation, and notations from different facets can be synthesized to express a complex topic. For example, one might express the topic "red plastic tables" with notational elements from the color, material, and type facets. The idea of facet analysis has also been adopted for the development of thesauri. Its advantage is that all topics do not have to be listed, and a notational subject statement may be built up in a way that is similar to constructing a sentence from component words in a natural language. Another faceted classification system is the *Bliss Bibliographic Classification* (devised by Henry Evelyn Bliss and edited by Jack Mills and Vanda Broughton), which is based on Ranganathan's theories and incorporates other advances from modern classification research.

The ability to search a database using notations as search terms means that the searcher does not have to know the human language that is used in the records. For example, using the *Dewey Decimal Classification* notation 636.8 ("cats") for searching a database in which each record has been assigned one or more notations will retrieve records in English, Spanish, Chinese, Russian, or any other natural language. The searcher does not have to know the word for "cats" and its synonyms in all these languages. This ability is particularly useful in multilingual information environments.

Nonstandardized Methods

Nonstandardized methods of knowledge organization have been developed and are used for accessing the content of an individual document. An abstract is a brief summary that contains only the most salient points from the document and is often written by a professional abstractor, not by the originator of the document. Abstracts are often included at the beginning of a journal article and, in an electronic environment, these abstracts can be searched to find words in uncontrolled vocabulary that are of interest to the searcher. Individual documents such as books often have an index that refers only to that document and its page numbers. These back-of-the-book indexes are created by professional indexers, and no standardized method has been developed. Each book also has a table of contents that includes the names of chapters and/or sections in order to help readers find what they want. In the case of both abstracts and back-of-the book indexes, searching with an uncontrolled vocabulary means that one can never be certain that all the relevant material has been retrieved or that the search has been comprehensive.

Producing Files in a Standardized Format

Individual surrogate records are entered into a file to create a manual or computerized catalog, list, directory, index, guide, or register that can be searched. In a manual (i.e., printed) file, the display format is usually established by a publisher (e.g., for a book) or by an institution (e.g., for a library catalog). For computerized resources (e.g., a database), information is encoded from descriptive standards such as AACR2, and the way this information is displayed can be customized. To encode information means to make it machine-readable. Institutions or individuals that want to exchange records can do so if they are using the same encoding standard or if a method has been developed to convert one standard format to another. Sharing records increases their accessibility for people who are trying to find information. Standardized encoding formats include, for example, Machine-Readable Cataloging (MARC) and Standard Generalized Markup Language (SGML), which allow data to be displayed in human languages. The MARC format is the oldest encoding standard and is used in many libraries. Markup languages such as SGML permit the structures of many different types of documents to be encoded. They show which elements are structural elements (e.g., a paragraph or a title) and which elements are content elements (e.g., the sentences in the paragraph). In addition, standards can be used to describe each other. For example, MARC records can be encoded with SGML.

Conclusion

Cataloging and knowledge organization systems have been developed to make it easier for people to find what they need within the complex worlds of information and knowledge. These systems are used in all kinds of information environments to improve access to actual and virtual documents in many formats, in many languages, and from many periods of history. The evolution of these systems is ongoing because information professionals are constantly striving to improve access for users of the systems.

See also: ARCHIVES, PUBLIC RECORDS, AND RECORDS MANAGEMENT; ARCHIVISTS; ARTIFICIAL INTELLIGENCE; BIBLIOGRAPHY; DEWEY, MELVIL; INTERNET AND THE WORLD WIDE WEB; KNOWLEDGE MANAGEMENT; KNOWLEDGE MANAGEMENT, CAREERS IN; LIBRARIANS; LIBRARIES, DIGITAL; LIBRARY AUTOMATION; MUSEUMS; RANGANATHAN, SHIYALI RAMAMRITA.

Bibliography

Chan, Lois Mai. (1994). *Cataloging and Classification: An Introduction,* 2nd edition. New York: McGraw-Hill.

Cutter, Charles Ammi. (1904). *Rules for a Dictionary Catalog,* 4th edition. Washington, DC: U.S. Government Printing Office.

DESIRE Consortium. (2000). "Welcome to the DESIRE Project." <http://www.desire.org>.

Dublin Core Metadata Initiative. (2001). "Overview." <http://www.dublincore.org>.

Getty Research Institute. (2001). "Art & Architecture Thesaurus Browser." <http://www.getty.edu/research/tools/vocabulary/aat/>.

Hensen, Steven L., comp. (1989). *Archives, Personal Papers, and Manuscripts: A Cataloging Manual for Archival Repositories, Historical Societies, and Manuscript Libraries,* 2nd edition. Chicago: Society of American Archivists.

Joint Steering Committee for Revision of AACR. (1998). *Anglo-American Cataloguing Rules,* 2nd edition. Chicago: American Library Association.

Lancaster, Frederick W. (1998). *Indexing and Abstracting in Theory and Practice,* 2nd edition. Champaign: University of Illinois, Graduate School of Library and Information Science.

Library of Congress, Cataloging Distribution Service. (1914–). *Library of Congress Subject Headings.* Washington, DC: Library of Congress.

Library of Congress, Cataloging Policy and Support Office. (1902–). *Library of Congress Classification.* Washington, DC: Library of Congress.

Library of Congress, Network Development and MARC Standards Office. (2001). "Dublin Core/MARC/GILS Crosswalk." <http://www.loc.gov/marc/dccross.html>.

Library of Congress, Network Development and MARC Standards Office. (2001). "Encoded Archival Description." <http://www.loc.gov/ead/ead.html>.

McKiernan, Gerry. (2001). "Beyond Bookmarks: Schemes for Organizing the Web." <http://www.public.iastate.edu/~CYBERSTACKS/CTW.htm>.

Mills, Jack, and Broughton, Vanda, eds. (1977–). *Bliss Bibliographic Classification,* 2nd edition. London: Butterworths.

Milstead, Jessica L. (1984). *Subject Access Systems: Alternatives in Design.* Orlando, FL: Academic Press.

Mitchell, Joan S.; Beall, Julianne; Matthews, Winton E., Jr.; and New, Gregory R., eds. (1996). *Dewey Decimal Classification and Relative Index,* 21st edition. Albany, NY: Forest Press.

Ranganathan, Shiyali Ramamrita. (1964). *Colon Classification,* 6th edition. Bombay, India: Asia Publishing House.

Vickery, Brian C. (1997). "Ontologies." *Journal of Information Science* 23(4):277–286.

CLARE BEGHTOL

CATHARSIS THEORY AND MEDIA EFFECTS

Is viewing violence cathartic? The large amount of violence in the mass media is often justified by the concept of catharsis. The word catharsis comes from the Greek word *katharsis*, which literally translated means "a cleansing or purging." The first recorded mention of catharsis occurred more than one thousand years ago, in the work *Poetics* by Aristotle. Aristotle taught that viewing tragic plays gave people emotional release (*katharsis*) from negative feelings such as pity, fear, and anger. By watching the characters in the play experience tragic events, the negative feelings of the viewer were presumably purged and cleansed. This emotional cleansing was believed to be beneficial to both the individual and society.

The ancient notion of catharsis was revived by Sigmund Freud and his associates. For example, A. A. Brill, the psychiatrist who introduced the psychoanalytic techniques of Freud to the United States, prescribed that his patients watch a prize fight once a month to purge their angry, aggressive feelings into harmless channels.

Catharsis theory did not die with Aristotle and Freud. Many directors and producers of violent media claim that their products are cathartic. For example, Alfred Hitchcock, director of the movie *Psycho*, said, "One of television's greatest contributions is that it brought murder back into the home where it belongs. Seeing a murder on television can be good therapy. It can help work off one's antagonism." More recently, in 1992, Paul Verhoeven, director of the movie *Total Recall*, said, "I think it's a kind of purifying experience to see violence."

The producers of violent computer games, like the producers of violent films, claim that their products are cathartic. For example, SegaSoft has created an online network containing violent games that claims to provide users an outlet for the "primal human urge to kill." In promotional materials for the fictional CyberDivision movement, the imaginary founder Dr. Bartha says, "We kill. It's OK. It's not our fault any more than breathing or urinating." Dr. Bartha claims that aggressive urges and impulses can be purged by playing violent video games. "It's a marketing campaign," said a SegaSoft spokesperson, "but there is some validity to the concept that you need an outlet for aggressive urges." Some people who play violent computer games, such as the following thirty-year-old video game player, agree: "When the world pisses you off and you need a place to vent, *Quake* [a violent video game] is a great place for it. You can kill somebody and watch the blood run down the walls, and it feels good. But when it's done, you're rid of it."

What do the scientific data say about the effects of viewing violence? Do violent media decrease or increase aggressive and violent behavior? Social

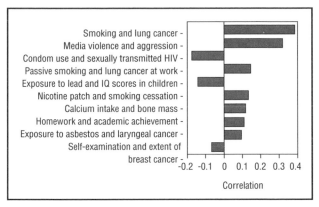

FIGURE 1. *Comparison of media violence effects from other domains.*

scientists have been very interested in this question since the late 1960s. The results from hundreds of studies have converged on the conclusion that viewing violence increases aggression. In fact, the U.S. Surgeon General came to this conclusion as early as 1972. The scientific evidence is overwhelming on this point. Viewing violence is definitely not cathartic—it increases rather than decreases anger and subsequent aggression.

Brad Bushman and his colleagues recently compared media violence effects with effects from other fields, and the results are displayed in Figure 1. A correlation can range from -1 to +1, with -1 indicating a perfect negative relation and +1 indicating a perfect positive relation. As the figure shows, all of the correlations for the studied effects are significantly different from zero. Note, however, that the second largest correlation is for violent media and aggression. Most people would agree that the other correlations displayed in Figure 1 are so strong that they are obvious. For example, most people would not question the assertion that taking calcium increases bone mass or that wearing a condom decreases the risk of contracting HIV, the virus that causes AIDS.

The correlation between media violence and aggression is only slightly smaller than that between smoking and lung cancer. Not everyone who smokes gets lung cancer, and not everyone who gets lung cancer is a smoker. But even the tobacco industry agrees that smoking causes lung cancer. Smoking is not the only factor that causes lung cancer, but it is an important factor. Similarly, not everyone who watches violent media becomes aggressive, and not everyone who is aggressive watches violent media. Watching violent media is not the only factor that causes aggression, but it is an important factor.

The smoking analogy is useful in other respects. Like a first cigarette, the first violent movie seen can make a person nauseous. Later, however, one craves more and more. The effects of smoking and viewing violence are both cumulative. Smoking one cigarette probably will not cause lung cancer. Likewise, seeing one violent movie probably will not turn a person into a psychopathic killer. However, repeated exposure to both cigarettes and violent media can have harmful consequences.

Catharsis theory is elegant and highly plausible, but it is false. It justifies and perpetuates the myth that viewing violence is healthy and beneficial, when in fact viewing violence is unhealthy and detrimental. After reviewing the scientific research, Carol Tavris (1988) concluded, "It is time to put a bullet, once and for all, through the heart of the catharsis hypothesis. The belief that observing violence (or 'ventilating it') gets rid of hostilities has virtually never been supported by research."

See also: VIDEO AND COMPUTER GAMES AND THE INTERNET; VIOLENCE IN THE MEDIA, ATTRACTION TO; VIOLENCE IN THE MEDIA, HISTORY OF RESEARCH ON.

Bibliography

Bushman, Brad J., and Huesmann, L. Rowell. (2000). "Effects of Televised Violence on Aggression." In *Handbook of Children and the Media*, eds. Dorothy G. Singer and Jerome L. Singer. Newbury Park, CA: Sage.

Geen, Russell G., and Bushman, Brad J. (1997). "Behavioral Effects of Observing Violence." In *Encyclopedia of Human Biology*, Vol. 1, ed. Renato Dulbecco. New York: Academic Press.

Smith, S. L., and Donnerstein, Edward. (1998). "Harmful Effects of Exposure to Media Violence: Learning of Aggression, Emotional Desensitization, and Fear." In *Human Aggression: Theories, Research, and Implications for Policy*, eds. Russell G. Geen and Edward Donnerstein. New York: Academic Press.

Tavris, Carol. (1988). "Beyond Cartoon Killings: Comments on Two Overlooked Effects of Television." In *Television as a Social Issue*, ed. Stuart Oskamp. Newbury Park, CA: Sage Publications.

BRAD J. BUSHMAN
COLLEEN M. PHILLIPS

CENSORSHIP

See: First Amendment and the Media; Intellectual Freedom and Censorship

CHAPLIN, CHARLIE (1889–1977)

Although his contributions to film extend from acting to directing, producing, and composing, it was his acting in silent films that brought Charlie Chaplin fame and made him the most widely recognized person of his era. He helped boost motion pictures from a novelty entertainment to a form of art, regularly breaking from convention to create fresh meaning.

Born in deep poverty in London, England, Charles Spencer Chaplin spent his early childhood in run-down housing, poorhouses, and even an orphanage. His music hall performer parents, Charles Chaplin and Lily Harley Chaplin, separated only a year after Chaplin was born. His father died in 1901 from liver complications as a result of his alcoholism, and his mother was placed in an asylum for the insane at about the same time.

Chaplin's acting career began when he was nine years of age. He soon left school and as a young teenager used his talent for entertaining to make living wages that were equivalent to those commonly earned by adults. Chaplin's brother, Sydney, got him a job in a comedy troupe in 1908. The touring troupe traveled to America, where Chaplin began to dream of working in the movie business. Mack Sennett, newly in charge of the Keystone Studios in Los Angeles, California, saw Chaplin's portrayal of a drunk with the comedy troupe and offered him a film-acting job in November 1913. His first film, *Making a Living* (1914), foreshadowed Chaplin's brilliant career as his creative impromptu comic antics stole the show and received accolades from audiences.

In only his second film, *Kid Auto Races at Venice* (1914), Chaplin invented his trademark jaunty slapstick "tramp" character (often called simply "Charlie") with baggy pants, a tight coat, big shoes, a small derby hat, and a cane. This costume (with some variations that still left it recognizably in tact) was used in most of the subsequent films that Chaplin would make—although the characterization of the tramp would change significantly. After acting in his first dozen or so films, Chaplin also began directing and codirecting many of the later Keystone films in which he appeared, mostly without the aid of a script.

In 1915, Chaplin achieved more artistic control and a much higher salary with a move to Essanay Studios, where he revealed new levels of character development and multidimensionality, showing a range of mood and personality elements in *The Tramp,* his sixth film with the company. The immortal characteristics of the tramp character, including his homelessness, his jaunty walk away from the camera, the lower stratum of society in which he moved, and the way the world always shunned him, first came together in this film. The character's persistent individuality, ability to overcome adversity and turmoil, and limitless empathy and compassion for another who was downtrodden have made this character into a social icon.

By 1916, Chaplin had again moved on, this time for a record $10,000 a week, to the Mutual Film Company. At Mutual, Chaplin had more time to make each movie, bigger budgets, and full artistic control. In his first Mutual film, *The Floorwalker* (1916), Chaplin began to emphasize the comedy's narrative structure or form. Instead of the gags and slapstick moves serving as the foundation around which a narrative is built, he began to create strong stories with elements of romance and pathos that are augmented by the comic elements. Other films of this nature that Chaplin made for Mutual include *The Vagabond* (1916), *Easy Street* (1917), and *The Immigrant* (1917).

Chaplin continued to emphasize romance and pathos in the eight films that he created at First National between 1918 and 1923, even though this was a very troubled period artistically and personally. *The Kid* (1921) was his most noted First National film, receiving accolades for the sensitivity that was expressed in the way the tramp became a reluctant father to an orphaned child. Some of his First National films, including the six-reel *The Kid,* stretched his work toward feature length. During this period, he also created his own Chaplin Studios.

Chaplin joined Douglas Fairbanks, Mary Pickford, and D. W. Griffith to form United Artists in 1919 (while he was still working at First National). This association of four of the top talents in Hollywood was designed to compete against the established studios that wanted to

A movie still shows Charlie Chaplin in the classic shoe-eating scene from The Gold Rush *(1925). (Bettmann/Corbis)*

monopolize the industry to keep salaries in check. It also offered Chaplin the opportunity to have utmost control over the films that he would make after fulfilling his contract with First National.

The Gold Rush (1925), a United Artists production, is most often considered to be Chaplin's greatest film, as well as one of the best films of the silent era. The scene in this film where the tramp character has a boiled shoe for dinner is a classic film moment. This film, which was a financial blockbuster for the financially strapped company, was the last Chaplin film to be finished before the advent of talking pictures.

When Chaplin moved to sound, he did so in gradual and masterful ways. Rather than purely embracing the new technology, he let it enhance the silent art, filming *City Lights* (1931) with no dialogue and *Modern Times* (1936) with very little, but both films had synchronized sound effects to enhance emotion and meaning. Chaplin's artistic greatness was solidified with his successful transition to "talkies" in *The Great Dictator* (1940). While the tramp remained silent, Chaplin adopted a new, boisterous tyrant persona as the dictator, Adenoid Hynkel, who was a representation of Adolf Hitler. Chaplin repeated this tyrant persona in *Monsieur Verdoux* (1947) and in *Limelight* (1952), the only other two talkies that he filmed in Hollywood.

Prior to the release of *Monsieur Verdoux*, Chaplin became the target of politicians during the "Red Scare" and his last two Hollywood films were ignored and boycotted. Chaplin left America for a trip to Europe in 1952 and, rather than answer U.S. Immigration Department questions about his political beliefs, chose to live out the rest of his life in Switzerland. He made two other movies, *A King in New York* (1957) and *A Countess from Hong Kong* (1967), but neither film lived up to the standards that he had set for himself in Hollywood.

Chaplin received a special Academy Award in 1972 for his contributions to the art of motion pictures. *Limelight* was also "officially released" and won an Oscar for best original dramatic score in 1973. Two years later, Queen Elizabeth II of England conferred a knighthood that made him "Sir Charles Chaplin." After a period of illness, Chaplin died at his home on Christmas day in 1977.

See also: FILM INDUSTRY, HISTORY OF; GRIFFITH, D. W.

Bibliography

Chaplin, Charles. (1964). *My Autobiography*. New York: Simon & Schuster.

Chaplin, Charles. (1975). *My Life in Pictures*. New York: Grosset & Dunlap.

Flom, Eric L. (1997). *Chaplin in the Sound Era: An Analysis of the Seven Talkies*. Jefferson, NC: McFarland & Company.

Maland, Charles J. (1989). *Chaplin and American Culture*. Princeton, NJ: Princeton University Press.

Robinson, David. (1985). *Chaplin: His Life and Art*. New York: McGraw-Hill.

Smith, Julian. (1984). *Chaplin*. Boston: Twayne.

Sobel, Raoul, and Francis, David. (1977). *Chaplin: Genesis of a Clown*. London: Quartet Books.

STEPHEN D. PERRY

CHARACTERS, ATTACHMENT TO

See: Attachment to Media Characters

CHIEF INFORMATION OFFICERS

The effective use of technology is an essential success factor in almost every aspect of the endeavors of any organization. As a result, the role of the chief information officer (CIO) grew and expanded rapidly in the 1980s and 1990s. This office began as the domain of engineering-based, technology-focused individuals who were able to make sense of the alphabet-soup world of technology jargon and equipment. By the beginning of the twenty-first century, however, this role had changed. The responsibilities of the CIO now focus on not only responsibility for the technology and information systems in an organization, but also on how the technology can be used to make the organization more effective and successful. The CIO must have both a strategic understanding of the workings and goals of the organization and a strategic understanding of technology. To be able to apply the technology to the workings of a specific business, industry, educational institution, or government agency, the CIO is most often a senior executive and a key player in the executive decisions of the entire organization.

Making Sure Technology Works for People

Peter DeLisi, founder and president of Organizational Synergies, has told a story that illustrates what a CIO position is *not*. Along a certain bus route in a big city, passengers who had waited patiently for a bus to arrive watched in disbelief as the bus driver smiled, waved, and drove along without stopping to pick them up. The boss asked the bus driver why he was not picking up any passengers. The driver replied that he would not be able to stay on time if he had to stop to pick up passengers, so he was skipping that part of the job. An organization does not care that their computer systems work well if those systems do not help people within the organization to accomplish their assigned tasks. The job of the CIO is to make sure that the technology works—the buses run on time—*and* that the technology is useful to the people in the organization—people are able to "get where they want to go" and get their work done.

The CIO is, of course, first of all expected to run an efficient information technology operation—the "buses" of the information technology system. The telephones, computers, networks, and all other technologies must be reliable and functional, and the staff who operates them must be customer-focused and helpful. This means that a CIO must know how to manage the technology procurement process and appropriately negotiate with suppliers. The CIO is responsible for buying the right technology for the organization at the best price. Often, he or she is the one who makes the decision about whether an organization should keep a certain technology function "in-house" (i.e., within the organization) or should buy that function from an outside company.

Frequently, one of the greatest areas of challenge for the CIO is determining and maintaining the technology infrastructure and architecture of an organization. Technology changes rapidly, and the network cables running through the walls of a building that were adequate for the computers of yesterday are often the wrong type for the new technology of today. The way the computers of an organization are networked together—the architecture of an information technology structure—often has to change as the company grows bigger, or is merged with another company that has a different system. At these times, the CIO is the individual responsible for keeping technology systems operational and integrated.

An Expanded Role

The CIO is responsible for a great deal more than just computer operations. For example, the CIO must be able to identify when a business or technology trend has the potential to radically redefine the way an organization does its work (i.e., improve its competitiveness and/or profitability). Then, the CIO must know how to assist the organization with that redefinition and how to obtain and implement the technology needed to make it all work.

More and more, business throughout the world is being done electronically, and the success of an organization often depends on "e-business" (or electronic commerce) opportunities and marketplaces. This means that the CIO is responsible for understanding the trends that are driving e-business at a particular time and how e-business is changing where an organization finds its customers.

Organizations are increasingly using information technology to share information and processes with business partners and customers so they can work together in new ways. The CIO is often assigned the key liaison role with these partners and customers and is responsible for determining both the processes and the technologies that must be designed and implemented to create an effective collaborative environment.

In the information age, any organization with the right information can effectively and aggressively compete with another organization. In the business world in particular, the information a

company has—about its customers, price–cost relationships, distribution models, and processes—is one of the most valuable assets of the company. The vast majority of this information is obtained and maintained in an electronic format, on computers. Collecting, analyzing, and protecting this information is often a key responsibility of the CIO, who is also responsible for maintaining the privacy and security of organizational information.

Educational and Professional Requirements

Because the CIO is generally one of the executives at the highest level of an organization, the educational and professional requirements for the position depend on what is expected of others at that level in the organization. For example, in the field of higher education, the CIO is generally expected to have advanced degrees and experience teaching or working in comparable colleges or universities. In the world of business and industry, the CIO is generally expected to have a strong business background and education, which may include management experience not only in technology but also in other aspects of the company's endeavors.

A "Big Picture" Job

The role of a CIO is one best suited for those who enjoy a "big picture" perspective. The CIO is in a better position than almost anyone else in an organization to understand the business from an enterprise-wide perspective. The CIO must appreciate and understand information technology, but he or she must be most enthusiastic about what the technology can do to help people and the organization accomplish their goals. Rather than behaving like the bus driver concerned about meeting a timetable, a good CIO must be interested in and working on the whole system—the buses, the routes, the timetables, picking up the passengers, knowing where they want to go, and getting them there on time. The position of chief information officer can be an exciting role for those who not only enjoy technology, but also understand its ability to transform the activities of an organization.

See also: ELECTRONIC COMMERCE; KNOWLEDGE MANAGEMENT; KNOWLEDGE MANAGEMENT, CAREERS IN; MANAGEMENT INFORMATION SYSTEMS; SYSTEMS DESIGNERS.

JOSÉ-MARIE GRIFFITHS

■ CHILDREN AND ADVERTISING

Most children have their first encounter with advertising messages while they are watching television. It is common for children to begin television viewing by the time that they are two years of age, long before they have developed the reading ability that is required to make advertising in print media accessible. Because children at this age lack the cognitive skills and abilities of older children or adults, they do not understand commercial messages in the same way as do more mature audiences, and hence they are more susceptible to the influence of advertising. A substantial body of research evidence documents age-related differences in how children understand and are affected by television advertising.

Children's Exposure to Television Advertising

It is estimated that the average child views more than forty thousand television commercials each year, most of which are fifteen to thirty seconds in length. Advertisers target the youth market because of its strong contribution to the consumer economy. According to 1998 data, children who are fourteen years of age and under spent $24 billion and influenced $188 billion in family purchases.

Approximately 80 percent of all advertising to children falls within four product categories: toys, cereals, candies, and fast-food restaurants. This pattern has remained remarkably stable since the 1970s. During the fourth quarter (October–December) of each calendar year, a seasonal shift in advertising practices occurs with toy commercials airing much more frequently during the pre-Christmas months.

The most common theme or appeal (i.e., persuasive strategy) that is employed in advertising to children is to associate the product with fun and happiness, rather than to provide any factual product-related information. For example, a commercial that features Ronald McDonald dancing, singing, and smiling in McDonald's restaurants, without any mention of the actual food products that are available, reflects a fun and happiness theme. This strategy is also found frequently with cereal advertisements, which often include the appearance of characters (e.g., Tony the Tiger, Cap'n Crunch) to help children identify the product. In contrast, most commercials fail even to mention the major grain used in each cereal unless it is included as part of the product name (e.g., Corn Flakes).

Another common feature of advertising to children is the use of product disclosures and disclaimers such as "batteries not included" or "each part sold separately." However, studies make clear that young children do not comprehend the intended meaning of the most widely used disclaimers. For example, Diane Liebert and her associates (1977) found that fewer than one in four kindergarten through second-grade children could grasp the meaning of "some assembly required" in a commercial; in contrast, the use of child-friendly language such as "you have to put it together" more than doubled the proportion of children who understood the qualifying message.

The phrase "part of a balanced breakfast" is a disclosure that is frequently included in most cereal advertisements to combat the concern that sugared cereal products hold little nutritional value for children. Consistent with the data on toy disclaimers, research by Edward Palmer and Cynthia McDowell (1981) shows that most children below seven years of age have no idea what the term "balanced breakfast" means. Rather than informing young viewers about the importance of a nutritious breakfast, this common disclaimer actually leaves many children with the misimpression that cereal alone is sufficient for a meal.

Children's Comprehension of Television Advertising

Children must acquire two key information-processing skills in order to achieve "mature" comprehension of advertising messages. First, they must be able to discriminate (at a perceptual level) between commercial and noncommercial content. Second, they must be able to attribute persuasive intent to advertising and to apply a degree of skepticism that is consistent with that knowledge to their interpretation of advertising messages. Each of these capabilities develops over time as a function of cognitive growth in conceptual and analytical ability.

Program-Commercial Discrimination

In their earliest years of television viewing, children do not yet recognize that there are two fundamentally different categories of television content: programs and commercials. Most children who are younger than four to five years of age exhibit low awareness of the concept of commercials, frequently explaining them as if they were a scene in the adjacent program. When this confusion diminishes, children first recognize the difference between programs and commercials based on either affective cues (e.g., "commercials are more funny than programs") or perceptual cues (e.g., "commercials are short and programs are long").

Most children's television shows include program–commercial separation devices (e.g., "We'll be right back after these messages") whenever a commercial break occurs. However, several studies indicate that these separators generally do not help child viewers to recognize advertising content. This likely occurs because most separation devices are not perceptually distinct from the adjacent programming that surrounds them; in fact, many separators feature characters who appear in the show that the commercial has just interrupted.

Popular program figures are frequently used in advertising that is directed to children. When an advertisement includes one of the same characters who is featured in an adjacent program, the practice is known as "host-selling." For example, Fred Flintstone appearing in an advertisement for "Fruity Pebbles" cereal that is shown during a break in the *Flintstones* cartoon show would be considered host-selling. A study by Dale Kunkel (1988) shows that this type of advertising makes the task of discriminating between program and commercial content particularly difficult for young children.

In sum, a substantial proportion of young children do not consistently discriminate between television program and commercial content. By about the time they are four or five years of age, however, most children develop the ability to distinguish between these two types of content quite well at a perceptual level. Still, this ability is only the first of two critical information processing tasks that young children must master in order to achieve mature comprehension of advertising messages.

Recognition of Persuasive Intent

The primary purpose of television advertising is to influence the attitudes and subsequent behavior of viewers. For adults, the recognition that a given message is a commercial triggers a cognitive filter or defense mechanism that takes

The use of characters in settings other than a television commercial, such as featuring Tony the Tiger in the Hot Air Balloon Fiesta in Albuquerque, New Mexico, is a subtle advertising technique designed to reinforce children's interest in the products that the characters represent. (*The Purcell Team/Corbis*)

into account factors such as the following: (1) the source of the message has other interests and perspectives than those of the receiver, (2) the source intends to persuade, (3) persuasive messages are biased, and (4) biased messages demand different interpretive strategies than do unbiased messages. When all of these considerations can be taken into account, then a child can be said to have achieved mature comprehension of the advertising process.

Young children, by virtue of their limited cognitive development, typically lack the ability to recognize the persuasive intent of television advertising until they reach seven to eight years of age. Prior to this point, children are generally egocentric and have difficulty taking the perspective of another person. This makes it difficult to recognize that commercial claims and appeals are likely to be biased or exaggerated in order to portray the advertised product in the most favorable light.

Some researchers, such as Thomas Donahue and his associates (1980), have argued that children may understand persuasive intent at a slightly earlier age. Such claims are made on the basis of evidence that indicates that younger children may report that a commercial wants the viewer to buy the advertised product. Such awareness, however, does not necessarily reflect an appreciation of persuasive intent. Just because a child understands that an advertisement seeks to sell a product, it does not automatically follow that the child will recognize the bias that is inherent in persuasive messages and therefore view advertising claims and appeals more skeptically. Overall, the weight of the evidence indicates that most children who are younger than about seven to eight years of age do not typically recognize that the underlying goal of a commercial is to persuade.

Effects of Television Advertising on Children

The effect of television advertising on children can be categorized according to both the intended and unintended effects that result from advertising exposure. For example, a cereal advertisement may have the intended effect of generating product purchase requests and increasing product consumption, but it may also contribute to unintended outcomes such as misperceptions about proper nutritional habits and/or parent–child conflict if a child's attempt to get a parent to purchase the product (i.e., purchase-influence attempt) is rejected.

Intended Effects

Many studies document the effectiveness of commercial campaigns at influencing child viewers' recall for the product, desire for the advertised product, and—depending on the age of the child—either purchase-influence attempts or actual purchase of the product.

Experimental studies that compare children who are shown a particular commercial with those who are not provide some of the most direct evidence of advertising effect. While it is typical for half or more of the children in a control group to report spontaneously a strong desire for a given toy or cereal (i.e., even without being shown a related commercial), exposure to an advertisement leads to statistically significant increases in children's desire for the advertised merchandise. From another perspective, survey research indicates that children who watch greater amounts of television (and hence are exposed to a higher volume of advertisements) tend to make a greater number of purchase-influence attempts when they are shopping with their parents at the supermarket.

Certain advertising strategies tend to enhance the effectiveness of advertising appeals to children. For example, advertising for cereals and fast-food meals often emphasize premium offers, such as a small toy figure included along with the product. In a study by Charles Atkin (1978), where researchers unobtrusively observed parents and children shopping at the supermarket, it was found that almost half of the children who were making product-purchase requests in the cereal aisle were influenced by premium offers.

Research also makes clear that children's purchase-influence attempts have a relatively high degree of success. Frequent parental yielding to children's purchase requests has been reported in studies that rely on parent self-reports as well as unobtrusive observation of behavior in the supermarket. In sum, although the process may be indirect, television commercials that are targeted at children are highly effective at accomplishing their intended goal of promoting product sales.

Unintended Effects

Although each advertisement may have as its primary purpose the goal of promoting product sales, the cumulative effect from children's long-term exposure to television advertising may exert far broader sociological influence. Some researchers have argued that one of the long-term effects of children's exposure to commercials is an increase in materialistic attitudes, although this is particularly difficult to establish because few children in the United States grow up without extensive media exposure, and thus no control group is available for comparative purposes. In other areas, however, several unintended effects of advertising have been more convincingly demonstrated.

One of the most visible of these unintended effects is the influence of television advertising on children's eating habits. Commercials for candies, snacks, sugared cereals, and fast foods represent a large proportion of the advertising that is presented during children's programs, while advertising for more healthy or nutritious foods is rare. Consequently, children tend to develop poor nutritional habits, mistakenly assuming that the products that they see advertised are an appropriate diet whenever they are hungry.

Advertisements for alcoholic beverages such as beer products, even though they are not intended for children, are nonetheless seen by many young viewers. Exposure to alcohol advertising exerts influence on young people's alcohol expectancies (e.g., when it is appropriate to drink; what happens when one drinks), which have in turn been shown to predict drinking behaviors later in life.

Another important area of unintended effects involves parent–child conflicts that emerge when children's purchase-influence attempts are refused. Parents obviously cannot honor all purchase requests that are triggered by television advertising. Studies have shown that a majority of children become angry, disappointed, or argumentative when purchase requests are denied. The frequent purchase requests that are associated with children's heavy exposure to television advertising may place a strain on parent–child interaction at times, an issue of consequence largely because of the sheer volume of commercials that are viewed by most children.

Conclusion

Children are a vulnerable audience, with limited information-processing capabilities that constrain their early understanding of the nature and purpose of television advertising. Because of these limitations, young children are more easily persuadable than are older children or adults. They are more trusting of advertising claims and appeals, and they are more susceptible to commercial persuasion. This situation has led over the years to varying legal restrictions on television advertising to children. Advertisers may air no more than 10.5 minutes of commercials during each hour of children's programming shown during weekends, and they may air no more than 12 minutes of commercials per hour during weekdays. In addition, certain advertising practices such as host-selling are prohibited by the Federal Communications Commission. Even with these policies in effect, this topic area remains controversial. Given the huge economic stakes that are associated with marketing to children, debates are likely to continue with regard to the need for further regulation to protect children's interests.

See also: ADVERTISING EFFECTS; ALCOHOL IN THE MEDIA; CHILDREN'S COMPREHENSION OF TELEVISION; NUTRITION AND MEDIA EFFECTS; PARENTAL MEDIATION OF MEDIA EFFECTS.

Bibliography

Adler, Richard; Lesser, Gerald; Meringoff, Laurene; Robertson, Tom; Rossiter, John; and Ward, Scott. (1980). *The Effects of Television Advertising on Children: Review and Recommendations.* Lexington, MA: Lexington Books.

Atkin, Charles. (1978). "Observation of Parent–Child Interaction in Supermarket Decision-Making." *Journal of Marketing* 42:41–45.

Blosser, Betsy, and Roberts, Donald. (1985). "Age Differences in Children's Perceptions of Message Intent: Responses to TV News, Commercials, Educational Spots, and Public Service Announcements." *Communication Research* 12:455–484.

Butter, Eliot J.; Popovich, Paula M.; Stackhouse, Robert H.; and Garner, Roger K. (1981). "Discrimination of Television Programs and Commercials by Preschool Children." *Journal of Advertising Research* 21(2):53–56.

Comstock, George, and Paik, Haejung. (1991). *Television and the American Child.* New York: Academic Press.

Donahue, Thomas; Henke, Lucy; and Donahue, William. (1980). "Do Kids Know What TV Commercials Intend?" *Journal of Advertising Research* 20:51–57.

Grube, Joel. (1993). "Alcohol Portrayals and Alcohol Advertising on Television: Content and Effects on Children and Adolescents." *Alcohol Health and Research World* 17(1):61–66.

Kunkel, Dale. (1988). "Children and Host-Selling Television Commercials." *Communication Research* 15:71–92.

Kunkel, Dale, and Gantz, Walter. (1992). "Children's Television Advertising in the Multi-Channel Environment." *Journal of Communication* 42(3):134–152.

Liebert, Diane; Sprafkin, Joyce; Liebert, Robert; and Rubinstein, Eli. (1977). "Effects of Television Commercial Disclaimers on the Product Expectations of Children." *Journal of Communication* 27(1):118–124.

Levin, Stephen; Petros, Thomas; and Petrella, Florence. (1982). "Preschoolers' Awareness of Television Advertising." *Child Development* 53:933–937.

Macklin, M. Carole. (1985). "Do Young Children Understand the Selling Intent of Commercials?" *Journal of Consumer Affairs* 19:293–304.

McNeal, James. (1992). *Kids as Customers.* New York: Lexington Books.

Palmer, Edward, and McDowell, Cynthia. (1981). "Children's Understanding of Nutritional Information Presented in Breakfast Cereal Commercials." *Journal of Broadcasting* 25:295–301.

Ward, Scott; Wackman, Daniel; and Wartella, Ellen. (1977). *How Children Learn to Buy: The Development of Consumer Information Processing Skills.* Beverly Hills, CA: Sage Publications.

Young, Brian. (1990). *Television Advertising and Children*. Oxford, Eng.: Clarendon Press.

DALE KUNKEL

■ CHILDREN'S ACADEMIC ACHIEVEMENT

See: Academic Achievement and Children's Television Use

■ CHILDREN'S ATTENTION TO TELEVISION

Understanding the nature of children's attention to television helps to clarify the fundamental nature of television viewing and its effect on children. As a practical matter, understanding when and how children pay attention to television has been useful in designing television programs for children (e.g., *Blue's Clues* and *Sesame Street*).

The term "attention" refers to selective perceptual and cognitive activities that are directed toward a restricted portion of a person's environment. Brain research shows that when a person pays attention to an object in the environment, brain activation associated with perception of that object is enhanced, whereas brain activation associated with perception of other objects in the environment is suppressed.

There is no direct way to measure attention to television; rather, attention must be inferred from behavior or from physiological measures. The indicator of attention to television that has been most commonly measured in research with children is looking at the television screen. A look begins when the viewer directs his or her gaze toward the screen and ends when the viewer looks away. In addition, a small scattering of studies have employed other measures, such as eye movements while looking at the screen, reaction times to a secondary task while watching television, changes in heart rate, and the time it takes to push a button to fix a disturbance in the audio portion of a television show.

The most basic observation is that looking at television is variable. Viewers may look at the screen and look away again many times in the course of a viewing session. When preschool children watch an age-appropriate television program in a room that contains toys with which they can play, other things to look at, or other children with whom they can interact, they look at and away from the screen approximately 150 times an hour, with looks averaging about 13 seconds in length (e.g., Anderson, Lorch, Smith, Bradford, and Levin, 1981). Similar patterns have been observed for older children and adults when they watch television in a setting that affords alternative activities besides television viewing (e.g., Burns and Anderson, 1993).

Looking at Television

Much of the research on attention to television has been directed at explaining why children initiate, sustain, and end looks at a television screen. The most straightforward factor that influences children's looking at a television program is the viewing environment. If children watch television in a quiet room that permits no other activities, then they look at the screen more than if there are toys available or other children present (e.g., Anderson, Lorch, Smith, Bradford, and Levin, 1981; Lorch, Anderson, and Levin, 1979).

Because children's homes afford a variety of activities in which viewers can engage while watching television, their looking at the screen is substantially less than 100 percent. Looking at television, moreover, varies with the age of the viewer. Infants under one year of age look at television less than 10 percent of the time they are within sight of a set that is in use. Thereafter, the level of looking steadily increases with age until it reaches a level of about 80 percent in late childhood, after which point it declines to about 60 percent during adulthood (Anderson, Lorch, Collins, Field, and Nathan, 1986).

What accounts for these age differences? For younger children, the comprehensibility of the programming is a central factor. For example, presenting attractive television content in a foreign language, or in backward English, or with the shots presented in random order dramatically reduces preschool children's looking (Anderson, Lorch, Field, and Sanders, 1981). Infants are able to understand little of what they see on television and, consequently, they pay little attention to the screen. What attention they do pay is probably elicited by movement and visual change (e.g., Richards and Gibson, 1997). Looking at television dramatically increases from one to three years of age as cognitive skills and receptive vocabulary grow.

As children mature, their increasing cognitive development and world knowledge allow more and more television programming to become understandable. Levels of looking at television therefore increase until late childhood, at which point most adult programs are fully comprehensible (Collins, 1983). The drop in levels of looking by adults is understandable because most of television is relatively simple for an adult to comprehend without paying full visual attention. Consequently, television is commonly timeshared by adults with chores, socializing, and reading (e.g., Anderson and Field, 1991).

When children watch a television program that is generally understandable to them, they tend to look more when the content is cognitively demanding or requires visual attention for full comprehension (e.g., Field and Anderson, 1985). It is not surprising that the personal relevance of the content itself is of the utmost importance in sustaining attention. For example, children look substantially more at children's programming than they do at adult programming, with the difference reaching a peak at about five years of age. From that point, the difference in favor of children's programming declines until about eleven years of age, after which there is a distinct attentional preference for adult programming (Schmitt, Anderson, and Collins, 1999). These changes, of course, correspond to children's changing interests as they approach adolescence. As another example of the importance of personal relevance, children of both sexes look more at female characters than they do at male characters (reflecting the influence of predominantly female caretakers of young children), until they achieve the concept of gender constancy (at about ages five to six years). Gender constancy is achieved when the child gains a substantial understanding that one's own and others' sex is permanent and immutable. After that time, they look more at characters of their own sex (Luecke-Aleksa, Anderson, Collins, and Schmitt, 1995).

Preschool children are highly similar to each other with respect to the points in television programs where they initiate looks at the screen. Children become even more similar as they get older. On the other hand, children are somewhat more idiosyncratic about the points at which they look away, and they become less similar to each other in this respect as they get older (Anderson, Lorch, Smith, Bradford, and Levin, 1981).

The use of puppets can serve to increase the amount of attention that children pay to television, which has been exemplified by the popularity of Jim Henson's characters, including "Ernie" and "Kermit the Frog," on Sesame Street since the 1970s. (Bettmann/Corbis)

Studies of the formal features of television have clarified the reasons for these findings. Formal features are aspects of television that can be described without specific reference to the content of the programming. These include editing and camera techniques such as cuts, pans, zooms, and dollies, as well as production techniques such as animation. Also included within the general concept of formal features are audio features such as sound effects, voice type (such as adult male voice), music, and applause. Additionally, character types (e.g., man, woman, child, animal, puppet) are often included in studies of formal features.

When a child is visually inattentive to the television, audio variations, such as change of speaker, sound effects, applause, peculiar voices, children's voices, and the onset of music, consistently attract looking at the television screen. The fact that, with viewing experience, children become more similar in terms of the points at which they initiate looks at television programs reflects their learning that these auditory features are cues to changing content and content of particular interest.

Visual movement and cuts sustain looking, as do child characters and puppets. Adult men, men's voices, and long zoom shots are associated with child viewers looking away from the television screen (e.g., Alwitt, Anderson, Lorch, and Levin, 1980). It is likely that many of these relationships of the visual features to looking are strongly related to the content with which the features typically appear. For example, adult men are ubiquitous on television (appearing much more frequently than women) and tend to be associated with adult-oriented content. Consequently, children associate men with less comprehensible and less personally relevant content. Familiar adult men associated with popular children's programs (e.g., Fred Rogers on *Mister Rogers' Neighborhood*; Steve Burns on *Blue's Clues*), on the other hand, are less likely to produce the negative relationship to children's attention. It is interesting that when content is controlled, there is no evidence that children look at animation more than live-action video (Schmitt, Anderson, and Collins, 1999). Nevertheless, when content is controlled, children look more at programming that is produced with formal features that are typical of children's television (Campbell, Wright, and Huston, 1987). Across all types of content and all ages of viewers, the formal features that have the most consistent relationships to looking are cuts and movement (e.g., Schmitt, Anderson, and Collins, 1999).

Studies with adults have observed that attention can be deployed with greater or lesser intensity. This appears to be true in the case of attention to television, and particularly in the phenomenon of attentional inertia. Attentional inertia was first described when it was shown that the longer a look at television is sustained, the less probable it is, in each successive second, that the viewer will look away. One consequence of this attentional inertia is that while typical looks are relatively short (i.e., less than fifteen seconds in length), there are some very long looks at television that are many minutes in duration, thus producing a highly skewed lognormal statistical distribution of look lengths. Attentional inertia in looking at television is not limited to adult viewers; it has been

found in infants and children as well (Burns and Anderson, 1993; Richards and Gibson, 1997). Investigations of attentional inertia reveal that as a look at television is sustained, viewers become progressively less distractible by stimuli that is external to the television, patterns of heart rate indicate progressively deepened attention, and memory for television content increases (e.g., Burns and Anderson, 1993; Richards and Gibson, 1997). It is likely that attentional inertia is not uniquely limited to television insofar as similar patterns of attention have been reported for children's toy play and reading. In any case, long periods of continuous looking at television indicate deeply engaged attention and increased information processing. Another consequence of attentional inertia during television viewing is that the viewer who has continuously looked at the screen for an extended period of time is more likely to keep looking at completely new content, such as a commercial (Burns and Anderson, 1993).

Listening to Television

Compared to looking, much less is known about auditory attention to television. Two studies have found that children better remembered dialogues if they were looking at the screen at the time when the dialogues occurred, suggesting that children tend to listen primarily when they are looking (Field and Anderson, 1985; Lorch, Anderson, and Levin, 1979). In addition, one study found that this link diminished from four to seven years of age, suggesting that older children are more likely to listen to the television even when they are not looking at it (Field and Anderson, 1985).

A study with adults found that they were progressively less likely to recognize snippets of audio from a program if they were not looking at the screen at the time the audio occurred. Moreover, the longer it had been since they had looked at the screen, the less likely they were to recognize the audio. This suggests that viewers progressively withdraw their auditory attention after withdrawing their visual attention (Burns and Anderson, 1993). Although the evidence suggests that viewers listen primarily when they look, there are some results that conflict with this interpretation. It is clear, as noted above, that young children are sensitive to auditory changes when they are not looking at the television. Additionally, in one study that required children to push a button to fix a distorted audio track, the researchers found that children were equally quick to fix the audio whether or not they were not looking at the television at the time when the distortion occurred (Rolandelli, Wright, Huston, and Eakins, 1991).

Basic Viewpoints about Attention

There are three main viewpoints on children's attention to television. The first, and simplest, is that children's attention is reflexively elicited by visual change and movement (Singer, 1980). While the evidence indicates that visual change and movement do help sustain attention, there are clearly many other factors that are as influential, if not more so.

The second viewpoint is that attention to television is primarily driven by the child's engagement with the content and that patterns of attention are largely in the service of comprehension (Anderson and Lorch, 1983). This perspective readily accounts for differing patterns of attention in relation to program comprehensibility and age. The theory falls short, however, in explaining the consistent effects of movement and visual change.

The third theory, which is more comprehensive, incorporates aspects of the other two perspectives (Huston and Wright, 1989). Taking into account the role of formal features in conveying content, this theory proposes that children learn how to watch television, gradually moving from a more reflexive form of attention to a more controlled and strategic form.

Conclusion

A number of writers who are concerned with children and education have argued that television produces mindlessly "mesmerized" children who become inattentive to language because of television's visual nature. The research, however, finds little to support these arguments. Children's attention to television is variable, cued by formal features, and sustained by engagement with the content, including language. To the degree that comparisons can be made, attention to television is comparable in many respects to the attention that children pay to other media and to their world in general.

See also: CHILDREN AND ADVERTISING; CHILDREN'S COMPREHENSION OF TELEVISION; CHILDREN'S PREFERENCES FOR MEDIA CONTENT; PARENTAL MEDIATION OF MEDIA EFFECTS; SESAME STREET; TELEVISION, EDUCATIONAL.

Bibliography

Alwitt, Linda F.; Anderson, Daniel R.; Lorch, Elizabeth Pugzles; and Levin, Stephan R. (1980). "Preschool Children's Visual Attention to Attributes of Television." *Human Communication Research* 7:52–67.

Anderson, Daniel R. (1998). "Educational Television Is Not an Oxymoron." *Annals of Public Policy Research* 557:24–38.

Anderson, Daniel R., and Field, Diane E. (1991). "Online and Offline Assessment of the Television Audience." In *Responding to the Screen: Perception and Reaction Processes*, eds. Dolf Zillmann and Jennings Bryant. Hillsdale, NJ: Lawrence Erlbaum.

Anderson, Daniel. R., and Lorch, Elizabeth Pugzles. (1983). "Looking at Television: Action or Reaction?" In *Children's Understanding of TV: Research on Attention and Comprehension*, eds. Jennings Bryant and Daniel R. Anderson. New York: Academic Press.

Anderson, Daniel R.; Lorch, Elizabeth Pugzles; Collins, Patricia A.; Field, Diane E.; and Nathan, John G. (1986). "Television Viewing at Home: Age Trends in Visual Attention and Time with TV." *Child Development* 57:1024–1033.

Anderson, Daniel R.; Lorch, Elizabeth Pugzles; Field, Diane E.; and Sanders, Jeanne. (1981). "The Effect of Television Program Comprehensibility on Preschool Children's Visual Attention to Television." *Child Development* 52:151–157.

Anderson, Daniel R.; Lorch, Elizabeth Pugzles; Smith, Robin; Bradford, Rex; and Levin, Stephan R. (1981). "The Effects of Peer Presence on Preschool Children's Television Viewing Behavior." *Developmental Psychology* 17:446–453.

Burns, John J., and Anderson, Daniel R. (1993). "Attentional Inertia and Recognition Memory in Adult Television Viewing." *Communication Research* 20:777–799.

Campbell, Toni A.; Wright, John C.; and Huston, Aletha C. (1987). "Form Cues and Content Difficulty as Determinants of Children's Cognitive Processing of Televised Educational Messages." *Journal of Experimental Child Psychology* 43:311–327.

Collins, W. Andrew. (1983). "Interpretation and Inference in Children's Television Viewing." In *Children's Understanding of Television: Research on Attention and Comprehension*, eds. Jennings. Bryant and Daniel R. Anderson. New York: Academic Press.

Field, Diane E., and Anderson, Daniel.R. (1985). "Instruction and Modality Effects on Children's Television Comprehension and Attention." *Journal of Educational Psychology* 77:91–100.

Healy, Jane M. (1990). *Endangered Minds: Why Our Children Can't Think.* New York: Simon & Schuster.

Huston, Aletha C., and Wright, John C. (1989). "The Forms of Television and the Child Viewer." In *Public Communication and Behavior,* Vol. 2, ed. George Comstock. Orlando, FL: Academic Press.

Lorch, Elizabeth Pugzles; Anderson, Daniel R.; and Levin, Stephan R. (1979). "The Relationship of Visual Attention and Comprehension of Television by Preschool Children." *Child Development* 50:722–727.

Luecke-Aleksa, Diane; Anderson, Daniel R.; Collins, Patricia A.; and Schmitt, Kelly L. (1995). "Gender Constancy and Television Viewing." *Developmental Psychology* 31:773–780.

Richards, John E., and Gibson, Therese L. (1997). "Extended Visual Fixation in Young Infants: Fixation Distributions, Heart Rate Changes, and Attention." *Child Development* 68:1041–1056.

Rolandelli, David R.; Wright, John C.; Huston, Aletha C.; and Eakins, Darwin. (1991). "Children's Auditory and Visual Processing of Narrated and Non-Narrated Television Programming." *Journal of Experimental Child Psychology* 51:90–122.

Schmitt, Kelly L.; Anderson, Daniel R.; and Collins, Patricia A. (1999). "Form and Content: Looking at Visual Features of Television." *Developmental Psychology* 35:1156–1167.

Singer, Jerome L. (1980). "The Power and Limitations of Television: A Cognitive–Affective Analysis." In *The Entertainment Functions of Television,* ed. Percy H. Tannenbaum. Hillsdale, NJ: Lawrence Erlbaum.

DANIEL R. ANDERSON

■ CHILDREN'S COMPREHENSION OF TELEVISION

Some critics of television have referred to the medium as a "plug-in drug" that causes children to become "zombie viewers" who take in information passively, rather than actively. However, research has shown that children actually are not passive while watching television. Rather, they are active viewers who engage in various forms of mental processing to construct an understanding of the programs they are watching.

Imagine, for instance, children watching a television program in which the detective hero investigates a mystery at a baseball stadium and (in a surprising twist ending) deduces that the pitcher's best friend is the one who stole his lucky cap. Numerous mental operations are necessary for viewers to make sense of and follow

this story correctly. On the most basic level, they must comprehend the dialogue and visual action presented. They must access their prior knowledge of baseball to grasp the context in which the action takes place. They must isolate information that is central to moving the plot forward from the incidental information that accompanies it. They must infer the motivations of the characters and reconcile the culprit's deceptive behavior as a "best friend" with his ulterior motives and crime. And many other operations must occur as well.

In cognitive psychology terms, television programs are complex audiovisual stimuli. To understand them, viewers must integrate a range of visual and auditory information: visual action, dialogue, gestures, intonation, and so on. In addition, comprehension of stories on television requires viewers to perform a variety of cognitive tasks and metacognitive tasks (i.e., tasks that monitor or control the process of comprehension), such as distinguishing between information that is central and incidental to the plot, organizing objects and events within scenes, integrating information across separate scenes, and drawing inferences about events, characters, and their motivations. The demands of this mental processing are compounded by the fact that, unlike reading, broadcast television is not self-paced. Television viewers cannot control the speed of the incoming information or review material that is difficult for them to understand; instead, the processing that underlies comprehension must fit the pace of the television program.

In light of the complexity of the incoming information and the challenges involved in making sense of it, it is not surprising that many studies have found consistent age differences in children's comprehension of television programs. Children under two years of age have been found to comprehend and imitate simple actions they have seen on a television screen. Yet, even second-grade children (i.e., eight-year-olds)—and in some respects, fifth graders—do not understand television programs as well as older children and adults. Research by W. Andrew Collins (1983) and his colleagues has shown that the deficits in young children's understanding stem primarily from several factors. While viewers of all ages draw on prior knowledge to help them understand material on television (and everything else in life), the recall exhibited by second-graders with regard to televised stories has been found to be fairly limited to stereotyped common knowledge (e.g., that police officers wear uniforms). Older viewers, on the other hand, are better able to recognize deviations from common knowledge and rely on information specific to the individual program or story (e.g., that a character without a uniform is a plainclothes police officer). In contrast to older viewers, second-grade children also have difficulty understanding the links between aggression on television and either its consequences or the motives of the characters involved, particularly when the motives, actions, and consequences are presented in separate scenes. (Indeed, this lack of understanding could contribute to children's imitating the aggressive behavior, since they may not understand its roots or consequences.) Finally, older viewers are more skilled at drawing inferences about events and the motives of characters; these differences have been most pronounced for inferences that are relatively abstract or require a greater number of inferential steps (e.g., recognizing an undercover police officer from the person's actions rather than from seeing a badge).

Factors Affecting Comprehension

Broadly speaking, children's comprehension of television rests upon three classes of factors: (1) characteristics of the viewing situation, (2) characteristics of the child, and (3) characteristics of the program. The "viewing situation" refers to the settings in which children watch television. For example, there may be distractions in the children's environment that draw their attention away from important parts of the program and reduce comprehension. Conversely, children may be watching with a parent or someone else who can point out important information in the program, thus helping to increase comprehension.

"Characteristics of the child" refers to the knowledge and cognitive abilities that children bring to the viewing experience and that help them make sense of the programs they watch. One obvious type of knowledge that children apply is their knowledge of the world around them; for example, it is probably easier for a viewer who knows a great deal about baseball (e.g., the rules of the game, the typical sequence of events in a game) to understand a television drama about a baseball game than it is for a viewer who has never seen a baseball game before. Such knowledge includes social knowledge (i.e., knowledge about the ways in which people interact) as well as more strictly "cognitive" knowledge. A second type of knowledge is program-specific knowledge regarding the characters, settings, and events in the particular program that a child is watching. Because regular viewers of a television series are already familiar with its format, the setting in which it takes place, and the relationships among its characters, this knowledge provides a base upon which they can build their understanding of each new episode. This provides a clear advantage over first-time viewers, who would have to construct all of this background knowledge from scratch while watching that same episode.

On a more abstract level, comprehension has been shown to be aided by prior knowledge of story schemas (i.e., the prototypical ways in which stories are structured). Similarly, comprehension can also be aided by a prior understanding of standard television conventions or "formal features," such as cuts, fades, or montage. These conventions convey narrative information in and of themselves; for example, sophisticated television viewers understand that the brief series of images presented in a montage might actually represent a large number of events or a longer passage of time.

Apart from their prior knowledge, children also bring a variety of cognitive abilities to the screen. One of these, as discussed above, is their skill at drawing inferences. Inferences are essential in understanding dialogue, creating mental representations of the physical settings in which the action occurs (e.g., where the characters are standing when only one of them is on-screen), grasping the motives of characters, linking information across scenes, and so on. Other sets of abilities include the same kinds of linguistic, visual, and information-processing skills that allow children to decode and make sense of visual and verbal information in face-to-face interactions. Finally, Gavriel Salomon (1983) showed that comprehension is also affected by the amount of mental effort viewers devote to the program; when children invest more mental effort (i.e., "work harder") in understanding a television program, their comprehension of the program is enhanced.

"Characteristics of the program" refer to features of the television program itself that can make it easier or more difficult for viewers to comprehend. Following from the discussion of inferences above, one relevant program characteristic is the degree to which important information is made explicit or must be inferred; explicit information is easier to comprehend, particularly for younger children. Another characteristic is the degree to which formal features are used to emphasize and draw the attention of viewers toward (or away from) information that is central to the plot, as when a close-up is used to highlight an important object in a scene. A third, related characteristic concerns the kinds of formal features that are employed in the program, and the ways in which they are used. For example, children below the age of six have been found to have difficulty understanding formal features that violate reality (e.g., thinking that an instant replay is a new event, rather than a repeat of something that has already been shown). A fourth characteristic centers on the relationship between visual and verbal information in the program; research has shown comprehension to be strongest when the same information is presented both visually and verbally at the same time. When different information is presented visually and verbally, children tend to show better comprehension for the visual material (a phenomenon that is referred to as the "visual superiority hypothesis").

Comprehension of Educational Television

The above discussion pertains to comprehension of all television programs. However, additional issues arise when considering children's comprehension of educational television programs. As Shalom Fisch (2000) has pointed out, viewers of educational television programs face even greater processing demands, because these programs typically present narrative content (i.e., the kind of story content discussed above) and educational content simultaneously. Thus, Fisch's "capacity model" proposes that the degree to which children comprehend the educational content depends on the ease or difficulty of comprehending the narrative as well as the educational content itself. In addition, the model argues that comprehension is affected by the degree to which the educational content is integral to the narrative or tangential to it. For example, in the mystery story discussed above, if the detective hero suddenly stopped to give a lesson on mathematical rate–time–distance problems, the mathematical content would be tangential to the narrative. On the other hand, if the hero used the rate–time–distance concept to prove that the pitcher's best friend was the only one close enough to have stolen the lucky cap (i.e., if it provided the key clue that solved the mystery), then the mathematical content would be integral to the narrative.

According to the capacity model, if the narrative and educational content are tangential to each other, the mental processing necessary for comprehension is generally devoted primarily to the narrative; thus, less mental resources are available for processing the educational content. However, if the educational content is integral to the narrative, then the two complement, rather than compete with, each other; the same processing that permits comprehension of the narrative simultaneously contributes to comprehension of the educational content. Thus, comprehension of educational content typically would be stronger when the educational content is integral to the narrative than when it is tangential to it.

When educational television is executed well, it can hold significant and long-lasting benefits for its viewers. Numerous studies have shown that preschool and school-age children comprehend and learn from educational television programs in areas such as literacy, mathematics, science, civics and social studies, and (among preschool children) more general school readiness. Moreover, these effects can last for years; Daniel Anderson, Aletha Huston, John Wright, and Patricia Collins (1998) found that children who had watched educational television as preschoolers demonstrated better school performance than nonviewers as late as high school. Presumably, the data reflect not just preschool children's learning of specific information from television but also the potential of educational television to contribute to an enduring love of learning.

See also: TELEVISION, EDUCATIONAL; VIOLENCE IN THE MEDIA, ATTRACTION TO.

Bibliography

Anderson, Daniel R.; Huston, Aletha C.; Wright, John C.; and Collins, Patricia A. (1998). "*Sesame Street* and Educational Television for Children." In *A Communications Cornucopia: Markle Foundation*

Essays on Information Policy, eds. Roger G. Noll and Monroe E. Price. Washington, DC: Brookings Institution Press.

Collins, W. Andrew. (1983). "Interpretation and Inference in Children's Television Viewing." In *Children's Understanding of Television: Research on Attention and Comprehension*, eds. Jennings Bryant and Daniel R. Anderson. New York: Academic Press.

Fisch, Shalom M. (2000). "A Capacity Model of Children's Comprehension of Educational Content on Television." *Media Psychology* 2(1):63–91.

Salomon, Gavriel. (1983). "Television Watching and Mental Effort: A Social Psychological View." In *Children's Understanding of Television: Research on Attention and Comprehension*, eds. Jennings Bryant and Daniel R. Anderson. New York: Academic Press.

SHALOM M. FISCH

CHILDREN'S CREATIVITY AND TELEVISION USE

The question about whether and how television viewing affects children's imagination has been debated since the medium became part of everyday life, and there is still no consensus on this issue. On the one hand, television viewing is believed to produce a passive intellect and reduce imaginative capacities. On the other hand, there has been enthusiasm about educational television viewing fostering children's imaginative skills.

Before reviewing the effects literature, it is necessary to define two aspects of children's imagination that have been addressed in earlier studies, namely imaginative play and creativity. In imaginative play, children pretend that they are someone else, that an object represents something else, or that they are in a different place and time. According to Greta Fein (1981), imaginative play usually emerges at around twelve months of age, reaches its height between five and seven years, and then gradually declines. Creativity is children's capacity to generate many novel or unusual ideas, for example, in drawings or stories. Creativity is believed to start at around five or six years of age.

Although there are some obvious differences between imaginative play and creativity, the two activities are related to each other. First, both imaginative play and creativity require the generation of ideas, and in both activities associative thinking plays an important role. Second, research suggests that children who exhibit a high level of

imaginative play in early childhood are more creative in the long term. Because imaginative play and creativity have so much in common, this entry discusses the effects that television viewing has on both imaginative play and creativity.

Researchers have advanced contradictory opinions about the influence of television on imaginative play and creativity. Some authors believe that television encourages play and creativity. This view is referred to as the stimulation hypothesis. Many others, however, argue that television hinders imaginative play and creativity. This view is referred to as the reduction hypothesis.

Stimulation Hypothesis

According to the stimulation hypothesis, viewing television enriches the store of ideas from which children can draw when engaged in imaginative play or creative tasks. Adherents of this hypothesis argue that television characters and events are picked up, transformed, and incorporated in children's play and products of creativity and that, as a result, the quality or quantity of their play and creative products is improved.

There is indeed evidence to suggest that children use television content in their imaginative play and creative products. However, this does not necessarily mean that children's play or creative products that are related to television content are more creative than play or products that are not related to television content. There is as yet no evidence that the quality or quantity of imaginative play or creative products is improved through television viewing in general. More specifically, none of the existing studies have as yet demonstrated that overall television viewing is positively related to imaginative play or creativity.

While a stimulating effect does not appear to be true of television viewing in general, it has been suggested that educational viewing might stimulate children's imagination. Two studies, by Jerome Singer and Dorothy Singer (1976) and Daniel Anderson and his colleagues (2001), have shown that that educational children's programs can promote imaginative play and creativity. Singer and Singer, for example, showed that preschoolers who had watched an episode of *Mister Rogers' Neighborhood* exhibited play with more "as-if" elements than did children who had not seen the show. However, although it is promising, the literature related to the beneficial effects that viewing educational televi-

A prominent feature of Mister Rogers' Neighborhood *was the Neighborhood of Make-Believe, through which children were encouraged to be creative and develop their imaginations. (Bettmann/Corbis)*

sion has on children's imaginative capacities is as yet too limited to justify decisive conclusions.

Reduction Hypotheses

Most research supports the contention that television reduces rather than increases creativity, but disagreement exists over the manner in which the reduction is brought about. In fact, six different types of reduction hypotheses have been proposed in the literature; displacement, passivity, rapid pacing, visualization, arousal, and anxiety. The first four hypotheses pertain to the effect of television viewing in general, whereas the latter two hypotheses are proposed to explain the effects of television violence on children's imaginative skills.

Displacement Hypothesis

The displacement hypothesis argues that children spend a considerable portion of their free time watching television at the expense of other leisure activities. In the case of imaginative play, the displacement hypothesis assumes that television viewing takes up time that could otherwise

be spent on imaginative play. In the case of creativity, it is argued that television viewing occurs at the expense of other leisure activities, such as reading, which are thought to stimulate creativity more than does television viewing.

The displacement hypothesis was tested in three studies conducted during the introductory stage of television, when households with and without television could still be compared. Although none of the studies investigated the effect of the arrival of television on the time devoted to imaginative play, they did investigate the consequences for playtime in general. The studies by Eleanor Maccoby (1951) and Wilbur Schramm and his colleagues (1961) found that television viewing did occur at the expense of playtime in general. Because on average approximately one-third of general play is spent on imaginative play, it is likely that television viewing had a reductive effect on imaginative play as well.

In the case of creativity, there is also reason to assume that the arrival of television resulted in a displacement of other media, such as comic books and radio (for a review see Valkenburg and van der Voort, 1994). It is, however, still unknown whether this displacement of other media leads to a reduction in creativity. Linda Faye Harrison and Tannis MacBeth Williams (1986) demonstrated that the arrival of television coincided with a decrease in children's creativity (as measured by the Wallach-Kogan creativity test), but this study did not check whether this was caused by a diminished use of radio and books by children.

Passivity Hypothesis

Adherents of the passivity hypothesis see television as an "easy" medium, requiring little mental effort. With a minimum of mental effort, the child viewer consumes fantasies produced by others. According to the passivity hypothesis, this leads to a passive "let you entertain me" attitude that undermines children's willingness to use their own imagination in play and creative products.

Despite popular stereotypes of children just sitting and staring at the screen, a study by Andrew Collins (1982) suggests that the child viewer is cognitively far from passive. Even very young children actively screen television offerings for attractiveness and understandability and make an effort to interpret television images in their own terms. This does not necessarily imply that the amount of mental effort children invest in processing television programs is large. Gabriel Salomon (1984) has demonstrated that for older elementary school children, television viewing requires less mental effort than does reading. There is some evidence then that television viewing requires relatively little mental effort. However, it has never been investigated whether this leads to a general tendency to expend little mental effort, including a diminished tendency to invest mental effort in imaginative play or creative activities. Of course, child viewers consume fantasies produced by others, but there is little reason to assume that this leads to reductions in fantasy play or creativity. Children who read a story, listen to a radio story, or watch a play also consume fantasies produced by others, but nobody has ever argued that print stories or theater hinder children's imaginative play or creativity. Therefore, there is little reason to assume that television's reductive effect on imaginative play and creativity is caused by a television-induced passive attitude of "let-you-entertain-me."

Rapid Pacing Hypothesis

The rapid pacing hypothesis attributes the reductive effect that television viewing has on imaginative play and creativity to the rapid pace of television programs. According to this hypothesis, the child viewer is confronted with images that must be instantaneously processed because scenes are presented in rapid succession. Children are thus allowed little time to process the information at their own rate or to reflect on program content. The hypothesis argues that rapidly paced television programs encourage cognitive overload, impulsive thinking, hyperactivity, and a nonreflective style of thinking (see Singer and Singer, 1990). Because both imaginative play and creative tasks require children to focus their attention for a longer period of time, the quality or quantity of imaginative play and creative products could be impaired.

Of course, rapidly paced programs leave children less room for reflection on program content than slowly paced programs. However, there are no indications that a rapid program pace per se leads to cognitive overload, impulsive thinking, and shortened attention spans. It is no surprise, therefore, that none of the existing studies have demonstrated that program pace affects children's imaginative play (see Valkenburg, 2000).

Visualization Hypothesis

The visualization hypothesis has been proposed and tested only with respect to creativity, not with respect to imaginative play. This hypothesis attributes the reductive effect of television on creativity to the visual nature of the medium. According to Patricia Greenfield and her colleagues (1986), television, unlike radio and print, presents viewers with ready-made visual images and leaves them little room to form their own images. When engaged in creative thinking, children find it hard to dissociate themselves from the images supplied by television, so that they have difficulty generating novel ideas.

Seven experimental studies have been designed to test the visualization hypothesis. In all of these media-comparison experiments, children were presented with either a story or a problem. The stories or problems were presented in either television (audiovisual), radio (audio), or print (written text) format. The text of the story or problem was usually kept the same, whereas the presentation modality was varied. After the presentation of the stories and problems, children were given a creative task. They were asked, for example, to find a solution for a problem, make a drawing, or complete a story that was interrupted just prior to the end.

With the exception of one study, which was conducted by Mark Runco and Kathy Pezdek (1984), these media-comparison studies showed that verbally presented information evoked more novel ideas than did television information. According to the authors, the television presentations led to fewer novel ideas than did the radio and print presentations because children in the video condition had difficulty dissociating themselves from television images during creative thinking.

Arousal Hypothesis

Like the rapid pacing hypothesis, the arousal hypothesis assumes that television viewing promotes hyperactive and impulsive behavior. However, the hyperactivity is not seen as a result of the rapid pace of television programs; it is attributed to the arousing quality of action-oriented and violent programs. This arousing quality is assumed to foster a physically active and impulsive behavior orientation in children, which in turn disturbs the sequential thought and planning necessary for organizing the plots of make-believe games and performing creative tasks.

Although television viewing appears to be generally associated with relaxation, Dolf Zillmann (1991) has found that violent programs can produce intense arousal in children. In addition, there is evidence that the frequency with which children watch violent and/or action-oriented programs is positively related to restlessness in a waiting room and impulsivity at school.

Because research does indicate that violent programs can induce an impulsive behavior orientation, it is no surprise that many studies have demonstrated that watching violent programs can adversely affect children's imaginative play and creativity. However, although there is convincing evidence that violent programs can hinder children's imaginative play and creativity, the studies failed to investigate whether it was the arousal provoked by television violence that was responsible for the reductions in imaginative play and creativity.

Anxiety Hypothesis

The anxiety hypothesis provides a plausible rival explanation for the reductive effect of television violence on children's imagination. This hypothesis also argues that violent programs hinder children's imaginative play, but the reduction effect is attributed not to the arousal that violent programs produce, but to the fright reactions they generate. According to Grant Noble (1970), television-induced fright leads to regression in behavior, which is expressed in a reduction in the quantity or quality of imaginative play.

Although the anxiety hypothesis has only been advanced with respect to the influence of television on imaginative play, it also provides a plausible explanation for reductive effects of violent programs on creativity. First, research by Joanne Cantor (1998) has shown that there is ample evidence that violent programs can induce intense fright reactions in children. Second, there are indications that high levels of anxiety can disrupt fantasy play and creativity. However, there is not yet any conclusive proof that television-induced fright is responsible for the reductive effects on imaginative play and creativity.

With regard to these final two reduction hypotheses, there is evidence that television violence has a negative effect on children's imaginative play and creativity, and that the mechanisms proposed by the arousal and anxiety hypotheses actually operate. However, researchers have not yet determined whether it is arousal or anxiety that is responsible for television-induced decreases in imaginative play and creativity. In fact, it is possible that both the arousal and the anxiety hypotheses are valid reduction hypotheses. It is widely recognized that different types of media violence evoke different reactions in different viewers. It could be that arousing programs, such as the *Power Rangers,* may affect imaginative play and creativity through arousal, whereas frightening movies, such as *The Exorcist,* which have been shown to disturb many young viewers, may reduce children's imaginativeness through fright.

Conclusion

Overall, research suggests that television viewing has a negative rather than a positive effect on children's creativity. However, most television studies conducted before the year 2000 examined the relation between television viewing and imagination as an input-output measure, without attempting to explore the mechanisms that might be responsible for the reductive or stimulating effects of television. Therefore, the research does not allow one to single out which of the hypotheses discussed in this entry are the most plausible ones. Future studies should pay closer attention to the question of how television may affect imaginative play and creativity. This is important, because only when people know how television influences imaginative play and creativity, will they be able to mediate its effects adequately.

See also: CHILDREN'S PREFERENCE FOR MEDIA CONTENT; RESEARCHERS FOR EDUCATIONAL TELEVISION PROGRAMS; SESAME STREET; TELEVISION, EDUCATIONAL.

Bibliography

Anderson, Daniel R.; Huston, Atletta C.; Schmitt, Kelly L.; Linebarger, Deborah L.; and Wright, John C. (2001). "Early Childhood Television Viewing and Adolescent Behavior: The Recontact Study." *Monographs of the Society for Research in Child Development* 66(1):1–134.

Cantor, Joanne. (1998). *Mommy I'm Scared: How TV and Movies Frighten Children and What We Can Do to Protect Them.* San Diego, CA: Harcourt Brace.

Collins, W. Andrew. (1982). "Cognitive Processing in Television Viewing." In *Television and Behavior: Ten Years of Scientific Progress and Implications for the Eighties,* eds. David Pearl, Lorraine Bouthilet, and Joyce Lazar. Washington, DC: U.S. Government Printing Office.

Fein, Greta G. (1981). "Pretend Play in Childhood: An Integrative Review." *Child Development* 52:1095–1118.

Greenfield, Patricia M.; Farrar, Dorathea; and Beagles-Roos, Jessica. (1986). "Is The Medium The Message? An Experimental Comparison of the Effects of Radio and Television on Imagination." *Journal of Applied Developmental Psychology* 7:201–218.

Harrison, Linda F., and Williams, Tannis M. (1986). "Television and Cognitive Development." In *The Impact of Television: A Natural Experiment in Three Communities,* ed. Tannis M. Williams. New York: Academic Press.

Maccoby, Eleanor E. (1951). "Television: Its Impact on School Children." *Public Opinion Quarterly* 15:421–444.

Noble, Grant. (1970). "Film-Mediated Aggressive and Creative Play." *British Journal of Social & Clinical Psychology* 9:1–7.

Runco, Mark A., and Pezdek, Kathy. (1984). "The Effect of Television and Radio on Children's Creativity." *Human Communication Research* 11:109–120.

Salomon, Gabriel. (1984). "Television Is 'Easy' and Print Is 'Tough': The Differential Investment of Mental Effort as a Function of Perceptions and Attributions." *Journal of Educational Psychology* 76:647–658.

Schramm, Wilbur; Lyle, Jack; and Parker, Edwin. (1961). *Television in the Lives of Our Children.* Stanford, CA: Stanford University Press.

Singer, Dorothy G., and Singer, Jerome L. (1990). *The House of Make-Believe.* Cambridge, MA: Harvard University Press.

Singer, Jerome L., and Singer, Dorothy G. (1976). "Can TV Stimulate Imaginative Play?" *Journal of Communication* 26:74–80.

Valkenburg, Patti M. (2000). "Television and the Child's Developing Imagination." In *Handbook of Children and the Media,* eds. Dorothy G. Singer and Jerome L Singer. Thousand Oaks, CA: Sage Publications.

Valkenburg, Patti M., and van der Voort, Tom H. A. (1994). "Influence of TV on Daydreaming and Creative Imagination: A Review of Research." *Psychological Bulletin* 116:316–339.

Zillmann, Dolf. (1991). "Television Viewing and Psychological Arousal." In *Responding to the Screen: Reception and Reaction Processes,* eds. Jennings Bryant and Dolf Zillmann. Hillsdale, NJ: Lawrence Erlbaum.

PATTI M. VALKENBURG

CHILDREN'S PREFERENCES FOR MEDIA CONTENT

Traditionally, research on the effects of television has assumed that children are passive recipients on whom television has a powerful influence. Since the mid-1970s, however, media-effects research has increasingly recognized the child viewer as an active and motivated explorer, rather than a passive receiver. Research now suggests that children are critical evaluators of what they see in the media. Even very young children have been shown to actively screen television offerings for attractiveness and understandability and to make an effort to interpret television images in their own terms.

Children might enjoy media content for a variety of reasons, including differences in experiences, differences in temperament, and differences in cognitive and emotional development. According to the research that has been conducted, two factors that have been shown to be important predictors of children's media preferences are their age, or developmental level, and their gender.

Early Childhood

Many theories of cognitive development distinguish the preschool and early elementary school years from the later elementary school years. Jean Piaget (1954) refers to the period between two and seven years of age as "preoperational," although many other researchers attribute specific characteristics to this age group without using Piaget's label. Although a two-year-old differs from a seven-year-old in many respects, preschoolers and young elementary school children do share certain cognitive-developmental characteristics that justify segmenting them in this way.

Unclear Fantasy-Reality Distinction

For preschoolers and young elementary school children, there is an unclear demarcation between fantasy and reality. Virtually anything is possible in the imagination of a child in this age range; a sponge can become a rock, bears can talk, and the wind can pick the child up and take him or her away. Research by Patricia Morrison and Howard Gardner (1978) has demonstrated that between the ages of three and ten years, children gradually become more accurate in distinguishing fantasy from reality on television. At first, children believe that everything on television is real. Young preschoolers sometimes even think the characters reside inside the television set. Leona Jaglom and Howard Garder (1981), for example, observed that two- and three-year-olds ran to get a paper towel to clean up an egg they saw break on television. In addition, most four-year-olds who participated in a study by Sue Howard (1998) were convinced that Big Bird and Bugs Bunny were real.

Children's failure to distinguish fantasy and reality can affect their preferences for media content in important ways. First, because fantasy and cartoon animals and characters are perceived as real, they can be just as engaging for young children as real-life characters. Second, some special effects or stunts, such as a character vanishing in a puff of smoke, can have a great effect. Because young children cannot put these events in perspective by understanding that they are cinematic tricks, they are more strongly affected by them.

Perceptional Boundedness and Centration

Another quality of thinking exhibited by preschoolers is the tendency to center attention on an individual, striking feature of an object or image, to the exclusion of other, less-striking features. Piaget (1954) and Jerome Bruner (1966) referred to this tendency as "centration" or "perceptual boundedness." A study reported by Dan Acuff (1997) is illustrative of this tendency of young children. In this study, girls were presented with three dolls. Two of the dolls were very expensive, had beautiful and realistic faces, and came with sophisticated mechanical effects. The third doll was cheaply made, but this doll had a big red sequined heart on her dress. To the surprise of the researchers, the majority of the girls preferred the cheap doll with the sequined heart. This choice is typical of children in this age group. When judging a product or media content, they focus their attention on one striking characteristic, and they therefore have little eye for detail. Similarly, their descriptions of television characters tend to fix on single, physical attributes, without integrating them into an overall picture. According to Jaglom and Gardner (1981), young children pay less attention to what characters are doing or saying and pay the most attention to simple, brightly colored visuals and colorful, uncomplicated, nonthreatening characters.

Responsiveness to Language, Rhymes, and Music

Children seem to have an innate tendency to respond to language. Long before infants talk, they are very responsive to human speech, and according to Robert Siegler (1991), they are especially attentive to a form of speech that is referred to as "motherese." Motherese is characterized by a slower cadence, a higher pitch, and exaggerated intonations. This preference lasts for several years. According to Patti Valkenburg and Joanne Cantor (2000), many audiovisual stories and programs for young children use motherese.

Young children also enjoy listening to songs, rhymes, and music. In a study by Margaret Cupitt and her colleagues (1998), almost half of the mothers of children who were two and one-half years of age reported that their children had imitated music, rhymes, or songs from television. This study also showed that nearly all of these children had interacted with television programs while watching—for example, by singing, dancing, or clapping hands. It is no surprise, therefore, that songs, rhymes, and music are often used successfully in educational and entertainment programs for young children.

Limited Cognitive Capacities

Because of their immature cognitive capacity, children in this age group need more time than adults to interpret and make sense of information

The toy industry often takes advantage of children's preferences for particular characters or programs, such as Blue's Clues, *to create and sell tie-in products. (Wilfred Tenaillon/Corbis)*

and television images. This is the reason why preschoolers often respond best to programs with a slow pace and with lots of repetition, for example *Barney and Friends* and *Mister Rogers' Neighborhood.* For the same reason, preschoolers often prefer familiar contexts and visuals and objects and animals that they can label, such as a cat, a dog, or a horse. According to Dafna Lemish (1987), they like to watch programs that show babies and young children, and they adore nonthreatening real or animated animals, such as kind birds, friendly dinosaurs, and babyish creatures like the *Teletubbies.*

By the time they are five or six years of age, children begin to develop a preference for more fast-paced programs. They also become more responsive to verbally oriented shows with more sophisticated forms of humor, such as the animated situation comedy *The Simpsons.* In addition, they often find slower-paced programs with friendly characters boring or childish, and they begin to prefer more adventurous themes located in foreign countries or in outer space and more complicated characters.

Middle Childhood

In contrast to preschoolers, the fantasies of children between eight and twelve years of age more often entail realistic and plausible themes. In this period, children develop a sincere, sometimes even exaggerated, interest in real-world phenomena. They can be highly critical of entertainment and commercials that lack realism. According to Keith Mielke (1983), children in middle childhood continue to like animals, but they are mainly interested in real-life animals. Because most fantasy characters have been demystified, children in this age group tend to become attached to real-life heroes, such as sports heroes, movie stars, and action heroes.

During middle childhood, children come to appreciate details. As explained above, a preschooler may focus on only one striking detail of a toy—a doll's clothing, for example. For the eight- to twelve-year-old child, many characteristics of a toy may be carefully observed, from the face and body to details of the doll's clothing to how it moves. At this age, children become progressively critical of television programs of low quality, such as those that are poorly produced or repetitious. They are no longer content with simple, salient characteristics, such as a colorful cartoon character. Unlike younger children, who are greatly impressed by special effects and characters with special powers, older children seem to agree that special effects by themselves are not enough.

Influence of the Peer Group

During middle childhood, peer interactions become increasingly sophisticated. Because children in this age group develop a strong sense of commitment and loyalty to the norms of their peer group, they are increasingly sensitive to the thoughts, opinions, judgments, and evaluations of other children, and they become very sensitive to what is "cool" and what is "in." They therefore become alert to how to behave in public and how to avoid being ridiculed with respect to what they wear or prefer to watch on television. For example, older children feel the need to demonstrate firmly their aversion to programs designed for younger children or for shows that feature characters younger than they are.

Gender Differences in Children's Media Preferences

Despite the fact that what it means to "be a girl" has changed considerably since the 1950s (and even the 1960s), there are still important differences in the way boys and girls typically think, what they value, and how they express themselves. Many researchers have observed that in the first two years of life, there does not appear to be any significant gender difference in play style and toy preference. Boys and girls in this age group also do not seem to differ in their liking for television characters, such as Barney versus the Teletubbies.

Significant gender differences in toy preference have been observed as early as two years of age, however. By the time they are three years old, boys and girls frequently participate in different activities, avoid toys that are perceived to belong to the opposite sex, and play primarily in same-sex groups. According to Eleanor Maccoby (1994), this so-called process of gender segregation is found in a variety of cultures and settings.

The emerging differences between boys and girls during the preschool years are clearly reflected in their preferences for media content. In comparison to preschool girls, preschool boys have a strong preference for action and violence in books and entertainment programs. They tend to prefer themes and content in entertainment, such as sports, violent fantasy themes, and more dangerous scenarios, involving, for example, dinosaurs and aliens. They also are attracted to heroic male characters, including superhumans (e.g., the Power Rangers, Hercules), sports stars, knights, soldiers, doctors, and policemen. Preschool girls are more interested in relationship-centered and nurturing themes. They prefer themes and contexts such as castles, dance studios, school, the circus, and farmyards. According to Acuff (1997), preschool girls generally focus on characters such as fashion models, ballerinas, dancers, good fairies, queens, and princesses.

Children's awareness of societal stereotypes for gender roles continues to increase with age, and in spite of the fact that cognitive flexibility increases in middle childhood and adolescence, the preferences of boys and girls diverge over time. Because children become increasingly involved with peers, there is greater pressure to conform to "gender-appropriate" behavior. It is not surprising, therefore, that differences in taste between boys and girls become stronger with age.

Elementary school boys and adolescent males still have a comparatively strong preference for action-oriented and violent programs. They become strongly attached to male action heroes and power figures, although the heroes are now more realistic (e.g., Arnold Schwarzenegger, Bruce Willis). Elementary school girls are in general more likely to react negatively to program scenarios that involve action, violence, horror, and swearing, possibly because girls report being frightened by violent media depictions more often than boys do.

What do girls like? Research on the preferences of girls for computer games suggests that girls are less object-oriented than males. They are less interested than boys in devices, such as lasers, buttons, and futuristic weapons. For girls, it is not so much about winning or killing the enemy. According to Jack Sanger and his colleagues (1997), girls like a story line; they like real-life situations; and they are more often interested in the development of relationships between characters. They also more often have a preference for family situations, and they enjoy serial dramas with realistic themes.

Finally, research by Patti Valkenburg and Sabine Janssen (1999) has found that girls attach more value than boys do to the comprehensibility of an entertainment program. This could be because girls are more interested than boys are in dramatic story lines. According to a study by Carrie Heeter (1985), teenage females are more eager than boys are to look for actors or actresses they recognize, invest more time in searching for information about shows and characters, and prefer to watch an entertainment show from start to finish.

Conclusion

Current media theories assume that children purposely select and expose themselves to television content to satisfy specific needs. They also assume that any effect of media content on children is enhanced or mitigated by how the child perceives it. Research has shown, for example, that the effect of television violence on aggressive behavior is mediated by the extent to which a child likes to watch violent programs. To understand media effects on children, then, it is crucial to gain insight into children's preferences for media content. While much research has already addressed how age and gender affect children's preferences, future research needs to focus on how other child characteristics, such as personality characteristics and emotional development, may affect children's media preferences and selective exposure to television content.

See also: CHILDREN'S COMPREHENSION OF TELEVISION; FEAR AND THE MEDIA; GENDER AND THE MEDIA; SESAME STREET; TELEVISION, EDUCATIONAL; VIOLENCE IN THE MEDIA, ATTRACTION TO; VIOLENCE IN THE MEDIA, HISTORY OF RESEARCH ON.

Bibliography

Acuff, Dan S. (1997). *What Kids Buy and Why: The Psychology of Marketing to Kids.* New York: Free Press.

Bruner, Jerome S. (1966). "On Cognitive Growth I & II." In *Studies in Cognitive Growth,* eds. Jerome S. Bruner, Rose R. Olver, and Patricia M. Greenfield. New York: Wiley.

Cupitt, Margaret; Jenkinson, Daniel; Ungerer, Judy; and Waters, Brent. (1998). *Infants and Television.* Sidney: Australian Broadcasting Authority.

Heeter, Carrie. (1988). "Gender Differences in Viewing Styles." In *Cableviewing,* eds. Carrie Heeter and Bradley S. Greenberg. Norwood, NJ: Ablex.

Howard, Sue. (1998). "Unbalanced Minds? Children Thinking About Television." In *Wired-up: Young People and the Electronic Media,* ed. Sue Howard. London: UCL Press.

Jaglom, Leona M., and Gardner, Howard. (1981). "The Preschool Viewer as Anthropologist." *New Directions in Child Development* 13:9–29.

Lemish, Dafna. (1987). "Viewers in Diapers: The Early Development of Television Viewing." In *Natural Audiences: Qualitative Research of Media Uses and Effects,* ed. Thomas R. Lindlof. Norwood, NJ: Ablex.

Maccoby, Eleanor E. (1994). "Commentary: Gender Segregation in Childhood." *New Directions for Child Development* 65:88–97.

Mielke, Keith W. (1983). "Formative Research on Appeal and Comprehension in 3-2-1 Contact." In *Children's Understanding of Television: Research on Attention and Comprehension,* eds. Jennings Bryant and Daniel Anderson. Hillsdale, NJ: Lawrence Erlbaum.

Morrison, Patricia, and Gardner, Howard. (1978). "Dragons and Dinosaurs: The Child's Capacity to Differentiate Fantasy from Reality." *Child Development* 49:642–648.

Piaget, Jean. (1954). *The Construction of Reality in the Child.* New York: Basic Books.

Sanger, Jack; Willson, Jane; Davis, Bryn; and Whittaker, Roger. (1997). *Young Children, Videos and Computer Games: Issues for Teachers and Parents.* London: Falmer Press.

Siegler, Robert S. (1991). *Children's Thinking,* 2nd edition. Englewood Cliffs, NJ: Prentice-Hall.

Valkenburg, Patti M., and Cantor, Joanne. (2000). "Children's Likes and Dislikes of Entertainment." In *Media Entertainment: The Psychology of Its Appeal,* eds. Dolf Zillmann and Peter Vorderer. Hillsdale, NJ: Lawrence Erlbaum.

Valkenburg, Patti M., and Janssen, Sabine. (1999). "What Do Children Value in Entertainment Programs? A Cross-Cultural Investigation." *Journal of Communication* 49:3-21.

PATTI M. VALKENBURG

COMMERCE, ELECTRONIC

See: Electronic Commerce

COMMUNICATIONS ACT OF 1934

The Communications Act of 1934 is the major, comprehensive legislation for the regulation of all nongovernmental wire and wireless telecommunication. It outlines specific laws that telecommunications operators must follow. It created the Federal Communications Commission (FCC) and enabled the commissioners to initiate further regulations that carry out the intent of the act. Most important, the act justifies the regulation of telecommunications, which is paradoxical, given the rights that are guaranteed to the press by the First Amendment.

Evolution of the Act

The Communications Act of 1934 grew out of the Radio Act of 1927, which was the first official attempt by the U.S. government at a comprehensive legislation for radio. The Radio Act of 1927 was passed by the U.S. Congress to help the U.S. Department of Commerce solve interference problems connected with the burgeoning number of new operating stations. Although this act gave First Amendment protection to broadcasting, it defined broadcasting as interstate commerce, a status that, according to the Constitution, gave Congress the power to control it. In addition, this act created the Federal Radio Commission (FRC), the precursor to the FCC, to govern licensing, frequency assignments, and station operations.

This 1927 act, though more comprehensive than its predecessors, still did not provide enough direction and justification for the regulation of the new media. In fact, it was not long after its inception that many of its powers, especially those involving the denial of a license, were challenged in court. Other court cases questioned the underpinnings of the 1927 act, including (1) whether the public-interest standard could be used to deny licenses on the basis of programming content and (2) whether broadcasting could even be considered interstate commerce. Finally, President Franklin D. Roosevelt wrote a letter to Congress asking for new legislation that would better harness the evolving industry of telecommunications, and Congress answered with the Communications Act of 1934.

Design of the Act

The Communications Act of 1934 acknowledges the First Amendment status of broadcasting, yet it also provides a rationale for regulation despite this status. This rationale is built on the premise that telecommunication operators must act "in the public interest, convenience, and necessity." The reason for this is twofold. First, the airwaves are considered to be a publicly owned natural resource. Therefore, as with any scarce resource, the government is entitled to ensure that this public property is used as a public service. The second part of this rationale argues that, because the airwaves are publicly owned, the operators of electronic media act not as owners but as trustees of the frequencies they use, thereby functioning as the public's proxy when managing this public resource. This rationale serves to justify the provisions of the act itself, but it also justifies electronic media regulation by the FCC beyond basic technological regulation.

The first paragraph of the act establishes the FCC as the independent regulatory agency that is charged with carrying out the intent of Congress and the act. Through this establishment, the act becomes the enabling legislation for the FCC, dictating the organization, enforcement measures, and procedural methods that the FCC must follow. Other sections of the act provide principles and initiatives that require specific regulatory action from the FCC in order to be implemented. For example, sections 303(o) and 303(p) of the act allow the FCC to assign call letters to stations and require that the stations publish "such call letters and other such announcements and data as in the judgment of the Commission . . . for the efficient operation . . ." of these stations. The latter part of this allowance entitled the FCC to create rule 73.1201, which requires stations to identify themselves during sign-on, sign-off, and natural breaks at every hour. This identification must include their call letters, the location in which they are licensed, and, for radio stations, their frequency. In this manner, the act empowers the FCC to create and execute rules, policies, and regulations based on the directives of the act.

Conjointly, the act also contains explicit regulations that the FCC must enforce. A prime example of this is found in the political communication provisions of section 315. Section 315, among other requirements, prohibits broadcast and cable operators from censoring the content of any political message. This means that broadcasters and cable operators cannot censor political advertisements, nor can the FCC ban a political spot based on questionable content. It is important to note, however, that although section 315 prohibits the banning of a political spot on the basis of content, even political messages are subject to the indecency and obscenity laws of the U.S. Criminal

Code (section 1464) and to the First Amendment tests for "clear and present danger" (as set forth in *Schenck v. United States,* 1919; *United States v. O'Brien,* 1968; and *Preferred Communications v. City of Los Angeles,* 1989). Nevertheless, this statute exemplifies one of the many explicit regulations of the act that must be enforced by the FCC.

Organization of the Act

The Communications Act of 1934 contains seven titles, or sections, each of which addresses a specific area of telecommunication. The first paragraph of Title I lays out the purpose of the act by first identifying wire and wireless communication as interstate and foreign commerce and then introducing the FCC as its regulatory enforcer. This first section also introduces the phrase "in the public interest, convenience, and necessity," the criterion for the discretionary regulatory authority that the government may hold over communications.

Title I also outlines the terms, organization, duties, and general powers of the FCC. It dictates the procedure for the appointment the five commissioners as well as the terms, qualifications, and restrictions that are required of the commissioner positions. It also outlines the various powers that Congress and the president of the United States have over the FCC, including the appropriation of operating funds for the agency. Application fees for the various communication services are listed, and related powers of the FCC are explained.

Title II addresses common carriers, such as telephone services. The first portion of the title requires common carriers to maintain reasonable charges for their services as well as justify these charges in a public inspection file. Other areas of regulation include the extension of lines, acquisition of equipment, and expansion of facilities or of the service area. Restrictions on the use of telephone equipment for various criminal or other infringing actions and requirements for disability access and blocking of offensive material are detailed. Finally, requirements, limitations, and other provisions are placed on existing or developing services.

Title III covers radio and television licensing and regulation, noncommercial and educational broadcasting, and maritime radio use. This is where the licensing procedures, conditions, and regulatory powers concerning all broadcast stations are written. It is also where the public-inter-est standard is formally addressed in a very tangible regulatory capacity. Enforcement powers and sanctions of the FCC are presented. Likewise, enforceable requirements of broadcasters are identified. Examples of the Title III broadcasting requirements include section 315, which demands that legally qualified candidates running for the same office receive an equal opportunity to use a given station, and section 335, which requires a direct broadcasting satellite (DBS) to carry educational and informational programming. Other sections in Title III cover assistance and provisions for public broadcasting, emergency or distress situations, and ship-to-shore communications.

Title IV lists procedural and administrative provisions that the FCC must follow. It begins with the establishment of the jurisdiction of the FCC to enforce the act and the possibility of court action against any violators of any order set forth by the commission. It then defines and explains the different procedures and types of evidence that may be used in conjunction with an FCC order or court action. These orders and enforcement issues are then expounded upon in the next title.

Title V addresses specific consequences, or penalties, that correspond with certain violations of the act or other FCC regulations, rules, or policies. Fines can be charged as a result of fraudulent contests or game shows, illegal acceptance of rebates or other money in exchange for transmission, and maritime safety violations. Penalties also include the confiscation of illegal or unauthorized telecommunications devices, which can then be sold by the confiscators as long as there is no potential for harming the public.

Title VI describes national policy for cable communication. Among its various provisions, it redefines the relationship between cable operator and franchising authority. In order to operate in a given community, a cable operator must obtain a franchise, which allows the operator to construct a cable system using public roads, or "right-of-way." The franchising authority is the community government or other government entity that grants a franchise to a cable operator, an action that is accompanied by a franchising agreement or contract with which the cable operator must comply.

In its definition of the cable-franchise relationship, the act gives the franchising authority the right to require a cable operator to designate a channel for educational, governmental, or other public use. In addition, the act requires cable operators to carry local television stations or low-power television stations in certain situations. Regarding the actual process of franchising, Title VI establishes franchising procedures, standards, and fee limitations that cable operators and franchising authorities must acknowledge and follow. Furthermore, the act governs franchise renewal procedures and provides for the protection of cable operators against wrongful denial of renewal. Other provisions of this title address the need for increased competition and public-interest obligations for the cable industry, and the establishment of common guidelines for federal, state, and local government in the regulation of cable.

The last title, Title VII, contains miscellaneous provisions that do not fall within the scope of the previous titles. Part of this title deals with the unauthorized publication and reception of communication. Another section outlines the powers of the president in times of war or national emergency. Services for the disabled, such as closed captioning and hearing-aid compatibility, are also addressed. Finally, the act ends with the establishment of a fund that will be used to promote competition, new technology development, employment and training, and the delivery of telecommunication services to all parts of the United States.

Major Amendments to the Act

Similar to the U.S. Constitution, the Communications Act of 1934 has had to evolve to accommodate new technologies and to ensure that the new and existing technologies were serving the public interest. In order to accomplish this, elements of certain sections were altered, expanded, or abolished in order to update the usefulness of the act. Also, from time to time, laws have been passed that added entire sections to the act. These sections were specific to particular areas of telecommunication, and they gave the FCC additional power and responsibilities.

One such modification to the Communications Act of 1934 is the Communications Satellite Act of 1962, which was enacted to regulate the long-term commercial use of satellites. This act created the Communications Satellite Corporation (COMSAT) to oversee this commercial use. That same year, the All Channel Receiver Act was passed to require all television receivers to receive both VHF and the new UHF signals, and the Educational Television

Facilities Act was enacted to provide money for the construction of educational stations.

The Educational Television Facilities Act of 1962 paved the way for the Public Broadcasting Act of 1967, which provided the first direct appropriation for noncommercial programming. More notably, it established the Corporation for Public Broadcasting, which has become the major founder of educational broadcasting facilities.

The next major legislation was the Cable Communications Policy Act of 1984. This act outlined the relationship between cable operator and local franchising authority as well as relaxed the franchise regulation of cable rates. However, the act was created during a time of deregulation, and it soon became apparent that the cable industry would need more conservative regulation. Thus, the Cable Television Consumer Protection and Competition Act of 1992 re-regulated cable by reevaluating the powers of the franchising authority over the cable operator, prohibiting exclusive program arrangements between cable operator and program supplier, and otherwise promoting competition.

Another piece of legislation passed in the same decade was the Children's Television Act of 1990. This act placed limitations on the amount of advertising as well as the use of advertising and other commercial acts during children's programming. It also detailed specific requirements for children's programming and made other suggestions on how communications operators could better serve the public interest.

Finally, the Telecommunications Act of 1996 was enacted as the largest-ever addition to the Communications Act of 1934. It gave the FCC new initiatives and challenges in the face of digital broadcasting and other dawning technologies, and it outlined further public-interest responsibilities that communicators in the new digital era would be obliged to adopt. In sum, the Telecommunications Act of 1996 amended and added provisions to the 1934 act in an effort to promote electronic media competition, provide universal service, and ensure that all future electronic media will serve "the public interest, convenience, and necessity."

Strengths and Weaknesses of the Act

The Communications Act of 1934 has been both praised and condemned for its various provisions and effects. One of its most notable strengths is its breadth in creating a single independent regulatory agency that has the power to regulate all electronic media. Likewise, the act can be admired for its design in that it includes the legislative, executive, and judicial branches of government in the execution and evaluation of its various provisions, similar to the laws establishing other regulatory agencies. A third strength is its interpretive quality in that it dictates initiatives that the FCC can interpret and then execute according to contemporary needs. This interpretive quality, however, has also been regarded as a weakness when certain provisions have needed further clarification in order to be effectively adopted.

Another criticism concerns the appointment method for filling commissioner positions, which leaves this process subject to political considerations that can take precedence over an appointee's qualifications. A related concern is the potential for Congress to refrain from approving the appointment of any or all commissioners or to delay appropriating an operating budget in an attempt to influence the functioning of the FCC.

However flawed the Communications Act of 1934 may be, its survival serves as a testament to its fundamental effectiveness. The act still stands as the first, and only, comprehensive regulatory legislation for all electronic media. It successfully solved the regulatory problems that were experienced by its predecessors, and it will continue to evolve with the evolving media, solving new problems as they arise.

See also: BROADCASTING, GOVERNMENT REGULATION OF; CABLE TELEVISION, REGULATION OF; CHILDREN AND ADVERTISING; FIRST AMENDMENT AND THE MEDIA; PUBLIC BROADCASTING; RADIO BROADCASTING; TELECOMMUNICATIONS ACT OF 1996; TELEVISION, EDUCATIONAL; TELEVISION BROADCASTING; SATELLITES, HISTORY OF.

Bibliography

Barnouw, Erik. (1966). *A Tower in Babel: A History of Broadcasting in the United States to 1933*. New York: Oxford University Press.

Barnouw, Erik. (1968). *The Golden Web: A History of Broadcasting in the United States 1933–1953*. New York: Oxford University Press.

Barnouw, Erik. (1970). *The Image Empire: A History of Broadcasting in the United States from 1953*. New York: Oxford University Press.

Kahn, Frank J., ed. (1978). *Documents of American Broadcasting*, 3rd edition. Englewood Cliffs, NJ: Prentice-Hall.

Smith, F. Leslie; Meeske, Milan; and Wright, John W., II. (1995). *Electronic Media and Government: The Regulation of Wireless and Wired Mass Communication in the United States*. White Plains, NY: Longman.

FRANCESCA DILLMAN CARPENTIER

■ COMMUNICATIONS DECENCY ACT OF 1996

The rise of new communications technologies, such as the Internet, poses a number of problems for policymakers. Perhaps the most vexing of these problems involves trying to balance (1) the First Amendment rights of those people who wish to communicate using the Internet with (2) ensuring that children who use the Internet are protected from adult-oriented material such as pornography. According to Timothy Zick (1999), millions of children access the Internet everyday despite the fact that approximately 70 percent of Internet traffic is sexually oriented in nature. Clearly, the World Wide Web differs from other media in that the availability of adult-oriented content is greater and restricting the distribution of that type of content is difficult at best.

Faced with the reality of children being able to view material that is intended for adults, the U.S. Congress passed the Communications Decency Act of 1996 as part of the Telecommunications Act of 1996. The Communications Decency Act was signed into law by President Bill Clinton on February 8, 1996. By the time the Communications Decency Act became law, however, it was already a highly controversial piece of legislation. For the first time, Congress had attempted to restrict what types of information could be put on the Internet.

Legislative Development

Faced with an explosion in the pervasiveness of digital communication by the early 1990s, Congress moved to update the various telecommunications laws that were in existence. This effort ultimately culminated in the passage of the Telecommunications Act of 1996. Essentially, the Telecommunications Act of 1996 updated the Communications Act of 1934 to include digital communication and to encourage market competition. This major reform effort was the subject of a great deal of congressional and public debate.

During the winter of 1995, as the Telecommunications Act of 1996 was taking shape, Senator Jim Exon of Nebraska introduced the Communications Decency Act as an amendment. A number of sources characterize this amendment as a last-minute addition to the Telecommunications Act of 1996. Exon built support for the Communications Decency Act by passing around a book that contained a variety of pornographic photographs that had been downloaded from websites. Certainly, the two acts essentially deal with different issues facing the same technological innovations. Because the nature of the Telecommunications Act of 1996 dealt with market conditions, new technology, and telecommunications policy, the Communications Decency Act broke new ground by attempting to regulate the content of digital communication. This fact led a significant number of senators to oppose the legislation initially. However, the Communications Decency Act encountered stronger opposition in the U.S. House of Representatives, which passed The Online Family Empowerment Amendment, a competing piece of legislation that had a similar purpose. In the end, a conference committee largely combined the two pieces of legislation into the version of the Communications Decency Act that ultimately became law.

In general, the Communications Decency Act sought to protect children from harmful material on the Internet. The act made it a crime to use any device to send "obscene, lewd, lascivious, filthy, or indecent communications with the intent to annoy, abuse, threaten, or harass another person." Specifically, the act made it illegal for one to "knowingly within the United States or in foreign communications with the United States by means of telecommunications device make . . . available any indecent communication in any form including any comment, request, suggestion, proposal, image, to any person under 18 years of age." The act stipulated that the penalty for indecent communication sent to minors would be a maximum fine of $100,000 and a maximum jail sentence of two years. The act further made it a crime for anyone to transmit patently offensive material to any specific minor, regardless of who initiated the communication. Perhaps most important, the act made it illegal to transmit such material in a way that could be accessed by a person under the age of eighteen.

This last portion of the Communications Decency Act became perhaps the most controversial aspect of the legislation because nearly any regular website can be accessed by anybody (whether child or adult) with an Internet connection.

Unconstitutionality of the Communications Decency Act

On the same day that President Clinton signed the Communications Decency Act into law, a number of groups sought and won—in *ACLU v. Reno* (i.e., *Reno I*)—a temporary restraining order in the U.S. District Court for the Eastern District of Pennsylvania to prevent enforcement of the act. Several other groups subsequently filed a similar lawsuit that was consolidated into one case at the U.S. Court of Appeals for the Third Circuit. The plaintiffs contended that the language contained in the act was overly vague, allowing regulators to restrict content that was ordinarily protected by the First Amendment. Moreover, enforcing the act might serve to restrict the First Amendment right of adults who choose to access adult-oriented material. The government argued that the Communications Decency Act was worded similarly to past U.S. Supreme Court decisions on indecency and obscenity. In addition, the government argued that there was a compelling interest in protecting children from dangerous material on the Internet.

The appellate court found in *Reno v. ACLU* (i.e., *Reno II*) that the Communications Decency Act was an unconstitutional violation of the First Amendment. The court relied on previous cases by noting that any law seeking to restrict content must pass "strict scrutiny." In other words, the law must serve a compelling governmental interest, and the law must be narrowly tailored to fix the problem at hand. Applying that standard, the court reasoned, the Communications Decency Act was unconstitutional because content that may have some literary or artistic merit but would be unsuitable for minors would be restricted. Hence, under the act, protected yet indecent speech may be restricted by the attempts of the law to curtail obscenity. The court further found that the Communications Decency Act was unconstitutional in that there were no technological means for ensuring that websites that featured adult-oriented content would be viewed only by adults. Finally, the court found that the interest of the government in protecting minors could be better served by enforcing already existing obscenity and pornography legislation than by risking the restriction of legitimate (protected) communication.

The U.S. Supreme Court agreed to hear *Reno II* with arguments presented during the spring of 1997. In a 7–2 decision, the Court ruled in June 1997 that the Communications Decency Act was unconstitutional. Justice Sandra Day O'Connor wrote a separate opinion in which she dissented in part and concurred in part. Chief Justice William H. Rehnquist joined O'Connor. Writing for the majority, Justice John Paul Stevens contended that the Communications Decency Act was too vague and overbroad in its scope and direction to be constitutional under the First Amendment. The first problem addressed by the Court was the notion of indecency versus obscenity. Sexual expression that is indecent but not obscene enjoys some First Amendment protection while obscene expression receives no such protection. The Communications Decency Act, however, at some points uses the terms interchangeably. According to the Court, this could result in confusion in interpreting the scope of the law. For example, a website developer who wishes to operate legally according to the framework of the Communications Decency Act would have extreme difficulty deciding exactly what kinds of depictions and descriptions to omit or include.

A second problem that the Court found with the Communications Decency Act is that because it is a criminal statute, the likelihood of chilling speech would be greater. A person who was afraid of large fines and a jail sentence might be less likely to communicate even though the expression might normally enjoy some constitutional protection. Perhaps most important was the employment of past precedent in the decision. In the case of *Sable Communications of California v. FCC* (1989), the Court held that a statute that prohibited the transmission of sexually oriented content via the telephone was unconstitutional in that it infringed upon the rights of adults in its attempt to protect children. In *Reno II*, the Court noted that the Communications Decency Act was similar to the statute tested by *Sable*. The telephone is similar to the Internet because it is less intrusive than other types of media. Unlike a television broadcast (where the viewer is the recipient of one-way communication), the telephone (and the Internet) gives the user more choice in terms of communicating. The caller chooses to dial a certain number with a par-

ticular result in mind, while a television viewer has less choice regarding specific programming offerings. The Court found that the mere fact that a statute is designed to protect children does not exempt that statute from judicial scrutiny. In fact, because the statute prohibited telephone communication in which it was normally legal for adults to participate, the statute was found to be an unconstitutional restriction of free speech.

Applying this logic to *Reno II*, the Court found that in attempting to protect children, the Communications Decency Act went too far by restricting the First Amendment rights of adults. Because there is no way to ensure absolutely that minors will not access adult-oriented websites, the effect of the Communications Decency Act might be to restrict all websites that contain material that is deemed inappropriate for children. The decision of the Court noted that the Communications Decency Act went too far to try to solve a problem that affected only one class of the population. The ruling of the Court in *Reno II* clearly indicates that if regulators at any level wish to restrict Internet content, they must design statutes that meet the highest level of scrutiny.

The Child Online Protection Act

The decision in *Reno II* did not end the controversy of governmental regulation of the Internet, however. Several main events occurred in the wake of that decision, and they affected how government attempts to regulate the Internet. First, existing obscenity laws have been employed to restrict the transmission of obscenity via computer. In the case of *United States v. Thomas* (1996), the first Internet obscenity case, obscenity laws that prohibit knowingly selling or transporting obscenity were successfully applied to computer-oriented communication. In *Thomas,* the U.S. Court of Appeals for the Sixth Circuit found that using a computer to transmit obscene material violated obscenity laws. In addition, the Child Pornography Act of 1996 has withstood judicial scrutiny (*United States v. Carroll*, 1997) of its provision outlawing Internet distribution of child pornography.

After the U.S. Supreme Court struck down the Communications Decency Act for being overly vague and too broad, Congress drafted and passed the Child Online Protection Act (COPA) in 1998. COPA was designed to survive judicial scrutiny by attempting to protect children from harmful material while protecting the First Amendment rights of adults. COPA differed from the Communications Decency Act in several key ways. First, COPA applied only to commercial websites, exempting private websites. COPA also did not use the word "obscenity" interchangeably with indecency. Instead, COPA sought to restrict websites that were deemed "harmful to minors." Specifically, COPA prohibited making "any communication for commercial purposes that is available to any minor and that includes any material that is harmful to minors" measured by "contemporary community standards." In addition, Congress attempted to define the key terms that were used within the wording of COPA. Finally, Congress strengthened the penalty for violating the law. Website operators in violation of COPA could be fined $50,000 per day. In order to prevent minors from accessing material intended for adults, COPA encouraged website operators to use some method designed to verify that the individual website visitor is indeed an adult. The suggested methods included requiring credit card numbers, having specific passwords generated, personal using identification numbers, and having debit accounts.

President Clinton signed COPA into law on October 21, 1998. The same groups that opposed the Communications Decency Act immediately filed a lawsuit to challenge COPA. On November 20, 1998, the U.S. District Court for the Eastern District of Pennsylvania granted a temporary restraining order that prevented enforcement of the law. Hearings on COPA began in February 1999, resulting in a preliminary injunction that prevented enforcement. Subsequently, on June 22, 2000, the U.S. Court of Appeals for the Third Circuit found in *ACLU v. Reno* (i.e., *Reno III*) that the law was unconstitutional. The employment in COPA of "contemporary community standards" was problematic according to the appellate court because website owners would have to conform with the community standards of the most conservative state in order to avoid prosecution. Since the web transcends geographic boundaries, the requirements of COPA served to restrict the expression of adults in less conservative states.

Because the appellate court could not identify a technological means of accomplishing what COPA set out to do (i.e., prevent certain websites from reaching certain groups of people in certain areas, while allowing access to those websites for certain groups in certain other areas), the court held that the law was an unconstitutional violation of free speech. An additional geographic issue involves the fact that the law would apply only to commercial websites that originated in the United States; it would not apply to foreign websites. Children could access many sexually oriented websites that originated from foreign countries and noncommercial entities, thus circumventing the intent and scope of COPA.

The court also found that websites that featured text containing nonsexual information that may be harmful to minors would be subject to age verification under COPA. The example that appeared throughout news accounts of the passage of COPA was the high degree of Internet traffic surrounding the release of the Starr report regarding President Clinton's activities in the White House. Under COPA, the rather graphic details of the Starr report would in the least necessitate the use of some age verification mechanism for the individuals who wish to access it. At worst, under the community standards clause of COPA, the Starr report might not have been legally posted, as the website operator would have to obey the most restrictive standards of the most conservative locality. Moreover, the court found that the remedies that were prescribed by COPA to ensure that only adults could access certain websites were problematic. Credit card verification would restrict websites to only those individuals who possessed a credit card number. In addition, credit card verification may be harmful to expression because the technology that is necessary to carry out this function is expensive to acquire. Finally, the court found that there are other, less restrictive means that are available to protect children from potentially harmful content. For example, the popularity of parental blocking software indicates that children can be protected without legislative action that may infringe upon the rights of adults.

The ruling of the appeals court in *Reno III* is a major event that relates directly to the Communications Decency Act. COPA was drafted as a direct result of the U.S. Supreme Court's ruling in *Reno II*. Despite the attempt of Congress to repair the Communications Decency Act, the courts still found that attempts to regulate the Internet, absent some technological solution to ensure that minors will not see information that is intended for adults, are unconstitutional restrictions on the First Amendment.

Conclusion

Regulating the Internet has turned out to be a controversial and vexing problem for Congress, despite the important interest in protecting children from potentially dangerous Internet sites. The lack of a technology that will simultaneously protect the well-being of the children and the constitutional rights of the adults will likely characterize this problem for some time.

See also: COMMUNICATIONS ACT OF 1934; DIGITAL COMMUNICATION; DIGITAL MEDIA SYSTEMS; FIRST AMENDMENT AND THE MEDIA; INTERNET AND THE WORLD WIDE WEB; PORNOGRAPHY; PORNOGRAPHY, LEGAL ASPECTS OF; TELECOMMUNICATIONS ACT OF 1996.

Bibliography

Doherty, Kelly M. (1999). "www.obscenity.com: An Analysis of Obscenity and Indecency Regulation on the Internet." *Akron Law Review* 32:259–300.

Hale, J. V. (1998). "*Reno v. American Civil Liberties Union:* Supreme Court Strikes Down Portions of the Communications Decency Act of 1996 as Facially Overbroad in Violation of the First Amendment." *Journal of Contemporary Law* 24:111–130.

Werst, Brian M. (1997). "Legal Doctrine and Its Inapplicability to Internet Regulation: A Guide for Protecting Children from Internet Indecency after *Reno v. ACLU.*" *Gonzaga Law Review* 33:207–240.

Zick, Timothy. (1999). Congress, the Internet, and the Intractable Pornography Problem: The Child Online Protection Act of 1998. *Creighton Law Review* 32:1147–1203.

PATRICK M. JABLONSKI

■ COMMUNICATION STUDY

Determining the beginning of interest in communication and human affairs is difficult—perhaps impossible. Prior to the fifth century B.C.E. Egyptian and Babylonian writings were already expressing an interest in the role of communication in human affairs.

The Roots of the Field

The first scholars to study and write about communication in a systematic manner lived in Ancient Greece. The culture of the times placed heavy emphasis on public speaking, so it is not surprising that the first theories of communication focused on speech. Perhaps the first theory of communication was developed in Greece by Corax, and later further refined by his student, Tisias. Their focus was on the role of communication as it could be used for persuasion in the courtroom, where many important events of the day transpired.

Both Aristotle and his teacher, Plato, were key figures in the development of early communication theory, but Aristotle was probably the most influential. He wrote extensively about communication—which was then termed "rhetoric." Aristotle thought about communication in terms of an orator, or speaker, constructing an argument to be presented in a speech to hearers—an audience. The goal and ultimate effect of communication was persuasion. He described the process as follows:

> [Communication] exists to affect the giving of decisions. . . . [The] orator must not only try to make the argument of his speech demonstrative and worthy of belief, he must also make his own character look right and put his hearers, who are to decide, in the right frame of mind [Roberts, 1924, p. 1377b].

Beginning with the formal study conducted by Aristotle and his contemporaries, communication came to be viewed as a process through which a speaker conveys messages to influence or persuade one or more receivers. In this paradigm, or perspective, emphasis is placed on the role of a source and on his or her intended message. This view of communication was helpful in many ways. It highlighted the key components in the communication process and emphasized the importance of messages in human behavior. It also emphasized that the source of a particular message can be important in determining the outcomes of the communication process.

In his writings, Plato provided a description of what he believed would be necessary for the study of rhetoric to contribute to a broader explanation of human behavior. He explained that the field would need to include the study of words and their nature, the study of human beings and their ways of approaching life, the study of the nature of order, and the study of the instruments by which human beings are affected.

Two other scholars, Cicero and Quintilian, also contributed to the development of communication thinking during this period. Similar to Plato and Aristotle, Cicero saw communication as a practical and academic subject, and Quintilian's contributions were as an educator.

During the classical period discussed so far, democracy and oral expression were valued and important aspects of the societies in which communication was studied. These values and the approach to communication that they implied were largely reversed in the medieval and Renaissance periods. At the close of the fourteenth century, most of the communication ideas that had been developed in rhetoric were instead being studied in religion.

The writings of Augustine led to a reemphasis on the earlier Greek approaches to communication study. His writings applied communication to the interpretation of the Bible and to the art of preaching.

During the eighteenth and nineteenth centuries, the focus of communication study was on written argument, persuasion, and literature. Speaking style, voice, pronunciation, and gestures also became topics of interest, and the National Association of Elocutionists was founded in 1892.

Speech and Journalism Emerge as Disciplines

The early twentieth century heralded the emergence of speech as a discipline. The Eastern States Speech Association—which later became the Eastern Communication Association—was formed in 1909, and the Speech Association of America—which later became the Speech Communication Association and then the National Communication Association—was established in 1914. One year later, the first issue of the *Quarterly Journal of Speech* was published.

Journalistic practice dates at least to the times of the early Egyptians, but the formalized study of the field did not begin until the early 1900s. In 1905, the University of Wisconsin offered what may have been the first journalism courses at a time when there were few published books on the subject.

Communication was also of interest in other fields, particularly philosophy, anthropology, psychology, and sociology, during the early part of the twentieth century.

Multidisciplinary Growth

In the 1940s, communication began to grow rapidly as a field as scholars from various subject areas pursued their interests in the topic. Psychologists studied communication and individual behavior, sociologists studied communication and social relations, anthropologists studied communication and language and culture, and political scientists studied communication and political activity.

At the same time, studies in rhetoric and speech contributed to a growing emphasis on speech and speech communication. Studies in journalism and mass media were providing the foundation for emergence of the study of mass communication.

By the end of the 1950s, a number of writings had appeared that linked speech and mass communication together under the heading of communication. During the middle of this decade, the National Society for the Study of Communication—which later became the International Communication Association—was established with the stated goal of bringing greater unity to the study of communication by exploring the relationship among speech, language, and media.

The 1960s brought many new integrating communication books to the field, particularly notable among them are *The Process of Communication* (1960), *On Human Communication* (1961), *The Science of Human Communication* (1963), *Pragmatics of Human Communication* (1967), and *Communication and Communication Systems* (1968). At the same time, many authors were applying communication concepts in various other fields and settings, laying the foundation for additional segmentation and specialization that would flourish in the years to come.

Growth and Segmentation

The expansion and specialization that began to emerge in the 1960s reached new heights during the 1970s. The topics of interpersonal communication, group communication, organizational communication, political communication, international/intercultural communication, and mass communication began to emerge as subfields within the larger discipline of communication. Meanwhile, interest in more traditional communication topics, such as rhetoric, public speaking, journalism, and mass media, continued to hold the interest of many scholars.

During the 1970s, 1,329 books were published with the word "communication" in the title. This is an amazing number when compared to the 20 such books published in the 1940s, the 61 books published in the 1950s, and the 329 books in the 1960s (Ruben, 1992).

The Information Age

The 1980s brought changes that resulted in the information age and continue to have a pervasive effect on the study of communication. The term "information age" refers to the fact that information and communication technology have come to have an influence on virtually every facet of the personal and occupational lives of individuals. Since the 1980s, information has come to be viewed as a commodity—an "economic" good—that can be bought and sold. The 1980s also marked the beginning of a trend toward consolidation and mergers among major communication and information providers and services.

Hybrid communication technologies began to be introduced in the 1980s. The video monitor, formerly associated with only the viewing of television programs, was beginning to be a common sight on desks in offices and other workplaces. Similarly, the keyboard, once simply a mechanical device that was an important part of a typewriter, was suddenly transformed into an electromechanical tool for inputting digital data. At the beginning of the information age, telephones were hard-wired to walls, "CD" only referred to certificates of deposit at the bank, "ATM" was an unfamiliar acronym, and videocassette recorders and modems were known only to technophiles. Telephone lines, previously used only for voice calls, were beginning to find use as channels to connect computers to other computers, to national networks, and to international networks. The rest, as they say, is history.

These many technological developments have had a huge effect on human communication practice and on communication study. Interest in communication, technology, and communication media has become common among a wide range of scholars, and the study of communication has become the study of message-related behavior. Communication study focuses on the ways in which individuals process information in order to adapt and influence, and in these endeavors, communication technology plays an ever-more central role. Where interpersonal communication was once thought of almost exclusively in terms of face-to-face communication, many who study this topic are now also interested in the role played by communication that is mediated by things such as the telephone, answering machines, and e-mail. Group communication studies may include studies of groups that exist electronically—"virtually"—as well as physically. The electronic group environments include Internet chat rooms and teleconference settings. The more traditional emphasis on the use of mass media, such as network television, radio, and newspapers, has now been expanded to give consideration to cable television, cell telephones, videocassette recorder usage, and the Internet.

Summary

As is apparent from the above discussion, communication is both an ancient and a newly emerging discipline. The core of contemporary communication thought has its origins in the writings of the Ancient Greeks in the area of rhetoric, but the twentieth century marked the emergence and growth of the field of communication as a social science and professional area of study. Through the intervening centuries, interest in the communication process has been strong in any number of related fields, including fields now known as psychology, sociology, cognitive science, political science, and management.

See also: CULTURE AND COMMUNICATION; EVOLUTION OF COMMUNICATION; GROUP COMMUNICATION; INFORMATION SOCIETY, DESCRIPTION OF; INSTRUCTIONAL COMMUNICATION; INTERPERSONAL COMMUNICATION; MODELS OF COMMUNICATION; NONVERBAL COMMUNICATION; ORGANIZATIONAL COMMUNICATION; PARADIGM AND COMMUNICATION; RHETORIC.

Bibliography

Berlo, David. (1960). *The Process of Communication.* New York: Holt.

Cherry, Colin. (1961). *On Human Communication.* New York: Science Editions.

Craig, Robert T. (1999). "Communication Theory as a Field." *Communication Theory* 9(2):119–161.

Harper, Nancy L. (1979.) *Human Communication Theory: History of a Paradigm.* Rochelle Park, NJ: Hayden Books.

Roberts, W. Rhys. (1924). *Works of Aristotle.* Oxford, Eng.: Clarendon Press.

Rogers, Everett M. (1997). *A History of Communication Study.* New York: Free Press.

Ruben, Brent D. (1992). *Communication and Human Behavior,* 3rd edition. Englewood Cliffs, NJ: Prentice-Hall.

Ruben, Brent D., and Stewart, Lea P. (1998). *Communication and Human Behavior,* 4th edition. Needham Heights, MA: Allyn & Bacon.

Schramm, Wilbur. (1963). *The Science of Human Communication.* New York: Basic Books.

Thayer, Leo. (1968). *Communication and Communication Systems.* Homewood, IL: R. D. Irwin.

Watzlawick, Paul; Beavin, Janet H.; and Jackson, Don D. (1967). *Pragmatics of Human Communication.* New York: W. W. Norton.

BRENT D. RUBEN

COMMUNITY NETWORKS

Community networks, often called "civic networks" or "free-nets," are computer networks that have been developed for public access in broad support of a geographic community. The developers of community networks hope to create long-lived public institutions that focus on digital communication much as public libraries, at least historically, have placed their focus on books and other printed material. Community networks apply the notions of free and uncensored access for everybody, both as producer and consumer, to the text, graphic, audio, and other resources found in cyberspace.

Although there is no precise definition of community networks, they have several common characteristics. Community networks aggregate a wide variety of information and communication services in a central, though "virtual," location, becoming, in effect a nonprofit "portal." Community networks are general purpose and strive to support the six "community core values," defined by Douglas Schuler (1996) as conviviality and culture; education; strong democracy; health and well-being; economic equity, opportunity, and sustainability; and information and communication. Furthermore, they generally do not charge for their services or make their money through advertising. In addition to performing the technical duties related to running a networked computer for a large community, community network developers typically engage in a wide range of other related activities including training, social activism, and advocacy.

The question of funding has plagued the community networks movement and the search for financial stability has been an overarching concern for community networks since their inception. Unlike public libraries, public broadcasting, and public access cable television, no universally adopted formula for sustained support has been found. Although many early developers believed that success was to be found through a business-oriented perspective, few (if any) community networks attained this. Many community networks have been kept alive only through long hours of unpaid volunteer labor and intermittent (and insufficient) foundation and government support. With the current lack of public and political support for government projects, it has been difficult to devise a model of financial viability. Also, as is discussed below, access to computer networks has become much more widespread and there are many websites offering free e-mail and other services that compete with community networks. Although it remains to be seen whether the advertising-based model will be viable over the long term, many community networking efforts have already ceased.

The Seattle Community Network

Community networks reflect the intent of their developers and users, and vary from community to community. The Seattle Community Network (SCN), however, can be considered somewhat representative. Launched in December 1992, SCN is a relatively successful and stable community network. SCN offers free e-mail (dial-up and web-based), free web space, and free list servers to anybody.

The SCN is a nonprofit membership organization that elects its board of directors. The board of directors works with members, users, and volunteers to maintain and expand the system according to the dictates of the principles and policies that the organization has adopted (and made available online). SCN may be something of an anomaly as it has been all-volunteer-based since its inception. Although SCN has received very little direct financial support from foundations or government, SCN has received strong nonfinancial support from another civic institution, the Seattle Public Library. Since its beginning, the Seattle Public Library

(SPL) has allowed SCN to house its computers in the same room as the SPL computers, to use the Internet connection of the library, to hold classes in SPL branch libraries, and to distribute SCN brochures in the library.

Although SCN first used a line-oriented menu system that was primarily accessed via dial-up telephone lines, it quickly became more oriented toward the World Wide Web. When a World Wide Web user accesses SCN (http://www.scn.org/), he or she will see the SCN logo, some announcements, and links to the thirteen subject areas of SCN (i.e., activism, arts, civic, earth, education, health, marketplace, neighborhoods, news, people, recreation, sci-tech, and spiritual). Although "activism" is listed first only by virtue of its alphabetic ordering, its placement highlights the focus of SCN on civic, citizen-led activities rather than activities that are commercially driven. Each section is managed by a volunteer subject-area editor who works with the information providers (IPs) in that subject area to make sure the information is readily accessible. The activism page has links to information on the World Trade Organization (the 1999 WTO Ministerial Meeting was held in Seattle), human rights, women's issues, and other concerns. The earth web-page has links to farmer's markets, environmental groups, and other organizations and projects related to the environment. The neighborhood web-page has links to one hundred neighborhood sites in Seattle and elsewhere in the region and beyond.

History

In the early days of the Internet, when access to computer networking services was restricted to academia and military research and development, several innovative pioneers developed projects aimed at the general community. Although most of these early community networks are no longer operational, they explored important new ground related to technology, community development, and the public sphere.

Community Memory of Berkeley, California, created by Efrem Lipkin, Lee Felsenstein, and Ken Colstad, was the world's first community network. Initially started in the mid-1970s after experiments on unmediated two-way access to a message database through public computer terminals, Community Memory was intended to help strengthen the Berkeley community. Their brochure stated that "strong, free, non-hierarchical channels of communication—whether by computer and modem, pen and ink, telephone, or face-to-face—are the front line of reclaiming and revitalizing our communities." Their commitment to serving those without ready access to information technology was demonstrated by numerous training programs and their insistence that all Community Memory terminals be in public places (e.g., libraries and laundromats) but could not be reached via modem or from the Internet. Moreover, all of the information on the system was community generated, such as the "Alameda County War Memorial Project," which contained information on every deceased veteran in Alameda County. Community Memory adopted a creative, direct approach to funding: They offered coin-operated terminals that were free to read, but required twenty-five cents to post an opinion or a dollar to start a new forum.

Big Sky Telegraph was designed to overcome some of the problems related to sparse population and long distances between communities in the rural American West. Frank Odasz (1991), working out of Western Montana University in Dillon, Montana, started the system in 1988 when he began electronically linking one- and two-room schoolhouses across Montana. Odasz used the telegraph metaphor, reflecting the influential communication technology of the nineteenth-century. According to their *Homesteading the Educational Frontier* brochure, "Teachers in rural Montana serving as Circuit Riders, Community Telegraphers, and Teletutors have used modems to overcome time, distance, and economic limitations to empower rural education and community survival." By the early 1990s, Big Sky Telegraph was a distributed system consisting of "Big Skies" and "Little Skies" that offered K-12 lesson plans and a "telecurricular clearinghouse" for K-12 projects running on networks all over the world.

The Public Electronic Network (PEN) in Santa Monica, California, a computer system designed to promote community-oriented participatory democracy, was one of very few government initiatives during that period. Through PEN, Santa Monica citizens could converse with public officials and city servants as well as with each other. PEN was established in 1989 and had over three thousand registered users and over five hundred user log-ons per month in the mid-1990s. PEN provided access to city government information such as city council agendas, reports, public safety tips, the online catalog of the library, and to government services such as obtaining permits. PEN also provided e-mail and conferences on a wide variety of local civic issues. PEN was an early testbed for many ideas related to "electronic democracy," and Pamela Varley (1991) has documented some of the problems PEN experienced.

The Cleveland Free-Net, the world's first free-net, was the most influential community network. With more than thirty-five thousand registered users and more than ten thousand log-ins per day, it was probably the largest as well. The model was developed by Thomas Grundner at Case-Western University and grew from his work on the public health information system, "St. Silicon's Hospital and Dispensary," an electronic question-and-answer forum devoted to medical topics. Doctors, lawyers, automotive mechanics, and others answered questions online on the Cleveland Free-Net, and this format persisted until the system was closed down in late 1999.

The free-nets employed a "city" metaphor to orient users; users go to the appropriate "building" to find the information or services they want. U.S. Supreme Court decisions, for example, were found in the "Courthouse." Free-nets were established in hundreds of locations around the world (although mostly in the United States and Canada) and were often members of the National Public Telecomputing Network (NPTN), an umbrella organization for free-nets that ceased operation in 1997.

Other notable early efforts include the New York Youth Network, which explored computer networking for disadvantaged youths; the Electronic Cafe project, developed by Kit Galloway and Sherrie Rabinowitz, which explored interactive encounters among people in the Los Angeles area and around the world using video and satellite technology; and Playing to Win, a popular educational effort, launched in New York City prisons and housing projects, that evolved over time into the Community Technology Centers Network (CTCNet), a coalition of several hundred computer centers in the United States.

Related Efforts

There is a wide range of efforts worldwide that promote the idea of "community networking" without necessarily being community networks.

Community technology centers provide physical places in communities all over the world. Proponents of these centers, like proponents of community networks, believe that access to digital communications, both as consumers and as producers, will be key to economic—as well as political—survival in coming years. The centers, unlike community networks, address the fact that many people worldwide do not own computers at home and need a place that is conveniently located where they can learn about and use computers.

No census of community networks worldwide—or even in the United States—is completely up-to-date or exhaustive. Community networks and institutions that promote community networking exist all over the world. The Association for Community Networking (AFCN) in the United States, the European Association of Community Networks (EACN) in Europe, and the Community Area Networks (CAN) forum in Japan all focus on community networking issues. Six community networks were launched in the late-1990s in Russia and similar projects are underway in Latin America and South America. Government support does exist in some cases. In the United States, the Telecommunications and Information Infrastructure Assistance Program (later the Telecommunications Opportunities Program) was launched in 1994 to provide assistance for innovative civic projects (including community networks) that use telecommunications technology, while similar projects exist within the European Union.

There were fifteen thousand Internet users when the Cleveland Free-Net started in 1986. Thirteen years later, when the system ceased operation, there were an estimated fifty million. What do community networks do when access is less of an issue, when the world, seemingly, is finding access to digital networking without their assistance, a world that is apparently willing to put up with advertisements to use Hotmail and other advertising-based networking services?

One answer is to concentrate less on the technological infrastructure and more on the idea of community networking in general—the idea of aligning communication technology to community needs in a noncommercial, inclusive way. Ann Bishop and her colleagues (1994) have been involved in several relevant projects. One example is the "Assets Mapping" project, which uses the insights of John Kretzmann and John McKnight (1993) to promote community development using community assets (rather than deficits) through the PrairieNet community network. Bishop and her colleagues have also worked with SisterNet, a local grassroots group, to develop web-based information services that address African-American women's health concerns.

Directions and Issues

The 1990s witnetssed major changes in political, economic, and other social forces, with the rise of global capitalism perhaps being the most dramatic. The accompanying changes in communication technology, such as the explosive growth of the Internet and its rapid commercialization, and the mergers of the world's largest media corporations, are also noteworthy. As the world has shrunk, so, too, as many have noted, have our problems increased. The possibility of global warming and other ecological disasters confront humankind collectively as does war, economic disparities, and our difficulties in addressing these problems collectively.

Robert Putnam (1995) of Harvard University has written about the decline of "social capital," based largely on declining membership in nearly all sectors of noncommercial and nongovernmental organizational life. At the same time, there was a phenomenal rise in the number of nongovernmental organizations worldwide between 1950 and 1999 (see Runyan, 1999) and in so-called virtual communities in cyberspace. Community networks are expressions of civic society whose objectives, unlike commercial systems, are complex and not intended to be judged in economic terms alone. They are alternatives to the commercial systems and often evolve to fit needs not met commercially, such as providing forums for voices that are often unheard or unrecognized. Community networks, though obviously no panacea, may ultimately become a meaningful institution for a new collective intelligence.

See also: COMPUTER LITERACY; COMPUTING; INTERNET AND THE WORLD WIDE WEB.

Bibliography

Agre, Philip E., and Schuler, Douglas, eds. (1997).Reinventing Technology, Rediscovering Community: Critical Explorations of Computing as a Social Practice. Greenwich, CT: Ablex.

Bajjaly, Stephen T. (1999). The Community Networking Handbook. Chicago: American Library Association.
Bishop, Ann, ed. (1994). Emerging Communities: Integrating Networked Information into Library Services. Urbana-Champaign: Graduate School of Library and Information Science, University of Illinois at Urbana-Champaign.
Castells, Manuel. (1996). The Information Age: Economy, Society and Culture. Malden, MA: Blackwell.
Cisler, Steve, ed. (1994). Ties that Bind: Building Community Networks. Cupertino, CA: Apple Library.
Kretzmann, John, and McKnight, John. (1993). Building Communities from the Inside Out: A Path Toward Finding and Mobilizing a Community's Assets. Evanston, IL: Center for Urban Affairs and Policy Research, Northwestern University.
Odasz, Frank. (1991). "Big Sky Telegraph." Whole Earth Review 71:32–35.
Putnam, Robert. (1995). "Bowling Alone: America's Declining Social Capital." Journal of Democracy 6(1):65–78.
Rheingold, Howard. (1993). The Virtual Community: Homesteading on the Electronic Frontier. Reading, MA: Addison-Wesley.
Runyan, Curtis. (1999). "The Third Force: NGOs." World Watch 12(6):12–21.
Schuler, Douglas. (1996). New Community Networks: Wired for Change. Reading, MA: Addison-Wesley.
Varley, Pamela. (1991). "What is Really Happening in Santa Monica?" Technology Review 94(8):42–51.

DOUGLAS SCHULER

COMPREHENSION OF TELEVISION
See: Children's Comprehension of Television

COMPUTER GAMES
See: Ratings for Video Games, Software, and the Internet; Video and Computer Games and the Internet

COMPUTER-HUMAN INTERACTION
See: Human-Computer Interaction

COMPUTER LITERACY

Computer literacy can be defined from two vantage points, each of which is informed by a dynamic mixture of skills that are needed to access and manipulate digitally encoded information. For an individual, it simply means being able to use the computer as a means to an end. A person who uses a vehicle to get from point *a* to point *b* must know how to drive, have a basic understanding of the need for automobile maintenance (such as having the oil changed), and demonstrate knowledge of the rules of the road. That person does not need any in-depth knowledge of how a car functions. In a similar fashion, attaining competence in using computers to perform personal or vocational tasks is the most rudimentary form of computer literacy. It is not essential that computer users know how the machine does what it does, although such knowledge might provide motivation for more sophisticated or increasingly efficient use or serve as a foundation for understanding how computers function in the social order. Hence, computer literacy can also be defined as one element of information literacy and as a collective concept that includes a grasp of the economic, social, and political consequences of widespread computer use.

Computers receive information as input by human beings. They then store, process, retrieve, and provide results in the form of displayed or printed output. All computer operations transpire in accordance with instructions that are written by human beings. At the most basic level, computer literacy means having the aptitude to manipulate these sets of instructions—rendered as programs or applications—to tell computers to process digital data in ways that serve human ends. Mastery of a word-processing program affords one the ability to create, edit, format, display, or print a document in record time. Computer literacy enables a person to exploit the computer's capacity for calculation and representation through use of spreadsheet and database applications. Computer literacy is critical for easy and immediate sorting, management, and association of a mixture of information that can be used for financial or inventory purposes. In their role as communication tools, computers serve to transfer information through programs that shift information from computer to computer, allowing it to be displayed as text or in graphic form. The concept can also include knowing how to connect to storehouses of information to satisfy curiosity or be entertained.

A person who is computer literate should be able to use computers to perform a few tasks such as writing letters or reports, calculating and comparing numbers or objects, or communicating via connections that support e-mail or (perhaps) a web-page, as personal, business, or educational circumstances require. A modest definition of individual computer literacy turns, therefore, on knowing how to use computers to personal advantage. It means using computers to do what they do best—storing, accessing, and repetitively and rapidly processing massive quantities of data for human interpretation, which adds value that turns data into information. The definition might include knowing how to connect to storehouses of information to satisfy curiosity or be entertained.

Computer literacy is not corroborated through a tidy checklist that enumerates how many and which functions an individual can complete using the tool. It occurs in the intersection of knowing how to do or find what one needs or wants in a particular place, at a particular time, for particular reasons. Similar to the driver's understanding of the need for basic car maintenance, a rudimentary definition of computer literacy would also include awareness of the basic elements of, and forces associated with, this machine. The coincidence of computer use and connectivity have brought about a changed atmosphere wherein users, regardless of their level of know-how, are aware that terms such as "hardware," "byte," "monitor," "modem," "bandwidth," "virus," and "protocol" have distinct meanings. Even if a user does not fully understand all of the vocabulary that comes with computer use, these words permeate public consciousness and emphasize a presumed need for computer literacy. Fundamental understanding of computer capabilities and configuration in networks suggests an expanded definition of computer literacy that recognizes the effect that computers have had on society. The notion of computer literacy thus grows to include access to means of improving one's computer skills through education or additional experience.

Within the United States, widespread computer use and networked exchange of information prompted the realization that most citizens should know how to work with applications that are used for writing, calculating, displaying, finding, and communicating information in digital form. A brief overview of the way in which computers became so pervasive in this, the information age, sets the stage for understanding collective computer literacy. By the mid-1970s, microcomputers

To increase their computer literacy and their familiarity with the use of specific software packages, many people take part in large instructional sessions, which are generally tailored to specific products. (Corbis)

were powerful enough and low enough in cost to be introduced into a variety of work settings. By the early 1980s, IBM had produced a personal computer that found its way into industry, schools, and homes. Other manufacturers modeled IBM, and micro (personal) computer use grew as prices decreased within an ever-expanding market. Computers became smaller and more powerful, replacing typewriters, cash registers, and (sometimes) human beings. Apple's Macintosh entered the market in 1984 with an easier-to-use, graphically based operating system that freed users from the need to input complex lines of instructions in order to tell the computer what to do. As a result, computer use continued to soar.

By the 1990s, the full force of networking—computers linked to one another so users could easily send and receive messages—could be felt throughout the world. In the United States, faster and cheaper networked computing moved out from under the umbrella of government and scholarship. More computers permeated the workplace, and more people had computers at home. Computers were linked in local-area networks in offices and factories and by wires and telephone lines from residence to residence. Worldwide connections ultimately flowed throughout the world to form the Internet—one massive network of computers that permits global exchange of information. With the conception of hypertext (providing fast links from one information source to another), graphical World Wide Web browsing capability (popularized in 1994 with the transcendence of Netscape), and the web's delivery of hypermedia, computer use and connectivity fused and heralded the need for computer literacy as a new competency to be addressed by educational and employment policies. These circumstances combined to spawn growing concern about how new generations could become conversant with the new information technology.

Concern for collective computer literacy is evident in America in the form of a succession of federal statutory and executive initiatives. As early as 1983, the need to ensure competence in computer use was set forth in *A Nation at Risk: The Imperative for Educational Reform*. This was an extended report on the quality of education, and it was prepared by the National Commission on Excellence in Education for the U.S. Department of Education. The report recognized the growth of technologically driven industry and the need to emphasize technological literacy among the mix of subjects to be taught in school. Among its recommendations for basic education, the report included the teaching of high school "computer science" so that students could (1) understand the computer as an information, computation, and communication device, (2) be able to use computers to study other fundamental subjects, (3) be able to achieve personal and work-related objectives, and (4) understand the effect of computers and attendant technologies on society.

The High-Performance Computing Act of 1991 declared that "advances in computer science and technology are vital to the Nation's prosperity, national and economic security, industrial production, engineering, and scientific advancement" and established the federally funded National Research and Education Network (NREN). Through NREN, researchers, educators, and students were afforded support for computer and scientific information resources and education. Although the act was not meant to advance computer use by the general public, it explicitly linked computer proficiency to economic progress and provided for coordination of federal agency activities and funding to support NREN. By 1993, the Clinton administration's *National Information Infrastructure: Agenda for Action* called for the establishment of "a seamless web of communications networks, computers, databases, and consumer electronics." This effort resulted in the alignment of government, industry, and general public interest in developing a National Information Infrastructure (NII), which came to be known as the "information highway" in popular culture.

The NII process activated a convergence of interests that can be interpreted as defining computer literacy characterized by both ability and access. Government, industry, and public-interest groups all became involved in an effort to create an enlarged concept of collective computer literacy at the end of the twentieth century. In 1995,

the National Telecommunications and Information Administration (NTIA) issued the results of the first in a series of investigations into the phenomenon of limited Internet and computer access among certain segments of the population. This issue has come to be called the "digital divide." The Telecommunications Act of 1996 produced the first major overhaul of telecommunications law since 1934 and authorized Federal Communications Commission oversight of a program whereby service providers would give reduced rates (or e-rates) for Internet service to schools, libraries, and health-care providers. Various federal agencies, including the NTIA and its Technology Opportunities Program (TOP, formerly TIIAP), initiated programs to support both computer connectivity and distribution of equipment and training. Interest groups and nonprofit organizations, such as Computer Professionals for Social Responsibility and the Benton Foundation, became active in the study and advocacy of ways and means of equitable and improved access to information technology.

In 1998, the Next Generation Internet Research Act amended the High-Performance Computing Act of 1991 and authorized federal interagency cooperation and funding for development and implementation of new and progressive networking capabilities. While this effort is again concentrated on a certain strata of scholarly and government users, the potential spin-off effects of all such legislation prompt continued discussion of what computer literacy means as a requirement for economic progress and participation. Computer literacy is an evolving concept that has rippled throughout society, reshaping thoughts on education, employment, intellectual freedom, privacy, and equality.

See also: COMMUNICATIONS ACT OF 1934; COMMUNITY NETWORKS; COMPUTER SOFTWARE; COMPUTER SOFTWARE, EDUCATIONAL; COMPUTING; FEDERAL COMMUNICATIONS COMMISSION; INTERNET AND THE WORLD WIDE WEB; LITERACY; TECHNOLOGY, ADOPTION AND DIFFUSION OF; TELECOMMUNICATIONS ACT OF 1996.

Bibliography

Beekman, George. (1999). *Computer Confluence: Exploring Tomorrow's Technology*. Reading, MA: Addison-Wesley.

COMPUTER SOFTWARE • 165

Benton Foundation. (1998). *Losing Ground Bit by Bit: Low-Income Communities in the Information Age.* Washington, DC: Benton Foundation.

Coyle, Karen. (1997). *Coyle's Information Highway Handbook: A Practical File on the New Information Order.* Chicago: American Library Association.

National Commission on Excellence in Education. (1983). *A Nation at Risk: The Imperative for Educational Reform.* Washington, DC: U.S. Government Printing Office.

National Telecommunications and Information Administration. (1999). *Falling Through the Net: Defining the Digital Divide.* Washington, DC: U.S. Department of Commerce.

TONYIA J. TIDLINE

■ COMPUTER SOFTWARE

Computer hardware, consisting mainly of the central processing unit (CPU), random access memory (RAM), and various peripheral devices, provides the physical components needed for computation, but hardware by itself can do nothing useful without the explicit step-by-step instructions provided by computer software.

Computer software consists of sequences of instructions for the CPU. A sequence of instructions for the CPU is typically referred to as a program. Programs vary in size and complexity and can be as simple as a utility that prints the current time and date on the screen or as large and complicated as a spreadsheet application or a full-featured word processor. Each instruction in a program directs the CPU to do one simple task, such as accessing the contents of a memory location, adding two numbers, or jumping to a different part of the program depending on the value contained in a register. Because individual instructions are so simple, it takes many of them to create a program. Complicated programs, such as word processors, contain literally millions of instructions and may require years of development time.

Historical Background

In 1944, the Hungarian-born mathematician John von Neumann developed the first practical way for computers to use software. The machine he designed to use this fundamental advance in computing was called the EDVAC (Electronic Discrete Variable Automatic Computer). All previous computers—including the Electronic Numerical Integrator and Computer (ENIAC), the first electronic digital computer—had to be rewired every time a different program was run. Obviously, this rewiring was a time-consuming, tedious, and error-prone task. With the EDVAC, programs could be loaded from external storage (typically by means of punched paper tape) exactly the same way as data. In fact, at the level of memory storage, programs were indistinguishable from data. By clever manipulation of the binary codes used to represent instructions as they resided in the computer memory, it was even possible to write programs that modified themselves as they ran. Such is the infinitely malleable and somewhat schizophrenic world of software that, for many individuals, makes it a fascinating and sometimes consuming passion.

During the very earliest years of general-purpose computing, programmers explicitly wrote all the instructions that the computer would execute in the course of running a program, including the instructions needed for input and output of the data on which the program performed its computations. This resulted in large numbers of programs that contained sections of identical code commonly used for reading data at the beginning of the run and writing results at the end. Programmers soon realized that these commonly used sections of code could be stored in a "library" that their programs could access whenever they needed to perform a common system-level function. For example, a library of routines to send output to the printer could be provided for programmers who were writing data processing software. The remainder of the code in each program would therefore be only that needed for the unique requirements of the specific task that the program was intended to perform. This allowed programmers to focus on the problem-solving, applied aspects of their programs and led the way not only for increased programmer productivity but also for the advent of software production and computing on a large-scale global basis.

Operating Systems and Applications

The two main types of software are system software and application software. As explained in the previous section, this fundamental division arose when programmers realized that they could be more productive, and their programs could be

Microsoft 2000, which is billed as an operating system for the high-priced, high-volume server computers that businesses use to run their networks, was unveiled by Bill Gates during a keynote address in San Francisco on February 17, 2000. (AFP/Corbis)

more reliable and efficient, with a layer of system-level software between their application programs and the computer hardware. System software consists mainly of the operating system and utility programs that help with its use.

The operating system is more than just routines to help with program input and output (I/O). Operating systems give application software access to the CPU, disk drives, modems, and any other hardware connected to the computer. The operating system governs the entire operation of the computer and supervises the behavior of application programs. It allocates CPU time to programs so that they use the resources of the computer efficiently. For example, in a multitasking operating system, one program can execute while another is waiting for an I/O operation to complete. The operating system also allocates memory to each incoming program, giving it a range of memory addresses to use. If a program

performs an illegal operation, such as attempting to access a part of memory outside of its allocated portion, the operating system aborts execution of the program, frees the resources it was using, and reports the problem to the user. This is one way in which the operating system prevents errant programs from disabling the entire computer or corrupting the data used by other programs.

Some operating systems are capable of very sophisticated memory management. The use of programs that require large amounts of memory has led to the development of virtual memory, in which the operating system uses a large hard disk to emulate a large RAM. As a program requests more and more storage, the operating system allocates more virtual memory to it, switching segments of memory between physical RAM and the disk as necessary. This is particularly economical because a hard disk of a given size is cheaper than a similar size of RAM, but the processing is slower than if the computer had that much physical RAM.

Those who use IBM-compatible personal computers probably use the operating system Microsoft Windows, or a version of it such as Windows 98 or Windows NT. Prior to about 1992, those using IBM-compatible personal computers probably used Microsoft's DOS (Disk Operating System). The operating system is usually supplied (or "bundled") with a new computer when it is sold to the user.

Operating systems such as Windows and Linux also provide support for the graphical user interface (GUI) that application programs use for screen displays and for reading input from the keyboard and mouse.

The operating system by itself, however, does not afford much in the way of useful work with a computer. For this, it is necessary to use an application such as a word processor for writing papers or a spreadsheet application for doing financial planning. Any given application is written for use with one particular operating system (sometimes referred to as a "platform") and can only be used with that operating system because it expects to find the specific services and function calls that that operating system provides. Thus, for example, a word processor written for Microsoft Windows will not run on a machine that has a DOS operating system.

As computer technology has progressed, the division of labor between operating systems and applications has become ever more important. New types of I/O devices, such as magnetic tape, magnetic disk, printers, monitors, keyboards, mice, and even network interfaces are all controlled through the operating system and never directly by application software. This is because each kind of device has unique control codes, and a single application could not be expected to anticipate every device that might be connected to the computer on which it runs. The operating system, therefore, provides applications with common ways of interacting with different types of devices. An application can, therefore, use one routine to write a file to a floppy disk, hard disk, or a remote disk connected through a network. This allows for device independence, which is crucial to the continued usability of existing software with new devices. If application programs had to know about the particulars and the operational details of each device that might be connected to a computer, not only would software development be far more expensive and time-consuming than it is already, but any device developed after that software was written would not work with the software.

When hardware vendors (e.g., printer manufacturers) introduce a new product, they typically provide "device driver" software with it. This is software that the operating system uses to communicate with and control the device on behalf of the application that requests the use of it. When the user selects the print command while using a word processor, for example, the word processor calls the operating system's print function and passes a copy of the current document to it. The print function in turn uses the device driver for that printer (and possibly other specialized software as well) to control the actual printing of the document. Having the operating system as a mediator, the word processor can print a document even though it does not know how to control the printer directly.

Programming Languages

A single CPU instruction does very little, and useful programs require thousands or even millions of instructions. If a programmer had to write each instruction individually, the task of developing software would be labor intensive and error prone. To expedite the development, as well as to improve the reliability of software, programmers use programming languages instead of writing machine instructions directly.

To see how a programming language can simplify the process of software development, consider the following sequence of machine instructions that adds two numbers. First, the computer loads the value stored at memory location X into a CPU register, then adds the number stored at memory location Y to it, and finally stores the result in memory location Z:

LOAD X

ADD Y

STORE Z

In a programming language such as FORTRAN (Formula Translator), for example, the programmer merely has to write $Z = X + Y$. This is easier for the programmer to write, but it is also easier for other programmers to read. This is important for the long-term maintenance of large systems, where a program may continue to go through development cycles years after the original programmer has left the company.

Even though most software is written using programming languages, computers still only understand CPU instructions. Thus, a special program called a "compiler" translates the programming language statements written by the programmer into the equivalent CPU instructions. Each programming language requires its own special compiler. Due to the generalized nature of programming languages, compilers are large, complicated programs that require months or even years of development time by teams of expert programmers. Developing a new programming language is therefore a long and expensive undertaking.

Hundreds of computer languages have been developed since the late 1950s, each with specialized purposes or particular kinds of users in mind. A few of the most common ones are briefly described below.

The first version of FORTRAN, which was developed for use in numerical and scientific applications, was released in 1958. LISP (List Programming), released the same year, was developed for use in artificial intelligence research. Both of these languages have been used extensively since that time and are still widely used.

COBOL (Common Business Oriented Language) was released in 1960 as a language to be used for business applications. It was designed to have an English-like structure and vocabulary so nonprogrammers (e.g., managers, accountants) could read it. While its effectiveness in this regard has been subject to debate, COBOL continues to be used extensively in business, particularly for large mainframe-based computer applications in banking and insurance.

Most programmers learn BASIC (Beginner's All-purpose Symbolic Instructional Code) as a first language. BASIC has an easy-to-learn syntax and does not require the use of complicated system software as do FORTRAN and COBOL. Because the syntax and resource usage of rudimentary versions of BASIC are so modest, it was the choice of microcomputer manufacturers in the early 1980s. At that point, the RAM supplied with such computers was as small as 8 kilobytes, and the BASIC interpreter and system software were permanently stored in read-only memory (ROM). More recent versions of BASIC take advantage of the larger capacity and increased speed of personal computers to offer more language features. Some versions of BASIC now resemble Pascal, a language that was developed in the late 1960s for programming education and that included sophisticated language features to help programmers avoid common errors in the structure of their programs.

During the 1980s, C became a widely used language. Although it has a sophisticated syntax, allowing programmers to write statements that would be very difficult and tedious to construct in machine language, it also allows the programmer to manipulate directly the register bits and memory addresses. Most other programming languages do not allow such direct manipulation. C was developed in 1972 at AT&T Bell Laboratories and was flexible and powerful enough that it was used to implement the UNIX operating system.

C continues to be used to implement operating systems and applications and is the principal language used to implement Linux, the freely distributed UNIX-like operating system developed by Linus Torvalds and other developers. The idea behind Linux is to provide computer users with a technically sophisticated alternative to other operating systems, particularly Microsoft Windows, and to do it in such a way that no large corporation or other centralized entity can control its licensing or otherwise dictate its terms of use.

Beginning in the late 1960s, attention turned to "object orientation" as a way to improve programmer productivity, software reliability, and the portability of programs between different operating systems. Object orientation allows programmers to think about program code and data much as individuals think about objects in the real world, with their inner workings being hidden and only the parts intended for user access being visible. An example of a real-world object that relates well to software objects is a portable radio; it is a self-contained object that has complicated inner workings but only presents a few simple controls to people. The radio is made to work by manipulating the external controls, not by tinkering with the complicated electronics inside of it. Software objects simplify software development by only allowing users (including programmers who use objects to build other programs) to manipulate the external attributes of objects. Only the developer of an object can tinker with its inner workings. Smalltalk, publicly released in 1980, was one of the first languages designed to be specifically object oriented, and it continues to be the model for object-oriented systems. C++ was developed as an object-oriented extension of C, but it has proved complicated and difficult to manage for large projects.

In 1995, Sun Microsystems introduced Java, an object-oriented language designed for developing Internet-based applications. Java's syntax is based on C, to encourage C and C++ developers to use it, and it does not require programmers who build network-aware applications to do complicated network programming. Java is also designed as a platform-independent language, allowing programmers to write code once and run it on any operating system and hardware. Java does this by running within a special environment that makes all platforms appear the same. Java "applets" are little programs that run in World Wide Web browsers and are often used as part of web-pages. Java "applications" run outside of web browsers, just like other applications do.

Influence of Software on Computer Markets

Even though people tend to think of computer hardware as the more substantial part of the computing package, software is often the more important consideration when buying a computer. Software is also more valuable because of the greater effort and expense involved in its development. Developing hardware is by no means trivial, but advances in hardware are typically manifested by increased speed and memory capacity. Advances in software are more difficult to measure, and they may only become apparent to users who have specialized needs or who are in particular circumstances.

Once users find software that satisfies their needs, they typically do not want to change, even when a new version or a competitor's version becomes available that may better serve them. The use of a particular piece of software represents not only an investment in that software and the hardware to run it, but also in training of the personnel who use it and do collaborative work with it. In this way, the use of particular kinds of software (as with any other tool) becomes enmeshed in the culture of the community that uses it. As time goes on, changing to a different system becomes more expensive. Therefore, the software company that establishes a greater market share first will most likely dominate the market thereafter.

This was the case with IBM, which dominated the computer hardware and software market from the 1950s through most of the 1980s, even though its hardware and software were not particularly advanced. They were sufficient to do the data processing jobs their customers required, and IBM's sales and service staff made up for any deficiencies that remained.

By the late 1990s, Microsoft had taken over the dominant position in the software market that IBM had once held. Microsoft uses its dominance in the operating system market to leverage sales of its application software, which it claims makes the best use of its operating system features. However, the extent to which Microsoft has pursued this dominance has caused them to have legal difficulties. Many competing software companies have successfully sued Microsoft for predatory business practices as well as for breach of licensing agreements. Most significantly, in late 1999, the U.S. Department of Justice found Microsoft in violation of antitrust statutes.

Conclusion

Computer software is an integral part of everyday life, not only in the use of personal computers but also behind the scenes of every business transaction, telephone call, and even in the use of everyday devices such as automobiles. Even devices that are not ostensibly computers may contain one or more small, embedded computers to enhance their operation in some way. All of these computers depend on the proper operation of software to accomplish their tasks. In certain respects, the operation of software is indistinguishable from the operation of the device that houses it, and some devices that were introduced in the late 1990s (such as DVD players and other digital media devices) would not even be possible without software.

Software will continue to be an ever more pervasive presence for the foreseeable future; it will become increasingly difficult, if not impossible altogether, to do anything without using software in some way. This presents challenges on a number of fronts, the most important being that the software be reliable and that people have control over how it is used, especially when it involves the transmission of personal information over data networks such as the Internet.

The Open Source Initiative (OSI), of which the Linux operating system is a part, seeks to improve the software development and distribution process by having a large and loosely knit group of developers write code that is freely available to all who use it, as well as freely modifiable by developers who discover bugs and other problems with the software. This is in contrast to the corporate model of software development, where only the company that produces the software maintains it and users of the software have no access to the source code.

See also: COMPUTER SOFTWARE, EDUCATIONAL; COMPUTING; DIGITAL COMMUNICATION; DIGITAL MEDIA SYSTEMS; INTERNET AND THE WORLD WIDE WEB; PRIVACY AND ENCRYPTION; STANDARDS AND INFORMATION; SYSTEMS DESIGNERS.

Bibliography

Harriger, Alka R.; Lisack, Susan K.; Gotwals, John K.; and Lutes, Kyle D. (1999). *Introduction to Computer Programming with Visual Basic 6: A Problem-Solving Approach.* Englewood Cliffs, NJ: Prentice-Hall.

Kraynak, Joe. (1998). *The Complete Idiot's Guide to PCs.* New York: Alpha Books.

Open Source Initiative. (2001). "OpenSource.Org." <http://www.opensource.org/.>

Perry, Greg M. (1993). *Absolute Beginner's Guide to Programming.* Indianapolis, IN: Howard W. Sams.

Perry, Greg M. (1994). *Absolute Beginner's Guide to C.* Indianapolis, IN: Howard W. Sams.

Schwartz, Randal L.; Christiansen, Tom; and Wall, Larry. (1997). *Learning Perl,* 2nd edition. Sebastopol, CA: O'Reilly & Associates.

ERIC JOHNSON

COMPUTER SOFTWARE, EDUCATIONAL

Educational computer software inherited from television the hope for revolutionizing educational practice. In addition to the audiovisual qualities found in educational television, computers offered learners interactivity, immediacy of feedback about responses, and control over learning experiences. Academic subjects such as mathematics, science, history, and reading could be taught to children in an efficient manner. Nonetheless, not all computer applications are alike in the educational opportunities that they afford children.

Basic Applications

In his book *Mindstorms: Children, Computers, and Powerful Ideas*, Seymour Papert (1980) advanced the idea that computers can teach children by serving as a tutor, a tool, or a tutee. As a tutor, the computer became an extension of teaching machines in which children learn by drill and practice. The computer tutors the child until the child masters that content. Lessons can be tailored to the knowledge bases of individual learners, and interactive contingent feedback allows children immediate knowledge about the accuracy of their responses. The research literature on computer-assisted instruction (CAI) demonstrates that drill and practice applications are effective in teaching children basic knowledge and even cognitive skills.

As a tool, computers can be used by children in their search for, and in their communication of, knowledge. Word processing packages are tools that children can use to meet their learning goals and objectives. Writing can be edited quickly and efficiently. Spell checkers automatically highlight words that are spelled incorrectly. Functions such as cut and paste, activities that were once done by hand with real scissors and tape, are now done electronically by computers. Children also use the computer as a tool for collaborating with others, particularly over the Internet.

Papert (1980) argued that the most powerful educational computer application, which is the least used option by children, is when the computer is a tutee. As part of this application, children tell the computer what to do. More specifically, children actively control the computer with their own programs, thereby mastering its codes and inner workings by engaging in cognitive activities such as logical thought, debugging, and planning. Research conducted by Yasmin Kafai (1995) demonstrated that child programmers use abstract cognitive skills when constructing logical flow charts to make fraction programs. Even so, other researchers, such as Diane Poulin-Dubois and her colleagues (1989) have found that learning a computer program designed to teach children geometry yielded specific skills but not general cognitive effects.

One way to foster children's involvement with computers is to embed the content in intrinsically interesting learning environments. In such applications, children become involved with the interactive software and master learning activities, such as reading along with a videodisc or a CD-ROM storybook or learning to read and write words within interesting computer simulations. Research by Carol Chomsky (1990) suggests that children are sometimes more motivated to learn in these interesting computer environments than when the same lesson is taught by a live teacher. More important, the research summarized by Sandra Calvert (1999a) shows that children learn and retain more of the educational material, recognizing new words or understanding complex concepts about how the brain works. These applications work for most children, including those with developmental difficulties such as autism.

Software Production Feature

Attractive formal production features from television can also be adapted to create intrinsically interesting computer environments. Formal features are audiovisual production features, such as action, sound effects, and language, that structure and represent the content that is to be learned. Formal features can be used to motivate, to focus attention selectively on important content, to provide visual and verbal modes to represent content, and to reward children for correct responses.

Moderate action has been a particularly useful feature for teaching children. According to research summarized by Calvert (1999b), when objects on a

Some educational software, such as Reader Rabbit, *helps young children learn to read by presenting the process in the context of a game.* (Wolfgang Kaehler/Corbis)

computer screen move rather than simply appear in still frame, children are more likely to select those objects, produce those object names, and remember those objects. Beneficial effects of action are most pronounced for young children and for those who have reading difficulties. These findings suggest that action is a developmentally appropriate mode that young or developmentally delayed children can use to represent content.

Production features, however, can also distract children from the learning task. For example, in one study summarized by Aletha Huston and John Wright (1998), first-grade boys became so interested in attractive CD-ROM production features that they rushed through an interactive story, later recalling less of the story material than children who saw the story without interactive capability.

Multimedia Teaching Methods

Anchored instruction is another method for creating intrinsically interesting learning environments for children. In anchored instruction, educational concepts are linked, or anchored, to entertaining, real-life material. For example, film situations such as Indiana Jones using his bullwhip to swing across a pit in *Raiders of the Lost Ark* are used to teach children math concepts. In addition to using the height of Indiana Jones and the length of the bullwhip to figure out how far he had to jump, the children can also apply this problem-solving approach to real-life problems that they encounter. According to research by Robert Sherwood and his associates (1987), such applications make learning fun while teaching children useful problem-solving strategies. Most of the research on anchored instruction was done with videodiscs, a device that has now been replaced by CD-ROMs.

The Internet provides academically oriented sites, including places to help children with their homework, to practice basic competency skills, and to explore areas that are of interest to them. Children collaborate online with other children throughout the world, including multinational efforts such as writing a joint newspaper.

Multimedia environments are emerging as a preferred method for teaching children. *Voyage of the Mimi*, a series developed by Bank Street College, was one of the first multimedia applications in which books, television, and computer software were used to teach science lessons. Such lessons were initially embedded within stories presented through books and television programs. The lessons could then be mastered by interacting with complementary computer software. These kinds of multimedia environments will become the norm as technologies converge, with the Internet delivering educational software applications and video content online to children in their schools and in their homes.

See also: CHILDREN'S CREATIVITY AND TELEVISION USE; COMPUTER LITERACY; COMPUTER SOFTWARE; EDUCATIONAL MEDIA PRODUCERS; INTERNET AND THE WORLD WIDE WEB; TELEVISION, EDUCATIONAL.

Bibliography

Calvert, Sandra L. (1999a). *Children's Journeys Through the Information Age*. Boston: McGraw-Hill.

Calvert, Sandra L. (1999b). "The Form of Thought." In *Theoretical Perspectives in the Concept of Representation*, ed. Irving Sigel. Hillsdale, NJ: Lawrence Erlbaum.

Chomsky, Carol. (1990). "Books on Videodisc: Computers, Video, and Reading Aloud." In *Cognition, Education, and Multimedia: Exploring Ideas in High Technology*, eds. Don Nix and Rand Shapiro. Hillsdale, NJ: Lawrence Erlbaum.

Huston, Aletha, and Wright, John. (1998). "Mass Media and Children's Development." In *Handbook of Child Psychology, Vol. 4: Child Psychology in Practice*, 5th ed., eds. William Damon, Irving Sigel, and K. Ann Renninger. New York: Wiley.

Kafai, Yasmin. (1995). *Minds in Play: Computer Game Design As a Context for Children's Learning*. Hillsdale, NJ: Lawrence Erlbaum.

Malone, Thomas W. (1981). "Toward a Theory of Intrinsically Motivating Instruction." *Cognitive Science* 4:333–369.

Papert, Seymour. (1980). *Mindstorms: Children, Computers, and Powerful Ideas*. New York: Basic Books.

Poulin-Dubois, Diane; McGilly, Catherine A.; and Shultz, Thomas R. (1989). "Psychology of Computer Use: Effect of Learning LOGO on Children's Problem-Solving Skills." *Psychological Reports* 64(3):1327–1337.

Sherwood, Robert D.; Kinzer, Charles K.; Bransford, John D.; and Franks, Jeffrey J. (1987). "Some Benefits of Creating Macro-Contexts for Science Instruction: Initial Findings." *Journal of Research in Science Teaching* 24(5):417–435.

SANDRA L. CALVERT

COMPUTER SOFTWARE, RATINGS FOR

See: Ratings for Video Games, Software, and the Internet

COMPUTING

Computers and computer networks have changed the way in which people work, play, do business, run organizations and countries, and interact with one another on a personal level. The workplace of the early twentieth century was full of paper, pens, and typewriters. The office of the early twenty-first century is a place of glowing monitor screens, keyboards, mice, scanners, digital cameras, printers, and speech recognition equipment. The office is no longer isolated; it is linked by computer networks to others like it around the world. Computers have had such an effect that some say an information revolution is occurring. This revolution may be as important as the printing revolution of the fifteenth century, the industrial revolution of the nineteenth century, or the agricultural revolutions of the ancient and medieval worlds.

The computer was invented to perform mathematical calculations. It has become a tool for communication, for artistic expression, and for managing the store of human knowledge. Text, photographs, sounds, or moving pictures can all be recorded in the digital form used by computers, so print, photographic, and electronic media are becoming increasingly indistinguishable. As Tim Berners-Lee (1998), developer of the World Wide Web, put it, computers and their networks promise to become the primary medium in which people work and play and socialize, and hopefully, they will also help people understand their world and each other better.

During the last half of the twentieth century, electronic digital computers revolutionized business, learning, and recreation. Computers are now used in newspaper, magazine, and book publishing, and in radio, film, and television production. They guide and operate unmanned space probes, control the flow of telecommunications, and help people manage energy and other resources. They are used to categorize and preserve the store of human knowledge in libraries, archives, and museums. Computer chips called "embedded microprocessors" are found in the control systems of aircraft, automobiles, trains, telephones, medical diagnostic equipment, kitchen utensils, and farm equipment. The effect on society has been so great that digital information itself is now exchanged more rapidly and more extensively than the commodities or manufactured goods it was originally supposed to help manage. Information has become an essential commodity and, some would argue, a necessary social good.

The history of computing is several stories combined. One is a hardware story—a tale of inventions and technologies. Another is a software story—a tale of the operating systems that enabled specific computers to carry out their basic functions and the applications programs designed to deliver services to computer users. A third story tells how computers provide answers to the problems of society, and how they in turn create new possibilities for society.

Computers and the Media

The computer has transformed print journalism and magazine and book production, changing the ways in which stories are researched, written, transmitted to publishers, typeset, and printed. Through computing and telecommunications, a news story breaking in Asia can be sent within seconds to North America, along with digital pictures. Word-processing software and more sophisticated desktop publishing programs allow authors to create and revise documents easily and to check them for spelling, grammar, and readability.

Copies of digital documents can be printed on demand, and because computers check for transmission errors, all the copies will be identical. While the first word-processing programs offered little more than typewriter-style characters, the introduction of graphical user interfaces (GUIs) in the 1980s and 1990s opened new design possibilities. Writers could choose from a variety of type fonts, select different page layouts, and include photographs and charts. Some feared that this might eliminate jobs since tasks performed by authors, editors, typesetters, proofreaders, graphic designers, and layout artists could all be performed by one person with a computer.

Laptop or notebook computers gave writers even more flexibility. A reporter on location could compose a story and transmit it immediately to a newspaper (using a modem and a hotel room telephone) on the other side of the globe and, perhaps, to wire news services such as The Associated Press or the Reuters news agency. Satellite uplinks, cellular phones, and infrared "beaming" between machines provide even more possibilities. Moreover, digital photography eliminates the time taken to develop photographs, and digital pictures can be transmitted as easily as text.

Computers have revolutionized radio, television, and film production as well. Computerized camera switching and special-effects generators, electronic music synthesizers, photographic exposure control, and digital radio and television programming are all examples. Computer graphics can be used to superimpose sports statistics over a picture of a game in progress or allow a commentator to explain a key play by drawing a diagram over a television picture. Computers have made it possible to produce the entire programming lineup of a radio station without relying on tape recorders except for archival materials or for recordings made in the field.

Digital sound editing can eliminate noise, mix voice and music, and give producers second-by-second precision in the assembly of programs. Computerized film processing can provide better quality images or allow images to be converted from color to black-and-white and vice versa. While movie animation has traditionally involved photographing thousands of separately drawn pictures or "cells," computer animation can use fewer drawings and produce thousands of variations. Special effects are much more convincing when the computer handles the lighting, perspective, and movement within the movie scene.

Speech recognition and dictating software can convert voice recordings directly to word-processed text, and translation programs can then rewrite the word-processed text into another human language. Musicians can compose new works at a computer keyboard and create a printed score from the finished version.

Even when an organization's primary medium is print, radio, or television, it has become common to provide more in-depth coverage on an associated website. While some radio and television networks simultaneously broadcast and webcast their programming, perhaps the most powerful potential will be found in ever-growing digital archives. Using search engines and, increasingly, programs called "intelligent agents," users can retrieve items from the archives, print fresh copies, or compare different accounts of the same event.

Most young people probably first use a computer for entertainment. Individual- and multiple-player games, online "chat" rooms, newsgroups, electronic mailing lists, and websites provide computer-mediated education and leisure activities that were never possible before.

At first, computer programmers wrote games to amuse themselves. The classic "dungeons and dragons" game, *Adventure,* invented by Will Crowther and Bob Woods, was a favorite. Players gave commands such as "go left" or "take lamp," and the computer printed replies such as "OK." There were no pictures. Simple games that used graphics, with names such as *Pong* and *Pacman*, became available during the 1970s. As personal computers and handheld games became practical to produce, an entire electronic games industry was born. Nintendo and Sega are two familiar games companies. Computerized video games and lottery ticket machines soon became such popular attractions in shopping malls and corner stores that critics began to warn that they might become addictive.

Research Databases

Computing has changed the way writers research and prepare scientific articles. During the early 1970s, a small number of databases containing "abstracts" (i.e., summaries of scholarly and popular articles) could be searched offline. Users submitted lists of subjects or phrases on coding forms. Keypunchers typed them onto computer cards, and operators processed them on mainframe computers. The answers would be available the next day. Library catalogs were printed on paper cards or computer output microform (COM). A microfiche is a transparent plastic slide, roughly the size of an ordinary index card, but it contains images of many pages of computer output.

The Library of Congress, and national libraries in other countries, had by this time converted most of the descriptions of the books they owned into machine-readable form. Toward the end of the 1970s, research databases and library catalogs were becoming widely available online. The Dialog database, and library services such as the Online Computer Library Center (OCLC), made it possible to search the contents of many journals or the holdings of many libraries at once. Standards such as the Machine-Readable Cataloging format (MARC) made it possible to exchange this information worldwide and to display it on many different types of computers. However, limits on computer disk space, telecommunications capacities, and computer processing power still made it impractical to store the full text of articles.

Because of the costs, researchers working for large institutions were the main users of these services. By the mid-1980s, when microcomputer workstations became widely available and compact disc read only memory (CD-ROM) became a practical distribution method, much research could be conducted without connecting to large central databases. Companies such as EBSCO and InfoTrac began licensing CD-ROMs to their subscribers. With better magnetic "hard" disks and faster microcomputer chips, full-text storage and retrieval finally became workable.

By the end of the twentieth century, databases and catalogs could be accessed over the Internet, on CD-ROM, or through dial-up connections. Some of the special databases include ERIC (for educational issues), Medline and Grateful Med (for medical issues), and Inspec (for engineering issues). Legal research was simplified by services such as Lexis and Westlaw, which allowed identification and cross-referencing of U.S. and international statute and case law. In one of the more interesting applications of computing technology, the Institute for Scientific Information in Washington, D.C., introduced its citation indexing services, which allow researchers to discover important authors and issues by revealing which authors quote one another. Some databases are free of charge, and some are available for a fee.

A researcher at a public library, in a television newsroom, or in a medical practice can perform searches against thousands of special databases and millions of sites on the World Wide Web. While this sort of research was possible with printed directories in the past, it was time consuming and labor intensive. However, searching for data electronically can have unexpected results. Because the computer does not really understand what the string of letters "Jim Smith" means, it will faithfully report any occurrence it finds, regardless of the context. Information retrieval theory and informetrics are two fields that study the implications.

The Computer Industry

In the late 1960s, some writers scoffed at the potential of computers. The mainframe machines of the time occupied entire rooms, and only large institutions could afford them. No computer ever conceived, suggested one writer, had ever weighed less than a human being or been capable of performing as many tasks.

Without the transistor and the integrated circuit, computers would still fill large rooms. Without the laser and improved plastics, optical storage media such as CD-ROMs and digital versatile discs (DVDs) would not be possible. Magnetic tapes and disks have also improved greatly over the years and can now store much more information than they could in the past. It is difficult to buy an item in the supermarket or to borrow a book from a library without that item having a barcode label on it. Credit and debit cards with magnetic strips make it easier to access bank accounts and make retail purchases. Inventions such as these are part of the story of computing, although they are often overlooked.

For example, a minicomputer of the mid-1980s could cost about $500,000 and could contain 64 kilobytes (kb) of random access memory (RAM). By the end of the century, a magnetic floppy disk containing 1.4 megabytes (Mb) of memory sold for less than a dollar, a CD-ROM disk that held 650 Mb was less than two dollars, and desktop microcomputers with 64 Mb of RAM were common household items.

As the industry grew, so did the legends of inventors who made fortunes or revolutionized the industry. William R. Hewlett and David Packard started their company in a garage. Graduate students David Filo and Jerry Yang developed the Yahoo! Internet directory in a dormitory room. Steve Jobs of Apple Computer, Bill Gates of Microsoft, and the heads of many other companies in California's Silicon Valley became known around the world.

Computer engineers and programmers have often exchanged their ideas openly, out of scientific duty. The Xerox Corporation hit on the idea of the graphical user interface (GUI), developed the "mouse," and then told everyone how to produce them. Linus Torvalds developed the Linux operating system as a personal project and then made it available for free. Universities also have a long history of developing software and computers and then sharing the knowledge.

The History of Computers

While digital computers are a relatively recent invention, analog devices have existed for thousands of years. The abacus, sometimes considered to be a computer, was used in medieval China and by the Aztecs of Central America, and earlier "counting boards" were found in ancient Babylon. Another analog device, the slide rule, continues to have a following because some engineers still prefer them to electronic calculators. Circular slide rules, called "dead-reckoning computers," were used by aircraft pilots well into the 1970s to perform navigational tasks.

During the Middle Ages, the Franciscan scholar Ramon Llull used circular disks that had letters and numbers (representing terms from philosophy) written on them. By turning the wheels, Llull could come up with new combinations of concepts. Llull's work continued to influence logicians. Gottfried Wilhelm von Leibnitz made it the topic of a treatise, *Dissertio de arte combinatoria*, in 1666.

During the industrial revolution, mass-production devices such as the Jacquard loom became common. Designs to be woven into cloth could be punched onto the cards that controlled the loom. Charles Babbage, working with Lady Ada Lovelace in the early nineteenth century, first thought of using punched cards to do mathematics. Their Analytical Engine wove numbers into tables the way the loom wove cloth from strands of thread. The modern Ada computer language commemorates their work. Toward the end of the nineteenth century, Herman Hollerith, who founded International Business Machines (IBM), developed the punched cards used in early digital computers.

In a 1936 paper, "On Computable Numbers," the British mathematician Alan Turing first suggested the idea of a general-purpose computing machine. With electronic digital computers, Turing's idea became realizable. Turing and the Hungarian-American mathematician John von Neumann are

Grace Hopper works on a 1944 manual tape punch, which was an early computer. (Bettmann/Corbis)

two of the many pioneers of digital computing. Turing designed machines called, individually, the Bombe and Colossus to break the "Enigma" cypher—a secret code used by Germany during World War II. He also proposed the famous "Turing test" for artificial intelligence. The Turing test suggests that if a person cannot tell the difference between responses from a computer and responses from a human, then the computer must be considered to be "intelligent."

The first generation of electronic computers, which included the Mark 1, the ENIAC, and other machines built with vacuum tubes, were huge, expensive, and apt to fail or "crash." Grace Hopper once repaired the U.S. Navy's Mark II computer by removing a moth from its circuitry. The term "debugging" is often associated with this incident.

The transistor made it possible to produce computers in quantity. However, mainframe computers such as the IBM 370 were still huge by modern standards, and only universities, govern-

ment agencies, or large companies could afford them. By the 1980s, with integrated circuits, a new generation of minicomputers was born. Digital Equipment Corporation (later Compaq), Hewlett-Packard, and Data General were some of the key manufacturers. These machines were about the size of a refrigerator.

By the end of the 1970s, desktop microcomputers began appearing in smaller offices and in ordinary people's homes. Beginning with the Osborne, the Commodore 64, the Apple, and the IBM PC, microcomputers and their software systems came to dominate the market. These machines used microcomputer chips—room-sized central processing units shrunk to less than the size of a penny. The Intel 8080 and the Motorola 6800 were among the very first such chips, appearing in the latter half of the 1970s. Many programmers joked about these new "toys." During the next decade, microcomputers would grow into powerful workstations—powered by chips from Intel and Motorola and built by companies such as Sun Microsystems, IBM, Apple, Dell, Toshiba, Sony, and Gateway, to name just a few.

Digital Information

Computing involves three activities: input, process, and output. Data enters the computer through a keyboard or mouse, from a camera, or from a file previously recorded on a disk. A program or "process" manipulates the data and then outputs it to a screen, printer, disk, or communications line.

Over the years, many different input devices have been used, including punched paper tape, punched cards, keyboards, mice, microphones, touch-screens, and video cameras. Output devices have included paper printouts, teletypewriters, and video monitors. The part of the computer that does the processing is known as the central processing unit (CPU). Collectively, everything other than the CPU, including memory boards, disks, printers, keyboards, mice, and screens can be thought of as peripheral devices, or just "peripherals."

There are two sorts of computer software. Operating systems, such as Microsoft Windows, Macintosh, or UNIX, allow machines to perform their basic functions—accepting input, running programs, and sending output to users. Applications programs, such as word processors, Internet browsers, electronic mail programs, or database management programs, do the work required by computer users.

Digital computers use data that has been encoded as series of zeros and ones—binary digits or bits. Text, images, sounds, motion pictures, and other media can all be represented as strings of zeros and ones and processed by digital computers. Programs—the instructions on how to manipulate data—also are represented in binary form. The earliest digital computers were designed to store and manipulate the numbers and letters of the alphabet that were found on typewriter keyboards. The American Standard Code for Information Interchange (ASCII) uses 128 combinations of bits to represent the letters, numbers, and symbols on a typewriter keyboard. Plain text worked well when computers were used primarily for mathematics.

Binary numbers can represent visual and audio information as well. By the end of the 1980s, designers had expanded the coding systems to store drawings, photographs, sounds, and moving pictures. Each dot on a screen is called a "picture element" (or "pixel"). To display graphics on the screen, computers use groups of binary numbers—ones and zeros—to represent the color, intensity of light, and position of each pixel.

Modern computers almost always use some type of GUI. Programmers use small graphics called "icons" to represent a program, a document, a movie, or a musical work. When a user selects an icon, the computer can open a file or program that is associated with it. This technique is object-oriented programming.

When the price of computers dropped, it became possible to distribute work among several machines on a network instead of using a large central computer. A piece of software called a "server" could now send information to smaller programs called "clients" located at the workstations. Shared files remain on large computers called "file servers," so several users can access them at once. Internet browsers, such as Netscape and Internet Explorer, are good examples of "client/server" design at work, where the browser is a client and an Internet site hosts the server software and the large files of information.

There are many programming languages, each better at addressing certain types of problems. The Formula Translation language (FORTRAN) was developed to handle scientific problems. The Beginner's All-purpose Symbolic Interchange Code (BASIC) and the Common Business-Oriented Language (COBOL) were better for office automation. The languages C, C++, Java, and Visual Basic use libraries of small, interchangeable programs that perform frequently required tasks, such as sorting items or displaying them on a screen. Programmers can combine these small programs into more complex systems, allowing programmers to build new applications quickly. Other languages, such as Prolog and LISP, were invented for work in artificial intelligence, while Ada was designed to address military needs.

Once personal computers were available, the demand for special software packages or "applications" increased. Spreadsheets, such as the early SuperCalc and Excel, have simplified accounting and statistical processes, and they allow users to try out various financial scenarios. If the costs or quantities of items change, the results will appear immediately on the screen. A whole range of database management packages, including dBase, FoxPro, Oracle, and Access, help users do inventories, maintain customer profiles, and more. Because records in databases can be matched against ones in different files, say a customer demographic file with a warehouse inventory file, businesses can predict supply and demand trends and improve the delivery of goods and services. Geographic information systems, online census data, and telephone directories make it easier to market products in areas where there is demand. Some critics argue that using data for reasons other than those for which it was collected is an invasion of privacy. In many countries, freedom of information and privacy protection laws have been passed to address these issues.

Computing and Knowledge

Computers have changed the world in which people live and work, and they have provided new ways of thinking about, and making sense of, that world. At the beginning of the twenty-first century, computer science is a mature academic discipline, with almost every university or college offering computer courses.

As an academic subject, computer science may involve information theory, systems analysis, software engineering, electrical engineering, programming, and information studies that examine the use of digital information. The founders of information theory, Claude Shannon and Warren Weaver, published *The Mathematical Theory of Communication* in 1949. The mathematician Norbert Wiener, who coined the term "cybernetics," showed how computing theories could be applied to problems of communication and control in both animals and machines. Ludwig von Bertalanffy founded general system theory because he saw that large complex systems did not necessarily behave in the same what that their individual components did. He is considered one of the founders of systems analysis.

Professional associations have also played important roles in the development of computing theory, practice, and standards. The Association for Computing Machinery, the Institute of Electrical and Electronic Engineers, the International Standards Organization, and the W3 Consortium are all agencies concerned with computing methods and standards. Less widely known groups, such as the International Society for Systems Sciences and Computer Professionals for Social Responsibility, concern themselves with professional ethics and the social effect of computing. Computing has its own journals and magazines that are aimed at special groups of professionals and at consumers.

Modern computing researchers come from many backgrounds. In turn, scholars from other areas apply computing theory and systems analysis to their own disciplines—from philosophy to psychology to social work. Centers such as the Media Lab at the Massachusetts Institute of Technology or the Xerox Corporation's Palo Alto Researcher Center bring together experts from many fields to design "neural networks" that simulate the human brain, to build smaller and faster machines, or to find better ways of managing digital information. Nicholas Negroponte, Marvin Minsky, and their colleagues at the Media Lab are associated with developments in artificial intelligence and robotics.

Some people fear that while computers relieve humans of repetitive tasks, they may also "deskill" workers who forget how to do such tasks by hand. Others suggest that having to cope with computers on the job adds extra stress, raises expectations of promptness, and requires ongoing retraining of workers. Because computing has made it possible to recombine and repackage stories, pictures, and sounds, some fear that the work of authors may one day be regarded as interchangeable, much like mechanical parts. In addition, as people depend more on computers, they become more vulnerable to system failure. If the world's computers should fail all at once, economic and social chaos might result. A series of Internet "worms" and "viruses" heightened concern over society's dependence on computers during 1999 and 2000. Governments, banks, companies, and individuals worried that the clocks in their computers might fail at the beginning of 2000, but the "Y2K" crisis they feared did not occur.

Computer designers and computer users think about computers in different terms, and they use different jargon. Hackers, who explore aspects of computers that designers could not have foreseen, have their own way of looking at and talking about computers. People who use computers for destructive purposes are more properly called "crackers." Finally, those people who do not have access to computers run the risk of economic and educational hardships.

The Internet and the Future

During the early 1980s, the Defense Advanced Research Projects Agency (DARPA)—the central research and development organization for the U.S. Department of Defense—commissioned work on a standard design for its wide area networks, computer connections that could link entire countries or continents. In response, communications standards called the Transmission Control Protocol and the Internet Protocol were published in 1981.

Many computer networks, with names such as Decnet, Usenet, and Bitnet, were already in operation, but within about a decade, the new standards were adopted around the world. At first, because there were no graphics, the Internet was used for electronic mail and discussions and for text-only directory services such as Gopher (from the University of Minnesota) and WAIS (wide area information service). Then Berners-Lee and his colleagues at CERN, the European nuclear research center in Switzerland, came up with a new set of protocols that could be used to mix pictures and sounds with text and let users locate any document on any network computer anywhere in the world. The result was the World Wide Web.

The Internet has created a new forum for expression and discussion of social issues. In April 2000, for example, the Dalai Lama, in New Delhi, India, was given a demonstration of a website that is intended to provide basic knowledge of a citizen's rights during a police complaint. (Reuters NewMedia Inc./Corbis)

Briefly, this is how the web works. Every computer on the Internet has a numeric Internet Protocol (IP) address, which looks like four groups of numbers separated by periods. Because humans would have trouble with addresses such as 123.12.345.1, websites also have "domain names," such as "wayne.edu" or "acme.com," which are easier to understand. Scattered around the world, domain name servers (DNSs) provide large telephone-directory style lists, which map the names to the numbers.

Every item on the web, whether a file of text, a picture, or a sound, can be found and retrieved by its uniform resource locator (URL). A URL contains the domain name of the computer on which the item is stored and, optionally, additional information about the file folders and file names on that computer. Documents on the web, called "pages," are written in the HyperText Markup Language (HTML) and exchanged using the HyperText Transmission Protocol (HTTP).

Berners-Lee (1998) believes that once most of human knowledge is made available over the Internet, and once the Internet becomes the primary way in which individuals communicate with one another, humans will have the wisdom to use computers to help analyze society and to improve it.

While the promise is bright, the Internet presents many challenges for information scientists. While URLs provide a way of locating individual documents anywhere on the network, the web is always in flux, and URLs are quite "volatile" or apt to change from day to day or even from minute to minute. In addition, because material on the web may look highly polished, it is sometimes hard for users to distinguish reliable information from unreliable information. Metadata—data about data—is one of the schemes proposed to reduce confusion. Metadata tags are similar to subject, author, and title entries in a library catalog, and can be written at the top of a web document.

Increasingly, the computer network is the medium through which scientists assemble and exchange knowledge from many sources and train future generations. The Human Genome Project and simulations to train surgeons or aircraft pilots are examples. Many scholars publish directly to the Internet by posting their discoveries to the World Wide Web, newsgroups, or mailing lists. This speeds the process of information exchange, but since such works are not examined by editors, it also increases the chances of error and makes it harder for readers to determine whether the information is reliable. The need to be able to index and describe web-pages has led to the development of metadata as a way of categorizing electronic documents. However, with millions of authors publishing to the web, the task of indexing and describing their work is staggering.

Computers continue to become smaller, less expensive, more powerful, and more essential to society. So far, dire predictions of de-skilled workers or massive unemployment due to an increased use of computers in the workplace have yet to materialize. In the future, computers will be still smaller and many times more powerful as engineers find ways to use nanotechnology to build microscopic machines. Some people predict that computers will eventually use individual molecules, or even subatomic particles, to store and manipulate the ones and zeros that make up digital information.

By building microprocessors into cars, aircraft, and even household devices such as microwave ovens, designers have produced a raft of "smart" devices. Steve Mann and his colleagues at MIT and the University of Toronto have even developed smart clothing, which can detect signs of sudden illness in the wearer. Increasingly, computers will be able to assist people with disabilities. Smart cars and smart houses have obvious social benefits. However, the same technologies can be used to produce smart weapons. Sensors in a smart office can prevent burglaries or announce guests. They can also monitor employees, minute by minute. Will ubiquitous computers have positive or negative effects on society? This is a question for which only the future can provide an answer.

See also: ARTIFICIAL INTELLIGENCE; COMPUTER SOFTWARE; COMPUTER SOFTWARE, EDUCATIONAL; DATABASES, ELECTRONIC; DIFFUSION OF INNOVATIONS AND COMMUNICATION; DIGITAL COMMUNICATION; DIGITAL MEDIA SYSTEMS; GEOGRAPHIC INFORMATION SYSTEMS; INTERNET AND THE WORLD WIDE WEB; KNOWLEDGE MANAGEMENT; LIBRARIES, DIGITAL; LIBRARY AUTOMATION; PRIVACY AND ENCRYPTION; RATINGS FOR VIDEO GAMES, SOFTWARE, AND THE INTERNET; RETRIEVAL OF INFORMATION; STANDARDS AND INFORMATION; TECHNOLOGY, ADOPTION AND DIFFUSION OF; WEBMASTERS.

Bibliography

Berners-Lee, Tim. (1998). "The World Wide Web: A Very Short Personal History." <http://www.w3.org/People/Berners-Lee/ShortHistory.html.>

Bertalanffy, Ludwig von. (1976). *General System Theory, Foundations, Development, Applications.* New York: G. Braziller.

Biermann, Alan W. (1997). *Great Ideas in Computer Science: A Gentle Introduction,* 2nd edition. Cambridge, MA: MIT Press.

Brookshear, J. Glenn. (1999). *Computer Science: An Overview.* New York: Addison-Wesley.

Carlson, Tom. (2001). "The Obsolete Computer Museum." <http://www.obsoletecomputermuseum.org>.

Gardner, Martin. (1982). *Logic Machines and Diagrams.* Chicago: University of Chicago Press.

Hiltz, Starr Roxanne, and Turoff, Murray. (1993). *The Network Nation: Human Communication Via Computer,* revised edition. Cambridge, MA: MIT Press.

Kidder, Tracy. (1997). *The Soul of a New Machine.* New York: Modern Library.

Negroponte, Nicholas. (1995). *Being Digital.* New York: Vintage Books.

Raymond, Eric S. (1998). *The New Hacker's Dictionary.* Cambridge, MA: MIT Press.

Shannon, Claude, and Weaver, Warren. (1949). *The Mathematical Theory of Communication.* Urbana: University of Illinois Press.

Sudkamp, Thomas A. (1996). *Languages and Machines: An Introduction to Theory of Computer Science.* New York: Addison-Wesley.

Turing, Alan M. (1936). "On Computable Numbers: With an Application to the Entscheidungsproblem." *Proceedings of the London Mathematical Society* (2nd series) 42:230–265.

Valovic, Thomas. (2000). *Digital Mythologies: The Hidden Complexities of the Internet.* New Brunswick, NJ: Rutgers University Press.

Wiener, Norbert. (1965). *Cybernetics; Or, Control and Communication in the Animal and the Machine,* 2nd edition. Cambridge, MA: MIT Press.

CHRISTOPHER BROWN-SYED

TERRI L. LYONS

■ CONFLICT AND GROUP COMMUNICATION

See: Group Communication, Conflict and

■ CONSERVATION

See: Archives, Public Records, and Records Management; Archivists; Conservators; Librarians; Libraries, Functions and Types of; Museums; Preservation and Conservation of Information

■ CONSERVATORS

Conservators are trained professionals who focus on the care and restoration of objects that have cultural or historical value. Such objects may include paintings and sculptures, fine prints, textiles, books, photographs, archival records and paper, and archeological artifacts. These artifacts are considered valuable sources of information for study and research, specifically in their original form. Conservators develop skills that allow them to examine an artifact, learn about its original form and purpose, and develop a plan for the care and maintenance it requires for continued use, study, and long-term preservation. Conservators receive training that specifically relates to this process and includes advanced study in artistic, historical, and scientific topics that provide a greater understanding of the materials with which they work.

A conservator determines what an artifact is composed of and what is required to preserve an artifact in its original form or as close to that original form as possible. A conservator must examine an artifact to determine the amount of damage or deterioration that has occurred. This examination often involves research concerning the history of an artifact and its cultural significance. Conservators also gather information through scientific analysis of the properties of an artifact—always ensuring that materials used in conservation treatments do not damage or destroy an artifact.

Conservators used computer technology in 1989 to help with the restoration of works by Tiziano Vecellio in Venice, Italy. (Vittoriano Rastelli/Corbis)

Professional conservators are trained to develop treatment methods that maintain the form, structure, and appearance of artifacts, to fix and repair damage to objects, and to develop treatments that stabilize, decrease, or halt further damage and deterioration. Treatment methods, most of which are done painstakingly by hand, may result in restoring an artifact to a close facsimile of its original appearance. Types of conservation treatments include cleaning and repairing tears in paper, creating envelopes or boxes to house artifacts (such as books), restoring paintings, removing mold and adhesives on objects, and developing recommendations for the proper storage of artifacts. When applying treatments, professional conservators are careful to make sure that any repairs or steps taken to stabilize an artifact do not alter or destroy its original form or historical integrity. For example, a conservator might repair a torn photograph or clean a photograph using appropriate solvents that do not cause staining, abrasions, or loss of the original image. Conservators also take steps to ensure that treatments or repairs made to an object can be reversed if necessary.

Conservators document the condition of an object before treatments are undertaken, the types of treatments they perform, and the condition of an object after treatment. Conservators also develop recommendations and guidelines for continued care or preventative care of artifacts and make recommendations concerning the type of storage environment that should be used to assure long-term preservation of an artifact. For example, a conservator can determine which type of storage enclosure will protect a photograph from dust and light, discuss proper handling methods, and recommend a long-term storage environment with temperature and humidity controls. In addition, conservators work with individuals who administer collections in order to assess conservation and preservation needs, to establish priorities for conservation work, and to develop cost estimates and budgets for conservation treatments.

All conservators are involved in the treatment and care of artifacts or collections of artifacts. There are specializations within the profession that allow an individual to develop skills that may adapt to the needs of a particular institution, focus on specific types of objects, or involve other conservation work such as preservation, administration, or education. Conservators may be employed in museums, libraries, archival repositories, or similar institutions. Alternatively, conservators may be employed on a contractual basis by institutions that do not have the resources to maintain a conservation laboratory or preservation department. Private collectors, as well as institutions such as libraries, archives, and museums may hire a conservator on such a contractual basis. Conservators may also choose to maintain their own businesses.

Individuals who are interested in conservation as a career must acquire the appropriate scientific, historical, and cultural knowledge that is necessary to become a practicing conservator. Those interested in a career as a professional conservator seek academic training in a graduate-level program. Coursework in conservation programs provides the theoretical and scientific background required for the application of conservation methods and treatments in a professional setting. Graduate programs typically include core classes in such areas as chemistry, studio art, art history, anthropology, archaeology, and related classes in the humanities and the sciences, as outlined by the American Institute for Conservation in "Conservation Training in the United States" (2000). Admission requirements and graduation requirements will vary depending on the program. Information about the individual prerequisites for graduate work in conservation is usually provided by academic institutions and by professional conservation associations.

Graduate programs in conservation are now recognized as the standard for training professional conservators, but internships are a valued and integral part of graduate coursework and research. Internships provide an opportunity for students to receive instruction in a variety of conservation methods, to see how these methods are practiced, and to have an opportunity for hands-on training. Internship opportunities allow a student to gain experience and training in an area most closely related to their interests. Individuals who are interested in conservation internships may find such opportunities through graduate programs, professional conservation organizations, or by contacting a conservator.

Once an individual becomes a practicing conservator, continued professional development is required, particularly in areas of technology, research, and conservation treatments. Participating in workshops, continuing education classes and seminars, attending conferences sponsored by professional conservation organizations, and reading current literature offer opportunities for professional development. Conservators also have a specific philosophy and set of guidelines that assist them in achieving a high standard of work. Conservators are encouraged to maintain a commitment to these standards and high levels of performance.

See also: ARCHIVES, PUBLIC RECORDS, AND RECORDS MANAGEMENT; ARCHIVISTS; LIBRARIES, FUNCTIONS AND TYPES OF; MUSEUMS; PRESERVATION AND CONSERVATION OF INFORMATION.

Bibliography

American Institute for Conservation of Historic and Artistic Works. (1991). *Guidelines for Selecting a Conservator.* Washington, DC: AIC.

American Institute for Conservation of Historic and Artistic Works. (1994). "AIC Code of Ethics and Guidelines for Practice." <http://aic.stanford.edu/pubs/ethics.html>.

American Institute for Conservation of Historic and Artistic Works. (2001). "AIC Conservation Training in the United States." <http://aic.stanford.edu/become/contrain.html>.

Clapp, Ann. (1987). *The Curatorial Care of Works of Art on Paper.* New York: Lyons and Burford.

Cunha, George Martin, and Cunha, Dorothy Grant. (1983). *Library and Archives Conservation: 1980s and Beyond.* Metuchen, NJ: Scarecrow Press.

Petherbridge, Guy, ed. (1987). *Conservation of Library and Archive Materials and the Graphic Arts.* Boston: Butterworths.

Swartzburg, Susan G. (1983). *Conservation in the Library: A Handbook of Use and Care of Traditional and Nontraditional Materials.* Westport, CT: Greenwood Press.

M. E. DUCEY

■ CONSUMER CULTURE

Any spectator of the contemporary visual landscape readily recognizes the prominence of material goods and their consumption in the increasingly global culture. Some observers argue that the landscape is "littered" with consumption icons and that it is a product of a larger project to create and sustain consumer culture. Other, less conspiratorial perspectives at least acknowledge the role that the "dream worlds" of the media play in perpetuating consumerism.

Defining Consumer Culture

There are many definitions of consumer culture. To begin, consumer culture should not be confused with two of its attributes: consumerism and materialism.

According to Yiannis Gabriel and Tim Lang (1995), consumerism has at least five distinct connotations. It is a moral doctrine, a means for demarcating social status, a vehicle for economic development, a public policy, and a social movement. Consumerism is defined here as the collection of behaviors, attitudes, and values that are associated with the consumption of material goods.

Materialism is another perspective that is prevalent in consumer culture. The term "materialism" also has a rich etymology. However, as it relates here, Russell Belk (1985, p. 265) defines materialism as "the importance a consumer attaches to worldly possessions." At the highest levels of materialism, possessions assume a central place in a person's life and are believed to provide the greatest sources of satisfaction and dissatisfaction. While one might readily think that materialism is a good synonym for consumerism, materialism, at least as it is defined here, only covers a part of consumerism. Namely, materialism deals only with the social value of material goods.

Consumer culture, which subsumes both consumerism and materialism, has been studied from the perspective of a variety of disciplines, including communication, cultural studies, theology, sociology, psychology, marketing, anthropology, and philosophy. Regardless of the disciplinary approach, a central feature of consumer culture is the relationship between people and material goods. Generically, consumer culture is a social arrangement in which the buying and selling of goods and services is not only a predominant activity of everyday life but also an important arbiter of social organization, significance, and meaning.

Origins of Consumer Culture

In a review of historical accounts of consumption and culture, Grant McCracken (1988) remarks that there is little consensus as to the origins of consumer culture. According to the perspective of Neil McKendrick and his associates

(1982), consumer culture began in eighteenth-century England with the commercialization of fashion precipitating a mass change in taste. According to these historians, the new predilection for style fueled a demand for clothing that was mass-produced through technical innovations in the textile industry and mass-marketed through innovations in printing technologies that afforded wide-scale advertising.

Another historian, Rosalind Williams (1982), claims that the consumer revolution began in late-nineteenth-century France, when the pioneering efforts of French retailers and advertisers transformed Paris into a "pilot plant of mass consumption" through the Paris expositions of 1889 and 1900. Williams argues that the expositions significantly contributed to the development of the department store and the trade show, key factors in the development of consumer culture.

Finally, McCracken (1988) suggests that it may be less useful to identify the specific points of origin for the consumer revolution than to note patterns of cultural change that foretold the radical restructuring of society. He identifies three moments in history that undergird the development of modern consumer culture. The first was Elizabethan politics in sixteenth-century England, where Queen Elizabeth I introduced the use of objects to her highly ceremonial court to communicate the legitimacy of her rule. The second was the increased participation of the masses in the marketplace in eighteenth-century Europe. As more members of the culture could participate in the marketplace because of the widespread prosperity of the industrial revolution, the marketplace expanded, creating an explosion of consumer choices. The gentry, the middle class, and the lower class perceived and adopted the social significance of goods and attempted to appropriate those significances for themselves. The third was the institutionalization of consumption through the emergence of the department store in the nineteenth century. The department store, McCracken argues, fundamentally changed the nature and the context of purchase activity as well as the nature of the information and influence to which the consumer was subjected.

Don Slater (1997) summarizes these thoughts by arguing that consumer culture began with a wide penetration of consumer goods into the everyday lives of people across social strata, that

consumption was ignited through a new sense of fashion and taste, and finally that the culture was cemented through the development of infrastructures, organizations, and practices that took advantage of the new markets, namely, the rise of shopping, advertising, and marketing.

The Role of the Media in Consumer Culture

From the beginning of consumer culture, the media, particularly print advertisements, were used to help inculcate demand for newly mass-produced goods. Stuart Ewen (1976) maintains that before the advent of mass production, industry had produced for a limited, largely middle- and upper-class market. However, with the revolution in production, particularly Fordism (i.e., the use of the assembly line to mass-produce consumer goods), industry required an equivalent revolution in consumption. The mechanism of mass production could not function unless markets became more dynamic, growing horizontally (nationally), vertically (into social classes not previously among the consumers), and ideologically. The media were used to encourage people to respond to the demands of the productive machinery. Ewen identifies "captains of consciousness," industry leaders and advertising executives, as the chief architects of the new social structure that privileged the consumption of mass-produced materials.

A structural concern of the "captains" was the provision of resources, namely time and money, for greater consumption by the masses. Ewen (1976) asserts that the general strategy to consumerize labor began in the 1920s as laborers were given higher wages in the hopes that they would purchase some of what they produced. They were also given more time in which to spend those wages because shorter work hours were made possible as a result of the greater efficiency of the production line. That labor movements were already pushing for these concessions made the job of the "captains" easier.

Once structural barriers to consumption were set aside, the industrialists needed to change the attitudes of the masses so they would be favorably disposed to purchasing the goods that they were constructing. Inspired by the social psychology of Floyd Henry Allport (1924), advertisers tried to grasp the nature of human motivation. They believed that if human "instincts" were properly understood, they could be manipulated not only to induce consumers to buy particular products but also to create in them a habitual desire to participate in the marketplace to extract social meaning. That is, not only might the consumers buy the advertised product, but they might also use the advertisement to understand their social selves, others, and the culture at large. Advertisements were to be the substance of mass culture's dreams. In such a case, the social control of the captain would be maximized (Ewen, 1976, p. 81).

As Ewen (1976) indicates, this project of social control was accomplished through the presentation of partial truths depicted through commercialized expression, namely art. Ewen states, "Artists, often gifted in their sensitivities to human frailties, were called upon to use those sensitivities for manipulation" (pp. 65–66). The images these artists produced painted industry as a benevolent fatherly figure that held society together, able to fulfill all of mass society's dreams by depicting perfect harmony, happiness, and opportunity for all.

In *Advertising the American Dream,* Roland Marchand (1985) provides a more neutral analysis of the early role of media in the promulgation of consumer culture. In doing this, he analyzed more than 180,000 advertisements, corporate archival data, trade journal articles, and even the minutes of advertising agency meetings during the period between 1920 and 1940. Marchand argues that advertisers in the 1920s assumed the dual function of "apostles of modernity"—heralds of modern technologies and missionaries of modern styles and ways of life—and "social therapists"—assuaging feelings of diminution and alienation stimulated by the fast pace of modern production and consumption. Advertisers presented a two-sided message about the good news of modernity. First, they praised the coming of a corporate, technologically sophisticated, urban civilization. Second, they reassured the masses that this civilization was a kind of self-correcting system that produced numerous products that were capable of solving the problems and calming the anxieties that it generated.

Marchand's analysis of the advertisements of the 1920s and 1930s revealed two categories of conventions. The first comprised a series of textual parables and the second a host of visual clichés that advertisers repeatedly used to advise

A 1920s advertisement for Welch's Grape Juice supports the notion of a growing consumer culture where people have time and money available for leisure activities such as picnics. (Bettmann/Corbis)

consumers of the promises and the perils of the times. In terms of parables, the first he discusses is that of the "first impression." This parable stresses the importance of external appearance in an impersonal society in which one is under the constant surveillance of strangers who judge character. These advertisements advised the consumer to avoid the disastrous consequences of body odor, bad breath, and other problems by using the advertised product. The second parable regards the "democracy of goods," which held that social equality was realized through the genuine opportunity of everyone to buy the same staple products (e.g., toothpaste, cereal, mattresses) that the wealthy purchase. Another parable, that of "civilization redeemed," reassured Americans that modernity would rescue itself from its own shortcomings. As an example, vitamin advertisements promised to supplement the nutrient-impoverished diets of people caught up in the fast pace of modern life. Finally, the parable of the "captivated child" offered consumer products as a way of placating even the most angry children, making other forms of coercion obsolete.

Advertisers also insinuated products into the consciousness of consumers by using visual clichés. The expanded technology for reproducing illustrations and using color made visuals an attractive alternative for advertisers. Because psychologists had regularly advised that pictures could best stimulate the basic emotions, the strategy was irresistible. Visual images also became the preferred modes of presentation because, as Marchand (1985, p. 236) states, of their utility "in cases where the advertiser's message would have sounded exaggerated or presumptuous if put into words, or where the advertiser sought to play upon such 'inappropriate' emotions as religious awe or thirst for power." Visual clichés include the office window through which a business executive gazes on a dynamic cityscape as the master of all that is surveyed, the family painted in soft focus, the towering and resplendent heavenly city of the future, and the harmonious world saved by modernity. Marchand suggests that advertisers appropriated sacred symbolism to imbue products with spiritual significance. Goods were presented in heroic proportions, towering over towns of consumers. Adoring throngs or smaller collections of worshipful attendants surrounded them. Often, products were juxtaposed against poignant moments, such as weddings, or were the object of radiant beams of light.

The Media in Contemporary Consumer Culture

If consumer culture was established at the beginning of the twentieth century, what role do the media play in its promulgation in the twenty-first century? With consumer culture established, the media are no longer tools of its development but rather transmit the culture to the young and reinforce the culture among adults. This process of transmission and reinforcement is referred to as socialization, and in the case of consumer culture, it is referred to as consumer socialization.

In the seminal work in this area, Scott Ward (1971, p. 2) defined consumer socialization as the "processes by which young people acquire skills, knowledge, and attitudes relevant to their functioning as consumers in the marketplace." He argued that in order to understand the consumer behavior of adults, one must first grasp the nature

of the childhood experiences of the adults, since those experiences shape patterns of cognition and behavior later in life. Ward sought to understand how children acquire attitudes about the "social significance" of goods, or how they learn that the acquisition of some kinds of products or brands of goods can be "instrumental to successful social role enactment" (p. 3).

The role of the consumer is defined by the skills, attitudes, and behaviors that are associated with consumption. Consumer skills include such practices as pricing goods before making a purchase decision, knowing the rights of the consumer, and budgeting. Consumer attitudes include the affective orientation toward goods, both general and specific, the value placed on the practice of consumption and the products consumed, and the evaluation of the marketplace. Consumer behavior simply refers to the consumption of goods.

Agents of consumer socialization can range from the small-town store clerk who teaches children to exchange bottles for money that they can use to buy candy, to the big-city billboard that depicts a liquor as a means to high social status and pleasure for adults. However, there are four agents of consumer socialization that have been formally studied in the literature: family, peers, mass media, and schools.

Whereas print advertisements were the medium of choice for establishing consumer culture, television has served a vital role in socializing new consumers and reinforcing consumerism among older ones. There are at least three different ways in which television may be related to consumer culture. The first way suggests direct effects through a learning model (e.g., social cognitive theory). It may be that individuals watch portrayals of consumerism and then model consumerist behaviors and adopt socially rewarded consumerist attitudes and values. Television also may be related to consumerism by influencing viewer perceptions of the world (e.g., cultivation theory). Finally, television may simply reflect the existing consumer culture.

Regardless of the mechanism, perhaps the most prevalent media messages for consumer socialization are television commercials. Interspersed between television programs, commercials are explicitly geared to prompt viewers to participate in consumer culture. Leslie Savan

(1994) reports that the average television viewer in America is exposed to approximately one hundred television commercials a day.

For the most part, the messages for consumer socialization found in television programming are not as explicit as those found in advertising. Nonetheless, they are present and add to the cumulative effect of the general consumption message of television. One manner by which consumer socialization messages are implicitly conveyed is through the presentation of a world of affluence. Early studies of television, conducted by Dallas Smythe (1954) and Melvin DeFleur (1964), for example, during the 1950s and 1960s found a strong bias toward portrayals of middle- and upper-class lifestyles in network programs. More recently, George Gerbner (1993) analyzed 19,642 speaking parts that appeared in 1,371 television programs (including cable) from the 1982–1983 season through the 1991–1992 season. The content analysis of these programs revealed that, on average, 92.3 percent of the characters were middle class, 1.3 percent were clearly lower class, and 4 percent were clearly upper class. Gerbner concluded that in the overwhelmingly middle-class world of television, poor people play a negligible role.

Another manner in which television conveys consumer culture is through its biased presentation of high-status occupations. Such occupations are esteemed at least in part because of the high incomes and consumption power that they wield. Nancy Signorielli (1993) conducted an extensive content analysis of the occupations presented in prime-time programming. She examined week-long samples of prime-time programs between the 1973 and 1985 television seasons. When compared to U.S. census reports, professionals were overrepresented by 66 percent on television. Doctors, lawyers, judges, and entertainers were some of the overrepresented occupations. Teachers, clerical and secretarial workers, sales workers, and other blue-collar workers—occupations that are generally associated with less than affluent lifestyles—were some of the underrepresented occupations.

Some work has been done on the effects of media messages on socializing people to consumer culture. As is true of most other areas, more work is needed to draw definitive conclusions about the nature of the relationship; however,

examples of work in the area that uses different methodologies indicate that the media play at least a modest role in promulgating consumer culture. Survey research has indicated that television viewing is related to consumer role conceptions (Moschis and Moore, 1978), and motivations to view television commercials are related to the adoption of materialistic values among adolescents (Ward and Wackman, 1971). Longitudinal research has indicated that exposure to television advertising leads to higher levels of subsequent (fourteen months later) materialism among adolescents who are not already materialistic or who do not discuss consumption issues with their families (Moschis and Moore, 1982). Finally, experimental research has shown that preschoolers who are exposed to advertising are more materialistic than their counterparts who are not exposed to advertising (Goldberg and Gorn, 1978). In this research, children who were exposed to advertisements were twice as likely as children who were not exposed to advertisements to choose to play with an advertised toy instead of playing with a playmate in a sandbox.

The research in the field as a whole does not permit definitive conclusions about the effect of the media on promulgating consumer culture. Many questions still need to be addressed to explain a relationship that is likely to be small and cumulative over time. What role do the media play in conveying other aspects of consumer culture to audiences? Through selective exposure, can audiences avoid consumer culture messages? How do the media reinforce consumer culture among adult audiences? These are just a few unanswered questions in an area that begs further exploration.

See also: ADVERTISING EFFECTS; CHILDREN AND ADVERTISING; CULTIVATION THEORY AND MEDIA EFFECTS; CULTURAL STUDIES; CULTURE AND COMMUNICATION; CULTURE INDUSTRIES, MEDIA AS; SOCIAL COGNITIVE THEORY AND MEDIA EFFECTS.

Bibliography

Allport, Floyd Henry. (1924). *Social Psychology*. Boston: Houghton Mifflin.

Baudrillard, Jean. (1983). *Simulations*. New York: Semiotext(e).

Belk, Russell W. (1985). "Materialism: Trait Aspects of Living in the Material World." *Journal of Consumer Research* 12:265–280.

Churchill, Gilbert A., and Moschis, George P. (1979). "Television and Interpersonal Influences on Adolescent Consumer Learning." *Journal of Consumer Research* 6:23–35.

DeFleur, Melvin L. (1964). "Occupational Roles as Portrayed on Television." *Public Opinion Quarterly* 28:57–74.

Ewen, Stuart. (1976). *Captains of Consciousness: Advertising and the Social Roots of the Consumer Culture.* New York: McGraw-Hill.

Ewen, Stuart. (1988). *All Consuming Images: The Politics of Style in Contemporary Culture.* New York: Basic Books.

Featherstone, Mike. (1991). *Consumer Culture and Postmodernism.* London: Sage Publications.

Gabriel, Yiannis, and Lang, Tim. (1995). *The Unmanageable Consumer: Contemporary Consumption and Its Fragmentation.* London: Sage Publications.

Gentile, Frank, and Miller, S. M. (1961). "Television and Social Class." *Sociology and Social Research* 45:259–264.

Gerbner, George. (1993). "Women and Minorities on Television: A Study in Casting Fate." A Report to the Screen Actors Guild and the American Federation of Radio and Television Artists, June 15. Philadelphia: Annenberg School for Communication, University of Pennsylvania.

Gerbner, George, and Gross, Larry. (1976). "Living with Television: The Violence Profile." *Journal of Communication* 26:173–199.

Goldberg, Mavin E., and Gorn, Gerald J. (1978). "Some Unintended Consequences of TV Advertising to Children." *Journal of Consumer Research* 5:22–29.

Jhally, Sut. (1990). *The Codes of Advertising: Fetishism and the Political Economy of Meaning in the Consumer Society.* New York: Routledge.

Lerner, Daniel. (1958). *The Passing of Traditional Society: Modernizing the Middle East.* Glencoe, IL: Free Press.

Marchand, Roland. (1985). *Advertising the American Dream: Making Way for Modernity, 1920–1940.* Berkeley: University of California Press.

McCracken, Grant. (1988). *Culture and Consumption: New Approaches to the Symbolic Character of Consumer Goods and Activities.* Bloomington: Indiana University Press.

McKendrick, Neil; Brewer, Neil; and Plumb, John Harold. (1982). *The Birth of a Consumer Society: The Commercialization of Eighteenth-Century England.* Bloomington: Indiana University Press.

Moschis, George P. (1987). *Consumer Socialization: A Life-Cycle Perspective.* Lexington, MA: Lexington Books.

Moschis, George P., and Moore, Roy L. (1978). "An Analysis of the Acquisition of Some Consumer Competencies among Adolescents." *Journal of Consumer Affairs* 12:277–291.

Moschis, George P., and Moore, Roy L. (1982). "A Longitudinal Study of Television Advertising Effects." *Journal of Consumer Research* 9:279–287.

Packard, Vance. (1960). *The Hidden Persuaders.* London: Penguin.

Riesman, David, and Roseborough, Henry. (1955). "Careers and Consumer Behavior." In *Consumer Behavior: The Life Cycle and Consumer Behavior,* ed. Lincoln Clark. New York: New York University Press.

Savan, Leslie. (1994). *The Sponsored Life: Ads, TV, and American Culture.* Philadelphia: Temple University Press.

Signorielli, Nancy. (1993). "Television and Adolescents' Perceptions about Work." *Youth & Society* 24:314–341.

Slater, Don. (1997). *Consumer Culture and Modernity.* Cambridge, Eng.: Polity Press.

Smythe, Dallas W. (1954). "Reality as Presented on Television." *Public Opinion Quarterly* 18:143–156.

Veblen, Thorstein. (1899). *The Theory of the Leisure Class: An Economic Study of Institutions.* London: George Allen and Unwin.

Ward, Scott. (1971). "Consumer Socialization." *Journal of Consumer Research* 1(2):1–14.

Ward, Scott, and Wackman, Daniel. (1971). "Family and Media Influences on Adolescent Consumer Learning." *American Behavioral Scientist* 14:415–427.

Ward, Scott; Wackman, Daniel; and Wartella, Ellen. (1977). *How Children Learn to Buy: The Development of Consumer Information Processing Skills.* Beverly Hills, CA: Sage Publications.

Williams, Rosalind H. (1982). *Dream Worlds: Mass Consumption in Late Nineteenth Century France.* Berkeley: University of California Press.

EMORY H. WOODARD

CONSUMER ELECTRONICS

"Everything that can be invented has been invented." This comment, commonly attributed to Charles H. Duell, commissioner of the U.S. Office of Patents in 1899, is intriguing, if not entirely accurate. At the end of the nineteenth century, it did seem as if everything that was absolutely necessary for a rural/agrarian or an urban/industrial mode of living had been invented. By the end of that century, transportation innovations including the railroad and the steamboat were flourishing, the nascent automobile had been developed, and experiments with flight were beginning to show promise. Communications systems had been advanced to include the telegraph, telephone, and radio telegraphy. Both factory owners and farmers benefited from machines that could do jobs faster and better than humans could do them. Few could have predicted the revolution to come that led the world beyond the industrial age and toward the information age. The twentieth-century innovations that would forever change almost every aspect and sphere of human behavior would not be foreseen until the final decades of the century, by which time they had spawned a multibillion-dollar consumer electronics industry.

History

The term "consumer electronics" encompasses a variety of products ranging from home theater systems to cellular telephones to personal computers. Though no one person can be identified as the "founder" of consumer electronics, Thomas Edison would be most deserving of the title. Edison's invention of the electric typewriter in 1872 and the phonograph in 1877 suggested the early potential of a new breed of business and entertainment devices. It was his discovery called the "Edison Effect," patented in 1883, that actually led to the creation of consumer electronics. Using the Edison Effect to control electricity, Edison opened his first experimental power station in the early 1880s. Though later perfected using the alternating current (AC) system, the electronics age commenced with Edison's power system. Over the course of the twentieth century, appliances and household devices were either redesigned or created to take advantage of modern electrical service to the home.

The radio, not the phonograph, can be considered the first consumer electronic device. Though the phonograph was invented and sold decades before the radio, it was initially marketed as a mechanical device, while radio was introduced to the public as a fully electrical device. Radio history is rooted in nineteenth-century wire transmission technologies that gave rise to the telegraph (1820s) and the telephone (1870s). Guglielmo Marconi, generally considered to be the inventor of radio, first transmitted telegraphic dots and dashes without the use of wires in the 1890s. In the early twentieth century, tremendous advances led to radio telephony that allowed voice and music to be transmitted without wires. Radio

sets of the 1900s and 1910s were limited to a growing number of tinkering enthusiasts. The general public did not own radios until the 1920s.

In 1920, the first radio stations began operation. Public displays that were held at department stores showed consumers the magic of the new device, with its ability to carry live music and information. These displays were effective and led to the initial acceptance of radio sets. Radio networks that were created later in the decade introduced programming that further advanced receiver sales, and radio supplanted the phonograph as the most popular consumer entertainment device. Much like the phonograph sales in the nineteenth century, radio sales did not take off until there was software that consumers found of value. The software of the phonograph was recorded music on discs and cylinders; the software of radio—and later television—was live programming.

One cannot underestimate the importance of the radio and the phonograph in the modern consumer electronics industry. These innovations had a direct effect on the development of a new breed of consumer electronic devices, including television, stereo systems, cassette and compact disc (CD) players, and home theater systems. By the end of the twentieth century, more than 98 percent of the U.S. population owned radios and televisions, and more than 90 percent owned videocassette recorders (VCRs). The information age had blossomed.

The Modern Marketplace

More than 250 million people lived in the United States by the end of the twentieth century. The Consumer Electronics Association (formerly the Consumer Electronics Manufacturing Association) reported in 1998 that the number of consumer electronic devices in the country was estimated at 1.6 billion, with annual sales exceeding $80 billion. The average person owned about six consumer electronic devices, with the average household spending about $1,000 annually on electronics. More than six million U.S. jobs were attributable to some aspect of the consumer electronics industry. This suggests the dramatic maturation of an industry in an extremely short time period.

Consumer adoption of new technologies is occurring faster than at any time in human history. The MP3 handheld music devices that down-

TABLE 1.

Penetration of Consumer Electronic Devices

Consumer Electronic Device	Penetration Rate (%)
Radio	99
Color Television	98
Videocassette Recorders	91
Cordless Telephone	73
Compact Disc Player	54
Personal Computer	44
Wireless Telephone	41
Camcorder	32
Pager	29
Home Theatre System	20

SOURCE: Consumer Electronics Manufacturing Association (1998).

load music files from the Internet became so popular in such a short amount of time that music distribution was forever altered virtually overnight. Digital satellite systems (DSS) and digital video, or versatile, discs (DVD) reached one million sales in a time period of eighteen and twenty-six months, respectively. It took fifteen years for cable television and four years for the VCR to reach that same mark of one million sales. Because consumers so quickly adopted a wide range of consumer electronic devices (see Table 1), the electronics industry introduced more consumer electronic devices and gadgets in the final twenty years of the twentieth century than it did during the first eighty years of the century. Some of these innovations have become commonplace; others failed to make an impression.

There are individuals who will buy almost any new gadget. They are referred to as "early adopters" because they want the newest and best consumer electronics gear. For products to be successful, however, they must reach a "critical mass" that includes a much wider base of consumers. This critical mass is divided into the "early" and "late" majority of buyers. A person who is the last to purchase a technology is referred to as a "laggard." Consumer electronics that reach a "critical mass" are considered to be successful, while those that are unable to sell beyond the early adopters are considered to be failures.

The DSS satellite dish, the DVD, and the MP3 player are examples of major success stories that occurred in the consumer electronics industry during the 1990s. However, for every success, failures litter the marketplace. The digital compact

cassette (DCC), Atari Jaguar video game system, digital video express (Divx), and a number of interactive television applications were among the misfires. It is difficult to explain why one technology succeeds where another fails. A body of research called "diffusion of innovations" helps to identify why consumers, over time, either accept or reject new consumer electronic items. Diffusion research suggests five important attributes affecting the success of a new technology: (1) relative advantage, (2) complexity, (3) reliability, (4) observability, and (5) compatibility.

The first four diffusion attributes are straightforward. The issue of relative advantage concerns how much better a new innovation is than the method that existed before it. The cellular telephone had an advantage over previous telephones because of its portability. Complexity deals with the ease of operation of the item. One of the chief advantages of radio was that the user interface was so simple, almost any family member could turn it on and make it work. Reliability is the measure of the consistency of the device over time. A 4-mm videotape system brought to market in the 1990s proved to be a failure, in part, because the tapes were easily damaged. As a result, the reliability questions were cited as a primary reason for the demise of the format.

Compatibility involves two different issues: (1) the technology's compatibility to the lifestyles of the consumers, and (2) the technology's interoperability with existing equipment. Consumers found that the time-shifting and video software playback features that were offered by the VCR were compatible with their busy lifestyles. As a result, the VCR became one of the most successful technologies of the 1970s. Interoperability of equipment is a more complex area that involves technical standards.

A consumer must determine if a particular computer peripheral or software works with an existing home system. The manufacturer usually places information on the packaging that explains compatibility issues. When groups of products work together, some form of technical standard has been established. Technical standards of consumer devices fall into several key categories, including first-agent standard, industry-wide agreement, and *de facto* standard.

With a first-agent standard, a single manufacturer or small group of companies will introduce a device, but they allow other companies to license the device. This type of industry agreement led to the widespread success of the CD player, which was jointly developed by Philips and Sony. The companies made one CD system available to the music industry in 1982, and consumers had a clear choice in the audio field. Consumers were able to buy CD music software and play it on any CD player.

An industry-wide agreement takes place when several companies that may be developing their own incompatible technologies agree to one standard device. Before the DVD was introduced, Sony and Philips had plans to release the MMCD (multimedia CD), while Toshiba was scheduled to release the similar, but incompatible, super density (SD) disc. The companies were urged by both the software industry and other manufacturers to agree to one DVD-type of system to avoid the compatibility problems of sustaining multiple formats. Industry-wide agreements can be fostered by congressional and/or Federal Communications Commission (FCC) actions. Government standards have been established for specific television set features, including closed-captioning and V-chips that screen out shows with violent content.

The *de facto* standard is established in the open marketplace. Consumers decide the format battle at the cash register. *De facto* standards have been developed with devices that include VCRs (VHS becoming the standard in many countries and supplanting the Beta format) and audiotape (the cassette defeating the eight-track, digital audiotape [DAT], and the DCC). Even after an industry-wide agreement was reached to release one format of DVD, Circuit City released the competing Divx format in 1998. The DVD became the *de facto* standard in 1999 when Divx was discontinued. Compatibility issues are a major factor in the ultimate success or failure of a consumer electronic device.

Trends

While it may have appeared to some by the end of the nineteenth century that everything necessary for leading a comfortable agrarian or industrial life had been invented, it will not so easily be accepted that everything needed to function in the information age has been introduced. Internet connectivity, cellular telephones, fax machines, laptop computers, and personal data assistants (PDAs) allow consumers to receive and send data instantaneously from almost anywhere in the

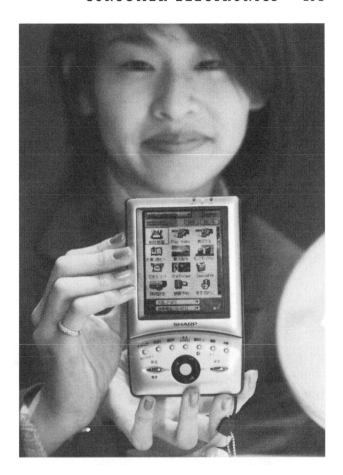

An Internet browser, an e-mail program, and an MP3 music player are all features of the Sharp Corporation's palmtop computer Zaurus MI-E1, which was first shown to the press on November 21, 2000. (AFP/Corbis)

world. Just as it was misguided to predict the end of change at the end of the nineteenth century, it would be a mistake to assume that innovation in the consumer electronics industry will cease in the near future. Several major trends continue to stimulate innovation in the electronics sector. Included in this list are miniaturization, digitization, and convergence.

Miniaturization

The modern consumer takes for granted the portability of electronics devices such as Walkmans, cellular telephones, pagers, and portable DVD players. Such portability of electronic devices has not always been the case. Early models of the radio, television, and computer were not considered portable. The processor of ENIAC, the first computer that was ever produced, included eighteen thousand vacuum tubes. As a result, ENIAC filled an entire room and generated a great amount of heat. Contemporary computers use semiconductor chips that are microscopic when compared to ENIAC's "brain." The widespread use of chips and transistors has allowed designers to create personal communication devices that are highly portable.

Cellular telephones, Palm Pilots, and laptop computers are among the items that have decreased in size while providing more options than ever before. This trend will continue as designers have unveiled prototype MP3 players that can be placed in a device the size of a wristwatch and in other wearable computer devices. Consumer electronics firms will continue to make "smarter" portable devices by packing miniature chips into devices that may include smart pagers and language translation devices.

Digitization

The gravitation of communications-related software and hardware away from analog and toward digital will continue to drive the consumer electronics industry. The recordable DVD and hard drive-based personal recorders such as TiVo and Replay are poised to replace the analog VCR, just as the CD basically replaced the vinyl record album. The broadcast industry is also undergoing a major transition from an analog-transmitted medium to a more dynamic digital medium. The conversion to high-definition television (HDTV) and digital audio broadcasting will hasten the demise of analog television sets and traditional AM/FM radios.

The conversion of entertainment and communications to digital ones and zeroes has made software more portable and easily transmitted. The MP3 has allowed music fans to download music with ease and to send music as e-mail attachments. Video-streaming concepts will be the next stage of development as people will be able to exchange home videos and video clips in the same manner as MP3s are exchanged. Digitization and the widespread sharing of digital files over cellular, satellite, and telephone lines does raise significant concerns about piracy of copyrighted material and issues that are related to the privacy of the individual who is receiving and sending digitized communication. However, the great advances that are offered by digital communication will continue without interruption as new generations of improved digital camcorders, personal computing devices, and still-frame cameras are introduced to the marketplace.

Convergence

Probably the most important trend for consumer electronics is that of convergence. The computer, the telephone, and broadcasting were always considered distinct from each other. The consumer electronics industry has long realized that devices that are useful to consumers could be created by combining the power of telecommunications with the power of computing. The rise of modems to provide Internet service on personal computers, cell telephones that provide e-mail and online services, and televisions that allow for Internet connectivity demonstrate the notion of convergence. The merger announced by AOL and Time Warner in 2000 lends further support to the fact that the boundaries within the various communication-related industries have been obliterated.

All technologies that were once considered "wired" are converging toward wireless delivery modes. Both telecommunication and Internet devices have become less dependent on traditional telephone lines. Cellular telephone systems use a series of radio transmitters to provide interconnectivity. The next wave of convergent devices may use the same type of system to provide increased interconnection. The most promising of the wireless standards is known as the "Bluetooth" standard. Bluetooth would allow for the wireless networking of television, home theater, and Internet equipment. Furthermore, Bluetooth could provide a wireless interconnection between MP3 players, Palm Pilots, pagers, and cell telephones. This would allow for the wireless transfer of entertainment and information between devices, thereby eliminating the wire connection. The ease of interoperability between electronic devices suggests a dynamic and convergent future for a new breed of consumer products.

See also: COMPUTER SOFTWARE; COMPUTING; COPYRIGHT; DIFFUSION OF INNOVATIONS AND COMMUNICATION; DIGITAL COMMUNICATION; EDISON, THOMAS ALVA; INTERNET AND THE WORLD WIDE WEB; MARCONI, GUGLIELMO; PRIVACY AND COMMUNICATION; PRIVACY AND ENCRYPTION; RADIO BROADCASTING, HISTORY OF; RADIO BROADCASTING, TECHNOLOGY OF; RECORDING INDUSTRY, TECHNOLOGY OF; TECHNOLOGY, ADOPTION AND DIFFUSION OF; TECHNOLOGY, PHILOSOPHY OF; TELECOMMUNICATIONS, WIRELESS; TELEPHONE INDUSTRY, TECHNOLOGY OF; TELEVISION BROADCASTING, TECHNOLOGY OF; V-CHIP.

Bibliography

Chandler, Al. (2001). *Inventing the Electronic Century: The Epic Story of the Consumer Electronics and Computer Industries*. New York: Free Press.

Consumer Electronics Association. (2000). *Digital America: U.S. Consumer Electronics Industry Today*. Arlington, VA: Consumer Electronics Association.

Consumer Electronics Manufacturing Association. (1998). "Market Overview: Consumer Electronics and the U.S. Economy." <http://www.ce.org/Market_Overview/Market_Overview_Overview.asp?client=public.>

Grant, August E. (2000). *Communication Technology Update*, 7th edition. Austin, TX: Technology Futures Inc.

Nixon, Richard. (1999). *Victory without War*. New York: Simon & Schuster.

Rogers, Everett M. (1986). *Communication Technology: The New Media in Society*. New York: Free Press.

DAVID SEDMAN

▰ CONVERSATION

See: Interpersonal Communication, Conversation and

▰ COPYRIGHT

Copyright is one of three types of intellectual property law, along with patents and trademarks. Copyright gives authors and creators a limited right to control the use of their expression. Expression is how people convey their ideas, and it can include books, drawings, paintings, sculptures, photographs, music, movies, sound recordings, and computer software programs. Copyright protects only expression, not the idea or fact that is being expressed. For example, a history book will include many base facts and ideas, as well as some original ideas that the author developed on his or her own. A second author (or filmmaker, etc.) can use any of the facts and ideas contained in the book but would need permission to copy the original author's expression.

Expression must be fixed (stored) in a tangible medium before it is protected by copyright. Recording music on a cassette tape, painting on a canvas, or saving text on a computer are all ways of storing expression. The copyright owner has the right to control the reproduction, distribution, public performance, and public display of the work that contains the expression, whether that work is a book, film, sculpture, and so on. In addition, the copyright owner can control derivative works (i.e., adaptations and transformations of the original work), as when a novel is turned into a movie.

A work is protected by copyright as soon as it is created. In many cases, the author sells or licenses the copyright to a media company, which then markets the work to the public. Huge media conglomerates such as AOL–TimeWarner, the Walt Disney Corporation, and the Sony Corporation own the copyrights to thousands of books, songs, films, and pictures. Computer software companies also own very important copyrights because computer programs are used in so many facets of modern day life. The duration of a copyright for a single-author work lasts for the life of the writer plus seventy years. The duration of a copyright for a corporate product is ninety-five years from the date of publication. After the copyright expires, the work falls into the public domain, and anyone may freely copy, distribute, or otherwise use the work.

Origins of Copyright

Before the development of the printing press in the fifteenth century, anyone could copy someone else's expression. Most books were written by hand, a very time-consuming process. The first European printers spent a lot of money setting up their presses and fonts, and they were concerned that rival printers would copy their books, causing them to lose money. Sometimes a government official would issue a special printing privilege, prohibiting other publishers from printing the same book. These privileges served two important purposes. First, they protected the young printing industry from competition. Second, they helped governments and the Roman Catholic Church to impose censorship on the publishing industry and control the spread of seditious and heretical books.

The first copyright law to give the author rather than the publisher initial control over how the work could be used was passed in England in 1710. Other European countries followed suit, and when the United States won its independence, the new nation modeled its first copyright law on the English statute. Copyright originally was a "Western" concept. Many countries in other parts of the world did not adopt copyright laws until the latter half of the twentieth century.

Justifications for Copyright

The primary purpose of copyright is to provide an economic incentive to create new works for the benefit of the public. Copyright law gives the author the ability to restrict access to the work in order to charge users and recoup his or her initial investment in creating the work. If competitors or consumers could copy and use the work without paying the author, the author might decide not to create the work in the first place. The dilemma for lawmakers is determining the appropriate amount of copyright protection. If the law grants more protection than necessary, the public will not have full access to the works that are created, reducing the public benefit of those works. If the law grants too little protection, fewer works will be created. Economists disagree about the degree of protection that is necessary to encourage creativity. On the one hand, creativity and expression flourished long before the first copyright law, suggesting that copyright protection is not necessary to encourage new works. On the other hand, more content is being produced than ever before, and that content is a significant portion of the world's economy, suggesting that copyright is beneficial to society.

In many countries, a second justification for copyright is to protect the moral rights of the author. This concept, sometimes referred to as *droit moral* for its basis in French copyright law, stems from the viewpoint that expression is the output of an author's distinct, individual personality and that authors deserve to be rewarded for their creative output. Moral rights typically include attribution of authorship (known as paternity) and protection for the integrity of the work. In countries that recognize a right of paternity, the author has the right to have his or her name associated with any work that the individual has created. The right of integrity gives the author control over how a work is altered to ensure that the work is not used in a way that would harm the author's reputation or distort the author's intent in creating the work. Moral rights, particularly the right of integrity, are limited in the United States because they sometimes conflict with free speech rights. Some commentators argue that authors deserve very strong copyright protection since they create new, original expression from their own minds. Other commentators argue that there are very few new or original ideas, and that most ideas come from the author's culture. These commentators believe that there should be very little copyright protection because the authors borrowed their ideas from the public domain in the first place.

Copyright in the United States

The U.S. Supreme Court has repeatedly stated that the purpose of copyright is to encourage creativity for the benefit of the public, not to reward authors for their labor. In an important 1991 ruling in *Feist Publications, Inc. v. Rural Telephone Service Company*, the Supreme Court said that the U.S. Constitution requires some degree of originality before expression can be protected by copyright. The fact that a work might be expensive and time-consuming to create (such as a telephone directory) does not mean that it deserves copyright protection.

Since copyright gives the author such a broad set of rights over how his or her expression is used (essentially granting the author a monopoly over the use of that expression), the law contains a number of limitations to ensure that the public can still gain reasonable access to the work. The most important limitation is known as fair use. Fair use allows someone to copy, without permission, portions of the author's expression in limited circumstances for purposes such as criticism, comment, teaching, news reporting, or research. Fair use eases the tension between copyright law and the First Amendment's protection of free speech.

Most of the other provisions of copyright law were created as compromises between the various media industries that exploit copyrighted works. For example, cable television companies pay a special fee for the right to retransmit the signals of local television stations. Musicians pay a special fee to record and distribute a new version of a different songwriter's song. Libraries and schools have been granted exemptions from many of the specific rules contained in copyright law since these institutions are supposed to make knowledge widely available to the public.

International Copyright

Copyright laws are designed primarily as a form of protectionism for the content industries, and international disputes play a major role in the development of each nation's domestic law. Problems of international piracy and lack of protection for foreign authors under the domestic copyright laws of most nations led to a major copyright treaty in 1886, the Berne Convention for the Protection of Literary and Artistic Works, which is administered by the World Intellectual Property Organization (WIPO). The Berne Convention outlines only the minimum standards of protection that each country must enact through its domestic laws. Thus, the potential for conflict between the laws of any two nations remains high.

The United States was precluded from joining the Berne Convention at first because the U.S. statute did not meet some of the minimum standards. From 1891 to 1955, the United States relied on bilateral agreements with individual nations. As intellectual property exports increased, the U.S. copyright industries (i.e., the publishing, film, music, and computer software industries) began to lobby more forcefully for U.S. involvement in international copyright treaties. In 1955, the United States joined the Universal Copyright Convention (UCC), which is administered by the United Nations Educational, Scientific, and Cultural Organization (UNESCO). The United States then joined the Berne Convention in 1989. The economic power of the copyright industries has made them forceful lobbyists for increased international and domestic copyright protection.

Copyright and Technological Change

Copyright law has changed dramatically as new technologies have been invented to create, store, and distribute copyrighted expression. With each new method of storing or transmitting expression, two key questions arise. First, does using the new technology infringe any of the rights of the copyright owner? For example, does playing a song on the radio count as a public performance of the song? Second, should the new technology itself be protected by copyright? For example, is the signal of a radio station protected by copyright? In the United States, the Copyright Act of 1976 attempted to answer these questions by granting protection to expression fixed in any tangible medium, no matter what technology is used. Yet the questions still persist. For example, does transmitting a song through the Internet count as a reproduction, distribution, public performance, or all three?

Technological advances such as photocopiers, videotape recorders, and cassette decks have made

In connection with one of the first cases to deal with copyright issues on the Internet, Napster founder Shawn Fanning (center) held a press conference in San Francisco on February 12, 2001, and said that his company would appeal a ruling by the Ninth Circuit Court of Appeals that said that Napster, an online music downloading service, must prevent subscribers from sharing copyrighted material. (Reuters NewMedia Inc./Corbis)

copying cheaper than ever before. All of these technologies have made it easy for consumers to make copies for their own personal use, resulting in lost sales by content creators. Yet it has proven impractical for copyright owners to try to enforce their legal rights in most cases involving such small-scale infringement.

The development of digital technology has increased the concerns of copyright owners. Unlike analog technology, digital technology creates perfect copies that are indistinguishable from the original work. In many instances, digital copies are also easier and cheaper to make than analog copies. For example, computer files can be copied almost instantaneously at the click of a button. While these attributes reduce the costs that are incurred by copyright owners in producing and distributing their works, they also significantly increase the amount of copyright infringement that takes place. Copyright owners increasingly have sought to use new technology to limit the ability of consumers to make copies. For example, cable and satellite television signals are often scrambled using encryption technology to prevent nonpayers from obtaining the content. In addition, much of the consumer electronic equipment that is used to play copyrighted content now contains special anticopying technology.

The Internet has dramatically exacerbated the threat of copyright infringement because computer networks are designed to facilitate the distribution of content. So now, not only are digital copies easy and cheap to make, they are also easy and cheap to distribute. This change in technology has led many commentators to question whether copyright law remains a useful concept. Copyright law has focused primarily on restricting the copying and distribution of the physical object that contains the expression. In a 1994 essay, John Perry Barlow suggested that copyright would quickly become anachronistic in a digital world where expression is created and distributed as digital bits on the Internet and where physical objects have less relevance.

The response of the copyright industries has been to rely more heavily on technological measures to control access to their content. The Digital Millennium Copyright Act (DMCA), a 1998 amendment to U.S. copyright law, makes it illegal to circumvent the technology used to protect a work or to develop or distribute devices that are designed to circumvent protection technology. Copyright owners claim that without these strong enforcement measures, the Internet will not reach its full potential as a distribution medium for copyrighted content. Many critics argue that copyright law is being expanded to grant copyright owners more control over their works than ever before, making it difficult for individuals to engage in fair use or gain access to the legally unprotected ideas contained in an author's expression.

Another important feature of the Internet is its global nature. The Internet allows users to send and receive information from almost anywhere on the planet. This creates additional challenges for copyright because each country has its own copyright law. A website that may be perfectly legal in the country where it was created is easily accessible from countries where that website would be considered copyright infringement. This problem is creating pressure for more conformity among the domestic laws of each nation. However, such conformity does not take into account the cultural differences and unique policy objectives of each nation. In the future, the World Intellectual Property Organization and the World Trade Organization will play an increasingly important role in shaping the balance of copyright between protecting content and providing access to information.

See also: FIRST AMENDMENT AND THE MEDIA; INTERNET AND THE WORLD WIDE WEB; PRINTING, HISTORY AND METHODS OF; WRITERS.

Bibliography

Barlow, John Perry. (1994). "The Economy of Ideas." Wired 2.03:84.

Bettig, Ronald. (1996). Copyrighting Culture. Boulder, CO: Westview Press.

Boyle, James. (1996). Shamans, Software, and Spleens: Law and the Construction of the Information Society. Cambridge, MA: Harvard University Press.

Ginsburg, Jane. (1995). "Putting Cars on the 'Information Highway': Authors, Exploiters, and Copyright in Cyberspace." Columbia Law Review 95:1466–1499.

Goldstein, Paul. (1994). Copyright's Highway: From Gutenberg to the Celestial Jukebox. New York: Hill and Wang.

Gordon, Wendy. (1993). "A Property Right in Self-Expression: Equality and Individualism in the Natural Law of Intellectual Property." Yale Law Journal 102:1533–1609.

Jackson, Matt. (2000). "The Digital Millennium Copyright Act of 1998: A Proposed Amendment to Accommodate Free Speech." Communication Law & Policy 5:61–92.

Landes, William M., and Posner, Richard A. (1989). "An Economic Analysis of Copyright Law." Journal of Legal Studies 18:325–363.

Leaffer, Marshall. (1995). Understanding Copyright Law, 2nd edition. New York: Matthew Bender.

Litman, Jessica. (1989). "Copyright Legislation and Technological Change." Oregon Law Review 68:275–361.

Litman, Jessica. (1996). "Revising Copyright Law for the Information Age." Oregon Law Review 75:19–48.

Patterson, L. Ray. (1968). Copyright in Historical Perspective. Nashville, TN: Vanderbilt University Press.

Saunders, David. (1992). Authorship and Copyright. London: Routledge.

Stewart, Stephen. (1989). International Copyright and Neighbouring Rights, 2nd edition. London: Butterworths.

MATT JACKSON

CREATIVITY

See: Children's Creativity and Television Use

■ CULTIVATION THEORY AND MEDIA EFFECTS

Cultivation analysis is the third part of a research strategy designed to examine the role of the media in society (see Gerbner, 1973). The first component, "institutional process analysis," investigates how media messages are produced, managed, and distributed. The second component, "message system analysis," examines images in media content. The third component, "cultivation analysis," studies how exposure to the world of television contributes to conceptions that viewers have about the real world. In its simplest form, cultivation analysis tries to ascertain if those who watch more television, compared to those who watch less but are otherwise comparable, are more likely to perceive the real world in ways that reflect the most common and repetitive messages and lessons provided by television programs.

Cultivation theory is not concerned with the "effect" of particular programs or with artistic quality. Rather, it looks at television as the nation's storyteller, telling most of the stories to most of the people most of the time. While these stories present broad, underlying, global assumptions about the "facts" of life rather than specific attitudes and opinions, they are also market- and advertiser-driven. Television's stories provide a "dominant" or mainstream set of cultural beliefs, values, and practices. Heavy viewing may thus override differences in perspectives and behavior that ordinarily stem from other factors and influences. In other words, viewers with varied cultural, social, and political characteristics should give different answers to questions about values, beliefs, and practices. These differences, however, are diminished or even absent from the responses of those who watch a large amount of television, while they exist for viewers who watch small amounts of television. Thus, television cultivates common perspectives; it fosters similar views and perspectives among those who, on the surface, should be very different.

The methods and assumptions behind cultivation analysis are different from those traditionally employed in mass communication research. Cultivation analysis begins with identifying and assessing the consistent images, portrayals, and values that cut across most programs, either by conducting a content (message system) analysis or by examining existing content studies. These findings are then used to formulate questions about people's conceptions of social reality. The questions juxtapose answers reflecting the television world with those that are more in line with reality. Questionnaires also measure television viewing, typically by asking how much time the respondent watches television on an "average day," and assess demographic variables such as age, gender, race, education, occupation, social class, and political orientation.

The cultivation questions posed to respondents do not mention television, and the respondents' awareness of the source of their information is seen as irrelevant. The resulting relationships, if any, between the amount of television viewing and the tendency to respond to these questions in the terms of the dominant and repetitive facts, values, and ideologies of the world of television (other things held constant) illuminate television's contribution to viewers' conceptions of social reality.

For example, one of the most examined features of television is gender-role stereotyping. Study after study has found that women are underrepresented and that most television characters are gender-typed (Signorielli, 1985; Signorielli and Bacue, 1999). Two cultivation analyses focusing on gender roles examined children's responses to questions that dealt with gender-role attitudes and behaviors (Morgan, 1987; Signorielli and Lears, 1992b). The questions that were related to gender-role attitudes asked if certain chores (i.e., wash or dry the dishes, mow the lawn, take out the garbage, help with the cooking, clean the house, help with small repairs around the house, and make the bed) should be done by boys only, girls only, or either girls or boys. Responses to these questions were analyzed to indicate whether or not they reflected traditional gender-role divisions of labor. The children's gender-role behaviors were also determined by asking which of these seven chores they did. In these studies, the "television answer" was the response that only girls should do "girl chores" (i.e., wash or dry the dishes, help with the cooking, clean the house, and make the bed) and that only boys should do "boy chores" (i.e., mow the lawn, take out the garbage, and help with small repairs around the house). With regard to the children's own behaviors, the "television answer" was indicating that they did those chores that were consistent with their gender. These studies found that those who watched more television typically gave more gender-stereotyped views about which chores should be done by boys and which should be done by girls.

The most well-known area of cultivation analysis has focused on the manifestation of television violence through the "mean-world syndrome" (see Signorielli, 1990). These questions (with the television answers in *italics*) included the following:

1. Would you say that most of the time people try to be helpful, or that they are mostly *just looking out for themselves?*

2. Do you think that most people would try *to take advantage of you* if they got a chance, or would they try to be fair?

3. Generally speaking, would you say that most people can be trusted or that *you cannot be too careful in dealing with people?*

Again, the results of these studies indicate that those who spend more time watching television's mean and dangerous world tend to have conceptions that the world in which they live is a mean and dangerous place.

Cultivation analyses have also examined relationships between viewing and the conceptions that people have about aging (i.e., those who watch more television tend to underestimate and undervalue the elderly population of society), occupations (i.e., those who watch more television want high-status and well-paying jobs but do not want to work very hard), and nutrition (i.e., those who watch more television tend to eat less healthy food) (e.g., Gerbner et al., 1980; Signorielli, 1993; Signorielli and Lears, 1992a).

As in most studies of media effects, the observable empirical evidence of cultivation tends to be modest in terms of its absolute size. In most national surveys a trivial, and demographically diverse, number of respondents (about 4% or less) say they do not watch television. Consequently, there are no real control groups. Even "light" viewers watch some television and live in the same cultural environment as "heavy" viewers. But, if one argues that the messages are stable, that the medium is virtually ubiquitous, and that it is accumulated exposure that counts, then it seems reasonable that almost everyone should be affected, regardless of how much television they watch. This means that the cards are stacked against finding evidence of cultivation. Therefore, the discovery of a systematic pattern of small but pervasive differences between light and heavy viewers may indicate far-reaching consequences. Indeed, in study after study, the evidence continues to mount as to the viability of cultivation theory in explaining the cumulative, long-term effects of watching television.

In summary, cultivation theory is an attempt to understand and explain the dynamics of television as a distinctive feature of the modern age. Cultivation analysis concentrates on the enduring and common consequences of growing up and living with television: the cultivation of stable, resistant, and widely shared assumptions, images, and conceptions that reflect the underlying dimensions, institutional characteristics, and interests of the medium itself. Cultivation analysis examines television as the common symbolic environment—the true "melting pot" of the twentieth and twenty-first centuries.

See also: ELDERLY AND THE MEDIA; FEAR AND THE MEDIA; GENDER AND THE MEDIA; NUTRITION AND MEDIA EFFECTS; VIOLENCE IN THE MEDIA, HISTORY OF RESEARCH ON.

Bibliography

Gerbner, George. (1973). "Cultural Indicators: The Third Voice." In *Communications, Technology and Social Policy,* eds. George Gerbner, Larry P. Gross, and William. H. Melody. New York: Wiley.

Gerbner, George; Gross, Larry P.; Morgan, Michael; and Signorielli, Nancy. (1981). "Health and Medicine on Television." *New England Journal of Medicine* 305:901–904.

Gerbner, George; Gross, Larry P.; Morgan, Michael; and Signorielli, Nancy. (1994). "Growing Up with Television: The Cultivation Perspective." In *Media Effects,* eds. Jennings Bryant and Dolf Zillmann. Hillsdale, NJ: Lawrence Erlbaum.

Gerbner, George; Gross, Larry P.; Signorielli, Nancy.; and Morgan, Michael. (1980). "Aging with Television: Images on Television Drama and Conceptions of Social Reality." *Journal of Communication* 30(1):37–47.

Morgan, Michael. (1987). "Television, Sex Role Attitudes, and Sex Role Behavior." *Journal of Early Adolescence* 7(3):269–282.

Signorielli, Nancy. (1985). *Role Portrayals and Stereotyping on Television: An Annotated Bibliography.* Westport, CT: Greenwood Press.

Signorielli, Nancy. (1990). "Television's Mean and Dangerous World: A Continuation of the Cultural Indicators Perspective." In *Cultivation Analysis: New Directions in Media Effects Research*, eds. Nancy Signorielli and Michael Morgan. Newbury Park, CA: Sage Publications.

Signorielli, Nancy. (1991). "Adolescents and Ambivalence toward Marriage. A Cultivation Analysis." *Youth & Society* 23(1):121–149.

Signorielli, Nancy. (1993). "Television and Adolescents' Perceptions about Work." *Youth & Society* 24(3): 314–341.

Signorielli, Nancy, and Bacue, Aaron. (1999). "Recognition and Respect: A Content Analysis of Prime-Time Television Characters Across Three Decades." *Sex Roles* 40(7/8):527–544.

Signorielli, Nancy, and Lears, Margaret E. (1992a). "Television and Children's Conceptions of Nutrition: Unhealthy Messages." *Health Communication* 4(4):245–257.

Signorielli, Nancy, and Lears, Margaret E. (1992b). "Children, Television and Conceptions about Chores: Attitudes and Behaviors." *Sex Roles* 27(3/4):157–172.

NANCY SIGNORIELLI

CULTURAL STUDIES

Cultural studies has become an increasingly difficult field of communication scholarship and political activism to define, mostly owing to the attempts of its adherents to transcend the confines of academic boundaries. As a result of this disciplinary and institutional resistance, cultural studies often is described in terms of the intellectual biographies of some of its leading scholarly figures (e.g., Raymond Williams and Stuart Hall in the United Kingdom, James Carey, Hanno Hardt, and Lawrence Grossberg in the United States, and Australians John Fiske, who now teaches in the United States, and John Hartley), as well as in terms of the geographical locations of cultural studies (e.g., the Birmingham School and the Glasgow School, both of British cultural studies; U.S. cultural studies at the University of Illinois and the University of Iowa; and cultural studies in Canada, including the work of Donald Theall and John Fekete). Dozens of spin-offs, reamalgamations, and reconfigurations of many disciplines in the humanities and social sciences, from postcolonial theory to queer theory, have become part of the landscape of cultural studies.

One mass communication theory text brackets cultural studies within a cultural turn as part of the last of five broad theoretical bases discussed, thus pointing out by its relation to other media theories the marginality of cultural studies (Baran and Davis, 1999). In a chapter on "critical cultural studies," British cultural studies is identified as one of the "contemporary schools of neo-Marxist theory." Cultural studies becomes a subtheory of "critical cultural studies," along with Marxist theory, textual analysis and literary criticism, the Frankfurt School, political economy theory, the media theories of Canadians Marshall McLuhan and Harold Innis, popular culture research, media as culture industries, and advertising as a cultural commodity, among others.

In resisting categories, cultural studies attempts to remain an open field, defying method and tradition. For example, Cary Nelson, Paula Treichler, and Lawrence Grossberg (1992) discuss cultural studies as defying research domains, methodologies, and an intellectual legacy of a tradition and language. They suggest that cultural studies averts being a traditional discipline and is even antidisciplinary. Cultural studies crosses domains, or disciplines, from Marxism and feminism to psychoanalysis and postmodernism. Cultural studies also has no identifiable methodology, best described as a "bricolage" of textual analysis, semiotics, deconstruction, ethnography, content analysis, survey research, and other methods. But while approaches may be methodologically diverse, it must be recognized that every method is applied self-reflexively and in context.

Despite the difficulties, Nelson, Treichler, and Grossberg attempt a general definition of cultural studies to include these elements of domain and methodology. Cultural studies is inter-, trans-, and counter-disciplinary, maintaining a tension between broad, anthropological concepts and narrow, humanistic concepts of culture. It studies primarily modern industrial societies, insists on treating high and popular culture as equals of cultural production, and compares these cultural products to other social and historical forms. It is "committed to the study of the entire range of a society's beliefs, institutions, and communicative practices." Culture itself is both conceptualized as a way of life and a set of cultural practices, the former including "ideas, attitudes, languages, practices, institutions and structures of power," and the latter including "artistic forms, texts, canons, architecture, mass-produced commodities" and so forth. In terms of its traditions, cultural studies has political aims, studying cultural change with the intent of intervening in it, although these aims differ in the British and U.S. versions. A frequent frame of analysis for cultural studies is race, gender, and class as culture and power are studied in tandem.

Searching for a definition of cultural studies, Hartley (1992) identifies the institutional and the genealogical levels of its identity. First, he finds cultural studies to be an "intellectual enterprise of the left" of the 1960s that was transformed, for the worse, into an "academic subject increasingly of the center" in the 1980s and 1990s. Second, cultural studies becomes a list of names of "prodigal parents" who begat a field that detests orthodoxy, avoids authority, and is committed to interdisciplinary work, but "it has no unified theory, textual canon, disciplinary truths, agreed methodology, common syllabus, examinable content or professional body."

Scholars Steven Best and Douglas Kellner (1991) situate cultural studies within their call for a multiperspective and multidimensional critical theory of the media and society, one that relates all dimensions of society, from the cultural to the social, political, and economic, to each other and to the dominant mode of social organization. Advertising, for example, not only would be studied under capitalism and its economic effects, but also as it adapts cultural forms and affects cultural life and as it has changed politics. Stressing multiple perspectives, Best and Kellner advocate using many approaches, theories, and disciplines, such as Marxism and feminism, critical theory and postmodernism, or economics, sociology, and philosophy. By multiple dimensions, Best and Kellner mean that each dimension of society is treated as relatively autonomous, thus inviting analysis from many disciplines or perspectives.

Given this whirlpool of contemporary versions of cultural studies and their instability, cultural studies might best be approached historically as part of a much wider cultural and critical turn in communication research after World War II. Reflecting on the divergent history of administrative and critical research in North America, the University of Iowa's Hanno Hardt (1992) groups U.S. cultural studies and critical theory together. Approaching communication as environments is one of the ideas of communication systems that is included in the cultural studies approach, where culture is the social context for creating meaning. In the longer history of U.S. mass communication research, critical theory and cultural studies are considered a radical branch.

Administrative Versus Critical Theory

The historical ground of the debate between mainstream administrative theory, or American empiricism, and critical theory, which is European theory, began as the two strains attempted a cross-fertilization in 1938. Paul Lazarsfeld brought Frankfurt School critical theorist Theodor Adorno to Princeton University's radio project (Slack and Allor, 1983). Lazarsfeld defined administrative research as carried out in the service of an administrative agency. He posed critical research as the study of the general role of media in the social system. His early attempts at convergence of these two approaches failed because he did not adequately appreciate the political and epistemological differences between the two. Adorno felt that administrative research was inherently narrow in scope and precluded the analysis of the system itself, and its cultural, social, and economic premises. He argued that the rift was more than a difference of theory and methods. Adorno wanted to study the process of communication critically. Administrative research was unable to confront the political and epistemological bases of the social order and its role in that order.

Slack and Allor contend that more recent attempts to accommodate the critical and administrative approaches have duplicated the same pitfalls that befell Lazarsfeld. They argue against casting administrative versus critical research in either (for the former) simple empirical, quantitative, functional, positivist, and effects-oriented dichotomies or (for the latter) qualitative, Marxist, structuralist, and owner/control-oriented dichotomies. They also argue against mainstream research adopting some critical theory aspects, such as communication context, ethical aspects, and multimethod approach. This convergence, critics say, amounts to co-optation of critical theory. Searching for the deeper boundaries separating administrative and critical approaches, Slack and Allor find that many models of communication developed in the administrative camp since the 1950s adhere to the basic linear causality reflected in the earliest sender-message-receiver model. Administrative research still treats communication as a process without context in which each element can be isolated. Adding bits of social context only adds a layer of sophistication to the simple linear terms.

The two authors view critical theory as encompassing a range of developing alternative approaches in such areas as international communication, new technologies, political economy, radical sociology, and cultural studies. The common thread is a critical perspective on the role of communication in the exercise of social power, a premise that leaves critical theory in opposition to liberal social theory. Critical approaches share a rejection of the linear causal model, adopting positions ranging from Marxist sociology to dependency theory and the Frankfurt School.

Slack and Allor argue that all critical approaches view media institutions and mass communication as intertwined with other social institutions, such as the family, the state, and the economy. Individuals are viewed as members of social groups defined by class, gender, race, and subculture. For example, Marxist studies looks at the complex and often contradictory interrelationships between politics, economics, and culture. This approach looks at the struggle over social meaning between dominant and oppressed groups. Using a structural approach, political economy studies look at the institutions involved in the production and distribution of communication. Cultural studies measures power in terms of hegemony, which is the idea of rule by consent. Hegemony describes the process by which oppressed classes come to experience the world in terms created by the ruling class. The authors see all these approaches to critical theory as offering an opportunity for communication research by redefining old research questions and opening new areas of inquiry. The challenge to the field is confronting the role of power and epistemology in communication institutions and research itself.

Canadian critical scholar Dallas Smythe and Tran Van Dinh (1983) assert that the ideological orientation of the researcher is inescapably linked to the choice of problems and methods. They argue that all researchers have a predisposition to either try to change the existing political–economic order or to preserve the status quo; value-free scientific inquiry is a myth. The two camps uneasily coexist in sharp, irreconcilable contrast as they define each approach in terms of problems, methods, and ideological perspective.

Administrative research focuses on how to make organizations more efficient—example, how to innovate word processors within a corporation, they argue. Administrative methods comprise neopositivist, behavioral theory applied to individuals. Administrative ideology means linking these problems and tools with results that either support or do not disturb the status quo. Conversely, critical theory researches problems of how to reshape or create institutions to meet the needs and achieve the values of the community. The critical method is historical, materialist analysis of the contradictory, dialectical processes of the real world. And critical ideology links these problems and methods with results that involve radical changes in the established order.

Smythe and Van Dinh stress the transdisciplinary scope of critical theory, including humanities, the arts, and social sciences. It must include criticism of the contradictory aspects of phenomena in systemic context, whether it is Marxist or not. The authors note that Marxist work was repressed in the United States until the 1960s, when research, teaching, and publishing spread rapidly.

On their agenda as objectives of critical research are the demystification of science and technology; the decentralization and democratization of media institutions; the formulation of praxis, where theory and practice intersect; and mass mobilization for action. Sketching needs for future critical research, Smythe and Van Dinh suggest researchers should study the communication theories and practices of independence, liberation, and revolutionary movements, the actions of multinational corporations, and Third World alternatives for horizontal media. Community research could involve projects to help people resist imposed communications systems. Researchers would work with labor, feminist, religious, and environmental groups as well as political parties.

Culture and media historian and sociologist Gaye Tuchman (1983) takes more of a middle ground in the critical versus administrative theory debate. Tuchman argues that theoretically and empirically sound studies of the "production of culture" can be done without adhering to a linear causality model. In other words, Tuchman's approach tries to accommodate the empirical demands of administrative research with the dialectics of critical research. Tuchman writes that the social movements of the 1960s made American media researchers expose themselves to ideas familiar to Europeans who looked at media as the study of the formation of consciousness. Tuchman's concern with consciousness forces consideration of dominant ideologies, the maintenance of power, the control and integration of social change, and the praxis for resistance to media hegemony. The circular model implicit in this perspective is that production influences content, which influences social behavior and structure, which influence production processes.

Hegemony and Ideology

False consciousness is the desired end product of the process of hegemony, which U.S. cultural historian Todd Gitlin (1980) and Williams (1977) both applied in relation to the mass media, as does the tradition of British cultural studies extended by Stuart Hall. According to Italian Marxist Antonio Gramsci, hegemony is the ruling class's domination through ideology and the shaping of popular consent. Hegemony unites persuasion from above with consent from below. The concept helps Gitlin's work and other cultural studies scholars explain the strength and endurance of advanced capitalism. In his study of the news media, Gitlin suggests that hegemony is secured when those who control the dominant institutions impress their definitions upon the ruled. The dominant class controls ideological space and limits what is thinkable in society. Dominated classes participate in their domination, as hegemony enters into everything people do and think of as natural, or the product of common sense—including what is news, as well as playing, working, believing, and knowing, Gitlin argues. Hegemonic ideology permeates the common sense that people use to understand the world and tries to become that common sense.

In capitalist society, the media and other institutions formulate the dominant ideology, Gitlin believes. The media also incorporate popular opposing messages into the dominant ideology, redistributing them through journalistic practices. Gitlin focuses on the struggle between the media, which uphold the dominant ideology, and groups out of power, which contest the ideology. The hegemonic ideology is reproduced in the media through media practices that stem from the ways journalists are socialized from childhood and then trained, edited, and promoted by media. Although journalists do not consciously consider ideology when they make news decisions, they tend to serve the political and economic elite's ideology by doing their jobs. Gitlin suggests the media remain free as long as they do not violate the essential hegemonic values or become too sympathetic to radical critiques. Opposition groups can exploit the contradictions in hegemonic ideology when elites conflict, but opposition groups and autonomous media will be muffled if the challenge to the hegemonic ideology is critical.

Gitlin contends that the media are controlled by corporate and political elites who bring media professionals into their social spheres. The ruling elites depend on the culture industry to advance their unity and limit competing ideologies. The media frame the ideological field within which the dominated classes live and understand their domination in order to perpetuate the hegemony of the elites. The elite economic class, however, does not produce and distribute ideology directly. Media workers do this within the culture industry, but only the media owners are directly linked to corporate and political leaders.

Gitlin suggests indirect control of the hegemonic ideology is difficult because liberal capitalism contains contradictions. The economic system generates ideologies that challenge and alter its own rationale. The hegemonic framework narrows the range of worldviews, preferring its version. To do this, the internal structures of the framework have to be continually re-created and defended, as well as challenged and adjusted superficially. The dominant ideology seems natural to media workers, who reproduce and defend it unconsciously. Gitlin says the media owners and managers reflect the ruling class's interest in private property, capital, the national security state, and individual success within the bureaucratic system.

The media also reproduce the discontinuity and detachment that characterize capitalism, Gitlin adds. Natural life rhythms are replaced by the artificial time of the workplace. Reading the newspaper or watching television reproduces the rhythms of capitalist production. The media reflect the production system's interchangeable time segments, such as the thirty-minute television show and the three-minute rock record. The fleeting images and abrupt changes of television socialize viewers into the discontinuity of the system. "Revolution" is co-opted in the changing of commodities, fashions, and lifestyles in a cycle that reflects the economic system. Individually, perpetual adaptation becomes the goal of comfort and status. The fast pace of consumer goods and advertising fuels the growth of new technologies and capital. This process culminates in a "tradition of the new."

The cultural-commodity process allows minor changes in the hegemonic ideology and may even require it, Gitlin argues. Contradictions within the ideology make it flexible enough to bend with the times and make opposition profitable. Opposition movements may be directed into other channels, from politics into culture and lifestyles, for example. The media balance, absorb, marginalize, and exclude to manage opposition or turn it into a commodity. The media may intensify change, but as long as the political economy provides goods that most people define as essential, the hegemonic system will prevail.

In Gitlin's analysis, ruling elites control media to spread a blanket of false consciousness over dominated classes, who are left with no room systemically for change. By contrast, Williams builds a hegemonic model that leaves more room for the emergence of a counterhegemony. Gitlin draws his concept of hegemony from Williams, who allows for the seeds of liberation and oppositional hegemony to grow. He identifies hegemony as a process rather than a system or structure. This approach to hegemony lets the process shape individual perceptions as a lived system of meanings and values that permeates all aspects of life. Hegemony defines reality for most people in the culture and sets the limit of reality beyond which it is difficult to think or move. However, as a complex process, hegemony does not passively exist as a form of dominance. It continually has to be renewed, defended, and adjusted. Because it is not absolute, hegemony is always resisted, challenged, and changed by counterhegemonies and alternative hegemonies that are produced by emergent social classes. A new class is always a source of emergent cultural practice, but as a subordinate class its practice is sporadic and partial. If the new class opposes the dominant social order, the new practice must survive attempts to co-opt it into the hegemonic ideology. As an example, Williams gives the emergence and successful incorporation, or co-optation, of the radical popular press in nineteenth-century England.

For Williams, the chink in the armor of the dominant ideology is that no hegemonic order includes or exhausts all human practice. Hegemonic ideology is selected from the full range of human practice, leaving the rest as the personal or private, natural or metaphysical. The danger of advanced capitalism is the media's seizure of these reserved areas of human practice. The dominant culture now reaches much further with mass media. Williams calls for resistance to the seizure of these private, personal human practices. He provides no program for resistance other than the study of the ownership and control of the capitalist media tied with wider analyses of capitalist structures. Williams helped create the strong commitment of cultural studies to a Marxist position as the only position that offers the potential of creating a new society. He also advocated the cultural studies assumption that culture is ideological.

Media Texts and Active Audiences

Cultural studies author John Fiske (1987) rejects "false consciousness" in the Marxist sense because the term implies a true consciousness. Fiske considers twentieth-century history as evidence that a society without ideology is impossible. He also argues that truth is a product of language and other cultural meaning systems, so truth is always a product of culture, society, and history. Fiske borrows neo-Marxist scholar Louis Althusser's concept of ideology as a process that is always reproduced in the way that people think, act, and understand themselves and society. Althusser contends that the relatively autonomous superstructure of the family, schools, media, political system, and other institutions shape norms of thought and action. The norms, however, are developed in the interests of the dominant groups who try to naturalize them as common sense. Social norms are ideological and accepted as natural even by classes whose interests are opposed by the norms. The institutions producing the dominant ideology share some characteristics, Fiske notes. They are patriarchal and concerned with wealth and possessions. They assert individualism and competition, yet they present themselves as neutral regarding class and interested in equality and fairness, despite their serving the white, male, middle class.

Fiske says cultural studies distinguishes between the individual, as a product of nature, and the subject, as a product of culture. Studying the subject-in-ideology is the best way of "explaining who (we think) we are." Social norms construct the subject's sense of self, society, and the world. According to this theory, a biological female can have a masculine subjectivity by adopting a patriarchal ideology; a black can have a white subjectivity; and a lower-class subject can have a middle-class subjectivity. Two more of Althusser's concepts, "hailing" and "interpellation," are used by cultural studies to describe the media's work. The media get a subject's attention by "hailing." This includes a social position for the subject to occupy. Interpellation is the larger process of providing social positions for all communicating parties. Fiske offers the television show *The A-Team* as interpellating the viewer as masculine, desiring power, and a team member.

Fiske argues that cultural studies should combine these concepts with Gramsci's theory of hegemony. The constant process of the dominant social groups constructing people as subjects-in-ideology is studied in the larger context of a constant process of struggle of the dominators to extend their power and the dominated to resist. Fiske reports that earlier cultural studies showed how the dominant ideology reproduced itself in popular television, but Stuart Hall's work introduced the idea that media texts are open to various interpretations. Hall also introduces the idea of the active audience that can interpret or read media texts in various ways. Hall's theory of "preferred reading" was developed to account for the correlation of various social meanings with social positions. Fiske summarizes Hall's three reading strategies: the dominant reading, the negotiated reading, and the oppositional reading. In the dominant reading, the viewer receives the intended ideological message in the social position of the dominant ideology. In the negotiated reading, the viewer may alter the media message to fit his or her social position. The third reading, the oppositional reading, is taken by those out of power and at odds with the dominant ideology.

Fiske offers two methodologies for use in cultural studies. He studies reading strategies about television and popular culture figures, such as the singer Madonna, through ethnography of fans' or viewers' responses, and semiotic and structuralist text analysis to analyze the signifiers in the text and the signifieds in the ideology of culture. Cultural studies has evolved to accommodate criticism of Hall's categories of reading as simplistic. French postmodernist Michel Foucault's discourse theory may be applied as a source for a media analysis model, treating discourse as a socially located way of making sense of a topic, according to Fiske. The media texts are discourses, and the consciousness of the audience is a discourse. The moment of reading takes place when these discourses meet, giving the audience's discourse equal weight in making meaning. The process involves the constant dynamic of agreement with the dominant ideology and resistance against it.

Fiske argues that the media audience is made up of diverse groups who actively read media to produce meanings that agree with their social experience. The television, and other media, text is capable of a variety of meanings, and is, in Fiske's word, "polysemic." The relationships between the television medium and content that comprise these polysemic messages are formed by three codes. First are the social codes of reality, including appearance, speech, and expression. Second, the technical codes of representation, including camera, lighting, editing, music and sound, transmit the conventional representational codes of, for example, narrative, conflict, character, action, and dialogue. Third, according to Fiske, ideological codes include individualism, patriarchy, race, class, materialism, and capitalism.

Culture, Society, and Postmodernism

U.S. cultural studies leading scholar James Carey (1989), who spent much of his academic career at the University of Illinois and has shaped the distinctively American and non-Marxist brand of cultural studies through his teaching and writing, suggests that mass communication research in America has erroneously overlooked the question at the heart of the mass culture debate of the 1950s: What is the relationship between popular art and other social forms, including the scientific, aesthetic, and religious, that popular art influences? American scholars generally have not, Carey suggests, examined the relationship between cultural, expressive forms, particularly art, and the social order. European scholars focus on this relationship. Culture is, in British sociology, the meaning people find in their experience through art, religion, and other expressive forms. Carey writes that culture must be regarded as "a set of practices, a mode of human activity, a process whereby reality is created, maintained, and transformed, however much it may subsequently become reified into a force independent of human action." One of his central contributions to the shift from the mainstream "effects" school of mass communication research in the United States to the cultural school is his development of a ritual model of communication, as opposed to a transportation model. In ritual communication, an entire sphere of cultural activity centers on the task of building community.

Cultural studies also may be seen as a linking bridge to postmodernist thinking, but its relationships to postmodernism are probably as varied as its approaches to cultural studies itself. However, a number of themes that are central to postmodern theory can be identified in reviewing the writing of cultural studies theorists about postmodernism. British sociologist Nick Stevenson (1995) contrasts the postmodern theories of French philosopher Jean Baudrillard, whose "rejection of ideology, truth, representation, seriousness, and the emancipation of the subject" embrace many issues of postmodernism, to the postmodern theories of U.S. cultural theorist Fredric Jameson (1991), whom Stevenson finds to be the "most sophisticated" postmodernist. In general, Jameson calls postmodernism the "cultural expression" or "logic" of "late capitalism." Fine and popular arts have been merged as the economic sector takes over the cultural sphere. Modernist culture has lost its subversiveness and contemporary cultural forms, like punk rock, are co-opted by the capitalist economic system.

For Jameson, the main themes of postmodernism include the absence of context and the uncertainty of interpretation; a growing concern with discourses; the end of the notion of individual style or the "death of the subject"; and a fragmentation of social meanings yielding "discursive heterogeneity" that best represents modern culture by parody or "pastiche," which Jameson calls a "blank parody" because the fragmenting of cultural styles has eroded social norms. The themes of postmodernism identified by Jameson and some other themes that rise among a group of cul-

tural studies scholars include: the death of individualism, as well as the end of Enlightenment thinking; fragmentation leading to parody and beyond to pastiche, with the loss of text and context and, more positively, the gaining of intertextuality; the focus on discourse and codes; the retrieval in postmodern thought of premodernism; the pointlessness of political action; and the concept of the "other."

Cultural studies absorption with issues of its own identities has helped lead not only to reevaluations of communication theory in the *Journal of Communication*, but also to a special 1997 issue of the University of Iowa's *Journal of Communication Inquiry*. Scholars debated the past, present, and future of cultural studies from a variety of perspectives, including calls for reclaiming its political activism and Marxist roots by Hardt. British scholar John Storey urges pursuing cultural studies as an academic discipline rather than as a political party. And still others contend that cultural critiques from the Third and Fourth Worlds centering on postcolonialism, multiculturalism, and globalization should be the focus of a reinvigorated cultural studies of the future that transcends the debate of its co-optation by academic institutions.

See also: CULTURE INDUSTRIES, MEDIA AS; INNIS, HAROLD ADAMS; JOURNALISM, PROFESSIONALIZATION OF; LAZARSFELD, PAUL F.; MCLUHAN, HERBERT MARSHALL; MODELS OF COMMUNICATION; NEWS PRODUCTION THEORIES; POLITICAL ECONOMY; SCHRAMM, WILBUR; SEMIOTICS; SOCIAL CHANGE AND THE MEDIA; WILLIAMS, RAYMOND.

Bibliography

Ang, Ien. (1996). *Living Room Wars: Rethinking Media Audiences for a Postmodern World.* London: Routledge.

Baran, Stanley J., and Davis, Dennis K. (1999). *Mass Communication Theory: Foundations, Ferment and Future,* 2nd edition. Belmont, CA: Wadsworth.

Baudrillard, Jean. (1983). *Simulations.* New York: Semiotext(e).

Best, Steven, and Kellner, Douglas. (1991). *Postmodern Theory: Critical Interrogations.* New York: Guilford.

Carey, James. (1989). *Communication as Culture: Essays on Media and Society.* Boston: Unwin Hyman.

Fiske, John. (1987). *Television Culture.* London: Methuen.

Gitlin, Todd. (1980). *The Whole World Is Watching: Mass Media in the Unmaking of the New Left.* Berkeley: University of California Press.

Hardt, Hanno. (1992). *Critical Communication Studies: Communication, History, and Theory in America.* London: Routledge.

Hartley, John. (1992). *The Politics of Pictures: The Creation of the Public in the Age of Popular Media.* London: Routledge.

Jameson, Fredric. (1991). *Postmodernism, Or, The Cultural Logic of Late Capitalism.* London: Verso.

Morley, David, and Chen, Kuan-Hsing, eds. (1996). *Stuart Hall: Critical Dialogues in Cultural Studies.* London: Routledge.

Nelson, Cary; Treichler, Paula A.; and Grossberg, Lawrence. (1992). "Cultural Studies: A User's Guide to This Book." In *Cultural Studies,* eds. Lawrence Grossberg, Cary Nelson, and Paula Treichler. New York: Routledge.

"Revisiting the Culture of Cultural Studies." (1997). *Journal of Communication Inquiry* 21(2), special issue.

Sardar, Ziauddin, and Van Loon, Borin. (1997). *Introducing Cultural Studies.* New York: Totem Books.

Silverstone, Roger. (1994). *Television and Everyday Life.* London: Routledge.

Slack, Jennifer Daryl, and Allor, Martin. (1983). "The Political and Epistemological Constituents of Critical Communication Research." *Journal of Communication* 33(3):208–218.

Smythe, Dallas, and Van Dinh, Tran. (1983). "On Critical and Administrative Analysis: A New Critical Analysis." *Journal of Communication* 33(3):117–127.

Stevenson, Nick. (1995). *Understanding Media Cultures: Social Theory and Mass Communication.* London: Sage Publications.

Thompson, John B. (1990). *Ideology and Modern Culture.* Stanford, CA: Stanford University Press.

Tuchman, Gaye. (1983). "Consciousness Industries and the Production of Culture." *Journal of Communication* 33(3):330–341.

Turner, Grame. (1990). *British Cultural Studies: An Introduction.* Boston: Unwin Hyman.

Williams, Raymond. (1962). *Communications.* Harmondsworth, Eng.: Penguin.

Williams, Raymond. (1977). *Marxism and Literature.* Oxford: Oxford University Press.

Williams, Raymond. (1992). *Television: Technology and Cultural Form.* Hanover, NH: Wesleyan University Press.

PAUL GROSSWILER

CULTURE

See: Consumer Culture; Cultural Studies; Culture and Communication; Culture Industries, Media as; Globalization of Culture Through the Media; Intercultural Communication, Adaptation and; Intercultural Communication, Interethnic Relations and; Organizational Culture

CULTURE AND COMMUNICATION

The term "culture" refers to the complex collection of knowledge, folklore, language, rules, rituals, habits, lifestyles, attitudes, beliefs, and customs that link and give a common identity to a particular group of people at a specific point in time.

All social units develop a culture. Even in two-person relationships, a culture develops over time. In friendship and romantic relationships, for example, partners develop their own history, shared experiences, language patterns, rituals, habits, and customs that give that relationship a special character—a character that differentiates it in various ways from other relationships. Examples might include special dates, places, songs, or events that come to have a unique and important symbolic meaning for two individuals.

Groups also develop cultures, composed of the collection of rules, rituals, customs, and other characteristics that give an identity to the social unit. Where a group traditionally meets, whether meetings begin on time or not, what topics are discussed, how decisions are made, and how the group socializes are all elements of what, over time, become defining and differentiating elements of its culture.

Organizations also have cultures, often apparent in particular patterns of dress, layout of workspaces, meeting styles and functions, ways of thinking about and talking about the nature and directions of the organization, leadership styles, and so on.

The most rich and complex cultures are those that are associated with a society or a nation, and the term "culture" is most commonly used to refer to these characteristics, including language and language-usage patterns, rituals, rules, and customs. A societal or national culture also includes such elements as significant historical events and characters, philosophies of government, social customs, family practices, religion, economic philosophies and practices, belief and value systems, and concepts and systems of law.

Thus, any social unit—whether a relationship, group, organization, or society—develops a culture over time. While the defining characteristics—or combination of characteristics—of each culture are unique, all cultures share certain common functions. Three such functions that are particularly important from a communication perspective are (1) linking individuals to one another, (2) providing the basis for a common identity, and (3) creating a context for interaction and negotiation among members.

The Relationship Between Communication and Culture

The relationship between communication and culture is a very complex and intimate one. First, cultures are created through communication; that is, communication is the means of human interaction through which cultural characteristics—whether customs, roles, rules, rituals, laws, or other patterns—are created and shared. It is not so much that individuals set out to create a culture when they interact in relationships, groups, organizations, or societies, but rather that cultures are a natural by-product of social interaction. In a sense, cultures are the "residue" of social communication. Without communication and communication media, it would be impossible to preserve and pass along cultural characteristics from one place and time to another. One can say, therefore, that culture is created, shaped, transmitted, and learned through communication. The reverse is also the case; that is, communication practices are largely created, shaped, and transmitted by culture.

To understand the implications of this communication–culture relationship, it is necessary to think in terms of ongoing communication processes rather than a single communication event. For example, when a three-person group first meets, the members bring with them individual thought and behavioral patterns from previous communication experiences and from other cultures of which they are, or have been, a part. As individuals start to engage in communication with the other members of this new group, they begin to create a set of shared experiences and ways of talking about them. If the group continues to interact, a set of distinguishing history, patterns, customs, and rituals will evolve. Some of these cultural characteristics would be quite obvious and tangible, such that a new person joining the group would encounter ongoing cultural "rules" to which they would learn to conform through communication. New members would in turn influence the group culture in small, and sometimes large, ways as they become a part of it. In a reciprocal fashion, this reshaped culture shapes the communication practices of current and future group members. This is true with any culture; communication shapes culture, and culture shapes communication.

Characteristics of Culture

Cultures are complex and multifaceted. As is apparent from the above discussions, cultures are complex "structures" that consist of a wide array of characteristics. The cultures of relationships or groups are relatively simple compared to those of organizations and, especially, societies. Edward Hall (1959, 1979) is one of the most significant contributors to the general understanding of the complexity of culture and the importance of communication to understanding and dealing with cultural differences at the societal level.

Cultures are subjective. There is a tendency to assume that the elements of one's own cultures are logical and make good sense. It follows that if other cultures—whether of relationships, groups, organizations, or societies—look different, those differences are often considered to be negative, illogical, and sometimes nonsensical. If, for example, an individual happens to be in a romantic relationship that is characterized by public displays of affection, that person might think that the behaviors of other people who have more reserved relational cultures may seem strange, even inappropriate. The person might wonder why a romantic couple would not be more open in displaying affection to one another in public. The individual might even be tempted to conclude that the "reserved" relationship lacks depth and intensity. This phenomenon is true in a variety of situations. People who are used to informal meetings of a group might think that adherence to formal meeting rules is strange and stilted. Employees in an organization where suits are worn every day may react with cynicism and questioning when they enter an organization where casual attire is standard practice. Someone from a culture that permits one man to have only one wife may find it quite inappropriate that another culture allows one man to have multiple wives.

With regard to culture, the tendency for many people is to equate "different" with "wrong," even though all cultural elements come about through essentially identical communication processes.

Cultures change over time. In fact, cultures are ever changing—though the change is sometimes very slow and imperceptible. Many forces influence cultural change. As indicated above, cultures are created through communication, and it is also through communication between individuals that cultures change over time. Each person involved in a communication encounter brings the sum of his or her own experiences from other (past or present) culture memberships. In one sense, any encounter between individuals in new relationships, groups, organizations, or societies is an intercultural communication event, and these varying cultural encounters influence the individual and the cultures over time. Travel and communication technologies greatly accelerate the movement of messages from one cultural context to another, and in small and large ways, cultures come to influence one another through communication. Phrases such as "melting pot," "world community," and "global village" speak to the inevitability of intercultural influence and change.

Cultures are largely invisible. Much of what characterizes cultures of relationships, groups, organizations, or societies is invisible to its members, much as the air is invisible to those who breathe it. Language, of course, is visible, as are greeting conventions, special symbols, places, and spaces. However, the special and defining meanings that these symbols, greetings, places, and spaces have for individuals in a culture are far less visible. For example, one can observe individuals kissing when they greet, but unless one has a good deal more cultural knowledge, it is difficult to determine what the behavior means in the context of the culture of their relationship, group, organization, or society. In other words, it is difficult to tell, without more cultural knowledge, if the kiss is a customary greeting among casual acquaintances or if such a greeting would be reserved for family members or lovers. As another example, beefsteak is thought of as an excellent food in some cultures. However, if one were a vegetarian or a member of a culture where the cow is sacred, that same steak would have an entirely different cultural meaning.

Glimpses of Culture

For the reasons noted above, opportunities to "see" culture and the dynamic relationship that exists between culture and communication are few. Two such opportunities do occur when there are violations of cultural conventions or when there is cross-cultural contact.

When someone violates an accepted cultural convention, ritual, or custom—for example, by speaking in a foreign language, standing closer than usual while conversing, or discussing topics that are typically not discussed openly—the other members of the culture become aware that something inappropriate is occurring. When "normal" cultural practices are occurring, members of the culture think little of it, but when violations occur, the members are reminded—if only momentarily—of the pervasive role that culture has on daily life.

When visiting other groups, organizations, and, especially, other societies, people are often confronted by—and therefore become aware of—different customs, rituals, and conventions. These situations often are associated with some awkwardness, as the people strive to understand and sometimes to adapt to the characteristics of the new culture. In these circumstances, again, one gains a glimpse of "culture" and the processes by which people create and adapt to culture.

The Role of Technology and Media

All institutions within society facilitate communication, and in that way, they all contribute to the creation, spread, and evolution of culture. However, communication media such as television, film, radio, newspapers, compact discs, magazines, computers, and the Internet play a particularly important role. Because media extend human capacities for creating, duplicating, transmitting, and storing messages, they also extend and amplify culture-building activities. By means of such communication technology, messages are transmitted across time and space, stored, and later retrieved and used. Television programs, films, websites, video games, and compact discs are created through human activity—and therefore reflect and further extend the cultural perspectives of their creators. They come to take on a life of their own, quite distinct and separate from their creators, as they are transmitted and shared around the increasingly global community.

Issues and Areas of Study

Understanding the nature of culture in relationship to communication is helpful in a number of ways. First, it helps to explain the origin of differences between the practices, beliefs, values, and customs of various groups and societies, and it provides a reminder of the communication process by which these differences came into being. This knowledge can and should heighten people's tolerance for cultural differences. Second, it helps to explain the process that individuals go through in adapting to new relationships, groups, organizations, and societies and the cultures of each. Third, it underscores the importance of communication as a bridge between cultures and as a force behind cultural change.

A number of questions also concern researchers and policymakers in this area. As communication increases between individuals, groups, and countries, does this mean that cultural differences and traditions will inevitably erode altogether? Will the cultures of individuals from groups, organizations, and societies that have great access to and control of communication media overpower those in cultures that have fewer resources and less access and control? Can knowledge be used to help individuals more comfortably and effectively adapt to new relationships, groups, organizations, and societies? The importance of these issues makes this area an important one for continued examination by scholars and practitioners.

See also: GLOBALIZATION OF CULTURE THROUGH THE MEDIA; GROUP COMMUNICATION; INTERCULTURAL COMMUNICATION, ADAPTATION AND; INTERCULTURAL COMMUNICATION, INTERETHNIC RELATIONS AND; INTERPERSONAL COMMUNICATION; LANGUAGE AND COMMUNICATION; ORGANIZATIONAL COMMUNICATION; RELATIONSHIPS, TYPES OF; SOCIAL CHANGE AND THE MEDIA; SOCIAL GOALS AND THE MEDIA; SOCIETY AND THE MEDIA; SYMBOLS.

Bibliography

Gudykunst, William B. (1991). *Bridging Differences: Effective Intergroup Communication.* Newbury Park, CA: Sage Publications.

Gudykunst, William B., and Kim, Young Y. (1984). *Communication with Strangers: An Approach to Intercultural Communication.* New York: Random House.

Hall, Edward T. (1959). *The Silent Language.* New York: Doubleday.

Hall, Edward T. (1979). *Beyond Culture.* New York: Doubleday.

Hunt, Todd, and Ruben, Brent D. (1992). *Mass Communication: Producers and Consumers.* New York: HarperCollins.

Kim, Young Y. (1988). *Communication and Cross-Cultural Adaptation.* Clevedon, Eng.: Multilingual Matters.

Ruben, Brent D. (1992). *Communication and Human Behavior,* 3rd edition. Englewood Cliffs, NJ: Prentice-Hall.

Ruben, Brent D., and Stewart, Lea P. (1998). *Communication and Human Behavior,* 4th edition. Needham Heights, MA: Allyn & Bacon.

Schiller, Herbert. (1989). *Culture, Inc.* New York: Oxford University Press.

BRENT D. RUBEN

■ CULTURE INDUSTRIES, MEDIA AS

In his essay "Culture Industry Reconsidered" (1975), Theodor Adorno recalls that Max Horkheimer and he first coined the term "culture industry" in their book *Dialectic of Enlightenment* (1972; first published in Amsterdam in 1947). The specific reference is to an essay entitled "The Culture Industry: Enlightenment as Mass Deception." Adorno points out that in early drafts of the essay they used the term "mass culture" but eventually replaced it with "culture industry" in order to "exclude from the outset the interpretation agreeable to its advocates: that it is a matter of something like a culture that arises from the masses themselves" (p. 12). Instead, Horkheimer and Adorno used the term to describe a commodified and industrialized culture, managed from above and essentially produced for the sake of making profits.

In "The Culture Industry," Horkheimer and Adorno laid out the basic framework for the study of culture under capitalism associated with the Frankfurt School of critical theory. The essay was part of a larger theoretical project begun with the founding of the Institute of Social Research at Frankfurt University, Germany, in 1924. Other important associates of the school were Erich Fromm, Leo Lowenthal, Herbert Marcuse, and Walter Benjamin. The institute's original mission was to serve as a sort of think tank for the German labor movement, but this soon changed with the rise of fascism.

Most of the members of the institute were Marxist and Jewish, and they managed to emigrate to the United States in the early 1930s. As they observed the continuing rise of European fascism, the Frankfurt School Èmigrés were compelled to compare these developments to their new environment. They found disconcerting tendencies toward totalitarianism in the United States similar to those they had left behind in Germany.

Although the U.S. culture industries—movies, music recording, radio broadcasting, newspapers, magazines, and books—were not directly controlled by a state ministry of information, their ownership structure and commercial nature made them function much like the state propaganda system of the Third Reich. They mobilized the working class to support causes against its own interests while at the same time demobilizing it through diversion. Rather than coming into consciousness and overthrowing the capitalist system, the working class had become more incorporated into it than ever, for which the culture industry was largely to blame.

The Frankfurt School shared some of the basic premises of mass society theory first laid out by European sociologists in the mid-nineteenth century. These theorists were trying to understand the nature of emerging industrialization and urbanization processes, including their effects on culture. With urban industrialization, people go from making their own living to working in factories where they must sell their labor to earn a living. This new way of making a living also involves the emergence of new forms of cultural life. Just as households began substituting mass-produced manufactured goods for homemade goods, the culture industry began substituting a manufactured and industrialized culture for the traditional cultural activities of rural society that revolved around family, community, and church.

The industrialization process results in a certain logic that governs the production and distribution of commodities. They are produced first and foremost for their exchange value (i.e., the profits they generate when sold to consumers). In consumer-goods markets, mass production has resulted in the output of increasingly homogeneous products that are artificially differentiated through advertising, providing the illusion of choice. The same has occurred with the industrialization of culture but the ramifications of homogenization seem more significant because of their fundamental role in helping shape the way reality is perceived. This is where the Frankfurt School becomes distinct from mass society theory. The culture industries are not ideological merely because they are controlled by economic and political authorities but rather primarily because their output is governed by the logic of capital. The result is formulaic and escapist entertainment that distracts and immobilizes agency for social change.

The Frankfurt School's Critique of the Culture Industry

By the late 1930s and early 1940s, when Horkheimer and Adorno began conducting their analysis of the U.S. culture industry, a small number of companies controlled each of the primary sectors of the mass media. Five companies controlled the production, distribution, and exhibition of movies in the United States. Since they owned their own theaters, screen time was guaranteed. The Great Depression had left four companies in charge of the recorded music industry. The music industry developed a symbiotic relationship with the radio broadcasting industry, which logically replaced live performances with cheaper recorded ones. This, in turn, helped the music industry sell its records. Prime-time radio programming belonged to two main networks, NBC and CBS, which through their owned-and-operated stations and affiliates, reached most of the nation.

The U.S. government helped establish NBC's parent company, RCA, after World War I to promote the development of a domestic radio industry. RCA went on to become one the of the media's first conglomerates. In addition to owning radio stations and the NBC network, RCA owned RKO, one of the five major film companies, and RCA Records, one of the four major recording companies. RCA also manufactured radios, record players, and theater sound systems, as well as car radios in a joint venture with General Motors.

The print media also underwent similar processes of concentration. For example, national magazines became primary outlets for the promotion of products and lifestyles, through both editorial content and advertisements. The book publishing industry also discovered the mass market, exploiting genres such as the romance novel, western, crime drama, and science fiction. The structure of the newspaper industry was also undergoing change. More and more communities found themselves with only one newspaper as advertisers logically shifted their advertising dollars to the newspapers offering the largest number of readers for the lowest price. These local monopolies, in turn, began to be bought up by regional and national newspaper chains that were pursuing the benefits of horizontal integration, such as pooling of news stories, sharing of presses, and selling of advertising space across a number of papers, thus lowering transaction costs to advertisers.

Horkheimer and Adorno (1972) provided one of the earliest frameworks for analyzing how this oligopolistic structure of the culture industry influenced the production, distribution, and consumption of entertainment and news. They identified several of the basic strategies used by the culture industry to sell itself and its products. First, though weak in comparison to the major industrial sectors of the day—steel, petroleum, electricity, and chemicals—consumers had come to see the culture industry as a producer of essential commodities. The wealth amassed by culture industry owners and the high salaries paid to culture industry executives seemed to validate the industry's contribution to the economy and society. Additionally, big-budget productions, what Horkheimer and Adorno called "conspicuous production," sought to demonstrate the apparent dedication of the industry to quality; that no expenses would be spared in the service of audience needs and desires. They recognized, of course, that the "varying budgets in the culture industry do not bear the slightest relation to factual values, to the meaning of the products themselves" (p. 124). Yet the hype surrounding the marketing of the blockbuster movie or record made it so compelling that audiences simply had to attend to it or feel left out.

The conspicuous production sought to attract the largest mass audiences. However, a second strategy of the culture industry aimed at carving up audiences on the basis of demographics and creating cultural content aimed at their specific needs and interests. Horkheimer and Adorno (1972) used the term "style" to describe what has more commonly come to be known as "genre."

Style represented the artificial differentiation of cultural products along prefabricated lines that had been designed to attract specific audiences identified by marketers. They equated the differing styles of Warner Brothers and Metro Goldwyn Mayer movies to the superficial differences among the lines of cars produced by Chrysler or General Motors and argued that due to the logic of oligopolistic markets, movies and automobiles tend to be "all alike in the end" (p. 123).

Styles and genres are, in turn, based on yet a third strategy of the culture industry: imitation and repetition. Each cultural product follows a formulaic structure, whether a movie romance comedy, three-minute pop song, or star biography. Horkheimer and Adorno (1972) did acknowledge that there had to be some variation to keep audiences interested, but the formulas could not deviate too greatly from audience expectations. The result, they argued, was "calculated mutations which serve all the more strongly to confirm the validity of the system" (p. 129). They also recognized that audiences derived pleasure from mastering the various formulaic codes of their favorite genres but that this pursuit of pleasure left them with little room for reflection about the content itself, particularly the ideological messages embedded within it.

The last, and perhaps most essential, strategy used by the culture industry to promote itself and the capitalist system as a whole involves the use of stars. For Horkheimer and Adorno (1972), stars not only guaranteed the sale of a certain number of theater tickets or records, their life stories and lifestyles helped promote the ideology of success and the habits of consumption. Their life stories provided audiences with hope that they too were just a chance away from being discovered by talent scouts. Their lavish lifestyles depicted in celebrity and fan magazines and on the movie screen gave audiences something to emulate while their advertising endorsements told consumers what to buy. Indeed, they argued, cultural products had become increasingly designed to "lend themselves to ends external to the work" (p. 163), particularly to the sale of consumer goods.

Horkheimer and Adorno concluded that the culture industry had undermined the normative role of art in society, which for them meant questioning the existing social order as well as offering alternative visions of the good life. All that remained of this tradition in the mid-twentieth century was found in the works of a handful of avant-garde artists, such as Samuel Becket, Franz Kafka, and Arnold Schonberg. These artists belonged to the high culture of the day, and their influence was not felt by the audiences of the culture industry.

Alternative Perspectives

The Frankfurt School's critique of the culture industry was not without internal dissent. In his essay "The Work of Art in the Age of Mechanical Reproduction" (1969), Benjamin put the culture industry of the early twentieth century in a more positive light, arguing that it had helped to demolish the "aura" surrounding works of high art and so to democratize aesthetic pleasure. More people could now learn to appreciate a variety of artistic forms provided by new media technologies, making the culture industry a potentially progressive force for social change. For Benjamin, the mechanical reproduction of art transformed the reaction of the masses toward art: "The reactionary attitude toward a Picasso painting changes into the progressive reaction toward a Chaplin movie" (p. 234).

In his book *One-Dimensional Man* (1964), Marcuse acknowledged that the consumption of mass-produced goods, including culture, brought pleasure to the masses. He argued, however, that this pleasure was based on "false needs" created by the consumer-goods and culture industries. This system provided consumers and audiences only with short-term gratifications, leaving their genuine needs unsatisfied and unfulfilled. Nonetheless, due to their total integration into this "one-dimensional society," the masses continued to pursue happiness in the form of consumption. In the essay "Art as Form of Reality" (1972), Marcuse concluded that artistic and intellectual creativity could only be truly free under socialism. Then it would no longer be a separate sphere of activity belonging to media capitalists and professionals, but one that was integrated into everyday life and in which everyone participated.

Another associate of the Frankfurt School, Jurgen Habermas, based his normative vision of a democratic communications system on the concept of the public sphere. In an essay titled "The Public Sphere" (1974), Habermas essentially reiterated the Frankfurt School position that the culture industry, including news and public-affairs programming, tended to promote the special interests of economic and political elites. The integration of big business, the media, and government undermined any possibility of democratic discourse about economic, social, and political issues because these institutions were not motivated by any general concern for the good of society and because they excluded genuine participation by the vast majority of the citizenry. Habermas concluded that establishing a new public sphere would require the dispersal of social and political power into the hands of a wide range of "rival organizations committed to the public sphere in their internal structure as well as their relations with the state and each other" (p. 55).

Hans Magnus Enzensberger, who had only a brief association with the Frankfurt School, criticized the culture industry approach for being too economically deterministic. In his book *The Consciousness Industry* (1974), Enzensberger argued that the ideological nature of the culture industry was determined more by the direct organization of consciousness by economic and political elites and not merely derivative of the commodification process. Indeed, he substituted the term "consciousness industry" for "culture industry" to underscore this point. The consciousness industry played an essential role in neutralizing the radical potential guaranteed to the citizenry of liberal democracies.

Enzensberger (1974) stressed that the ruling class had to work to gain the consent of the dominated classes, and that culture industry workers played a primary role in helping it to do so. However, he also saw them as the weak link in the system of domination. He believed that culture industry workers could play a vital role in undermining this consent from within the media system because media capitalists were ultimately dependent on human artistic and intellectual creativity for delivering the ideas and products from which they earned their profits. Media owners were aware of this and had developed a range of tactics to suppress this potential, from "physical threat, blacklisting, moral and economic pressure on the one hand, [to] overexposure, star-cult, co-optation into the power elite on the other" (p. 14). Nevertheless, Enzensberger concluded that the relative autonomy of artists and intellectuals held the greatest potential for inspiring social change through the media.

Among the contemporaries of the Frankfurt School were English scholars F. R. Leavis, Richard Hoggart, and Raymond Williams. They sought to reconsider the negative connotations associated with mass culture as an industrial product imposed from above, by shifting the focus to how audiences actually used the products of the culture industry. In his book *The Uses of Literacy,* (1957), Hoggart found that the British working classes of the mid-twentieth century were quite selective in their consumption of the products of the culture industry, and actually relied much more heavily upon oral and local forms of culture left over from the beginning of the century to adapt to their ever-changing urban industrial environment. However, Hoggart concluded that the growing influence of the culture industry, and the seduction of consumerism, was gradually undermining traditional working-class culture. Finally, like the Frankfurt School, he viewed the increasing commercialization of the culture industry as a threat to any potential for its "progressiveness" and "independence" because it was required by its very nature to "promote both conservatism and conformity" (p. 196).

In his book *The Long Revolution* (1958), Williams agreed that the development of mass media technology was progressive to the extent that the working class had managed to gain some control over media output, for example, the working-class press. Furthermore, the increasing democratization of education and the spread of literacy gave the working classes new means by which to organize and express their interests. Williams stripped the critique of the cultural industry of its mass society roots and its nostalgia for some pure age of artistic and intellectual freedom, and refused the escape into high art. His response to mass society theory was simply that "there are no masses, only ways of seeing people as masses" (p. 289). His response to cultural elitism was just as simple: "creation is the activity of every human mind" (p. 17) and every human being therefore possesses artistic abilities that can be cultivated. He agreed that the industrialization culture had generally stifled this potential, especially the professionalization of intellectual and artistic creativity, which had produced an increasing division between producers and consumers of culture. Like Marcuse, Williams insisted that the separation of artistic and intellectual creativity

from daily life had to be resolved, and this could only occur with the extension of public ownership of the means and systems of communication, along with the means of production in general.

Developing Perspectives on the Culture Industries

The debates about the role of the culture industry among the Frankfurt School and its contemporaries continued to influence media theory and research through the late twentieth century. These scholars, among others, not only generated the central questions for the study of the culture industry, they also opened the space for such an inquiry by providing criticisms of the dominant research paradigm guiding studies of mass communication from the 1930s through the 1960s, based primarily on survey and laboratory research on media uses and effects. They argued that prioritization of such empirical approaches to the study of the media were too narrow to generate any thorough understanding of the role of communications in society. Indeed, Adorno's involvement with quantitative research efforts led him to write an essay on "Scientific Experiences of a European Scholar in America" (1969) in which he concluded that the application of purely empirical methods to the study of cultural phenomena was "equivalent to squaring the circle" (p. 347).

The Frankfurt School also criticized the dominant paradigm for its orientation toward so-called administrative research, mainly its privileging of survey and laboratory studies on consumer and voter opinions and behavior produced primarily for use by business and government. This administrative orientation served two purposes for mass communications scholars. First, within the academy, it helped to establish the field of communications studies as a distinct and legitimate field of social science. Second, outside the academy, it facilitated efforts to attract funding from industry and government sources. While mass communications scholars could claim to be neutral and objective social scientists following the methods of normal science, their research agendas had turned the discipline into another pillar of support for the existing political–economic structure.

In an essay entitled "Historical Perspectives of Popular Culture" (1950), Lowenthal called for a critical alternative to the study of audiences as markets beginning with the still-unanswered and

One of the major products of the Hollywood star system was Elizabeth Taylor, who was later able to use that studio success to her own personal commercial advantage with the launch of a perfume line in 1987. (Bettmann/Corbis)

essential question: "What are the functions of cultural communication within the total process of society?" Lowenthal continued that a critical alternative would then proceed to two more specific yet vital questions: "What passes the censorship of the socially powerful agencies? How are things produced under the dicta of formal and informal censorship?" (p. 331). To broadly generalize, cultural studies has taken up the former question and political economy the latter.

Within the cultural studies perspective, a focus on culture industries follows the tradition of Hoggart and Williams and echoes the critical theory of Benjamin and Enzensberger. This approach tends to emphasize the relative autonomy of culture industry workers, media texts, and media audiences. It reasserts the position that the inherent tension between profitability and creativity allows culture industry workers significant space for advancing messages that challenge the status quo, but it also highlights media producers working outside the dominant communications systems,

such as grassroots and alternative media resisting the processes of commodification.

The cultural studies approach to culture industries also insists on making the analysis of media content a specific mode of inquiry. This is based on the view that news and entertainment products are not simple reflections of media industry structures and practices. Rather, for a number of reasons—from the ambiguity of language and divisions among political and economic elites, to the aforementioned tension between profit and creativity—media texts contain within them many layers of meaning and therefore many potential interpretations that must be explored on their own terms. Some texts, such as news photo captions, leave little room for interpretation. Others, such as rock-music videos, are deliberately left open to interpretation. Accordingly, how audiences interpret the products of the culture industry must also be taken as a separate problem.

In their research on culture industries, cultural studies scholars employ audience reception theory to explore the actual interpretations made by audiences of media texts. Their research confirms that audiences are indeed capable of producing a variety of readings of news and entertainment content, sometimes even in opposition to the intended meaning of the producer. In addition to examining how audiences actually read texts, the cultural studies approach uses ethnographic research methods to look at ways in which audiences use the media in their daily lives. These studies demonstrate that subcultures are capable of making a variety of uses of culture industry output, again often in ways not intended by their producers. The results of studying audience interpretations and uses of media texts demonstrate that a variety of factors beyond the structure of the text are at work in shaping the responses of audiences, including class, gender, race, ethnicity, age, and so on.

The political economy approach has built on the critique of the culture industry laid out by Horkheimer and Adorno in the 1940s. The analysis of the structure and marketing strategies of the culture industry therefore remains central to this approach. This includes continuing to document the tendency toward concentration in the culture industry, which accelerated in the late twentieth century as the industry became dominated by a handful of global multimedia conglomerates. This period also saw the increasing convergence between media, computer, and telecommunications companies and a tightening of the vertical integration between producers and distributors of informational and cultural products.

This global culture industry continues to use the same basic strategies identified by Horkheimer and Adorno: the star system, style, genre, formula, and imitation. It also relies increasingly on remakes, sequels, spin-offs, and the recycling and repackaging of entertainment products. Additionally, the conglomerate structure of the culture industry facilitates the cross-promotion of cultural products through a variety of outlets. A feature-length movie comes packaged with a music video, a movie soundtrack, a novelization, a magazine review, and a promotional website, all produced under the same corporate umbrella. These practices are simply the logical result of culture industry owners and executives seeking to minimize risk and maximize profit. However, from the normative perspective of political economy, they also deprive audiences of a genuinely diverse range of informational and cultural output, first by crowding the media marketplace with similar products, and second, by deterring potential voices through oligopolistic control of production, distribution, and marketing.

From the political economy perspective, the commodification and industrialization of intellectual and artistic creativity significantly circumscribes the relative autonomy of culture industry workers, media texts, and audiences. Culture industry workers are constrained not only by the mandate to produce profitable commodities but also by the interventions of media owners seeking to protect or promote their specific economic and political interests, as well as the general interests of the capitalist class to which they belong.

Additionally, advertisers have significant influence over culture industry content. Advertisers shape both the structure and content of the media marketplace by the way they allocate their advertising expenditures. Advertising dollars tend to go to media outlets that reach audiences with the specific traits desired by advertisers, leaving undesirable audiences under-served. Advertising also affects media form, be it the layout of a magazine or newspaper, the dramatic structure of a prime-time television program, or a radio format based on three-minute songs. Finally, advertising affects media content. Producers of advertiser-supported entertainment and news cannot alienate either their sponsors or audiences due to the risk of losing advertising revenues. They are also expected to help promote consumerism. A magazine, for example, will specifically tie its editorial content directly to an advertisement in the same issue, while prime-time television must generally keep audiences in a buying mood and assure them that their problems can be solved through consumption.

The political economic critique of the structure and practices of the culture industry lead to the obvious conclusion that commodification of culture and information, intervention by economic and political elites, and the influence of advertisers result in the production of media texts that tend to reinforce the status quo rather than promote social change. Furthermore, audiences are predisposed toward the preferred interpretations intended by producers because the culture industry fails to provide them with the alternative perspectives required to generate oppositional readings.

Both cultural studies and political economy have sought answers to the central question posed by the Frankfurt School: What is the role of the culture industry within the social totality? From the cultural studies perspective, it can serve as a force for social change because there is much that escapes what Lowenthal (1950) called the "censorship of the socially powerful agencies" (p. 331). For political economists, the culture industry continues to be too interwoven into existing structures of economic and political domination to play any significant role in social change. Therefore, artistic and intellectual creativity cannot be truly free and spontaneous without the transformation of the social totality within which it is produced.

See also: ADVERTISING EFFECTS; CULTURAL STUDIES; CULTURE AND COMMUNICATION; FILM INDUSTRY; GLOBALIZATION OF CULTURE THROUGH THE MEDIA; GLOBALIZATION OF MEDIA INDUSTRIES; MAGAZINE INDUSTRY; NEWS EFFECTS; NEWSPAPER INDUSTRY; POLITICAL ECONOMY; PUBLISHING INDUSTRY; RADIO BROADCASTING; RECORDING INDUSTRY; WILLIAMS, RAYMOND.

Bibliography

Adorno, Theodor W. (1969). "Scientific Experiences of a European Scholar in America." In *The Intellectual Migration: Europe and America, 1930–1960*, eds. Donald Fleming and Bernard Bailyn. Cambridge, MA: Harvard University Press.

Adorno, Theodor W. (1975). "Culture Industry Reconsidered," tr. Anson G. Rabinbach. *New German Critique* 6:12–19.

Benjamin, Walter. (1969). "The Work of Art in the Age of Mechanical Reproduction." In *Illuminations*, ed. Hannah Arendt, tr. Harry Zohn. New York: Shocken Books.

Enzensberger, Hans Magnus. (1974). *The Consciousness Industry*. New York: Seabury Press.

Habermas, Jurgen. (1974). "The Public Sphere." *New German Critique* 3:49–55.

Hoggart, Richard. (1957). *The Uses of Literacy: Changing Patterns in English Mass Culture*. Fairlawn, NJ: Essential Books.

Horkheimer, Max, and Adorno, Theodor W. (1972). *Dialectic of Enlightenment*, tr. John Cumming. New York: Seabury Press.

Lowenthal, Leo. (1950). "Historical Perspectives of Popular Culture." *American Journal of Sociology* 55:323–332.

Marcuse, Herbert. (1964). *One-Dimensional Man: Studies in the Ideology of Advanced Industrial Society*. Boston: Beacon Press.

Marcuse, Herbert. (1972). "Art as Form of Reality." *New Left Review* 74:51–58.

Williams, Raymond. (1961). *The Long Revolution*. London: Chatto and Windus.

RONALD V. BETTIG

■ CUMULATIVE MEDIA EFFECTS

Researchers who study the effects of the mass media typically focus on the immediate, short-term effects of a particular program or movie. However, many of the effects of media exposure occur over the long term, with repeated exposure over time. One important area in which there is extensive evidence for cumulative effects is media violence.

By the 1970s, scholars concurred that early childhood exposure to media violence caused children to be more aggressive. As Leonard Eron and his associates wrote (1972, p. 262), "the weight of evidence . . . supports the theory that during a critical period in a boy's development, regular viewing and liking of violent television lead to the formation of a more aggressive life style." The consensus of scholarly opinion in this area prompted the U.S. Surgeon General to issue a warning in 1972 about the cumulative effects of viewing violence in the media.

While short-term stimulating effects of media violence have been found in people of all ages, cumulative long-term effects have generally only been observed in children. Although the processes that underlie these cumulative effects were unclear in 1972, they have since been elaborated. The five major processes are as follows: observational learning of behaviors and scripts, observational learning of attitudes and beliefs, emotional desensitization, cognitive justification processes, and cognitive cueing and priming.

Observational Learning of Behaviors and Scripts

Observational learning theory, as originally developed by Albert Bandura and his colleagues (1963, 1986), proposes that children develop habitual modes of behavior through imitation and vicarious reinforcement. Identification with the model, the perception that the behavior is realistic, and the perception that the model possesses valued characteristics, influence whether a child will imitate the model. Furthermore, direct reinforcement of the child's own behavior leads to a continuation of imitated behavior patterns and resistance to extinction.

More recently, Rowell Huesmann (1998) extended the concept of observational learning to include the learning of social scripts, which are "programs" that children may employ automatically when they are faced with social problems. Often, after a script is suggested by an observation, the child fantasizes about behaving that way—making the use of the script even more likely.

Observational Learning of Attitudes and Beliefs

Television shapes schemas about how hostile the world is. Viewing television cultivates a sense of personal risk in the real world, according to George Gerbner and Larry Gross (1976). Compared to viewers who watch a small amount of television, viewers who watch a large amount of television are more anxious about becoming victims of violence (e.g., carrying weapons for protection), are less trusting of others, and are more likely to perceive the world as being a dangerous, mean, hostile place. Kenneth Dodge and Nicki Crick (1990) have demonstrated that such attributional biases foster a misinterpretation of the actions of others as being hostile and thus promote aggressive interactions.

Television violence changes normative beliefs about violence. In the United States and elsewhere, a "culture of violence" is said to exist, and a number of studies have shown that more aggressive children are less likely to believe that aggression and violence are wrong. Moreover, longitudinal studies have shown that early childhood exposure to television violence is related to normative beliefs that are more accepting of violence—even fifteen years later, during young adulthood.

Television violence produces a cognitive desensitization to violence. An inhibiting factor of aggressive and violent behaviors in socialized humans is that individuals are simply not "used" to violence. However, the more that individuals are exposed to it or even think about it, the more accustomed to it they become. Psychologists call this a cognitive desensitization to violence, and repeated exposures to television violence facilitate this process.

Emotional Desensitization

Just as repeated exposure to television violence has been shown to cause cognitive desensitiza-
tion, emotional desensitization can also occur. In one quasi-experimental field study conducted by Victor Cline and his colleagues (1973), boys who regularly consumed a heavy diet of television displayed less physiological arousal in response to new scenes of violence than did control subjects. In another study, Ron Drabman and Margaret Thomas (1974) demonstrated that children who watched violence responded less emotionally afterward to other scenes of violence and tolerated such violence more. For most people, the arousal that is naturally stimulated by observing violent behaviors is unpleasant and, therefore, inhibits aggressive actions. However, once this arousal habituates, aggression is no longer inhibited.

Cognitive Justification Processes

The justification process is a psychological phenomenon that explains why people who are aggressive like to watch violent television. A child's own aggressive behaviors normally should elicit guilt in the child because of the responses of others. However, for the child who watches a lot of television violence, this guilt is reduced by the recognition that "everyone is doing it." The child who has behaved aggressively and watches violent television programs feels justified and does not try to stop behaving aggressively.

Cognitive Cueing and Priming

An important element of the cumulative effects of exposure to violence is the increase in the number of cues that become associated with violence for the viewer who watches a large amount of television. While the observational learning process explains how exposure to media violence leads to the acquisition of violent scripts, priming theory explains why such violent scripts are more likely to be used. Leonard Berkowitz and his colleagues (1967, 1984, 1993) have proposed that any cues that appear in violent videos become associated with violence and in the future can "prime" aggressive scripts. Just the sight of objects that have often been associated with violence, such as guns, primes the retrieval of aggressive scripts. Furthermore, as Wendy Josephson (1987) has shown, even an innocuous object (e.g., a walkie-talkie) that has been observed in a violent scene can subsequently stimulate aggression in a future encounter.

Longitudinal Research

The five processes described above help explain why the cumulative effects of media violence can be so strong for children. As Huesmann and his associates (1986, 1997, 1999) have shown in two separate studies, children who grow up watching a steady diet of media violence are significantly more at risk to behave violently as young adults than are comparable children who watch less violence. In one study, the children (at eight years of age) who watched more violence behaved more violently ten years later (when they were eighteen years of age), and again twelve years after that (when they were thirty years of age). In a second study, the children (six to eleven years of age) who watched more violence behaved more violently fifteen years later (when they were between the ages of twenty-one and twenty-six).

Conclusion

The five major processes that were discussed above probably account for most of the cumulative long-term effects of television violence on the behavior of a viewer. The processes are well-understood psychological processes that operate in all humans. The outcome of such processes is highly predictable: an increase in the likelihood that the child who repeatedly watches violent television will behave more violently when he or she grows up.

See also: AROUSAL PROCESSES AND MEDIA EFFECTS; DESENSITIZATION AND MEDIA EFFECTS; RATINGS FOR TELEVISION PROGRAMS; SOCIAL COGNITIVE THEORY AND MEDIA EFFECTS; VIOLENCE IN THE MEDIA, ATTRACTION TO; VIOLENCE IN THE MEDIA, HISTORY OF RESEARCH ON.

Bibliography

Bandura, Albert. (1986). *Social Foundations of Thought and Action: A Social–Cognitive Theory.* Englewood Cliffs, NJ: Prentice-Hall.

Bandura, Albert; Ross, Dorthea; and Ross, Sheila A. (1963). "Imitation of Aggression through Imitation of Film-Mediated Aggressive Models." *Journal of Abnormal and Social Psychology* 66:3–11.

Berkowitz, Leonard. (1984). "Some Effects of Thoughts on Anti- and Prosocial Influences of Media Events: A Cognitive–Neoasociation Analysis." *Psychological Bulletin* 95(3):410–427.

Berkowitz, Leonard. (1993). *Aggression: Its Causes, Consequences, and Control.* New York: McGraw-Hill.

Berkowitz, Leonard, and LePage, Anthony. (1967). "Weapons as Aggression-Eliciting Stimuli." *Journal of Personality and Social Psychology* 7:202–207.

Cline, Victor B.; Croft, Roger G., and Courrier, Stephen. (1973). "Desensitization of Children to Television Violence." *Journal of Personality and Social Psychology* 27:360–365.

Dodge, Kenneth A., and Crick, Nicki R. (1990). "Social Information–Processing Bases of Aggressive Behavior in Children." *Personality and Social Psychology Bulletin* 16(1):8–22.

Drabman, Ron S., and Thomas, Margaret H. (1974). "Does Media Violence Increase Children's Toleration of Real-Life Aggression?" *Developmental Psychology* 10:418–421.

Eron, Leonard D.; Huesmann, L. Rowell; Lefkowitz, Monroe M.; and Walder, Leopold O. (1972). "Does Television Violence Cause Aggression?" *American Psychologist* 27:253–263.

Gerbner, George, and Gross, Larry. (1976). "Living with Television: The Violence Profile." *Journal of Communication* 26:172–199.

Huesmann, L. Rowell. (1998). "The Role of Social Information Processing and Cognitive Schemas in the Acquisition and Maintenance of Habitual Aggressive Behavior." In *Human Aggression: Theories, Research, and Implications for Policy,* eds. Russel G. Geen and Edward Donnerstein. New York: Academic Press.

Huesmann, L. Rowell. (1999). "The Effects of Childhood Aggression and Exposure to Media Violence on Adult Behaviors, Attitudes, and Mood: Evidence from a 15-Year Cross-National Study." *Aggressive Behavior* 25:18–29.

Huesmann, L. Rowell, and Eron, Leonard D. (1986). *Television and the Aggressive Child: A Cross-National Comparison.* Hillsdale, NJ: Lawrence Erlbaum.

Huesmann, L. Rowell; Moise, Jessica; and Podolski, Cheryl-Lynn P. (1997). "The Effects of Media Violence on the Development of Antisocial Behavior." In *Handbook of Antisocial Behavior,* eds. David Stoff, James Breiling, and Jack Masser. New York: Wiley.

Josephson, Wendy L. (1987). "Television Violence and Children's Aggression: Testing the Priming, Social Script, and Disinhibition Predictions." *Journal of Personality and Social Psychology* 53(5):882–890.

L. ROWELL HUESMANN
ANGIE C. BEATTY

■ CURATORS

Curators work in museums and similar institutions that serve as repositories for objects that document and explain the artistic, historical, or scientific conditions of human existence. Such settings can be thought of as distinct types of "information systems" that exist to disseminate the kind of knowledge that resides in representative objects or specimens. Like books, documents, or records, museum objects are made useful when they are arranged according to particular principles and are disseminated on the basis of their context and communicative capacity. Within a museum setting, it is the curator who performs this function, using professional expertise to generate vital associations among objects to satisfy the curiosity of the general public and to meet community educational and scholarly needs. Curators are found in art museums, children's museums, history museums, maritime museums, and science and technology museums, in botanical gardens and arboretums, and in cultural societies and zoos. The curator oversees selection, acquisition, organization, preservation, and presentation of museum objects and collections.

Like their information professional peers—librarians and archivists—curators make sure their particular information system responds to its environment by applying specific organizing conventions and interpretive sensibilities to museum collections. They do this by carrying out research about museum objects and by making sure artifacts are displayed in exhibitions in ways that are meaningful to museum patrons. The curator thus establishes or reinforces the circumstances of the existence of artifacts, their relationship to life, culture, or custom, and their relevance both to the museum's mission and its audience. In doing this, the curator guarantees the institution's survival and its commitment to the purpose for which it was created.

In addition to applying rules of organization by creating exhibitions that display and interpret museum collections, curators are in charge of collection development, selecting items that fit the institutional mission. They also direct conservation and preservation of museum objects. Curators are frequently involved in the public relations and fund-raising activities of their museums. They may supervise the creation of flyers, brochures, webpages, or other descriptive and educational materials that accompany exhibitions. Curators may need to write grants to secure funding for museum projects. They frequently attend, speak at, or manage fund-raising or other special events

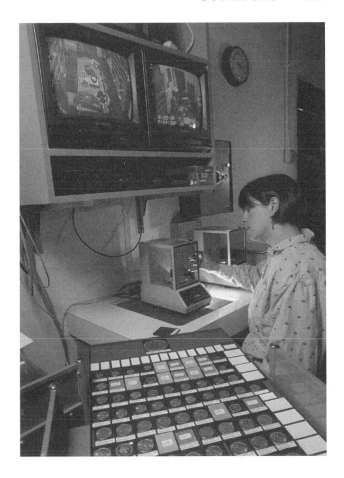

A curator for the Numismatic Vault at the Smithsonian National Museum of American History in Washington, D.C., weighs gold coins. (Richard T. Nowitz/Corbis)

that help their institutions maintain a positive public image. Consequently, curators need to be well informed and have a range of communication skills, which come from a mixture of education and experience.

Undergraduate school may be the place where a future curator begins to develop the subject expertise in art, history, or science that leads to work in a specific museum environment. Graduate education provides training in organizational principles that are appropriate to their craft and introduces future curators to the range of possible job responsibilities. Like librarians, archivists, and other information professionals, curators must learn organizational principles that reflect a mixture of museum purpose, the unique characteristics of the type of information found in museums, and best practices for making this kind of information available. Although some colleges and universities offer undergraduate education in the study of museums, or museology, curators typically gain expertise and credentials in graduate programs of museum or cultural studies or of museum science.

Graduate programs offer instruction in museum administration and management, preservation of materials, collection management, exhibition design, interpretation, public programming, and museum education. Courses emphasize the history, function, and philosophical and societal roles of museums. They also cover different museum types, review issues of contemporary museum practice and professional concern, analyze the technical aspects of museum work, and examine monetary or other resources available to museums. Future curators get instruction in the planning, design, and production of exhibitions, become skilled in translating museum exhibition concepts into detailed plans or models, and learn about preservation and restoration strategies. Classes in museum education teach the students how to create and deliver successful museum-based instruction to a variety of audiences.

Requirements for a graduate degree in museum or cultural studies or in museum science usually include an internship or practicum component that gives students experience with regular museum activities. Students get to work in an actual museum setting where they have the opportunity to put their classroom knowledge of collection development strategies, exhibition design, conservation techniques, and administrative protocols into action. They may get direct insight into museum research and grant-writing efforts and get to do this kind of work as well. An internship or practicum also affords students the chance to meet future colleagues. Moreover, graduate education generally helps develop the level of analytical, decision-making, and communicative skills that curators need to do an effective job for their institution.

Organizations such as the American Association of Museums, the Institute of Museum and Library Services, and the International Council of Museums advocate for or provide services or funding to museums. These entities give guidance and support for continuing education and professional development activities for curators and other museum staff. They offer or suggest programs that help curators stay abreast of the best practices in object acquisition, conservation, interpretation, and presentation. These programs may feature advice about working with members of the museum's board, other members of the museum's staff, and members of the museum's community. The American Association of Museums, the Institute of Museum and Library Services, and the International Council of Museums also help make curators aware of funding opportunities related to museum activities. The American Association of Museums issues standards for museum accreditation. Their standards prescribe appropriate education and expertise for curators and other staff members. The Institute of Museum and Library Services, established by the United States Museum and Library Services Act of 1996, works in cooperation with the American Association of Museums on museum assessment and conservation assessment programs. Curators are likely to be involved in determining the eligibility of their museums for these programs. The International Council of Museums, which counts museums of all types and from various countries among its membership, maintains a committee devoted to recommending educational standards and has adopted a code of ethics for curators and other museum professionals.

See also: ARCHIVISTS; LIBRARIANS; MUSEUMS.

Bibliography

Buckland, Michael. (1991). *Information and Information Systems.* New York: Praeger Publishers.

Orosz, Joel J. (1990). *Curators and Culture: The Museum Movement in America, 1740–1870.* Tusculoosa: University of Alabama Press.

Pearce, Susan M. (1991). "Collecting Reconsidered." In *Museum Languages: Objects and Texts,* ed. Gaynor Kavanagh. Leicester, Eng.: Leicester University Press.

Rubin, Richard. (1998). *Foundations of Library and Information Science.* New York: Neal-Schuman Publishers.

TONYIA J. TIDLINE

DATABASE DESIGN

"Database design" is the term that is commonly used to refer to a wide variety of functions that are associated with database generation within organizations that are involved in the electronic publishing of data or information collections that are intended for search and retrieval or other manipulation by computer. Database design can be interpreted narrowly, broadly, or anywhere in between. This entry uses a broad interpretation; it assumes that design is seldom a one-person effort and may require a team of experts in order to provide the necessary technical, management, human resources, financial, and subject expertise. Design is not a one-time activity even though many people think of it as occurring only prior to the creation of a database. In a broad sense, database design involves the continued improvement of database products. The principal designer or leader of the design team is unlikely to be an expert in all aspects of design, so he or she must call on and interact with others to accomplish a good, flexible, expandable design.

Database design involves the organization and presentation of data (where the term "data" is understood to refer to data or information or facts of any type) so it can be easily located, accessed, and used. It includes a wide variety of functions and activities that range from selection and acquisition of raw, reduced, or otherwise processed data to a variety of value-adding activities.

Design involves specification of criteria for limiting the type of content by subject matter (i.e., its breadth and depth—often referred to as "horizontal" and "vertical," respectively—in connection with an information system), language, type of data (e.g., abstracts, full text, numeric data, images, audio data), geographic location, file size, and so on. In general, database design covers all aspects of what needs to be accomplished both manually and by computer in preparing, processing, and maintaining a database. Design must include documentation of all of the parameters and activities discussed in this entry.

Content and Value Adding

Database content is roughly determined by the visionary who proposed the product and by amplifications that are made by a design team of experts who will have checked appropriate reference sources and experts to gain further understanding of the user needs and sources for the data. Details will depend on the subject matter or functions that will be served by the proposed database. The methods for organizing and indexing (or otherwise making access points to the data) will dictate the type of format that is appropriate and the standards that should be considered. Content is the most important element of the database, but next to that is the added value that may determine the uses to which the data can be put and the attractiveness of the database.

Adding value applies to virtually any aspect of the database. It applies to basic production processes as well as enhancements that improve, for example, the content, accessibility, appearance, usability, of databases. Value-adding activities include the following:

- reducing data (where needed),
- formatting data in accordance with standards,
- enhancing, expanding, merging with other data or data records,
- categorizing, classifying, indexing, abstracting, tagging, flagging, and coding to improve accessibility,
- sorting, arranging or rearranging, putting the information into one or more forms that will satisfy users,
- creating visual representations of data (especially for numeric data),
- updating, correcting errors,
- adhering to production schedules, and
- putting the data into searchable form with appropriate access points (and links to other databases and application packages) for search, retrieval, manipulation, and use by users.

These and many more activities are all considered to be a part of adding value to the product.

Computers and Information Technology

Database design includes the recommendation and eventual selection of appropriate information technology for processing, storing, and manipulating data, as well as the selection of the media for processing and storing data on site and for distribution of data to customers. The database may be produced in several different media (e.g., CD-ROM, DVD, diskettes, hand-held devices, or any new technology that may appear in the marketplace), depending on the type of product that is needed by customers. Any organization that produces databases must remain alert to the development of new technologies that may be of use to the organization for (1) processing, storing, distributing, and using their data, (2) management of the various functions, or (3) generation of reports. Computer selection is important because of its centrality to the entire process of database production and use.

Software for Processing, Management, and Search/Retrieval

Database design includes the development of, or acquisition of, software for managing the flow of data and records through all steps of the process—from acquisition and processing of data, to generating management reports about the data flowing through the system, to delivery to customers or making data accessible to users online. Software is required for search/retrieval processes, as well as for manipulation of the data (e.g., using spreadsheets, sorting, rearranging, running statistical programs on data) and the generation of reports in compliance with user requests.

In general, a database design is created for a master database from which a variety of products can be produced. The products can have exactly the same content, and they can be produced in the same format or in differing formats. The products created from the master database can be made available on different media for distribution. The master database can also be used to create subsets of the same data to meet specific customer needs. Subsets of the data can be merged with outside data to create new products, or the records in the master database may have additional data elements added in order to increase the value for specific customers.

Quality Assessment and Control

When designing a database, quality is an important consideration. The designer or design team must indicate the areas where quality should be monitored, determine how it can be monitored, and establish methods for controlling quality. The quality of a database product involves many different aspects of the database, such as reliability of the medium for distribution/access, accuracy of data, timeliness, inclusion of essential data elements in every record, and additional elements that may or may not be present because of the variability of data sources. Customers and users judge databases according to many objective and subjective factors. Accuracy of data, clarity of presentation and ease of using the front end to the information system, and adherence to time schedules are a few of the objective factors. The subjective factors include such things as acceptability of price in relation to the user's budget and how good a match there is between the user's need and the database design.

Market Analysis, Pricing, and Marketing

Designers must determine the target market for a given database product in terms of potential size, characteristics, geographic location, language, spending limits, needs/wants for data, and current information use patterns. Much of this would depend on a "user needs assessment" that should be done prior to the design phase or as the first step of the design process. Designers must analyze the potential market, review the competition, compare both the positive and negative aspects of competitor products with the planned database product, estimate prices for types of lease, license, and online use of the database, estimate likely levels of sales from a reasonable fraction of the market, and estimate the design, production, and operating costs. These various types of market data become a part of the business plan for the database. The designers must consider methodology for marketing the database, including the use of site visits, telephone contacts, attendance at conferences/meetings, advertising, and websites that have two-way links to appropriate databases.

Business Plan

When a new database is designed, the design documentation or proposal for creating the database should include a business plan as a part of the general design. Producer organizations normally require detailed cost data for any new product. Three-year or five-year projections (sometimes more) of costs for selected methods for marketing, along with identification of the named sources, targets, and links, should be included in the text description and in the spreadsheets of the business plan. The plan must also include detailed discussion of all aspects of the database, including source material (where will the data come from and what will it cost) required for the data, quality assessment and control, analysis, and all planned aspects of adding value.

The total cost information that is provided for the business plan should include the estimated cost of designing and testing a sample database and the cost of gearing up for production, as well as revenue projections for a specified number of years. By using a computer-generated spreadsheet application (e.g., Excel or Lotus), it is easy to make adjustments in pricing—for example, to see how the adjustments affect the projected costs to the producer and the projected revenue from the customers.

Legal Considerations

The design of a database must take into account the legal problems that are associated with the intellectual property rights, copyrights, and use rights that belong to the author of the original data contained in the database; the rights of the users to have open access to information; the rights and liabilities of the database producer who makes a collection of data available to a wide audience; and the responsibilities that the producer has to the sources of information as well as to the customers who use the database. These aspects, plus financial consideration and pricing, are put into legal contracts (prepared by an attorney for the producer) that are executed between the database producer organization and the data sources and between the producer and the customers. In large organizations, there is generally an attorney to handle such matters, and in small organizations, a consulting attorney is employed to develop contracts. The design team should have a knowledge of where the problems lie and should be able to convey the necessary information to the attorney.

See also: CATALOGING AND KNOWLEDGE ORGANIZATION; COMPUTER SOFTWARE; COMPUTING; DATABASES, ELECTRONIC; KNOWLEDGE MANAGEMENT; LIBRARIES, DIGITAL; LIBRARY AUTOMATION; MANAGEMENT INFORMATION SYSTEMS; RETRIEVAL OF INFORMATION; SYSTEMS DESIGNERS.

Bibliography

Arnold, Stephen E. (1989). "Online Pricing: Where It's at Today and Where It's Going Tomorrow." *Online* 13(March):6–9.

Berghel, Hal. (1996). "HTML Compliance and the Return of the Test Pattern." *Communications of the ACM* 39(2):19–22.

Jacsó, Péter. (1997). "Content Evaluation of Databases." In *Annual Review of Information Science and Technology*, Vol. 32, ed. Martha E. Williams. Medford, NJ: Information Today, Inc.

Lipinski, Tomas A. (1998). "Information Ownership and Control." In *Annual Review of Information Science and Technology*, Vol. 33, ed. Martha E. Williams. Medford, NJ: Information Today, Inc.

Mason, Richard O.; Mason, Florence M.; and Culnan, Mary J. (1995). *Ethics of Information Management*. Thousand Oaks, CA: Sage Publications.

McGarty, Terrence P. (1989). *Business Plans that Win Venture Capital*. New York: Wiley.

Mirchin, David. (1999). "Protecting and Using Intellectual Property on the Internet: Exploding the Myth." In *Proceedings of the Twentieth National Online Meeting*, ed. Martha E. Williams. Medford, NJ: Information Today, Inc.

Oppenheim, Charles. (1990). "Marketing of Real-Time and Bibliographic Databases." In *Proceedings of the 14th International Online Meeting, London, 11–13 December 1990*, ed. David I. Raitt. Oxford, Eng.: Learned Information, Ltd.

Tenopir, Carol. (1993). "Priorities of Quality." In *Quality and Value of Information Services*, ed. Reva Basch. London: Ashgate.

Tenopir, Carol. (1995). "Authors and Readers: The Keys to Success or Failure for Electronic Publishing." *Library Trends* 43:571–591.

Webber, Sheila. (1998). "Pricing and Marketing Online Information Services." In *Annual Review of Information Science and Technology*, Vol. 33, ed. Martha E. Williams. Medford, NJ: Information Today, Inc.

Williams, Martha E. (1994). "Implications of the Internet for the Information Industry and Database Providers." *Online & CD-ROM Review* 18(3): 149–156.

MARTHA E. WILLIAMS

DATABASES, ELECTRONIC

Electronic databases are organized collections of data, or information, that are stored in computer-readable form. In general, electronic databases are of two types: those that can be accessed by large mainframe computers and those that can be accessed by small personal computers. However, this distinction is becoming less important as small (in physical size) computers continue to increase in power. In general, mainframe databases—most of which are highly specialized—are maintained by large businesses, institutions, and government agencies. Databases can be either publicly available or private. Private databases can be accessed only by employees of the organization that maintains the databases. Public databases are designed for access by the public. Databases for personal computers typically are created and used by individuals, small businesses, and units within large businesses; they can be used for a wide variety of purposes.

Definitions

The term "database" is used in two senses. One refers to the organized collection of data that is created, maintained, and searched. The other refers to the software that is used to create and maintain the data. Database management systems are often simply called "databases." This entry concentrates on large, publicly available databases, together with the services that make them available.

The term "data" refers to facts, numbers, letters, and symbols that describe an object, idea, condition, situation, and so on. Data elements, which are the smallest units of information to which reference is made, are combined to create records. Data elements in a bibliographic reference include the names of the author or authors, the title of referenced work, the journal name, the pagination, the volume number, the issue number, and the date of publication. A data set is a collection of similar and related data records or data points that have not yet been organized for computer processing. A data file is an aggregation of data sets or records treated as a unit. While databases are also collections of related data and information, the difference between a data file and a database is that a database is organized (by a database management system) to permit the user to search and retrieve or process and reorganize the data.

The data in a database may be predominantly:

- word oriented (e.g., textual, bibliographic, directory, dictionary, full text),
- numeric (e.g., properties, statistics, time series, experimental values),
- image—both fixed images (e.g., photographs, drawings, graphics) and moving images (e.g., a film of microbes under magnification or time-lapse photography of a flower opening), or
- sound (e.g., a recording of the sound of a tornado, wave action, or an explosion).

The discussion in this entry is concerned primarily with digital data, although a large portion of raw data is recorded as analog data, which also can be digitized. Digital data are represented by the digits zero to nine. In the case of analog data, numbers are represented by physical quantities (e.g., the lengths obtained from a slide rule, the measurements of voltage currents). These physical quantities can be converted to digital data through an analog-to-digital converter. Because word-oriented, numeric, image, and sound databases differ, they are processed by different types of software that are specific to each type of data. Digital data may be processed or stored on various types of media, including magnetic media (e.g., tapes, hard drives, diskettes, random access memory) and optical media (e.g., CD-ROMs, digital video discs). Users can access the data either through portable media or, more generally, through online sources.

The term "data" can refer to raw data, processed data, or verified data. Raw data consist of original observations (e.g., those collected by satellite and beamed back to Earth) or experimental results (e.g., laboratory test data). Raw data are subsequently processed or reduced to make them more useable, organized, or simplified. Large data sets need to be cleaned, processed, documented, and organized to enable their use. These activities are occasionally called "curation." In general, the more curated the data are, the more broadly useable they become to users outside the original research group or subdiscipline. Verified data are data whose quality and accuracy have been assured. For experimental data, this means that the original test or experiment has been duplicated and the same data have been produced. For observational data, it means that either the data have been compared with other data whose quality is known or the instrument through which the data were obtained has been properly calibrated and tested.

Many databases are used to retrieve and extract specific data points, facts, or textual information for use in building a derivative database or data product. A derivative database, which is the same as a value-added database or a transformative database, builds on a preexisting database and may include extractions from multiple databases as well as original data. When dealing with derivative databases, the question of intellectual property rights arises and must be resolved.

Availability of Online Public Databases

The range of public databases has grown to the extent that it is now possible to find data on almost any subject. Databases have been created for nearly every major field and many subfields in science, technology, medicine, business, law, social sciences, politics, arts, humanities, and religion as well as for news (worldwide, regional, or subject-related), problems (specific to topics and organizations), missions (such as transportation, defense, shipping, robotics, oil spills, solid waste), and consumer interests such as shopping and automobile repair.

The first comprehensive database directory, *Computer-Readable Databases* (CRD), was com-

piled and edited by Martha E. Williams and was published in 1976 by the American Society for Information Science. CRD originally covered 301 publicly available databases, but by the mid-1980s, the number of publicly and commercially available electronic databases that were listed in CRD had grown to more than three thousand. Gale Research, Inc. (which became the Gale Group in 1999) acquired CRD in 1987 and continued to publish it until 1992, when they renamed it the *Gale Directory of Databases* (GDD). By the year 2000, GDD had grown to include more than twelve thousand databases. Both CRD and GDD included all types of public, commercial databases (i.e., word-oriented, number-oriented, picture-oriented, and sound-oriented databases), as well as multimedia, which include combinations of these types.

Access Services

When a database is developed for public use, it is usually made accessible to users through a telephone connection to the host computer ("online") where it resides; wireless access, however, is gaining importance as a technology for access. Database services may be provided by the producer of the database or, more commonly, by a separate organization that offers online searching of one or more databases.

In order to find information online, one needs to know which database is likely to contain that information. There are several ways of identifying specific databases. One way is through the use of printed directories such as GDD. Another way is through online directories that are maintained by search services for those databases on their systems. Yet another way is through the various search engines on the World Wide Web. Search engines may use various methods to index or catalog website contents. Web crawlers robotically go from website to website and index their contents. Examples of web crawlers include AltaVista, Excite, Hot-Bot, Magellen, and WebCrawler. Some search engines, such as Yahoo, Lycos, and LookSmart, use directories that are generated by humans who intellectually catalog websites. Metacrawlers check many search engines to produce a single list of databases so that the user does not have to check each search engine individually.

Organizations that provide online search services are also called online vendors. They have the computers and software (computer programs) that allow outside users to search databases themselves for data and information, whether it is in the form of numeric data, text, images, sounds, or a mixture of these formats.

Users and Access

Users of public databases include most groups of people whose profession, business, and educational activities require quick access to information. This includes scientists, lawyers, doctors, stockbrokers, financial analysts, librarians, executives, students, and other researchers. Some public databases and search services are focused on consumer needs, providing access to such information as flight schedules, merchandise catalogs, movie reviews, theater schedules, restaurant information, and hotel/motel availability and reservation services. In addition, there are financial, bibliographic, and other services that were initially developed for professional and business users.

Online access to a database usually requires that the user has computer access to an account with a search service that offers such access, a password to log onto the service, knowledge of how to use the service, and information about specific features of the database.

Procedures that users need to know in order to take full advantage of search services and the databases to which they provide access vary widely in complexity. This complexity depends on the type of stored information and the user that the database was designed to serve. For example, searching a database for physical or chemical properties of a certain class of substance requires a different and less widely held kind of knowledge than does searching a database for the names of theaters in a given geographic area. Similarly, an online system intended for professional researchers who use the system daily can be very complex and therefore will contain more useful features than one aimed at occasional end users. Some database producers and/or vendors offer their services to users over the Internet, providing access to all or a sampling of their database product, either for free or for a fee.

Types of Databases

Databases are organized and maintained in different ways for different types of information (i.e., words, numbers, sounds, and images). Each infor-

mation type has a distinctive machine representation and requires a distinct kind of software. Word-oriented databases contain words, phrases, sentences, paragraphs, or text as their principal data. The principal data in numeric databases, often called "databanks," consist of numbers and symbols that represent numbers, statistics, experimental values, time series (i.e., events or phenomena observed over a span of time), tables of numbers, graphs that are based on such tables, and similar material. Pictorial databases, many of which are constructed for scientific or engineering purposes, may contain representations of virtually any multidimensional structure (e.g., chemical structures, nuclear particles, graphs, figures, photographs, architectural plans, and geographic maps). Moving picture databases can represent virtually anything shown in motion. Audio databases, which contain sounds, can represent music, voices, sounds of nature, and anything than can be heard.

Alphabetic and alphanumeric strings of characters cannot be handled by numeric processing software. In other words, these strings cannot be added, subtracted, multiplied, or divided. Therefore, they require software that is designed specifically for handling character strings. Word-oriented databases allow the users to search the database for strings of characters that match the strings of characters in, for example, names, titles, and keywords. Most of these databases allow the user to search using partial words (i.e., truncated words that use a wildcard symbol such as an asterisk to permit multiple endings on the word stem). For example, a user who conducts a single search using the string or partial word "bridg*" would be able to retrieve information related to "bridge," "bridges," "bridged," "bridging," and other similar words or phrases. Word-oriented databases were the earliest publicly available electronic databases They were introduced in the 1960s and contained predominantly information related to science, engineering, technology, and medicine. These early databases contained bibliographic references to published scientific and technical literature, and there were initially only a few dozen of them. They have since multiplied into the thousands.

Bibliographic databases range in size from small files such as the Acid Rain database (with approximately four thousand citations) and the AgeLine database (with approximately fifty thousand citations) to large files such as Medline (with more than eleven million citations in the biomedical and health sciences fields). Chemical Abstracts Service produces several databases, which in the year 2000 collectively included more than twenty-two million document citations to documents.

Full-text databases provide access to the texts of such documents as legal cases and statutes, wire services, journal articles, encyclopedias, and textbooks. Except for the Lexis-Nexis service, which has a large set of legal databases that are mostly grouped in "libraries" of databases, most of the full-text databases were established after 1980. The first full-text database, Lexis, was established in 1973 by Mead Data Central (which later became the Lexis-Nexis service). Lexis-Nexis is one of the world's largest word-oriented database services, and among services that have legal databases, it is approached in size only by Westlaw, a legal database service established in 1975 by West Publishing Company (which later became the West Group). The Westlaw service includes billions of pages of information in thirteen thousand databases in a few dozen "libraries" (all represented as a few dozen entries and umbrella entries in GDD).

Online newspapers, newsletters, journals, and textbooks are among the numerous full-text databases that are available online. Examples include the United Press International and Associated Press wire services, *The New York Times* and *Wall Street Journal* newspapers, and *U.S. News and World Report* and *Newsweek* magazines. Examples of electronic journals are the *Harvard Business Review* and many of the American Chemical Society journals. Electronic encyclopedias include the *Academic American Encyclopedia and Encyclopaedia Britannica.*. Among the many thousands of medical textbook databases are *Gray's Anatomy*, *Textbook of Surgery*, and *Principles and Practices of Emergency Medicine.*

In numeric databases, numbers and symbols are the principal data that are stored and processed. Generally, compared to word-oriented databases, numeric databases involve less fetching and character-string matching and more processing. Most of the programming for a numerical database involves manipulating the data mathematically and presenting it in reports that are formatted and labeled in forms that are familiar to the specific class of users for which the database is designed. Statistical routines, time series, and other programs for manipulating data mathematically work in the same way for numeric data regardless of whether the data relate to sociology, economics, finance, chemistry, or any other field. One example of a large time series database is the National Online Manpower Information Systems (NOMIS), which is produced by the University of Durham in England and has more than twenty billion time series records in its databases.

Pictorial databases are relatively specialized and are fewer in number. Their data consist chiefly of specifications for shapes, distances, geometrical relationships (including three-dimensional relationships), colors, and the like. The computer processing of pictorial data (including photographs and videos) requires sophisticated programs for such functions as video pattern matching, coordinate matching, and extraction of specific features of photographs, maps, videos, or other pictorial representations. Computer processing of sounds has its own set of requirements for matching and analyzing sounds (e.g., by parsing and other techniques).

Production and Distribution

Databases are produced by a wide variety of commercial, governmental, academic, and non-profit organizations. The way in which a database is created depends on whether it is a primary database (e.g., containing the text of an original article) or a secondary database (e.g., providing references, abstracts, or index entries associated with an original article). To prepare a secondary database, the producers cull the primary literature for source material, books, journals, dissertations, government reports, and conference proceedings in order to identify items that are relevant to the subject area of the database. For each item selected for mention in the secondary database, the producers prepare a bibliographic record that lists the names of the author or authors, the title of the article or book, and further information that is needed in order to find the cited publication. The record is then entered into the database, and individual data elements (e.g. author, title, date of publication, journal name, volume number, issue number, page range, and so on) are identified by a specific code or position in the record. In some bibliographic databases, the records include index terms and/or keywords for the articles and books that are referenced. Other bibliographic databases also include abstracts of the articles.

Most large databases are updated periodically (e.g., monthly, weekly, continuously). These updates may be put on magnetic tape and shipped, they may be transmitted directly to search service organizations for incorporation, or they may be made available for downloading from the producer's website. Some small databases are issued on floppy disks or CD-ROMs for use on personal computers. Other small databases are sold as a part of handheld devices that contain both information and searching capabilities. Some large databases are sold or leased to government agencies and corporations for in-house use. Other large databases are sold or licensed to online search services where they are reformatted by the search service's software or search engine in order to allow searching by their customers.

Electronic databases are accessed mainly through online search services (i.e., database vendors) and/or directly through the Internet. These services provide online databases together with software for search and retrieval, data manipulation, and modeling. They are sometimes called "information utilities," because, like electric or gas utilities, an online search service serves a widely distributed network of users. Several hundred such services in the United States and Europe provide access to more than twelve thousand databases and databanks worldwide with billions of records.

If a database is part of a commercial online service, anyone with a microcomputer, a modem, and a telephone can have access to it for a fee. The search fee includes charges for accessing the database itself and for the use of its search software. There may also be charges for printing or downloading search results.

The fees required for using search services vary widely from service to service and from database to database. Many services charge only for the actual use of the service. Others require subscription fees, monthly or yearly minimum payments, and the like. Information that is available at websites on the Internet may be entirely free, or it may require a payment.

Charges usually are based on usage or on units accessed, retrieved, or delivered. Usage is measured in terms of connect time (i.e., the number of minutes that are used to carry out an online search), or in terms of the number of records accessed, viewed, retrieved, downloaded, or printed, or in terms of computer resource units. Resource units measure the amount of the computer facility (including machine time and storage capacity) that is used in a search. The units accessed, retrieved, or delivered may be, for example, bibliographic references in a bibliographic database, individuals identified in an employment database, or time series in a time series database. The units may be displayed on the user's terminal, printed out by the search service and sent to the user, or, more commonly, downloaded by the user for local printing and use.

Among the commercial online services for searching numeric databases are Standard & Poor's DRI (Data Products Division), GE Information Services, The WEFA Group, and the Oxford Molecular Group (Chemical Information System). All of these except Chemical Information System provide mainly business-oriented databases; Chemical Information System provides mainly scientific databases. Among the vendors of word-oriented databases are Lexis-Nexis, The Dialog Corporation (DIALOG Information Services, Inc.), the U.S. National Library of Medicine, West Group (Westlaw), CompuServe Information Service, America Online, Inc., and Dow Jones and Company, Inc.

DIALOG, the largest of the online search services that provide mostly bibliographic databases, began offering commercial search services in 1972. At that time, it featured two government-produced databases—ERIC (Educational Resources Information Center) and NTIS (National Technical Information Service). By the year 2000, DIALOG had several hundred databases with nine terabytes of data. The U.S. National Library of Medicine began its search service in 1971, offering the Medline database with 147,000 records. By the year 2000, the U.S. National Library of Medicine had dozens of databases with about eleven million records. Lexis-Nexis, the largest service to provide mostly textual databases, introduced its commercial online service in 1973 with a database of 208,000 documents or 2.5 billion characters. By the year 2000, it had burgeoned to more than 2.8 billion searchable documents or 2.6 trillion characters of data.

See also: BIBLIOGRAPHY; CATALOGING AND KNOW-LEDGE ORGANIZATION; COMPUTER SOFTWARE; COMPUTING; DATABASE DESIGN; INFORMATION INDUSTRY; INTERNET AND THE WORLD WIDE WEB; KNOWLEDGE MANAGEMENT; LIBRARIES, DIGITAL; LIBRARY AUTOMATION; MANAGEMENT INFORMATION SYSTEMS; SYSTEMS DESIGNERS.

Bibliography

Faerber, Marc, and Nagel, Erin, eds. (2000). *Gale Directory of Databases*, 2 vols. Detroit, MI: Gale Group.

Williams, Martha E. (1985). "Electronic Databases." *Science* 228:445–456.

Williams, Martha E. (1994). "Implications of the Internet for the Information Industry and Database Providers." *Online & CD-ROM Review* 18(3): 149–156.

MARTHA E. WILLIAMS

■ DECISION MAKING AND GROUP COMMUNICATION

See: Group Communication, Decision Making and

■ DEMOCRACY AND THE MEDIA

In modern societies, it is impossible to talk intelligently about democracy without considering the role played by print and electronic media in disseminating political messages to the public. Especially following the creation of electronic media in the twentieth century, the connections between democracy, political campaigns, public opinion, and journalistic practices have become the focus of great attention and anxiety among communication scholars. Each new media innovation is evaluated for its potential effect on democratic politics, and media professionals are regularly criticized for practices that are perceived in one way or another as being antidemocratic. Also, as media have allowed politicians and political candidates to address large audiences, Richard E. Neustadt's contention in his book *Presidential Power* (1980)—that the real power of the U.S. president is the "power to persuade"—has become increasingly intuitive, with presidents and other politicians acquiring more and more channels through which to reach their constituents, in addition to their normal interactions with other appointed and elected policymakers.

The relationship between democracy and the media has been a regular topic of discussion ever since the emergence of liberal democratic theory as an intellectual force in Europe. In the seventeenth century, John Milton's *Aeropagitica* provided a libertarian argument for the right of free discussion, as such discussion presumably would lead to the rejection of false and unsound opinion and the discovery of truth. Although the free press guarantee in the Bill of Rights of the U.S. Constitution received surprisingly little attention at the time of the adoption of the First Amendment, that guarantee has been the object of much debate ever since. In part because of frustration with the early Federalists, Thomas Jefferson and other anti-Federalists were passionate defenders of the free press in the early days of the American republic. In the nineteenth century, the English philosopher John Stuart Mill articulated a fully developed justification for free speech and a free press, as silencing anyone might prevent the truth from being told and would run the risk that errors would not be discovered.

The modern media has only been able to convey up-to-date political information to the public for a little less than two centuries, thanks largely to technological innovations in print media and the rapid development of electronic media forms. Furthermore, German sociologist Jürgen Habermas explains in his book *The Structural Transformation of the Public Sphere* (1962) that the rise of the politically oriented public sphere in parts of Europe and the United States was fundamentally linked to the development of the media. In the emerging democratic societies of Europe and North America, newspapers became not only reporters of news but shapers of public opinion. However, as newspapers became increasingly dependent on commercial advertising for support, economic considerations meant that newspaper editorial policy and journalistic practice could also be influenced by those who controlled financial resources. The result, as described by Habermas, is that wealthy individuals or those who control wealth have more influence over public opinion and, ultimately, over what policies are changed than do members of the lower and middle classes. Other scholars also have worried that, in addition to the economic forces that might distort public debate, the heavy reliance of the modern media on governmental sources of information might lead in some cases to less scrutiny and criticism of governmental policies.

As the relationship between democracy and the media has been considered throughout the twentieth century, much attention has been given to the extent of media effects, especially following the experience with government-produced propaganda during two world wars. If media coverage of politics and political campaigns has little influence on public attitudes and behaviors, then presumably people need not be concerned over the quantity and quality of attention that is paid to politics in the media. However, if media coverage of politics and political campaigns has a moderate or strong influence on public attitudes and behaviors, then protecting democratic government requires careful review—and possibly governmental regulation—of media, whether print or electronic, mainstream or alternative. Historically, some scholars have maintained at one time or another that the media have almost no effect or that the media have a strong, direct effect on audiences, but the vast majority of contemporary scholars believe that the media have some, usually moderate, effects on some audiences in some situations.

Further complicating the relationship between democracy and the media has been the emergence of computer-based interactive media, including the Internet, and other new technologies, such as facsimile machines. New media forms provide ordinary people with unparalleled opportunities to distribute information quickly and inexpensively to large numbers of their fellow citizens. The democratic potential of such new media is sometimes described as being a way to compensate for the ownership of traditional media forms (e.g., newspapers) by fewer and fewer large corporations, given the concern that this trend to "media monopolies" has or will reduce the diversity of opinions that are expressed in established media. However, the proliferation of Internet sources has meant that the information provided on the Internet often is not accurate or, at the very least, Internet information has not been properly checked for accuracy. Additionally, while some political observers have discussed the potential of Internet voting and campaign material distribution to rejuvenate interest in voting and in political activism, others have argued that the tendency of Internet websites to engage in shallow political humor and parody is more likely to foster cyni-

cism than to combat it. Of course, given the rapid development of the Internet and its steady increase in availability and ease of use, the political implications of emerging electronic media are far from certain, whether in historically democratic societies or in authoritarian nations where governments are struggling, usually with uneven success, to restrain the free flow of information.

Moral Obligations of Media Professionals

The obligations or duties of media professionals as those duties relate to life in a democracy have been far from clear as new media technologies have become available. By the eighteenth century, liberal democratic theory as developed in Europe and North America suggested that opinion and deception were inevitably going to be part of a free society, but such theories also maintained that truth would emerge in the end after vigorous debates about public policy issues. In the latter half of the nineteenth century, however, slipshod journalistic practices and highly partisan editors and publishers (including Joseph Pulitzer and William Randolph Hearst) led many observers to become increasingly uncomfortable with media that frequently published exaggerated stories that came complete with an obvious political slant.

In response to such excesses, alternative theories of the relationship between democracy and the media were considered. Specifically, what eventually was called the social responsibility theory of the media emerged by the mid-twentieth century in the United States, most noticeably in the 1947 report of the Hutchins Commission on Freedom of the Press. While still embracing the notion of a free press, social responsibility theory suggested that the special freedoms that were given to media in democratic societies meant that media had a responsibility to report accurately and objectively the multiple perspectives on matters of public relevance. This argument was used with particularly great force against radio and television broadcasters who were allowed to use a public resource, broadcast frequencies, for their individual gain. Because media have an obligation to inform the public about politically relevant information, for example, some members of the Hutchins Commission even speculated that the failure of media to meet their public obligations might require further governmental regulation to see that this obligation was met. While government surveillance and regulation of media content along the lines discussed by the Hutchins Commission never took place, prevailing sentiment among media professionals who reported political news favored some version of the social responsibility theory for the latter half of the twentieth century.

Even as social responsibility theory was gaining acceptance among journalists, modern political campaigns increasingly were required to rely heavily on media for contact with prospective voters in nations such as France, Great Britain, and the United States. Even the ancient practice of political speech making, as Kathleen Hall Jamieson observes in her book *Eloquence in an Electronic Age* (1988), became relatively more intimate, conversational, and television-friendly by the late twentieth century. In addition to "paid media," or media messages that were distributed in the form of paid advertisements, for example, political candidates sought to capitalize on the advantages of "free media" exposure by soliciting favorable media attention in one way or another, even by staging media events, or "pseudo-events," whose only purpose was to attract the attention of print and electronic journalists.

While media effects research in the 1940s and 1950s often indicated that the influence of media on prospective voters was minimal, more recent research suggests that media coverage of political campaigns may have some worrisome and, ultimately, undemocratic effects. In U.S. presidential campaigns, for example, some scholars have argued that the tendency of many media outlets is to emphasize the "horse race" component of the contest itself, rather than focusing on the issues that are being discussed by the various candidates. In presidential primaries, the tendency of media professionals to give the vast majority of their attention to the best-known candidates and to put great importance on performance in a few early primaries or caucuses means that the choices of those professionals may have an enormous effect on the outcome of the campaign. Furthermore, even when media outlets talk about issues, those issues may concern campaign issues (e.g., the age of a political candidate) rather than policy issues (e.g., income tax reductions). Another complaint is that some electronic media, most notably television, address a diverse mass audience that discourages candidates from taking any meaningful or controversial positions for fear of alienating some voters.

As a result of these observations, some scholars conclude that the media have not met their obligations to the public by providing relevant information about the public policies that are preferred by different candidates. In contrast, defenders of media campaign coverage point out that people learn about issues and policy preferences from media outlets. If voters do learn relatively little about issues, it may be because candidates themselves take few substantive policy positions during campaigns. Perhaps the most optimistic way to interpret the current situation is described by Roderick P. Hart in his book *Seducing America* (1994). According to Hart, one way to interpret the relationship between democracy and the media is that television, at least, is an imperfect and frequently shallow source of political information, but it teaches something about politics to even the most apathetic citizen and encourages the best citizens to learn more about politics and even to become politically active. The problem for Hart, unfortunately, is that television, the primary source of political information for most people, is a passive medium designed for personal entertainment, rather than encouraging political action and a sense of civic responsibility. Only the exceptional individual is inspired by television to take an active and personal interest in politics, let alone in political campaigns.

One clear example of the controversial and complex relationship between democracy and the media is found in research on campaign debates. Beginning with the famous Kennedy–Nixon U.S. presidential debates in 1960, campaign debates involving two or more political candidates have become an increasingly important part of political campaigning. Presidential candidates have no choice but to participate in such debates if they wish to be perceived as being capable and qualified, and candidates in state and even local political campaigns are likely to be invited to participate in one or more debates. Certainly, the available evidence suggests that, whatever their previous levels of information, voters acquire more knowledge about political candidates after watching a debate, in which voters are able to compare the policy platforms and personal attributes of the major-party candidates. When compared to traditional campaign speeches, debates may be more informative and rightly deserve the large amount of media attention that they get. However, media coverage

One of the turning points in terms of media influence on democracy was the television broadcast of the 1960 presidential debates between Richard Nixon and John F. Kennedy. (Bettmann/Corbis)

of and participation in campaign debates has been repeatedly criticized. First, media are sometimes said to influence public perceptions of those debates by focusing on competitive concerns, namely who "won" or "lost" a given debate. The result is that public policy concerns addressed in those debates are given relatively little attention. Second, as media professionals sometimes ask questions of the candidates or serve as moderators during the debates, their participation in the debates is subject to great scrutiny. For example, one study published by Frances R. Matera and Michael B. Salwen (1996) found that journalists who asked lengthy questions of candidates during presidential debates, especially questions with multiple parts, might contribute to the tendency of candidates to give long-winded answers that ignore part or all of the original question. As long as media representatives continue to participate in such debates, there will be a need to assess their contributions to campaign debates, along with the performances of the candidates themselves.

The increasing importance of media in political campaigns has also led to a rise in the use of professional political consultants by candidates. While such consultants could be found by the mid-nineteenth century in the United States, only since the 1960s have consultants dealing with scientific polling and various media outlets become a fixture in all but the most local of political campaigns. Candidates and their professional advisers became increasingly sophisticated in their targeting of certain groups of voters, and, by the 1990s, President Bill Clinton would be described as the most poll-driven and public-opinion-sensitive politician in the nation's history. Consultants are depicted as constantly attempting to "spin" the perceptions of U.S. voters in a way that is favorable to the candidate, and some critics of political consulting believe that consultants are responsible for a shift to an increasingly superficial style of political campaigning. However, defenders of consulting argue that voter cynicism is most directly attributable to disenchantment with political parties and with widely reported political scandals. Furthermore, consultants reject any strategy or approach that would alienate key groups of voters. In the end, consultants design and create campaign messages not to anger voters but because they believe those messages have a good chance of working. Finally, if political consultants are guilty of unethically manipulating media professionals and the public, then it is the job of media professionals and the public to uncover and point out those attempts at manipulation.

Social-Scientific Theories of the Media

Several different social-scientific theories of media effects have important implications for the creation and modification of public opinion in democratic societies. Some of the most successful and well-known contemporary media theories are related to agenda setting, the knowledge gap, news diffusion and information flow, and the spiral of silence.

The Agenda-Setting Effect

As originally explained by Maxwell E. McCombs and Donald L. Shaw (1972), media may not be able to tell people what to think, but they are able to tell audiences what to think about. In other words, media may set the public agenda by saying which concerns are important and which are not. Hundreds of studies of the agenda-setting effect suggest that media exposure encourages individuals to agree more closely on what public issues are most important at any given time. This finding is important because it suggests that media gatekeepers (e.g., editors) may help to determine what issues will find their way onto the public agenda. Also, most people are only able to remember and describe a few issues at a time, so issues to which the media pay attention are quite likely to displace or crowd out other potentially worthy issues that receive less media attention. Once an issue is perceived as important by ordinary citizens, politicians and political candidates are more likely to address this issue in their public statements and/or to work for social and political changes that will resolve the public policy problems with which that issue is linked. Other organizations and people outside the media, of course, also work to set the agenda in a democratic society. Media act as only one force among many in determining what issues get attention and what issues are ignored.

Consistent with contemporary theories of indirect media effects, the relative importance of the agenda-setting effect depends on the situation in which the effect is measured. For example, a strong agenda-setting effect is more likely when the relevant audience believes that the source of the media message is highly credible, since a highly credible source is more likely to be persuasive. Furthermore, heavy media exposure may result in a stronger agenda-setting effect than when media use is fairly light.

The Knowledge Gap Hypothesis

Democratic theory requires that citizens be informed about political candidates and public policy debates in order to make reasoned decisions, and from this perspective, the media in a democratic society are obligated to provide appropriate information to the public. However, some researchers have maintained that providing a larger quantity of information does not necessarily reduce the "gap" in the amount of knowledge that is possessed by some groups when compared to others. Early versions of this thesis, called the knowledge gap hypothesis, maintained that higher socioeconomic status groups would acquire knowledge at a faster rate than lower socioeconomic status groups. Some studies suggest that knowledge gaps exist for other reasons as well. For example, a group that is highly motivated will gain knowledge more quickly than a group that is not motivated, and highly educated groups will acquire knowledge more quickly than will less educated groups. Situational factors and the source(s) of information may also determine the nature and extent of knowledge gaps.

If such knowledge gaps sometimes persist despite efforts to distribute information to all members of society, then these gaps suggest that some groups are better equipped to influence public policy than others. Such a conclusion is obviously troubling in democratic societies. Some knowledge gap researchers have tried to isolate strategies for reducing knowledge gaps, such as finding ways to increase motivation among groups that have a lower socioeconomic status.

News Diffusion and Information Flow

Scholars have periodically attempted to determine how members of the public learn about breaking news stories, what media are turned to for information, and what sorts of information are actively sought by the public. Various labels have been used for research of this sort, including "news diffusion," "news seeking," "information seeking," "flow of information," and "news learning." While these various research projects have differed in some important ways, all seek to explain how information is acquired in various contexts. For example, when a crisis or catastrophic event occurs, such as the assassination of a prominent politician, people are likely to turn to the media they most often use to acquire information. However, especially if people find a certain event to be upsetting, they are apt to talk about it with others, which can result in additional people learning about that event. As a result, when almost everyone knows about an event, the majority of those who are familiar with the event will have heard about it via interpersonal communication. For events that are less well known, those who are familiar with the events are more likely to have learned about them from the media.

Some research on this topic, not surprisingly, suggests that contextual factors such as prior knowledge determine the extent of learning that takes place when information is provided by the media. Where information-seeking is concerned, a study by Walter Gantz, Michael Fitzmaurice, and Ed Fink (1991) found that people are most likely to seek regular weather information from news sources, but people seek information on other topics, including politics, much less frequently. While this finding is not particularly encouraging in a democratic society, it is not surprising that ordinary people in a heterogeneous society would not actively seek political information on a regular basis. Where television newscasts are concerned, some researchers have suggested that, to help people recall and understand more news programming, including programming that deals with politics, the ideal news program should include fewer stories, explain those stories in more detail, and eliminate distracting visual images.

The Spiral of Silence Theory
Elisabeth Noelle-Neumann (1974) has argued that people who hold a minority viewpoint about an issue or political candidate often feel pressured to keep silent, while people who hold a majority viewpoint are more likely to express that viewpoint. The explanation for this behavior is that people in the minority will doubt their own critical thinking abilities and, ultimately, question their own beliefs as they try to avoid isolating themselves socially. In contrast, people who are in the majority will become increasingly self-confident in the rightness of their beliefs and, as a consequence, will talk about their beliefs with ever-greater frequency. As such talk increases, it can tend to silence those who hold minority views. The implications of this phenomenon, in which overt opposition to prevailing beliefs becomes less and less likely, are obvious, as public opinion is a measure more of people's desire to be on the winning side than of which set of arguments is most persuasive. As a result, the spiral of silence theory predicts that media can influence public opinion by creating perceptions about which opinions are in the majority or are gaining influence and which are in the minority or are losing influence. Rather than public opinion being the product of rational debate about the best course of governmental action, as described by some democratic theorists, the spiral of silence theory depicts public opinion as the product of essentially undemocratic choices that are made by media professionals.

Obviously, if the spiral of silence theory always worked in the way outlined by Noelle-Neumann, there would only be one prevailing public opinion on each subject to which the media paid attention. As the existence of social movements and pressure groups proves, however, there are still many minority groups that loudly and repeatedly demand social change. The available evidence suggests that, for some people and in some situations, people who perceive that their opinion is in the majority are slightly more likely to express their opinion than people who are in the minority. However, other factors may lead people in the minority to speak or people in the majority to remain silent, so the spiral of silence theory, by itself, is not sufficient to explain how public opinion is created and maintained. Also, the theory is not particularly good at describing how public opinion shifts from month to month or year to year, as examples exist of minority positions that later become majority positions.

Conclusion

In one way or another, many theories of media now claim that objectivity is not a feasible goal for media in a democratic society because political "facts" typically are based on subjective experiences and impressions. From this perspective, media help, however unintentionally, to determine how people perceive the political realities of the world in which they live, and the demand for objective reporting that is central to social responsibility theory simply cannot be met. When a woman or man watches a television news program, for example, she or he is not simply collecting information about a local school bond issue. Instead, that woman or man is learning what matters and what does not in society and is being told how legitimate (or illegitimate) a specific political perspective is. If media coverage of an issue does have a real chance of shaping people's perceptions of reality, then the goal must be for people to become active listeners and readers in their assessments of media messages. Unfortunately, the trend in the United States favors a lack of interest in politics. Surveys indicate that American citizens knew no more about politics in the 1990s than they did in 1940, despite the fact that the U.S. population had far more education on average in the 1990s than it did fifty years earlier. Demanding a more critical audience that would carefully analyze media messages about politics seems unduly optimistic. However, the experience of other democratic countries with democracy and the media has often differed from that of the United States, and voter participation in elections, at least, remains comparatively high in many of those countries. The experience of other countries with democracy and the media needs to be considered before coming to pessimistic conclusions on the basis of the U.S. experience alone.

Another contemporary concern that was not envisioned by the creators of social responsibility theory in the mid-twentieth century is the widespread availability of multiple media channels for conveying information to the public. Different media channels are perceived differently by users, so that the interactive experience of using the Internet poses a sharp contrast to the passive experience of watching television. The most famous example of these differences in experience with media channels involves the 1960 Kennedy–Nixon presidential debates. One study found that those who listened to the debates on the radio thought that Nixon had won, while those who watched the debates on television thought that Kennedy had won. Those people who research the relationship between democracy and the media must deal with the challenges that are posed by several different channels, with each channel affecting the perception of information in different ways.

Obviously, the relationship between democracy and the media remains complex. Many citizens of democratic societies do not want any government control of major media because they fear that governmental regulation of media would be incompatible with democracy, yet these citizens very much hope that media will restrain themselves voluntarily and act in a responsible fashion that facilitates and promotes democracy. Of course, what key terms in the last sentence mean, including "democracy" and "responsible," will continue to be debated. Also, as media sources are no longer provided only by full-time professionals using incredibly expensive equipment, more and more individuals with little commitment to careful research will be able to make their views known on the Internet or using inexpensive desktop-publishing software programs and personal computers. As society continues to be introduced to new and exciting communication technologies, the goal for individuals should be to become more critical receivers and users of the various media outlets. Only by carefully analyzing the sources of information and the arguments made by those sources can people reach thoughtful conclusions on the political issues that matter in their everyday lives. Whether most media professionals are proponents of big government or apologists for big corporations—both of which charges are made by media critics—the final responsibility for judging the performance of the media rests with ordinary people.

See also: BROADCASTING, GOVERNMENT REGULATION OF; BROADCASTING, SELF-REGULATION OF; ELECTION CAMPAIGNS AND MEDIA EFFECTS; FIRST AMENDMENT AND THE MEDIA; GLOBALIZATION OF CULTURE THROUGH THE MEDIA; GLOBALIZATION OF MEDIA INDUSTRIES; HEARST, WILLIAM RANDOLPH; INTERNET AND THE WORLD WIDE WEB; JOURNALISM, HISTORY OF; JOURNALISM, PROFESSIONALIZATION OF; NEWS PRODUCTION THEORIES; OPINION POLLING, CAREERS IN; PIRATE MEDIA; PROPAGANDA; PUBLIC BROADCASTING; PULITZER, JOSEPH; SOCIAL CHANGE AND THE MEDIA.

Bibliography

Cobb, Roger W., and Elder, Charles D. (1983). *Participation in American Politics: The Dynamics of Agenda-Building*, 2nd edition. Baltimore, MD: Johns Hopkins University Press.

Davis, Dennis K. (1990). "News and Politics." In *New Directions in Political Communication: A Resource Book*, eds. David L. Swanson and Dan Nimmo. Newbury Park, CA: Sage Publications.

Edelman, Murray. (1988). *Constructing the Political Spectacle*. Chicago: University of Chicago Press.

Friedenberg, Robert V. (1997). *Communication Consultants in Political Campaigns: Ballot Box Warriors*. Westport, CT: Praeger.

Gantz, Walter; Fitzmaurice, Michael; and Fink, Ed. (1991). "Assessing the Active Component of Information-Seeking." *Journalism Quarterly* 68:630–637.

Glynn, Carroll J.; Hayes, Andrew F.; and Shanahan, James. (1997). "Perceived Support for One's Opinion and Willingness to Speak Out: A Meta-Analysis of Survey Studies on the 'Spiral of Silence.'" *Public Opinion Quarterly* 61:452–463.

Habermas, J¸rgen. (1962). *The Structural Transformation of the Public Sphere: An Inquiry into a Category of Bourgeois Society*, trs. Thomas Burger and Frederick Lawrence. Cambridge, MA: MIT Press.

Hart, Roderick P. (1994). *Seducing America: How Television Charms the Modern Voter*. New York: Oxford University Press.

Jacques, Wayne W., and Ratzan, Scott C. (1997). "The Internet's World Wide Web and Political Accountability." *American Behavioral Scientist* 40:1226–1237.

Jamieson, Kathleen Hall. (1988). *Eloquence in an Electronic Age: The Transformation of Political Speechmaking*. New York: Oxford University Press.

Jamieson, Kathleen Hall. (1992). *Dirty Politics: Deception, Distraction, and Democracy*. New York: Oxford University Press.

Lemert, James B. (1993). "Do Televised Presidential Debates Help Inform Voters?" *Journal of Broadcasting & Electronic Media* 37:83–94.

Matera, Frances R., and Salwen, Michael B. (1996). "Unwieldy Questions? Circuitous Answers?: Journalists as Panelists in Presidential Election Debates." *Journal of Broadcasting & Electronic Media* 40:309–317.

McCombs, Maxwell E., and Shaw, Donald L. (1972). "The Agenda-Setting Function of Mass Media." *Public Opinion Quarterly* 36:176–187.

Neustadt, Richard E. (1980). *Presidential Power: The Politics of Leadership from FDR to Carter*. New York: Macmillan.

Noelle-Neumann, Elisabeth. (1974). "The Spiral of Silence: A Theory of Public Opinion." *Journal of Communication* 24(2):43–51.

Paletz, David L. (1998). "The Media and Public Policy." In *The Politics of News, the News of Politics*, eds. Doris Graber, Denis McQuail, and Pippa Norris. Washington, DC: Congressional Quarterly.

Siebert, Fred S.; Peterson, Theodore; and Schramm, Wilbur. (1956). *Four Theories of the Press*. Urbana: University of Illinois Press.

Viswanath, K., and Finnegan, John R., Jr. (1996). "The Knowledge Gap Hypothesis: Twenty-Five Years Later." In *Communication Yearbook, Vol. 19*, ed. Brant R. Burleson. Thousand Oaks, CA: Sage Publications.

Wanta, Wayne, and Hu, Yu-Wei. (1994). "The Effects of Credibility, Reliance, and Exposure on Media Agenda-Setting: A Path Analysis Model." *Journalism Quarterly* 71:90–98.

Warnick, Barbara. (1998). "Appearance or Reality?: Political Parody on the Web in Campaign '96." *Critical Studies in Mass Communication* 15:306–324.

BRIAN R. MCGEE

■ DEPENDENCE ON MEDIA

Millions of Americans, and no doubt many more millions of people around the world, believe that television viewing can be addictive. Although only 2 percent and 12.5 percent of American adults in two separate surveys believed that they were addicted, 65 percent to 70 percent believed that others were addicted (McIlwraith, 1990; McIlwraith, Jacobvitz, Kubey, and Alexander, 1991). Many millions more appear to experience some misgiving about how much they view. According to a 1990 Gallup poll, 42 percent of adult Americans reported spending "too much time watching television"—up from 31 percent in the late 1970s.

Although it is tempting to use a term such as "addiction" when referring to individuals who report more than sixty hours of viewing each week, the term connotes different things to different people, and it is likely that less confusion will result if more care is taken in the choice of words.

The prime diagnostic manual used by psychotherapists throughout North America, the American Psychiatric Association's *Diagnostic and Statistical Manual of Mental Disorders* (DSMV-IV, 1994), does not even use the term "addiction." Instead, the committees that wrote the DSM preferred the term "substance dependence." Still, there are researchers and clinicians who use the term "addiction." As a result, this entry also uses that term from time to time.

How the Viewing Habit Is Formed

Giving thought to how people's viewing habits are formed can be helpful. Among the primary experiences that people report when viewing television is "relaxation," but research suggests that the relaxed and passive bodily and mental states that are associated with television viewing may also make it difficult for many people to turn the set off. According to Robert Kubey and Mihaly Csikszentmihalyi (1990), the passivity of viewing appears, for many people, to continue after the set is turned off (i.e., the feeling of passivity spills over into how they feel afterward).

As noted by Gary Steiner (1963), it is critical to know that many people also use television to escape negative and unpleasant moods. In fact, according to Robert McIlwraith (1990), adults who called themselves "TV addicts" were significantly more likely than "nonaddicted" viewers to report using television to cope with negative moods such as loneliness, sadness, anxiety, and anger.

Self-labeled "addicts" also say that they are particularly likely to use television when they have nothing to do and when they need to fill open time (McIlwraith, 1990). In comparison with viewers who watch less than two hours of television a day, viewers who watch more than four hours of television per day generally report feeling worse when they are alone and when they are in unstructured situations, such as when they are waiting in line or when they are "between" activities (Kubey, 1986). These findings suggest that dependence on television develops in some people partly as a function of their need to fill the unpleasant emotional voids that accompany solitude and/or open time.

In both the United States (Smith, 1986) and Canada (McIlwraith, 1990), researchers have found that self-reported television "addicts" score significantly higher than "nonaddicts" on measures of mindwandering, distractibility, boredom, and unfocused daydreaming. This all presents the possibility of a vicious circle. Negative moods and thoughts that people experience when they are alone and when they are in unstructured situations can be quickly and easily escaped by viewing television. However, as a result of spending many hours viewing television over many years, some people may become unpracticed in spending time alone, entertaining themselves, or possibly even in readily and simply directing their own attention. This could, in turn, lead some people to experience negative moods and thoughts when they are alone or in unstructured situations—resulting in

their returning to television viewing for escape and comfort.

People who live alone and/or feel lonely appear to be particularly inclined to turn to television viewing and may become even more uncomfortable when alone and left without the quasi-social experience the medium offers. Viewers who watch a large amount of television do tend to have more time on their hands and spend more time alone than do viewers who watch only a small amount. The demographic groups that tend to have higher proportions of people who watch a large amount of television are the elderly, the unemployed, and people who are recently divorced or separated.

Television viewing also helps people relax, and anecdotal reports indicate that it relaxes them quickly. Within moments of sitting or lying down and pushing the power button of a television set, many viewers report feeling more relaxed than they did before. Because the reinforcement of relaxation occurs quickly, people readily learn to associate viewing with relaxation. The association is then repeatedly reinforced through simple operant conditioning because viewers remain relaxed throughout viewing but not afterward (unlike a general feeling of passivity that does seem to last after viewing) (Kubey and Csikszentmihalyi, 1990).

The quick onset of relaxation is particularly telling when compared to the use of certain drugs that prove to be habit-forming or "addictive." According to Alvin Swonger and Larry Constantine (1976, p. 235), "The attribute of a drug that most contributes to its abuse liability is not its ability to produce tolerance or physical dependence but rather its ability to reinforce the drug-taking behaviors." This is why both the speed with which a drug takes effect and how quickly it leaves the body can be critical factors as to whether or not dependence occurs. Reinforcement does not need to be experienced consciously for dependence to occur.

Some tranquilizers, for example, those whose effects do not last as long as the effects of other drugs, are often more habit-forming precisely because the user is more aware that the effects of the drug are wearing off. When one starts feeling bad again rather quickly after the drug's effect is no longer experienced, the tendency to turn to the drug again for relief will be greater than if its effects were to have worn off more gradually.

Similarly, or even more notably, the change in mood that one experiences when one suddenly stops viewing television can be abrupt. Many people will report a subtle sense of having given something up when they first turn the set off. Many parents find it easier to get children to turn off the set if the parents can interest the children in another activity.

According to Kubey (1984), viewing begets more viewing because one must generally keep watching in order to keep feeling relaxed. In short, relative to the other possible means that are available to bring about distraction and relaxation, television is among the quickest, and certainly among the least expensive. Unlike engaging in conversation or playing games, one does not need anyone else to be present in order to watch television. With the incredible ubiquity of television and other media, self-control over one's viewing habits may be more of a challenge in the contemporary environment than it was in the not-so-distant past.

Using DSM-IV as a guide can be illuminating, and the case has been made by Kubey (1996) that were television a substance, there is little question that people could legitimately be given diagnoses of dependence. Indeed, Dr. Allen J. Frances, who oversaw the 1994 revision of the manual concluded that "Under the broader definition, many kinds of compulsive behavior could be considered addictive, including obsessive sex or compulsive television viewing" (Goleman, 1990, p. C8).

DSM-IV lists seven possible criteria for making a diagnosis of substance dependence. Only three of the criteria must apply in order to make a diagnosis of "dependence." However, five of the seven diagnostic criteria might readily be applied to television viewing and its concomitant behaviors and effects.

One of the most interesting questions to consider is whether people experience anything akin to withdrawal if and when they stop viewing or using other media. In 1963, Steiner presented the following fascinating individual accounts of what happened when a family lost the use of a television set due to a technological malfunction (in a time when many families had only one set): "The family walked around like a chicken without a head." "It was terrible. We did nothing—my husband and I talked." "Screamed constantly. Children bothered me and my nerves were on edge."

Tried to interest them in games, but impossible. TV is part of them" (p. 99).

Charles Winick's (1988) review of studies of families whose television sets were in repair led him to the following conclusion:

> The first three or four days for most persons were the worst, even in many homes where viewing was minimal and where there were other ongoing activities. In over half of all the households, during these first few days of loss, the regular routines were disrupted, family members had difficulties in dealing with the newly available time, anxiety and aggressions were expressed, and established expectations for the behavior of other household members were not met. People living alone tended to be bored and irritated. Over four-fifths of the respondents reported moderate to severe dislocations during this period. . . . The fifth to eighth day represented, in many cases, some form of readjustment to the new situation. . . . By the second week, a move toward adaptation to the situation was common [pp. 221–222].

Video Games, Computer Games, and the Internet

Contemporary concerns are focused as often on computer and video games and Internet habits as they are on television viewing. There has been much less research on video games, but it is not difficult to use many of the explanations regarding television dependence to help explain people's affinity for video games. As with television, the games offer the player an escape and distraction, and as with television, players quickly learn that they momentarily feel better when they play the games—leading to a kind of psychological reinforcement.

Computer and video games also have particular characteristics that make children and adults especially likely to report that they are "addicted" to them. First, there is the general challenge posed by the game and the wish to overcome it and succeed—something largely or entirely missing with television viewing. Second, there is the critical characteristic that the games are designed to increase the level of challenge and difficulty as the player increases his or her playing ability.

The rows of computer games in a game center in Osaka, Japan, illustrate the variety of challenges that are available and that can keep some people involved in trying to "defeat" them. (Michael S. Yamashita/Corbis)

Psychic pleasure accompanies the improvement of one's skills and the increased mastery of most any human endeavor. In being programmed to challenge players at their current ability, video and computer games offer a nearly perfect level of difficulty for the player who enjoys such challenges. One may search for months or even years to find another tennis or chess player who has a very comparable ability, but many programmed games will provide a near-perfect matching of challenge with player skill. Thus, computerized games also make extended play extraordinarily common because one is feeling neither bored by too easy an opponent nor too anxious by not being able to match the level of competition.

Computer and video games offer all the essential features that are likely to result in a "flow" experience. This term refers to a period of intense, enjoyable, high concentration and involvement resulting from being engaged in an activity where skills and challenges are closely matched and where rapid feedback is available regarding one's

performance (Csikszentmihalyi, 1975; Kubey and Larson, 1990). The games give the player nearly instantaneous feedback as to whether the last activity (shot, jump, run, or whatever) was successful. In computer play, as with sports, musical performance, and certain hobbies, the feedback is quick and clear, and insofar as it often occurs at the height of one's own personal level of performance, it is no wonder that the games are extremely engaging and, perhaps, "addictive."

The latest media "addiction" to be proposed both popularly and in academic and clinical circles is so-called Internet addiction. Few journal articles using scientific methodologies and subjected to the rigors of peer review have been published. Much of the existing work has been published on websites. There is little question, though, that as with other media before it, a wide variety of Internet activities have a very strong "pull" or "hold" on users (Young, 1998).

What appears to distinguish the Internet most from the usual media that are examined in terms of dependence is that the Internet is interactive and that it can be readily used to sustain or form social relationships. Playing computer games on the "net" can doubtlessly entail forms of involvement and/or dependency that are very much akin to those related to video games. People may also become dependent on the Internet in connection with hobbies, whether it be genealogy or baseball card collecting. However, insofar as people can communicate readily online with friends, relatives, and professional colleagues—regardless of distance or time—this relatively new technology provides a whole new array of social possibilities. If people have been dependent on the telephone for social contact, it is no wonder that the Internet adds all manner of new possibilities. Being connected with others when one is alone—at any time of day and at very little expense—is very attractive, and there can be little doubt that some individuals are becoming dependent on the Internet. Future research will undoubtedly provide important insights related to this phenomenon.

Dependence on Pornography

A final important consideration is the phenomenon of pornography, a media form that also has often been cited as being addictive. Indeed, with the huge growth in the availability of pornography that has accompanied the availability of video playback technology in the home since the early 1980s, and now with the development of interactive pornography available via CD-ROM and the Internet, the concern over the potentially addictive properties of pornography will undoubtedly be an issue for some time.

It must be noted that research and reporting on the effects of pornography have long been politicized, and thus it is more difficult to weigh the validity and veracity of some contributions to the literature. As with other debates that are related to media effects, it is very difficult to disentangle cause from effect when dealing with pornography. Still, a number of researchers and clinicians report significant evidence for dependence and addiction.

Authorities often find large private pornography collections in the residences of people who are arrested for sexual crimes (Cline, 1994; Reed, 1994), especially pedophiles (Lanning and Burgess, 1989). At a minimum, it can be said that a relationship between the frequent use of pornography and problematic sexual disorders exists for some individuals. Whether the pornography is merely symptomatic of the disorder or plays a causal role is very difficult to establish.

For some observers, there is little doubt that both negative effects and pornography addiction do indeed occur. M. Douglas Reed (1994), a practicing psychiatrist, is explicit in his presentation of specific criteria that he believes would constitute an addiction to pornography. He notes that DSM-IV itself recognizes that many paraphilias (i.e., compulsive sexual deviances) frequently involve the use and collection of pornography. Reed lists thirteen paraphilias and how they are related to the use of pornography.

Victor Cline (1994), a clinical psychologist who has treated hundreds of people who have sexual disorders, describes a four-step process in the involvement of his patients with pornography. First, Cline describes an "addiction effect" wherein the person comes back repeatedly for more material because it provides "a very powerful sexual stimulant or aphrodisiac effect followed by sexual release most often through masturbation" (p. 233). Second, Cline describes an "escalation effect" in which there is an "increasing need for more of the stimulant to get the same effect [that had been obtained initially]" (p. 233). Third, Cline observes "desensitization" in which things that might have once seemed shocking become less so and are thereby legitimized. Fourth, Cline claims that there is an "increasing tendency to act out sexually the behaviors viewed in the pornography" (p. 234).

A number of other psychological and physiological mechanisms have been suggested for how pornography addiction might develop. Among the most common is that sexual gratification is a powerful reinforcer (Lyons, Anderson, and Larson, 1994). For Cline, and for many other observers, pornography provides powerful occasions in which modeling and imitative learning can occur.

Dolf Zillmann (1994) has proposed that in many instances, "initial sexual dissatisfaction drives exposure to pornography" and a vicious circle then ensues. With consumption of pornography, the dissatisfaction grows stronger and draws the person into further consumption. It is important to point out that video recorders and the Internet have led to an explosion in pornographic materials and that such materials are far more accessible to people, including children and adolescents, than they have ever been before. This is important since, if a pornography habit—or addiction—can indeed develop, it would seem more likely to develop if pornographic materials can be easily obtained and if the use of such materials is socially sanctioned.

See also: Pornography; Pornography, Legal Aspects; Ratings for Video Games, Software, and the Internet; Video and Computer Games and the Internet; Violence in the Media, Attraction to; Violence in the Media, History of Research on.

Bibliography

American Psychiatric Association. (1994). *Diagnostic and Statistical Manual of Mental Disorders*, 4th edition. Washington, DC: American Psychiatric Association.

Cline, Victor B. (1994). "Pornography Effects: Empirical and Clinical Evidence." In *Media, Children, and the Family: Social Scientific, Psychodynamic, and Clinical Perspectives*, eds. Dolf Zillmann, Jennings Bryant, and Aletha C. Huston. Hillsdale, NJ: Lawrence Erlbaum.

Csikszentmihalyi, Mihaly. (1975). *Beyond Boredom and Anxiety: The Experience of Play in Work and Games*. San Francisco: Joseey-Bass.

Goleman, Daniel. (1990). "How Viewers Grow Addicted to Television." *The New York Times*, Oct. 16, pp. C1, C8.

Kubey, Robert. (1984). *Leisure, Television, and Subjective Experience*. Doctoral dissertation, University of Chicago.

Kubey, Robert. (1986). "Television Use in Everyday Life: Coping with Unstructured Time." *Journal of Communication* 36(3):108–123.

Kubey, Robert. (1996). "Television Dependence, Diagnosis, and Prevention: With Commentary on Video Games, Pornography, and Media Education." In *Tuning in to Young Viewers: Social Science Perspectives on Television*, ed. Tannis MacBeth. Newbury Park, CA: Sage Publications.

Kubey, Robert, and Csikszentmihalyi, Mihaly. (1990). *Television and the Quality of Life: How Viewing Shapes Everyday Experience*. Hillsdale, NJ: Lawrence Erlbaum.

Kubey, Robert, and Larson, Reed. (1990). "The Use and Experience of the New Video Media among Children and Young Adolescents." *Communication Research* 17:107–130.

Lanning, Kenneth V., and Burgess, Ann W. (1989). "Child Pornography and Sex Rings." In *Pornography: Research Advances and Policy Considerations*, eds. Dolf Zillmann and Jennings Bryant. Hillsdale, NJ: Lawrence Erlbaum.

Lyons, John S.; Anderson, Rachel L.; and Larson, David B. (1994). "A Systematic Review of the Effects of Aggressive and Nonaggressive Pornography." In *Media, Children, and the Family: Social Scientific, Psychodynamic, and Clinical Perspectives*, eds. Dolf Zillmann, Jennings Bryant, and Aletha C. Huston. Hillsdale, NJ: Lawrence Erlbaum.

McIlwraith, Robert. (1990). "Theories of Television Addiction." Talk presented to the August meeting of the American Psychological Association, Boston.

McIlwraith, Robert; Jacobvitz, Robin Smith; Kubey, Robert; and Alexander, Alison. (1991). "Television Addiction: Theories and Data Behind the Ubiquitous Metaphor." *American Behavioral Scientist* 35:104–121.

Reed, M. Douglas. (1994). "Pornography Addiction and Compulsive Sexual Behavior." In *Media, Children, and the Family: Social Scientific, Psychodynamic, and Clinical Perspectives*, eds. Dolf Zillmann, Jennings Bryant, and Aletha C. Huston. Hillsdale, NJ: Lawrence Erlbaum.

Shotton, Margaret. (1989). *Computer Addiction?: A Study of Computer Dependency*. London: Taylor & Francis.

Smith, Robin. (1986). "Television Addiction." In *Perspectives on Media Effects*, eds. Jennings Bryant and Dolf Zillmann. Hillsdale, NJ: Lawrence Erlbaum.

Steiner, Gary. (1963). *The People Look at Television*. New York: Knopf.

Swonger, Alvin K., and Constantine, Larry L. (1976). *Drugs and Therapy: A Psychotherapist's Handbook of Psychotropic Drugs*. Boston: Little, Brown.

Williams, Tannis MacBeth, ed. (1986). *The Impact of Television: A Natural Experiment in Three Communities*. New York: Academic Press.

Winick, Charles. (1988). "The Functions of Television: Life without the Big Box." In *Television as a Social Issue*, ed. Stuart Oskamp. Newbury Park, CA: Sage Publications.

Young, Kimberly. (1998). *Caught in the Net: How to Recognize the Signs of Internet Addiction and a Winning Strategy for Recovery*. New York: Wiley.

Zillmann, Dolf. (1994). "Erotica and Family Values." In *Media, Children, and the Family: Social Scientific, Psychodynamic, and Clinical Perspectives*, eds. Dolf Zillmann, Jennings Bryant, and Aletha C. Huston. Hillsdale, NJ: Lawrence Erlbaum.

Robert Kubey

DESENSITIZATION AND MEDIA EFFECTS

Desensitization is a psychological process that has often been involved in explaining viewers' emotional reactions to media violence. Research on emotional reactions to violent messages has been concerned with the possibility that continued exposure to violence in the mass media will result in desensitization, that is, that exposure to media violence will undermine feelings of concern, empathy, or sympathy that viewers might have toward victims of actual violence.

To understand the effects of repeated exposure to violence, researchers have suggested that viewers become comfortable with violence that is initially anxiety provoking, much as they would if they were undergoing exposure therapy. According to Gordon Paul and D. A. Bernstein (1973), exposure therapy is widely regarded as the most effective clinical therapy for training individuals to engage in behaviors that were previously inhibited by anxiety responses. Originally, researchers emphasized a therapeutic counterconditioning technique known as "systematic desensitization," in which the patient was gradually and systematically exposed to a graded series of anxiety provoking objects or situations. Many researchers, including Edna B. Foa and Michael J. Kozak (1986), have demonstrated that simply exposing a patient to frightening stimuli, regardless of whether it is presented in graduated form, will significantly diminish the anxiety or negative affect that the stimulus once evoked. This logic may be applied to the effects of repeated exposure to media violence.

Most of the early work on desensitization to media violence, such as that conducted by Victor B. Cline and his colleagues (1973) and Margaret H. Thomas and her colleagues (1977), involved exposure to rather mild forms of television violence for relatively short periods of time. These studies indicated that viewers who watched large amounts of media violence showed less physiological reactivity to violent film clips, compared to viewers who watched only small amounts, and that general physiological arousal decreased as viewers watched more violent media. Children as well as adults are susceptible to this effect.

More recently, Daniel Linz, Edward Donnerstein, and Steven Penrod (1984, 1988) measured the reactions of adult men to films that portrayed violence against women, often in a sexual context. The viewings took place over a period of several days, and comparisons of first-day reactions and last-day reactions to the films showed that, with repeated exposure, initial levels of self-reported anxiety decreased substantially. Furthermore, the research participants' perceptions of the films also changed from the first day to the last day. Material that was previously judged to be violent and degrading to women was considered to be significantly less so by the end of the exposure period. Participants also indicated that they were less depressed and enjoyed the material more with repeated exposure. These effects generalized to responses to a victim of sexual assault in a mock trial presented to the men at a later time. Men who had been exposed to the sexually violent films, compared to a no-exposure group, rated the victim as being less severely injured. The men who had been exposed to the violent film, again compared to men in a no-exposure control group, were also less sympathetic to the rape victim portrayed in the trial and less able to empathize with rape victims in general. These effects did not emerge following exposure to a single film. Longer film exposure was necessary for it to affect the violence-viewing participants' general empathetic response. Linz and his colleagues (1984, 1988) suggested that the viewers were becoming comfortable with anxiety-provoking situations much as they would if they were undergoing desensitization therapy. Carol Krafka and her associates (1997) observed these same effects for women who viewed sexual violence. Linz and his colleagues (1989) also showed that a reduction in physiological responsiveness accompanies repeated exposure to sexualized violence and that viewing violent films results in less sympathy for victims of domestic violence as well as rape victims.

Most recently, Charles R. Mullin and Linz (1995) demonstrated that viewers who show a desensitization toward victims of violence in non-media contexts following exposure to media violence may recover sensitivity rather quickly provided they are not exposed to additional violent depictions. An experiment was conducted to examine the effects of repeated exposure to sexually violent films on emotional desensitization and callousness toward domestic abuse victims. Results indicated that emotional responses, self-reported physiological arousal, and ratings of the extent to which the films were sexually violent all diminished with repeated film exposure. Three days following exposure to the final film, participants in the experiment expressed significantly less sympathy for domestic violence victims and rated their injuries as being less severe than did a no-exposure control group. Five days after the final film exposure, the participants' level of sensitivity to the victims of domestic violence rebounded to the baseline levels that were established by the no-exposure comparison group.

In conclusion, exposure to violence in the mass media may result in a desensitization effect in which viewers experience diminished feelings of concern, empathy, or sympathy toward victims of actual violence. Research has shown that viewers who watch large amounts of media violence show less physiological reactivity to violence in other contexts. Men and women who are exposed to sexual violence in the media also show less sympathy toward rape victims portrayed in other contexts and are generally less able to empathize with rape victims. However, resensitization to victims after desensitization may occur given a sufficient rest period.

See also: AROUSAL PROCESSES AND MEDIA EFFECTS; PORNOGRAPHY; VIOLENCE IN THE MEDIA, ATTRACTION TO; VIOLENCE IN THE MEDIA, HISTORY OF RESEARCH ON.

Bibliography

Cline, Victor B.; Croft, Roger G.; and Courrier, Stephen. (1973). "Desensitization of Children to Television Violence." *Journal of Personality and Social Psychology* 27:360–365.

Foa, Edna B., and Kozak, Michael J. (1986). "Emotional Processing of Fear: Exposure to Corrective Information." *Psychological Bulletin* 99:20–35.

Krafka, Carol; Linz, Daniel; Donnerstein, Edward; and Penrod, Steven. (1997). "Women's Reactions to Sexually Aggressive Mass Media Depictions." *Violence Against Women* 3(2):149–181.

Linz, Daniel; Donnerstein, Edward; and Adams, Steven M. (1989). "Physiological Desensitization and Judgments About Female Victims of Violence." *Human Communication Research* 15:509–522.

Linz, Daniel; Donnerstein, Edward; and Penrod, Steven. (1984). "The Effects of Multiple Exposures to Filmed Violence Against Women." *Journal of Communication* 34(3):130–147.

Linz, Daniel; Donnerstein, Edward; and Penrod, Steven. (1988). "Effects of Long-Term Exposure to Violent and Sexually Degrading Depictions of Women." *Journal of Personality and Social Psychology* 55:758–768.

Mullin, Charles R., and Linz, Daniel. (1995). "Desensitization and Resensitization to Violence Against Women: Effects of Exposure to Sexually Violent Films on Judgments of Domestic Violence Victims." *Journal of Personality and Social Psychology* 69(3):449–459.

Paul, Gordon L., and Bernstein, D. A. (1973). "Anxiety and Clinical Problems: Systematic Desensitization and Related Techniques." In *Behavioral Approaches to Therapy*, eds. Janet T. Spence, Robert C. Carson, and John W. Thibaut. Morristown, NJ: General Learning Press.

Thomas, Margaret H. (1982). "Physiological Arousal, Exposure to a Relatively Lengthy Aggressive Film and Aggressive Behavior." *Journal of Research in Personality* 16:72–81.

Thomas, Margaret H.; Horton, R. W.; Lippincott, E. C.; and Drabman, R. S. (1977). "Desensitization to Portrayals of Real-Life Aggression As a Function of Exposure to Television Violence." *Journal of Personality and Social Psychology* 35:450–458.

Ullman Leonard P., and Krasner, Leonard. (1969). *A Psychological Approach to Abnormal Behavior*. Englewood Cliffs, NJ: Prentice-Hall.

Wolpe, Joseph. (1958). *Psychotherapy by Reciprocal Inhibition*. Stanford: Stanford University Press.

DANIEL LINZ

■ DESIGNERS

See: Database Design; Systems Designers

■ DEWEY, JOHN (1859–1942)

A native of Burlington, Vermont, John Dewey received his B.A. from the University of Vermont in 1879 and his Ph.D. from Johns Hopkins University in 1884. Except for a brief appointment at the University of Minnesota, he taught at the University of Michigan from 1884 to 1894.

In 1894, Dewey joined the faculty of the University of Chicago as head of the department of philosophy, psychology, and pedagogy. While at Chicago, he founded an experimental elementary school that came to be known as the "Dewey School." Among the major influences on his theory of communication during this period were his colleague George Herbert Mead and Jane Addams (the founder of Hull House).

In 1904, Dewey resigned from the University of Chicago and accepted a position at Columbia University where he was appointed professor emeritus of philosophy in residence in 1930 and professor emeritus in 1939. He traveled widely, presenting

John Dewey. (Bettmann/Corbis)

lectures in Japan, China, Mexico, Turkey, and Russia, among other places. Politically active, he was an energetic promoter of the American Civil Liberties Union, The American Association of University Professors, and the women's suffrage movement. Dewey died at his home in New York City on June 1, 1952. An urn containing his ashes is interred at the University of Vermont.

In 1896, Dewey published his watershed essay "The Reflex Arc Concept in Psychology"(EW.5.96), in which he attempted to replace the received model of a stimulus–response arc with the model of an adjustive circle or spiral. He rejected the idea that stimuli exist as already complete in a world external to a passive subject and that they impinge on the subject in ways that effect a response. In place of this view, he advanced the idea that stimuli are selected by an active subject. They are properties of the interaction between a subject and its environing conditions rather than properties of a world external to the subject. Applied to a situation involving communication between two subjects, for example, this means that when A asks B to bring him or her some-

thing and points to it, the stimulus for B is neither A's asking nor A's pointing, but the anticipation that B has as a result of the cooperative situation that is shared with A. In order for there to be a stimulus at all, B must have already entered into a cooperative situation by placing him- or herself in the position of A, thus viewing the situation from A's standpoint. This cooperative situation is what Ludwig Wittgenstein would later call a "language game."

The most succinct formulation of Dewey's philosophy of communication is in chapter five of his book *Experience and Nature* (1925). In this material, Dewey criticized what he considered to be reductionist theories of communication. On one side, he rejected supernaturalist and other transcendentalist views that locate the origin or measure of communication in a *logos* beyond human conduct. He thought that this had been the error of the Athenian Greeks and their heirs, the medievals. They had mistaken the structure of communication for the structure of things.

On the other side, he rejected views that drive a wedge between internal states and external expression by locating language and meaning in a private, subjective world. He thought that this had been the error of philosophers of the modern period, beginning with René Descartes. They had failed to recognize that language is a social product. Further anticipating the work of Wittgenstein, Dewey argued that there can be no private language.

He thus rejected the view that communication consists of fixed messages that move through inert media, much as water through a pipe, to be delivered fully intact to passive recipients. His rejection of this absolutist notion—that communication is the transmission of fixed ideas—was balanced with his rejection of the opposite view, namely, the nominalist notion that communication is a purely arbitrary social construct. He argued that nominalism cannot account for the fact that communication is both organized and objective. Meanings are organized by language, which is the tool of tools. Further, meanings become objective as they are grounded in the natural interactions—including those that are social—of which they are by-products.

Dewey's view of communication is perhaps best understood as a variety of social behaviorism. When an organism becomes capable of understanding an expression as meaningful from the standpoint of another organism, meanings are made common to at least two centers of behavior.

Meanings then "copulate," as he put it, breeding new and more enriched meanings. Signs and significance come into existence not intentionally but as a kind of overflow or by-product of communication. In articulating this view, Dewey drew heavily on the work of Mead.

In what is perhaps his most precise characterization of the term, Dewey wrote that communication is "the establishment of cooperation in an activity in which there are partners, and in which the activity of each is modified and regulated by partnership" (LW.1.141). Such partnerships can be formed between and among humans, between humans and other organisms, and even between humans and inorganic materials. Artists, for example, can be said to communicate with their materials when they take them into account in ways that express and enlarge the meanings of the materials. Dewey characterized intelligence as the ability to engage in such activities. A corollary of his view is that meanings are properties of behavior first, and properties of objects only derivatively.

Dewey described communication as "uniquely instrumental and uniquely final." It is uniquely instrumental in the sense that it organizes events in ways that render them more meaningful, thus affording liberation from what is dangerous, debilitating, or boring. It is uniquely final in the sense that when meanings are shared and thereby enriched, an enhanced sense of community with the human and nonhuman environment is achieved. The separation of these two functions is infelicitous because what is only instrumental remains thin and partial and what is only final tends to be either corrupting or trivial. In true communication, instrumental and final functions cooperate. Meanings are enriched and a corresponding growth of the organism is produced. "Of all affairs," he wrote, "communication is the most wonderful" (LW.1.132).

See also: MEAD, GEORGE HERBERT; SOCIETY AND COMMUNICATION; SOCIETY AND THE MEDIA.

Bibliography

Alexander, Thomas M. (1987). *John Dewey's Theory of Art, Experience, and Nature: The Horizons of Feeling.* Albany: State University of New York Press.
Boydston, Jo Ann, ed. (1970). *Guide to the Works of John Dewey.* Carbondale: Southern Illinois University Press.
Campbell, James. (1995). *Understanding John Dewey: Nature and Cooperative Intelligence.* Chicago: Open Court.
Dewey, John. (1969–1991). *The Collected Works of John Dewey, 1882–1953*, ed. Jo Ann Boydston. Carbondale: Southern Illinois University Press. [Published in three series as *The Early Works* (EW), *The Middle Works* (MW), and *The Later Works* (LW). "LW.1.14," for example, refers to *The Later Works*, volume 1, page 14. The pagination of the print edition has been preserved in *The Collected Works of John Dewey, 1882–1953: The Electronic Edition*, ed. Larry A. Hickman (1996). Charlottesville, VA: InteLex.]
Garrison, Jim, ed. (1995). *The New Scholarship on Dewey.* Dordrecht, The Netherlands: Kluwer Academic.
Hickman, Larry A. (1990). *John Dewey's Pragmatic Technology.* Bloomington: Indiana University Press.
Rockefeller, Steven C. (1991). *John Dewey: Religious Faith and Democratic Humanism.* New York: Columbia University Press.
Schilpp, Paul Arthur. (1939). *The Philosophy of John Dewey.* Evanston, IL: Northwestern University.
Westbrook, Robert B. (1991). *John Dewey and American Democracy.* Ithaca, NY: Cornell University Press.

LARRY A. HICKMAN

DEWEY, MELVIL (1851–1931)

An educational reformer and librarian, Melvil Dewey was born in Adams Centre, New York, on December 10, 1851 (a "decimal" date, he later boasted to friends), the fifth and last child of Joel and Eliza Greene Dewey. He attended rural local schools and early in life determined that his "destiny" was to become a "reformer" in educating the masses. In September 1870, he enrolled in Amherst College in Massachusetts.

In 1872, Dewey began working in the college library. There he discovered a site for his reforming interests, which by that time had also extended to simplified spelling, use of shorthand, and metric conversion. After he graduated in 1874, Amherst College hired Dewey to manage the library and reclassify the collections. For two years Dewey worked out a new scheme that superimposed a system of decimals on a structure of knowledge first outlined by Sir Francis Bacon and later modified by William Torrey Harris. In 1876, Dewey copyrighted the "decimal classification," moved to

Melvil Dewey. (Library of Congress)

Boston, and in the summer of 1876 helped found the Spelling Reform Association, the Metric Bureau, and the American Library Association (ALA). He also became managing editor of a new periodical—*Library Journal*—which was introduced in October 1876 at the first ALA conference. For each organization, Dewey also authored a constitution and served as the first secretary, a post from which he exercised close control.

Lacking sufficient capital to push for reforms, however, Dewey soon merged the treasuries of all of these organizations into a single account and (without informing any of them) used that account as collateral against which to borrow money to fund initiatives that he was pushing in each. He continued this practice as president of the private Readers and Writers Economy Company (RWEC) that he started in 1879. In 1880, when other RWEC investors discovered what he was doing, they obtained a court injunction that denied him access to these funds. Because the injunction prevented him from accessing the accounts of reform organizations he had founded,

he had to tell them about his unorthodox business practices. An out-of-court settlement enabled him to restore access to organizational treasuries, but by that time "Dui" (in 1879 he had changed the spelling of his last name to a more simplified, phonetically accurate form) had lost substantial credibility with all of the organizations. In March 1881, he established the Library Bureau and, as president, resumed efforts to increase the efficiency of library services and to advance spelling and metric reform.

In May 1883, "Dewey" became librarian-in-chief at Columbia College, an all-male institution, and, at the urging of his new employers, reverted to the original spelling of his name. Quickly implementing changes that he had been marketing through the Library Bureau, Dewey consolidated, by 1887, more than fifty thousand poorly cataloged and lightly used volumes housed in nine separate campus locations into a central facility classified by the decimal system. In January of that year, Dewey opened the world's first library school, and against the opposition of many faculty members and most of the university board members, he included seventeen women in the first class of twenty students. The friction he caused by this and other acts eventually led Dewey to accept an offer in December 1888 from the Regents of the University of the State of New York (USNY) to become their secretary and the New York State librarian. All parties also agreed to let Dewey move the library school with him to Albany.

As secretary, Dewey crafted his office into a powerful force to lobby the legislature for higher education, to increase funding for New York libraries, and to eliminate bogus diploma mills. He also began to use the growing number of public libraries in New York as sites where USNY instructors would teach courses that would enable local residents to obtain a USNY degree. To help with this endeavor, he organized the New York Library Association in 1890, set up extension sites in public libraries, and created departments within the State Library that provided traveling and interlibrary loan services and issued bibliographies of "best books" recommended for purchase by local libraries. In 1892, Dewey convinced the legislature to provide matching grants to the public libraries of New York if their collections passed inspection by a State Library employee. Because he irritated a number of politicians in the process of pushing for all these reforms, he also became an obstacle to efforts to merge New York's separately run common school and higher education systems. In part to remove himself from unification politics and in part because he wanted to avoid charges of conflict of interest (for helping a family member whose proprietary school operated in violation of a university charter that Dewey had responsibility for enforcing), he resigned as secretary of the USNY in 1899. However, he remained the state librarian.

While in Albany, Dewey did not neglect his other reform interests. As president of the American Library Association in 1893, he organized an annual conference for the Chicago World's Fair that exhibited a 5,000-title "model library" that his New York Library School students and faculty had put together. He then got the U.S. Bureau of Education to publish the model library as a bibliographic guide that librarians across the country could obtain as a government document. In the 1890s, his Library Bureau also developed a card-index system that reduced record-keeping costs for banks and insurance companies. Most of the money Dewey realized by this venture he rolled back into other reforms, including a private Lake Placid Club that he and his wife Annie started in 1894 as an exclusive rest and recreation facility in the Adirondack Mountains. From the beginning, however, the club admitted no Jews or ethnic or racial minorities. In 1905, several prominent New York City Jews protested, and under the pressure, Dewey resigned as state librarian. About the same time, several library school alumnae and ALA women threatened to bring a vote of censure against Dewey for sexual harassment of females at ALA conferences. In 1906, they forced him out of active ALA participation.

Dewey then channeled his efforts to improve the Lake Placid Club, which in the next twenty years grew from a central clubhouse to a 10,000-acre complex with scores of buildings, five golf courses, and twenty-one tennis courts. The club also cultivated winter sports and by 1930 had become so popular as a site that the International Olympic Committee chose the village of Lake Placid to host the 1932 Winter Olympics. By that time, Dewey had started a second club in Florida with the same exclusionary rules as its northern counterpart. All assets from both clubs were left to the Lake Placid Education Foundation, an organization Dewey and his wife had established to carry on reform efforts in areas such as metric conversion and simplified spelling.

In the twentieth century, the decimal classification system that Dewey copyrighted in 1876 (and which had gone through several editions) became the common organizing system for hundreds of thousands of libraries of all types in the United States and throughout the world. In addition, the jurisdictional boundaries of library science that he had defined in the late nineteenth century became a formal professional structure. This system gave a privileged position to information process over content and focused on developing the library as an information agency where library professionals exercise the expertise and management skills that are necessary to run it efficiently. The American Library Association that he helped to found grew into the largest such association in the world, and the bibliographies of "best books" that he fostered evolved into a system of guides upon which librarians relied to develop their collections. Finally, his activities as secretary for the University of the State of New York significantly improved the quality of higher education in New York and became a model that other state systems emulated. Dewey died in Florida on December 26, 1931.

See also: CATALOGING AND KNOWLEDGE ORGANIZATION; LIBRARIES, HISTORY OF; LIBRARY ASSOCIATIONS AND CONSORTIA.

Bibliography

Comaromi, John Phillip. (1976). *The Eighteen Editions of the Dewey Decimal Classification.* Albany, NY: Forest Press.
Dawe, Grosvenor. (1932). *Melvil Dewey, Seer: Inspirer: Doer.* Lake Placid, NY: Lake Placid Club.
Garrison, Dee. (1978). *Apostles of Culture: The Public Librarian and American Society, 1876–1920.* New York: Free Press.
Rider, Fremont. (1944). *Melvil Dewey.* Chicago: American Library Association.
Stevenson, Gordon, and Kramer-Greene, Judith, eds. (1983). *Melvil Dewey: The Man and the Classification.* Albany, NY: Forest Press.
Vann, Sarah K., ed. (1978). *Melvil Dewey: His Enduring Presence in Librarianship.* Littleton, CO: Libraries Unlimited, Inc.
Wiegand, Wayne A. (1986). *The Politics of an Emerging Profession: The American Library Association, 1876–1917.* Westport, CT: Greenwood Press.

Wiegand, Wayne A. (1996). *Irrepressible Reformer: A Biography of Melvil Dewey*. Chicago: American Library Association.

WAYNE A. WIEGAND

DIFFUSION OF INNOVATIONS AND COMMUNICATION

The diffusion of an innovation is the spread of a product, process, or idea perceived as new, through communication channels, among the members of a social system over time. Innovations can be a new product or output, a new process or way of doing something, or a new idea or concept. The "newness" of an innovation is subjective, determined by the potential adopter.

Diffusion Processes

Generally, the diffusion, or cumulative adoption, of an innovation over time follows an S-curve: that is, slowing growing initially, then accumulating quickly, then flattening out as the maximum level of adoption is reached. Portions of this diffusion curve (i.e., standard deviations of the normal curve) can be characterized as types of adopters. The first 2.5 percent of adopters within a social system are innovators, the next 13.5 percent are early adopters, the next 34 percent are early majority, the next 34 percent are late majority, and the final 16 percent are laggards. Innovators and early adopters are usually distinguished by high levels of "innovativeness," a general disposition toward change and trying new things, as well as higher education and higher income, among other factors.

Diffusion and adoption can be measured in a variety of ways: number or percentage of adopters at a certain time, number or percentage of organizational units adopting, average duration of usage, number of innovation components adopted, number of units sold or implemented, level of system usage (such as number of log-ons, messages sent, files stored, records processed), level of satisfaction, acceptance, diversity of planned uses, number of new uses, and so on.

Crucial to all diffusion patterns is the achievement of a "critical mass," or the number of adopters sufficient to foster sustained adoption beyond that point. This concept of critical mass is especially relevant to interactive communication innovations, such as the telephone or electronic mail. This is because the value of the overall system (the telephone system, the Internet) grows exponentially as each additional user adopts, so that later adopters perceive and obtain much greater value than do early adopters. Further, with communication innovations, there are typically competing channels already in place, so that early adopters have to use multiple channels while non-adopters, or late adopters, have to choose only one of the competing channels. Thus, it is important to provide early adopters extra incentives, or to target clusters of early adopters who have special needs for, or who can gain particular benefits from, the new innovation. Unless critical mass is achieved early, the new communication channel will likely falter. Indeed, considering time as a crucial element of diffusion, different innovations may take very different lengths of time to achieve widespread adoption. For example, in the United States, it took more than half a century to obtain broad residential adoption of the telephone, while compact disc has been quickly adopted as the standard for audio music recording and distribution.

An intriguing extension of critical mass is the concept of adoption thresholds. The idea here is that each individual has a (possibly variable) threshold for adopting a particular innovation. From a social and critical mass perspective, initial adopters have low thresholds—they may have sufficient resources, high innovativeness, unique relative advantages, and low need for social influence. Thus, they are likely to be innovators and early adopters within their social systems. Later adopters have higher thresholds, but, as more and more innovators adopt the innovation, these higher thresholds are more likely to be met. Thus, as initial innovators adopt, those close to them in the social network will now have achieved their just-slightly-higher thresholds, and also adopt. This in turn makes it more likely that others with even-slightly-higher thresholds will soon adopt. The implication here is that innovation implementers must be able to identify those with low initial thresholds and enable those to communicate soon after with those having slightly higher thresholds.

There are several interim stages in the adoption decision process: knowledge or awareness of the innovation, persuasion (reactions to and evaluations of the innovation), decision (to obtain, purchase, try out), implementation (acquiring, adjusting, applying, including a "fair trial" period), and confirmation (including public display of the adoption, and recommending the innovation to others).

Within organizations, there are five major stages as well: agenda-setting (a general definition of the initial rationale or problem statement, which may be more or less "rational" or well-informed), matching (alternative solutions are identified, evaluated, and compared to the agenda), redefining (the attributes of the innovation are defined relative to the needs of the organization, but the alternative solutions may also lead to recasting the initial agenda), structuring and interconnecting (where elements of the current social system and/or the innovation are redesigned to integrate the innovation within appropriate procedures and processes, through both formal and informal negotiations and peer pressure), and routinization (where the innovation becomes a part of normal organizational operations).

There are, of course, many other factors influencing the success, failure, or rate of diffusion of an organizational innovation. These include the justification for the initial agenda rationale; the geographic location and closeness of potential adopters; the complexity, size, and culture of the organization (decentralized, small organizations may be much better at initiating innovations, while centralized, large organizations may be more successful at implementing them); the personalities and power bases of the organizational actors; changes in political agendas, resources, and goals that affect the nature and evaluation of the innovation; different stakeholders becoming activated by different stages in the lifecycle of the innovation; external organizational environments, including changing competitors, regulatory environments, economic resources; and technological changes, rendering a current innovation incompatible or inappropriate.

Indeed, there are many important examples where the wider economic, regulatory, and social environment heavily determine the success or failure of an innovation. "Positive feedbacks," "positive network externalities," or "complementarities" are, respectively, benefits associated with an innovation that accrue to later adopters rather than early adopters, benefits that increase the value of early versus later innovations, and serv-

ices and other innovations that arise due to the success and features of an earlier innovation. For example, the Microsoft Windows operating system has extensive positive externalities because, since it is the dominant operating system, most other companies design their software applications for use under Windows. This, in turn, raises the value and market centrality of Windows. Another example is the design of the typewriter (and, thus, computer keyboard) keys. The QWERTY system (named because of the sequence of the top left-hand row of letters) was initially designed to slow down typing speed because the early metal typewriter mechanisms would become jammed if pressed too quickly. By the time that manufacturing innovations allowed for faster mechanisms (especially consider modern computer keyboards), the infrastructure surrounding the typing industry (manufacturing processes, repair, training, secretarial skills) made it too expensive (socially, organizationally, personally) to switch to a different, more efficient keyboard layout (such as the DVORAK design). Thus, initial adoption patterns can heavily constrain or influence later diffusion (an example of path dependence), often institutionalizing initial innovations that are in fact less technologically or socially innovative or effective.

Another time-based factor in the diffusion process is the "chasm" between early and later innovation design and adoption. Initial development of an innovation tends to be technology-driven, as widespread uses and critical mass have not yet been established. Here, developers attempt to design sufficient performance, features, and quality to satisfy early adopters, who are often willing to pay more (and become initial subscribers), and to tolerate poorer design, in return for new technological features and the status of "innovators" and "early adopters." However, "early" and "late" majority adopters are not typically interested in the technological aspects, but are more concerned about relative advantage, compatibility, and low complexity. Thus, the technology itself is not perceived as important; rather, usable devices, commodities, services, and content become more valued. The challenge for the developer and implementer, then, is to cross this "chasm," knowing when to emphasize technology and when to emphasize the general marketplace.

E-mail, one of the most rapidly diffused innovations of the late-twentieth century, continues to change with the introduction of products such as 3Com's "Audrey" Internet appliance, which became available in January 2001 and offers three ways to send e-mail: typical message, handwritten message, and voice message. (Reuters NewMedia Inc./Corbis)

Because of these several stages in the individual and organizational adoption process, and the wide and complex range of factors affecting diffusion, an innovation may not be rejected initially, but still may be discontinued at any stage of the diffusion process.

Innovation Attributes

Generally, potential adopters assess five main attributes of an innovation. Relative advantage is the extent to which the innovation provides greater benefits, and/or fewer costs, than the current product or process. Compatibility is the extent to which the innovation fits in with existing habits, norms, procedures, and technical standards. Trialability is the extent to which potential adopters can try out components, instead of the entire innovation, or can try out the innovation through pilot demonstrations or trial periods, but

decide to return to their prior conditions without great cost. Complexity is the extent to which potential adopters perceive the innovation as difficult to understand or use. Finally, observability or communicability is the extent to which potential adopters can observe or find out about the properties and benefits of the innovation. Every innovation has positive and negative aspects of each of these attributes.

Consider, for example, electronic mail (e-mail). Clearly, a general critical mass of users has been achieved, especially within communities of certain online information services, but certain subgroups have low overall levels of adoption so would not experience critical mass. E-mail has relative advantages over a face-to-face interaction because one can send the message at any time, regardless of where the other person is or how difficult it would be to actually meet up with them. To many people, e-mail is still somewhat incompatible with traditional social norms such as sending holiday greetings, but it is highly compatible with other work and computer applications. With trial subscriptions or even free e-mail now offered, it is relatively inexpensive to try out electronic messaging, but one still has to have purchased a modem and communication software. Regardless of how simple advertisements make using e-mail appear, the various functions and interconnections with other applications still make e-mail fairly complex to understand and use. It is fairly easy to communicate the basic features, uses, and benefits of e-mail to others, but it might be hard to actually observe some of those benefits, or even one's own e-mail, without taking the time and effort to check the e-mail system. However, developments such as accessing one's e-mail by WebTV or a standalone e-mail appliance for the kitchen will make the benefits of e-mail more compatible and observable and less complex.

A major development in the conceptualization of an innovation was the realization that an innovation is not a fixed, static, objective entity. Rather, it is contextual, flexible, and dynamic. It may be adapted and reinvented. A reinvention is the degree to which an innovation is changed by the adopter(s) in the process of adoption and implementation, after its original development. A reinvention may involve a new use or application of an already adopted innovation, or an alteration in the innovation to fit a current use. Reinventions may be categorized based on intentionality—whether they are planned (intentional) or vicarious (learning by other's mistakes)—and source—whether they are reactive (solving a problem generated by the innovation itself) or secondary (solving unintended consequences elsewhere in the organization or innovation due to the reinvention). The four levels of reinvention include unsuccessful adoption (low integration), successful adoption (clockwork systems), local adaptation (expanding systems), and systemwide adaptation (high-integration systems).

One significant distinction within organizational settings is between administrative (managing organization processes) and technical (specific manufacturing or service processes) innovations, each fostered by different influences and each having different consequences. Another distinction, often found in consumer studies of innovations, is the extent to which the innovation is perceived as being part of a "cluster" of already adopted products, processes, or ideas. A marketer or implementer can attempt to determine these innovation clusters, and then position the proposed innovation as having relative advantage to, yet compatibility with, things already familiar and valued. So, for example, while designers of desktop videoconferencing thought that users would perceive this innovation as similar to face-to-face interaction, they typically perceive it as more similar to the telephone. Thus, design, marketing, implementation, and pricing efforts should take this into consideration.

Another major factor influencing both the initial agenda rationales, relative advantage, observability, and management of organizational innovations is the extent to which the innovation is information-based as opposed to material-based. Information is difficult to completely own because it is easily copied and distributed to others. Furthermore, some uses and values of information are unpredictable, and can only be determined through usage by specific adopters. Because all the benefits of information-based innovations cannot easily be appropriated by the innovator, it is not economically rational to fully invest in innovations. Thus, the legal and economic infrastructure of copyright, patents, licenses, disclosure agreements, royalties, and so on has been developed to help guarantee innovators that their ideas, and the benefits associated with them, accrue to the developers during a specific period. Furthermore, it is difficult to identify, much less estimate, all the long-term benefits associated with information-based innovations, so initial agenda rationales based on traditional return-on-investment calculations will suppress the adoption of many innovations. Thus, specific institutions have arisen, such as universities, government and other funding agencies, incubator organizations, and "skunkworks" in protected units within organizations, to foster the development of innovations.

Communication Channels

Communication channels also play an important role in diffusion. Because the innovation is a new product, process, or idea, it must be communicated to potential adopters in order for them to assess its attributes and decide whether to try out and eventually adopt it. Very broadly speaking, mediated communication and interpersonal communication play complementary, but different, roles. Electronic mass media channels such as television and radio are useful for raising awareness about the innovation, but cannot provide much detail (except for specialty radio programs). They can provide images and brand name identification, helping the attributes of compatibility and observability. Print mass media channels such as newspapers and magazines (and, to some extent, the Internet) are useful for explaining conceptual and technical details, helping out with the attributes of relative advantage and complexity. New media such as the World Wide Web can provide interesting mixtures of image, explanation, and demonstrations, thus also fostering trialability.

Interpersonal communication is especially important in changing opinions and reducing uncertainty about the innovation, as potential adopters turn to credible and important sources to provide first-hand experiences and legitimization of the new idea. Much innovation research shows the significant role that social influence, peer pressure, and social learning plays in affecting not only the final adoption decision, but also the evaluation of the attributes of the innovation. This is particularly important when initial relative advantages are low (high adoption costs or low observability), critical mass has not yet been achieved (thus representing higher learning and adoption costs for early adopters), or when the innovation is not obviously compatible with current social or group norms. In such cases, certain innovation roles become crucial.

The "cosmopolite" is a member of a social system who travels more, communicates and uses the media more, attends more conferences, and is generally more aware of the external environment, than other members. Thus, the cosmopolite is a valuable source to the social system for innovations. Within particular groups or organizational units, this role may be filled by a "technical gatekeeper," who seeks out and brings into the group relevant facts and practices, freeing the rest of the group to focus on the group's task but also keeping it informed of innovative ideas. Within a social system, the "opinion leader" plays the valuable role of evaluating and legitimizing new ideas, especially normative ideas that fit in with the general social context of the group. The opinion leader must be fairly similar to the rest of the group in order to represent the central norms and values of the group, but tends to be just slightly more educated and experienced, and receives more communication, than the other members. Different types of innovations or social norms may be regulated by different opinion leaders. For example, political, religious, and agricultural innovations would probably be discussed and evaluated by different (if somewhat overlapping) social groupings and opinion leaders. Thus, an important diffusion strategy is to identify the appropriate opinion leader for the type of innovation, communicate the relative advantage and compatibility of the innovation for that social system, and then provide incentives and communication channels for the opinion leader to diffuse the idea to other members.

Radical or "taboo" innovations are highly incompatible with the norms and practices of a social system, so an opinion leader will quickly reject such suggestions, even presuming the leader will have been exposed to the idea. Thus, the social "isolate" (who is not heavily constrained by group norms) or the cosmopolite who has many "weak ties" (infrequent, somewhat distant, or diverse communication with others outside the social group) are necessary to ensure that social groups become exposed to, and eventually try out, innovations. For example, highly traditional or conservative groups are unlikely to find out about, much less try, radical or taboo innovations, largely because of their social structure and use of communication channels. A well-known example is the adoption of family planning within Korean villages. The concept was so taboo that husbands and wives did not communicate about it, and it certainly was not discussed in public meetings or media. However, relatively isolated individual "mother's clubs" with innovative leaders began talking about and practicing family planning, motivated by face-to-face communication with change agents. Adoption spread within the boundaries of these small social systems, and, with increasing evidence of relative advantage, began to diffuse through the more-normative mother's clubs. However, clubs that did not have the active support of their opinion leaders were either late adopters or nonadopters.

The diffusion of innovations is a rich, complex, challenging, and rewarding area for communication and information research and practice.

See also: INTERNET AND THE WORLD WIDE WEB; ORGANIZATIONAL COMMUNICATION; TECHNOLOGY, ADOPTION AND DIFFUSION OF.

Bibliography

Arthur, W. Brian. (1990). "Positive Feedbacks in the Economy." *Scientific American* 262(February):92–99.

Brown, Lawrence. (1981). *Innovation Diffusion: A New Perspective*. London: Methuen Press.

Damanpour, Fabriz. (1991). "Organizational Innovation: A Meta-Analysis of Effects of Determinants and Moderators." *Academy of Management Journal* 34:555–590.

Gattiker, Urs. (1990). *Technology Management in Organizations*. Newbury Park, CA: Sage Publications.

Hagerstrand, Torsten. (1967). *Innovation Diffusion as a Spatial Process*. Chicago: University of Chicago Press.

Hiltz, S. Roxanne, and Johnson, Kenneth. (1989). "Measuring Acceptance of Computer-Mediated Communication Systems." *Journal of the American Society for Information Science* 40:386–397.

Kimberly, John. (1981). "Managerial Innovation." In *Handbook of Organizational Design*, Vol. 1, eds. Peter Nystrom and William Starbuck. New York: Oxford University Press.

Kuczmarski, Thomas. (1992). *Managing New Products: The Power of Innovation*, 2nd edition. Englewood Cliffs, NJ: Prentice-Hall.

Markus, M. Lynne. (1987). "Toward a 'Critical Mass' Theory of Interactive Media: Universal Access, Interdependence and Diffusion." *Communication Research* 14:491–511.

Moore, Gary, and Benbasat, Izak. (1991). "Development of an Instrument to Measure the Perceptions of Adopting an Information Technology Innovation." *Information Systems Research* 2(3):192–222.

Norman, Donald A. (1998). *The Invisible Computer: Why Good Products Can Fail, the Personal Computer Is So Complex, and Information Appliances are the Solution.* Cambridge, MA: MIT Press.

Rice, Ronald E., and Johnson, Bonnie McDaniel. (1987). *Managing Organizational Innovation.* New York: Columbia University Press.

Rogers, Everett M. (1996). *Diffusion of Innovations,* 4th edition. New York: Free Press.

Rosegger, Gerhard. (1986). *The Economics of Production and Innovation,* 2nd edition. Oxford, Eng.: Pergamon.

Senge, Peter. (1994). *The Fifth Discipline Field Book: Strategies and Tools for Building a Learning Organization.* New York: Doubleday Currency.

Sunbo, Jon. (1998). *The Theory of Innovation.* Cheltenham, Eng.: Edward Elgar.

Tornatzky, Louis G., and Klein, Katherine J. (1982). "Innovation Characteristics and Innovation Adoption-Implementation: A Meta-Analysis of Findings." *IEEE Transactions on Engineering Management* 29(1):28–45.

Valente, Thomas. (1995). *Network Models of the Diffusion of Innovations.* Cresskill, NJ: Hampton Press.

Valente, Thomas, and Davis, Rebecca. (1999). "Accelerating the Diffusion of Innovations Using Opinion Leaders." *Annals of the American Academy of Political and Social Science* 566(November):55–67.

RONALD E. RICE

DIGITAL COMMUNICATION

In order to understand the notion of digitizing information, it must first be understood that everything in nature, including the sounds and images one wishes to record or transmit, is originally analog. The second thing to be understood is that analog works very well. In fact, a first-generation analog recording can be a better representation of the original images than a first-generation digital recording. This is because digital is a coded approximation of analog. With enough bandwidth, a first-generation analog videotape recorder (VTR) can record the more "perfect" copy.

Binary Systems

Digital is a binary language represented by zeros (an "off" state) and ones (an "on" state), so the signal either exists ("on") or does not exist ("off"). Even with low signal power, if the transmitted digital signal is higher that the background noise level, a perfect picture and sound can be obtained—"on" is "on" no matter what the signal strength.

Digital uses its own language that is based on the terms "bits" and "bytes." Bit is short for binary digit and is the smallest data unit in a digital system. A bit is either a single 1 or a single 0. A byte consists of a series of bits. The most common length for a byte "word" is 8 bits, although there can be other lengths (e.g., 1, 2, 10, 16, 24, 32).

In an 8-bit system, there are 256 discrete values, ranging from 0 to 255. The mathematics are simple because the number of discrete values is equal to the number 2 (as in binary) raised to the power of the number of bits. In this case, 2 raised to the power of 8 equals 256. The two extreme bytes in the 8-bit system are 00000000 and 11111111, which are calculated as follows:

$$00000000$$
$$= 0 \cdot (2^7) + 0 \cdot (2^6) + 0 \cdot (2^5) + 0 \cdot (2^4) + 0(2^3) + 0 \cdot (2^2) + 0 \cdot (2^1) + 0 \cdot (2^0)$$
$$= 0 \cdot (128) + 0 \cdot (64) + 0 \cdot (32) + 0 \cdot (16) + 0 \cdot (8) + 0 \cdot (4) + 0 \cdot (2) + 0 \cdot (1)$$
$$= 0 + 0 + 0 + 0 + 0 + 0 + 0 + 0$$
$$= 0.$$

and

$$11111111$$
$$= 1 \cdot (2^7) + 1 \cdot (2^6) + 1 \cdot (2^5) + 1 \cdot (2^4) + 1(2^3) + 1 \cdot (2^2) + 1 \cdot (2^1) + 1 \cdot (2^0)$$
$$= 1 \cdot (128) + 1 \cdot (64) + 1 \cdot (32) + 1 \cdot (16) + 1 \cdot (8) + 1 \cdot (4) + 1 \cdot (2) + 1 \cdot (1)$$
$$= 128 + 64 + 32 + 16 + 8 + 4 + 2 + 1$$
$$= 255$$

An example of an 8-bit value between the two extremes is 10100011, which is calculated as follows:

$$10100011$$
$$= 1 \cdot (2^7) + 0 \cdot (2^6) + 1 \cdot (2^5) + 0 \cdot (2^4) + 0(2^3) + 0 \cdot (2^2) + 1 \cdot (2^1) + 1 \cdot (2^0)$$
$$= 1 \cdot (128) + 0 \cdot (64) + 1 \cdot (32) + 0 \cdot (16) + 0 \cdot (8) + 0 \cdot (4) + 1 \cdot (2) + 1 \cdot (1)$$
$$= 128 + 0 + 32 + 0 + 0 + 0 + 2 + 1$$
$$= 163.$$

On January 29, 2001, Matsushita unveiled the digital video camcorder Digicam NV-MX2000, which features a set of three 380,000-pixel CCDs (light-sensitive picture elements) on its image sensor and a 2.85-28.5 mm zoom lens equipped with an optical image stabilizer system.(AFP/Corbis)

The more bits in the byte, the more distinct the values. For example, a gray scale can be represented by 1 bit. This would give the scale two values (2 raised to the power of 1): 0 or 1. Therefore, the gray scale would consist of white and black. A 2-bit gray scale has four values (2 raised to the power of 2): 0, 1, 2, and 3. In this case, 0 = 0 percent white (black), 1 = 33 percent white, 2 = 67 percent white, and 3 = 100 percent white. As the number of bits is increased, a more accurate gray scale is obtained. For example, a 10-bit system has 1,024 discrete values (2 raised to the power of 10), providing a more detailed gray scale. With each additional bit, the number of discrete values is doubled, as is the number of values for the gray scale.

Digital Video and Audio

In digital video, black is not at value 0 and white is neither at value 255 for 8-bit video nor 1,023 for 10-bit video. To add some buffer space and to allow for "superblack" (which is at 0 IRE while regular black is at 7.5 IRE), black is at value 16 while white is at value 235 for 8-bit video. For 10-bit video, black is at value 64 while white is at value 940.

While digital is an approximation of the analog world—the actual analog value is assigned to its closest digital value—human perception has a hard time recognizing the fact that it is being cheated. While a few expert observers might be able to tell that something did not look right in 8-bit video, 10-bit video looks perfect to the human eye. Digitizing audio, however, is a different story. Human ears are not as forgiving as human eyes; in audio, most people require at least 16-bit resolution, while some experts argue that 20-bit, or ultimately even 24-bit, technology needs to become standard before recordings will be able to match the sensitivity of human hearing.

To transform a signal from analog to digital, the analog signal must go through the processes of sampling and quantization. The better the sampling and quantization, the better the digital image will represent the analog image.

Sampling is how often a device (such as an analog-to-digital converter) samples (or looks at) an analog signal. The sampling rate is usually given in a figure such as 48 kHz (48,000 samples per second) for audio and 13.5 MHz (13.5 million samples per second) for video. For television pictures, 8-bit or 10-bit sampling systems are normally used; for audio, 16-bit or 20-bit sampling systems are common, though 24-bit sampling systems are also used. The International Telecommunications Union–Radiocommunication (ITU-R) 601 standard defines the sampling of video components based on 13.5 MHz, and the Audio Engineering Society/European Broacasting Union (AES/EBU) defines sampling based on 44.1 and 48 kHz for audio.

Quantization, which involves assigning a more limited scale of values to the sample, usually occurs after the signal has been sampled. Consequently, it defines how many levels (bits per sample) the analog signal will have to force itself into to produce a digital approximation of the original signal. As noted earlier, a 10-bit digital signal has more levels (thus higher resolution) than an 8-bit signal.

Errors at this stage of digitizing (called quantization errors) occur because quantizing a signal only results in a digital approximation of the original signal. Errors can also occur because of loss of signal or unintended changes to a signal, such as when a bit changes its state from "off" to "on" or from "on" to "off." Just how large the error will be is determined by when that change occurred and how long the change lasted. An error can last briefly enough not to even affect one bit, or it can last long enough to affect a number of bits, entire bytes, multiple bytes, or even seconds of video and audio.

Errors

In an 8-bit byte, for example, the 1 on the far right represents the value 1. It is the least significant bit (LSB). If there is an error that changes this bit from 1 ("on") to 0 ("off"), the value of the byte changes from 163 to 162—a very minor difference. Error increases as problems occur with bits more toward the left of the byte word.

In contrast, the 1 on the left that represents the value 128 is called the most significant bit (MSB). An error that changes this bit from 1 (on) to 0 (off) changes the value of the byte from 163 to 35—a very major difference. If this represented

the gray scale, the sample has changed from 64-percent white to only 14-percent white.

If the error occurs in the LSB, chances are that the effect will be lost in the noise and will not even be noticed. An MSB error may result in a pop in the sound or an unwanted dot in the picture. If the error occurs in a sync word (i.e., the part of the digital signal that controls how a picture is put together), a whole line or frame could be lost. With compressed video, an error in just the right place could disrupt not only one frame but a long string of frames.

One of the benefits of digital is that through a process called "error management," large errors can become practically invisible. When things go wrong in the digital world, bits are corrupted and the message can become distorted. The effect of these distortions varies with the nature of the digital system. With computers, there is a huge sensitivity to errors, particularly in instructions. A single error in the right place, and it becomes time to reboot. With video and audio, the effect is more subjective. Error management can be broken down into four stages: error avoidance, error detection, error correction, and error concealment.

Error management, error avoidance, and redundancy coding constitute a sort of preprocessing in anticipation of the errors to come. Much of this is simply good engineering, such as preventative maintenance for errors. For example, technicians check to make sure that there is enough transmit power and a strong enough antenna to ensure an adequate signal-to-noise ratio at the receiver.

Next comes redundancy coding, without which error detection would be impossible. Detection is one of the most important steps in error management. It must be very reliable, because if an error is undetected, it does not matter how effective the other error management techniques are.

Redundancy codes can be extremely complex, but the simple parity check illustrates the principle. As with all redundancy codes, the parity check adds bits to the original data in such a way that errors can be recognized at the receiver. Certain bits in a byte, when their representative values (1 for "on" or 0 for "off") are added together, must always be an odd or an even number. If the receiver sees that the redundancy code is incorrect (i.e., odd when it should be even, or vice versa), the receiver can request a retransmission of that part of the data.

Of course, every system has its limits. Large errors cannot be corrected. However, it is possible to interleave data (i.e., send the data out of sequence) during transmission or recording to improve the chances of a system to correct any errors.

No matter how elegant the coding, errors will occur that cannot be corrected. The only option is to conceal them. With digital audio, the simple fix is to approximate a lost sample by interpolating (averaging) a value from samples on either side. A more advanced method makes a spectral analysis of the sound and inserts samples with the same spectral characteristics. If there are too many errors to conceal, the only choice is to mute.

With digital video, missing samples can be approximated from adjacent samples in the same line or adjacent lines, or from samples in previous and succeeding fields. The technique works because there is a lot of redundancy in a video image. If the video is compressed, there will be less redundancy, so concealment may not work as well. When both correction and concealment capabilities are exceeded in video, the options are either to freeze the last frame or to drop to black.

To make digital video more affordable for both professionals and consumers, compression is used. The trade-off is quality because compression "throws away" some of the signal. For example, high definition is compressed to approximately 18 Mbits per second (18 million bits per second) for digital television transmission, a compression ratio of almost 55:1.

There are two general types of compression algorithms: lossless and lossy. As the name suggests, a lossless algorithm gives back the original data bit-for-bit on decompression. Lossless processes can be applied safely to a checkbook accounting program, but their compression ratios are usually low—on the order of 2:1. In practice, these ratios are unpredictable and depend heavily on the type of data in the files. Alas, pictures are not as predictable as text and bank records, and lossless techniques have only limited effectiveness with video.

Virtually all video compression uses lossy video compression systems. These use lossless techniques where they can, but the really big savings come from throwing things away. To do this, the image is processed or "transformed" into two groups of data. One group will, ideally, contain all the important information. The other gets all of the unimportant information. Only the important data needs to be kept and transmitted.

Lossy compression systems take the performance of the human eye into account as they decide what information to place in the important pile and which to discard in the unimportant pile. They throw away things that the eye does not notice or will not be too upset about losing. Because human perception of fine color details is limited, for example, chroma resolution can be reduced by factors of two, four, eight, or more, depending on the application.

Video compression also relies heavily on the correlation between adjacent picture elements. If television pictures consisted entirely of randomly valued pixels (noise), compression would not be possible. Fortunately, adjoining picture elements are more likely to be the same than they are to be different. Predictive coding relies on making an estimate of the value of the current pixel based on previous values for that location and other neighboring areas. The rules of the estimating game are stored in the decoder, and, for any new pixel, the encoder need only send the difference or error value between what the rules would have predicted and the actual value of the new element. The more accurate the prediction, the less data needs to be sent.

The motion of objects or the camera from one frame to the next complicates predictive coding, but it also opens up new compression possibilities. Fortunately, moving objects in the real world are somewhat predictable. They tend to move with inertia and in a continuous fashion. With the Motion Picture Experts Group (MPEG) standard, where picture elements are processed in blocks, quite a few bits can be saved if it can be predicted how a given block of pixels has moved from one frame to the next. By sending commands (motion vectors) that simply tell the decoder how to move a block of pixels that is already in its memory, resending of all the data associated with that block is avoided.

As long as compressed pictures are only going to be transmitted and viewed, compression encoders can assign lots of bits into the unimportant pile by exploiting the redundancy in successive frames. This is called "interframe" coding. If, on the other hand, the video is destined to undergo further processing such as enlargement or chromakey, some of those otherwise unimportant details may suddenly become important, and it may be necessary to spend more bits to accommodate what postproduction equipment can "see." To facilitate editing and other postprocessing, compression schemes that are intended for postproduction usually confine their efforts within a single frame and are called "intraframe." It takes more bits, but it is worth it.

Ratios

Ratios such as 4:2:2 and 4:1:1 are an accepted part of the jargon of digital video, a shorthand that is taken for granted and sometimes not adequately explained. With single-channel composite signals, such as the National Television System Committee (NTSC) and Phase Alternate Line (PAL) signals, digital sampling rates are synchronized at either two, three, or four times the subcarrier frequency. The shorthand for these rates is 2fsc, 3fsc, and 4fsc, respectively.

With three-channel component signals, the sampling shorthand becomes a ratio. The first number usually refers to the sampling rate that is used for the luminance signal, while the second and third numbers refer to the rates for the red and blue color-difference signals, respectively. Thus, a 14:7:7 system would be one in which a wideband luminance signal is sampled at 14 MHz and the narrower bandwidth color-difference signals are each sampled at 7 MHz.

As work on component digital systems evolved, the shorthand changed. At first, 4:2:2 referred to sampling luminance at 4fsc (about 14.3 MHz for NTSC) and color-difference signals sampled at half that rate, or 2fsc. Sampling schemes based on multiples of NTSC or PAL subcarrier frequency were soon abandoned in favor of a single sampling standard for both 525- and 625-line component systems. Nevertheless, the 4:2:2 shorthand remained.

In current usage, "4" usually represents the internationally agreed upon sampling frequency of 13.5 MHz. Other numbers represent corresponding fractions of that frequency. Thus, a 4:1:1 ratio describes a system with luminance sampled at 13.5 MHz and color-difference signals sampled at 3.375 MHz.

The shorthand continues to evolve. Contrary to what one might expect from the discussion above, the 4:2:0 ratio that is frequently seen in discussions of MPEG compression does not indicate a system without a blue color-difference component. Here, the shorthand describes a video stream in which there are only two color-difference samples (one red, one blue) for every four luminance samples. Unlike 4:1:1, however, the samples in 525-line systems do not come from the same line as luminance; they are averaged from two adjacent lines in the field. The idea was to provide a more even and averaged distribution of the reduced color information over the picture.

See also: CABLE TELEVISION, SYSTEM TECHNOLOGY OF; DIGITAL MEDIA SYSTEMS; RECORDING INDUSTRY, TECHNOLOGY OF; TELEVISION BROADCASTING, TECHNOLOGY OF.

Bibliography

Panasonic. (1999). *The Video Compression Book*. Los Angeles: Panasonic (Matsuchita Electronic Industrial Co., Ltd., Video Systems Division).

Silbergleid, Michael, and Pescatore, Mark J., eds. (2000). *The Guide to Digital Television*, 3rd edition. New York: United Entertainment Media.

MICHAEL SILBERGLEID
MARK J. PESCATORE

■ DIGITAL MEDIA SYSTEMS

The conversion from analog to digital technology is one of the most fundamental and dramatic changes in modern media. Digital technology is displacing analog at every stage of the production-distribution-exhibition (PDE) process. At the exhibition level, consumers already have a variety of digital devices in their homes, offices, and cars. The computer is the most prominent, but by no means the only, example; compact discs (CDs) have replaced vinyl records, and the digital cell telephone has displaced its analog predecessor. Handheld minicomputers or personal digital assistants (PDAs) are required technology for some executives; answering machines, still cameras, and home video cameras have all made the jump to the digital binary language of zeros and ones. At the production and distribution levels, most media sectors, including broadcast and cable television, the recording industry, and even print media, have been deeply involved in the process of converting to digital. This has all set the stage for what many see as the eventual melding, or convergence, of these previously distinct channels of communication.

There are a number of reasons for the switch to digital. In the analog world, reproduction and distribution of information usually requires some form of copying, such as making additional prints of films or copies of audiotapes. Every time an analog copy is made, however, the quality of the image or sound deteriorates. The more copying that is done from one generation to the next, the greater the loss in original fidelity. Digital communication does not suffer from this handicap. When the equipment is working properly, the last copy in the chain retains all the quality of the original. Converting information to the language of computers also makes it almost infinitely malleable. Audio, video, and textual information that are distinct in the real world are converted into the same currency of digital bits in the computer world, where they can be combined in ways that are limited only by the human imagination. Sights and sounds can be altered, enhanced, created, and destroyed.

Video Production

Traditional analog methods of electronically capturing, assembling, and storing images involved the use of either videotape or film. For image capture, digital cameras began replacing their analog predecessors in the 1990s. While the signals that they generate can be stored and edited on tape, disk storage, which is faster at accessing and transferring material, is usually preferred.

Editing analog videotape, as has been done in television news and entertainment, involves a laborious process of copying segments of images from the original master tape and assembling them into a coherent story, or package. The process requires a sequential, or linear, assembly of shots, like creating a railroad train by adding one car at a time. It does not allow the insertion of one car between two others, nor one scene between two existing shots, without re-editing the full piece. Digital, or nonlinear, editing frees the editor from this constraint. Shots can be arranged and rearranged like a giant jigsaw puzzle with little technical effort. Different compositions can be quickly attempted, discarded, or accepted. Televi-

sion news uses digital technology to increase dramatically the speed of creating video packages for the evening news.

Film Production

In the motion picture industry, 35-mm film is likely to remain the staple for major studio production and exhibition for many years, largely because of the superior quality of the analog image that is prized by most filmmakers. Nonetheless, many see a day when a large-screen, digital video format will displace film. Rather than making physical copies, or prints, of film for shipment to theaters, some see the instant electronic distribution of digital "films" to multiplexed screens around the world. Meanwhile, filmmakers make use of digital technology in a variety of other ways. Rough cuts, a kind of rough draft of a finished film, can be edited much more quickly using nonlinear editing, with the digital product serving as a guide for the splicing of film for the finished product. Computer-generated special effects are among the most easily recognized digital applications. Nearly any part of a movie or television show can be digitally created or transformed, extending the creative range of television and film artists. *Star Wars I: The Phantom Menace*, for example, featured extraterrestrial characters that were fabricated through the use of computer animation. In television and film, entire sets, the background setting for a program, can be generated digitally so that an actor or television news anchor appears to be standing in a forest or on a busy city street when in fact he or she is standing in an empty studio.

Home Video and Audio

The power of digital video production is available for home users as well. Digital still-cameras that store images on a disk instead of film are common. On home computers, these images can be cropped, sized, or otherwise altered in hundreds of ways before being printed or sent by e-mailed. Home computers that have the appropriate software can also be used to edit home video, shot on either digital or analog cameras. These digital home movies, edited using the same nonlinear techniques as those that are employed by professionals, can be stored on videotape and played in the family videocassette recorder (VCR). Consumers also can create their own video CDs.

The versatile CD has become the vehicle of choice for many applications. It is the primary medium for recorded music and commercial computer software, and it is increasingly being used in place of videotape for home viewing of theatrical films. In the latter case, manufacturers have adopted the term "DVD" (meaning either digital videodisc or digital versatile disc, depending on the manufacturer). The standard analog videotape player also has a digital companion in the personal video recorder (PVR), which uses computer hard drives to allow a viewer to record and watch a television program, with the full functionality of a VCR (including pause, rewind, and automatic commercial deletion), even while the program is being aired.

For the recording industry, CDs have been supplemented by several other digital technologies, including minidiscs, digital audiotape, and MP3 players that download music from the Internet.

Broadcast Television

The distribution of radio and television programming began migrating to a digital format in 1998 when television stations began their initial digital transmissions. The change means several things. Broadcasters, over time, have to give up their old analog frequencies for the new digital channels and invest hundreds of millions of dollars in new equipment. Because the traditional analog television set cannot use digital signals, every analog television set must eventually be replaced. Converter boxes that translate digital signals into usable analog signals will ease the transition, allowing consumers to make the change at their leisure.

There are a number of benefits for both broadcasters and the public. Digital images, coupled with high-resolution transmission formats, provide sharper, more detailed images. One of the applications of digital television technology is high-definition television (HDTV), which improves the clarity and detail of the home picture. High definition also changes the aspect ratio of television images from the 3 X 4 (three units high by four units wide) dimensions of analog sets to a wider 9 X 16 frame that mirrors the dimensions of a movie screen.

Through digital compression, broadcasters can squeeze more information into their signal and thereby offer new services. For example, programs

Multiple product uses are incorporated in Fuji Photo Film's FinePix40i (a 155-gram, 4.32 million pixel camera), which was unveiled in June 2000 and allows its user to listen to both high-quality MP3 music files using a smart media card and earphones and to use it as a standard compact digital camera. (Reuters NewMedia Inc./Corbis)

can be simultaneously broadcast in multiple languages for different audiences. Detailed textual information, such as baseball statistics that viewers can access on-screen during the game, can be fed with the normal programming. Broadcasters can also offer datacasting services, such as paging and Internet access, completely separate from traditional television programming. Digital compression also allows broadcasters to transmit multiple program channels, instead of just one.

Digital Radio

Radio broadcasting has lagged behind television in the migration to digital, but new industry standards for digital radio will, as with television, mean the eventual replacement of all analog receivers in homes and automobiles. Unlike television, however, digital radio will use the same channels as existing analog service, with broadcasters transmitting both digital and analog during the transition period. Conversion to digital means CD-quality sound and allows broadcasters to transmit information about the music, including title, artist, and label, for display on a small screen. Station call letters and formats are also available, and programmable receivers allow drivers to lock automatically onto successive regional jazz stations as they drive across the country. Digital radio technology can also datacast information such as stock market quotes, sports scores, and traffic updates.

In addition to traditional terrestrial broadcasters, nationally distributed satellite digital radio services have emerged. These subscription services beam dozens of audio channels from dedicated communications satellites. Similar to older cable audio services, the channels are divided into special-interest categories from country and western to jazz to opera. Web-based radio stations are also proliferating, and wireless receiving units for them are being developed.

Digital Cable

In the late 1990s, cable television operators began adding digital capacity to their systems, increasing channel capacity and interactivity. Just as in digital broadcasting, cable operators can take a channel that had carried one analog signal and use it to carry multiple digital signals. The increase in channel capacity has meant an increase in consumer program choices. The Discovery Channel, for example, created specialty channels for children, health, aviation, science, and other niche interests. Premium movie services such as Home Box Office and Encore also developed themed or multiplexed channels in categories such as mysteries, westerns, romance, and family entertainment. Digital technology means more pay-per-view movie choices as well. The cable and satellite industry envisions a digital future in which films will be placed on high-capacity servers and customers will be able to order those films whenever they want. Customers need only press a button on their remote control to invoke this video-on-demand (VOD) service. Moreover, the service will provide full VCR functionality; the subscriber will be able to start, stop, and rewind the movie at his or her convenience. Some people see more programming moving to this VOD model, allowing subscribers to order reruns of their favorite old shows, music videos, documentaries, and other material whenever they choose.

Using video streaming—the playing of movies and other video material from digital servers—Internet companies already provide a variety of similar video-on-demand services, although the quality of the image delivered over a standard telephone modem is very poor. Communications companies of all types are looking to marry broadband delivery platforms, such as cable, with video-streaming technology to make instant, on-demand programming a reality.

Digital service also means greater integration of video programming with data for broadcasters, satellite television, and cable operators. Viewers can call up baseball statistics during the game, as noted above, but even greater interaction is possible. In addition to detailed statistics, the living room fans may be able to request a picture-in-picture screen that shows favorite players in old games, or they may be able to change camera angles to watch only the outfielder. Using computer-like pull-down menus, viewers will be able to order tickets to the next game or buy home-team hats and tee-shirts.

Digital Publishing

Newspaper, magazine, and book publishing have all been affected by the digital revolution. One of the most prominent manifestations is their use of the Internet, from the delivery of additional or enhanced content in the case of newspapers, magazines, and journals to book-buying online. Nearly every magazine and newspaper has its own website that features material culled from their print editions and supplemented with additional information, searchable archives, audio and video feeds, and hot links to related sites.

Reinventing the backroom, or production process, in publishing was one of the pioneering steps in digital communications. Newspapers began replacing typewriters with computers in the 1970s, converting over the next two decades to systems in which stories were written, edited, and set in type all within the confines of the computer. In the 1990s, newspaper and magazine photographers began switching from film to digital imagery. Film, which at one time had to be shot in the field, carried back to the newspaper, developed in the lab, printed in the darkroom, and edited physically, can now be transmitted electronically to the newspaper, edited in the computer, and placed in print in a fraction of the time.

The development of "desktop publishing"—which relies on home computers, sophisticated word processing and publishing software, packages full of clip art, and inexpensive digital scanners—has turned millions of hobbyists into home publishers, churning out newsletters, pamphlets, and minimagazines for their schools, churches, and civic clubs.

For years, newspaper publishers, and to a lesser extent magazine publishers, sought a means of delivering their product electronically using small, portable wireless readers or flat screens to replace paper. Flat-panel technology is still evolving and may merge with other developing wireless devices. The book publishing industry has also developed electronic book readers. "E-books" can be purchased on disk or downloaded from the World Wide Web and played back, or read, on the flat-screen device that is designed to emulate the sense and feel of a real book. The industry has also considered a "books-on-demand" system in which titles are stored electronically and printed as needed at a local outlet. Using this system, publishers would no longer have to guess about consumer demand and press runs, saving time, money, and natural resources, and there would no longer be such a thing as an out-of-print book.

Wireless

The ubiquitous cell telephone is being replaced by a digital cellular unit, sometimes called a personal communications system (PCS). In addition to improving the clarity of the telephone call, small, built-in screens allow these units to be used for data communication. Users can check their e-mail, trade stocks, or buy gifts online. For more powerful web surfing, the digital telephones serve as wireless modems for laptop computers. Wireless PDAs such as Palm Pilot and two-way, Internet-enabled pagers offer similar tetherless features. Global digital telephone systems that use low-Earth-orbiting satellites are extending this power all over the world.

The Digital Home

The digital future is a switched, broadband, highly interactive information and communication system. A variety of industries, including telephone, cable, television satellite, and even power companies, will vie to provide consumers with bundled packages of telephone service, Internet access, paging, and television programming and present one bill for everything at the end of the month. In the home, it will likely mean high-resolution display screens in as many rooms as the owner wishes. While screens will vary in size—large ones in the family room, small ones in the den—each will have similar capacities to view movies, surf the Internet, look at e-mail, or order dinner. While most home devices may be wired, wireless technologies will be common for any mobile application, from surfing the web on the patio to reviewing voicemail in the car or at the airport. In short, digital technology is changing the way people work, play, and socialize.

See also: CABLE TELEVISION, PROGRAMMING OF; CABLE TELEVISION, SYSTEM TECHNOLOGY OF; DIGITAL COMMUNICATION; FILM INDUSTRY, TECHNOLOGY OF; INTERNET AND THE WORLD WIDE WEB; RADIO BROADCASTING, TECHNOLOGY OF; RECORDING INDUSTRY, TECHNOLOGY OF; SATELLITES, COMMUNICATION; SATELLITES, TECHNOLOGY OF; TECHNOLOGY, ADOPTION AND DIFFUSION OF; TECHNOLOGY, PHILOSOPHY OF; TELECOMMUNICATIONS, WIRELESS; TELEPHONE INDUSTRY, TECHNOLOGY OF; TELEVISION BROADCASTING, TECHNOLOGY OF.

Bibliography

Brinkley, Joel. (1998). *Defining Vision*. San Diego, CA: Harcourt.

Case, Dominic. (1997). *Film Technology in Post Production*. Woburn, MA: Butterworth-Neinemann.

Covell, Andy. (1999). *Digital Convergence: How the Merging of Computers, Communications and Multimedia is Transforming Our Lives*. Newport, RI: Aegis.

Dholakia, Ruby Roy; Mundorf, Norbert; and Dholakia, Nikhilesh. (1996). *New Infotainment Technologies in the Home: Demand-Side Perspectives*. Mahwah, NJ: Lawrence Erlbaum.

Dizard, Wilson, Jr. (2000). *Old Media, New Media: Mass Communications in the Information Age*, 3rd edition. New York: Longman.

Dupagne, Michel, and Seel, Peter. (1997). *High Definition: A Global Perspective*. Ames: Iowa State University Press.

Grant, August. (1998). *Communication Technology Update*, 6th edition. Woburn, MA: Butterworth-Heinemann.

Negroponte, Nicholas. (1995). *Being Digital*. New York: Knopf.

Pavlik, John V. (1996). *New Media and the Information Superhighway*. Boston: Allyn & Bacon.

Robin, Michael. (2000). *Digital Television Fundamentals*, 2nd edition. New York: McGraw-Hill.

Rubin, Michael. (2000). *Nonlinear: A Guide to Digital Film and Video Editing*, 4th edition. Gainesville, FL: Triad.

Silbergleid, Michael, and Pescatore, Mark, eds. (1999). *The Guide to Digital Television.* New York: Miller Freeman.

Whitaker, Jerry. (1999). *DTV: The Revolution in Digital Video.* New York: McGraw-Hill.

PATRICK R. PARSONS

■ DISNEY, WALT (1901–1966)

Born in Chicago to Elias Disney (an Irish Canadian) and Flora Call Disney (a German American), Walt Disney, who was one of five children in the family, spent most of his early life in Missouri (first in Marceline and later in Kansas City). After serving in Europe as an ambulance driver in Europe at the end of World War I, Disney returned to Kansas City, where he worked with Ub Iwerks at the Kansas City Film Ad Company. The two decided to set out on their own in 1922 and founded Laugh-O-gram Films. Although working at their own company allowed them to fine-tune a method of combining live action with animation, distribution problems led to the demise of Laugh-O-grams in a year. In 1923, Disney moved to Hollywood and founded the Walt Disney company with his brother Roy. Iwerks later joined them as a key animator. The company's first contract was to produce the short, animated, live-action Alice Comedies.

In 1927, Disney created the cartoon character Oswald the Lucky Rabbit, which proved to be popular with audiences. However, Disney later learned that Universal, his distributor, owned full rights to the Oswald character, a hard-learned lesson that pushed Disney to create a new character, Mickey Mouse, who was featured in *Plane Crazy* (1928) and *The Gallopin' Gaucho* (1928). On November 18, 1928, *Steamboat Willie*, which featured Mickey and his companion, Minnie Mouse, was the first Mickey cartoon to be released, premiering at the Colony Theatre in New York City. This was the first synchronized sound cartoon, and while Disney auditioned many people for the voice of Mickey, he chose to provide the high-pitched voice himself. Disney won an Academy Award in 1932 for the creation of Mickey Mouse, and he continued to provide the voice until the late 1940s.

The summer after *Steamboat Willie* was released, Disney kicked off his Silly Symphony series with *The Skeleton Dance* (1929), which won acclaim for its synchronized sound and movement. Other Silly Symphony cartoons followed, including *Flowers and Trees* (1932), which was the first full-color cartoon and the first animated film to win an Academy Award. Disney's use of Technicolor saved this unproven commodity and garnered Disney an exclusive three-year contract with Technicolor, giving him an edge over his competitors. The Academy Award-winning *Three Little Pigs* (1933), another in the Silly Symphony series, was praised for character development, and the cartoon's theme song—"Who's Afraid of the Big Bad Wolf?" by Frank Churchill—was popular with Depression-era audiences.

As Disney prepared for the creation of the first full-length animated film, he started exploring new techniques in animation photography. His third Academy Award-winning Silly Symphony, *The Old Mill* (1937), was the first short subject to use the multiplane camera technique. Disney also won a special Academy Award for the design and application of the multiplane camera, a device that photographed up to six sheets of glass held several inches apart, thereby producing animation with a greater sense of depth and dimension. That same year, *Snow White and the Seven Dwarfs* (1937) premiered at the Carthay Circle Theater in Los Angeles as the first full-length animated feature film. It won critical and popular acclaim and broke ground for the future of animated films. The film capitalized on Disney's animation achievements to date and took great leaps in the creation of well-developed cartoon characters who exhibited a wide range of emotions and could evoke emotions from the audience as well.

Disney is known for other firsts in animated feature films. *Fantasia* (1940), which features visual interpretations of orchestral classics, was the first animated film to use Fantasound, a multitrack sound system that paved the way for stereophonic sound. *The Reluctant Dragon* (1941) combined animation with live action. *Lady and the Tramp* (1955) was the first animated feature film to use the widescreen projection process CinemaScope, while *Sleeping Beauty* (1959) was the first animated feature film to use the widescreen projection process Technirama 70. Other notable animated features that were produced by Disney Studios during Disney's lifetime include *Pinocchio* (1940), *Dumbo* (1941), *Bambi* (1942), *Cinderella* (1950), *Alice in Wonderland* (1951), *Peter Pan*

In 1939, Shirley Temple presented a special Academy Award—one big statue and seven little ones—to Walt Disney for his accomplishments on Snow White and the Seven Dwarfs. (Bettmann/Corbis)

(1953), *One Hundred and One Dalmatians* (1961), and *The Sword in the Stone* (1963). *The Jungle Book* (1967) was the last animated film that Disney was personally involved in, although it was released after his death. Disney believed in education for animators, which was the impetus for the establishment of an animation school at his Hollywood studio in 1932. The excellent training that his animators received not only improved the quality of Disney films but upgraded industry standards. Later, in 1961, Disney led the establishment of the California Institute of the Arts in Valencia as a college-level professional school that specialized in creative and performing arts.

On July 19, 1950, Disney Studios released the live-action feature *Treasure Island*, which was the first of sixty-three live-action films that Disney oversaw before his death. Other notable live-action Disney classics include *Davy Crockett, King of the Wild Frontier* (1955), *Old Yeller* (1957), *The Shaggy Dog* (1959), *Pollyanna* (1960), *Swiss Family Robinson* (1960), *The Absent-Minded Professor*

(1961), *The Parent Trap* (1961), and *The Incredible Journey* (1963). *Mary Poppins* (1964), which was acclaimed for its combined use of animation and live action in a key sequence and is often considered to be Disney's last great film, won five Academy Awards.

Disney also made his mark in television. In 1950, his first television show, *One Hour in Wonderland*, was broadcast on Christmas Day. During the early 1950s, after the success of his first show, the networks began pursuing Disney to create a weekly show, but he was focused on opening his Anaheim, California, theme park, "Disneyland." Finally, in 1954, Disney agreed to supply a series to ABC if the network would provide a loan to begin construction of the park. Disney used the series to promote the park, which was well publicized through the show by the time it opened on July 17, 1955. In 1961, Disney moved the series to NBC and began producing the series in color, changing its name to *Walt Disney's Wonderful World of Color*; the series was eventually called

The Wonderful World of Disney. Meanwhile, Disney's *Mickey Mouse Club*, which ran from 1955 to 1959, was another television venue that the creator used to bolster interest in the theme park. "Walt Disney World," a similar, yet much larger, park opened in Orlando, Florida, in 1971.

Although Disney left his mark as a film innovator, he was also a savvy entrepreneur. His keen sense for what audiences wanted helped him to created many types of media that would satisfy—and continue to satisfy—the American public. Under his leadership, Disney's studio won hundreds of awards, including forty-eight Academy Awards, seven Emmy Awards, and two Grammy Awards.

See also: FILM INDUSTRY, HISTORY OF.

Bibliography

Holliss, Richard, and Sibley, Brian. (1988). *The Disney Studio Story*. New York: Crown Books.

Jackson, Kathy Merlock. (1993). *Walt Disney: A Bio-Bibliography*. Westport, CT: Greenwood Press.

Maltin, Leonard. (1995). *The Disney Films*, revised edition. New York: Hyperion.

Schickel, Richard. (1997). *The Disney Version: The Life, Times, Art, and Commerce of Walt Disney*, revised edition. New York: Simon & Schuster.

Smith, Dave. (1998). *Disney A to Z: The Official Encyclopedia*, revised edition. New York: Hyperion.

Thomas, Bob. (1958). *Walt Disney: The Art of Animation*. New York: Simon & Schuster.

Thomas, Bob. (1994). *Walt Disney: An American Original*, revised edition. New York: Hyperion.

Thomas, Frank, and Johnston, Ollie. (1984). *Disney Animation: The Illusion of Life*. New York: Abbeville Press.

TRACY LAUDER

■ DURKHEIM, ÉMILE (1858–1917)

Émile Durkheim was one of the founding figures of sociology. His work is important to students of communication because of the central, though often implicit, role of communication processes in his sociological analyses. In current Durkheimian theory, communication, broadly conceived, is the fundamental social process. As a result of communication, biological beings become civilized human beings, psychological dispositions take the shape of cultural forces, and material and economic life takes meaningful shape as community and society. Durkheim himself was never so explicit about such large claims, and he was writing before the development of the modern vocabulary of communication theory. Nevertheless, interested readers have no difficulty seeing that signs, symbols, representations, rituals, myths, symbolic interaction, and other modes and media of communication are the underlying processes of his theoretical explanations of social order and process.

Durkheim was born in Épinal in the Lorraine region of France. His family expected him to become a rabbi, but Durkheim opted instead for secular scholarship. He studied philosophy at the École Normale Supérieure in Paris and spent a year in Germany (1885–1886) studying the new social sciences. In 1887, he took a post in education and sociology at Bordeaux; this was the first professorship in sociology in France. In 1902, he was given a professorship at the Sorbonne in Paris. At both universities Durkheim surrounded himself with a busy group of talented students. Together they conducted research, planned courses, wrote books and articles, and edited one of the world's first journals of sociology, *L'Année Sociologique*. Three of the four books published in his lifetime—*The Division of Labor in Society* (1893), *The Rules of Sociological Method* (1895), and *Suicide* (1897)—appeared in rapid order during the Bordeaux years and cemented his reputation as an important, if controversial, thinker. *The Elementary Forms of the Religious Life* (1912) was completed and published fifteen years later, following a prolific production of articles, reviews, courses, and lectures. Course notes and essays were compiled and published posthumously. He died in November 1917 while recuperating from a stroke suffered after leaving a war information meeting the previous year. It is commonly reported that the heartbreak and strain of the war—in which his only son and many of his students were killed—contributed directly to his death.

The first step in Durkheimian social theory is the claim that society, or the social, represents a distinct and separate type of reality. Durkheim said the social was *sui generis* (i.e., unique, individual) and set it alongside physical, biological, psychological, and economic realities. This entails, then, that social reality has a degree of autonomy vis-à-vis physical, biological, psychological, and economic circumstances and that it follows some of its own rules of cause and consequence. Sociology, then, as the science devoted to social realities, needed to have its own concepts, logic, and method, as it too would make a *sui generis* contribution to the academy. Modern students of communication can read Durkheim's work as an early movement toward the later establishment of communication studies, cultural studies, and the textual turn throughout the social sciences.

The next step in Durkheimian social theory is to posit social forces as the causal explanation for the socialized behavior of individuals and the endurance of social organizations and order. In Durkheim's early work, on the division of labor and on suicide, for example, the nature of these social forces was sometimes mysterious. Because he often deduced the evidence for their existence through argument by elimination—showing first that biological, psychological, and economic explanations were inadequate—the nature of the social forces was in important ways left undefined. In *The Elementary Forms of the Religious Life,* Durkheim offers his most substantive analysis of social forces, and it becomes clear that they exist and work through processes of communication. In the analysis of religious symbol and ritual that is the centerpiece of that work, Durkheim shows how the ordinary material objects and body movements of religious ceremony carry special meanings and powers for the social group that is practicing the ritual. They actually represent the group to itself, and thus the ritual objects and practices are the symbols and media of the group's power over the individual.

One of the most general propositions of Durkheimian theory is that group activities strengthen the group by expressing and representing social forces, and thus reinforcing their presence in individual minds. Normally socialized adults, for example, feel social norms in their own consciousness, whether as spontaneous desires or as uncomfortable social pressures. Normative social interaction reinforces the ubiquity, utility, and taken-for-grantedness of those norms. Language, logic, aesthetic preferences, rules of interaction, taken-for-granted political beliefs, and religious practice and belief all share these characteristics with social norms. Durkheim described this class of phenomena as "things in us, not of us," as instances of the social within the mind of the individual.

Émile Durkheim. (Bettmann/Corbis)

These ideas have become commonplace. No one doubts that social interaction, communication, and culture are fundamental to socialization, and that the outcome of socialization is such that much of a person's conscious thought is a social product, even as it is his or her own individual experience. That does not diminish Durkheim's innovation. At the time, this was a fundamentally new approach to sociology, tantamount to the invention of social psychology. It is of further importance to students of communication because it puts symbolic processes at the heart of social theory and points toward "communication-centric" analyses of culture, politics, and social life.

For example, the practices of modern democratic politics—campaigning, voting, swearing in, parades, saluting the flag, holidays, monuments, speeches—can be analyzed as the ritual of a modern social religion. Much political activity that appears purposeless or irrational can be shown to be ritually important. The entertainment, leisure, and consumer goods industries, for another example, also have a ritual and normative element, since they provide the material resources for the modern cult of the individual. In modern society, each person must be a distinct individual; the social norm is to be one's self. Choices in entertainment, leisure activities, and consumer goods are media for the expression of that identity, rituals of each individual's adherence to the norm. As these examples indicate, there is room in contemporary communication, cultural, and social theory for a distinctive Durkheimian contribution.

See also: CULTURE INDUSTRIES, MEDIA AS; ELECTION CAMPAIGNS AND MEDIA EFFECTS; GROUP COMMUNICATION; LANGUAGE AND COMMUNICATION; SOCIETY AND THE MEDIA; SOCIOLINGUISTICS; SYMBOLS.

Bibliography

Durkheim, Émile. (1893 [1984]). *The Division of Labor in Society,* tr. W. D. Halls. New York: Free Press.

Durkheim, Émile. (1895 [1982]). *The Rules of Sociological Method,* tr. W. D. Halls. New York: Free Press.

Durkheim, Émile. (1897 [1966]). *Suicide,* trs. John A. Spalding and George Simpson. New York: Free Press.

Durkheim, Émile. (1912 [1995]). *The Elementary Forms of the Religious Life,* tr. Karen E. Fields. New York: Free Press.

Lukes, Steven. (1972). *Émile Durkheim, His Life and Work: A Historical and Critical Study.* New York: Harper & Row.

Pickering, W. S. F. (1984). *Durkheim's Sociology of Religion: Themes and Theories.* London: Routledge and Kegan Paul.

ERIC W. ROTHENBUHLER

■ DYNAMICS OF GROUP COMMUNICATION

See: Group Communication, Dynamics of

E

▮ ECONOMICS OF INFORMATION

Though economists often talk in terms that seem impenetrable, what they study is very simple and basic. The "economy" is how resources are distributed throughout society. Since the 1960s, the world has been described as an information economy, rather than an industrial or agricultural economy. Buying, selling, and using information are at the heart of economic activity for businesses and consumers, as well as for the governments that regulate them.

Development of the Field

In ancient hunter-gatherer or small-scale agricultural societies, most economic activity was governed by tradition. When a global economy first began to develop in the fifteenth and sixteenth centuries, however, the need to plan for activities that would be coordinated over vast distances and the need to account for the effects of weather and events in faraway places on domestic availability of food and goods led to the articulation of theories about how the economy works. Each subsequent change in the nature of the economy has similarly stimulated the development of new economic ideas, first with industrialization and then with "informatization."

The subfield of the economics of information emerged as several distinct strands of research and theory that dealt with very different aspects of information began to be considered together. Neoclassical economic theory, the economic ideas that dominated most of the decision making (whether of government or of corporations) during the twentieth century started from a set of five assumptions: (1) that everyone has access to the same information, (2) that everyone has perfect information about prices and goods in the marketplace, (3) that purchasing decisions are made solely for economic reasons, (4) that the histories and habits of consumers have no influence on individual buying decisions, and (5) that power and influence play no role in how the market works. Historical work that contributes to the way in which economists understand information dealt with matters as different from each other as optimization of flows through a communication system, decision theory, research and development, prices, organizations as economic entities, and risk.

Over the course of the twentieth century, however, the growth in the importance of information goods and services to the economy forced reconsideration of many of these inherited economic ideas. In the 1930s, Ronald Coase pointed out that the very reason corporations form is to reduce the transaction cost (i.e., the cost of getting knowledge about prices for necessary things). One important implication of this insight, he noted, was that businesses should not be seen as solid and stable structures; rather, they should be seen as incompletely connected networks of information flows. By the 1960s, Fritz Machlup and Kenneth Boulding started identifying industries that fell within the "information sector" of the economy. In the 1970s, Uri Porat offered a framework for statistically analyzing trends in the information sector. This framework was taken up by the U.S. government and subsequently by other governments around the world, leading to the creation of the body of statistics related to the enormous growth in the percentage of the work force involved in "information work," the contributions of information industries to the national economy, and so on.

Subsequently, a great deal of work began to be done to investigate how neoclassical economic ideas applied to information creation, processing, flows, and use. A number of problems were identified. It is difficult to break information into units, so it is therefore difficult to quantify it. Information is not appropriable; while it can be owned, that ownership is rarely exclusive. Information is thus said to be "leaky" because when it is transferred it may go not only from seller to buyer but also to third parties who may be in the vicinity and acquire the information solely through, for example, overhearing it, viewing it from afar, or accessing it through web-based means. Information is heterogeneous in nature, so it often is valued in widely differing ways by different people. This is illustrated by the fact that "old" information is useless to corporate decision makers, but it is invaluable to historians. In most cases, value is put not on information itself but in its material packaging—the book, the classroom, or the television set. Economists use the term "commodities" to identify things that are bought and sold that are fixed in time and space, but informational goods and services are not necessarily fixed in time and space. Where, for example, would one locate the site of the purchase of information processing in a transaction that involves a buyer in one country, a seller in a second, and a computer in a third? Despite these problems, it has been necessary to come up with some way of understanding economic processes as they take place within an economy that is (1) clearly ever-more reliant on information technologies for the production, distribution, and use of all kinds of goods and services and (2) composed of an ever-larger proportion of informational goods and services.

What Is "The Information Economy"?

The earliest way of understanding the information economy was set forth in the 1960s. According to this product-based theory, an information economy operates just like any other economy except for the simple difference that there is a larger proportion of informational goods and serv-ices being bought and sold. This approach continues to underlie most governmental decision making, and it is the approach that is used to generate statistics to describe the growth of the information economy. This approach is useful as far as it goes, and it has the advantage of permitting decision makers to continue to work with the kinds of analytical tools that they have always used. However, people in the business world increasingly began to feel that this approach did not adequately capture what was going on in the contemporary economy—where value was being created and money was being made.

By the 1970s, some people began to look for an alternate understanding of the information economy because of the problems that were associated with treating information as a commodity and with the social inequities that resulted from differential access to information. This led to a domain-based theory that said the information economy resulted from the expansion of the boundaries of the economy itself through commodification of forms of information that had never before been treated as a commodity. Some of the forms of information newly commodified could be public, as when governmental databases such as those generated by the U.S. satellite surveillance system are turned over to the private sector. Some of it is private, as in the example of the details of one's personal life that are now bought and sold. Again, there is some truth in the insights offered by this approach. However, it has been limited in its influence upon policymaking because it has not offered alternative analytical tools that can help policymakers solve problems.

In the early 1990s, a third way of defining the information economy appeared, focused not on products or on the domain but on how the economy functions. Led by Cristiano Antonelli, proponents of this approach argue that the contemporary economy is an information economy because it operates in qualitatively different ways from how the economy operated in earlier stages. Antonelli and others argue that in the information economy, cooperation and coordination are as important as competition for long-term economic success. Because different types of economic, political, and social entities are so intertwined in all of their activities, these economists argue that there is little that actually still takes place in the market as idealized by the neoclassical economists of the late nineteenth century. Rather, most economic activity takes place via the "harmonization" of different types of information systems with each other.

While all three of these perspectives are used to support decision making by various groups, both public and private sector decision makers are gradually shifting from the most traditional approach to an appreciation of the unique informational features of what many now call the "network economy." Corporations are changing because they are finding that traditional ways of thinking do not account for what they are experiencing. Governments are changing in order to remain competitive with other types of organizations—such as transnational corporations—in contemporary struggles for power.

Economic Analysis of Information

Information is important economically both as a good (i.e., an object that can be bought and sold, such as a book) and as a service (i.e., a process that can be bought and sold, such as data processing). One of the reasons it has been so difficult to deal with information in economic terms has been that it is more difficult to deal with the economic features of commodities that are intangible than with those that are material, or tangible.

Consumers tend to think most of primary or final information goods and services, those that are bought by users in the form in which they are produced. Movies, television programs, databases, books, and magazines are all examples of information as a final good. In the contemporary economy, however, informational goods and services are also important in secondary or intermediate form, meaning that they are not products bought and sold in the retail market. Rather, they are inputs into the production of other types of goods and services. For example, data about marketing and sales trends is an important input into the production of goods for sale. Data about the functioning of the global information infrastructure through which the communications of the Internet flow is another example of information as a critically important secondary good. Information as a secondary good may be in the form of raw data, as in these examples. It is also said to be embedded in advanced technologies that embody information because they are the outcome of lengthy research processes that produce information. It is also embedded in the people who use those technologies as a form of what is called "human capital."

One of the first problems economists faced in thinking about information was defining the information sector of the economy (i.e., those industries involved in working with information) so they could be analyzed separately from other types of economic activities. This is not a problem with a precise and fixed solution because many companies are involved in both information-based and materials-based businesses and new information businesses are being created all the time. Generally, the information sector is defined as those industries that have a primary focus of producing, distributing, processing, or storing information. Important examples of industries that belong to the information sector include education, media (e.g., television, radio, book and magazine publishing, and film), Internet companies, telephone companies, libraries, database providers, and data processors.

It is precisely because so many new businesses are being created all the time that it is difficult to draw clear lines between different information industries. For example, a film archive may become a content producer, a law firm may launch a data processing venture, and a radio station may make money transferring data files as a side business. Furthermore, many of the new types of businesses that are emerging, such as Internet service providers and cable television, do not quite fit into the previously standard ways of categorizing industries.

Historically, an economic analysis of an industry would have focused on the activities of individual corporations, what economists call the "firm." Accounting systems—and the governmental regulation for which they provide the framework—have long been in place, and they support the continued reliance on such an approach. However, economists are developing analytical techniques that look at the long-term project rather than the firm as the unit of analysis because so much activity in the network economy takes place not within single firms but within a network of interdependent organizations of different types that interact in a multitude of ways.

The Information Production Chain

The fundamental principle of the economics of information is that value is added every time information is processed. Donald Lamberton, a key figure in the development of the subfield, points out that the division of labor involved in information processing—the way in which processes are broken up into small pieces for handling—may be the most fundamental form of the division of labor. Awareness of this has led to the use of models of an "information production chain" as a way of identifying the different points at which value is added and as a means by which information commodities can be distinguished from each other.

While different industries and governments break up the steps of the information production chain in different ways, work by Machlup and Boulding suggests a basic model that includes the following stages: information creation (*de novo,* or through generation or collection), processing (algorithmic [computerized] or cognitive [human]), storage, transportation, distribution, destruction, and seeking. Those who think about the informational value of production chains for other types of goods and services often think of each stage of manufacturing and distribution as spinning off an informational "value chain."

This emphasis on distinctions among types of information processing as a source of economic value has another consequence, exacerbated by the fact that ongoing technological innovation processes continue to offer new opportunities to entrepreneurs. Though, historically, analysis of functions within the firm were organized around the product, the task, or the job description, economists, led by Roberto Scazzieri, are learning to analyze activities within individual and networked firms in terms of their processes. Thinking in terms of an information production chain also heightens awareness of the value of information as a resource.

Creating Information Goods and Services

In the agricultural and industrial economies, fundamental resources were material. In order to have more (whether it was, for example, land, oil, or iron ore), more had to be found physically, or new ways of getting at known resources had to be invented. In the information economy, however, the discovery of new resources is conceptual. Distinctions among types of information processing and the informational states they produce must be understood in a new way so that a new type of

product or service niche becomes available. It is this emphasis on thinking as a way of creating new products that has made it possible for so many young people to have succeeded so well in information businesses. In the past it might have taken years for an entrepreneur with a good idea to accumulate the needed capital and capacities, but today, even someone who is very young can come up with a new way of thinking about ways to create, process, distribute, and use information and turn that into a business.

Creativity is needed in order to form a successful information-based business, but economists are able to offer a number of basic generalizations regarding how best to think about information from a business perspective. These approaches begin by segmenting the market into different niches, each of which can be served with a different product. Marketing equipment and software for web access to the elderly population that would use it primarily for family correspondence, for example, might stress features that would be very different from the ones emphasized in marketing the same equipment and software to teens who might be more interested in games, music, and other web-based activities. Through product differentiation, different products are developed for each niche. Versioning, or developing several different versions of the same product, is a popular approach to product differentiation for information goods and services. A different version can be developed for each market segment. If such a breakdown is not evident, information economists Carl Shapiro and Hal R. Varian suggest that a business should create three versions because psychologically, the market will at the least break down into those segments that are attracted to each of the extremes and to the central choice. Versions can be distinguished from each other along a number of dimensions, depending on which are most important to the specific good or service involved. Shapiro and Varian identify the following as possibilities: delay, interface (e.g., nature of and ease of use), convenience (e.g., how long does it take to learn to use it, how troublesome is it), image resolution, speed of operation, flexibility of use, capability, features and functions, comprehensiveness, annoyance, and support.

The cost of producing information is independent of the scale on which it is produced; that is, the cost of producing information is the same whether it results in one commodity for sale or a million. The difference between the "first unit cost" and subsequent reproduction means that there can be enormous "economies of scale" in the information industries. This is the reason for the economic appeal of mass market products such as television programs, films, and books to those who produce and sell them.

The features of information technologies are critical to understanding the economics of information. Two features worth mentioning here are those of "lock-in" and "network externalities." Lock-in reflects the fact that the "sunk costs" involved in building any specific communications network are so high that it is hard to change technologies once the network is built. (This is also called "path dependence.") Lock-in makes decision making even more difficult during a period in which innovation is constant and experience with existing and new technologies is so thin that it is difficult to know how to evaluate various technologies relative to each other. One way to reduce the risks associated with lock-in is to respond to network externalities (i.e., the characteristic that the greater the number of individuals and organizations using a network good or service, the greater will be the value of that service). The greater the market for an informational product, the more likely it will be that users will develop an experiential base that facilitates use, that maintenance systems will be in place, and that complementary goods and services will be available.

Lock-in also facilitates what antitrust law refers to as "tying" and those in the information industries refer to as "bundling"—linking together different informational goods and services for joint purchase and use. One of the discoveries of experimentation within the newly emergent information economy has been that many types of informational goods previously thought of as discrete and unique entities can themselves be "unbundled," or broken down into their parts, for separate sale and use. Vendors of magazines, for example, have realized that in the digital environment they can sell article titles, summaries, texts, references, and tables of contents separately. A very famous example of unbundling was the result of the 1983 insistence by the antitrust division of the U.S. Department of Commerce that AT&T divest itself—separate off and sell—local telephone services, which had always historically been bundled with long-distance telephony in one service package.

While ownership of material goods, land, capital, and resources remains important in the information economy, many would say that property rights in information and ideas have become the most important form of property. Intellectual property rights law determines the nature of property rights in information. In the United States, there are several different types of intellectual property. The most important are copyright (i.e., ownership of the expression of ideas), patent (i.e., ownership of the expression of ideas in an invention), trademark (i.e., the right to control the use of symbols), and working papers (i.e., privacy for and control over the results of information processing conducted in the course of completing a work process).

Policymakers struggle with adapting the intellectual property rights system to the contemporary technological environment. It has been difficult, for example, to figure out just how to deal with computer software from an intellectual property rights perspective. Should it be covered by copyright or by patent? Which kinds of software programs should be available to everyone and which kinds should have to be purchased? These problems are made even more difficult by the need to reach international agreement on these matters, since the global nature of the information infrastructure means that property rights issues that arise anywhere are global in nature.

The Limits to Information as a Commodity

While both governments and corporations make policy based on economic analyses of information and the processes by which it is created, stored, distributed, and used, the same matters can be analyzed from political, social, cultural, or ecological perspectives. The greatest value can be derived from economic analyses when they are placed within the wider context. From this point of view, the weaknesses as well as the strengths of the economic approach can be identified.

One of the most striking features of the last half of the twentieth century was the way in which forms of information never before treated as economic goods and services were commodified, or turned into something that could be bought and sold. Examples of such newly commodified forms of information include those that are most private, such as what thoughts are in one's mind, or what chemicals are in one's urine. They also include those that had historically been most public, such as databases put together by governments in order to serve the public interest or the traditional stories that ensure survival of ancient cultures. The fact that such forms of information can be commodified, however, does not mean that they should be. Growing numbers of economists, policymakers, and communities have begun to realize that the pursuit of the economic value of information must be balanced with the pursuit of other types of important value. Even when information is treated as a commodity, it remains important in other ways—as knowledge structures and as a constitutive force in society. Information is critical to the social construction of reality—to the ways in which people together build the social world. Information policy for a thriving political culture and creative expressive environment may have to temper economic profit with other social values.

Even within the economically defined world, the unique characteristics of the network economy make clear that competition is not the only important way of relating to others for long-term economic survival. Cooperation and coordination are important as well. Incorporation of this knowledge into planning is to some degree just a shift in the way planners are thinking. For example, while in the short term it may be economically inefficient to let the children of illegal immigrants attend public school in the United States, the U.S. Supreme Court has realized that, considering the long-term costs to the community as a whole should those children not receive an education, it makes more sense economically to permit those children into the schools.

The problem of differences in access to information, including the ability to use it once it is acquired, is as important to economists as it is to society as a whole because research consistently shows that those differences are often due to differences in economic class. In the Internet environment, this is known as the problem of the "digital divide." With this in mind, policymakers struggle to ensure that access to the Internet is equal within and across communities. The problem is, of course, not unique to the Internet environment. Before there was any such thing as a digital divide, sociologists were studying the effects of the "knowledge gap" as it played out between the poor and the rich, the rural and the urban, the uneducated and the educated, the female and the male, and the black and the white.

Summary

The economics of information is a subfield of the general field of economics. It has risen in importance because of the shift to an information economy that is best described as a network economy. Economists are still learning how to adapt economic theory to apply to the new information environment, which seems to operate differently from economic environments of the past. In particular, cooperation and coordination have joined competition as all-important strategies for long-term economic success. The goal of such success, however, must be combined with other important social, cultural, political, and ecological goals to determine just what types of information policy are most desirable.

See also: COPYRIGHT; ELECTRONIC COMMERCE; ETHICS AND INFORMATION; INFORMATION INDUSTRY; INFORMATION SOCIETY, DESCRIPTION OF; MACHLUP, FRITZ; PRIVACY AND ENCRYPTION; USE OF INFORMATION.

Bibliography

Antonelli, Cristiano, ed. (1992). *The Economics of Information Networks.* Amsterdam: Elsevier Science Publishers.

Babe, Robert E. (1996). *Communication and the Transformation of Economics: Essays in Information, Public Policy, and Political Economy.* Boulder, CO: Westview Press.

Boulding, Kenneth E. (1966). "The Economics of Knowledge and the Knowledge of Economics." *American Economic Review* 56(2):1–13.

Braman, Sandra. (1999). "The Information Economy: An Evolution of Approaches." In *Information and Organization*, eds. S. Macdonald and J. Nightingale. Amsterdam: Elsevier Science.

Coase, Ronald J. (1937). "The Nature of the Firm." *Economica* 4:386–405.

Lamberton, Donald M. (1994). "The Information Economy Revisited." In *Information and Communication in Economics*, ed. Robert E. Babe. Boston: Kluwer Academic.

Machlup, Fritz. (1979). "Uses, Value, and Benefits of Knowledge." *Knowledge* 1(1):62–81.

Mansell, Robin, and Wehn, Uta, eds. (1998). *Knowledge Societies: Information Technology for Sustainable Development.* Oxford, Eng.: Oxford University Press.

Marschak, Jacob. (1968). "Economics of Inquiring, Communicating, Deciding." *American Economic Review* 58(2):1–18.

Porat, Marc Uri. (1977). *The Information Economy: Definition and Measurement.* Washington, DC: Office of Telecommunications, U.S. Department of Commerce.

Scazzieri, Roberto. (1993). *A Theory of Production: Tasks, Processes, and Technical Practices.* Oxford, Eng.: Clarendon Press.

Shapiro, Carl, and Varian, Hal R. (1999). *Information Rules: A Strategic Guide to the Network Economy.* Cambridge, MA: Harvard Business School Press.

SANDRA BRAMAN

ECONOMY, POLITICAL

See: Political Economy

EDISON, THOMAS ALVA (1847–1931)

Thomas Alva Edison was a master of combining ideas into working systems and overcoming technical hurdles that seemed insurmountable. He developed the notion of using teams of specialists in well-equipped laboratories to invent new devices. With the possible exception of the lightbulb, the inventions for which he was best known were in the field of communication.

Edison was born in Ohio; his father moved the family to Michigan when Thomas was seven years old. His father was looking for a town that would prosper in a country newly connected more by railroads than canals. It was on the new railroad lines in Edison's early teenage years that he first became entranced with communication technology.

In addition to selling newspapers on the trains, Edison began to print his own railroad newspaper called the *Weekly Herald.* He gathered some of his news stories from reports coming over the railroad telegraphs. At the age of fifteen, he was taught telegraphy by a railroad stationmaster and soon began to experiment with modifications to the telegraph itself. He worked on systems to send multiple messages simultaneously over the telegraph and on automatic telegraphy. During this work, he even reported finding electromagnetic waves, though he did not know what this "etheric force" was and took the discovery no further than reporting it. Other work on the telegraph led to

the invention of the mimeograph machine and to improvements to the telephone.

In 1877, Edison discovered that it was possible to record sound, and this had a dramatic effect on the future of communication. He first developed a paraffin paper strip that would pass under a needle, much like a magnetic tape slides across a magnet in a modern tape recorder. This "telephonic repeater" recorded crude sounds of voices. From this, he began work on his first phonograph. Edison sketched out a crude design for a working phonograph recorder and gave the assignment to make the device to John Kruesi, one of his workmen. About a week later, the finished device, which placed grooves in tin-foil wrapped around a drum, recorded human voices on the very first try. Edison also made a disc model that used tin-foil to record sounds, but he soon set aside the phonograph to work on the electric lightbulb.

Ten years later, Edison made his next major improvement on the phonograph when he developed a solid wax cylinder that replaced the tin-foil medium for recording. He developed "The Improved Edison Phonograph" and then "The Perfected Edison Phonograph" machines. Edison sold the Edison Phonograph Company for $500,000 in 1887 to the North American Phonograph Company, which immediately began employing the devices in business for dictation purposes. Edison continued to work on development of the phonograph, however, under a company named Edison Phonograph Works. This company produced talking dolls and musical cylinders for entertainment. Initially, there was no way to reproduce (or duplicate) a cylinder; each recording was an original. However, methods of limited mechanical reproduction were soon devised, and Edison eventually developed a method of reproduction in 1898 that used a molded wax cylinder—enabling the mass production of individual recordings. Edison also developed electronic and spring-wound versions of the phonograph for business and home use, respectively. Most of the recordings lasted two minutes each, and the spring-wound phonographs could play up to six cylinders without being rewound.

Edison was not the only person working in this area by the end of the nineteenth century; he had plenty of competition from other phonograph companies. The North American Phonograph Company had granted territories to franchisees

Thomas Edison sits beside his speaking phonograph for an 1878 photograph. (Bettmann/Corbis)

for selling phonograph equipment. One of these was the Columbia Phonograph Company, which developed many versions of phonographs to compete directly against those designed by Edison. Columbia and several other companies also produced many of their own musical cylinders. In particular, Emile Berliner created a flat, hard shellac disc that had better sound quality and could be stored more easily than a wax cylinder. This development, adopted by the Victor Talking Machine Company, eventually replaced the Edison cylinder as the dominant version of the phonograph.

During much of the time that Edison was working on the phonograph, he was also developing another major invention, or rather series of inventions, that would dramatically influence the future of communication. With no background in photography, Edison plunged into the study of how to capture and use a rapid series of pictures to approximate live motion. He encouraged George Eastman to adapt his photographic process so that it could be used on flexible film, which could then be used for Edison's idea of approximating motion with a series of pictures. Following Eastman's success, Edison developed and patented in 1893 the Kinetograph, a camera that could capture a rapid sequence of pictures on flexible film that was perforated at the edge. Laboratory assistant William Dickson was his chief assistant on the project. While others, such as Eadweard Muybridge, had captured a short series of pictures using multiple cameras and had played them back as a repeating sequence, Edison's camera was more practical, so it provided a leap forward in the field.

His camera was followed by the invention of the Kinetoscope, a one-person machine that allowed fifty feet of film to loop continuously through a viewing device that magnified the image for the patron. For a nickel, patrons could watch the simple acts of gymnasts, jugglers, and acrobats who had performed for the cameras in Edison's Black Maria film studio. The studio was built on a revolving platform with a roof that opened to allow the sunlight in so the scene could be illuminated effectively. Large numbers of these films were made for use in the Kinetoscope machines, but most of them have been lost to posterity because he failed to copyright the ones made before 1896. Copyrighting films required the deposit of a print on paper in the U.S. Copyright office, thus providing a record of the film on a permanent medium, while early filmstock allowed the images to fade away with time. At one point, Edison linked the Kinetoscope to the phonograph, thereby creating an early version of talking pictures, but this innovation did not catch on for general use.

The Kinetoscope, which limited viewing to one person at a time, finally gave way to Edison's more refined 1896 invention of the Vitascope, a projector that used an arc lamp to light up the photographs and project them onto a screen—thereby allowing multiple viewers to see the images at the same time. The Vitascope drew the film in intermittent jumps in front of a rapidly opening and closing shutter. Each time the film paused, the shutter allowed a burst of light through the opening, thereby projecting one frame of the film. When the image changed at a rapid rate, such as forty-eight frames per second (the standard speed that is used in modern motion pictures), the human eye was unable to detect the momentary gap between the images. Therefore, because of this phenomenon (called "persistence of vision"), the constant barrage of pictures in rapid succession fooled the eye into seeing constant motion.

Beyond the development of the mechanical elements of motion pictures, Edison's employees also advanced the art of motion pictures, conceiving elements of story, editing, cross-cutting, and moving the camera. However, Edison's own contribution basically ended at the mechanical operation of the machinery. He left it to others to pursue the art of motion pictures.

See also: FILM INDUSTRY, HISTORY OF; FILM INDUSTRY, TECHNOLOGY OF; RECORDING INDUSTRY, HISTORY OF; RECORDING INDUSTRY, TECHNOLOGY OF.

Bibliography

Bryan, George S. (1926). *Edison: The Man and His Work*. Garden City, NY: Garden City Publishing.

Dickson, W. K. L., and Dickson, Antonia. (1970). *History of the Kinetograph, Kinetoscope & Kinetophonograph*. New York: Arno Press.

Garbedian, H. Gordon. (1947). *Thomas Alva Edison: Builder of Civilization*. New York: Julian Messner.

Hendricks, Gordon. (1966). *The Kinetoscope: America's First Commercially Successful Motion Picture Exhibitor*. New York: Theodore Gaus' Sons.

Koenigsberg, Allen. (1969). *Edison Cylinder Records, 1889–1912: With an Illustrated History of the Phonograph*. New York: Stellar Productions.

Phillips, Ray. (1997). *Edison's Kinetoscope and Its Films: A History to 1896*. Westport, CT: Greenwood.

Runes, Dagobert D., ed. (1948). *The Diary and Sundry Observations of Thomas Alva Edison*. New York: Philosophical Library.

Wachhorst, Wyn. (1981). *Thomas Alva Edison: An American Myth*. Cambridge, MA: MIT Press.

STEPHEN D. PERRY

▌■ EDITORS

Editors are people who prepare the writing of others for publication. They may supervise a range of functions, from planning content to preparation for a press run or website launch. They make long-range plans, consider ideas, solicit authors, make assignments, schedule manuscripts, order illustrations and photographs, have copy typeset, read and correct galley proofs, and correct final proofs. The specific activities of editors vary given the nature of the publication or publishing firm for which they work. It is possible that the title "senior editor" in one firm refers to a person who must edit manuscripts, while the same title in another firm refers to an executive who assigns work to other editors, selects material, or gives directions to staff.

A minimum of a bachelor's degree is required, and a specialization in the liberal arts is preferred. Depending upon into which area in publishing one wishes to enter, additional areas of study may be required (e.g., marketing, production, business, or journalism). Several universities, including Denver University, offer short-term, non-degree-granting courses in publishing.

Types of Editors

There are many types of editors. Some editors handle managerial or administrative tasks, while others are more "hands-on" in their work. Editors can work for a company as a regular employee or as a freelance, or contract, employee. There is considerable overlap between editorial duties as one moves between demands of book, journal, and

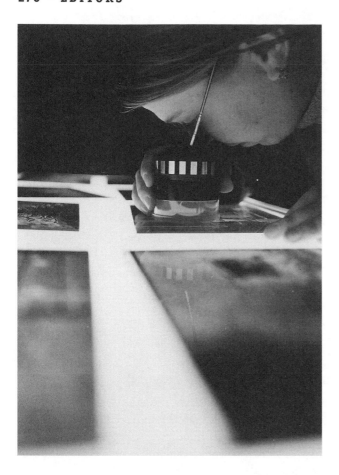

A photo editor examines images on a light table before making final selections. (Timothy Fadek/Corbis)

news publishing. However, there will also be duties that are unique to each of those areas.

A managing editor is responsible for the content and quality of the publication. Managing editors ensure that staff writers and freelance writers complete their articles on time, they check on the art layouts, they proofread materials, and they sometimes write materials themselves. Managing editors also have managerial and budget responsibilities. Managing editors are found in the worlds of books, journals, and newspapers.

An acquisitions editor works with authors whose book manuscripts he or she is interested in publishing. If the publishing house also publishes or distributes journals or monographs, the acquisitions editor will work with the editors of those journals or the board members of the sponsoring organizations. A financial or marketing background is often required.

A sponsoring editor, who is sometimes the same person as the acquisitions editor, has the broadest, most general responsibility for a book once it has been accepted. As the liaison between the publisher and the author, everything done to the book by other departments, including jacket design, promotional copy, copyediting, and press proofs, must be signed off on by the sponsoring editor. The sponsoring editor is the author's advocate from the day the book is signed until the book goes out of print.

Contributing or guest editors appear in series, journal, or newspaper publications and may have their names featured on the publication masthead. A contributing editor may receive a regular salary, an honorarium, or no compensation.

Copy editors edits for the overall style or tone of the publication after a manuscript or article has been accepted for publication. Articles often have to be revised, corrected, polished, or improved for clarity, but the amount of copyediting can vary from one manuscript to the next. If, for example, the editor wants to avoid the use of jargon in a publication, the copy editor may make drastic revisions. However, if it is agreed that an author's style is to remain "untouched," then the copy editor will review the material only for grammatical and spelling errors.

Although a good editor publishes important, useful, and original works that contribute to an existing body of knowledge or expand knowledge and insights about a discipline, nowhere is this gatekeeper role more apparent than in the role of the academic or scientific journal editor.

The scientific journal and its de rigueur practice of peer review began in 1753 with the British Royal Society journal *Philosophical Transactions* (Merton, 1973, p. 463). Journal editors and the referees who advise them must offer critical evaluation, constructive criticism, and a thorough review of manuscripts in order to ensure quality. To do this, a journal editor needs to have access to a broad range of reviewers in a variety of specialties and methodological and theoretical orientations in a discipline.

Photo editing is very different from text editing and is found in all publishing areas. Because images range from the very powerful to the purely informational, selecting the best photograph to illustrate a particular piece takes skill. A good picture editor also guides projects through the publication process. Just as a manuscript editor can improve the quality of the materials produced by a writer, a good photo editor can improve the quality of the illustrations through judicious selection of images.

A freelance editor may find himself or herself "ghosting" (i.e., writing without credit) for another author, writing critiques of manuscripts, helping authors write nonfiction proposals, or working as an agent for another author. Freelance work is often found through agent, editor, and author contacts that a person may have acquired during previous employment or through referral agencies.

Trends

Successful book and journal editors see the development of trends and plan for publications to emerge just when readers (and the market) are most receptive. However, the work of "breaking issues" is complicated by the fact that these editors often work a year or more in advance of actual publication dates. In the life of a newspaper or news photo editor, "breaking issues" occur on a daily basis. It is up to them to decide quickly, perhaps in a matter of minutes, what to publish and how to frame it. A good editor knows how to package and deliver a product that generates a profitable revenue stream.

Changing trends affect not only the content but also the mechanics of publication. Technology continues to push its way into the editor's daily routine, from layout and production systems to the rise of electronic publishing, with its access to information archives, real-time dissemination of conferences and forums, and widespread distribution of publications.

See also: MAGAZINE INDUSTRY; MAGAZINE INDUSTRY, CAREERS IN; MAGAZINE INDUSTRY, PRODUCTION PROCESS OF; NEWSPAPER INDUSTRY; NEWSPAPER INDUSTRY, CAREERS IN; PUBLISHING INDUSTRY; PUBLISHING INDUSTRY, CAREERS IN; WRITERS.

Bibliography

Cortada, James W., and Woods, John A. (1996). "The Story Behind the Book: Using Quality Practices to Create the Quality Yearbook." *TQM Magazine* 8(5)27–31.

Gross, Gerald C. (1993). *Editors on Editing: What Writers Should Know about What Editors*. New York: Grove/Atlantic.

Mandell, Judy. (1995). *Book Editors Talk to Writers*. New York: Wiley.

Merton, Robert K. (1973). *The Sociology of Science*. Chicago: University of Chicago Press.

Morris, John G. (1998). "Get the Picture: A Personal History of Photojournalism." *Knifeman Reports* 52(2):32–38.

Patterson, Benton R., and Patterson, Coleman E. (1997). *The Editor-in-Chief: A Practical Management Guide for Magazine Editors*. Ames: Iowa State University Press.

Simon, Rita, and Fyfe, James J. (1994). *Editors as Gatekeepers*. Rowman & Littlefield.

Wills, Matthew, and Wills, Gordon. (1996). "The Ins and Outs of Electronic Publishing." *Journal of Business and Industrial Marketing* 11(1):90–104.

ARDIS HANSON

EDUCATIONAL MEDIA PRODUCERS

A variety of programming opportunities may be pursued by a person who is interested in becoming an educational media producer. They all involve hard work (e.g., researching a topic, interviewing experts, writing scripts, blocking shots, shooting footage, editing the footage, promoting the finished product, and ultimately airing the program), but they all provide the opportunity to work creatively on a fulfilling enterprise.

Educational Television Programming

There are many outlets for educational television programming, including Nickelodeon, the Disney Channel, the History Channel, the Arts and Entertainment Network (A&E), and the Public Broadcasting Service (PBS). In fact, there are dozens of channels that want good "educational" programming. Getting into the business, however, is difficult. For some students, there may be hidden opportunities.

PBS stations are licensed in four ways: to the community, to the state, to a technical college, or to a university. For those stations that hold a technical college or university license, the station is generally affiliated with the local university or technical college. For students who are obtaining a degree in the television production or communication arts arenas, there may be employment opportunities at these local PBS stations. Coming out of any undergraduate program with experi-

As part of the creation of a 1996 educational documentary, the producer (left) and cameraman film Ecuadorian painter Oswaldo Guayasamin (center) in his studio in Quito. (Pablo Corral V/Corbis)

ence at a local PBS station gives students a valuable advantage over other applicants.

Students generally can work at these television stations as a studio crew person. They can operate studio cameras, control room switchers, and teleprompters, or they can floor manage the productions. They might assist in lighting studio and/or remote locations, or they might help with scenic design. They might also work as a production assistant, where they log tapes and assist with tasks—such as setting up shoots—that every producer must learn. For students who show promise, these production houses often allow for the opportunity to produce segments under supervision. This provides a training ground where students can sort out whether they want to produce programs or go into other, more technical fields such as sound recording or videography/editing, or whether they might be more suited for graphic design and/or animation work. There are also "enhanced television" arenas that deal with websites and the Internet. All of these areas, no matter

how technical, still require creativity and ingenuity in putting programs together. All of them demand advanced computer skills and a bachelor's degree.

Instructional Programming

Teachers often use videos in the classroom to assist with lessons from geography to history, or when dealing with more sensitive issues such as diversity.

Producing educational media for the classroom is an option for someone who wants to teach children but who does not want to be a classroom teacher. A double major in education and communication arts would be good preparation for such a career. Work in this area will require a familiarity with state educational standards—standards that students must meet before graduating from high school. A producer of classroom videos needs to work with an advisory board that consists of teachers, state education department staff, and other professionals with appropriate areas of expertise. In other words, producing a series on geography, on history, on math, or on diversity necessitates engaging expert educators (e.g., local university professors) from those specific areas. A familiarity with curriculum development, which is possessed by anyone who has a degree in education, is also helpful when producing instructional videos. However, the field is not limited to just those individuals who have degrees in education. Expertise in a particular subject area may be just as valuable. For example, someone who has a double major consisting of science and a communication arts may be ideally suited for the creation of science videos. This idea of double majors can be extended to almost any other subject area.

Most research shows that successful educational programs for children incorporate interactivity. Instructional programming for the classroom deals with more than a series of videos on a specific topic; it requires ancillary materials that stretch into Internet functions and employ website design, HTML editing, online courseware, teacher guides, and/or CD-ROM or DVD media. It all comes as a package, and thus the media producer becomes a multimedia producer.

Industrial Educational Media

In any given region, there are hundreds of jobs that require video production. Rather than investing in their own video production facilities, the individual companies will instead look to outsiders to produce the desired videos. This "industrial" educational media production provides a more commercial environment in which to work.

The subject matter with which they will be asked to deal is extremely varied. It could cover anything from television advertisements for a company that just came out with a new, technologically innovative software program; to hospitals that need to demonstrate new surgical procedures; to mental-health facilities that model new treatment techniques for social-service providers. It might be a university women's studies department that has funds to produce tapes for women in rape crisis situations, or a social-work department that is producing a tape about teaching high-risk students, or maybe an engineering department that has a grant with outreach requirements that can be fulfilled through the distribution of a video production.

The pace for the creation of industrial educational media and the nature of the final product might be somewhat different from other educational products, but there is definitely less bureaucracy involved with the production of industrial media. What may be more important for some, the opportunities provided by the production of industrial educational media can help driven individuals to create their own production companies.

Changing Technologies

It must be recognized that people are no longer simply just watching television. With the arrival of digital television and other communication advancements, producers must begin to reach out to people wherever they are. Online and on video, in words and in music, educational media producers must extend educational programming into homes, into classrooms, into libraries, and into the workplace. Therefore, the opportunities for using creativity to improve education will continue to expand as new technologies continue to develop.

See also: COMPUTER SOFTWARE, EDUCATIONAL; PUBLIC BROADCASTING; SESAME STREET; TELEVISION, EDUCATIONAL.

Internet Websites

CollegeView Partners. (2001). "Education Index." <http://www.educationindex.com/>.
Gateway to Educational Materials. (2001). "GEM Project Site." <http://www.geminfo.org/>.
Lightspan. (2001). "Online Learning for School and Home." <http://www.lightspan.com>.
U.S. Department of Education. (2001). "Office of Educational Technology." <http://www.ed.gov/Technology/>.

KAY F. KLUBERTANZ

EDUCATIONAL TELEVISION
See: Educational Media Producers; Researchers for Educational Television Programs; Television, Educational

EFFECTS
See: Advertising Effects; Arousal Processes and Media Effects; Catharsis Theory and Media Effects;

Cultivation Theory and Media Effects; Cumulative Media Effects; Desensitization and Media Effects; Election Campaigns and Media Effects; Mood Effects and Media Exposure; News Effects; Nutrition and Media Effects; Parental Mediation of Media Effects; Social Cognitive Theory and Media Effects; Sports and Media Effects; Tobacco and Media Effects

ELDERLY AND THE MEDIA

The population of people who are more than sixty-five years of age (often labeled "older adults") is estimated to grow to 37 million in the United States by 2015, an increase of 78 percent over the size of the population in the mid-1970s. As this age group expands, so does interest in the leisure activities and lifestyles of older adults. In part because watching television is the leisure activity that occupies the most time per week for older adults, media researchers have investigated the patterns and effects of media use in this age group.

Aging and Levels of Viewing

It is generally accepted that elderly adults watch more television than any other age group. According to Nielsen data, the average level of viewing among adults who are sixty-five years of age or older is between four and five hours per day—compared to two to three hours for younger adults. Although these comparisons seem relatively straightforward and uncontroversial, comparing averages in this way is a simplification that deserves further discussion.

First, viewing levels and the predictors of viewing are more variable among older adults than among younger age groups (Chayko, 1993). The average of five hours says relatively little about how much time most older adults spend watching television, whereas the average of two to three hours represents the viewing of the majority of younger adults. In fact, there are some older adults who watch for many hours a day, others who watch moderate amounts, and some who watch virtually no television at all.

Second, it is unclear what causes age differences in average levels of viewing. One of the most common explanations put forward by authors such as Robert Bower (1985) is that elderly adults watch more television because they have the time and opportunity. That is, most people watch as much as they are able, and elderly adults are able to watch more because they are more likely to be retired. A similar argument proposed by Alan Rubin and Rebecca Rubin (1982) is that elderly adults watch television because it fills needs created by retirement and increasing infirmity, such as information, companionship, and entertainment. Both of these accounts are maturational explanations. That is, age differences in viewing are assumed to reflect the life events of individuals such as getting a job, getting married, having children, and retiring.

James Danowski and John Ruchinskas (1983) have an alternative explanation: Maybe individuals remain relatively constant in amount of television viewing across the life span, but earlier generations watch more than recent generations. Those early generations watch more because television became widely available when they were in their midlife peak of purchasing power and interest in new technologies. According to this account, cross-sectional comparisons (e.g., between young, middle, and older adults) that seem to find age differences, really reveal variation between generations.

Various studies have been conducted using large-scale national data sets to try to resolve these issues, with inconsistent results. Clearly, age, generation, and time of measurement all play roles in determining viewing levels, but the relative sizes of the roles vary by the country in which viewing was measured and by the way in which viewing was measured (e.g., single-item versus multi-item measures; preelection viewing versus overall television viewing).

What Do Older Adults Watch?

The most striking characteristic of the viewing habits of older adults is how heavily they are dominated by factual (rather than fictional) content. In numerous surveys conducted between 1970 and 1999 (e.g., Goodman, 1990), older adults reported that their favorite content consisted of news, documentaries, public affairs programming, and game shows. According to ratings information from the Simmons Market Research Bureau in 1991, adults over sixty-five were the largest single audience for local and network prime-time news. Although older adults were less likely to have cable television than younger age groups, when they did have cable they formed the largest audience for community access programming.

Of course, there are important variations in viewing by subgroups of elderly adults. For example, in a survey by Norbert Mundorf and Winifred Brownell (1990), elderly males listed sporting events among their favorite content, and elderly women listed soap operas and dramas. John Burnett (1991) also reported differences based on income. Affluent older adults were more likely (than the less-affluent older adults) to have cable and to report watching premium cable channels, CNN, and PBS. Less-affluent older adults were more likely (than the more-affluent older adults) to report watching prime-time movies, late-night reruns, and religious programs.

Why should nonfictional content form such a large part of the television diet of older adults? Older adults, like younger adults, report that their primary motive for watching television is to be entertained, so, on the face of it, their emphasis on nonfictional content is surprising. One explanation may be that fictional content often contains sexual and violent material. In a number of surveys, older adults reported finding such material offensive. Although news programming also contains high levels of violence, older adults may perceive it as less gratuitous.

Another explanation for the emphasis on non-fictional programming may be that the majority of characters in fictional television content are young (as discussed below), and therefore the plots of fictional content typically revolve around concerns and issues related to young adults. There is some evidence that older adults prefer to see older characters both in fictional and factual content if given the opportunity. Jake Harwood (1997) analyzed the age distribution of characters in the top ten prime-time Nielsen-rated shows for ages two to eleven, eighteen to fifty-four, and over sixty-five. He reported that all viewer age groups watched a television population of leading characters that was skewed in favor of their own age, even overrepresented compared to their presence in the real-world population. There was the same, somewhat weaker, pattern for supporting characters. In an experimental examination of age-based preferences for content, Marie-Louise Mares and

Joanne Cantor (1992) gave older adults synopses of nonfictional television programs that varied in terms of the age of the main characters. When asked to rate how much they would like to see each program, the respondents gave higher ratings to programs featuring older characters.

Other Media Use

Older adults spend less time listening to the radio (typically between one and two hours per day) than do younger adults. James Robinson and Tom Skill (1995) suggested that age differences in time spent listening may be explained by the fact that most people listen to the radio while they are working and driving—and older adults tend to spend less time at these activities. According to ratings information from the Simmons Market Research Bureau in 1991, older adults listened to country music, talk radio, news, and nostalgia programming, generally on daytime AM rather than FM stations. They were significantly more likely to listen to news or talk radio than were young adults. Burnett (1991) found that, as with television, gender and financial status played a role in favorite radio content. More-affluent older adults preferred easy-listening music, whereas less-affluent older adults listened to country music, gospel music, and religious programming. Men were much more likely than women to listen to radio sports programming.

Newspaper reading increases with age, until age sixty-five—when it starts to decrease slightly (presumably partly due to vision impairments associated with aging). Overall, adults who are more than fifty-five years of age are significantly more likely to read one or more newspapers per day than are younger adults. As with television viewing, it is probable that cross-sectional comparisons of averages reflect generational as well as aging effects, and that earlier generations spent more time reading newspapers than more-recent generations.

Portrayals of the Elderly on Television

James Robinson and Tom Skill (1995) conducted a content analysis of prime-time network fictional programming aired in 1990. Their results replicated two decades of reports by researchers such as George Gerbner on portrayals of age on television. First, Robinson and Skill reported that elderly adults continued to be underrepresented

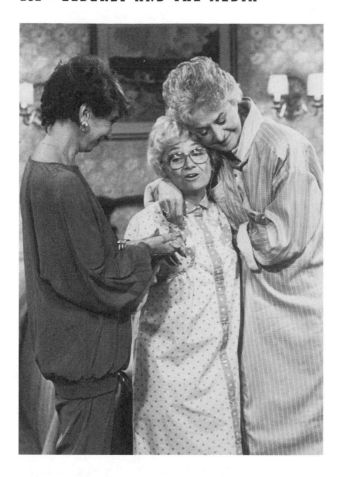

The Golden Girls, *a hit television series in the 1980s featuring Bea Arthur (right) and Estelle Getty (center), was one of the most successful series to feature an entire cast of older women. The show dealt both with topics related to aging and with topics related to caring for an aging parent. (Bettmann/Corbis)*

on television, compared to real-world demographics. Less than 3 percent of characters were sixty five years of age or older (that is, 34 characters out of a total of 1,446). Moreover, only 3 of the older adults shown were major characters (9 percent of older characters compared to 19 percent for the total sample). Nearly 90 percent of older characters were white; the remainder were African American. There were no Latino or Asian-American adults over sixty-five years of age.

Prior research reports had indicated that older male characters tended to outnumber older female characters. Robinson and Skill found that among characters who were sixty-five years of age or older, women outnumbered men, reflecting real-world demographics. However, among characters who were between fifty and sixty-four years of age, there were nearly three times as many men as women. Men who were more than fifty years of

age were more likely than older women to be depicted as married rather than widowed or divorced, and were depicted as more financially secure. Finally, adults who were more than fifty years of age were much more likely than younger adults to be shown as having a religious affiliation.

Robinson and Skill did not report on more qualitative aspects of the portrayals. Research conducted during the 1970s by George Gerbner and his associates (1980) reported that elderly characters were often portrayed as foolish and eccentric and that they were typically comedic figures who were not treated with respect or courtesy.

Effects of Age Depictions on Younger Viewers

If old age is accorded such little attention and respect on television, what effect does this have on the younger viewers' images of old age? Unfortunately, much of the existing research is dated and merely involves comparing attitudes toward aging among viewers who watched heavy amounts of television and viewers who watch light amounts. Overall, though, the research suggests that television viewing perpetuates stereotypes about old age.

Gerbner and his associates (1980) reported that people who watched a heavy amount of television were more likely than similar groups of people who watched a light amount of television to think that older people were not open-minded, adaptable, alert, or good at getting things done. They also believed that the proportion of older people in the population was declining, that older people were less healthy than previous generations of older adults, and that people were not living as long as they did in the past. The relationship between viewing and negative stereotypes of old age was strongest for those who were between eighteen and twenty-nine years of age. Finally, people who watched a heavy amount of television perceived "old age" as beginning sooner (i.e., at fifty-one years of age) than people who watched a light amount of television, who, on average, thought that old age began at fifty-seven years of age. Moreover, a higher proportion of people who watched a heavy amount of television agreed that women become "old" before men do.

Effects of Age Depictions on Older Viewers

Felipe Korzenny and Kimberly Neuendorf (1980) surveyed older adults and reported that those who viewed for escape reasons also tended to have relatively negative images of themselves. Although the direction of causality could not be determined from this survey, the authors suggested that television viewing contributed to negative self-concepts because of the infrequent but stereotypical images of old age. Other research suggests that the results of viewing are more complex.

One reason for the complexity is that, as Harwood (1997) reported, older adults (like all age groups) are adept at finding images of their own age group on television. A second reason is that older adults often have more-positive perceptions of the portrayals of old age than do communication researchers. Elliot Schreiber and Douglas Boyd (1980) reported that the elderly adults in their sample generally thought that elderly characters in television commercials were positively portrayed. Similarly, Richard Hofstetter and his colleagues (1993) found that 80 percent of their elderly sample disagreed that television news portrayed older adults less favorably than younger adults. Between 60 percent and 70 percent disagreed that talk shows and television dramas had less-favorable portrayals of old age than of youth. Moreover, people who watched more television overall, and more news in particular, had more-positive perceptions of portrayals of old age. The subset of respondents who perceived unfavorable stereotyping in television content were generally those who were less physically able, were less mobile, and were more depressed. That is, those who had reason to be dissatisfied with their own aging were more sensitive to negative images of aging on television.

It is not surprising that many elderly adults focus on the few salient positive portrayals of old age and choose to disregard the less-favorable portrayals. John Bell (1992) examined the title sequences of five prime-time programs that were most popular with older audiences in 1989 (*Murder She Wrote*, *Golden Girls*, *Matlock*, *Jake and the Fatman*, and *In the Heat of the Night*). These programs all featured elderly characters portrayed as powerful, affluent, active, admired, and often quite physically attractive. The characters were mentally competent, often solving mysteries that puzzled younger adults.

Even when older adults do see negative images of old age, the effects may not be uniformly negative. Mares and Cantor (1992) found that older

adults may sometimes use portrayals of old age to provide information about how well they are faring relative to other people their age. In their study, lonely older adults reported feeling better after they watched a documentary about a sad, socially isolated man, possibly because the program allowed them to reassess their situation and decide that they were doing relatively well. In contrast, other lonely older adults continued to feel sad after watching a version of the documentary in which the old man was depicted as happy and socially integrated, possibly because the program made their own situation seem sorrier by comparison. Nonlonely adults responded more empathically to the two versions, feeling worse after seeing the sad man and remaining positive after seeing the happy man.

Conclusion

Emotional responses to portrayals of old age are not homogeneous. As always, it is important to note differences by subgroups of older adults, rather than assuming that the population of people who are more than sixty-five years of age is an undifferentiated group.

See also: CULTIVATION THEORY AND MEDIA EFFECTS; NEWS EFFECTS.

Bibliography

Bell, John. (1992). "In Search of a Discourse on Aging: The Elderly on Television." *Gerontologist* 32(3):305–311.

Bower, Robert T. (1985). *The Changing Television Audience in America*. New York: Columbia University Press.

Burnett, John J. (1991). "Examining the Media Habits of the Affluent Elderly." *Journal of Advertising Research* 31(5)33–41.

Chayko, Mary. (1993). "How You 'Act Your Age' When You Watch TV." *Sociological Forum* 8(4):573–593.

Danowski, James A., and Ruchinskas, John E. (1983). "Period, Cohort, and Aging Effects: A Study of Television Exposure in Presidential Election Campaigns, 1952–1980." *Communication Research* 10(1):77–96.

Gerbner, George; Gross, Larry; Signorielli, Nancy; and Morgan, Michael. (1980). "Aging with Television: Images on Television Drama and Conceptions of Social Reality." *Journal of Communication* 30(1):37–48.

Goodman, R. Irwin. (1990). "Television News Viewing by Older Adults." *Journalism Quarterly* 67(1):137–141.

Harwood, Jake. (1997). "Viewing Age: Lifespan Identity and Television Viewing Choices." *Journal of Broadcasting and Electronic Media* 41(2):203–213.

Hofstetter, C. Richard; Schultze, William A.; Mahoney, Sean M.; and Buss, Terry F. (1993). "The Elderly's Perception of TV Ageist Stereotyping: TV or Contextual Aging?" *Communication Reports* 6(2):92–100.

Korzenny, Felipe, and Neuendorf, Kimberly. (1980). "Television Viewing and the Self Concept of the Elderly." *Journal of Communication* 30:71–80.

Mares, Marie-Louise, and Cantor, Joanne. (1992). "Elderly Viewers' Responses to Televised Portrayals of Old Age: Empathy and Mood Management Versus Social Comparison." *Communication Research* 19:459–478.

Mundorf, Norbert, and Brownell, Winifred. (1990). "Media Preferences of Older and Younger Adults." *Gerontologist* 30(5):685–692.

Robinson, James D., and Skill, Tom. (1995). "Media Usage Patterns and Portrayals of the Elderly." In *Handbook of Communication and Aging Research*, eds. John Nussbaum and Justine Coupland. Mahwah, NJ: Lawrence Erlbaum.

Rubin, Alan M., and Rubin, Rebecca B. (1982). "Contextual Age and Television Use." *Human Communication Research* 8:228–244.

Schreiber, Ellen S., and Boyd, Douglas, A. (1980). "How the Elderly Perceive Television." *Journal of Communication* 30(4):61–70.

Simmons Market Research Bureau. (1991). *The 1990 Study of Media and Markets*. New York: Simmons Market Research.

MARIE-LOUISE MARES

■ ELECTION CAMPAIGNS AND MEDIA EFFECTS

For most people living in established democracies and societies that are in transition to democracy, election campaigns are primarily experienced through the media. Politicians know that far more people turn to the media for information than turn out for political rallies in local town squares. The daily campaign activities are thus primarily designed to meet the constraints and deadlines of the major news outlets. Therefore, there are two important contexts to consider when thinking about the effects of the media in election campaigns. One is the context of the campaign or the potential media effect on the campaigns of candidates, which can be described as the institutional level of media effects. The other is the context of the potential media effect on individual voters or citizens, which can be described as media effects at the individual level.

Institutional Contexts and Effects

The institutional effects of the media on the campaigns of candidates may vary depending on the type of electoral system, the rules and regulations governing campaign coverage, and other institutional characteristics of the political and media systems. In the United States, for example, where the race for the presidency begins a year prior to the election with candidates declaring their candidacy and then moves into the primary season when Republicans and Democrats vote in each state to select the ultimate nominees for the parties, the media play a very important role in shaping expectations and judging outcomes. In the year leading up to the actual election, the media pass judgement on the viability of the candidates based on the indicators that the media decide are important.

One of the most important indicators has been the amount of money a campaign has raised, and another is the professional background of the candidate's campaign managers. These two factors have led to some candidates withdrawing from the race even before the primary season begins, so voters are never even given a chance to pass judgement on those particular candidates. In the 2000 race for the presidency, money raised was used as the major indicator of the viability of George W. Bush, and any challengers on the Republican side were considered to be marginal until the primary season began. The surprise victory of Senator John McCain in the 2000 New Hampshire Republican primary was all the more powerful because it exceeded expectations, and momentum provided by that win generated more than six million dollars in campaign donations via the Internet. The Internet has made campaign donations much faster, and its use in campaigns may further fuel the momentum provided by unexpected outcomes. In other countries where money is not an important indicator of candidate viability because of different campaign finance rules, or where the professionalism of electioneering is a more recent phenomenon, there may be less opportunity for media to have an effect on the campaigns of parties and candidates.

The shaping of expectations is very important—sometimes more important than actual outcomes. In the New Hampshire primary in 1992, for example, Bill Clinton finished second after Paul Tsongas. That fact is difficult for most people to remember because the media coverage of that primary named Clinton the real winner because he did much better than expected. As this shows, one does not have to win a primary in order to be labeled the winner.

Media coverage, of course, is not determined by journalists alone. It is a product of the efforts of politicians and their advisors, the so-called spin doctors who talk with journalists. To what extent do politicians have control over the news agenda? A comparative study of news coverage of elections in Great Britain and the United States in the 1980s and how it was produced showed that British politicians had considerably more opportunity to influence television news coverage than U.S. politicians did and that U.S. television journalists exerted considerably more discretion in shaping the news agenda than their British counterparts did. Holli Semetko, Jay Blumler, Michael Gurevitch, and David Weaver (1991) provided evidence for this conclusion with a variety of content analysis indicators. These indicators included the following:

- the amount of space used in the main evening news program for coverage of election news (more in Great Britain than the United States),
- the amount of news devoted to politicians' "soundbites" (considerably more in Great Britain),
- extent to which the main topics of news stories were initiated by politicians or journalists (more party-initiated news in Great Britain, more media-initiated news in the United States),
- the proportion of political stories in which politicians or parties were the main focus (greater in Great Britain than the United States), and
- extent to which reporters offered evaluations of political participants (more in the United States than in Britain).

Whereas British reporters were more likely to offer only descriptive comments on politicians' activities on the campaign trail, U.S. reporters were more likely to evaluate candidate performance. The only instance in which politicians in both countries were on equal footing in terms of their ability to influence the news agenda was in the domain of visuals. Politicians in both countries initiated the majority of key visuals in election news stories, and the vast majority of these visuals were favorable. In the United States, however, positive visuals were far more likely to have been accompanied by critical voiceover commentary by reporters; in Great Britain reporters were more likely to describe the scene in a neutral way. A look at television coverage of elections in the two countries in the 1990s suggests that while British reporting may be moving in the direction of the U.S. coverage, there is still some gap between the two.

Other institutional contexts of importance include the balance between public and commercial (private) broadcasting, the political autonomy of broadcasting from government and political parties, the rules and traditions that surround party access to broadcasting, and the extent of partisanship in the printed press. In theory, television (whether the channel is public or private) is expected to provide impartial coverage of politics, and this is deemed to be of particular importance at election time. Research by Semetko (1996) has shown that in practice, the meaning of "balance" in election news varies not only across countries but also across news organizations within a particular country.

In the United States and other countries, for example, parties of government and the president or prime minister continue to conduct the business of government during the official election campaign as well as in the weeks preceding it. It is up to reporters and journalists, as well as political partisans, to label any such event or activity as "campaigning." U.S. television reporters have been more ready than their colleagues elsewhere to label as campaigning any incumbent activity at any time during an election year, regardless of the gravity of the event or situation. For example, Jimmy Carter's "Rose Garden strategy" in the final weeks of the 1980 election during the U.S. hostage crisis and George H. W. Bush's 1988 visit to Florida (a "key" state in that presidential campaign) to provide government relief to the victims of Hurricane Andrew were both connected by journalists to vote-getting strategies. As a contrast, in the final days before the 1990 election in Germany, the first national election after the fall of the

The U.S. national conventions, where each political party is given exclusive prime-time television coverage, serve as the official transition from the state party primaries to the national interparty competition for the election of the President and the Vice-President of the United States. (Joseph Sohm; ChromoSohm Inc./Corbis)

Berlin Wall and the unification of the eastern and western parts of the country, television news coverage failed to mention that Chancellor Helmut Kohl's meetings with heads of state were "photo opportunities" or in any way connected to enhancing his image as a leader.

These cross-national contrasts in reporting styles are changing, however. David Swanson and Paolo Mancini (1996) have argued that most countries had by the 1990s moved in the direction of the United States with respect to campaigning techniques and strategies, as well as with respect to an increased number of television channels and thus more competitive media markets. This brings with it a tendency for reporting to become more ratings-dependent and star-oriented coverage. One indication of this trend was the decision in 1999 to have Klaus-Peter Siegloch anchor the main evening news on Germany's Second German Television channel (ZDF), one of the country's two public service broadcasters. Siegloch was a

well-known figure because of the reports that he had been filing from Washington, D.C., during the previous five years. As a result, he brought his personal credibility to the program, along with a more American style of anchoring, and he incorporated many of the format features found in U.S. evening television news. The result was increased ratings for the program.

One very popular form of broadcast access to election information is the debate between party leaders. A debate is arguably the single most important unifying event of a campaign, if only because millions of electors share the experience. While debates are a tradition in U.S. presidential elections, they are less common in other countries. Debates can be the centerpiece of the campaign, and they can have important effects on the candidate image, perceptions of who is winning, and ultimately voter participation. Although debates can produce more voter involvement in elections and are therefore quite welcome, there is no guarantee that debates will take place. For example, debates between the party leaders were common in Germany in the 1970s and 1980s, and Peter Schrott (1990) has shown that the perceived winners of the debates won more election votes than the perceived losers of the debates. However, there were no debates in the Bundestag elections of 1990, 1994, and 1998 because the incumbent chancellor, Kohl, was running for re-election as the leader of the Christian Democratic Party (CDU) and was not interested in participating in debates.

Individual Contexts and Effects

Media effects on individuals may be short-term or long-term effects. They may be cognitive (i.e., effects on political knowledge), attitudinal (i.e., effects on political opinions) or behavioral (i.e., effects on actual voting). Despite the fact that television has transformed the electoral process, it has proven difficult to isolate exposure or attention to television as a significant variable in determining vote choice. In the 1990s, a number of studies explored media effects in one or another of these domains in the national elections of a variety of countries. Richard Johnston and his colleagues (1992) studied Canada. For Great Britain, William Miller (1991) studied the 1987 general election, John Curtice and Semetko (1994) studied the 1992 general election, and Pippa Norris and her colleagues (1999) studied the 1997 general election. Semetko and Julio Borquez (1991) studied the effects of the media in the 1988 presidential election in France, while Semetko and Klaus Schoenbach (1994) studied the first national election in German after the 1990 unification.

The United States has the longest history of election research, and it dates back to the 1940s. The media became a central focus of some election research in the 1960s and 1970s, and they have been the central focus of many more studies since then. Some important examples include Thomas Patterson (1980, 1994), who has written seminal books on media effects in the 1976 presidential election and has conducted a long-term study of changes in news coverage of presidential campaigns, Marion Just and her colleagues (1996), who have studied how people interpret election information, and Russell Dalton and his colleagues (1998), who have studied the way in which metropolitan newspapers mediated the 1992 campaign. Two of the most well-known con-

cepts in media effects research on political attitudes, agenda-setting and priming, provide a way of looking at questions of effects of news and information on public opinion and the influence of politicians on news content.

The notion of an all powerful media—with direct effects injected as if by hypodermic needle—was an important part of mass society theorists' explanation of the experience of Nazi Germany. The propaganda model of the 1920s later led social scientists in the United States to study the power of the media in democracy and the electoral process. However, the early empirical evidence suggested only a limited ability of the media to influence the public's political attitudes and voting behavior. Empirical research into media effects on partisan preferences in U.S. elections in the 1940s brought the so-called "reinforcement" model of media influence into fashion. According to this model, exposure to news during the campaign did not change vote choice for most people; it simply reinforced preexisting partisan preferences. By the 1970s and 1980s, the news media became major players in the presidential selection process. As a consequence, a broader view of media influence, known as the "limited effects" model, emerged.

The concept of "agenda-setting" refers primarily to the process by which issues in the news become important in public opinion. It brings scholarship back to the notion of a powerful media, but one which does not have electoral outcomes or the vote as its primary focal point. It has become one of the most important concepts in public opinion and media effects research. Since the term itself was first coined by Maxwell McCombs and Donald Shaw (1972) in their community study of media agenda-setting in the 1968 U.S. presidential campaign, hundreds of empirical studies have been published on the subject (see Protess and McCombs, 1991). The majority of these studies focus on the effect of news agendas or media agendas on public opinion. As in the year-long study by David Weaver and his colleagues (1981), many of these studies involve data collected during election campaigns. Taken together, these studies provide a substantial body of evidence that the news media can and do influence public perceptions of the importance of issues.

A number of studies have also failed to support the agenda-setting hypothesis, however. The study conducted by Miller (1990) of the 1987 British general election and the study conducted by Norris and her colleagues (1999) of the 1997 general election found little or no significant agenda-setting effects over the four-week campaign period. Similarly, in Germany's 1990 election, Semetko and Schoenbach (1994) found that the most visible issues in the news were not those that were most important with regard to public opinion. These studies provide important evidence to suggest that agenda-setting, as it was originally and narrowly defined in terms of media effects on issue salience, was not operating. However, the studies also found evidence of other significant media effects, particularly in the domain of public evaluations of political parties and top candidates. Agenda-setting therefore should not be taken as the sole or the primary indicator of a powerful news media. The absence of evidence to support the agenda-setting hypothesis in an election does not mean that other important effects on opinions are entirely absent.

A related concept is priming, which refers to the ability of what is emphasized in the news to alter the standards by which citizens evaluate political leaders. By emphasizing some issues and by ignoring others, the news media may "prime" the public to think about those issues when judging the performance of politicians (see Iyengar and Kinder, 1987; and Iyengar, 1991). Jon Krosnick and Donald Kinder (1990) show that, indeed, exposure to news about Attorney General Ed Meese's announcement concerning U.S. involvement in the Iran-Contra Affair directly and immediately led to changes in the issues that were used by the public to evaluate President Ronald Reagan's performance.

One of the earliest findings of agenda-setting research established variation in effects; not all of the people are influenced all of the time. One of the most important developments in agenda-setting and priming research has been the identification of the contingent conditions under which influence can occur. Two of the most commonly discussed conditions are interest and knowledge. A number of studies have established that effects can be modified by the public's interest in information or knowledge about a subject. In these studies, the more knowledgeable people are distinguished from those who have little or no knowledge. Generally speaking, those who are

least susceptible to agenda-setting and priming effects are those who have some independent store of knowledge. This knowledge enables people to argue against what they see in the news. These studies therefore offer a rather disturbing conclusion from the perspective of democracy. Shifts in public opinion about the president most commonly occur in those who are the least informed or knowledgeable, as those who know the least and have weak or no attachments to political parties are most likely to be influenced by the news.

Political Advertising and Media Effects

Although scholars and practitioners alike agree that political advertising is important for election campaigns, there is no clear agreement on the effects of political advertising on electoral outcomes. Political advertisements on television and radio count for much more in U.S. elections than in many other countries such as Great Britain, for example, where the purchase of broadcast advertising is prohibited and the forms of television advertisements are regulated. There are far more advertisements in U.S. elections than in elections abroad, and as Lynda Lee Kaid and Ann Johnston (1991) have shown, the percentages of negative advertisements in U.S. election campaigns has increased over the years. Negative advertisements take various forms; at the core they involve criticism of a candidate, a policy position, or past performance. An overview of research by Kaid (1999) has shown that exposure to advertisements does influence public perceptions of the candidates. However, a meta-analysis (i.e., an empirical study of all the studies published to date specifically on the effects of negative advertising) led Richard Lau and his colleagues (1999, p. 851) to question "why negative political advertisements have become so popular in practice when there is so little evidence that they work especially well."

Despite these doubts on the effectiveness of such advertising, debate continues over the question of whether negative advertising mobilizes or demobilizes the electorate. For example, it has been argued that "going negative" actually discourages people from going to the polls to vote and diminishes confidence in the political system (Ansolabehere and Iyengar, 1995; Ansolabehere, Iyengar, and Simon, 1999), but analysis of similar data resulted in the view that such conclusions cannot be sustained (Wattenberg and Brians,

1999). Research by Steven Finkel and John Geer (1998) on the effects of attack advertisements have also cast doubt on the idea that they demobilize the electorate.

Research methods are often at the core of the debate, although different campaign settings, for example, whether it is a presidential, congressional, or local election, can also influence conclusions about the power of negative advertisements and negative information. Kim Kahn and Patrick Kenney (1999) showed that in the 1990 U.S. Senate elections, for example, voters were able to distinguish between "mudslinging" and "legitimate criticism," and when the latter (but not the former) increased, citizens were more likely to vote. The effect was especially strong for those who had low interest in politics, little knowledge about politics, and lacked attachments to the main parties or described themselves as independents.

Conclusion

Much of what is now known about the media in election campaigns comes from research conducted in the United States. There is a considerable amount of scholarship in Germany on media content and its uses and effects in elections, as well as a growing body of literature in Canada, Australia, Great Britain, Italy, Spain, Scandinavia, and The Netherlands. However, data remain extremely limited for many other advanced industrial societies. It has only been relatively recent that the topic has become the focus of scholarship in Latin America, largely because of the rise of television as a major source of political information, candidates' strategic use of the news media, and the growth of public opinion polling in that region. In Russia, Eastern Europe, the new republics, and other societies in transition to democracy, research on elections and the media is still in its infancy.

The institutional contexts of elections in these other countries can be quite different from the United States. The main challenge for research on individual-level effects is to identify the contingent conditions under which effects occur. In other words, researchers need to identify the specific characteristics of media contents and media audiences that lead to specific types of effects, and they need to determine how the institutional contexts enhance or diminish these effects.

See also: DEMOCRACY AND THE MEDIA; NEWS EFFECTS; PROPAGANDA; SOCIAL CHANGE AND THE MEDIA; SOCIAL GOALS AND THE MEDIA; SOCIETY AND THE MEDIA.

Bibliography

Ansolabehere, Stephen, and Iyengar, Shanto. (1995). *Going Negative: How Political Advertisements Shrink and Polarize the Electorate.* New York: Free Press.

Ansolabehere, Stephen; Iyengar, Shanto; and Simon, Adam. (1999). "Replicating Experiments Using Aggregate and Survey Data: The Case of Negative Advertising and Turnout." *American Political Science Review* 93:901–909.

Curtice, John, and Semetko, Holli. (1994). "Does It Matter What the Papers Say?" In *Labour's Last Chance?*, eds. Anthony Heath, Roger Jowell, and John Curtice. Aldershot, Eng.: Dartmouth.

Dalton, Russell J.; Beck, Paul A.; and Huckfeldt, Robert. (1998). "Partisan Cues and the Media: Information Flows in the 1992 Presidential Election." *American Political Science Review* 92:111–126.

Finkel, Steven E., and Geer, John G. (1998). "A Spot Check: Casting Doubt on the Demobilizing Effect of Attack Advertising." *American Journal of Political Science* 42:573–595.

Iyengar, Shanto. (1991). *Is Anyone Responsible?* Chicago: University of Chicago Press.

Iyengar, Shanto, and Kinder, Donald R. (1987). *News that Matters: Agenda-Setting and Priming in a Television Age.* Chicago: University of Chicago Press.

Johnston, Richard; Blais, Andre; Brady, Henry E.; and Crete, Jean. (1992). *Letting the People Decide: Dynamics of a Canadian Election.* Stanford, CA: Stanford University Press.

Just, Marion; Crigler, Ann; Alger, Dean; Kern, Montague; West, Darrell; and Cook, Timothy. (1996). *Crosstalk: Citizens, Candidates, and the Media in a Presidential Campaign.* Chicago: University of Chicago Press.

Kaid, Lynda Lee. (1999). "Political Advertising: A Summary of Research Findings." In *The Handbook of Political Marketing*, ed. Bruce I. Newman. Thousand Oaks, CA: Sage Publications.

Kaid, Lynda Lee, and Johnston, Ann. (1991). "Negative Versus Positive Television Advertising in US Presidential Campaigns, 1960–1988." *Journal of Communication* 41:53–64.

Kahn, Kim F., and Kenney, Patrick J. (1999). "Do Negative Campaigns Mobilize or Suppress Turnout? Clarifying the Relationships Between Negativity and Participation." *American Political Science Review* 93:877–889.

Krosnick, Jon A., and Kinder, Donald R. (1990). "Altering the Foundations for Support for the President Through Priming." *American Political Science Review* 84:497–512.

Lau, Richard R.; Sigelman, Lee; Heldman, Caroline; and Babbitt, Paul. (1999). "The Effects of Negative Political Advertisements: A Meta-Analysis Assessment." *American Political Science Review* 93:851–877.

McCombs, Maxwell, and Shaw, Donald. (1972). "The Agenda-Setting Function of the Mass Media." *Public Opinion Quarterly* 36:176–187.

Miller, William L. (1991). *Media and Voters: The Audience, Content, and Influence of the Press and Television in the 1987 General Election.* Oxford: Clarendon Press.

Norris, Pippa; Curtice, John; Sanders, David; Scammell, Margaret; and Semetko, Holli A. (1999). *On Message: Communicating the Campaign.* London: Sage Publications.

Patterson, Thomas. (1980). *The Mass Media Election.* New York: Praeger.

Patterson, Thomas. (1994). *Out of Order.* New York: Vintage.

Protess, David, and McCombs, Maxwell, eds. (1991). *Agenda-Setting: Readings on Media, Public Opinion and Policymaking.* Hillsdale, NJ: Lawrence Erlbaum.

Schrott, Peter R. (1990). "Electoral Consequences of 'Winning' Televised Campaign Debates." *Public Opinion Quarterly* 54:567–585.

Semetko, Holli A. (1996). "Political Balance on Television: Campaigns in the US, Britain, and Germany." *Harvard International Journal of Press/Politics* 1:51–71.

Semetko, Holli A.; Blumler, Jay G.; Gurevitch, Michael; and Weaver, David. (1991). *The Formation of Campaign Agendas.* Hillsdale, NJ: Lawrence Erlbaum.

Semetko, Holli A., and Borquez, Julio. (1991). "Audiences for Election Communication." In *Mediated Politics in Two Cultures: Presidential Campaigning in the United States and France,* eds. Lynda Lee Kiad, Jacques Gerstle, and Keith Sanders. New York: Praeger.

Semetko, Holli A., and Schoenbach, Klaus. (1994). *Germany's "Unity Election": Voters and the Media.* Cresskill, NJ: Hampton Press.

Swanson, David, and Mancini, Paolo, eds. (1996). *Politics, Media, and Modern Democracy.* New York: Praeger.

Wattenburg, Martin P., and Brians, Craig L. (1999). "Negative Campaign Advertising: Demobilizer or Mobilizer?" *American Political Science Review* 93:891–899.

Weaver, David H.; Graber, Doris A.; McCombs, Maxwell E.; and Eyal, C. E. (1981). *Media Agenda-Setting in a Presidential Election: Issues, Images, and Interest.* New York: Praeger.

HOLLI A. SEMETKO

■ ELECTRONIC COMMERCE

Although use of the term "electronic commerce" (or "e-commerce") dates back only to the 1970s, broadly interpreted it includes all commercial transactions that use any electronic communications facilities. Used this way, its origins extend back to the commercial use of the telegraph in 1861. However, the term was widely adopted in the 1990s to describe business transactions involving the Internet. There is, nonetheless, historical continuity between earlier technologies and the Internet since Internet-based commerce is rooted in prior technologies, policies, and business practices.

The Emergence of Electronic Commerce

During the first half of the twentieth century, the use of the telephone and the introduction of office machines such as the typewriter, adding machine, cash register, mimeograph, and Teletype transformed previous ways of doing business, creating a new paradigm based on mechanical automation. Then, following its development during World War II, the computer became commercially available in 1951. Early computers were large, sensitive, expensive devices for storing and manipulating data. These "mainframe" computers were subsequently connected in closed (nonpublic) proprietary networks by large corporations, research universities, and governmental departments. These networks often used leased telecommunications facilities to transport their data.

By the late 1960s, such networks, called Value-Added Networks (VANs), served a variety of purposes, such as timesharing of mainframe computing, electronic messaging, and data transfer. Companies could acquire electronic data services by leasing the networking services of telephone companies, and by acquiring leased computer time offered by the large in-house shops of companies such as General Electric (GE) and International Business Machines (IBM). Independent companies began to offer packages of combined communications and data processing services, forcing the Federal Communications Commission (FCC) in 1971 to decide whether such providers were telephone "common carriers," and thus subject to extensive regulation. The FCC, in a decision with subsequent critical effect on the development of the Internet, decided they were not.

In the 1970s and 1980s, businesses extended their networks to include suppliers and customers, electronically sending and receiving purchase orders, invoices, and shipping notifications. This kind of communication is called Electronic Data Interchange (EDI). In the 1980s, vendors such as McDonnell Douglas and General Motors introduced computer-aided design, engineering, and manufacturing over these communications networks. During the same period, banks developed a closed system for the management of electronic funds transfers (EFTs). The first consumer-directed network of automatic teller machines (ATMs) was introduced in 1970. Thus, a significant volume of commercial transactions was being conducted over private, digital networks well in advance of the widespread availability of the Internet.

A related development was the improved capability and availability of U.S. and international telecommunications infrastructures, including the gradual introduction of digital technologies. At the same time, the arrival of competition into long-distance telecommunications services and customer-owned communications equipment, and the breakup of the American Telephone and Telegraph (AT&T) monopoly under a 1982 consent decree, provided an environment of increased competition and innovation (especially for service to profitable business customers).

The Advanced Research Projects Agency Network (ARPANET), which was eventually transformed into the Internet, was originally created in 1969 to provide military and university research centers with a digital communications system that was able to self-repair by quickly rerouting packets of data in the event of damage to part of the system. By adopting the set of software instructions developed in 1972 by the Inter-Networking Group, other networks could interconnect to ARPANET in a way that was transparent to the user. The first description of this network of networks as "the Internet" apparently appeared in 1974. This network evolved through the 1970s primarily under the direction and supervision of the U.S. government through the National Science Foundation (NSF), which operated it on a noncommercial basis. Notwithstanding this, there were early pioneers of commercial-type services before the Internet, such as The Source, which started in 1979. However, the technology of the time was cumbersome and daunting to nonexpert users.

This trend—experimentation with technology and services—continued through the 1980s. It has been estimated that there were some two thousand commercial online offerings attempted in the United States during the 1980s. The idea of commerce over a network with a wide consumer base was also initiated in France, with the "Minitel" service, first introduced in 1982. The necessary infrastructure for expansion—high-speed digital transmission facilities and large dedicated computers for storing and forwarding packets of data—all were put into place. The FCC, following the logic of its 1971 decision, ruled that the Internet, and Internet service providers (ISPs), were not subject to common carrier regulation. However, it took some additional developments to make large-scale Internet e-commerce feasible.

By the early 1990s, several factors began to make the idea of commerce over the Internet both feasible and attractive. Networked microcomputers were replacing mainframes and were generally accessible to businesses. Uniform packaged software platforms (operating systems) were widely adopted. The Internet began to establish itself as a global network, and in 1991, the set of instructions underlying the World Wide Web (WWW) were written. This allowed both the display of graphics as well as text on Internet web-pages and the introduction of "hyperlinks," allowing easy movement from one web-page or site to another. This was further enhanced in 1993 by the development of Mosaic, the first "browser" (and predecessor to Netscape Navigator). With these changes, the Internet became more "consumer friendly." Then, in 1995, the NSF surrendered its role in managing the Internet to private enterprise, opening up its full commercial potential.

Subsequently, use of the Internet by businesses as both a substitute for, and complement to, closed EDI networks and public telecommunications facilities rapidly evolved. Websites became more sophisticated, new business models evolved, and an array of new business intermediary services appeared. It also became apparent that the new information technologies would drive a major restructuring of corporate enterprises. By 1997, the phenomenon of Internet-based electronic commerce was thoroughly launched, with wide-ranging implications for businesses, consumers, and society.

A view of the Amazon.com distribution center in Milton Keynes, England, on July 7, 2000, gives a visual "measurement" of the volume that can be involved in electronic commerce, at least in the case of J. K. Rowling's Harry Potter and the Goblet of Fire, *which became the biggest seller in the history of online book sales. (Reuters NewMedia Inc./Corbis)*

Measuring Electronic Commerce

Before addressing the changes that the Internet-as-business-tool has brought about, a few words about the concept of "electronic commerce" and its measurement may be useful in putting industry statistics into context.

There is no single, universally accepted definition of "electronic commerce." Definitions range from extremely inclusive to a narrow requirement that the entire transaction, including payment and delivery, be conducted over the Internet. In its most common usage, e-commerce refers to a transaction some part of which has been conducted over the Internet (although this does not usually reflect transactions in which the Internet was used to collect information used to consummate a transaction elsewhere). This lack of a universal definition is one, but not the only, challenge in interpreting studies purporting to measure "electronic commerce." The amount of e-commerce varies depending on the scope of what is

being measured. For example, one estimate released in early 2000 estimated that there would be $7.29 trillion in e-commerce transactions by the year 2004. However, such large numbers can be misleading.

The Internet is most often used as a substitute for another form of communication (e.g., EDI, telephone, facsimile). Thus, in many cases, there may be little or no net new business occurring, just the same old business being conducted through a new medium. The real benefits to companies of doing business online are more difficult to measure: increased efficiency, fewer errors, lower cost, smaller inventory, elimination of paper, and better relationships with customers.

Furthermore, electronic commerce is typically divided into two kinds: business-to-business and business-to-consumer (some also add consumer-to-consumer and consumer-to-business). These "virtual" divisions mirror physical reality in that business-to-business transactions represent eight to ten times the dollar volume of business-to-consumer transactions. In overall statistics, these numbers are often combined. Moreover, these figures say nothing about profitability. As of 2000, the businesses primarily receiving profits from use of the Internet were companies facilitating electronic commerce, rather than the online businesses themselves.

It is clear nonetheless that there is an extraordinary expansion of e-commerce around the world. This global growth of electronic commerce has raised significant regulatory and legal issues at the national and global levels. The resolution of these issues may either facilitate or hinder the growth of e-commerce.

Electronic Commerce and Globalization

The period following World War II saw a steady growth in the volume and importance of international trade. In the mid-1980s, large parts of the world experienced a "sea change" in their view of the relationship of government and business. Many governments moved from a highly regulatory and national protectionist posture to one of deregulation, privatization, and the opening of domestic markets. The result was the globalization of markets, corporations, finance, banking, and consumerism. The collapse of the bipolar political world with the breakup of the Soviet Union emphasized the dominant role of the United States. The United States was the leader in Internet development, is the home of the largest number of commercial websites, and stands to be the largest gainer from increased global electronic commerce, at least in the short term. Consequently, the United States has adopted a very aggressive policy position in international forums insisting that the global Internet be free from regulation, tariffs, and new taxes. The majority of the developed nations generally support this view. A number of lesser-developed nations do not support this view, because they see "globalization" as a euphemism for "Americanization" and as a threat to their sovereignty and interests.

The organization that most embodies the open-market approach in the trade arena is the World Trade Organization (WTO). Through a series of market-opening agreements, it has been able to reduce or eliminate many tariff barriers to trade, particularly in telecommunications and electronic equipment. This, along with the liberalization of banking and investment rules, helped lay the foundation for a system of electronic global trade.

At the same time, since the Internet is inherently global, cross-border electronic trade raises many policy issues that can only be addressed by international bodies. These include issues of consumer protection, privacy and encryption, advertising, intellectual property, the protection of children, and harmful content. Several international organizations have taken up these themes. These included the WTO, the International Telecommunications Union (ITU), the Organization for Economic Cooperation and Development (OECD), and the World Intellectual Property Organization (WIPO), among others. Some issues have proven quite contentious, such as the differing views on an individual's right of privacy that are held in Europe and in the United States.

These developments also create new challenges (or opportunities) for lawyers. Unresolved legal issues include jurisdiction (who can be sued where), uniform commercial codes, contract law, recognition of digital signatures and digital documents, and uniform consumer protection laws. The process of resolving these issues is ongoing.

Another area vexing governments has been taxation. There is as yet no easy and reliable mechanism for taxing transactions over the Internet. Countries that rely on a value-added tax (such as most European countries) are concerned about possible loss of revenues, as are countries (and states of the United States) that rely heavily on sales-tax revenues and fear losing them—and sales—to enterprises outside their taxing jurisdictions. Some new tax concepts, such as a "bit tax" on the number of bits transferred, have been suggested, but so far, they have all been rejected. Both among nations and within the states of the United States there is a search underway for "global" solutions—uniform taxes across jurisdictions for Internet transactions.

Effects on the Business Enterprise

It is easiest to explain the business effects of electronic commerce by emphasizing two main areas: (1) the website itself and (2) the implications of integrated information technology for the structure of the enterprise (called "e-business"). They are not antithetical but complementary. There is also a general, underlying condition for the continued rapid growth of electronic commerce that is summed up in the word "trust." In this context, it means businesses being able to trust one another, consumers being able to trust businesses, and all of them trusting that the system is both reliable and secure. Attacks on websites, or on the Internet, that erode this trust deter electronic commerce in two ways: (1) by reducing its use and (2) by reducing investment that will support future growth. Thus, stock market dips directed at Internet-based ("dot-com") companies tend to follow negative publicity about security breaches or technical difficulties.

The Website

A company's website is its virtual storefront, which can be designed with varying degrees of sophistication, complexity, and interactivity. It can be a catalog, providing product information; it can permit real-time transactions (purchase, payment, and, if an electronic product, delivery); and it can provide a window for customers into the enterprise.

Although considerably lower in dollar volume than business-to-business e-commerce, much publicity has been focused on sales through retail websites, called "e-tailing." The U.S. Department of Commerce estimates that there was $5.3 billion in Internet sales during the 1999 holiday season. Impressive as it may sound, this represents only about 0.64 percent of all retail sales—but the trend line suggests continued rapid growth.

There are numerous models for websites, typically involving some kind of catalog, a search capability, "shopping carts," and payment systems. Some websites allow for "click to talk," which can put customers directly in touch with a customer service agent. Some websites use other approaches, such as auctions and barter.

For many commercial websites, third-party advertising is perceived as a significant source of revenue—a part of the process of "monetizing the traffic," that is, converting site visits ("clicks" or "hits") into a revenue stream. The measurement and evaluation of the advertising value of traffic to a website remains problematic, but it is receiving intense study by the advertising community. Some commercial websites use "cookies," small bits of software that are implanted by a website into the computer of a visitor and are then used for tracking purposes. Websites that aggregate traffic either vertically (one industry) or horizontally (general purpose), which are used as start points or consistent return points, are called "portals." Other important sites for electronic commerce are called "search engines" (e.g., Yahoo, AltaVista, Lycos), which help potential customers locate resources online.

Doing retail business online has also produced a new set of intermediaries, companies that provide ancillary, but useful or necessary, services to facilitate electronic commerce. These services include privacy codes, security verification, payment systems, networked advertising, order fulfillment, and digital certificates (authentication of identity). There are numerous techniques for attracting consumers to a website, and a variety of possible payment systems, both online and offline, for purchases.

The rapid growth of "dot-com" companies in the late 1990s was fueled by heavy speculative investment in their stocks. While company managers focused on developing market share instead of traditional profits, investors focused on future expectations of earnings, sometimes to a degree inexplicable by past investment theories. The belief seemed to be that a few dominant websites would develop early in each area (the "first mover" advantage), called "category killers," which would be so well known they would dominate the field. Established companies with known brands often have not been among the first to move to e-tailing, for a variety of reasons. However, almost all major retailers are now making the Internet at least a part of their strategy.

The Internet does not seem to be equally hospitable to all kinds of retail commerce. In 1999, the top five categories—computers/software, travel, financial/brokerage, collectables, and music and videos—constituted 75 percent of the dollar volume of sales.

The fundamental lessons for successful websites so far seem to be the importance of (1) creating a brand, (2) building a sense of community with customers, and (3) adding value to the experience of the users.

E-Commerce and the Structure of the Enterprise

Entry into electronic commerce over the Internet is almost inevitably connected with the realization that the introduction of the information technology necessary to provide a full-purpose website also has major implications for the structure of the business enterprise. This transformation has already been initiated in some corporations, often under the name "business process reengineering." It typically involves increased outsourcing, a flattened management structure, reordering of the channels of supply and distribution, and a greater sense of customer orientation. Consulting companies and others offer products for "enterprise resource planning" that integrate all of the functions of the enterprise under one information system.

Social Implications

Concerns have been raised by a number of groups about possible adverse effects of the spread of electronic commerce. These include nationalists, who fear loss of sovereignty to multilateral organizations and global corporations; labor unions, which fear a loss of jobs and a "race to the bottom" as capital migrates freely while labor does not; environmentalists, who fear that "dirty" production facilities will move to countries with the lowest environmental requirements; child-protection organizations, which fear that the search for the lowest-cost production will lead to exploitation of minors; and the traditional political left, which sees the further erosion of the role of the government as provider for the common good and the social safety-net.

Collectively, these groups represent a minority in most developed countries, but when organized together, they create a powerful political statement, as occurred at the December 1999 meeting of the World Trade Organization in Seattle, Washington, where protests and civic disturbances caused the meeting to fail. Following that, there were signs that the United States began to recognize that the views of these groups needed to be heard.

Conclusion

The use of the Internet for business transactions between and among businesses and with consumers is gradually becoming the norm, bringing with it major changes in corporate structure and a reordering of the chains of supply and distribution. There remain significant technical, regulatory, and political issues that could present impediments to further growth. Barring unforeseen catastrophic failures, electronic commerce will become the new business model, moving from a focus on the office machine in the early twentieth century to a focus on information flows in the early twenty-first century.

See also: ADVERTISING EFFECTS; COMMUNITY NETWORKS; COMPUTER LITERACY; ECONOMICS AND INFORMATION; INTERNET AND THE WORLD WIDE WEB; PRIVACY AND ENCRYPTION.

Bibliography

Amor, Daniel. (2000). *The E-Business (R)evolution: Living and Working in an Interconnected World.* Upper Saddle River, NJ: Prentice-Hall.

Canton, James. (1999). *Technofutures: How Leading-Edge Technology Will Transform Business in the 21st Century.* Carlsbad, CA: Hay House.

Fellenstein, Craig, and Wood, Ron. (1999). *Exploring E-Commerce, Global E-Business, and E-Society.* Upper Saddle River, NJ: Prentice-Hall.

Kalakota, Ravi. (1999). *E-Business: Roadmap for Success.* Reading: Addison-Wesley.

Keen, Peter; Balance, Craigg; Chan, Sally; and Schrump, Steve. (2000). *Electronic Commerce Relationships: Trust by Design.* Upper Saddle River, NJ: Prentice-Hall.

Kelly, Kevin. (1998). *New Rules for the New Economy: Ten Radical Strategies for a Connected World.* New York: Viking.

"Shopping Around the Web: A Survey of E-Commerce." *Economist,* February 26, 2000, special section, pp. 1–54.

Tapscott, Don; Lowy, Alex; and Ticoll, David, eds. (1998) *Blueprint to the Digital Economy: Wealth Creation in the Era of E-Business.* New York: McGraw-Hill.

U.S. Department of Commerce. (1998). "*The Emerging Digital Economy.*" <http://www.ecommerce.gov/emerging.htm>.

U.S. Department of Commerce. (1999). "The Emerging Digital Economy II." <http://www.ecommerce.gov/ede/>.

White House. (1997). "*A Framework for Global Electronic Commerce.*" <http://www.ecommerce.gov/framewrk.htm>.

Westland, Christopher J., and Clark, Theodore H. K. (1999). *Global Electronic Commerce: Theory and Case Studies.* Cambridge, MA: MIT Press.

World Trade Organization. (1998). *Electronic Commerce and the Role of the WTO.* Geneva: World Trade Organization.

Wigand, Rolf T. (1997). "Electronic Commerce: Definition, Theory, and Context." *Information Society* 13:1–16.

RICHARD D. TAYLOR

ELECTRONICS

See: Consumer Electronics

ENCRYPTION

See: Privacy and Encryption

ETHICS

See: Ethics and Information; Interpersonal Communication, Ethics and; Psychological Media Research, Ethics of

ETHICS AND INFORMATION

The shortest definition of ethics is "moral decision making." What is moral? Morality encompasses people's beliefs and practices about good and evil. If something is moral, that implies conformity to the sanctioned codes or accepted notions of right and wrong, the basic moral values of a community. Morals can be local and/or universal. When individuals use reason to discern the most moral behavior, then they are practicing ethics.

Information ethics focuses on information, not just life. Information gains a prominent role because of its crucial importance to the health of human cultures. In other forms of ethics, only animals and people deserve to be the proper center of moral claim. However, with information at the focal point, the privacy, security, ownership, accuracy, and authenticity of information, as well as access to information, become values in themselves.

The rise in information ethics has not occurred in a vacuum. There exist biomedical ethics, nuclear ethics, and numerous other branches of ethics to coincide with two phenomena: (1) the challenges of new technologies and (2) the breakdown of historical ethical traditions and of common assumptions.

Narrowly construed, information ethics would appear to be a field for librarians. However, people grapple with thorny ethical issues daily in entertainment, news media, nonprofit organizations, governments, businesses, and the population as a whole. The ubiquity of computers means that many people make vital decisions about information on an almost constant basis.

Caring and trust are essential values to develop in a just society. In the field of information ethics, the word "trust" appears repeatedly. Trust is relying with confidence on something or someone. In a healthy society, people should be able to trust information.

Information ethics deserves special attention because of the rather human ability to view personal actions in the intangible, virtual world of information technologies as being less serious than personal actions in the real world. Among the issues open to debate are exporting software, releasing viruses on the Internet, defining copyright and fair use, and combining data from global information systems with other databases, thereby pinpointing people in ways that were never before possible.

In information ethics, a moral agent is a person or artificial agent who works or participates in the information environment and could improve it. Whether any information process is moral or immoral is judged on how the process affects the essence of the information. Information welfare, in other words, is what ought to be promoted by extending information quantity, improving information quality, and enriching the level of information in general.

The Main Areas of Concern about Information

The following example contains the most critical information issues: privacy, accuracy, authenticity, security, access, and ownership.

If a person was speeding down the highway and got stopped by the police, the resulting traffic ticket would contain true but potentially harmful information about that person. Because of the ticket, the driver's insurance policy premium might increase and other friends and relatives might lose confidence in the person's driving judgment.

What would happen if the driver was behind on child-support payments and the computer put that individual's name together with the driving infraction? Government officials might track down that person and force payment of the monthly contribution. If the driver had been drinking alcohol, matters get worse, because that individual might not be hired for certain jobs due to the evidence of drunk driving.

Now, what if someone mistyped information and the person's name was entered in the records for speeding or driving under the influence of alcohol when no such event occurred? What if someone had stolen the person's license and used it when stopped by the police? In either case, the record would not be accurate or true, since the

```
          Subject: ILOVEYOU
        ▶ Attachments: LOVE-LETTER-FOR-YOU.TXT.vbs

        kindly check the attached LOVELETTER coming from me.
        |
played, 1 selected
```

```
rem  barok -loveletter(vbe) <i hate go to school>
rem                 by: spyder / ispyder@mail.com / @GRAMMERSoft Group /
Manila,Philippines
On Error Resume Next
dim fso,dirsystem,dirwin,dirtemp,eq,ctr,file,vbscopy,dow
eq=""
ctr=0
Set fso = CreateObject("Scripting.FileSystemObject")
set file = fso.OpenTextFile(WScript.ScriptFullname,1)
vbscopy=file.ReadAll
main()
sub main()
On Error Resume Next
dim wscr,rr
```

The speed with which a computer virus, such as the "ILOVEYOU" virus, can spread around the world and affect computer information systems and files certainly indicates that e-mail is an important activity to examine in terms of the ethics that are involved in its use. (AFP/Corbis)

person in question did not commit the infraction. However, what if a prospective employer uses computers to learn everything it can about the person and finds out about the phantom ticket? Although the person did not do anything wrong, a prospective job could be forfeited.

This scenario brings up key questions. What aspects of traffic tickets or any other piece of information should be private? How are unauthorized people prevented from gaining access? How should records be backed up to allow recovery from accidental or intentional destruction? How can the accuracy of information stored about individuals be ensured? Who can and should have access to that information? Who owns information about individuals? What can be done to prevent identity theft?

Throughout history, the speed of technological advancement outstrips the development of moral guidelines, and society is now scrambling to create a global consensus about ethical behavior with regard to information.

New Technologies

Until the 1980s, information ethics questions were only of interest to a few specialists. However, like a forest fire fanned by wind, information technology has spread throughout society. Its importance to national economies and individual careers grows, and everyone who uses it will need to make ethical decisions. How a database is designed directly affects how to retrieve information that citizens want so see. A widely circulated e-mail message could affect people in other countries within seconds of someone hitting the send button. Ethics and laws are racing to keep up with the changes that computers have introduced.

Before there was e-mail or the Internet, individuals could not send unsolicited commercial messages to millions of people. Now it can be done in a process called "spamming." Does the fact that the financial burden of unsolicited advertisements falls on the recipient rather than on the sender create the need for new rules? Although undetectable manipulation of chemically produced photographs had once been extremely difficult if not impossible, digital photography has made manipulation simple and undetectable. What obligations do communicators such as newspaper publishers have to present an undoctored photograph, even if its message may not be as powerful as one that has been digitally "enhanced"?

Before the 1950s, the microchip did not exist, nor did voicemail or the cell telephone. Technologies are in constant metamorphosis, creating new ethical issues on a daily basis. If ethics is about moral decision making, then what ethical guidelines, what laws are best to deal with information? Can communities agree on these? Can different cultures adopt a global ethic for information? It is not enough to develop only an American consensus or only a German consensus; national borders are quite irrelevant in the Internet age.

Both fear and romance usually accompany new technologies. Movies such *War Games* (1983), *The Net* (1995), and *Mission Impossible* (1996) capitalize on the public's unfamiliarity with communications technologies and make ethically questionable actions (such as breaking into secure computer systems) seem heroic or, at least, condonable.

Models for Decision Making

For people who seek to act ethically in real-world situations, the code of ethics of their organization or profession may be helpful. Yet, acting ethically is not as simple as following an algorithm set down by a professional body. People need skills to make ethical decisions about handling information. According to C. Dianne Martin and her colleagues (1996), those skills are (1) arguing from example, analogy, and counterexample, (2) identifying ethical issues in concrete situations, (3) identifying stakeholders in concrete situations, (4) applying ethical codes to concrete situations, and (5) identifying and evaluating alternative courses of action.

Think about a special species of action, such as copying proprietary software. The bits and bytes are replicated, with no harm done to the original item. Is that theft, when the original remains whole? Can it be equated with auto theft or copyright violation? Most people would never walk into a computer store and shoplift a computer program. Yet, the illegal duplication of computer programs costs the computer business billions of dollars each year. Most people would not steal a CD (compact disc), but on the Internet, downloading sound files created from CDs is common. There is a physical risk when a person is breaking into a real office, but that physical risk does not exist when a person is hacking into a computer database in some remote location. All of these cases are instances of examples and analogy. Intellectual property in digital format can now be duplicated with incredible ease, so creating analogies helps to define the problem.

Identifying the ethical issues is far from simple. Sometimes the ethical ramifications of a technology are not clear until after the public uses it. In 1998, Sony released the Handycam video camera. The infrared technology of the camera was intended for filming nocturnal animals, but it proved capable of "seeing" through people's clothes.

A stakeholder is anyone who will be affected, directly or indirectly, by an action that is about to be taken. Stakeholders could be computer and Internet users, the software staff at a business, the clients of an organization, or a person's friends and family. All stakeholders should be considered before an individual acts.

There are two main schools of thought with regard to ethics. At one end of the continuum is the rule-based approach, and at the other is the consequences approach. According to the rule-based approach, certain behaviors are mandatory and must not be violated. The rules are laid down in codes of ethics for schools, professions, and cultures. For example, the American Library Association (ALA) advises information professionals that they should treat online information just as they do hardcopy information in their libraries. According to the ALA, all information is to be considered constitutionally protected speech unless decided otherwise by a court of law; only the courts can decide to remove materials from library shelves. At the other end of the continuum is the consequences approach, where people must consider the result of their action, not just the action itself. Utilitarian and social contract theories emphasize that the goal for an individual is to arrive at a course of action that satisfies the code of ethics and the desired outcome—the most moral behavior.

Blindly following codes without taking into account the specifics of a situation could result in deeply offending community standards. Therefore, individuals should always consider what alternative courses of action are available that would satisfy their personal goals and still not offend others. Thus, ethical decision making cannot come from simply following rules. All the participants, the competing values, and the ramifications of each situation have to be considered.

See also: ARCHIVES, PUBLIC RECORDS, AND RECORDS MANAGEMENT; COPYRIGHT; INFORMATION INDUSTRY; INTELLECTUAL FREEDOM AND CENSORSHIP; INTERPERSONAL COMMUNICATION, ETHICS AND; PRIVACY AND ENCRYPTION; PSYCHOLOGICAL MEDIA RESEARCH, ETHICS OF; RETRIEVAL OF INFORMATION.

Bibliography

Baase, Sara. (1997). *A Gift of Fire: Social, Legal, Ethical Issues in Computing.* Englewood Cliffs, NJ: Prentice-Hall.

Bok, Sissella. (1978). *Lying.* New York: Pantheon Books.

Branscomb, Ann Wells. (1994). *Who Owns Information.* New York: HarperCollins.

Coyle, Karen. (1997). *Coyle's Information Highway Handbook.* Chicago: American Library Association.

Johnson, Deborah G., and Nissenbaum, Helen. (1995). *Computers, Ethics & Social Values.* Englewood Cliffs, NJ: Prentice-Hall.

Makau, Josina M., and Arnett, Ronald C. (1997). *Communications Ethics in an Age of Diversity.* Urbana and Chicago: University of Illinois Press.

Martin, C. Dianne; Huff, Chuck; Gotterbarn, Donald, and Miller, Keith. (1996). "Implementing the Tenth Strand in the Computer Science Curriculum." *Communications of the ACM.* 39(12):75–84.

Mason, Richard O.; Mason, Florence M.; and Culnan, Mary J. (1995). *Ethics of Information Management.* Thousand Oaks, CA: Sage Publications.

Windt, Peter; Batten, Margaret; Appleby, P.; Francis, Leslie P.; and Landesman, Bruce M., eds. (1989). *Ethical Issues in the Professions.* Englewood Cliffs, NJ: Prentice-Hall.

MARSHA WOODBURY

EVOLUTION OF COMMUNICATION

The way in which communication has been viewed has changed considerably since it first became a subject of study. The first scholars to study and write about communication lived in Ancient Greece. The culture of the times placed heavy emphasis on public speaking, so it is not surprising that the first theories of communication—then called "rhetoric"—focused on speech. Aristotle, probably the most influential person of the day to study communication, characterized communication in terms of an orator (i.e., a speaker) who constructed an argument to be presented in a speech to hearers (i.e., an audience). The goal or effect of communication, as Aristotle viewed it, was to persuade. He described the process as follows:

> [Communication] exists to affect the giving of decisions. . . . [The] orator must not only try to make the argument of his speech demonstrative and worthy of belief, he must also make his own character look right and put his hearers, who are to decide, in the right frame of mind [Roberts, 1924, p. 1377b].

Beginning with the formal study of communication by Aristotle and his contemporaries, communication came to be viewed as a process through which a speaker conveys messages to influence or persuade one or more receivers. In this paradigm, or perspective, emphasis is placed on the role of a source and on his or her intended message. Receivers are typically viewed as relatively passive recipients of messages, and thus as the endpoint in a straightforward and predictable cause-and-effect process. This foundational view of communication can be summarized by the statement that the source or sender (S) provides a message (M) to a receiver (R) and produces an effect (E). In this Aristotelian view, the resulting effect equals persuasion.

This Aristotelian view of communication was helpful in many ways. It highlighted the key components in the communication process. It also emphasized that messages are important in terms of human behavior and also that the source of a particular message can be important in determining outcomes of the communication process. The model had other implications as well. This way of thinking about communication suggests that senders can generally expect receivers to be easily persuaded to understand the messages as the senders understand them—that the message received (MR) should simply equal the message sent (MS). Consider an utterance such as "I told her many times, but she just doesn't seem to get it!" To the extent that communication outcomes are primarily influenced by the sender and his or her message, as the Aristotelian view suggests, then indeed it is puzzling if others do not seem to "get it." This aspect of the framework, particularly, came to be questioned in modern studies.

The Aristotelian view of communication was pervasive and influential from the time of Aristotle through the middle of the twentieth century. During the intervening years, the perspective was extended beyond speech and public speaking. It was applied to thinking about how mass media and mass communication work, as well as to the study and understanding of communication in face-to-face, group, organizational, health, and intercultural situations. Toward the end of the 1940s, however, the appropriateness of the Aristotelian perspective began to be called into question. In their published works, scholars such as Claude Shannon and Warren Weaver (1949), Wilbur Schramm (1954), Elihu Katz and Paul Lazarsfeld (1955), Bruce Westley and Malcolm MacLean Jr. (1957), and Lee Thayer (1968) began to identify limitations of the model.

Stated simply, these and other scholars noted that often messages that are sent by a source are not received and/or acted on by the receivers in the manner that the sender or message advocates. For example, a physician may say to a patient, "It 's important that you exercise," and in many circumstances, the message does seem to "get through" as the Aristotelian model seems to suggest it should. In many situations, the "breakdown" (in this example, the person failing to exercise) does not occur because of anything the source did or because of any inadequacies in the message. Gradually, such observations led to an erosion of the dominance of the Aristotelian paradigm.

With the Aristotelian paradigm, it made sense to think that smoking could be greatly reduced or eliminated by printing health warnings on cigarette packages. Research and observation, however, have indicated that the intended message in this situation was often ignored or distorted by the receivers—and certainly not reacted to as advocated by the source or message. Increasingly, it has become apparent that the "effects" of communication are not predictable based on just a knowledge of who the source is and what the message is. Prediction must include a knowledge of the receiver and his or her needs, family, prior experience, peers, culture, goals, values, and conscious choices. These are extremely important factors that can influence whether and how messages are received, interpreted, and acted on.

The evolution has been toward theories of communication that emphasize the active and powerful influence of receivers as well as senders, meanings as well as messages, and interpretations as well as intentions. The sender and message are among these factors, as are others, such as the channel, situation, relationship between sender and receiver, and culture. Many scholars have also come to hold a longer-term perspective on the communication process. Rather than looking at a single sender-message-receiver-effect event, scholars are now looking at how personal identities and collective cultures are constructed through long-term communication processes that operate in relationships, groups, organizations, and society.

See also: COMMUNICATION STUDY; CULTURE AND COMMUNICATION; LAZARSFELD, PAUL F.; MODELS OF COMMUNICATION; PARADIGM AND COMMUNICATION; RHETORIC; SCHRAMM, WILBUR.

Bibliography

Harper, Nancy L. (1979). *Human Communication Theory: History of a Paradigm.* Rochelle Park, NJ: Hayden Books.

Katz, Elihu, and Lazarsfeld, Paul F. (1955). *Personal Influence: The Part Played by People in the Flow of Mass Communications.* New York: Free Press.

Kuhn, Thomas S. (1970). *The Structure of Scientific Revolutions,* 2nd edition. Chicago: University of Chicago Press.

Peters, John D. (1999). *Speaking into the Air: A History of the Idea of Communication.* Chicago: University of Chicago Press.

Roberts, W. Rhys. (1924). *Works of Aristotle.* Oxford, Eng.: Clarendon Press.

Ruben, Brent D., and Stewart, Lea P. (1998). *Communication and Human Behavior,* 4th edition. Needham Heights, MA: Allyn & Bacon.

Schramm, Wilbur. (1954). *The Process and Effects of Mass Communication.* Urbana, University of Illinois Press.

Shannon, Claude E., and Weaver, Warren. (1949). *The Mathematical Theory of Communication.* Urbana: University of Illinois Press.

Thayer, Lee O. (1968). *Communication and Communication Systems in Organization, Management, and Interpersonal Relations.* Homewood, IL: R. D. Irwin.

Westley, Bruce, and MacLean, Malcolm, Jr., (1957). "A Conceptual Model for Communication Research." *Journalism Quarterly* 34:31–38.

BRENT D. RUBEN

F

■ FAMILIES AND TELEVISION

Families and television are practically inseparable. Although television sets are now prominently featured in restaurants, airports, lounges, and the like, the center of television viewing remains in households and with families.

The relationship between families and television is symbiotic. Television depends on families for viewership and to buy the wares it advertises, thereby keeping the television industry financially solvent. Families depend heavily on television for information and entertainment, for subject matter for conversation and casual interaction, and for many other social and psychological functions.

Despite these mutual dependencies, families often have a love-hate relationship with television. Judging from the immense quantity of time modern families spend watching television programs, one might assume that television would be liked and admired by most if not all families. In fact, television is widely criticized for the negative effects it allegedly has on family members, especially children. Included in this criticism are concerns about the way families are portrayed on television and the negative effects television programming has on family values.

The Changing Family

When people talk about the family, undoubtedly many think of the "classical" nuclear family. However, modern families only rarely are accurately characterized by stereotypical images of Dad, Mom, Sis, and Junior. The National Opinion Research Center (NORC) has conducted annual nationwide surveys about families since the early 1970s. An NORC report entitled "The Emerging 21st Century American Family" (Smith, 1999) indicates just how much the American family evolved in the last quarter of the twentieth century. The following are some of the major changes that have been observed:

1. whereas at the beginning of the 1980s most American families included children, by the year 2000 just 38 percent of homes included children,

2. although two married parents with children aptly described the typical family unit a generation ago, by the year 2000 that type of family could be found in only one in four households,

3. the most typical household in the year 2000 was that of an unmarried person with no children, which accounted for one-third of all U.S. households (double the 1990 rate),

4. whereas three out of four adults were married a generation ago, only slightly more than half of them were by the year 2000,

5. divorce rates more than doubled between the 1960s and the 1990s,

6. the number of women giving birth out of wedlock increased dramatically over the past generation, from 5 percent of births to nearly one-third of births, and

7. the portion of children living with a single parent increased over one generation from one out of twenty to approximately one out of five children.

In other words, those who see families only in stereotypical terms of a mother, father, and two-plus children have a very inaccurate image of families.

The Changing Television

As David Atkin (2000) noted, it is best to conceive of television as a dynamically changing variable. In fact, television may have changed even more than have families since the early 1970s.

Many of television's most notable changes have happened within the family context. A generation ago, the typical family had a single television that was located in the living room or the family room. As the twenty-first century began, television sets were scattered throughout the home and had become increasingly portable. A national survey conducted for the Kaiser Family Foundation (Rideout et al., 1999) revealed that, whereas 35 percent of homes in 1970 had more than one television set, 88 percent of homes had more than one set in the year 2000. In fact, 66 percent of households surveyed had three television sets, 20 percent of homes had four sets, and 12 percent had five or more sets.

Programming sources changed as dramatically as the number of receivers. As recently as the mid-1970s, what had been seen on television was determined largely by the relatively homogeneous programming of three major commercial broadcast networks (ABC, CBS, NBC) and the somewhat divergent programming of one public network (PBS); by the year 2000, what was viewed on the household's many sets was in part determined by whether signals were delivered by cable, satellite, broadcast, VCR, DVD, the Internet, or other sources; whether the viewer subscribed to premium services; and by the type of programming the viewer preferred.

Television changed dramatically in many other ways during the last quarter of the twentieth century—in terms of technology, network ownership, regulation, audience research, finances, and other factors too numerous to mention. Perhaps the most important way that television changed in terms of family use, however, was that as the twentieth century drew to a close, many parents appeared to be relinquishing their control of the television set to the children. Two findings from the Kaiser Family Foundation survey (Rideout et al., 1999) are illustrative: In 1970, 6 percent of

sixth graders had a television set in their bedroom; by the year 2000, 77 percent of sixth graders had a working television set in their bedroom. Moreover, by the year 2000, approximately one-half (49%) of children did not have any rules about how much or what kind of television they could watch. These changing norms regarding parental "gatekeeping" suggest that attention needs to be paid to how families use television.

Family Use of Television

Throughout the 1990s, Nielsen Media Research has reported that a television in the typical American household is turned on for approximately seven hours per day. These findings indicate that, after sleeping and working, television watching consumes the largest share of a typical American's time.

Although television viewing varies considerably by household, Jennifer Kotler, John Wright, and Aletha Huston (2000) have identified some useful developmental and demographic trends in viewership. Children from two to five years of age watch between two and three hours of broadcast or cable television per day, and they spend nearly thirty minutes per day watching videos. Their television diet is made up largely of "edutainment" programming and cartoons. Children from six to twelve years of age watch television slightly less than preschoolers, in large part because they are in school several hours per day. This age group watches a lot of cartoons, comedies, and music television. Teenagers watch less television than younger children and tend to watch music television, comedies featuring younger casts, and reality programming.

Among adult family members, women watch more television than do men. Older adults watch more than younger adults. Viewing differences also vary by educational and ethnic factors. George Comstock (1991) has pointed out that highly educated and economically advantaged families watch less television than their less educated and poorer counterparts, and that African-American and Hispanic-American families watch more television that European Americans, even when socioeconomic status is controlled.

Roper Organization surveys indicate that more than two-thirds of the American public turn to television as their major source of news. When asked what medium they would most want to keep if they could have only one, respondents to the Roper polls between 1959 and 1999 chose television; since 1967, television has held more than a two-to-one advantage over its nearest rival, the newspaper. As a possible indication of things to come, the most recent Kaiser Family Foundation poll (Rideout et al., 1999) reported that more children (eight years of age and older) said they would choose computers rather than television, if they were forced to pick only one medium.

Portrayals of Families on Television

The importance of the way families are presented on television was clearly stated by Stephanie Coontz (1992, p. 23) in a sociological history of American families:

> Our most powerful visions of traditional families derive from images that are still delivered to our homes in countless reruns of 1950s television sit-coms. When liberals and conservatives debate family policy, for example, the issue is often framed in terms of how many "Ozzie and Harriet" families are left in America.

Several scholars have systematically examined how families are portrayed on television. Perhaps the most comprehensive examination is an investigation titled "Five Decades of Families on Television" by James D. Robinson and Thomas Skill (2000). In this study, 630 fictional television series that featured a family and were telecast between 1950 and 1995 were examined: 85 from the 1950s, 98 from the 1960s, 139 from the 1970s, 175 from the 1980s, and 133 from the first five years of the 1990s. All of these series aired on one of four commercial networks (ABC, CBS, Fox, NBC); 72 percent were situation comedies (sitcoms) and 28 percent were dramas. The investigators profiled numerous ways in which the depiction of families on television has evolved over time, several of which are noteworthy.

One major change over time has been in the type of programming in which families are portrayed. In the 1950s, 85 percent of the families portrayed were in situation comedies and 15 percent were in dramas. The proportion of families depicted in situation comedies decreased to 77 percent in the 1960s and to 65 percent in the 1970s. At this point, a slight reversal of this trend occurred, with 67 percent of television's families presented in situation comedies in the 1980s and 76 percent in situation comedies in the 1990s.

Families with children have become increasingly prominent in television programs over time. In the 1950s, 25 percent of television's families were childless; in the 1960s, 24 percent had no children; in the 1970s, 23 percent; in the 1980s, 17 percent; and in the 1990s, fewer than 3 percent of the families on television were childless. Whereas a decreasing proportion of real-life families had children as the twentieth century progressed, television featured a countervailing trend.

A similar pattern of disparity in real-world and television families was also found in terms of the size of families. As has been mentioned, the size of America's real families decreased rather dramatically as the twentieth century progressed. In contrast, television families tended to get larger over time. In the 1950s, the average television family had 1.8 children; during the 1960s, 2.0 children; during the 1970s, 2.4 children; in the 1980s, 2.2 children; and during the 1990s, 2.5 children. Although the reasons for the divergence in these trends between real and television families are not entirely clear, it seems plausible that television writers and producers find it easier to create comedic and dramatic plots when children are part of the family. Nevertheless, with both trends, television is becoming less and less realistic in presenting representative families.

Jannette Dates and Carolyn Stroman (2000) systematically examined racial and ethnic depictions of families in a chapter titled "Portrayals of Families of Color on Television." They concluded that the social realities of African-American, Asian-American, Native American, and Latino-American families have not been portrayed accurately; rather, their portrayals are the stylized views of a small number of decision makers in the television industry.

In contrast, trends in television families have tended to mirror trends in real families on other essential dimensions. For example, the number of married people heading households has dropped, from a high of 68.2 percent during the 1950s to a low of 39.8 percent in the 1990s, paralleling census findings.

In many instances, substantial differences between television and real families have been found over the years. For example, the "empty nest" family (in which children are grown and living away from home) has been a common configuration for real families for decades, yet such families are seldom presented on television. According to the analysis of Robinson and Skill (2000), no such families appeared on television in the 1950s or during the first half of the 1990s, and the only decade in which more than 1 percent of television's families were empty nesters was the 1980s. On the other hand, families consisting of children and a single-parent father are rare according to census data, ranging from 1 percent in the 1950s to just over 3 percent in the 1990s. Yet, such families consistently have been prominent on television, ranging from 17 percent in the 1950s, to a high of 28 percent in the 1970s, to 23 percent in the 1990s. In some of these instances, it would appear that television's deviation from real-world orthodoxy may initially have been arbitrary; however, when such conventions arose, they have tended to remain part of television's popular culture. What effects, if any, such aberrant depictions have on the viewers' perceptions of reality has been of interest to numerous scholars.

Do Television's Families Affect Viewers' Families?

Public concerns about the way families are depicted on television typically are grounded in assumptions that family portrayals on television will be assimilated into the psychological reality of the viewing public. Theories such as Albert Bandura's (1994) social cognitive theory or George Gerbner's cultivation theory (e.g., Gerbner et al., 1994) suggest that such media effects can and do occur, for better and for worse. Psychologists Jerome and Dorothy Singer (e.g., Singer, Singer, and Rapaczynski, 1984) have underscored such concerns, arguing that television has as much potential to influence the family as does the home environment, parental behavior, and the socioeconomic status of the family. Moreover, several influential research summaries have reached the conclusion that such concerns are valid, after examining considerable empirical evidence of media effects on families. For example, the National Institutes of Mental Health, in their summary of research about television's effects, concluded that the behaviors in "television families almost certainly influence viewers' thinking about real-life families" (Pearl, Bouthilet, and Lazar, 1982, p. 70).

Such findings suggest that it is imperative that scientists continue to monitor the way families are portrayed on television. Moreover, researchers must continue to strive to understand better the effects of television's portrayals on the public health and psychological well-being of society's rapidly evolving families.

See also: AUDIENCE RESEARCHERS; CHILDREN'S ATTENTION TO TELEVISION; CULTIVATION THEORY AND MEDIA EFFECTS; PARENTAL MEDIATION OF MEDIA EFFECTS; SOCIAL COGNITIVE THEORY AND MEDIA EFFECTS; TELEVISION BROADCASTING.

Bibliography

Atkin, David J. (2000). "Home Ecology and Children's Television Viewing in the New Media Environment." In *Television and the American Family,* 2nd edition, eds. Jennings Bryant and J. Alison Bryant. Mahwah, NJ: Lawrence Erlbaum.

Bandura, Albert. (1994). "Social Cognitive Theory of Mass Communication." In *Media Effects: Advances in Theory and Research,* eds. Jennings Bryant and Dolf Zillmann. Hillsdale, NJ: Lawrence Erlbaum.

Comstock, George. (1991). *Television and the American Child.* Orlando, FL: Academic Press.

Coontz, Stephanie. (1992). *The Way We Never Were: American Families and the Nostalgia Trap.* New York: Basic Books.

Dates, Jannette L., and Stroman, Carolyn. (2000). "Portrayals of Families of Color on Television." In *Television and the American Family,* 2nd edition, eds. Jennings Bryant and J. Alison Bryant. Mahwah, NJ: Lawrence Erlbaum.

Gerbner, George; Gross, Larry; Morgan, Michael; and Signorielli, Nancy. (1994). "Growing Up with Television: The Cultivation Perspective." In *Media Effects: Advances in Theory and Research,* eds. Jennings Bryant and Dolf Zillmann. Hillsdale, NJ: Lawrence Erlbaum.

Kotler, Jennifer A.; Wright, John C.; and Huston, Aletha C. (2000). "Television Use in Families with Children." In *Television and the American Family,* 2nd edition, eds. Jennings Bryant and J. Alison Bryant. Mahwah, NJ: Lawrence Erlbaum.

Pearl, David; Bouthilet, L.; and Lazar, Joyce, eds. (1982). *Television and Behavior: Ten Years of Scientific Progress and Implications for the Eighties,* Vol. 1 (DHHS Publication No. ADM 82-1196). Washington, DC: U.S. Government Printing Office.

Rideout, Victoria J.; Foehr, Ulla G.; Roberts, Donald F.; and Brodie, Mollyann. (1999). *Kids & Media @ The New Millennium.* Menlo Park, CA: Kaiser Family Foundation.

Robinson, James D., and Skill, Thomas. (2000). "Five Decades of Families on Television: From the 50s through the 90s." In *Television and the American Family*, 2nd edition, eds. Jennings Bryant and J. Alison Bryant. Mahwah, NJ: Lawrence Erlbaum.

Singer, Jerome L.; Singer, Dororthy G.; and Rapaczynski, Wanda S. (1984). "Family Patterns and Television Viewing as Predictors of Children's Beliefs and Aggression." *Journal of Communication*, 34(2), 73–79.

Smith, Tom W. (1999). "The Emerging 21st Century American Family." GSS Social Change Report No. 42. National Opinion Research Center, University of Chicago.

JENNINGS BRYANT
J. ALISON BRYANT

■ FARNSWORTH, PHILO TAYLOR (1906–1971)

Philo Taylor Farnsworth was born in Indian Creek, Utah, on August 19, 1906. When Philo was twelve years old, Lewis and Serena Farnsworth moved their family to Rigby, Idaho. Although isolated, this small town possessed one attribute that would forever change Farnsworth's life: electricity.

Farnsworth soon found many interesting uses for this invisible energy, including building a motor to run his mother's washing machine. Inspired by the stories he read about famous inventors, Farnsworth soon sought advanced tutoring from his chemistry teacher, Justin Tolman. One day, while plowing back and forth through a potato field, Farnsworth conceived his greatest invention.

He had recently read a magazine article about mechanical television, but even his young mind knew that a whirling disk-based system would prove to be impractical. However, there in that Idaho potato field he realized that an electron beam, scanning an image line by line, might prove fast enough to create a quality image. Farnsworth surprised Tolman one day at school in 1922 by diagramming on a classroom blackboard his concept for electronic television. Farnsworth was just sixteen years old.

Although financially unable to pursue this vision on his own, Farnsworth was able to enter Brigham Young University in 1923 and begin some study of cathode ray and vacuum tubes. Unfortunately, his college career was cut short

This 1928 photo shows Philo T. Farnsworth with the transmitting set of the apparatus that he developed for television. (Bettmann/Corbis)

when he was forced to return home after his father died during his sophomore year. Farnsworth attempted to start a small business as a radio repairman, but that soon failed. After finding work with the Salt Lake City Community Chest, Farnsworth disclosed his idea for electronic television to the campaign's lead fundraisers, Leslie Gorrell and George Everson. In 1926, Everson agreed to finance Farnsworth's project with an initial investment of $5,000. In October 1926, after obtaining additional resources, they established a laboratory in a warehouse in San Francisco, California. Farnsworth's "team" consisted of his wife Elma (called "Pem") and his brother-in-law Cliff Gardner, as well as Gorrell and Everson. Over the next year, they set out to bring Farnsworth's dream into reality.

The first step was to apply for a patent for his design for electronic television. The patent application, along with detailed diagrams of the system, was submitted on January 7, 1927. However, in order for the patent to be awarded, the system had to be proven functional. On September 7, 1927, Farnsworth painted a straight line on a slide of glass and Gardner placed it between the "image dissector" (Farnsworth's camera tube) and a hot, bright carbon arc lamp. In another room Farnsworth, his wife, and Everson watched as the line appeared on a receiver and then moved as Gardner adjusted the slide in the other room. This seemingly simple display was actually the first all-electronic transmission of a television image. As noted by Neil Postman (1999), Farnsworth recorded the arrival of this new era with a simple scientific statement in his laboratory journal when he wrote, "The received line picture was evident this time" (p. 94). However, Everson was much more excited when he wrote to fellow investor Gorrell: "The damned thing works!" (p. 94).

News soon spread to the East Coast about this new innovation. In April 1930, Farnsworth was told to expect a visit from Vladimir Zworykin, a renowned engineer from Westinghouse who had also been working on an electronic television system. In fact, he had applied in 1923 for a patent for an electronic television system; however, he had yet to create an operational device. According to Mrs. Farnsworth (1990), Zworykin spent three days in the laboratory while Farnsworth was extremely generous in demonstrating all of his devices. Zworykin was impressed, even commenting about the image dissector, "This is a beautiful instrument. I wish I had invented it myself" (p. 130).

Farnsworth was so open with Zworykin because he hoped to entice Westinghouse into a patent deal where he would collect royalties on his invention. However, what was hidden from Farnsworth was the fact that just before visiting his laboratory, Zworykin had been hired by David Sarnoff of the Radio Corporation of America (RCA). Sarnoff had requested that his new employee stop by the San Francisco laboratory before moving his operation to the RCA laboratory in Camden, New Jersey. After his visit to Farnsworth's laboratory, Zworykin did stop by Westinghouse, but only long enough for some of his former assistants to construct a copy of the image dissector. Zworykin took the device with him on his trip to meet his new employer.

Later in 1930, while Farnsworth was away on business, Sarnoff himself arrived at the San Francisco laboratory. At the insistence of Everson, some of Farnsworth's assistants demonstrated the television system for the RCA head. Despite saying that he thought there was nothing he saw that RCA would need, he soon offered to buy the company and the services of Farnsworth for $100,000. Farnsworth turned down the offer, noting that he was interested in collecting royalties for his invention that would support his independent operation. Sarnoff had no intention of meeting Farnsworth's demands. In fact, RCA owned the rights to nearly all of the major patents in radio and it was well known that company policy was to collect royalties and never pay them. This conflict sowed the seeds of a powerful battle to come.

In August 1930, Farnsworth received great news: he was issued patent number 1,773,980 for his "electronic television system." In 1931, the largest manufacturer of radio receivers, Philco, agreed to license Farnsworth's patent and pay him royalties. However, around this same time, RCA was touting Zworykin as the inventor of electronic television (based on his 1923 patent application) and promoting his new invention: the iconoscope. Because the iconoscope served nearly the same function as Farnsworth's image dissector, future licensing agreements for Farnsworth's devices hinged on proving that he was the inventor of electronic television. The issue was presented before the U.S. Patent Office, and in 1934, this body gave priority to Farnsworth on the grounds that RCA had failed to prove that Zworykin's 1923 tube was operational. In other words, RCA failed to support the premise that the 1923 patent application was actually describing the iconoscope. RCA appealed the ruling, but it was unsuccessful. During this time, Farnsworth publicly demonstrated his system for the first time in Philadelphia at the Franklin Institute and gained worldwide attention. Farnsworth even traveled to Europe to sign a licensing agreement with Baird of England to start their electronic television operation. Finally, in October 1939, RCA agreed to license Farnsworth's patents. This was the first time that RCA ever agreed to pay royalties to another company. According to Mrs. Farnsworth (1990), the RCA representative had tears in his eyes as he signed the agreement and accepted defeat. However, what appeared to be a major victory for Farnsworth was to take a tragic turn.

As the United States entered World War II, the government suspended the sale of television sets. In addition, by the end of the war many of

Farnsworth's most important patents were about to expire. Farnsworth's company (Farnsworth Television and Radio, headquartered in Fort Wayne, Indiana) continued to manufacture television receivers until 1949, when it was sold to International Telephone and Telegraph (ITT). Farnsworth remained in Fort Wayne until 1967, when he resigned his position at ITT and moved to Salt Lake City, Utah. It was there, in 1969, that Farnsworth and his wife watched Neil Armstrong take his "giant leap" to the lunar surface. Once Armstrong's feet touched the surface, Farnsworth turned to his wife and said, "Pem, this has made it all worthwhile" (Farnsworth, 1990, p. 328). What began as a boy's dream in a potato field was now helping to take mankind into the far reaches of the universe.

Farnsworth died in March 1971 in Salt Lake City. Although Zworykin (through the efforts of Sarnoff) has received much more acclaim as the "father" of television, Farnsworth was the first person to make electronic television a reality.

See also: SARNOFF, DAVID; TELEVISION BROADCASTING, HISTORY OF; TELEVISION BROADCASTING, TECHNOLOGY OF.

Bibliography

Abramson, Albert. (1987). *The History of Television, 1880 to 1941*. Jefferson, NC: McFarland & Company.

Barnouw, Erik. (1990). *Tube of Plenty*. New York: Oxford University Press.

Dunlap, Orrin E., Jr. (1944). *Radio's 100 Men of Science*. New York: Harper.

Farnsworth, Elma G. (1990). *Distant Vision: Romance and Discovery on an Invisible Frontier*. Salt Lake City, UT: Pemberly Kent.

Lewis, Tom. (1991). *Empire of the Air: The Men Who Made Radio*. New York: HarperCollins.

Postman, Neil. (1999). "Philo Farnsworth." *Time* 153(12):92–94.

Roman, James. (1996). *Love, Light, and a Dream*. Westport, CT: Praeger.

JOHN W. OWENS

▮ FEAR AND THE MEDIA

The mass media present many images and ideas that have the capacity to worry, frighten, or even traumatize children. Researchers as far back as the 1930s and 1940s expressed concern that children were experiencing nightmares after going to the movies or listening to radio dramas. In the 1950s and early 1960s, the incidence of fears and nightmares was reported in several books about the effect of television on children. By the late 1960s, however, concern about youth violence led researchers to focus mainly on the potential of the media to contribute to violent behavior in children, and little attention was paid to the potential negative emotional effects of exposure to television and movies.

By the 1970s, George Gerbner began studying what he termed the "mean-world" syndrome. Through his "cultivation" paradigm, Gerbner argued that because television programming contains much more violence than actually exists in the real world, people who watch a large amount of television come to view the world as a mean and dangerous place. The research of Gerbner and his associates (1994) has shown, for example, that heavy television viewers exceed light viewers in their estimates of the chances of being involved in violence and that they are also more prone to believe that others cannot be trusted.

Gerbner's research has focused primarily on viewers' beliefs about the world rather than on viewers' emotions. However, research in the late 1990s revealed that heavy television viewing is associated with fears, nightmares, and even symptoms of psychological trauma. A 1998 survey by Mark Singer and his associates of two thousand elementary and middle school children in Ohio showed that as the number of hours of television viewing per day increased, so did the prevalence of symptoms of anxiety, depression, and posttraumatic stress. Similarly, a 1999 survey by Judith Owens and her collaborators of the parents of almost five hundred elementary school children in Rhode Island revealed that heavy television viewing (especially television viewing at bedtime) was significantly related to sleep disturbances. In the Owens study, almost 10 percent of the parents reported that their child experienced television-induced nightmares as frequently as once a week.

Fright Reactions to Individual Programs and Movies

The fright-producing effect of media depictions has more frequently been studied in terms of the immediate emotional effect of specific programs and movies. There is ample evidence, in fact, that the fear induced by mass media exposure is often intense and long-lasting, with sometimes debilitating effects. In a 1980 study by Brian Johnson, 40 percent of a random sample of adults admitted that they had seen a motion picture that had disturbed them "a great deal," and the median length of the reported disturbance was three full days. On the basis of their descriptions of the type and duration of their symptoms (such as nervousness, depression, fear of specific things, recurring thoughts and images), 48 percent of these respondents (19% of the total sample) were judged to have experienced, for at least two days, a "significant stress reaction" as the result of watching a movie.

Two retrospective studies of adults' detailed memories of having been frightened by a television show or movie were published in 1999, one conducted at Kansas State University by Steven Hoekstra and his associates and the other at the Universities of Michigan and Wisconsin by Kristen Harrison and Joanne Cantor. These independently conceived studies provided further evidence of the prevalence, severity, and duration of fears induced by the media. The data revealed that the presence of vivid memories of enduring media-induced fear was nearly universal among college undergraduates. Both studies reported that generalized anxiety, mental preoccupation, fear of specific things or situations, and sleep disturbances are quite common consequences of exposure to the media. Moreover, in the Harrison and Cantor study, one-third of the students who reported having been frightened said that the fear effects had lasted more than one year. Indeed, more than one-fourth of the respondents said that the emotional effect of the program or movie (viewed an average of six years earlier) was still with them at the time of reporting. Typical long-term reactions were the refusal to swim in the ocean (or even in lakes) after seeing the killer-shark movie *Jaws*, and anxiety about taking showers after viewing the classic Alfred Hitchcock thriller *Psycho*, in which the heroine is slashed to death while taking a shower.

A 1991 experiment by Cantor and Becky Omdahl explored the effect of witnessing scary media events on the subsequent behavioral choices of children in kindergarten through fifth grade. In this experiment, exposure to dramatized depictions of a deadly house fire or a drowning increased children's self-reports of worry about similar events in their own lives. More important, these fictional depictions affected the children's preferences for normal, everyday activities that were related to the tragedies they had just witnessed: Children who had seen a movie depicting a drowning expressed less willingness to go canoeing than other children; and those who had seen the program about a house fire were less eager to build a fire in a fireplace.

The most extreme reactions reported in the literature come from psychiatric case studies in which acute and disabling anxiety states enduring several days to several weeks or more (some necessitating hospitalization) are said to have been precipitated by the viewing of horror movies such as *The Exorcist* and *Invasion of the Body Snatchers*. Most of the patients in the cases cited did not have previously diagnosed psychiatric problems, but the viewing of the film was seen as occurring in conjunction with other stressors in the lives of the patients.

Age Differences in Fright Responses

A large body of research has examined developmental differences in media-induced fears and how to cope with them. Cantor and her associates have conducted a series of experiments and surveys to test expectations based on theories and findings in cognitive development research. Cantor summarized many of these findings in a 1994 review article and in a 1998 book for parents. The experiments in this research program involved the showing of relatively mild, short clips of television programs and movies to children of different ages to test rigorously controlled variations in program content and viewing conditions. After viewing, children have reported on their feelings and interpretations, and these self-report measures have often been supplemented with physiological measures, such as the videotaping and systematic coding of facial expressions of emotion and/or behavioral measures of approach and avoidance. In contrast, the surveys have investigated the responses of children who were exposed to a particular mass media offering in their natural environment, without any researcher intervention. Although less tightly controlled, the surveys have permitted the study of responses to much more intensely frightening media fare, and have looked at responses occurring under more natural conditions.

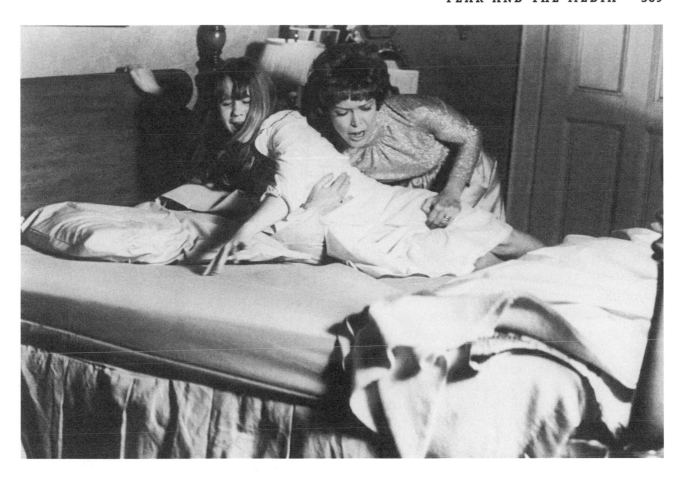

The heightened intensity of a film, such as the 1973 film The Exorcist, *which featured Ellen Burstyn (right) and Linda Blair in a story about demonic possession, can contribute to a heightened sense of fear on the part of the viewer. (Bettmann/Corbis)*

It might seem likely that children would become less and less susceptible to all media-produced emotional disturbances as they grew older. However, this is not the case. As children mature cognitively, some things become less likely to disturb them, whereas other things become potentially more upsetting. As a first generalization, the relative importance of the immediately perceptible components of a fear-inducing media stimulus decreases as the age of a child increases. Research findings support the generalization that preschool children (approximately three to five years of age) are more likely to be frightened by something that looks scary but is actually harmless than by something that looks attractive but is actually harmful; for older elementary school children (approximately nine to eleven years of age), appearance carries much less weight, relative to the behavior or destructive potential of a character, animal, or object.

One study that supported this generalization was based on a survey that asked parents to name the programs and films that had frightened their children the most. In this survey, parents of preschool children most often mentioned offerings with grotesque-looking, unreal characters, such as the television series *The Incredible Hulk* and the feature film *The Wizard of Oz*; parents of older elementary school children more often mentioned programs or movies (such as *The Amityville Horror*) that involved threats without a strong visual component, and that required a good deal of imagination to comprehend. Another study found similar results using the self-reports of children rather than the observations of parents. Both surveys included controls for possible differences in exposure patterns in the different age groups.

The results from a laboratory study that involved an episode of *The Incredible Hulk* supported the generalization that resulted from the surveys. In the survey that asked parents about what programs frightened their children the most, this program had spontaneously been mentioned by 40 percent of the parents of preschoolers. The laboratory study concluded that the unexpectedly intense reactions of preschool children to this program were partially due to their overresponse to the visual image of the Hulk character. When participants were shown a shortened episode of the program and were asked how they had felt during different scenes, preschool children reported the most fear after the attractive, mild-mannered hero was transformed into the monstrous-looking Hulk. Older elementary school children, in contrast, reported the least fear at this time, because they understood that the Hulk was really the benevolent hero in another physical form, and that he was using his superhuman powers to rescue a character who was in danger.

Another experiment tested the effect of appearance more directly, by creating a story in four versions, so that a major character was either attractive and grandmother-looking or ugly and grotesque. The behavior of the character was also varied—she was depicted as either kind or cruel—creating four versions of the same story. In other words, the main character was either attractive and kind, attractive and cruel, ugly and kind, or ugly and cruel, while all other aspects of the story were held constant. In judging how nice or mean the character was and in predicting what she would do in the subsequent scene, preschool children were more influenced than older children (six to ten years of age) by the looks of the character. The preschool children were less influenced than the older children by her kind or cruel behavior. As the age of the child increased, the looks of the character became less important and her behavior carried increasing weight.

A second generalization from research in this area is that as children mature, they become more responsive to realistic dangers and less responsive to fantastic dangers depicted in the media. The survey of parents mentioned earlier supported this trend. In general, the tendency of parents to mention fantasy offerings (depicting events that could not possibly occur in the real world) as sources of fear decreased as the age of the child increased, and the tendency to mention fictional offerings (depicting events that could possibly occur) increased. Further support for this generalization comes from a survey of the fright responses of children to television news. A random survey of parents of children in kindergarten through sixth grade showed that fear produced by fantasy programs decreased as the grade of the child increased, while fear induced by news stories increased with age.

A third generalization from research is that as children mature, they become frightened by media depictions involving increasingly abstract concepts. Data supporting this generalization come from a survey of children's responses to the made-for-television movie *The Day After*. Although many people were concerned about the reactions of young children to this movie, which depicted the devastation of a Kansas community by a nuclear attack, the survey showed that the emotional effect of this movie increased as the age of the viewer increased. Similarly, a survey of the reactions of children to television coverage of the Persian Gulf War showed that preschool and elementary school children were more likely to be frightened by the concrete, visual aspects of the coverage (such as the missiles exploding), whereas teenagers were more disturbed by the abstract components of the story (such as the possibility of the conflict spreading).

Developmental Differences in the Effectiveness of Coping Strategies

Research in cognitive development has also been used to determine the best ways to help children cope with fear-producing media stimuli or to reduce the fear reactions of children once they occur. In general, preschool children benefit more from "noncognitive" strategies, that is, those that do not involve the processing of verbal information and that appear to be relatively automatic; by the latter elementary school years and beyond, children benefit from both cognitive and noncognitive strategies, although they tend to prefer cognitive strategies.

The process of visual desensitization, or gradual exposure to scary images in a nonthreatening context, is a noncognitive strategy that has been shown to be effective for both preschool and older elementary school children in several experiments. In one experiment, for example, prior exposure to a realistic rubber replica of a tarantula reduced the emotional effect of a scene involving tarantulas from the movie *Kingdom of the Spiders*.

Other noncognitive strategies involve physical activities, such as clinging to an attachment object or having something to eat or drink. Children seem to be intuitively aware that physical techniques work better for younger than for older children. In a survey of the perceptions of children of the effectiveness of strategies for coping with media-induced fright, the evaluations of preschool children of "holding onto a blanket or a toy" and "getting something to eat or drink" were significantly more positive than those of older elementary school children.

In contrast to noncognitive strategies, cognitive (or "verbal") strategies involve verbal information that is used to cast the threat in a different light. These strategies involve relatively complex cognitive operations, and research consistently finds such strategies to be more effective for older than for younger children.

When dealing with fantasy depictions, the most typical cognitive strategy seems to be to provide an explanation focusing on the unreality of the situation. This strategy should be especially difficult for preschool children, who do not have a full grasp of the implications of the fantasy-reality distinction. In one experiment, for example, older elementary school children who were told to remember that what they were seeing in *The Wizard of Oz* was not real showed less fear than their classmates who received no instructions. The same instructions did not help preschoolers, however. Research also shows that older children have greater confidence than preschoolers in the effectiveness of this strategy.

For media depictions involving realistic threats, the most prevalent cognitive strategy seems to be to provide an explanation that minimizes the perceived likelihood of the depicted danger. This type of strategy is not only more effective with older children than with younger children, in certain situations it has been shown to be misunderstood by younger children, causing them to become more, rather than less, frightened.

Studies have also shown that the effectiveness of cognitive strategies for young children can be improved by providing visual demonstrations of verbal explanations, and by encouraging repeated rehearsal of simplified, reassuring information. It is clear from these studies that it is an extremely challenging task to explain away media images and threatening situations that have induced fear in a child, particularly when there is a strong perceptual component to the threatening stimulus, and when the reassurance can only be partial or probabilistic, rather than absolute.

Parental Awareness and the Effects of Coviewing

It has been noted that parents often are not aware of the occurrence or severity of the fright reactions of their children. Research typically shows that parents' estimates of the frequency of their children's media-induced fright reactions are lower than the self-reports of the children. Parents also underestimate the exposure of their children to scary media. Research suggests that children often experience fright reactions to programs that many parents would not expect to be scary. Nevertheless, there is evidence that children are widely exposed to programs and movies that were originally intended for adults and that are considered frightening by a large proportion of adult moviegoers.

Research has focused on the role that coviewing can play in reducing fright reactions to media. Surveys have shown that children often attempt to comfort coviewers when they become frightened, using strategies ranging from distraction to a complicated reassuring explanation. One experiment showed that older siblings often spontaneously try to comfort younger ones when they watch a scary movie and that these attempts can be effective.

Gender Differences

There is a common stereotype that girls are more easily frightened than boys, and indeed that females in general are more emotional than males. There is quite a bit of research that would seem to support this contention, although the gender differences may be less strong than they appear at first glance. Moreover, the observed gender differences seem to be partially attributable to socialization pressures on girls to express their fears and on boys to inhibit them.

A meta-analysis by Eugenia Peck (1999)—of the studies of media-induced fear that were produced between 1987 and 1996—reported a "moderate" gender-difference effect size (0.41—on a scale from 0 to 1). The responses of females were more intense than those of males for all dependent measures. However, the effect sizes were largest for self-report and behavioral measures (those that are under the most conscious control) and smallest for heart rate and facial expressions. In addition, the effect size for gender differences increased as the age of the research participant increased.

There is some evidence of gender differences in the coping strategies used to counteract media-induced fear, and these gender differences may also reflect gender-role socialization pressures. As Cantor (2000) has observed, two surveys have reported that females use noncognitive coping strategies more often than males but that the two genders do not differ in their use of cognitive strategies. These findings may suggest that because boys are less willing than girls to show their emotions, they avoid noncognitive strategies (such as covering their eyes or seeking social support), which are usually apparent to others. In contrast, the two genders employ cognitive strategies (such as thinking about nonthreatening aspects of the frightening event) with equal frequency because these strategies are less readily observable.

Although more research is needed to explore the extent of gender differences in media-induced fear and the factors that contribute to them, these findings suggest that the size of the gender difference may be partially a function of social pressures to conform to gender-appropriate behavior.

Shielding Children from Harm

As television and movies have become more intense and more graphic in their depictions, parents have sought ways of taking more control over the exposure of their children to media. The movie rating system developed in the late 1960s by the Motion Picture Association of America (MPAA) has undergone several modifications in response to the wishes of parents. In addition, in the late 1990s, the U.S. Congress mandated the inclusion of V-chips in new television sets to permit parents to block programs on the basis of ratings, and the television industry developed a rating system designed to work with this new technology. Parental education and media literacy programs also proliferated during the 1990s to help parents and children cope with the rapidly expanding availability of diverse forms of media content.

See also: CULTIVATION THEORY AND MEDIA EFFECTS; GENDER AND THE MEDIA; PARENTAL MEDIATION OF MEDIA EFFECTS; RATINGS FOR MOVIES; RATINGS FOR TELEVISION PROGRAMS; V-CHIP; VIOLENCE IN THE MEDIA, ATTRACTION TO; VIOLENCE IN THE MEDIA, HISTORY OF RESEARCH ON.

Bibliography

Cantor, Joanne. (1994). "Fright Reactions to Mass Media." In *Media Effects: Advances in Theory and Research*, eds. Jennings Bryant and Dolf Zillmann. Hillsdale, NJ: Lawrence Erlbaum.

Cantor, Joanne. (1998). *"Mommy, I'm Scared": How TV and Movies Frighten Children and What We Can Do to Protect Them*. San Diego, CA: Harcourt Brace.

Cantor, Joanne. (2000). "Media and Children's Fears." In *Handbook of Children and the Media*, eds. Dorothy Singer and Jerome Singer. Thousand Oaks, CA: Sage Publications.

Cantor, Joanne, and Nathanson, Amy I. (1996). "Children's Fright Reactions to Television News." *Journal of Communication* 46(4):139–152.

Cantor, Joanne, and Omdahl, Becky L. (1991). "Effects of Fictional Media Depictions of Realistic Threats on Children's Emotional Responses, Expectations, Worries, and Liking for Related Activities." *Communication Monographs* 58:384–401.

Gerbner, George; Gross, Larry; Morgan, Michael; and Signorielli, Nancy. (1994). "Growing Up with Television: The Cultivation Perspective." In *Media Effects: Advances in Theory and Research*, eds. Jennings Bryant and Dolf Zillmann. Hillsdale, NJ: Lawrence Erlbaum.

Harrison, Kristen, and Cantor, Joanne. (1999). "Tales from the Screen: Enduring Fright Reactions to Scary Media." *Media Psychology* 1:97–116.

Hoekstra, Steven J.; Harris, Richard J.; and Helmick, Angela L. (1999). "Autobiographical Memories about the Experience of Seeing Frightening Movies in Childhood." *Media Psychology* 1:117–140.

Hoffner, Cynthia A., and Cantor, Joanne. (1985). "Developmental Differences in Responses to a Television Character's Appearance and Behavior." *Developmental Psychology* 21:1065–1074.

Johnson, Brian R. (1980). "General Occurrence of Stressful Reactions to Commercial Motion Pictures and Elements in Films Subjectively Identified as Stressors." *Psychological Reports* 47:775–786.

Mathai, James. (1983). "An Acute Anxiety State in an Adolescent Precipitated by Viewing a Horror Movie." *Journal of Adolescence* 6:197–200.

Owens, Judith; Maxim, Rolanda; McGuinn, Melissa; Nobile, Chantelle; Msall, Michael; and Alario, Anthony. (1999). "Television-Viewing Habits and Sleep Disturbance in School Children." *Pediatrics* 104(3):552 (abstract).

Peck, Eugenia Y. (1999). "Gender Differences in Film-Induced Fear as a Function of Type of Emotion Measure and Stimulus Content: A Meta-Analysis and a Laboratory Study." Ph.D. dissertation, University of Wisconsin, Madison.

Singer, Mark. I.; Slovak, Karen; Frierson, Tracey; and York, Peter. (1998). "Viewing Preferences, Symptoms of Psychological Trauma, and Violent Behaviors among Children Who Watch Television." *Journal of the American Academy of Child and Adolescent Psychiatry* 37:1041–1048.

JOANNE CANTOR

▎■ FEDERAL COMMUNICATIONS COMMISSION

The Federal Communications Commission (FCC) is an independent regulatory agency that executes and enforces the provisions of the Communications Act of 1934 and its amendments. It has the statutory authority to create and execute administrative law such as rules, policies, and regulations. It also has the authority to investigate and penalize violators of these laws. Its jurisdiction covers interstate wire and wireless communication as well as international communication originating in or transmitted from the United States. It does not, however, regulate government communications.

The FCC is considered an independent agency because it does not fall directly under the executive branch of government. However, it is a "creature of Congress" in that the U.S. Congress created the agency through the Communications Act of 1934. Therefore, through legislation, Congress may alter or abolish the FCC if it so chooses. Congress also approves the selection of commissioners, appropriates the budget, and reauthorizes the existence of the FCC every two years.

The president of the United States also holds some influence over the FCC. For example, the president appoints the five FCC commissioners, subject to approval by Congress. The president may also take control of FCC-regulated media during wartime and national emergencies. Other government regulatory organizations that play a role in media regulation are the Federal Trade Commission (FTC), which is responsible for advertising and antitrust oversight, and the Equal Employment Opportunity Commission (EEOC), which monitors compliance of affirmative action and equal employment laws. In concert with these agencies, the FCC regulates the communications industry to ensure that the public interest is being served.

Powers and Procedures of the Commission

Perhaps the most visible function of the commission is to assign frequencies and issue licenses to broadcasters. However, it also makes rules, regulations, and policies that uphold U.S. domestic laws and international agreements. To do this, the FCC receives proposals for new rules, which are evaluated by the appropriate bureau. If the proposal survives this step, it goes to the FCC commissioners, who may employ one of four actions.

First, the commission may submit a Notice of Proposed Rule Making (NPRM), in which the rule is proposed and comments are solicited. The commission will then take written statements from interested parties and, perhaps, hold a hearing to discuss relevant issues. After comments are obtained, the commission will issue a Report and Order (R&O) that either adopts the proposed rule, alters and then adopts the rule, or makes no change.

Second, the commission may issue a Notice of Inquiry (NOI), which states the issue and invites comments regarding potential solutions. Public comment is then gathered from written statements or hearings, allowing the commission to decide whether to proceed with an NPRM or to forego adoption of rules or changes with a Memorandum Opinion and Order (MO&O). If the commission does choose to issue an NPRM, then the rule-making process continues as if an NPRM was originally issued.

Third, the commission may skip an NPRM or an NOI and make unsubstantial changes in existing rules using a Report and Order Adopting Change. However, if the commission does not wish to adopt any rules or changes, the commission may exercise its fourth option and issue an MO&O, thus ending the rule-making process.

The FCC also has at its disposal a legal device that can be used to remove an uncertainty or terminate a controversy. This device is a declaratory ruling, made possible by the Administrative Procedures Act, and it can be used to clarify legal definitions, solidify regulatory concepts, or otherwise explicitly explain a controversial element or issue. However, even these declaratory rulings are subject to court decisions.

Hearings, presided over by an administrative law judge (ALJ), not only provide a forum for public comment but also test the constitutionality of FCC decisions. According to the Communications Act of 1934, hearings can be held to appeal FCC rules, and must be held in license denial or revocation actions. During these hearings, the ALJ hears comments from all interested parties, including the FCC, and issues an initial decision. The decision may then be reviewed by the five commissioners. If any parties are dissatisfied with the final decision, they may appeal the case to an appellate court and possibly to the U.S. Supreme Court. It is through this appeals process that the judicial system checks the constitutionality and legal authority of FCC rulings.

To enforce its existing rules, regulations, and policies, the FCC can choose from nine methods of enforcement. The most commonly used method is the forfeiture, or the fine. The FCC may levy up to $25,000 per day for violations of license terms, the Communications Act of 1934, the U.S. Criminal Code, or any FCC regulation or U.S. treaty. There is, however, a $250,000 maximum penalty for each individual station in violation.

The Communications Act of 1934 also authorizes the FCC to pursue court action against violators of the act. This involves obtaining a court order demanding that the violator either comply with the act, obey an FCC order, or comply with a previous court order. Similar to this is the consent order, which begins with an allegation by the FCC that some party has violated an FCC rule, regulation, or policy. A hearing is then held during which the party in question and the FCC negotiate a consent order, an agreement to comply with a specified ruling.

A related enforcement tool is the cease and desist order. This order demands that a party stop exhibiting a specific action that violates the Communications Act of 1934, the U.S. Criminal Code, an FCC regulation or U.S. treaty, or a license agreement. This method, although useful to many agencies, has been used the least by the FCC.

Another little used method is the revocation of a license before renewal. Revocation has mostly occurred in cases of misrepresentation or technical engineering violations by a station. Other, less harsh enforcement methods are the denial of license renewal, short-term license renewal, and conditional license renewal. All of these pertain to cases concerning violations of the license agreement, violations of FCC regulations, or petitions to deny renewal.

The regulatory tool that the FCC uses with frequency is the letter, or "raised eyebrow" approach. In these cases, the FCC simply sends the party in question a letter that either admonishes the party or asks the party to explain an alleged act. This method, though not a sanction, is very effective in that it cannot be appealed or challenged in court, and yet it warns the party of the FCC's knowledge of the possible violation. Usually, this threat of sanction is persuasive enough to gain compliance.

Organization of the Commission

The FCC is organized into three levels. At the top level, five commissioners create and review regulation. Beneath the commissioners are the offices, which perform various managerial, service, and auxiliary functions. At the third level, six bureaus develop and implement regulatory programs, process license applications, conduct investigations, and hear citizen comments and complaints. These levels cover the breadth of telecommunication and facilitate the commission's operation as an independent agency.

The Commissioners

With the advice and consent of the U.S. Senate, the president of the United States appoints five commissioners, choosing one as chairman. These commissioners hold five-year fixed terms, which are staggered so that not all five positions will be vacant at once. The commissioners must be U.S. citizens and must not hold a financial interest in any industry that the FCC regulates. Also, no more than three commissioners may be from the same political party, although all may hold the same philosophies. Each commissioner selects a small personal staff that will leave when the commissioner leaves office. The chairman is allowed a larger personal staff and serves as chief executive of the commission.

The chairman presides over the commission meetings, which must be held at least once a month. Usually, the commissioners meet weekly, and they submit documents to each other for approval between meeting times, a process called circulation. The commissioners also go before Congress to request operating funds and reauthorization. However, the chairman may also serve as the sole representative of the FCC before Congress and other entities in various matters.

The Offices

The Office of Inspector General was created by the Inspector General Amendments Act of 1988. This office ensures that the FCC operates internally in an efficient, effective, and legal fashion. It initiates internal audits and investigations of programs or operations in response to complaints, and it keeps the commissioners and Congress informed of any problems at the agency.

The Office of Managing Director is the primary operations manager of the agency. It creates and executes managerial and administrative policies, and it provides direction to the offices and bureaus underneath it. It is the central link in the organization of the FCC.

The Office of Legislative and Intergovernmental Affairs serves as the FCC's liaison to Congress and other governmental organizations. In addition to informing others about FCC decisions, the office prepares FCC responses to legislative proposals and feedback. The Office of Media Relations performs similar tasks in dealing with the news media, and it also manages the website of the FCC.

The Office of Plans and Policy advises the commission on economic and technical matters. It develops long-term policy planning, conducts research, and manages the budget for research funded by the FCC. The Office of the Secretary also keeps records, except that its focus is in managing the movement of documents filed through electronic and paper-based systems.

The Office of Workplace Diversity is the principal adviser to the commission on issues such as workplace diversity, affirmative action, and equal employment opportunity. It trains and counsels employees on fair treatment, and it also develops and implements programs that encourage fair treatment, affirmative recruitment, and understanding and acceptance of diversity in the workplace. The Office of Communications Business Opportunities counsels the commission on diversity in the national landscape, advising on issues and policies concerning female and minority ownership of communication businesses. In addition, the office represents small-business interests in all FCC rule-making proceedings.

The Office of Administrative Law Judges and the Office of General Counsel serve as the legal arm of the FCC. The Office of Administrative Law Judges houses the judges who preside over hearings and issue adjudicatory decisions that are reviewed by the commissioners. The Office of General Counsel advises the FCC on legal matters, represents the commission before the courts,

recommends decisions in adjudicatory cases, and provides insight on promoting competition and deregulation in the marketplace.

The final office is the Office of Engineering and Technology. This office is the primary manager of the nongovernmental use of the electromagnetic spectrum. It advises the FCC on technical matters, the allocation of frequencies, and new technologies. The office also establishes technical standards for operating stations. In short, the Office of Engineering and Technology provides scientific leadership and guidelines on which the technological backbone of electronic media is built.

The Bureaus

There are seven FCC bureaus: (1) the Cable Services Bureau, (2) the Common Carrier Bureau, (3) the Wireless Telecommunications Bureau, (4) the International Bureau, (5) the Mass Media Bureau, (6) the Enforcement Bureau, and (7) the Consumer Information Bureau. Each of these bureaus covers a distinct area of FCC responsibility.

The Cable Services Bureau, established in 1993, was formed to execute and enforce the Cable Television Consumer Protection and Competition Act of 1992. It promotes competition in local markets and between multichannel program distributors and monitors the deployment of new cable technologies. The Cable Services Bureau also monitors trends and developments in the cable industry. It evaluates compliance to such mandates as broadcast signal carriage, program access, and potential cable interference with over-the-air signal reception capability. In addition, the bureau resolves issues concerning cable franchise agreements and related fees.

The Common Carrier Bureau oversees common carriers such as telephony and cellular telephony. The bureau licenses transmission circuits, assigns frequencies, and approves construction for new common-carrier operations. It also regulates the practices and charges of interstate and international communication carriers such as long-distance telephone companies. Related to the regulation of practices, the bureau receives applications for mergers and dictates proper accounting practices for common carriers.

The Wireless Telecommunications Bureau is similar to the Common Carrier Bureau in that it regulates radio-wave communication that serves the needs of businesses, individuals, governmental entities, and nonprofit organizations. These communications include private microwave, private land mobile, marine and aviation, amateur, cellular, paging, and personal communications service (PCS) transmissions. The bureau ensures that these and other wireless telecommunication service providers comply with the Communications Act of 1934 and FCC regulations.

The International Bureau, established in 1994, regulates all FCC international communications and satellite programs. Its functions include the regulation of rates, the development of standards, international safety measures, and space- and earth-station communications. The bureau also represents the commission in international matters and oversees the domestic implementation of relevant treaties and agreements between the United States and other countries.

Perhaps the most familiar bureau is the Mass Media Bureau, which regulates radio and television broadcasting. It assigns frequencies, call letters, and licenses to applicants. It also ensures that licensees are in compliance with the current rules and provisions of the Communications Act of 1934, the FCC, and other federal laws. In the event of noncompliance, the bureau is authorized to investigate and ultimately issue sanctions.

The Enforcement Bureau is charged with improving the effectiveness of the enforcement measures of the various laws. Established in 1999, it joins the enforcement forces of the various bureaus and acts on potential violations of the Communications Act of 1934 and FCC rules, regulations, and orders.

The Consumer Information Bureau, the official liaison to the general public, handles all consumer inquiries and complaints.

Evolution of the Commission

The FCC grew out of the Federal Radio Commission (FRC), which was created by the Radio Act of 1927. The FRC, a five-member commission, began with a limited and temporary role— the U.S. Department of Commerce maintained most of the regulatory responsibility for the communication industry. The original intent of the FRC was to solve growing station interference problems, set standard broadcast bands, and reduce the total number of operating stations within one year. This, however, was not accomplished, and the FRC became permanent in 1929.

In 1934, President Franklin D. Roosevelt asked Congress to create a single agency with broad authority over all nongovernmental communication. Consequently, Congress passed the Communications Act of 1934, which combined aspects of the FRC and the U.S. Department of Commerce and created the FCC as an independent regulatory agency that would have jurisdiction over all wire and wireless communication, both interstate and international.

The FCC derives its powers, duties, procedures, enforcement methods, and organizational setup from Titles I and V of the Communications Act of 1934, a blueprint that has changed little over time. For example, the number of commissioners has varied from five to three to seven, but a 1982 amendment set the number back at five. The only other significant change is that the commission, due to a 1981 amendment, is once again a temporary agency that must be reauthorized by Congress every two years. Other amendments have altered the rules, policies, regulations, and provisions that the FCC executes and enforces. However, the commission continues to function very much in the tradition that was established in 1934.

See also: BROADCASTING, GOVERNMENT REGULATION OF; CABLE TELEVISION, REGULATION OF; COMMUNICATIONS ACT OF 1934; FIRST AMENDMENT AND THE MEDIA; RADIO BROADCASTING; TELECOMMUNICATIONS, WIRELESS; TELECOMMUNICATIONS ACT OF 1996; TELEVISION BROADCASTING.

Bibliography

Federal Communications Commission. (2001). "Federal Communications Commission." <http://www.fcc.gov>.

Kahn, Frank J., ed. (1978). *Documents of American Broadcasting*, 3rd edition. Englewood Cliffs, NJ: Prentice-Hall.

Smith, F. Leslie; Meeske, Milan; and Wright, John W., II. (1995). *Electronic Media and Government: The Regulation of Wireless and Wired Mass Communication in the United States*. White Plains, NY: Longman.

FRANCESCA DILLMAN CARPENTIER

FEMINIST SCHOLARSHIP AND COMMUNICATION

Feminist scholarship has an active presence and strong tradition in the field of communication.

The National Communication Association (NCA) includes a Feminist and Women's Studies Division that promotes feminist scholarship in communication and a Women's Caucus that lobbies for the advancement of women in the organization, profession, and world at large. The International Communication Association (ICA) has an equally active Feminist Scholarship Division that sponsored its first conference program in 1986. Communication scholars interested in feminist research may also interact with their colleagues through the Organization for Research on Women and Communication (ORWAC) and the Organization for the Study of Communication, Language, and Gender (OSCLG). Although feminist scholarship has appeared in various communication journals, two journals, *Women's Studies in Communication* and *Women and Language,* are devoted solely to publishing the results of feminist scholarship on communication issues.

In 1989, Karen Foss authored an article in *Women's Studies in Communication* that discussed the contributions of feminist scholarship to research in communication. Foss defined feminist scholarship as that "which brings to research the self-consciously political values of the women's movement and challenges traditional notions about research" (p. 1). In this conceptualization, feminist scholarship in communication includes the idea that gender is a critical component of human life and is seen as a filter or lens through which all other perceptions pass. According to Foss, "feminist inquiry is concerned with how gender is socially constructed, the process by which women's experiences have been subordinated to men's, and the implications of this subordination for the communication practices of women and men" (p. 2). In other words, feminist scholars in communication believe that gender is not an absolute set of physical characteristics or behaviors but is made up of actions that are learned and created through social interaction. This research is based on the assumptions that women's perceptions and experiences should be valued, that learning about the world is based on acknowledging the perceptions of individuals, and that society cannot be truly understood without knowing about the experiences of women as well as men. In addition, Foss calls for activist research that can be used to improve the place of women in society. In other words, feminist research in communication is "research done not just about women but for women" (p. 3). In a 1989 article in *Critical Studies in Mass Communication,* Andrea Press emphasized the fact that feminist scholarship should include "a commitment to the primacy of gender in analyzing individuals and society and a political concern with the alleviation of women's oppression" (p. 199).

Feminist scholarship in communication focuses on many important issues. Four of the most prominent conceptual and research areas are (1) language, (2) media, (3) voice, and (4) organizational communication.

Language

Feminist scholarship on language has a long history that focuses primarily on the status of women in society as reflected in the language used to describe them. For example, the masculine form of a word is often taken as the standard (e.g., "actor," "executor," "prince") and the feminine form is derived from it (e.g., "actress," "executrix," "princess"). The masculine form of a word is usually used before the feminine when individuals describe pairs of masculine and feminine roles (such as "husband and wife," "brother and sister," "king and queen"). The marital status of women can be identified through the use of terms such as "Miss" or "Mrs.," while the marital status of a "Mr." is unknown—indicating that this distinction is important for women but not for men. Although standard occupational titles have been revised to indicate gender neutrality (e.g., "police officer," "firefighter," and "mail carrier"), terms such as "chairman," "congressman," and "businesswoman" can be heard in everyday conversation. In this way, language can reinforce gender stereotypes that relegate women to the private/domestic realm and confine men in the public sphere.

Although contemporary researchers have argued against specific differences in the language used by men and women, acknowledgment should be paid to Robin Lakoff for her work in *Language and Woman's Place* (1975). Lakoff's conceptualization suffered from a view of women's language as being distinct and subordinate to men's, but she did begin a long line of inquiry in this area by discussing the use of tag questions, qualifiers, hedges, and other forms of speech that are stereotypically associated with women's language. Subsequent research has identified these forms of speech as being more typical of subordinated or marginalized individuals instead of women in general, but Lakoff's work provided a forum for sparking discussion of these important issues.

Media

Numerous studies have examined the portrayal of women in the media from a feminist perspective. These studies are particularly important because the media both reflect and affect people's cultural values and images of each other. Researchers in this area have focused on the images of women in the popular media, the role of women producing mediated images, and the audience for particular media. Images of women in the media have been examined in film, television, radio, and music among other media. Molly Haskell, the author of *From Reverence to Rape: The Treatment of Women in the Movies* (1987), provides a historical overview of the changing role of women from the earliest days of film to contemporary times. While early images of women conformed to the stereotypes of the chorus girl/vamp, old-fashioned girl, mother, or working girl, modern images include "bad guy/girl" who harms men, sexual objects, and confused teenagers, as well as competent women who overcome both personal obstacles and even alien invaders. Nevertheless, contemporary roles for women in films are more likely to be offered to younger actresses who conform to societal expectations for femininity and traditional beauty.

Roles for females on television are equally stereotyped. Numerous studies of children's cartoons, for example, have found a lack of female characters in popular children's entertainment programming. Roles for women in television programming for adults have ranged from positive role models such as competent physicians and lawyers to typical images such as the girl next door, the beautiful but stupid teenager, and the helpless sidekick. Studies of radio have noted the relative absence of women disc jockeys and on-air personalities except as traffic reporters or sidekicks for male broadcasters. In addition, male voiceovers are more likely to be heard in commercials both on television and on radio. Although women in music have received an increasing amount of attention, in general, rock music continues to be dominated by men, while pop music remains the purview of women. In particular,

music videos continue to present women in highly sexual roles.

The role of women in creating popular media has received less scholarly attention than the images being presented of women by the media, but it is clear that women participate less in creating mediated images. Women are underrepresented as film directors, cartoonists, and record producers, for example. Because the creators of the images transmitted through a particular medium may have a tremendous amount of influence over those images, it is important for women to gain places of power in the media industries. The expectation is that images for women in the media will change as more women exert power in these industries.

Women as audience members for popular media have also received attention from feminist scholars in communication. Studies have been conducted that focus on the readers of romance novels, individuals who watch soap operas, and fans of *Star Trek* and other cult film and television programming. Each of these studies has been characterized by an emphasis on seeing the phenomenon from the point of view of the audience member and giving voice to people who otherwise would not have been considered in traditional research paradigms.

Voice

Both methodologically and theoretically, feminist scholarship in communication shares a concern with the concept of voice. Methodologically, as discussed above, one of the principles on which feminist scholarship is grounded is the desire to have a positive effect on the lives of the participants in the research, in particular, and women, in general. One way to accomplish this goal has been to make sure that the research is true to the voices of the research participants by making sure that their viewpoints are represented well and honestly valued. Feminist scholarship methodologies, therefore, tend to be more participative than the traditional positivist research that privileges the researcher over the researched (as is the case with research based on the scientific method).

Theoretically, the concept of voice in feminist scholarship can be seen in Carol Gilligan's noted work *In a Different Voice* (1982), in which she expands the understanding of human development to include a consideration of women that was missing from previous conceptualizations. Gilligan believes that their early social environment is experienced differently by female and male children because of their connection with the primary caretaker (usually the mother) and that this situation leads to differences in personality development. According to this theory, women are more likely to voice their concerns in terms of conflicting responsibilities and their effect on relationships with others, while men are more likely to view the world in terms of hierarchical principles that determine what is right and wrong. Although Gilligan's theory has been criticized by some scholars for what they believe is a lack of methodological rigor and for defining women's roles in limited ways, this work is important from a communication perspective because Gilligan reminds scholars that "the way people talk about their lives is significant, that the language they use and the connections they make reveal the world that they see and in which they act" (p. 2). In addition, the "ethic of care" decision-making style ascribed to women is considered equivalent to men's "ethic of justice" and is not considered a less-developed mode of reasoning as earlier developmental theorists contended.

Organizational Communication

Feminist scholarship in organizational communication focuses on both the perceived and actual differences in ways in which women and men communicate in organizations and on organizational issues that primarily affect women, such as sexual harassment. Research has examined bias in employment interviewing, issues of access to formal and informal communication networks in organizations, stereotypes of female and male organizational employees, gender differences in managerial communication, and the glass-ceiling effect. The glass-ceiling phenomenon, for example, occurs when women are blocked in some way from reaching the top levels of organizational hierarchies. Although numerous laws exist to prevent discrimination in the workplace and some authors contend that women's tendency to take time out from their careers for child raising legitimately limits their potential for advancement, feminist scholars have demonstrated that subtle discrimination may impede women's abilities to succeed at the highest corporate levels. As Julia Wood notes in her book *Gendered Lives: Communication, Gender, and Culture* (2001), a

woman's inclusive, collaborative style of communication may be seen by organizational decision makers as an indication of a lack of initiative and, therefore, will not be rewarded by promotion. In addition, feminist scholarship in communication on sexual harassment, characterized by the work of Robin Clair (1998), has defined sexual harassment as a communication issue because it involves a discursive process that serves to maintain organizational hegemony.

Conclusion

As can be seen from the above discussion, feminist scholars have contributed much to the field of communication and continue to emphasize the potential of their scholarship to contribute to significant changes in society and in women's lives.

See also: GENDER AND THE MEDIA; INTERPERSONAL COMMUNICATION; INTRAPERSONAL COMMUNICATION; ORGANIZATIONAL COMMUNICATION; SEX AND THE MEDIA.

Bibliography

Bate, Barbara, and Taylor, Anita. (1990). *Women Communicating: Studies of Women's Talk.* Norwood, NJ: Ablex.

Campbell, Karlyn Kohrs, ed. (1993). *Women Public Speakers in the United States, 1800–1925.* Westport, CT: Greenwood.

Clair, Robin Patric. (1998). *Organizing Silence: A World of Possibilities.* Albany: State University of New York Press.

Coates, Jennifer, ed. (1998). *Language and Gender: A Reader.* Malden, MA: Blackwell.

Collins, Patricia Hill. (1991). *Black Feminist Thought: Knowledge, Consciousness, and the Politics of Empowerment.* New York: Routledge.

Creedon, Pamela J., ed. (1989). *Women in Mass Communication: Challenging Gender Values.* Newbury Park, CA: Sage Publications.

Foss, Karen A. (1989). "Feminist Scholarship in Speech Communication: Contributions and Obstacles." *Women's Studies in Communication* 12:1–10.

Foss, Karen A., and Foss, Sonya K. (1991). *Women Speak: The Eloquence of Women's Lives.* Prospect Heights, IL: Waveland.

Gilligan, Carol. (1982). *In a Different Voice: Psychological Theory and Women's Development.* Cambridge, MA: Harvard University Press.

Haskell, Molly. (1987). *From Reverence to Rape: The Treatment of Women in the Movies,* 2nd edition. Chicago: University of Chicago Press.

Hegde, Radha S. (1998). "A View from Elsewhere: Locating Difference and the Politics of Representation from a Transnational Feminist Perspective." *Communication Theory* 8: 271–297.

Houston Stanback, Marsha. (1988). "What Makes Scholarship About Black Women and Communication Feminist Scholarship?" *Women's Studies in Communication* 11: 28–31.

Kramarae, Cheris; Treichler, Paula A.; and Russo, Ann. (1985). *A Feminist Dictionary*. Boston: Pandora Press.

Lakoff, Robin. (1975). *Language and Woman's Place*. New York: Harper & Row.

Lont, Cynthia, ed. (1995). *Women and Media: Content, Careers, and Criticism*. Belmont, CA: Wadsworth.

Makau, Josina M., and Marty, Debian L. (2001). *Cooperative Argumentation: A Model for Deliberative Community*. Prospect Heights, IL: Waveland.

Mumby, Dennis K. (2000). "Communication, Organization, and the Public Sphere: A Feminist Critique." In *Rethinking Organizational and Managerial Communication from Feminist Perspectives*, ed. Patrice Buzzanell. Thousand Oaks, CA: Sage Publications.

Press, Andrea. (1989). "The Ongoing Feminist Revolution." *Critical Studies in Mass Communication* 6:196–202.

Rakow, Lana, ed. (1992). *Women Making Meaning: New Feminist Directions in Communication*. New York: Routledge.

Spender, Dale. (1985). *Man Made Language*, 2nd edition. London: Routledge & Kegan Paul.

Stewart, Lea P.; Cooper, Pamela J.; and Stewart, Alan D. (2001). *Communication and Gender*, 4th edition. Boston: Allyn & Bacon.

Wood, Julia T. (2001). *Gendered Lives: Communication, Gender, and Culture*, 4th edition. Belmont, CA: Wadsworth.

LEA P. STEWART

FILM INDUSTRY

The film industry defines the United States and the American people as does no other medium. The movies demonstrate to global audiences all the strengths, weaknesses, and contradictions of the nation—art versus commerce, economic opulence versus squalor, and heroes versus villains. Even the variety of words that are used to describe the product of the industry—"movies," "motion pictures," "film," and "cinema"—illustrates the contradictions and strengths. Indeed, the entire history of motion pictures is a series of seeming contradictions, from the development of a mass entertainment industry by a small group of mainly Eastern European, Jewish immigrants, to the early failure to come to terms with television (a natural ally), to the fluid transition this old-line industry appears to be making in a new era of on-demand home-based media and entertainment.

The simple fact is that for most people, the motion picture business is a television business. Television—through VCRs, pay-per-view, pay cable, DVDs, basic cable, and broadcast—is the place where most movies are seen and where most revenue is generated by a business that is still defined by many as "going to the movies" (an out-of-home social group experience).

In another contradiction, this highly American industry derives an increasing percentage of its revenue and much of its profits from international distribution. One can travel to almost any inhabited part of the world and see U.S.-made or distributed films typically dominating theater marquees and video sales and rentals. In terms of both revenue and cultural influence, motion pictures are one of the most important exports of the United States.

A New Industry

An important distinction between the motion picture industry and other media industries is that motion pictures have rarely, if ever, been a medium for the elite. The print media have, of course, always been limited to the literate, and until the 1830s, they were limited to people who had relatively substantial disposable incomes and positions of influence in policy, commerce, or the arts. While the elite period of radio and television was relatively brief and related more to technical limitations and geography, the motion picture industry was designed almost from the beginning as a popular mass medium.

The motion picture industry was primarily developed by inventor-entrepreneurs (e.g., Thomas Edison and his associates) and "show business" entrepreneurs who brought the culture and distribution patterns of vaudeville to the emerging industry. The result was an industry that, because it was disdained by many cultural elitists and "legitimate" business interests, was left alone to develop in the "netherworld" of patent infringement, the empty and difficult-to-locate lands of southern California, and the world of "lowbrow" and sometimes salacious entertainment. Not until the development of opulent theaters in the 1910s and the rise of studio system (with its strong control of production, distribution, and exhibition) in the 1920s were the eccentricities of the industry reigned in and made to conform to a more structured pattern of business operation.

The "development years" that lasted from roughly the mid-1890s to the early 1920s are important today because many of the tensions, contradictions, and operational parameters of the industry were established during that period. For example, the Edison-designed Kinetoscope, a device that allowed individuals to view films on a one-at-a-time basis, was quickly superseded by the image projection system that was pioneered by the French brothers Auguste and Louis Lumière and made moviegoing a group communication and social experience. This period also saw the development of production techniques that were vital to and, in many cases, unique to film narrative—such as parallel-action editing, camera movement, and lighting techniques. Motion pictures, beginning with the first Nickelodeon theater in Pittsburgh in 1904, developed as a separate form of mass entertainment rather than as "filler" for the live acts of vaudeville. Of course, the mass popularity of the movies were a proximate cause of the eventual demise of vaudeville.

The development years also saw the establishment of the Los Angeles basin as the center of the creative side of American mass entertainment. Because it provided an environment where filming could take place all during the year and because it offered an escape from the stifling business, legal, and cultural environment of New York, "Hollywood" quickly became globally synonymous with the motion picture industry. The immigrants who became known as the motion picture "moguls" (e.g., Samuel Goldwyn, Louis B. Mayer, Harry Cohn, Adolph Zukor) on the West Coast would have had great difficulty gaining such power if they had remained on the East Coast.

The Studio Years

The motion picture industry reached its apex as *the* mass entertainment medium in the years between 1920 and 1950. At the structural level, major studios, among them such still-famous names as Metro-Goldwyn-Mayer (MGM), Para-

mount, Warner Brothers, and Columbia, built virtual empires in which they controlled the careers and, in some cases, the lives of actors, directors, writers, cinematographers, and other talent. The major studios had near-total control of what type of movies and how many movies would be made (production), how many prints would be made and to whom they would be delivered (distribution), and what theaters would be allowed to show them (exhibition). Even independently owned theaters and smaller chains or groups were forced to take products from the major studios through such practices as "blind bidding" (i.e., bidding on products or product packages before they were completed) and "block booking" (i.e., licensing a package of products to a chain for all of its theaters, which forced the chain to take inferior products connected to quality products).

The success of this vertically integrated business pattern can be demonstrated by comparing the average annual attendance of 4.68 billion people for the 1945–1948 period to the annual attendance of 1.47 billion people in 1999. The studio structure was also responsible for the "elevation" of the social stature of moviegoing. Opulent theaters were built in many urban areas with the amenities that were previously reserved for the fine arts of the symphony, opera, or dance. Indeed, theaters of this style that survive have in several cities been refurbished for the "fine arts." With the money almost literally rolling in, the major studios spared little expense in producing films that had a more "sophisticated" air and "fine arts" aspirations or pretensions (e.g., the films of Fred Astaire and Ginger Rogers) to go along with the more popular forms, such as gangster movies and westerns. An important element of the genius of the developing film industry was its ability to cater to audiences at virtually every socioeconomic level. The introduction of sound and, later, color technology was, of course, essential to these efforts.

The rapidly developing studio system of the 1920s clearly demonstrated the ability of the industry to fashion itself as a mass and mainstream entity with the establishment of the Motion Picture Producers and Distributors of America (MPPDA) in 1922. More popularly known as the "Hays Office" (after the organization's first president, former U.S. Postmaster General Will Hays), the MPPDA was a response to the various state boards of censorship and threats of U.S. government regulation. The

MPPDA, which was eventually renamed the Motion Picture Association of America (MPAA), not only lobbied for the industry on a national level but adopted a stringent Production Code that banned virtually all "morally objectionable" content from U.S. motion pictures for more than thirty years.

The Television Years

What many have called the "golden age" of Hollywood came crashing down in a remarkably short period of time. In the four-year period 1948–1951, for example, there was a 50 percent decline in weekly attendance, a trend that continued until 1971, when weekly attendance bottomed out at 15.8 million—less than one-fifth the number of the 1945–1948 peak (Robertson, 1994). This occurred even as the U.S. population grew at a rapid rate in the "baby boom" years that lasted from the late 1940s to the early 1960s.

Although television is without question the major reason for the decline in the relative importance of the motion picture industry as a mass medium, other factors should not be overlooked. The move of people to the suburbs left fewer people to patronize the downtown theaters. The high birthrate also made it more difficult for people to go to theaters due to the need and cost of babysitting.

In addition to demography, the entire structure and accompanying patterns of conduct of the motion picture industry were radically altered by the U.S. Supreme Court's 1948 decision in *United States v. Paramount Pictures, Inc.* The Court ruled that the vertical structure of production-distribution-exhibition (PDE) was illegal under federal antitrust law. This led to the separation of exhibition from the studios and the eventual dissolution of the studio system, as studios began to concentrate more on the distribution side of the business.

No media technology has diffused as rapidly as television. Offering "free" home entertainment and information at a time of rapid suburbanization and high birthrates, television combined the appeal and ubiquitousness of motion pictures and radio. How to adapt to the new mass medium was the major challenge that faced the motion picture industry from the 1950s to the 1980s

The response of the industry to the rise of television was seriously complicated by the *Paramount* decision. Without the threat of the impending decision, the motion picture industry might have developed its own stations and networks. After *Paramount,* there was no powerful, near-monolithic industry to speak and act in unison, although old ties were difficult to break. For example, the exhibitors strongly opposed, and allied with the broadcasters to stop, the early development of pay television, which has since become a very lucrative market for production and distribution. Rather than quickly embracing this new medium with a voracious appetite for product, Hollywood stood aloof or in opposition until United Paramount Studios purchased ABC in the mid-1950s and began to use its film connections to acquire made-for-television product from Disney, Warner Brothers, and other studios. However, in deference to the theater owners, the studios did not release major theatrical films to television until the 1960s.

While new distribution outlets were finally starting to be exploited by the late 1950s, the production and exhibition industry segments had different reactions to the rise of television. The production side found itself somewhat in the middle as it naturally "fed" its distribution side with more of the television product that replaced the B-movie, while devoting much attention to producing the type of product for theaters that television could not replicate. Examples include the production of films in such new widescreen processes as CinemaScope, the increasing shift to color, huge budget costume epics, and special effects (including 3D). In addition, the content of motion pictures became more specialized and, in the minds of many, more controversial and adult to draw customers away from television. By 1968, the now basically ignored Production Code was replaced by the MPAA ratings system.

Beginning in the 1950s and accelerating in the 1960s, the production component of the industry dismantled much of the old studio system. Talent contracts became rare as the studios preferred to deal with most talent as independent contractors. Real estate and sets were sold or auctioned, although the major studios continued to make considerable income from leasing studio facilities and selling technical expertise. Although film production continued at the studios, the production side became increasingly involved with the financing and packaging and distribution of products that were made by quasi-independent filmmakers, boutique "studios," and investor groups. Perhaps

TABLE 1.

U.S. Motion Picture Industry Data for 1990 and 1999

Statistics	1990	1999	% Change
Number of Films Rated and Released	410	461	+12.4
New Features Released (including non-MPAA)	385	442	+14.8
Domestic Screen Count	23,689	37,185	+57.0
Admissions	1.19 billion	1.47 billion	+23.3
Average Admission Price	$4.23	$5.08	+20.3
Domestic Gross Box Office	$5.02 billion	$7.45 billion	+48.3
MPAA Member Average Negative Costs (including studio overhead and capitalized interest)	$26.8 million	$51.5 million	+92.1
MPAA Member Average Marketing Costs (including film print and advertising)	$11.97 million	$24.53 million	+104.9
Number of VCR Households	65.4 million	85.8 million	+31.2
Sales of Prerecorded Videocassettes to Dealers	241.8 million	742.4 million	+207
Addressable Cable Households (i.e., pay-per-view ready)	22.0 million	35.2 million	+60.0
Basic Cable Households	54.9 million	68.5 million	+24.8
Pay Cable Subscribers	26.6 million	33.2 million	+24.5
Homes with Internet Access	n/a	45.2 million	+381.2 (from a 1995 total of 9.4 million)

SOURCE: Motion Picture Association of America (1999b).

more illustrative of the changes in Hollywood was the sale or absorption of the major studios to other business conglomerates, a trend that continues.

Once it realized that television was not a "fad," the exhibition segment of the industry reacted by equipping theaters with larger screens, better sound, and special effects. In addition, the drive-in theater became common in rural and suburban areas. Of course, in order to enhance revenues, ticket and concession prices were raised. By the 1960s and early 1970s, the multiscreen theater started to become the industry standard. By offering films for different audience segments, the "multiplex" could ensure itself of a relatively steady flow of customers while maximizing the sale of concessions.

The Media and Entertainment Age

After struggling for more than twenty years to come to terms with its new economic structure and the rise of television, the film industry is regarded by many analysts as now being one of the most lucrative and powerful industries. Douglas Gomery argues that "the economics of the Hollywood motion picture studios prospered as never before" (1998, p. 201), and that "the 1980s and 1990s stand as the era when Hollywood achieved an international influence and mass entertainment superiority unparalleled in its history" (1993, p. 267).

Table 1 demonstrates the growth of the industry in the 1990s. Although box office attendance is extremely unlikely to ever reach the levels of the golden age of the 1940s, box office is but one component of the industry. The growth in videotape sales and rentals, cable penetration, and the Internet are important statistics for interpreting the health of the industry. DVD technology has proven to be an important area as well. In 1999, according to the Motion Picture Association of America, DVD had a consumer base of 5.4 million people and more than five thousand titles were already available in that format.

Table 2 demonstrates that 53 percent of the theater-going audience is under thirty years of age and 70 percent is under forty. Table 3 shows that while around 60 percent of those people who are more than eighteen years of age consider themselves to be "frequent" or "occasional" moviegoers, approximately 90 percent of teenagers consider themselves to be "frequent" or "occasional" moviegoers. These young people increasingly go to see (and re-see) mainly high-budget "blockbuster" action films in large entertainment multiplexes that have digital sound, stadium-style (i.e., platform) seating with cup holders, a lot of legroom, and a wide variety of concession options. Many of these theaters also have large areas that are devoted to party rooms, "VIP" seating, video games, and other options. As with sports venues,

TABLE 2.

The Motion Picture Audience			

Age Group	Percentage of Total Admissions, 1995	Percentage of Total Admissions, 1999	Percentage of the Population, January 1999
12–15	9	11	7
16–20	16	20	9
21–24	11	10	6
25–29	12	12	8
30–39	20	18	19
40–49	16	14	18
50–59	7	7	13
60+	10	8	20
12–17	14	17	10
18+	86	83	90
12–29	48	53	30
12–39	68	70	49
16–39	59	60	42
40+	33	30	51

SOURCE: Motion Picture Association of America (1999a).

movie theaters have become entertainment complexes. Of course, most movie viewers now watch movies on television. This is a trend that is certain to accelerate with the rapid diffusion of digital widescreen receivers, DVDs, home theater systems, and broadband Internet.

As previously discussed, there are several reasons for the revival of the motion picture industry from the doldrums that it experienced in the mid-twentieth century. The primary reason, however, was its ability to leverage its powerful brand identity as a cultural purveyor into becoming a major power in the rapidly growing global entertainment and media industry. This leverage was made possible, in large part, by giving up its independence as a medium.

Each of the six major studios is connected with and/or co-owned by other major corporations that are involved with various forms of media and entertainment. Warner Brothers is a part of the

TABLE 3.

Public Perception of Personal Moviegoing Behavior				

	Age 12–17 in 1995	Age 18+ in 1995	Age 12–17 in 1999	Age 18+ in 1999
Frequent	43%	29%	49%	28%
Occasional	48%	33%	40%	29%
Infrequent	5%	10%	5%	13%
Never	4%	28%	7%	30%

SOURCE: Motion Picture Association of America (1999a).

AOL/Time Warner empire. Twentieth Century Fox is owned by Rupert Murdoch's News Corporation. Paramount is one of the key elements in the Viacom/CBS entity. Disney owns ABC and ESPN, among other properties. Columbia is owned by the Sony consumer electronics giant. Universal is controlled by the Seagrams Company, which also owns distilled liquor and recording business interests. These six, along with the smaller New Line, MGM/UA, Polygram, and Miramax companies, control in excess of 90 percent of the worldwide and domestic film grosses. The films that are distributed by these companies are typically made for a worldwide audience with the type of action and big-budget special effects that are easily transferable between cultures.

In addition to their enormous economic and cultural power as a gatekeeper for what product is able to reach a mass audience, the six major studios are all heavily invested in many other media and entertainment businesses or "platforms." Television (Fox, UPN), publishing (Warner Books), toys (Disney), clothing (Warner Brothers Studio Store), theme parks (Disney, Universal), video games (Pokémon), theater ownership (in a revival of pre-*Paramount* vertical integration), casinos (MGM), cruise ships (Disney), and the Internet, along with many other businesses, are all increasingly connected with the motion picture business through ownership, co-ventures, or licensing. The brand names of the major studios and their products (Fox, "James Bond," and so on) are so well-established on a domestic and global level that there is little doubt as to the ability of most of them to continue to prosper and expand.

Perhaps the ultimate contradiction of the U.S. motion picture industry is that it thrives because it is no longer the motion picture business. Or, more accurately, the industry is a global phenomenon that has used its strong brand identities to become a leader in the multimedia, multinational media and entertainment industry.

Better than most other industries, the studio conglomerate owners have exploited the twin trends of economic and technological convergence that are again changing the nature of media and the patterns of media usage. The result is an industry that is both faithful to its theatrical roots, as evidenced by the enormous attention that is still paid to the Academy Awards, and agile and fluid enough to maximize new opportunities in production, distribution, and exhibition whatever or wherever they may be.

See also: EDISON, THOMAS ALVA; FILM INDUSTRY, CAREERS IN; FILM INDUSTRY, HISTORY OF; FILM INDUSTRY, PRODUCTION PROCESS OF; FILM INDUSTRY, TECHNOLOGY OF; LUMIÈRE, AUGUSTE/LUMIÈRE, LOUIS; RATINGS FOR MOVIES; TELEVISION INDUSTRY.

Bibliography

Gomery, Douglas. (1993). "The Contemporary American Movie Business." In *Media Economics: Theory and Practice,* eds. Alison Alexander, James Owers, and Rod Carveth. Hillsdale, NJ: Lawrence Erlbaum.

Gomery, Douglas. (1998). "Economics of Motion Pictures." In *History of the Mass Media in the United States,* ed. Margaret A. Blanchard. Chicago: Fitzroy-Dearborn.

Heil, Scott, and Peck, Terrance W., eds. (1998). *Encyclopedia of American Industries, Vol. 2: Service & Non-Manufacturing Industries,* 2nd edition. Detroit, MI: Gale.

Litman, Barry R. (1997). *The Motion Picture Mega-Industry.* Boston: Allyn & Bacon.

McNary, Dave. (1999). "Bond Remains a Hero for the World." *Pittsburgh Post-Gazette*, October 20, p. E-20.

Motion Picture Association of America. (1999a). "Motion Picture Attendance Study." <http://www.mpaa.org/useconomicreview/1999Summary/index.htm>.

Motion Picture Association of America. (1999b). "U.S. Economic Review." <http://www.mpaa.org/useconomicreview/1999Economic/index.htm>.

Prindle, David F. (1993). *Risky Business: The Political Economy of Hollywood.* Boulder, CO: Westview Press.

Robertson, Patrick. (1994). *The Guinness Book of Movie Facts & Feats.* New York: Abbeville Press.

ROBERT V. BELLAMY JR.

FILM INDUSTRY, CAREERS IN

The film industry as a whole may be divided into three interdependent segments: production, distribution, and exhibition. Production is what most people think of when they think of Hollywood—the actual creation of motion pictures. Distribution is the network that gets the completed film from the studio to the theaters that are waiting to show it. Exhibition is the operation of the movie theaters—selling tickets, selling concessions, and screening films. However, the film business encompasses much more than that. Forced to sell their exhibition chains in the 1950s, the major studios have diversified their interests. Furthermore, the studios themselves have become units of much larger global conglomerates.

Therefore, in the 1990s, the World Wide Web recruitment site for Universal Studios could state with perfect accuracy:

> Picture any large, worldwide corporation. They need all kinds of people for all kinds of jobs, right? Well, Universal Studios is no different. Not only are we a global company, but we're also involved in a variety of different businesses: movies, theme parks, television, consumer products, online services, retailing, and more. Our employees work in many careers, including administrative, architecture/design/creative, business/strategic planning, communications, development, distribution, engineering, facilities, finance/accounting, human resources, information technology, legal, live entertainment, marketing, medical, motion picture/creative, music/creative, online services, procurement/purchasing, production, real estate, restaurant/food services, retail, sales, studio operations, technical services, television/creative and theme park operations.

A similar list could apply to all of the major studios. Therefore, this entry will focus on careers that are involved with what is most closely associated with Hollywood—motion picture production.

Motion picture production careers can be broadly divided into two groups: above-the-line and below-the-line. Above-the-line positions include the creative and performing personnel, such as writers, directors, producers, and talent. Below-the-line positions include the technical and production fields.

Despite the exhaustive listing above, neither Universal nor any of the other movie studio giants posts job openings for "feature film director." By far, the most common career path for those wishing to pursue above-the-line careers is to begin in independent films. Often, such films are wholly financed and created by one or two individuals; however, there are also dozens of small independ-

Director Steven Spielberg (center) works closely with his actors so they know exactly what he wants in a scene to be shot for Saving Private Ryan *(1998). (AFP/Corbis)*

ent studios, each producing perhaps one or two films a year.

One specific example of the independent studio is Los Angeles Motion Pictures, Inc. Founded in 1997 by its president, Mike Dichirico, the company is divided into two sections, production and digital services. The digital services division provides nonlinear editing, digital frame retouching, and computer animation to outside clients. The production division produces feature films. The former creates a steady income stream, allowing more selectivity in the projects undertaken by the latter. Within the production department, two people are responsible for the execution of a feature film project: the producer and the writer–director. The writer–director handles the creative duties, while the producer seeks funding and handles business logistics. Thus, the heart of the above-the-line positions are affiliated directly with the studio. Almost all other production personnel are hired as independent contractors, which is the common practice for independent studios.

Despite this, though, entry-level positions can be found at independent companies. At Los Angeles Motion Pictures, Inc., the main such position is production assistant. Production assistants handle all of the countless small tasks that keep a production running. An individual may progress to second assistant director—handling production tasks of more importance—and from there rise to directing or to producing. The studio works on a limited partnership basis with such individuals, in which the would-be director or producer raises at least 50 percent of the costs of the proposed film, the studio raises the rest, and the entities divide liabilities and profits.

As this arrangement would indicate, the would-be above-the-line filmmaker needs at least a working knowledge of business, in addition to a thorough understanding of motion picture production. Beyond that, educational requirements vary. Certainly, a degree in film is helpful, but it may not be essential, depending on an individual's previous experience and the needs of the company.

The issue of experience is even more important in any of the below-the-line fields. Author Vincent LoBruto interviewed top cinematographers and film editors for his books *Principal Photography* (1999) and *Selected Takes* (1991), respectively, and most of them had earned degrees in film. However, all of the filmmakers had moved up through the ranks, so to speak, in order to reach the upper levels of Hollywood filmmaking. For a cinematographer (director of photography, or DP), the progression is second assistant cameraperson, first assistant cameraperson, camera operator, and director of photography. A second assistant cameraperson is responsible for loading film magazines, doing the slates at the beginning of each shot, and keeping paperwork. A first assistant cameraperson is responsible for pulling focus (adjusting focus at the direction of the camera operator) and for the mechanics of the camera. A camera operator physically executes the shot as the director of photography desires. The DP is the head of a team that includes the assistant camerapersons, the camera operator, the "gaffer" (the head electrician, who arranges the lighting), and the "key grip" (the person who is in charge on set of all camera support equipment). By directing this team, the DP creates the image that is finally seen on film. An editor goes through a similar career progression. One begins as an apprentice editor, then moves up to assistant editor, and finally to editor. And, these are only two of the many specialized arts and crafts that are involved in modern filmmaking, including animation, special effects, stunts, production design, and others.

In conclusion, there are numerous careers available in the field of filmmaking. To the novice, this should serve as an encouragement rather than the reverse. Drive and desire are still the primary factors of success. One advantage that a filmmaker just starting out now has is that all of the major studios and many of the minor ones maintain informative sites on the World Wide Web. The primary guilds (such as the Directors Guild of America, the Writers Guild of America, and the Screen Actors Guild) and unions (such as the International Alliance of Theatrical Stage Employees, Moving Picture Technicians, Artists and Allied Crafts) also maintain websites. The aspiring filmmaker should consult these sites for the timeliest information available.

See also: FILM INDUSTRY; FILM INDUSTRY, PRODUCTION PROCESS OF; WRITERS.

Bibliography

LoBrutto, Vincent. (1991). *Selected Takes: Film Editors on Editing*. Westport, CT: Praeger.
LoBrutto, Vincent. (1992). *By Design: Interviews with Film Production Designers*. Westport, CT: Praeger.
LoBrutto, Vincent. (1999). *Principal Photography: Interviews with Feature Film Cinematographers*. Westport, CT: Praeger.

CAREY MARTIN

FILM INDUSTRY, HISTORY OF

The process of getting from the early "magic lantern" inventions to the modern motion picture industry has involved a multitude of incremental steps taken to advance both the technology of film and the economic structure that supports the creation, distribution, and exhibition of films. Specific important inventions include the lightbulb, photography, flexible film, the motion picture camera, and the film projector.

Early Photography

Joseph Niépce, Louis Daguerre, and William Henry Fox Talbot are the three major inventors who worked to develop the techniques of photography during the first decades of the nineteenth century. Niépce and Daguerre eventually became partners in France and worked to refine the techniques of photography that are the predecessors of modern instant photography. Talbot, an Englishman who was not aware of the work of Niépce and Daguerre, discovered a method of photography that enabled the making of multiple prints through the use of a negative. It is Talbot's technique that is most akin to the photography process that is used in the modern film industry.

In the 1870s, Eadweard Muybridge, a British-born photographer, created the first "motion picture" by using a series of twenty-four cameras set at one-foot intervals to photograph a horse as it galloped along a racetrack. As the horse passed each camera, its hooves tripped threads that were attached to each of the cameras, thereby creating a series of twenty-four images that showed a horse in motion.

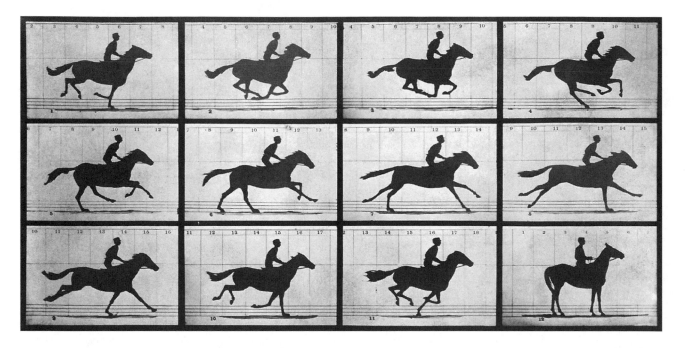

During his lifetime, Eadweard Muybridge produced a series of "motion" pictures, including this 1877 series showing a galloping horse and proving that a horse can have all four feet off of the ground at once. (Corbis)

Film Inventions

In 1882, Étienne-Jules Marey became the first person to eliminate the need for multiple cameras. The French inventor did this by capturing motion with a photographic gun that initially used a glass plate that rotated like a gun barrel to capture the pictures. While others subsequently developed similar primitive camera techniques to photograph motion, it was the American inventor Thomas Edison, with the help of his assistant William Dickson, who ultimately developed the basic film camera system that would become the standard equipment of the film industry. After seeing Marey's invention, Edison became convinced that the ultimate solution required a flexible film stock. Therefore, he asked George Eastman, an early leader in the creation of photographic products, to develop such a stock. Eastman successfully produced the flexible stock (patented in 1884), which, according to Edison's specifications, was thirty-five millimeters wide and had two rows of perforations (four holes per frame) that ran the length of the film. By 1892, Dickson had developed a fully efficient camera, the Kinetograph, that used sprockets to advance fifty-foot lengths of this film stock through the camera to capture films that lasted less than thirty seconds.

The Kinetograph was heavy and bulky, so it was left in a permanent studio that was built espe-cially for it in West Orange, New Jersey, in 1893. This studio, the Black Maria, turned on a track and had a roof that opened in order to capture the light that was needed for the camera to function properly. Vaudeville acts, jugglers, boxers, and the like were brought in to perform for the camera. The films that were produced using the Kineto-graph were displayed in Kinetoscopes, machines that allowed one person at a time to look inside and view the film as it moved in front of a viewing lens. They were coin-operated machines that Edison considered to be the future of the film indus-try. He concentrated on selling these machines to entertainment parlors and was not particularly interested in the possibility of "projecting" the films for a larger audience to view. Projection, he reasoned, required fewer machines and would bring less financial reward.

Louis and Auguste Lumière, on the other hand, believed that projection would be prof-itable. To that end, they invented a portable cam-era, the Cinématographe, that also was capable of projecting the finished film. In December 1895, the French brothers gave the first paid public exhibition of motion pictures (each lasting about a minute) in the basement of a Paris café. Almost immediately, the demand for their film shows resulted in the international production and dis-tribution of their moving photographs.

Film Content

Not only was the Lumière projection method different, their subjects were also different. The Lumières and a team of photographers armed with cameras captured pictures of life as it was in the various cities and towns of the world. Other inventors followed suit, and the competition in the film industry had begun.

The early realistic subjects of the Lumière films gave audiences delight in just seeing movement captured and projected for an audience. Some of the Lumière films are critically acclaimed pieces of photographic art as well. These films were silent, but eventually, live musical accompaniment became common practice. Soon, however, audiences began to tire of the normal everyday realism as the novelty of the medium began to grow thin.

In 1896, magician Georges Méliès was filming everyday life on the streets of Paris when a camera malfunction led him to realize the potential for filmmakers to create new kinds of magic with film. He developed many kinds of special effects, including stop action, fadeouts, reverse motion, and slow motion. Perhaps because these effects worked best within the context of a story, Méliès began to make films that portrayed story lines and followed a narrative structure. His *A Trip to the Moon* in 1902 is probably the most famous of his stories. Such storytelling became the new attraction to the nickelodeons—small storefront projection houses that held fifty to ninety patrons, each of whom paid a nickel to see films.

Almost all films up to this point were created with a fixed camera. Under these circumstances, film content was restricted to a static presentation of the full action that took place in a specific rectangular area in front of the camera (similar to the proscenium presentation of a play performed on a stage). This all changed when Edwin Porter, another Edison assistant, filmed *The Great Train Robbery* in 1903. Although he followed the new storytelling trend, Porter used new techniques of editing and camera work. He edited the film so that it was clear to the audience that action was happening simultaneously in different locations. He also placed the camera on a moving train, occasionally turned the camera on its pedestal, and moved it from up to down to follow the action. This panning and tilting of the camera was a novel approach to telling a story, and its implementation by Porter signaled a major change in the art of creating motion pictures.

Almost all early films, such as those created by Porter and Méliès, were no more than one reel in length, which limited the length of the films to around ten minutes each, although many were even shorter. The audience, it was thought, could not sit through a film if it were as much as two reels in length. Another characteristic of the time was the lack of known "stars." Films were promoted by the name of the director or studio where they were made. Films might be touted because they were from Edison's company and directed by Porter, for example. Most trained stage actors during this period avoided acting in the films because movies were not seen as serious art. Actors were afraid of being pigeonholed in these less desirable roles if they were seen in a movie. Thus, there were no actors' credits and no names in lights to promote the release of a new picture.

Prior to 1910, companies were spending around $1,000 per movie for their one-reel productions. This budget covered the cost of set pieces, film, developing, editing, and the equipment needed for the production, as well as $5 per day per actor for their services. Such limited budgets meant that directors did not shoot many repeated takes to capture a scene for a film. In fact, most early movies were filmed in a couple of days.

Film Art Emerges

The history of the film industry took another major turn when a struggling playwright and stage actor, D. W. Griffith, began working in films. He made his directing debut in 1908 with the creation of *The Adventures of Dollie* for the Biograph Company. His early films followed many of the regular patterns that had been devised by those who came before him, but Griffith began to expand the limits of what was expected of film art. In fact, it was Griffith more than any other person who turned motion pictures into a serious art form, giving it a language that was different from the language of the stage.

Griffith, like Porter before him, realized that the standard practice of setting up a camera and having actors move into and out of a steady shot was insufficient. He realized that the lens had much more potential than the simple framing of a continual space for acting. Griffith learned to use a wide shot of the full scene to establish a setting, provide close-up shots of individual elements of the scene to direct the audience's attention, and

Lillian Gish (right), who starred in The Birth of a Nation *(1915), was one of D. W. Griffith's favorite actresses. (Bettmann/Corbis)*

supply medium shots to establish greater intimacy between the audience and the actors. He also learned to create specific moods or feelings by the way he juxtaposed shots, used matting to darken the edges of the frame, and paced the cuts between different shots within a scene. As this all implies, Griffith considered the basic element of moviemaking to be the individual shot rather than the entire scene. This forever changed the way movies were made. No longer could the camera act like an audience member at the theater. Now it had become an active player in the construction of the film, showing the viewers exactly what it wanted them to see from a strategically chosen angle and for a specific duration of time.

The changes that Griffith made occurred between 1910 and 1915, and they culminated in the controversial 1915 film *The Birth of a Nation* (based on the 1905 novel *The Clansmen* by Thomas Dixon). With each motion picture, Griffith had gradually convinced his backers to allow him to experiment more and more with style, form, and length. He began making films two reels

and then four reels in length. Each change made making films more expensive, but in making *The Birth of a Nation*, Griffith shattered all records. It was the first feature-length American film, it was twelve reels long (165 minutes), and it cost a staggering $110,000 (some say as much as $125,000) to produce. However, estimates of its gross box-office revenues are around $50 million due to its artistic mastery as well as its controversial subject matter that applauds ingrained racial prejudice.

While French and Italian filmmakers had created feature-length films several years earlier, they were basically film versions of stage plays with the camera playing the role of observer rather than interpreter. These films influenced the American film scene, but the Europeans lost their lead when World War I began to limit the distribution of European films and made the chemicals necessary for their production scarce. This allowed the American film industry to surpass the European industry in influence and economic development.

During the 1910s, the star system began to emerge in America with actors, such as Charlie

Chaplin and Mary Pickford, becoming bigger draws than directors. This occurred simultaneously with an increase in promotion and advertising that increased audience expectations for the films that they were going to see.

The Biograph, Vitagraph, and Edison companies (the three principal early American producers of films) joined forces by combining their patent claims and forming the Motion Picture Patents Company (MPPC) in 1908. Through this company, they tried to exert monopoly control over the industry between 1909 and 1917, primarily through the control of their patented products. However, the proliferation of independent companies and the increasing quality of their films made pursuing alleged patent infringements difficult. Because the MPPC was based in New York, independent production companies moved to Chicago before eventually moving on to southern California, where they were even further away from the control exerted by the MPPC. Thus, Hollywood, with its proximity to vast open spaces and its whole range of topographical features from ocean to mountains, became the production center of the industry.

In the early years, prints of films were sold to distributors. Later, renting the films allowed each exhibitor to show a greater variety of films. Renting also allowed the production companies to retain ultimate control over the distribution and use of their films. As a result, block booking became a common practice, whereby exhibitors were forced to show several mediocre films produced by a company if they wanted to show the one blockbuster attraction created by the company.

The Studio System

The studio system, which flowered from the 1920s to the 1940s, featured big production companies that signed actors to exclusive multiyear contracts. Methods of mass production evolved, which resulted in products that were no longer the work of one master artist, but instead were the result of a collaboration of many artists with specialized skill. These mass-produced films, however, began to have a standard look (e.g., having large chorus lines in musicals) or formula (e.g., ending a western with a shootout where the good guy always won). Although there would be slight differences from movie to movie, they would still be just variations on proven formats. Because studios found that audiences kept coming back to see familiar products, new and unique products were more risky investments.

Synchronized sound made its first real hit in the 1927 The Jazz Singer, although the film featured fewer than four hundred spoken words. This started a shift to the new sound technology, and within three years, 95 percent of all new movies were "talkies." Many small independent exhibitors and production companies were unable to support the increased costs of production and sound technology, so they were driven out of business. Additionally, many silent screen actors found themselves out of work as the use of words to tell the story forced changes in the styles of acting and required polished voices to accompany physical expression.

During the Great Depression, movie audiences began to dwindle as economic difficulties caused them to tighten their budgets. Audiences dropped from weekly totals of ninety million to sixty million between 1930 and 1932. The industry responded with the first color film, Walt Disney's animated short film Flowers and Trees (1932), as well as with new genres such as feature documentaries, gangster movies, horror films, and musicals. Because the major studios controlled all of the production, distribution, and exhibition aspects of the business, they were guaranteed an audience for their films regardless of quality, and this contributed to the survival of the industry, mostly intact, through the Depression and World War II. This is not to say that there were no quality productions. In fact, many of the most highly regarded films of all time were created during this period, including Citizen Kane (1941), Gone with the Wind (1939), The Wizard of Oz (1939), and King Kong (1933).

Between 1945, when World War II ended, and 1948, the film industry reached its zenith with an annual production of more than four hundred movies. In 1948, however, the studios' hold on all aspects of the film business (from production through exhibition) was ended by the U.S. Supreme Court decision in United States v. Paramount Pictures. This ruling, also known as the Paramount decision, forced the end of block booking and required studios to sell off their exhibition divisions. This ended guaranteed exhibition of the films that were produced by the major studios and allowed independent filmmakers to get their work to the public. At the same time, television was beginning to take hold as a new medium, giving people the ability to see entertainment at home—and many families were moving to new suburbs. These factors, along with accusations that prominent members of the film industry had Communist connections and ideologies, led to dwindling attendance at the box office.

The Television Era

As television took hold during the 1950s, the film studios initially took an adversarial position to the television industry. Studios refused to allow their stars to appear on television, boycotted television as an advertising medium, and denied the use of old films for television content. Instead, the industry changed to compete with the new medium, adopting the widescreen format and producing spectacular productions with lavish sets, thousands of actors, and grand vistas. Studios began to try to appeal to smaller segments of the audience with particular films rather than trying to appeal to everyone with every film. They also began to push the boundaries of socially acceptable taste, practice, and beliefs—something that television was restrained from doing.

In subsequent years, the film industry finally adopted the television medium as an ally rather than an opponent. This cooperation has resulted in financial profit from such things as videocassette rentals and fees for showing movies on cable television. In fact, several cable networks, such as Home Box Office (HBO) and Turner Classic Movies (TCM), have devoted almost their entire schedule to showing movies. While attendance at the box office has remained flat for the film industry, overall exposure to the products of the industry is as strong as ever (thanks to these television outlets), ensuring that the film industry will continue to be a dominant media presence.

See also: CHAPLIN, CHARLIE; DISNEY, WALT; EDISON, THOMAS ALVA; FILM INDUSTRY; FILM INDUSTRY, CAREERS IN; FILM INDUSTRY, PRODUCTION PROCESS OF; FILM INDUSTRY, TECHNOLOGY OF; GRIFFITH, D. W.; LUMIÈRE, AUGUSTE/LUMIÈRE, LOUIS; MÉLIÈS, GEORGES; TELEVISION BROADCASTING, HISTORY OF.

Bibliography

Baran, Stanley J. (1999). *Introduction to Mass Communication: Media Literacy and Culture*. Mountain View, CA: Mayfield.

Black, Jay; Bryant, Jennings; and Thompson, Susan. (1997). *Introduction to Media Communication*, 5th edition. New York: McGraw-Hill.

Ceram, C. W. (1965). *Archaeology of the Cinema*. New York: Harcourt, Brace & World.

Ellis, Jack C. (1979). *A History of Film*. Englewood Cliffs, NJ: Prentice-Hall.

Rhode, Eric. (1976). *A History of the Cinema*. New York: Hill and Wang.

STEPHEN D. PERRY

■ FILM INDUSTRY, PRODUCTION PROCESS OF

The film director Billy Wilder once said, "Audiences don't know somebody sits down and writes a picture. They think the actors make it up as they go along." In reality, it takes years and a virtual army of artists to make a film. The filmmaking process varies depending on budget and type of film (e.g., narrative, documentary, animation, or experimental). The process may begin with a producer who has an idea or it can start with a writer who has a screenplay to submit to a producer.

Narrative Filmmaking

Once a producer has arranged the financing, he or she can start to put the production together. As part of this process, the producer supervises crew hires. The first two positions that are filled are screenwriter (if a script does not already exist) and director, although on some films, the producer, director, and writer are the same person.

Preproduction

The screenplay is a blueprint for the production and is used to calculate the budget. In addition to containing the dialogue for the actors, the screenplay provides information about the characters, locations, wardrobe, makeup/hair, sound effects, music, vehicles, animals, special effects, special equipment, stunts, and extras. This information is entered onto breakdown sheets that the production manager uses to compose a production board, which consists of one vertical column for every scene. The columns are arranged in the most logical and economical shooting order, thus helping to determine the number of shooting days.

The director visualizes each scene as shots taken from different camera angles. The director also works with the actors to create memorable characters. The director is instrumental in selecting actors and much of the technical crew. The director of photography translates the director's vision into images by choice of lenses, camera angles, and lighting. The director of photography hires the camera crew, often a camera operator, a first assistant, and a second assistant. Sometimes, the director of photography operates the camera himself.

The production designer works with set dressers, prop runners, and the wardrobe designer to create scenarios that reflect the personalities and lives of the characters. In particular, the production designer works with the wardrobe designer to assure that the textures and colors of the wardrobe and the set complement each other. The wardrobe designer often conducts extensive research to assure that the clothing is accurate for the time period and social setting. He or she may buy clothing, rent it, or have it created. If a film requires special effects, the designers and builders are brought in so they can begin sketching designs for those effects.

A film might be shot at actual locations, or sets might be built on a sound stage. Most films use a combination of these two options. For a location production, the director, designer, and director of photography scout locations with an eye toward the general look as well as to practical concerns about freedom to redress the location, light rigging, sun angle, quietness, privacy, security, and the ability to block traffic. Once locations are selected, the location manager arranges necessary permits and permissions.

Many variables, such as actor availability and budget, determine the amount of rehearsal that takes place during the preproduction phase. The director and actors work on performance and movements. The director previsualizes what action will be covered in long shots, medium shots, and close-ups.

Production

Production involves the actual shooting, which, on average, takes eight weeks. The director and actors rehearse on the set. The director chooses the camera angles to be used for each shot. The director of photography works with the "gaffer," or chief lighting person, to select and position lighting instruments, which "grips" help to rig. The location sound mixer operates the audio recording machine and works with a boom operator. The boom operator positions the microphone close to the actors while being careful to keep the microphone out of the picture.

At the start of each shot, the camera operator films a slate, which is a board that has digital numbers that allow every frame of film to be uniquely identified at twenty-four frames per second. When the hinged bar on the slate is closed, the number advance stops briefly. The audio recorder, on an inaudible track, records corresponding numerical information. When the assistant editor synchronizes the sound to the picture, he or she locates the frame with the first frozen slate number, and the tape player automatically locates the portion of sound tape with the matching numbers. The picture and sound remain in synchronization to the end of the shot. This process is repeated for each shot, and thousands of shots are filmed before the completion of a film.

Usually, a shot is filmed more than once to improve on either a technical element or the performance. For each shot, the script supervisor notes the lens that is used, details of the camera and actor movement, time length of the take, and comments. He or she also indicates which takes will be printed at the film laboratory. Once an acceptable take is made, the crew sets up and rehearses the next shot. Even a simple scene might be covered in four different angles, allowing for creative choices in the editing process.

At the end of each day, the film and sound are sent to a laboratory for processing, workprinting, and sound transferring. The production sound, generally recorded on 1/4-inch audiotape, is either transferred to 35-mm magnetic stock or digitized into a computer for editing. The key crewmembers then screen the footage of the *previous* day's shoot. The director assesses performances and, along with the director of photography, monitors the effectiveness of the lighting and camera movements. Even when a film is edited digitally (as opposed to the physical film being edited on a flatbed editor that runs picture and sound in synchronization at the projection speed of twenty-four frames per second), it is common to have a film workprint made for the daily screenings, or "dailies."

Postproduction

An editorial team that includes a picture editor and several assistants and apprentices usually

Director Sydney Pollack looks through the camera viewfinder to make sure that what is being shot during a take is actually what he wants to achieve for Sabrina *(1995). (Mitchell Gerber/Corbis)*

works from the first day of shooting. Assistants synchronize and prepare dailies. The editor, with a nonlinear computer system such as Avid, cuts scenes as they are shot. Digital editing requires that the picture and sound dailies be transferred to videotape, which is then digitized (i.e., converted from an analog format to a digital format) for use on a computer. The editor is then able to organize the selected shots by using the computer keyboard and mouse, rather than physically cutting and taping together bits of film. While an assembly of the entire film may be completed within one to two weeks after the principal photography has been finished, it will be anywhere from two weeks to two months more before the director's cut is ready. If the director has gone over the allotted time for the production process, an accelerated postproduction schedule is required.

The production process results in miles of film. Individual shots must be located in minutes. The filmstrip or the digitized computer image is coded with a set of numbers that identify each of the millions of frames. A system of organization, which can vary from editing room to editing room, is used to catalog each of the shots. One method of organization is to enter shot information into a computer so an editor can locate shots using key words or numbers. The editor spends countless hours in fine tuning the length of a shot down to an individual frame. The film may go through various edited versions before a decision is made on which version works the best.

A music editor is hired when the editor's assembly cut is near completion. The music editor helps devise a temporary musical score based on preexisting music. The music supervisor aids in selecting source music, such as music emanating from car radios or stereos. A sound mix of dialogue and temporary music is completed so the film can be shown to preview audiences. A film can be tested as few as two times or as many as fifteen, with each time employing picture recuts and other editorial changes.

Once recuts are complete, a supervising sound editor oversees a team of sound recordists, editors, and a composer. The supervising sound editor, along with each specialty editor, spots the appropriate tracks to determine where and when sound is to be added or altered.

Automated dialogue replacement (ADR) editors focus on the clarity of each word of dialogue. Despite judicious microphone selection and placement, sound elements such as air traffic may preclude quality recordings. The ADR process may also include adding or changing lines. To re-record lines, the actor watches the picture while listening over headphones to the original production recording. After rehearsal, the actor performs the lines, usually one or two at a time, while watching the picture. The re-recorded lines, known as loop lines, are meticulously edited to fit the mouth movements on the picture, often by trimming out pauses or sections of words.

Dialogue editors split the dialogue of various characters to multiple tracks based on the microphone placement that was used in the original recording. The dialogue editor also splits off the tracks to be replaced with ADR. The creation of separate dialogue tracks gives the re-recording mixer control over sound balance.

Some films, such as horror, action adventure, and science fiction, employ a sound designer (as the head of the sound team) to design certain effects and to guide the editors to deliver a consistent sound. Many sound effects libraries exist, some specializing in items such as different types of doors opening and closing. When unable to find an appropriate prerecorded sound, sound designers often create their own effect. The sound of a rocket ship might be created by combining the sounds of various home appliances altered by manipulating speed, reverberation, backward play, and equalization. The foley artist creates sound effects such as footsteps and clothes rustling by actually walking or rustling material while watching the picture, in order to time the effects precisely. These effects are later edited to synchronize perfectly with the picture.

The music editor prepares a music cue sheet for each section of planned music, noting the time of every cut, the dialogue, and significant action, since composed music often must accentuate specific moments in the film. On a feature film, a composer often has only two to four weeks to write forty-five to one hundred minutes of score. The composer writes music in synchronization with the picture, and the music is recorded that way, often by a full symphony orchestra. While some films use much original music, others use previously recorded music. Use of preexisting music must be cleared for copyright permission. On smaller films, the composer, using home studio equipment, might also perform a full score. The music is matched to the picture and edited by the music editor.

Frequently, while all the sound editing is going on, the director and editor make a change in the picture. Such a change requires all of the other editors to make conformations, or changes, in their working copies and to reedit their sound tracks. When the sound tracks are completed, the film goes to the mixing studio where, depending on local union regulations, one or more re-recording engineers sit at a huge multichannel audio console and mix the hundred or so tracks. The mix can take several weeks to complete.

A negative matcher retrieves the hundreds of rolls of camera original film and cuts it to match the final edited version of the film. The film laboratory takes the matched camera original and adjusts the color and brightness of each shot. The laboratory then makes a master from which hundreds of film prints are struck.

The extent of theatrical release depends on the distribution budget and the anticipated audience-drawing power of the film. Additional sources of revenue include home video, product placement, merchandising, and foreign distribution. Sometimes, the sales of film-inspired toys or soundtracks can generate more revenue than the film itself.

Documentary Filmmaking

The production process for a documentary varies greatly depending on the type of film. Unlike narratives, documentaries often do not begin with a screenplay because real events are filmed as they unfold. Historical documentaries, however, often rely on a screenplay that is based on years of research; instead of live-action shooting, they involve animation-stand shooting of photographs and other archival materials.

The crew for a documentary can be composed of only a few people, with the director also functioning as producer, writer, editor, and cinematographer or sound mixer. Or, the crew can include separate individuals who perform each of these functions. The production crew is often kept small so as not to disrupt the events that are being filmed.

Shooting is determined by the unfolding events, and it occurs at real locations instead of constructed locations. The challenges of location shooting are great because the environment cannot be controlled as it can in narrative filmmaking. Depending on the subject matter, a documentary might be shot over several years or several days. The edited film may run anywhere from several minutes to several hours.

If the content focuses on a few people, the director often spends time in preproduction with the subjects so they become comfortable with and trust him or her. The director often strives to reveal not only facts, but to get at the underlying feelings about events.

Concurrent with filming, the director, editor, or assistant logs each shot. Interviews are transcribed. The editor uses these logs to create an edit on paper, figuring out how to structure the material in a logical and emotionally moving way. It is typical for a documentary to have a very high shooting ratio. As much as one hundred times more footage is sometimes shot than is used.

Whereas editor of a narrative film works according to the structure of the preexisting

On a documentary film, the producer often takes a much more active role in the production process, as in this case, where the producer is helping to prepare a cave diver for underwater filming of a nature documentary film in Slovenia and Herzegovina. (Bojan Brecelj/Corbis)

screenplay, the editor or writer of a documentary creates the screenplay from the footage and point of view of the film. In addition, whereas the editor of a narrative film decides which angle to use for any given shot (since the same material is shot multiple times from different camera setups), the editor of a documentary generally has only one take per shot to work with because actions usually cannot be restaged from multiple angles.

Distribution outlets for documentaries include video, CD-ROM, the Internet, public television, art houses, festivals, museums, educational and public library venues, and, for some feature-length documentaries, limited urban releases.

Experimental Filmmaking

Experimental films generally explore alternative content and forms. Often compared to poetry and to the other plastic arts, experimental films deal with a wide variety of subject matter, from personal issues and interior psychological states to the very nature and ontology of the film image.

Experimental films are usually independently produced, with one individual often acting as producer, writer, director, sound mixer, and editor.

Photographic equipment employed in experimental films ranges from a state-of-the-art 35-mm camera to a child's toy camera. Some filmmakers bypass the camera completely and draw, scratch, or otherwise work directly on the celluloid, or they construct their films from found or archival footage. A film might be scripted down to the individual frame, or it might be spontaneously and instinctively shot, much in the manner of abstract expressionist painting. One film might have a different image on each frame, while another might consist entirely of one long shot taken by a static, stationary camera.

Though generally short, due to the financial exigencies of independent filmmaking, experimental films might run a few minutes, a few hours, or be virtually endless as in the case of film loops. Experimental films can cost less than $100, or they can cost many thousands of dollars. Distribution outlets for experimental films are similar to, but often more limited than, those for documentary films.

The Future

The process of filmmaking has changed more since the early 1980s than it did in the preceding eighty years. Changes from analog to digital technology have increased the variety of ways in which images and sounds are recorded, manipulated, and edited. There is no longer (if there ever was) one standard process for making a film. The only certainty about the future is that further changes are inevitable.

See also: FILM INDUSTRY; FILM INDUSTRY, CAREERS IN; FILM INDUSTRY, HISTORY OF; FILM INDUSTRY, TECHNOLOGY OF.

Bibliography

Brown, Blaine. (1995). *Motion Picture and Video Lighting*. Newton, MA: Focal Press.

Dmytryk, Edward. (1984). *On Screen Directing*. Newton, MA: Focal Press.

Goodell, Gregory. (1998). *Independent Feature Film Production*. New York: St. Martin's Press.

Hollyn, Norman. (1990). *The Film Editing Room Handbook*. Beverly Hills, CA: Lone Eagle Publishing.

Holman, Tomlinson. (1997). *Sound for Film and Television*. Newton, MA: Focal Press.

Katz, Steven D. (1991). *Film Directing Shot by Shot*. Studio City, CA: Michael Wiese Productions (in conjunction with Focal Press).

Kerner, Marvin. (1989). *The Art of the Sound Effects Editor*. Newton, MA: Focal Press.

Laybourne, Kit. (1998). *The Animation Book*. New York: Three Rivers Press.

Madsen, Roy Paul. (1990). *Working Cinema*. Belmont, CA: Wadsworth.

Mamer, Bruce. (2000). *Film Production Technique*. Belmont, CA: Wadsworth.

Miller, Pat P. (1990). *Script Supervising*. Newton, MA: Focal Press.

Murch, Walter. (1995). *In the Blink of an Eye*. Los Angeles: Silman-James Press.

Rabiger, Michael. (1997). *Directing the Documentary*. Newton, MA: Focal Press.

Rosenblum, Ralph, and Karen, Robert. (1980). *When the Shooting Stops . . . the Cutting Begins*. New York: Penguin Books.

Rosenthal, Alan. (1996). *Writing, Directing, and Producing Documentary Films and Videos*. Carbondale: Southern Illinois University Press.

Seger, Linda, and Whetmore, Edward Jay. (1994). *From Script to Screen*. New York: Henry Holt.

Singleton, Ralph S. (1984). *Film Scheduling*. Beverly Hills, CA: Lone Eagle Publishing.

Viera, David. (1993). *Lighting for Film and Electronic Cinematography*. Belmont, CA: Wadsworth.

Wiese, Michael, and Simon, Deke. (1995). *Film and Video Budgets*. Newton, MA: Focal Press.

LILLY ANN BORUSZKOWSKI

▣ FILM INDUSTRY, RATINGS FOR
See: Ratings for Movies

▣ FILM INDUSTRY, TECHNOLOGY OF

During the preproduction stages of a feature film, the screenwriter, director, production designer, and cinematographer may have widely differing visions concerning the ultimate look and sound of the film. Each scene has a series of variables that must be addressed prior to setup and shooting. Decisions about the technology that is to be used during the principle shooting will affect what the audience ultimately sees at the multiplex. Though the director is responsible for the finished product, the key players on the production team are hired for their expertise in the technical craft of filmmaking.

Format and Film Stock

The first decision to be made regarding the technology of a feature film centers on the screen format, which is the ratio of a film's width to its height (i.e., the aspect ratio). All pre-1952 films and most non-high-definition television (non-HDTV) programs have aspect ratios of 1.33:1—or 4 (width) by 3 (height)—which is the same aspect ratio as traditional television screens. It would be unusual for a contemporary film to be shot using the 1.33:1 format, given that contemporary movie theater screens are made to accommodate wider screen formats. Films shot on digital camcorders, including Michael Moore's documentary *The Big One* (1997), are exceptions. Moore's decision to use the digital camcorder in his guerilla-style documentary led him to use the 1.33:1 aspect ratio.

The more common format choices are the CinemaScope ratio (2.33:1) and the non-anamorphic ratio (1.85:1). The content of the film has much to do with the ultimate decision about format. The film *Titanic* (1998), which featured complex action sequences, virtually required the use of the 2.33:1 format. Conversely, *American Pie* (1999) was a teenage comedy that kept its characters in tightly framed shots. Therefore, the non-anamorphic ratio was deemed better suited for that film's format. In addition to film content, the equipment that is available will be a factor that helps to determine the final screen format.

Prior to shooting, the director and cinematographer must make a technical decision concerning what film stock to use. The film stock will have a significant effect on the look and feel of the film. *Blair Witch Project* (1999) combined video and grainy 16-mm film to create a realistic, low-budget look. A more traditional approach is to shoot in the Super 35-mm (Super35) format to reduce grain and capture superior contrast ratios. Lower budget films and documentaries might be shot on Super 16-mm (Super16) film.

A decision might also be necessary if a film is going to mix daytime and nighttime scenes. Some cinematographers prefer to use the same film stock throughout the production and use filters to create night sequences during daylight hours. Other cinematographers are adamant about shooting night sequences at night, so they may decide to mix, for example, 200-speed film for the daytime sequences with 500-speed film for the nighttime sequences. Technical decisions about formats and film stocks may seem mundane, compared to other aspects of the filmmaking process, but the choices made in this area will have a direct effect on the decisions that must then be made about cameras, lenses, and lighting.

Cameras and Lenses

Camera selection may appear to be a difficult procedure; however, the choices that are available to filmmakers are somewhat limited. There are only a handful of professional camera makers. The major camera manufacturers include Panavision, ≈aton, and Arriflex. Once the format decision is made, the cinematographer looks at what cameras are available. The ultimate decision will be made based primarily on the cinematographer's experience and preference. With camera and format in mind, lens choice is the next major issue.

Several lenses are used on a feature film, and the decision to use a specific lens is based on the action, composition, and lighting of a particular scene or shot. Unlike cameras, there are many makers of lenses and a wide variety of lens types. The primary companies that produce lenses are Angénieux, Zeiss, and Leitz. For many directors, the decision to shoot Super35 film is based on being able to use spherical lenses. Introduced in the late 1980s, these lenses have great depth of field, feature very wide contrast ranges, and have exceptional resolution performance. The Primo spherical lens has had such a profound effect that its inventors were awarded a Scientific and Engineering Award from the Academy of Motion Pictures Arts and Sciences in 1998. In addition to spherical lenses, a wide variety of fixed-focus lenses and special-purpose lenses can be used by the cinematographer, with the final decision being based on the needs of the director in a given scene. The director, cinematographer, and lighting director must determine, as well, the number of cameras to be used on the shoot.

Prior to the 1980s, almost every motion picture was shot using the single-camera method. The single-camera approach is exacting and methodical. The first step in the process is to shoot the master scene that captures all of the essential action and dialogue. More detailed shots, including close-ups, medium close-ups, and reaction shots, are then shot individually. Each new camera setup is time consuming. A large number of lighting changes and camera setups can often lead to production delays. Throughout the 1990s, the pressure to reduce the shooting schedules of feature film projects led to the increased use of the multicamera technique.

The multicamera technique allows the director to shoot a scene with two or more cameras. Recording the master scene and close-ups simultaneously can make the editing process much easier and generally saves setup time. The multicamera method places demands on the lighting director to light the scene in a manner that accommodates two or three cameras that are shooting simultaneously. When used effectively, the multicamera approach can help the director to trim days from the shooting schedule. While the orchestration that is involved with moving two or more cameras is important, lighting is the key component of the multicamera method.

Lighting

It is safe to say that lighting style and technique set the mood of a scene and can direct the attention of an audience to some desired element within the frame. The depth of field, or number of elements that can be held in focus by the camera, is largely dependent on the lighting. Table 1 provides some of the most common lighting devices and their uses. The lighting crew is responsible for all aspects of lighting technology during production.

The lighting crew consists of the lighting director, who has the primary responsibility for creating the look that is called for by the director; the gaffer, who is the electrician who sets up the lights; and the best boy, who assists the gaffer. Their job collectively is to control the lighting that falls into the camera frame.

The color quality, or the relative amount of red and blue of a light, is measured in color temperature. The color temperature emitted by all light sources, natural or human made, has an effect on the look of the scene. Film stock and lights have been created to take advantage of various color temperatures. Color-negative film stock is designed for exposure at a color temperature of 3,200 degrees Kelvin (K). Many spotlights, called Fresnels, produce the required 3,200-K light. Natural, outdoor light is generally about 5,600 K. Commonly used metal halide arc (HMI) lights produce light at 5,600 K and, therefore, equate natural light. If the camera crew is told to produce an indoor scene at 3,200 K, it could opt to use only Fresnel lighting fixtures and block out all other light sources. It is more common for the crew to work with Fresnels, HMIs, and natural light pouring through existing windows. In such mixed lighting situations, the crew will use gels, reflectors, flags, and a number of other accessories to balance the color temperature of all sources to the desired level. Controlled, professional lighting is generally the key to a professional-looking project.

Sound

To *Star Wars* creator George Lucas, sound is 50 percent of the film. When the sound system fails at a movie theater, people complain vociferously. The art of sound for motion pictures is challenging. A single action sequence in *Titanic* might feature a mixture of realistic ship sounds, crisply recorded dialogue, background cries of passengers, and original music that establishes the mood of the scene. The mixing of audio is handled so expertly that it may belie the fact that almost all of these sound elements were created separately, rather than as part of the actual filming.

TABLE 1.

Common Lighting Devices

Type	Description
Fresnel	A spotlight that is used as a main source of illumination.
Soft Light	Any lighting fixture that reflects light to fill in shadows caused by Fresnels.
Kicker	A smaller light that highlights one aspect of a set or an actor.
Barndoor	A four-leaved metal attachment to a light that restricts the light's direction.
Scrim	A wire mesh screen that is placed in front of a light to restrict the light's intensity.
Gel	Plastic material that is placed over a light source to alter its color or temperature.
Reflector	Large, flat device that is used to bounce light from one source to another
Gobo/Flag	Large, usually black, objects that are used to block light from entering the set.
C-Stand	A clamp device that is designed to hold reflectors, gobos, or other devices.
Light Meter	A device that is used to measure the light in a given scene.

During the production, the sound crew uses audio technology to meet their initial goals of consistency of audio and clarity of dialogue. To capture dialogue, the crew may employ tiny, wireless lavaliere microphones that are worn by actors, or they may decide to use the more common boom microphone. The boom operator's job is to ensure that the boom microphones are directionalized toward the actor, yet do not enter the frame of the shot. They must also be consistent in the distance that they establish between the microphone and the actor throughout each take of each scene.

All of the location film sound is recorded on a digital audio recorder and on film. This process is referred to as the double system. It allows the audio team to work on mixing dialogue, music, and sound effects independently in postproduction. Because many scenes in a film may be shot without sound, the supervising sound editor has the responsibility of creating a realistic audio mix for the audience. While the audio postproduction team is working on sound stages, dub stages, and audio control rooms, another team of artists works on the visuals.

Editing and Visual Effects

Once the film is shot, two separate processes will generally occur with the acquired film. The first is editing. Few directors still cut actual film. Steven Spielberg is one exception to this rule. He uses Moviola and/or Steenback film editors to cut

A computer animator at Boss Films designs computer-animated penguins for A Day in the Life of Hollywood *(1995). (Galen Rowell/Corbis)*

together a final "master" print. However, this is becoming increasingly rare. The most common technology that is used in contemporary film editing is a computer-based, nonlinear editor. The film is "digitized" or transferred from film to computer data. Many film editors use the Avid brand of nonlinear editing. The Avid systems and similar computer-based editors provide a series of editing options, including cuts, fades, and dissolves. The nonlinear system allows directors and editors to make last-minute changes with ease because changes can be made with literally one or two keystrokes at the computer workstation.

The craft known as visual effects was at one time primarily associated with science fiction and high-budget films. It has since become commonplace to use computer-based visual effects in almost every type of film. The possibilities are limitless to a visual-effects team. The processes of color-correcting elements within a scene, removing scratches from a film or adding scratches for effect, and "airbrushing" out unwanted elements from a scene pose little problem with modern technology.

When reshooting a scene is impossible, the visual team can save it in postproduction. For example, in one scene in the film *Braveheart* (1995), it appears as if thousands of extras are storming across the battlefield. A visual-effects team took the somewhat limited-looking groups of extras that were actually filmed and simply copied and pasted the extras digitally until the battlefield appeared full. The result is both convincing and one of the film's highlights. More complex films, such as *The Matrix* (1999), feature a dizzying array of visual effects. Many of the film's key sequences were shot with actors in front of green screens. The effects team had to use digital compositing to create futuristic and compelling action sequences. The death of a performer during production, such as when Brandon Lee died on the set of *The Crow* (1994) or when Oliver Reed died during the production of *Gladiator* (2000), might force a studio to terminate or recast a project. In these two cases, however, the scenes that remained to be shot for these two actors were completed with the use of computer-generated "virtual" actors.

The pace of computing technology has been so remarkable that entire films are being created on the computer desktop. *Toy Story 2* (1999) is an example. The film's preproduction, production, and postproduction all took place in the digital domain. The film was even projected at some theaters from a computer hard-drive that was connected to a filmless digital light processing (DLP) projector. The progression of film away from analog toward a digital base is one of several key trends for the industry.

Trends

Several key developments in film technology are changing the production and postproduction process in contemporary filmmaking. These trends are affecting the very heart of the films seen at the multiplex.

Cameras

The physical size of film cameras continues to decrease. This allows directors much more flexibility in obtaining the shots that they need. Because cameras are lighter than ever before, hand-held shots are being used more effectively than at any other time in the history of cinema. The audience may not realize that shots are hand-held, thanks to improvements made in Steadicam products that counterbalance the motion of the camera operator. Smaller cameras can also be attached to radio-controlled devices to follow the action of a scene. As cameras become smaller, the types of shots that are possible increase dramatically.

Video assists are being used more commonly to monitor camera shots. Instead of waiting for the "dailies" to return from the developing lab, directors watch a video monitor to see if a shot is acceptable. Some video assists have a freeze-frame capability that allows the director to call up a previously shot scene and reset all of the scenic elements and actors to ensure continuity from take to take.

A closely followed area in camera technology is that of the "filmless" camera. High-definition cameras are being tested that record images either on digital videodiscs (DVDs) or directly to hard drives. The use of such cameras would allow for instantaneous review and preliminary editing of material while eliminating film and developing costs. Studio pressure to release film content at a faster pace could lead some directors toward digital film acquisition in the field.

Audio

In the realm of sound, film continues to move closer to an immersive experience for audience members. Three formats of digital audio bring six or more channels of audio to moviegoers. The three formats are:

1. Digital Theater Sound (DTS), which is a six-channel digital audio system that reproduces audio from a separate compact disc (CD) that is synchronized to the film,

2. Sony Dynamic Digital Sound (SDDS), which was originally a six-channel digital audio system but was expanded to an eight-channel system in the late 1990s, and

3. Dolby Digital Surround, or Spectral Recording-Digital (SR-D), which, following the trend toward more immersive audio, improved the original six-channel system by adding speakers at the back of the theater.

Audio engineers continue to experiment with innovations that might result in audio emanating from the ceiling and floor of the theater.

Digitization

The progression of film toward a more fully digital medium seems obvious. Audio production, postproduction, and exhibition continue to be largely digital. Visual effects, titles, and editing are almost predominantly handled at the computer desktop. Filmless DLP projection systems have proven successful in theaters. Home video continues its progression toward DVD and Internet-delivered film content. As a result, the only major analog component of the filmmaking process is the actual shooting of the film. It is not inconceivable that the film technology of tomorrow will be fully digital.

See also: DIGITAL COMMUNICATION; DIGITAL MEDIA SYSTEMS; FILM INDUSTRY; FILM INDUSTRY, CAREERS IN; FILM INDUSTRY, HISTORY OF; FILM INDUSTRY, PRODUCTION PROCESS OF; RECORDING INDUSTRY, TECHNOLOGY OF.

Bibliography

Brinkmann, Ron. (1999). *The Art and Science of Digital Compositing*. San Francisco, CA: Morgan Kaufmann Publishers.

Eastman Kodak Company. (2001). "Entertainment Imaging." <http://www.kodak.com/US/en/motion/index.shtml>.

Happé, L. Bernard. (1971). *Basic Motion Picture Technology*. New York: Hastings House.

Jones, Stuart Blake; Kallenberger, Richard H.; and Cvjetnicanin, George D. (2000). *Film Into Video: A Guide to Merging the Technologies*. Boston: Focal Press.

Rickitt, Richard. (2000). *Special Effects*. New York: Watson-Guptill Publications.

Salt, Barry. (1999). *Film Style & Technology: History and Analysis*, 2nd edition. New York: Samuel French Trade.

Yewdall, David L. (2000). *The Practical Art of Motion Picture Sound*. Boston: Focal Press.

DAVID SEDMAN

FIRST AMENDMENT AND THE MEDIA

The courtship between the First Amendment and the mass media can trace its roots back to Colonial America. The mechanical printing press, invented in the fifteenth century, had come across the ocean and was being employed by the American colonies for the dissemination of many messages, some of which were political. England, angered that these certain messages openly criticized their government of the New World, sought to inhibit free speech. The three mechanisms that they used, government censorship, taxation, and seditious libel, comprised America's first encounter with prior restraint.

Early Prior Restraint

The first mechanism of prior restraint in the American colonies was government censorship. This practice, though not shared by all colonies, was a younger brother of England's mandatory licensing of all printing presses. The English licensing, introduced in 1530, required that all persons wishing to run a press meet certain criteria, mainly to refrain from criticizing the church or state. Those persons who published any material without a license were subject to severe penalties. Across the ocean, the American colonies did not require official licensing of newspapers and the like. However, some colonies still exercised the philosophy that printing was under state jurisdiction.

The second mechanism of prior restraint was the 1712 Stamp Act, which England imposed on the colonies. With this act, effective until 1855, publishers had to pay taxes on all newspapers, pamphlets, advertisements, and the paper itself. This meant that not only did the government know who was printing, via tax records, but the government also had monetary control over who could afford to print. Unlike the licensing philosophy, American colonists strongly objected to the taxation, the objection of which manifested itself in several acts of revolt.

The third mechanism of prior restraint was the punishment of seditious libel. Seditious libel was the printed criticism of any people in authority, be they government officials or leaders of the English Church. Consequences for this were so severe that many publishers refrained out of fear from printing anything controversial about an official. However, one man would prompt the colonies to rethink this accepted restraint. John Peter Zenger, publisher of the *New York Weekly Journal,* printed a negative piece about Governor William Crosby. Crosby reacted to the article by accusing Zenger of seditious libel, thus taking Zenger to court. Before the jury, Zenger, represented by Alexander Hamilton, admitted his "guilt" in publishing criticisms of the governor. However, Hamilton argued that these criticisms were true, in which case the truth should acquit Zenger from any wrongdoing. In the end, the jury decided to release Zenger on the basis that his message, though critical of an official, was nonetheless true. The acquittal of Zenger was the first stepping stone in a series that would finally lead to the birth of the First Amendment. After the American Revolution was fought and won, the new *Constitution of the United States* was created, and in 1791, the First Amendment was accepted. This first amendment (part of the Bill of Rights) simply stated:

> Congress shall make no law respecting an establishment of religion, or prohibiting the free exercise thereof; or abridging the freedom of speech, or of the press, or the right of the people peaceably to assemble, and to petition the Government for a redress of grievances.

It is unlikely that the writers of this simple sentiment, that "Congress shall make no law . . . abridging the freedom of speech, or of the press," could foresee the intricate web of arguments that would surround the amendment's interpretation. However, history shows that several competing philosophies and many court decisions would cause this "freedom" to take on different meanings for each new medium.

A nonchalant glance at modern media regulation quickly reveals a disparity between regulation of print media and regulation of electronic media—mainly that there is much less regulation of print media than there is of electronic media. This is because the electronic media, and broadcasting in particular, were treated differently by the U.S. Congress at their inception. The rationale for this difference in treatment for broadcasting was that the airwaves were a scarce, public resource, and that messages traveling on these public airwaves could potentially reach, and indeed affect, a great many more people than print messages. Therefore, the government thought that, in the public interest, it was necessary to regulate broadcasting. Furthermore, broadcasting was seen as a form of interstate commerce, which, under Article I, Section 8, of the U.S. Constitution, Congress had the authority to regulate. Other electronic media were categorized similarly and are regulated under the Communications Act of 1934 as amended by the Telecommunications Act of 1996. Print, however, is only regulated under the ownership, antitrust, and criminal laws shared by all businesses in the United States.

Despite these regulatory differences, all forms of media, be they print or electronic, are subject to the courts. Unfortunately, it is difficult to say with certainty how the courts will interpret the First Amendment for a given media case because the judicial system has frequently changed its philosophies regarding the amendment throughout media history. However, four theories regarding free speech have taken turns influencing judicial decisions, and they continue to influence judges and lawmakers. These theories are the marketplace of ideas, political speech absolutism, absolute expression, and public access.

Theories of Free Speech

The marketplace of ideas theory, introduced in 1644 by John Milton in his book *Areopagitica,* suggests that all ideas should be allowed to be disseminated into the public marketplace. These ideas would then be individually weighed and compared to other ideas in the marketplace. The result would be a forum through which the available ideas would be debated and from which the proverbial truth would emerge. For practical purposes, it is assumed that the public would be able to choose, from the multitude of ideas, which idea would be the most suitable or valid for its time. Because it assumes an open forum, the marketplace of ideas implies that the government should either adopt a *laissez-faire* policy toward media content or promote diversity among mediated messages.

The second theory regarding free speech concerns the absolute freedom of political speech. Championed by Alexander Meiklejohn in the early 1960s, the idea of absolute freedom of political speech proposed that the government should under no circumstances inhibit or interrupt any speech regarding the regulation of the country, community, or self. This speech included scientific, artistic, political, social, and moral or religious speech. It did not, however, include personal, private speech.

The third theory takes Meiklejohn's idea to its limits. This absolutist interpretation of the First Amendment draws its fuel from a U.S. Supreme Court decision (*United States v. Washington Post Co.,* 1971), in which Justice Hugo L. Black, supported by Justice William O. Douglas, wrote:

> Both the history and language of the First Amendment support the view that the press must be left free to publish news, whatever the source, without censorship, injunctions or prior restraints.

This stance was translated as the endorsement for the U.S. government to refrain from any and all interference with public or private speech, absolutely. This absolutist interpretation of the First Amendment was too extreme for many to support.

The fourth popular interpretation of freedom of the press is the public access theory that was argued by Jerome Barron in 1967. This theory assumes that the purpose of the First Amendment is to allow the public to openly voice the various opposing views surrounding a public issue. This assumed purpose, whose roots can be seen in the marketplace of ideas and the absolute political speech theories, therefore implies that the general public should be guaranteed access to the different media in order to voice these views. This theory is arguably the most visibly manifested theory in broadcast regulation, as evidenced by the Fairness Doctrine (officially set forth in 1949 by the Federal Communications Commission as *In the*

Reporters gather near pacifists David A. Reed, David P. O'Brien, David Benson, and John A. Phillips as they burn their draft cards at a Vietnam War protest in Boston on March 31, 1966. (Bettmann/Corbis)

Matter of Editorializing by Broadcast Licensees) and other Communications Act of 1934 stipulations that required broadcasters to provide equal opportunity to air the various sides of public issues. Print media, however, were never subjected to access rulings, and broadcasting later received a similar reprieve when the Fairness Doctrine was abolished in 1987.

Tests for Possible Violations of the First Amendment

Regardless of which theory was popular at any given moment, there have always been media messages that would cause such controversy as to require the court system to test their validity against the First Amendment. Therefore, in answer to this periodic need, three main tests eventually evolved that were used widely in U.S. Supreme Court decisions when possible violations of the First Amendment were involved. These tests were the clear and present danger test, the O'Brien test, and the strict scrutiny test.

Clear and present danger has historically been the popular standard for whether the First Amendment has been violated. Seen as early as 1917, clear and present danger is based on the premise that the government may protect citizens from messages that would "create a clear and present danger that they will bring about the substantive evils that Congress has a right to prevent." This statement, written by Justice Oliver Wendell Holmes in *Schenck v. United States* (1919), was used to convict two men who had circulated print messages against the draft during World War I. It is interesting to note that the same judge later amended his earlier position to specify in *Abrams v. United States* (1919) that messages must show a purposeful and immediate intent to cause danger.

In 1968, another case gave birth to a new First Amendment test. *United States v. O'Brien* involved a young man, David O'Brien, who was convicted of burning his draft card in front of a Massachusetts courthouse in 1966. O'Brien appealed his conviction on the grounds of free speech, and he won the review of the U.S. Supreme Court. The Court evaluated the case under three grounds. First, the conviction was tested to see if it aided a substantial government interest. Second, the substantial government interest was tested to see if it was necessarily tied to the suppression of free speech. Third, the government's actions were tested to see if they were no more severe than needed to further the substantial interest. This three-pronged test, which led the Court to uphold O'Brien's conviction and subsequently came to be referred to as the O'Brien test, is still used by federal and state courts to decide many First Amendment cases that involve government interference.

A more stringent test of government interference and violation of the First Amendment is the strict scrutiny test, which was first applied in *Preferred Communications v. City of Los Angeles* (1989). This test mirrors the O'Brien test, but there are two major changes. First, the government interest that the O'Brien test claimed should be "important" or "substantial" must, under strict scrutiny, be "compelling." Second, the way in which the government furthers this compelling interest must be in the least restrictive manner possible, as opposed to "no greater than necessary." The strict scrutiny test is employed whenever a government restriction directly affects First Amendment protections. In contrast, the O'Brien test is used in cases where First Amendment rights are indirectly affected by government involvement. Consequently, the government usually prefers the use of the O'Brien test over the strict scrutiny test because it is easier to prove that an interest is "substantial" rather than "compelling," and it is much easier to argue that an imposed restriction is "no more severe than needed" rather than "the least restrictive manner possible."

Of course, these three tests, which apply to all media, only constitute a fraction of the tests that may apply to broadcasting. Whereas print media enjoy relatively few restrictions and regulations, the electronic media must operate with substantial regulation. For example, section 1464 of the U.S. Criminal Code prohibits the broadcasting of "obscene, indecent, or profane language."

Restrictions on Electronic Media

Through the years, definitions of "indecency" and "obscenity" have evolved as a result of various court decisions, including *Federal Communica-*

tions Commission v. Pacifica Foundation (1978) and *Miller v. California* (1973), respectively. In both instances, the definitions include an aspect that references current community standards as a guide to identifying indecency or obscenity. Other aspects of the definitions include the identification of such material as offensive, sexual in nature, and devoid of any social value. Clearly, the definitions still require considerable interpretation, as does the First Amendment itself. Therefore, the application of these definitions will change according to the times, morals, and community standards in which the questionable messages are disseminated. Profanity, or the utterance of irreverent words, is not deemed to be seriously offensive, and consequently, cases involving profanity are not often seen in the courtroom.

Many of the historic regulations restricting the First Amendment privileges of the electronic media are still in place. Examples of this include section 312 and 315 of the Communications Act of 1934. Section 312 requires that broadcasters provide airtime to legally qualified candidates during federal elections. Section 315 requires that media outlets that give one political candidate media time must provide an equal opportunity for all other competing political candidates who wish to have media time. Other regulations that restrict the First Amendment rights of the electronic media are more recent, such as the Children's Television Act of 1990, which restricts certain advertising practices and imposes certain programming requirements for children's viewing. However, the general trend appears to be a relaxing of First Amendment restrictions and a more equal interpretation of the First Amendment with respect to both print and electronic media.

An example of the relaxing of restrictions for radio is the landmark case *Federal Communications Commission v. WNCN Listeners Guild* (1981). This case upheld the commission's policy that it would not become involved in the decision of a radio station to change its programming format. Radio could choose its programming strategy without government oversight.

Regarding broadcasting in general, *League of Women Voters v. Federal Communications Commission* (1982) found that the decades-old ban on broadcast editorializing was unconstitutional. In a similar vein, the 1987 repeal of the Fairness Doctrine furthered the freedom of speech of broadcasting by lifting the previous requirement to air opposing viewpoints of controversial public issues in a balanced manner. As a result of these changes, broadcasters gained more control over the content that was aired.

An example of relaxed restrictions for cable television is the outcome of *Federal Communications Commission v. Midwest Video Corporation* (1979). In this case, the U.S. Supreme Court officially struck down the commission's requirement that larger cable systems provide a certain number of public-access channels. The resulting effect of this court decision was to allow cable operators greater freedom in selecting channel line-ups and in acquiring programming.

Other media, such as digital cable, satellite television, digital broadcasting, and the Internet, remain somewhat ambiguous in terms of their First Amendment status. These media, of course, have First Amendment protection. However, recalling the disparate treatment between broadcasting and print, it is uncertain how the newer media will eventually be treated by the government and the judicial system. The merging of broadcast and print characteristics in the various new media will undoubtedly muddy the interpretive waters even more, rendering definitive decisions extremely difficult. Nevertheless, despite conflicts between protection of the public interest and freedoms of speech and press, the relationship between the First Amendment and the media will continue to evolve and shape the messages that are heard.

See also: BROADCASTING, GOVERNMENT REGULATION OF; CABLE TELEVISION, REGULATION OF; COMMUNICATIONS ACT OF 1934; PORNOGRAPHY; PORNOGRAPHY, LEGAL ASPECTS OF; TELECOMMUNICATIONS ACT OF 1996.

Bibliography

Barron, Jerome. (1967). "Access to the Press: A New First Amendment Right." *Harvard Law Review* 80:1641–1678.

Kahn, Frank J., ed. (1978). *Documents of American Broadcasting,* 3rd edition. Englewood Cliffs, NJ: Prentice-Hall.

Meiklejohn, Alexander. (1961). "The First Amendment Is an Absolute." *Supreme Court Review* 1961:245–266.

Pember, Don R. (1992). *Mass Media in America,* 6th edition. New York: Macmillan.

Smith, F. Leslie; Meeske, Milan; and Wright, John W., II. (1995). *Electronic Media and Government: The Regulation of Wireless and Wired Mass Communication in the United States.* White Plains, NY: Longman.

FRANCESCA DILLMAN CARPENTIER

■ FRANKLIN, BENJAMIN (1706–1790)

A printer, author, library organizer, inventor, diplomat, scientist, philanthropist, and statesman, Benjamin Franklin was born in Boston on January 17, 1703, the fifteenth child of Abiah and Josiah Franklin. At that time, more than half of the booksellers in the New World were within a quarter of a mile of his birthplace. It is little wonder, then, that Franklin learned to read early in life ("I do not remember when I could not read"). He spent many hours poring over the works of authors such as John Bunyan and Cotton Mather, works he found in the small libraries of his father and his friend Matthew Adams. The life-story record Franklin left of his eclectic reading interests demonstrates that it was always socioculturally mediated, no matter what his stage of life or his location. From these works it appears that he developed the sense of duty, self-improvement, and moralism that characterized his adult life. In the works of Enlightenment thinkers, he developed a faith in reason and order and cultivated an interest in science and benevolence.

In 1718, Franklin was apprenticed as a printer to his brother James, publisher of *The New England Courant.* Under the pseudonym "Silence Dogood," Franklin penned a series of letters in 1722, and although the readers received them favorably, his brother was annoyed. In 1723, Franklin fled Boston (with three years left on his apprenticeship) and shortly thereafter took up residence in Philadelphia to work as a compositor in the printing establishment of Samuel Keimer. In 1728, Franklin formed a printing partnership in Philadelphia with Hugh Meredith, and over the years, he became the official printer for several colonial legislatures. Generally, Franklin confined his printing business to practical materials of immediate use and market potential and avoided efforts to produce fine printing.

In 1730, Franklin acquired the *Pennsylvania Gazette* (which Keimer had founded two years earlier), and this newspaper became the centerpiece of his printing business. He made it lively and local, yet balanced enough in his coverage of colonial politics to be open to all parties. "In the Conduct of my Newspaper I carefully excluded all Libelling and Personal Abuse," he later wrote in his autobiography. His "open press" strategy—as much economic as political—became the model most Middle Colonies printers followed in the first half of the eighteenth century. It enabled Franklin to print polemical pamphlets on most sides of any debate. One example of this practice was manifest in the printing opportunities sparked by George Whitefield's Great Awakening revivals of 1739–1741. At his own risk, Franklin published devotional books that Whitefield had recommended, and between 1740 and 1742, he printed forty-three books and pamphlets—both for and against Whitefield and his revivals. By advertising for subscribers in the *Gazette,* he was able to generate cash in advance of producing copy. In 1741, Franklin began publishing *General Magazine* (a 70- to 76-page duodecimo monthly modeled after London's *Gentleman's Magazine*), which carried reports of the proceedings of colonial legislatures and other public issues. Due to lack of interest, however, *General Magazine* ceased after six issues.

In 1732, Franklin issued the first edition of his *Poor Richard's Almanack,* a small tome consisting of well-known aphorisms that Franklin first appropriated and then modified for a New World audience. "I endeavor'd to make it both entertaining and useful," he said later, "and it accordingly came to be in such Demand that I reap'd considerable Profit from it." It became an immediate bestseller, sold out ten thousand copies shortly after it was published, and made Franklin a celebrated author at home and (eventually) abroad. Franklin also experimented with printing German-language materials, but he ultimately financed Anton Ambruster to run a separate office for this market.

Although Franklin profited most from his newspaper, almanacs, and job printing, he also engaged in what he called "book work." Franklin's printing office doubled as a bookshop where customers could peruse works that Franklin had printed and published, or imported. The latter usually consisted of Bibles and testaments or primary education schoolbooks that generated a steady but not heavy demand. Most bookstore sales came from his own publications.

A 1790 profile engraving from Massachusetts Magazine *memorializes Benjamin Franklin. (Corbis)*

In 1727, Franklin organized the Philadelphia Junto, a group of twelve like-minded individuals who were interested in self-improvement through discussion of politics, morals, and natural philosophy. Because the Junto was regularly frustrated over a lack of information on which to ground meaningful debates, Franklin recommended in 1730 that the membership begin "clubbing our Books to a common Library" so that each would have "the Advantage of using the Books of all the other Members, which would be nearly as beneficial as if we owned the whole." The experiment was short-lived, however. Too many Junto members despaired of the care and arrangement afforded their textual treasures.

Franklin was undeterred. In 1731, he "set on foot my first Project of a public Nature" and organized the Library Company of Philadelphia, which decades later he referred to as "the Mother of all N. American Subscription Libraries now so numerous." Shares were sold to provide capital to buy books (most of which were ordered from London); annual dues provided for ongoing purchases. Company members were, for the most part, merchants interested in practical information for self-improvement. Franklin served as "librarian" from December 1733 to March 1734, as secretary to the Library Company from 1746 to 1757, and remained a member his entire life. By 1776, at least eighteen social libraries existed in the colonies, all of which were modeled after the Library Company. By the end of his life, Franklin was convinced that social libraries had "improved the general conversation of the Americans."

By the time he had started the Library Company of Philadelphia, Franklin had already perceived British North America's potential as a political and cultural unity and, in part, facilitated movement toward this potential—at least in the culture of print. He did this by fostering an informal network of printers (stretching from South Carolina to Massachusetts) who modeled his precedents. As the deputy postmaster of Philadelphia (1737–1753) and as deputy postmaster-general for the Colonies (1753–1774, serving with William Hunter), Franklin also worked to improve communication and information transfer in the New World.

Franklin, who retired from publishing in 1748 to devote himself to other interests, spent a large portion of his later life living in England and France—serving as the colonies' official emissary to France during the American Revolution. While in Europe, he solicited gifts for the American Philosophical Society (which he had founded in 1743) and negotiated exchange agreements with similar European societies for the society's *Transactions*. After he returned to the newly founded United States of America, Franklin served as a delegate to the convention that framed the U.S. Constitution in 1787.

Few people in colonial America were as influential as Franklin in establishing a culture of print that functioned as a primary agency to facilitate communication and information creation, storage, and dissemination. Franklin married Deborah Read on September 1, 1730, and by her had two children; he also fathered two illegitimate children. When Franklin died on April 17, 1790, his library contained 4,276 volumes. He once joked that he wanted his epitaph to read "B. Franklin, Printer"; the final inscription, however, read "Benjamin and Deborah Franklin."

See also: LIBRARIES, HISTORY OF; PRINTING, HISTORY AND METHODS OF.

Bibliography

Buxbaum, Melvin H. (1988). *Benjamin Franklin: A Reference Guide,* 2 vols. Boston: G. K. Hall.

Clark, Ronald William. (1983). *Benjamin Franklin: A Biography.* New York: Random House.

Hawke, David Freeman. (1976). *Franklin.* New York: Harper & Row.

Labaree, Leonard W., et al., eds. (1959–2000). *Papers of Benjamin Franklin,* first 35 vols. New Haven, CT: Yale University Press.

Lemay, J. A. Leo, ed. (1993). *Reappraising Benjamin Franklin: A Bicentennial Perspective.* Newark: University of Delaware Press.

Miller, Clarence William. (1974). *Benjamin Franklin's Philadelphia Printing, 1728–1776; A Descriptive Bibliography.* Philadelphia: American Philosophical Society.

Van Doren, Carl. (1938). *Benjamin Franklin.* New York: Viking Press.

Wright, Edmond. (1986). *Franklin of Philadelphia.* Cambridge, MA: Belknap Press of Harvard University Press.

WAYNE A. WIEGAND

FUNCTIONS OF THE MEDIA

Robert Merton introduced a form of functionalism in his 1949 book *Social Theory and Social Structure,* and that form has been widely adopted by media researchers. His "functional analysis" detailed how the study of social artifacts (such as media use) could lead to the development of theories explaining their "functions." Merton derived this perspective from earlier forms of structural-functionalist theories that were used in anthropology and sociology. Functional analysis argues that a society can best be viewed as a "system in balance," consisting of complex sets of interrelated activities, each supporting the others. All forms of social activity play a part in maintaining the system as a whole.

The apparent value neutrality of functional analysis appealed to many media scholars because much early media theory characterized media and media consumption as either "good" or "bad." Functionalists reject this good-bad dichotomy, arguing instead that only objective, empirical research can identify the functions and dysfunctions of media, leading to a systematic appraisal of media's overall effect on society. Functionalist theorists believed that scientists had neither the right nor the need to make value judgments about media when they conducted their research.

Functionalists view activity that contributes to maintaining the society as functional, not good. Disruptive activities are, by definition, dysfunctional, not evil. Some social activities might be found to be functional in some respects but dysfunctional in others. Functionalists also distinguish between manifest functions (i.e., those consequences that are intended and easily observed) and latent functions (those consequences that are unintended and less easily observed).

Functional analysis provided the foundation for many theories of media effects and of much of the related research during the 1950s and 1960s. Researchers found that functional analysis can be very complicated. Some forms of media content can be functional or dysfunctional for society as a whole, for specific individuals, or for various subgroups in the society. Thus, entertaining network television crime shows might be functional for the viewing audience as a whole but dysfunctional for children who learn that aggression is a good way to deal with problems. The functions for society (the larger audience) may be offset by the dysfunctions for an individual child or for a particular group of viewers (children).

This example highlights a major problem with functional analysis. It does not permit the development of definitive conclusions about the overall functions or dysfunctions of media. Researchers can easily avoid drawing controversial conclusions by noting that dysfunctions are balanced by functions. In 1961, for example, Wilbur Schramm, Jack Lyle, and Edwin Parker wrote in their book *Television in the Lives of Our Children* that although viewing of some forms of violent television content encouraged some children to be aggressive, this was more than offset by the fact that most children show little postviewing aggression. Some kids might even learn how to deal with aggressive playmates. Therefore, as far as the social system is concerned, violent television content does not make much difference despite being dysfunctional for a few children.

Sociologist Charles Wright directly applied functionalism to mass communication in his 1959

book *Mass Communication: A Sociological Perspective.* He wrote that media theorists "noted three activities of communication specialists: (1) surveillance of the environment, (2) correlation of the parts of society in responding to the environment, and (3) transmission of the social heritage from one generation to the next" (p. 16). Wright added a fourth, entertainment. These became known as the "classic four functions of the media."

Wright's particular contribution was to draw a distinction between the intended purpose of media activity and its consequences (its functions). Nonetheless, for most communication scholars, functions became synonymous with the aims or goals of the media industries themselves. As a result, many critics saw functionalism as doing little more than legitimizing the status quo. For example, surveillance of the environment refers to the collection and distribution of information by the media. People know the fate of the government appropriations bill because they saw it on the news. Correlation of parts of society refers to the interpretive or analytical activities of the media. People know from the newspaper that the bill's failure to pass means no raises for teachers this year. Transmission of the social heritage refers to the ability of the media to communicate values, norms, and styles across time and between groups. What were typical attitudes toward racial minorities in the 1950s? People can see them manifested in old movies and television shows. Finally, entertainment refers to the ability of the media to amuse or entertain.

These are obvious aims of the media, but they may not necessarily be the functions served for the people who consume those media. For example, a television network might air a violent police drama with the aim of entertaining, but the actual function served for the audience might be learning how to solve conflicts. In other words, the aim is not always the ultimate or only function. Critics contend that restricting the study of functions to functions intended by media practitioners (their aims) is likely to ignore many negative effects.

Surveillance activity and its effects on democracy offer an example of how functionalism should be applied to media studies. In their intention to survey the environment, the mass media devote significant resources to the coverage and reporting of political campaigns. But if citizens ignore this coverage, the intended function fails to occur—the environment has not been surveyed despite the efforts of the media. But if citizens do consume the reports, then the intended function—surveillance of the environment—does take place. For surveillance to occur, the transmission of news about important events must be accompanied by audience activity that results in learning about and understanding those events. Simply put, aims become functions only when the interrelated parts of the system operate to produce those functions.

This proper use of functionalism opens the media-society interrelationship to more robust questioning. Might not the frequently shallow, entertainment-oriented coverage of politics by the media actually contribute to dysfunctional media use, as citizens become less involved in the political process because they are turned off not only by the nature of the coverage but by its content? Might not the manifest function served by the media and audience interrelationship actually produce a latent function, the pacification of a citizenry that might otherwise demand real change from its government and politicians? This allowance for dysfunctions and latent functions has resulted in a renewed interest in functionalism among researchers who are skeptical of theories that they consider to be too apologetic or forgiving of routine media practice.

See also: ADVERTISING EFFECTS; AROUSAL PROCESSES AND MEDIA EFFECTS; CATHARSIS THEORY AND MEDIA EFFECTS; CULTIVATION THEORY AND MEDIA EFFECTS; CUMULATIVE MEDIA EFFECTS; DESENSITIZATION AND MEDIA EFFECTS; ELECTION CAMPAIGNS AND MEDIA EFFECTS; ETHICS AND INFORMATION; MOOD EFFECTS AND MEDIA EXPOSURE; NEWS EFFECTS; PARENTAL MEDIATION OF MEDIA EFFECTS; SOCIAL CHANGE AND THE MEDIA; SOCIAL COGNITIVE THEORY AND MEDIA EFFECTS; SOCIAL GOALS AND THE MEDIA; SOCIETY AND THE MEDIA.

Bibliography

Merton, Robert K. (1949). *Social Theory and Social Structure.* Glencoe, IL: Free Press.

Schramm, Wilbur; Lyle, Jack; and Parker, Edwin. (1961). *Television in the Lives of Our Children.* Stanford, CA: Stanford University Press.

Wright, Charles R. (1959). *Mass Communication: A Sociological Perspective.* New York: Random House.

KIMBERLY B. MASSEY